NORTHERN EDITORIALS
ON SECESSION

PREPARED AND PUBLISHED UNDER THE DIRECTION OF THE AMERICAN HISTORICAL ASSOCIATION FROM THE INCOME OF THE ALBERT J. BEVERIDGE MEMORIAL FUND.

FOR THEIR ZEAL AND BENEFICENCE IN CREATING THIS FUND THE ASSOCIATION IS INDEBTED TO MANY CITIZENS OF INDIANA WHO DESIRED TO HONOR IN THIS WAY THE MEMORY OF A STATESMAN AND A HISTORIAN.

The American Historical Association

NORTHERN EDITORIALS
ON SECESSION

EDITED BY

HOWARD CECIL PERKINS, Ph.D.

Bradley Polytechnic Institute

Volume I

D. APPLETON–CENTURY COMPANY
INCORPORATED

NEW YORK · · LONDON

TO MY MOTHER AND THE
MEMORY OF MY FATHER

PREFACE

This compilation of northern editorials is presented as a selection of representative newspaper opinions on different aspects of the secession crisis of 1860–1861. It is designed to suggest the diversity of thought and feeling from which there later emerged an aggressive northern policy and a fair degree of northern unity. Readers may find that the testimony of witnesses induces a deeper realization that the preservation of the Union, as a northern policy, was emphatically not an instinctive response to southern ordinances of secession. Actually, prospective disunion evoked in the North not a public opinion but countless private opinions, which soon tended to assume party lines. Some of these sentiments, expressed at various stages and on significant phases of the crisis, comprise this collection of editorials.

The main text in these volumes is preceded by an introduction and followed by a newspaper index and a general index. The introduction discusses the politics of the secession crisis, describes the northern press of the period, and explains the selection and classification of editorials. The newspaper index includes a geographical listing of quoted editorials, the names of editors and other persons associated with each paper at the time, and information on name-changes, mergers, and suspensions within the period. The general index is intended as a guide to editorial sentiments, and for that reason does not cover the introduction.

The *Manual of Style* of the Beveridge Memorial Fund Committee of the American Historical Association has been followed wherever possible. It has provided welcome guidance, and, on occasion, even mandates, as on the lower case writing of "northern" and "southern" in the preface and introduction. Yet, neither the *Manual* nor any other style book affords much assistance in the editing process itself. A number of rules, therefore, had to be formulated. In these, fidelity to the original has been constantly in mind, but the reader has been spared the review of mere discoveries in bad typography. All matters on which the author himself was conceivably in error, however, are presented to the reader for his judgment.

The editing rules may be stated briefly. Italics and small and large capitals, used for emphasis, are presented as in the original. Except for modernization of editorial titles, capitalization is reproduced, inconsistent as it is both between and within editorials. This practice entails the use of lower case letters in beginning many quotations. Older forms of spelling are retained, as, for example: "embassador," "cotemporary," "phrensy," "harrass," "Sumpter," "negociation," "seige," and "loth." Some words, now used as one, were then often written separately, as "can not," "them selves," "every where," and "for ever," and are retained in that form. Marks of quotation and punctuation, unless otherwise indicated, are kept as in the original, except that the occasional device of beginning each line of quoted material with quotation marks is discarded. Punctuation is thus frequently at variance with recent practice, especially in the handling of quotations and the placing of commas. Ellipses are inserted in eight editorials to indicate omissions; all others are presented in their entirety. All titles are unchanged, but fabricated ones are added in brackets to editorials originally printed without heads. Following the newspaper name in the date line of each editorial there is given in brackets the presidential candidate supported by the paper in the election of 1860. A few footnotes are inserted to present relevant information.

This work was begun at Yale University in a seminar of the last students to complete their graduate work under the direction of the late Ulrich B. Phillips. Through the good offices of Professor Phillips, then chairman of the Beveridge Memorial Fund Committee, opportunity was offered to continue the study of northern editorial sentiment on secession and coercion. Materials used in a doctoral dissertation were thereupon greatly expanded, providing the basis of the present selection and, it is hoped, of an eventual interpretative volume.

Professor Phillips, as his students know so well, was a constant source of friendly guidance. His successor as chairman of the Beveridge Committee, Professor Roy F. Nichols, of the University of Pennsylvania, has also been helpful in many ways. His sympathy with the editor's conviction that a selection of representative editorials must rest on the groundwork of an almost exhaustive reading of northern newspapers has permitted the editor a period of research extending beyond original calculations. Professors Arthur C. Cole, of Western Reserve University, and J. G. Randall, of the University of Illinois, both sometime members of the Beveridge Committee, and the present chairman, Professor Richard H. Shryock, of the University of Pennsylvania, have all contributed welcome counsel.

The editor is indebted to the many librarians and newspapermen whose helpfulness has made research a double pleasure. Indeed, without their favors, many of the editorials in these volumes would never have appeared. The staffs of the following institutions are remembered for their especial kindness: the University of Vermont; the Athenaeum, Boston; Harvard University; the American Antiquarian Society; the Worcester Public Library; Yale University; the New York State Library; the Troy Public Library, New York; the Oneida Historical Society, Utica; the Utica *Observer-Dispatch;* the Camden Historical Society; the Library of Congress; the Pennsylvania State Library; the Allentown *Morning Call;* the Washington *Reporter and Tribune,* Pennsylvania; the Ohio Archeological and Historical Society; Indiana University; the Indiana State Library; the Grand Rapids Public Library; the Newberry Library, Chicago; the Chicago Historical Society; the Galena *Gazette;* the Belleville Public Library, Illinois; the Burlington Public Library, Iowa; the Iowa Historical Society; the Historical, Memorial and Art Department of Iowa; the Carnegie-Stout Library, Dubuque; and the Minnesota Historical Society.

Acknowledgments are also due Miss Bertha E. Josephson, technical editor of Beveridge Fund publications, for her coöperation throughout. She has shown a constant willingness to share the wealth of her editorial experience. Mr. Hubert M. Hawkins and Mr. Clarence L. Weaver, assisting Miss Josephson, have both read these volumes in proof. Helen Hart Metz, of Elmwood, Illinois, has read the proofsheets and has, in addition, performed the ultimate kindness of preparing the index. Colleagues at Bradley have aided through the reading of confused passages in the text, the criticism of the introduction, and the verification of Latin quotations.

The editor must also acknowledge the assistance of his sister, Arlene Perkins Newcomer, then a student at Findlay College, in carding and indexing photostats, and of Kathryn Gaver Ferguson, also of Findlay College, and of Marion Putnam Bohner, of Bradley Polytechnic Institute, in preparing and checking the manuscript. Finally, and above all, he wishes to thank his wife, Mary Sutherland Perkins, for her continuous and efficient help: she has written hundreds of letters to assemble the data in the newspaper index and to clarify indistinct passages in photostatic materials; and she has twice read every sentence in these volumes, excepting only this one.

H. C. P.

Bradley Polytechnic Institute
November 25, 1941

CONTENTS

PAGE

VI. CONCILIATION AND COMPROMISE

PAGE

VII. MEASURES FOR PEACE

CONTENTS

CONTENTS xxi

XII. THE ''CHIVALRY''

200. THE ERA OF LIBERTY. Chicago *Daily Democrat,* October 31, 1860 508

201. SECESSION NOT FAVORABLE TO THE LUXURY OF SAFE VIOLENCE. *Daily Boston Traveller,* November 20, 1860 . . 509

202. AMERICA, OR AUSTRIA? Cincinnati *Daily Commercial,* December 1, 1860 510

203. SOUTHERN ATROCITIES UPON NORTHERN MEN. Chicago *Daily Tribune,* December 13, 1860 513

204. WAR IN THE EVENT OF SECESSION. Bellefontaine (O.) *Republican,* December 15, 1860 516

205. SOUTHERN TREATMENT OF NORTHERN CITIZENS. Davenport *Daily Gazette,* December 19, 1860 518

206. LAWLESSNESS ON A GIGANTIC SCALE. Philadelphia *North American and United States Gazette,* February 4, 1861 . . 520

207. THE TREASON AND THE TRAITORS. Quincy (Ill.) *Daily Whig and Republican,* March 7, 1861 522

208. "BLOOD WILL TELL." Detroit *Daily Advertiser,* April 4, 1861 524

209. SOUTHERN CHIVALRY. New Haven *Daily Palladium,* April 29, 1861 525

210. NORTHERN HOMAGE TO SOUTHERN HUMBUG. Peoria *Daily Transcript,* May 8, 1861 528

211. THE SEPOYS OF MONTGOMERY. Albany *Evening Journal,* May 10, 1861 530

212. ARE WE ONE PEOPLE? Burlington (Vt.) *Daily Times,* May 14, 1861 531

213. THE ASHES OF WASHINGTON STOLEN! Boston *Herald,* May 17, 1861 533

214. THE MORALITY OF THE COTTON CONFEDERACY. Paris (Me.) *Oxford Democrat,* May 31, 1861 534

215. CHIVALRY. Columbus *Daily Ohio State Journal,* June 3, 1861 535

Index i

XIII. THE MISSISSIPPI

XIV. THE ECONOMICS OF UNION

CONTENTS

PAGE

XV. INAUGURALS SOUTH AND NORTH

XVII. THE STRATEGY OF SUMTER

XIX. POST-SUMTER PLEAS FOR PEACE

XX. OBJECTS OF THE WAR

xxviii CONTENTS

XXI. THE BORDER STATES

XXII. WESTERN VIRGINIA

CONTENTS

XXVII. MORAL AND SPIRITUAL VALUES

NORTHERN EDITORIALS
ON SECESSION

NORTHERN EDITORIALS ON SECESSION

INTRODUCTION

The four hundred and ninety-five editorials contained in the two volumes of *Northern Editorials on Secession* have been selected from the files of eight hundred newspapers scattered among one hundred and forty libraries and newspaper offices in seventeen states and Washington, D. C. Of the hundred thousand editorials originally examined, perhaps five thousand were subjected to study. Those finally selected represent one hundred and ninety newspapers. The papers consulted were published in an area containing the northern free states of 1860 and, in addition, the District of Columbia, that part of Virginia which subsequently became West Virginia, and Kansas, after its admission as a state in January, 1861. Except for California, Oregon, and the territories, the editorials of these volumes speak for that portion of the United States not represented in Professor Dwight L. Dumond's *Southern Editorials on Secession,* also a Beveridge Memorial Fund publication.

The editorials presented here have been taken exclusively from the English language press and from what might be called the "political" or "news" press. Accordingly, trade, professional, and religious papers have been excluded. A number of abolitionist "sheets" were examined, notably the *Liberator* and the *National Anti-Slavery Standard,* but with a single exception no editorials from them have been included. This exclusion appears justified by the great length of the better editorials, the general availability of the files, and the probability that most of their readers were also subscribers to other journals. The exception to the rule of exclusion is an editorial from a rare issue of James Redpath's *Pine and Palm.*

The files of northern newspapers of the secession period have survived in remarkable number. There are fewer than a dozen incomplete files of the daily newspapers of the twelve or fifteen largest cities, each of which had from four to eight dailies. Most notable of the papers with broken files are the Chicago *Times,* the Chicago *Democrat,* the Philadelphia *Evening Journal,* and the New York *Day-Book.* Files of the Philadelphia *Evening Argus* and the Cincinnati *Courier* appear to be unknown. The surviving volumes of county-seat and village

3

weeklies are almost beyond number. While there are only ten or twelve extensive newspaper libraries in the North, nearly every city has files of local papers in the public library or in a city or county historical society collection. Yale and Harvard have the only large holdings belonging to universities, but a number of state historical societies possess important collections, some of which are readily accessible to graduate schools. Three of these deserve special mention: those of Wisconsin, Ohio, and Pennsylvania. There are good collections in the public libraries of Boston and New York, in the Library of Congress, and at the American Antiquarian Society. In some states local files have been deposited with county auditors or clerks of courts. Most newspaper offices have preserved their own papers, and some have acquired the files of defunct rivals. Winifred Gregory's *Union List of Newspapers,* published in 1937, is an accurate and helpful guide to newspaper depositories.

The editorials in these volumes express the sentiments of northern editors during what were perhaps the most crucial ten months since the winning of American independence. In that brief time, events moved rapidly. September, 1860, opened the active phase of the presidential campaign, and editors wrote of secession and the preservation of the Union and perhaps of coercion, just as they had in 1852 and 1856, but nobody in the North bought a gun or refused a southern order for goods. By the following June all was different. From the confusion of counsel emerged the resolution to impose the northern will by force of arms. The rapidity of the transition left some editors dismayed, others prayerful, still others buoyant, but none speechless. As one of them remarked, "We have lived a century in six months." June closed with a rising clamor for "traitors' blood." Within three weeks the northern press coerced the administration into the battle at Bull Run.

The search for the solution to such a riddle of human conduct leads to the exploration of the documents of those startling days: the letters, diaries, public records, sermons, magazines, and newspapers. In all of them together may be found the best answer, not the perfect but the best possible answer. Newspaper editorials, for their part, reveal the sentiments of northern editors, not the sentiments of the North. It seems, however, that the editors of 1860–1861, free from copyrighted sentiments and newspaper chains, representing every rural and urban section of the North, every political party, every economic and religious group, must have been almost "representative" in their thoughts and feelings. In small population centers their offices were the favored exchanges of "local intelligence," and almost invariably the editors themselves paired off to cross quills in provincial politics. Many became party leaders by way of editorial exposition; others became editors to make vocational capital of party leadership. Most of them had the common touch: What else could have sold the bleak sheets of 1860? They were certainly far better spokesmen of their times than are the editors of modern newspapers; and the conclusion seems warranted that they were the best spokesmen of their day.

— The transition from peace to war suggests many questions: questions concerning the promises and fears of each party in the presidential campaign, the evaluation of secession threats, the impact of the ordinances of secession, the acceptance or rejection of compromise, the feasibility of peaceable separation, the score of conciliation proposals, the conduct of Buchanan, Davis, and Lincoln, the restiveness and hopefulness of the North during the apparently policyless months of February and March, the gradual realization of the administration's decision to coerce, the challenge at Sumter, the early confusion in the public's resolution to support the administration, the emergence of a consolidated northern Unionism, and the fanciful strategy of composing-room generals. In the gifted language of Horace Greeley and in the rustic phrase of printer-editors, free-state journals urged their answers to all these and like questions of the sectional crisis. Their editorials are historical documents filled with the emotionalism of one of the greatest tragedies in history: hate, hope, greed, charity, resolution, resignation, humor, even humor. The authors were the northern editors who experienced the metamorphosis of 1860–1861 that is the subject-matter of these volumes.

The secession crisis may be said to have begun with the Democratic National Convention of 1860, meeting on April 23 at Charleston, South Carolina. The convention adopted a platform which reaffirmed the Cincinnati resolutions of 1856 and promised to abide by future decisions of the Supreme Court on the status of slavery in the territories. Then, finding it impossible to nominate a presidential candidate under the rule requiring two-thirds of a full convention, it adjourned to meet in Baltimore on June 18. At Baltimore the forces of Stephen A. Douglas controlled the seating of delegates and preferred the claims of newly elected Douglas delegates to those of delegates originally accredited to the Charleston convention. The southern-rights men, including some Northerners, withdrew, and in a separate assembly nominated John C. Breckinridge and Joseph Lane on a platform which asserted the constitutional obligation of Congress to protect slavery in the territories. Meanwhile, the Douglas party had nominated Douglas and Herschel V. Johnson. It retained the Charleston platform but added a resolution again to pledge its support of all decisions that might be handed down by the Supreme Court on the status of slavery in the territories.

Two other parties with their nominees had already entered the campaign. The new National Constitutional Union party, representing twenty-four states but dominated by the border slave states, met in Baltimore and nominated John Bell and Edward Everett. Its platform was simply a vow to support "the Constitution of the country, the union of the States, and the enforcement of the laws." In May the Republicans at Chicago had nominated Abraham Lincoln and Hannibal Hamlin. Their platform denounced the principle of popular sovereignty, denied the power of Congress or territorial legislatures to sustain slavery in the territories, condemned secession as treason, and approved the homestead measure which had already passed the House of Representatives.

Early in the campaign, a so-called Fusion movement appeared in all of the northern states, but was especially active in the East. Its sponsors endeavored to combine the opposition to the Republicans in order to maneuver Lincoln out of a majority in the electoral college and thus throw the election into the House of Representatives. There—in balloting by states—it was hoped that a compromise Democratic-Unionist candidate might be elected. Fusion was actually effected in only four states: New York, New Jersey, Pennsylvania, and Rhode Island.

The campaign itself was vigorous and colorful. Orators of all parties crossed and recrossed the land, speaking in music halls, opera houses, and from specially built platforms in public squares. Torch-light processions led by Lincoln "Wide-Awakes" caught the popular fancy and evoked parades of equally glamorous "Little Giants." The candidates themselves were everywhere acclaimed by the shouting faithful. Despite the volleying and thundering and viewing with alarm, few nonpartisan editors attributed to the election that crucial and decisive character that historians have assigned to it. The confident Republicans swore by the Constitution and the laws, and so did the other parties. The Democrats deplored the schism that foretold defeat, but they vowed party reunion and victory in 1864. Campaign tactics were not more reprehensible than on earlier occasions, the Springfield *Republican* even declaring that the country had achieved new and higher standards of political sportsmanship.

The issues of the campaign were confused. The status of slavery in the territories, supposedly the dominant issue, was subject not only to the fortunes of the election but also to the actions of the Supreme Court. The Republicans pledged themselves to a program apparently declared unconstitutional in the Dred Scott case. Just how was that decision to be reversed? The Douglas Democrats and the Constitutional Unionists pledged themselves to the rulings of the court, whatever those might be. The Breckinridge Democrats accepted the Dred Scott decision, but denied the validity of a possible reversal. Thus, control of the Executive and Congress would in itself be insufficient to enable any party to choose and enact a particular territorial policy. The tariff was a local issue, and neither Republicans nor Democrats had identical principles in Iowa and Pennsylvania. The Republicans were emphatic in support of homestead legislation, but Douglas himself had repeatedly championed homestead proposals. Republicans appealed to labor votes by emphasizing the unfairness of the competition of free and slave labor, while to win the same votes Democrats pictured the migration of hordes of free Negroes from the cotton states to northern mill towns. Charges of corruption against the Buchanan administration, particularly of the Department of War, and condemnation of the "Lecompton fraud" provided grist for party mills, but honesty in public office did not figure in the debates between Douglas men and Lincoln men, for the Buchanan blessing had gone to Breckinridge, and he alone was called upon to defend the administration. The feelings between Douglas and Buchanan were bitter.

All parties appealed to the robust American nationalism, everywhere interpreted as "Unionism." On this issue the Republicans, strictly a northern party, were on the defensive, yet they insisted that the only assurance of perpetual union lay in the triumph of the Republican candidate, and they urged his election to defeat the sectionalism which they attributed to Douglas and Breckinridge. Thus, while Lincoln editors denounced Breckinridge Democracy as disunionism, Douglas Democracy as treason, and Bell Unionism as evasion, they preached the preservation of the Union through the destruction of the slave power in the councils of the nation. Slavery, they argued, was sectional, freedom was national; the victory of freedom, therefore, was the victory of nationalism. They declared that they harbored no intentions of invading the legal rights of the southern states and that they sought only to use the authority that would be assigned to Congress when the Supreme Court correctly interpreted the Constitution. They professed to believe that southern rights would remain uninjured so long as Congress worked within constitutional limitations, as it must. In answer to this contention the Democrats repeatedly pointed out that either the Republican party would prove false to its antislavery platform or it would declare war on southern rights, for the greatest of those rights was that of maintaining and cherishing the institution that supported southern economy and the southern social system.

The Douglas press, next to the Republican the most powerful in the North, declared that a Douglas victory was the one guarantee of the Union. Popular sovereignty alone, its journals asserted, offered the inhabitants of a territory an opportunity to determine their own institutions, and it alone was loyal to the sacred American principle of government by consent of the governed; it was the golden mean between the Breckinridge ultimatum of slavery protection and the Republican mandate of abolition. To the Douglas Democracy, Republicanism was offensive northern sectionalism, Breckinridge Democracy was equally offensive southern sectionalism, and Bell Unionism was without principle, conviction, or hope.

Breckinridge editors paraded the grievances of the South and frequently pointed out extenuating factors in slavery. They denounced abolitionism and all its prophets and implored Americans to see that southern institutions and southern economy would collapse if the country accepted the leadership of northern politicians who aimed at political revolution. Not in the South and not in Breckinridge Democracy, they declared, but in the North and in Black Republicanism lay the peril to the Union. The Constitution, they insisted, was the ark of safety and union when correctly understood. To them, of course, a correct understanding meant the acceptance of the Dred Scott decision.

The Bell journals exalted the Union, glorified the Constitution, and pleaded for a return to the good old days of harmony and national pride. The crisis was to them a matter of feeling and not of measures; and for its alleviation they asked a change of heart and not an array of acts and resolutions. The Bell strength was in the Border States and was popularly regarded as including a disproportionately large number of older men. John Bell himself was sixty-three and his running mate was sixty-six.

The Union-saving professions of all four parties when the preservation of the Union was itself not a formal issue prompted questions on the underlying intentions of party leaders and on the eventual result of party programs: disunion might be a secret ambition or it might be an unlooked-for consequence. Thus the voters of 1860 developed a general suspicion and confusion of mind; devoted to the Union as they were told they should be, they sensed a fundamental moral issue, but only individually could they translate it into right and wrong ways of voting. This elusive moral issue concerned the theory of the Union, the

right of self-government, and the "arrogance" of the "slaveocracy."
Somehow, government by consent of the governed and majority rule
did not square, yet both were part and parcel of the American faith.
If "the destiny of the republican model of government" were "staked
on the experiment intrusted to the hands of the American people," as
Washington declared, how would an American of 1860 vote to sustain
republicanism? Did the Declaration of Independence, presumably rejecting slavery, take precedence over the Constitution, accepting slavery?
Was "popular sovereignty" a territorial right or only a national privilege? Did minorities have any rights that majorities were bound to respect? Was the "arrogance" of southern "Bombastes Furiosos" a threat
to republicanism or a resolution to defend republicanism? Surely, in all
this, there was a moral issue. What was it?

Widely branded as abolitionists who preferred disunion to slavery,
the Republicans defended themselves by insisting upon the identity of
Republicanism and Unionism. Northern voters, they realized, must not
be permitted to regard votes for Lincoln as votes for disunion. It was
true that Northerners hated slavery, but equally true that many of
them were resolved that there must be no encouragement of a party
which, if elected, might violate southern rights and provide moral if
not constitutional grounds for secession. Consequently, Republican editors had no choice but to deny the seriousness of southern threats to
withdraw from the Union in the event of Lincoln's election. Almost
unanimously they responded to secession threats with charges of "humbug," "bullying game," "scare stuff," "empty sham," and "chronic disease." The attitude of the *Central Illinois Gazette,* of Champaign City,
was representative. On November 7 it declared that after "some sharp
crimination and recrimination among the Quattle bums . . . all will
be quiet and peaceful, and the Union will be safe—not having been
in danger."

Douglas editors, on the other hand, sought to blast Republican
chances by insisting that the secession threats of southern journals were
the pronouncements of desperate men and that Lincoln's election would
bring disunion. To these editors, secession was an imminent danger
which they implored the North to avert. They took up the cries of
compromise, concession, peaceable separation, each in its own setting
of circumstance. Perhaps to win reconciliation through northern envy,
perhaps to intimate the unthinkableness of coercion, they pictured the
prosperity of a southern confederacy. They always laid the crisis to the
sectionalism of the Republicans, and they frequently blamed New England Republicans in particular. The attitude of the Douglas press was

fairly stated by the Bedford *Gazette*, of Pennsylvania, on October 12: "No man with a thimblefull of brains in his head can fail to see that the triumph of a sectional party, whose avowed object is to make war upon the other half of the Confederacy, leads inevitably to a dissolution of the Union."

The Breckinridge press divided in responding to charges of disunionism. Some of their organs, like the Boston *Post* and the Hartford *Times*, denied that the southern states intended secession and termed disunion threats a "panic game" begun by the Republicans. Other Breckinridge papers, like the New Haven *Register* and the Philadelphia *Pennsylvanian*, expected secession to follow Lincoln's election. Bell editors generally feared the secession threats.

With the approach of November 6, a Republican victory became a foregone conclusion. Douglas editors urged their fellows to courage and industry, but their bitterness against the Breckinridge Democracy suggested expectations of defeat. Following the election, Republicans described secession threats as called bluffs and dismissed Carolinian steps toward a state convention as moves to save face. They expected separationist brag to "fizzle out" as it had on many occasions since the bitter debates on the Missouri Compromise, and they looked to see southern hot-heads overwhelmed by southern Unionism. With the growing realization that secession was more than idle talk, Republican editors divided their admonitions to the South between "be gone and good riddance" and "a million men will spring to arms to defend the Union." The opposition parties, now merging into a compromise front, implored the Republicans to choose their course with patriotism rather than partisanship.

The editorial discussions of southern policy led naturally to appraisals of the "right of secession." During the weeks following the election, editors of all parties assumed that secession as a constitutional right was not in question, for they had not yet arrived at the point where they sought legal justification for coercion. On the contrary, the southern claim to a right of peaceable withdrawal was countenanced out of reverence for the natural law principle of government by consent of the governed. This response constituted another rejection of "coerced allegiance," a rejection proclaimed countless times during the months preceding the outbreak of war. With many editors, however, changing tempers later produced a willingness to oppose the southern course with whatever arguments were available, and of those the denial of secession as a constitutional right ranked first among a people with a stubborn faith in legal processes. The southern program, editors then asserted, actually invoked not a right of secession but the right of revolution. To this doctrine northern editors without exception gave lip service, but almost unanimously they declared that it could be exercised only for proper cause. The determination of the propriety of the cause they reserved to themselves; such an argument, of course, denied the right of revolution. Thus, without ever having admitted the right of secession, many editors veered from acquiescence to opposition on the practical question of peaceable separation.

During late November and early December, editors of all parties looked with eagerness to President Buchanan's approaching message to Congress. Yet the message, like Buchanan himself, never had a chance. Editorial pens, dipped in party ink, were poised on December 5 as they were later on March 4. Buchanan supporters were too few; their approval was lost in the clamor of Lincoln and Douglas editors who denounced as a fallacy the President's contention that the absence of a constitutional right of secession did not imply a right of executive coercion.

The winter months of 1860–1861 produced bitter argument on the appropriate policy of the government. As topics germane to the controversy, editors wrote at length on the economics and morality of slavery, the attitude of foreign powers in the event of disunion, the rôle of the tariff in the economics of the nation, sectional resources, Andrew Jackson's disposition of the South Carolina nullification venture, the meaning of the Constitution, the interpretation of Lincoln's inaugural, and countless others. Democratic journals urged conciliation and compromise and almost frantically approved most of the many "plans"; Republican journals, with few exceptions, rejected the principle involved in "concession" and opposed all specific measures aimed at reconciliation. Repeatedly, a host of Democrats and a few Republicans pleaded for "peaceable separation," while just as often Republicans demanded "the enforcement of the laws." In their fight for northern concessions Breckinridge Democrats and Douglas Democrats stood side by side, and the Bell Unionists, already without even the sentimental integrity present during the presidential campaign, stood with them. Pleas for compromise and pleas for peaceable separation appeared in the same journals at about the same moment. Always, Democratic editors preferred compromise and Union to disunion, but when it appeared that the Republicans might eschew all settlement proposals and choose between peaceable separation and coercion, the choice of most Democrats was peace and disunion. When changing prospects suggested that the issue was compromise or peaceable separation, then the Democrats rejected disunion and fought for compromise. It was altogether a matter of getting the best that could be had.

Northern editors took little notice of the firing on the *Star of the West,* the successive ordinances of secession, or the organization of the Confederate States of America. They were more interested in the progress of southern military measures and in the expropriation of federal properties in the South. Still more, however, they were concerned with the reports of southern bombast and trickery, and those reports, extravagant and inciting as they were, they fashioned to partisan ends.

Inevitably, President Lincoln's inaugural evoked Republican praise and Democratic censure. Later, his taking of the northern pulse by a reported decision to abandon Fort Sumter disclosed the reluctance of Republicans to yield to Confederate pretensions and the eagerness of Democrats to taunt the administration with charges of retreat. The response of the Democrats may have figured significantly in suggesting a conditional quality to their peace professions. On the appearance in early April of an apparent willingness on the part of the administration to attempt coercion, Democratic editors with virtual unanimity protested, but Republican editors acclaimed the impending struggle as a "mission for humanity."

Lincoln's attempt to provision Fort Sumter was widely interpreted in the northern press as revealing a decision by the administration to force the issue of submission or war. The Confederates accepted the challenge. The Republicans at once gave the war full support; many Democrats, however, withheld their approval until President Lincoln's call for troops on April 15 made the war policy explicit rather than implicit. The issue was then one of loyalty, and the response was overwhelmingly in support of the administration. Most Democratic journals announced support of the war but at the same time proclaimed its needlessness, its wickedness, or its futility. They would not be traitors, they insisted, but they would remember and punish the war guilt of the Republicans. Here and there, however, a powerful journal called upon the Republicans to reverse the war policy; a few sought to arouse opposition.

The general acceptance of the administration's leadership neither rested upon nor immediately inspired a common view of the purposes of coercion. In rapidly mounting numbers, however, editors accepted the objective of the preservation of the Union, but differed widely as to the meaning of the phrase. It did not commonly have the geographical connotation that it has to-day; to many it was a political or legal term, and it meant the maintenance of sovereignty, stability, prestige, or

honor. Its power vindicated, some editors argued, the federal government could honorably permit disunion. A few contended that it should
then even compel the withdrawal of the disaffected states. Other editors
viewed the abolition of slavery rather than reunion as the condition of
peace. With this discussion of war aims the country was fairly launched
into civil war.

The Southerners of 1860–1861, in seeking to alter the *status quo,* had
to choose a line of action before the North could formulate a policy
in response to that action. Thus, while the course of at least seven
southern states was set with the adoption of their ordinances of secession and became almost unalterable on the organization of the Confederacy on February 4, at the time of the latest of these events northern
newspapers were filled with discussions of the right of revolution, peaceable separation, the enforcement of the laws, compromise proposals, the
Republican platform, and a hundred other subjects related to the crisis.
So far as northern editorials reveal it, there was no northern "stand"
on February 4, 1861, or even on the inauguration of Lincoln a month
later. The bulk of significant southern editorials on the secession crisis
therefore appeared before the ordinances of the Gulf states; the bulk of
northern editorials followed them.

The determination of northern policy was not left to argument alone:
emotionalism was as real throughout the Secession Winter as in any
crisis in American history. A free press exploited its freedom to print
and broadcast a thousand inciting rumors taken from "correspondence
to the editor" and frequently purporting to reveal the experiences of "a
gentleman lately traveling in the South." Editors, like tradesmen and
farmers, rallied to the defense of long cherished interests and ideals,
frequently, of course, concealing punitive and selfish purposes with the
nobler arguments of constitutional and moral "rights" and "duties."
On many occasions, however, they spoke straight from the heart—spoke
bitterly about plots to assassinate the President-elect or to capture the
city of Washington, about obstruction of the Mississippi, abuse of Northerners in the South, the cruelty of slavery, grandiose schemes of southern
empire and monarchy, free-trade competition, repudiation of southern
debts, confiscation of federal property, southern alliances with European
powers, denial of the suffrage and representative government in the
South, and countless other "wrongs," actual or rumored. These revela-
tions of feeling, lacking the logic and dignity of constitutional argument, were nevertheless very much a part of northern newspaper sentiment and must be included in a selection of representative editorials.

While northern editors were often concerned with the legality of the right of secession and with the morality of the right of revolution, their denial of either or both of these did not inevitably lead to a support of coercion. A thousand incidents of fact and fancy divorced the question of coercion, compromise, or separation from abstract and dispassionate constitutionality and morality. Consequently, few northern journals presented any consistency through the secession months. A declaration for coercion or for peaceable separation on one date offered scarcely more than a presumption as to the attitude of the editor on a later date. An extreme but not an isolated example was Horace Greeley's shift from his "depart in peace" benediction of November to his "death to traitors" invocation of March.

By virtue of its numbers and the influence of certain of its members, the leading party press in the northern states during the Secession Winter was the Republican. Its journals outnumbered those of the combined opposition; and it dominated the presses of the four largest urban centers: New York and Brooklyn, Philadelphia, Boston, and Cincinnati.

In the New York area, the *Tribune,* the *Times,* the *Evening Post,* the *Courier and Enquirer,* and the *Commercial Advertiser* were Lincoln papers. In addition, the Brooklyn *City News,* the *Advertiser* and the *Mercury* of Newark, and the *Courier and Advertiser* of Jersey City, all in the New York urban area, were Republican. The newly established New York *World* professed independence but expressed radical Republican sentiments.

Philadelphia had three Republican organs: the *Daily News,* the *Evening Bulletin,* and the old and influential *North American and United States Gazette.* Boston had five: the *Advertiser,* the *Atlas and Bee,* the *Journal,* the *Traveller,* and the *Saturday Evening Gazette.* Cincinnati had two: the *Gazette* and the widely quoted *Commercial.*

Here and there, outside these urban areas, other journals of importance carried the Republican banner. In New England the leading ones were the Portland *Advertiser,* the Providence *Journal,* the Springfield *Republican,* the Hartford *Courant,* the Hartford *Evening Press,* the New Haven *Journal and Courier,* and the New Haven *Palladium.* Outside of New England in the East were the Albany *Evening Journal,* the *Commercial Advertiser* and the *Express* of Buffalo, the Rochester *Evening Express,* the Syracuse *Journal,* the Harrisburg *Telegraph,* the Pittsburgh *Gazette,* and the *National Republican,* established in early 1861, in Washington, D. C. The *Intelligencer* in Wheeling; the *Leader* and the *Herald* in Cleveland; the *State Journal* in Columbus; the *Journal* in Indianapolis; the *Advertiser* and the *Tribune* in Detroit; the *Tribune,* the *Journal,* and the *Democrat* in Chicago; the *State Journal* in

Springfield; and the *Sentinel* and the *Wisconsin* in Milwaukee—these belong in the roll of the more important Republican journals of the nation. Still smaller cities, covering the North from Bangor to Des Moines, had able and locally influential Republican organs.

The prominent Douglas papers of the North were the Boston *Herald,* the Providence *Post,* the Albany *Atlas and Argus,* the Buffalo *Courier,* the Buffalo *Republic,* the Brooklyn *Evening Standard,* the Philadelphia *Press,* the Washington *States and Union,* the Pittsburgh *Post,* the Cincinnati *Enquirer,* the Cleveland *Plain Dealer,* the Indianapolis *Sentinel,* the Detroit *Free Press,* the Chicago *Times,* the Springfield *Register,* and the Milwaukee *Press and News.* Only the religious *Sun* and the weekly *Leader* supported Douglas in New York City. The Boston *Herald* early approved coercion; and the editor of the Philadelphia *Press,* John W. Forney, sold out to Lincoln, as earlier, abandoning Buchanan, he had sold out to Douglas. The Chicago *Times,* the Cincinnati *Enquirer,* and the Providence *Post* proved the stanchest of Douglas journals.

The leading organs of the Breckinridge Democracy were the New York *Herald,* the New York *Journal of Commerce,* the New York *News,* and the Brooklyn *Eagle.* All of these, however, were lost to the Breckinridge candidacy—not to the Breckinridge platform—when they joined in the Fusion anti-Republican clamor and then later accepted the Fusion ticket. More persevering Breckinridge papers were the Boston *Post,* the Newark *Evening Journal,* the Philadelphia *Pennsylvanian,* and the Washington *Constitution.* The *Journal* opposed the war even after Sumter, while the *Pennsylvanian* and the *Constitution* ceased publication before that date. The editor of the *Constitution,* William M. Browne, became assistant secretary of state in the Confederacy. Lesser Breckinridge organs were the Bangor *Daily Union,* the Concord *Democratic Standard,* the Hartford *Daily Times,* the Syracuse *Courier and Union,* the Harrisburg *Patriot and Union,* the Columbus *Capital City Fact,* and the Cleveland *National Democrat.* With the exception of the Madison, Wisconsin, *Argus and Democrat,* there was no influential Breckinridge paper west of Ohio. The Bangor *Daily Union,* the Concord *Democratic Standard,* and the Cleveland *National Democrat* died before the close of 1861; the Madison *Argus and Democrat* disappeared in 1862 and the Columbus *Capital City Fact* in 1864. Thus, only five of the twelve leading northern papers loyal to Breckinridge in 1860 survived the Civil War.

The leading Bell papers were the Washington *National Intelligencer,* the Boston *Courier,* the Philadelphia *Evening Journal,* the Cincinnati *Times,* and the Jersey City *American Standard.* The *Intelligencer* was one of the most respected journals in the country; the *Courier* was supposedly popular with Harvard people; the *Evening Journal* failed to survive the War; the *Times* was early won to coercion; the *Standard* was clamoring against war long after Sumter. The Troy *Whig* also supported Bell.

It was not only in these metropolitan and larger city journals, however, that the thoughts and sentiments of the North were expressed; they were presented in the papers of a score of smaller cities: Burlington, Lynn, Roxbury, Worcester, Lowell, Newport, Utica, Trenton, Camden, Reading, Erie, Toledo, Fort Wayne, Grand Rapids, Peoria, Quincy, Davenport, Dubuque, Des Moines, St. Paul, and many lesser centers of population. Perhaps, as they stood between the metropolitan centers of the day on the one hand and the villages and farms on the other, these small cities most fairly represent the United States of secession times.

The editorials of the secession months came from the pens of some of the greatest figures in the history of American journalism. It was indeed a propitious moment for editorial greatness, for personal journalism was in its heyday: the cheap press with its wide circulation had arrived, but stock-company ownership and staffs of editorial writers were uncommon, and syndicated features were unknown. The New York *Tribune,* for instance, was "Horace Greeley's paper" and had been for almost twenty years. Other New York journals were likewise the personal organs of their editors and always they were linked: Henry J. Raymond with the *Times,* James Gordon Bennett with the *Herald,* James Watson Webb with the *Courier and Enquirer,* Gerard Hallock with the *Journal of Commerce,* and William Cullen Bryant with the *Evening Post.*

Even outside of New York City there were editors of national reputation: William Winston Seaton of the Washington *National Intelligencer,* Joseph Medill of the Chicago *Tribune,* Samuel Bowles of the Springfield, Massachusetts, *Republican,* John Forney of the Philadelphia *Press,* Thurlow Weed of the Albany *Evening Journal,* and Murat Halsted of the Cincinnati *Commercial.* The editors were legion whose reputations extended the length and breadth of their own states and frequently beyond. There was George Lunt of the Boston *Courier,* Morton McMichael of the Philadelphia *North American,* Charles Gordon Greene of the Boston *Post,* James Hawley of the Hartford *Evening Press,* James Gray of the Cleveland *Plain Dealer,* Samuel Medary of the Columbus *Crisis,* Edward McLean of the Cincinnati *Enquirer,* John Wentworth of the Chicago *Democrat,* E. W. McComas of the Chicago

Times, and James Sheahan of the Chicago *Post.* Scores of other editors of the secession period have surviving local reputations. The men behind all of the newspapers quoted in these volumes are listed at the close of the second volume.

Northern Editorials on Secession has been compiled with particular regard to the faithfulness with which it presents the sentiments of the northern press and, within that press, the sentiments of the journals of the various sections and parties of the North. The editorials of this selection are therefore apportioned among the states in the ratio of the distribution of population in 1860 and among parties in the ratio of the popular vote in the election of the same year. While two factors —the varying size and number of cities in the respective states and the Fusion vote in four states—complicate this distribution, it is relatively accurate. The District of Columbia, Rhode Island, and, to a lesser degree, Massachusetts, are somewhat overrepresented, due to the number of good newspapers and the relatively small population in each. Indiana, on the other hand, is underrepresented because it had a population disproportionately large for the number of its urban inhabitants. In the party distribution, the Breckinridge press is overrepresented at the expense of the Douglas press, a disparity arising from the situation in the New York metropolitan area. The Fusionists are not regarded as a party, but their supporting newspapers are credited to the candidates which they favored before Fusion was effected. Only by this classification can the attitude of the papers toward slavery be indicated.

The subjects chosen for this selection are those most relevant to the theme of the transition from peace to war. They are listed in whatever of chronological order may be possible, and within each subject-group the editorials also are presented in chronological sequence. The subjects, twenty-seven in number, may be defined as follows:

I. *The Campaign of 1860*—Discussions of the issues of the election by Lincoln, Douglas, Breckinridge, Bell, and independent editors. Lincoln journals numbered fully half the newspapers of the North; and Douglas, Breckinridge, and Bell papers followed in decreasing numbers. "Fusion" won sporadic support in most states, particularly in the East, and powerful support in metropolitan New York. Important independent journals numbered fewer than half a dozen.

The main formal issue in the election was the status of slavery in the territories, but editors adopted far-reaching implications of that issue as the subject matter of their editorials. They ventured into discussions of secession, the morality of slavery, alleged southern and Republican conspiracies to disrupt the Union, and a host of related matters. Not-

withstanding the height of party feeling, the campaign itself was regarded by the press as not more bitter than certain earlier ones. On
October 2 the Springfield *Republican,* of Massachusetts, declared that
the freedom of the campaign from personalities and vituperation demonstrated the capacity of democratic governments for spiritual growth.

II. *The Prospect of Secession*—Speculations on the future of the
secession movement in the southern states. These editorials fell within
the period between the election and the secession of South Carolina;
and they discussed the possibility and consequences of actual recourse
to ordinances of secession in an attempt to withdraw from the Union.
In them Republican editors continued their preëlection skepticism into
December, whereas Democrats hailed developments in the South as the
vindication of their campaign warnings. In addition to speculations on
the resort to secession ordinances, editors advanced guesses on the course
of the federal government in the event of the adoption of such ordinances, they painted both bright and somber pictures of the future of
a southern nation, and they raised questions about the attitude of foreign powers toward a free-trade, cotton-growing American republic.
Frequently, editors asserted that the South should not be coerced into
allegiance. The classic statement of this sentiment came from Horace
Greeley on November 9: "We hope never to live in a republic whereof
one section is pinned to the residue by bayonets."

III. *Buchanan's Message to Congress*—Reviews of that portion of
President Buchanan's Message to Congress on December 5 which dealt
with the sectional crisis and the prospective secession of South Carolina
and other southern states. The President charged the North with aggressions on the South, and in a narrowly legalistic interpretation of
the Constitution denied both the right of secession and the right of
the President to coerce states of the Union. He pleaded with the North
to cease its attacks upon slavery and the South, and he urged the repeal
of the Personal Liberty Acts enacted by a number of the northern states.
This stand was denounced as cowardly, inconsistent, and traitorous by
practically every Lincoln paper and by most Douglas journals. The
speech was approved in the North by the Breckinridge press, a few
Douglas papers, an occasional Bell organ, and a few independent journals, notably the Providence *Evening Press.*

IV. *Secession: Right or Revolution?*—Characterizations of secession
through unilateral action as a "right" and as "revolution," drawn from
the period between November 6 and December 20. Editorials before November 6 were written with the prime object of winning votes, whereas
after December 20 they were written in an atmosphere that was already

filling with rumors and criminations that made consideration of the
right of secession increasingly less abstract. In the six weeks between the
presidential election and the secession of South Carolina, northern editors most closely approached an objective contemplation of the right of
secession asserted by southern constitutionalists. Through a supposed
identity with the principle of government by consent of the governed,
many northern editors, including Republicans, at first gave acceptance
to the right of secession; soon, however, they began to qualify their
acceptance with stipulations of procedure; and they concluded by denying the right *in toto*. This course, step by step, was followed again and
again by northern editors. A perfect example was provided by the Indianapolis *Journal;* another, almost as good, was presented by the New
York *Tribune.*

V. *"The Enforcement of the Laws"*—Appeals for the restoration of
federal authority in the seceded states. "The Enforcement of the Laws,"
a phrase suggestive of law and order and good citizenship, was the battle-
cry of editors prepared for a resort to arms. "Have We a Government?"
and "Is the Union a Rope of Sand?" were likewise popular among "coercionist" editors. These editorials first appeared in large number in
mid-December as the compunction against "coerced allegiance" lost its
flush; they continued in strength until on the eve of Fort Sumter the
war preparations of the administration set for their authors the congenial labors of justifying the employment of military force and proclaiming the objectives of coercion. It was a truly exceptional Lincoln
paper, like the Fort Wayne *Times* or the Newburyport *Herald,* that was
not thoroughly coercionist by the time that the war policy of the administration became apparent. The four great Lincoln dailies of New
York City were then coercionist: the *Tribune,* the *Times,* the *Evening
Post,* and the *Courier and Enquirer.* An occasional Douglas paper, like
the Boston *Herald,* and an occasional Bell paper, like the Cincinnati
Times, were ready for war before the engagement in Charleston harbor.

VI. *Conciliation and Compromise*—Discussions of the principle involved in proposals to restore the Union by granting some of the demands of the seceded states. "Conciliation," suggestive of reasonableness
and good will, was an approving Democratic word; "compromise," suggestive of abandoned morality, was a disapproving Republican word.
Some Lincoln editors, however, would accept "conciliation," but by the
word they meant little more than a willingness to point out the error
of southern ways. "Concession" had the same flavor as "compromise,"
and so was unacceptable to Republican editors. The Chicago *Tribune*
waged the most relentless campaign in the northern press against the

relinquishment of any part of the Chicago Platform; and even Greeley, in the New York *Tribune,* announced that he preferred the platform to fifty Unions. The prevailing Republican attitude was one of resolute opposition to the principle of conciliation and compromise; occasionally, however, editors promised more friendly consideration for compromise proposals once southern acceptance was assured. Democratic editors, of both Douglas and Breckinridge leanings, and Bell editors were generally favorable to compromise.

VII. *Measures for Peace*—Analyses of specific proposals for averting both secession and war. These editorials suggest the possible results of compromise programs and then pass judgment on their acceptability. On any particular proposal the attitude of the editors of the various parties was just about their stand on the principle of compromise: Republicans demurred and Democrats approved.

Measures for peace were at times mere proposals for setting up the machinery of negotiation. Examples of such measures were a national convention and the Washington Conference Convention. Other proposals dealt with concrete issues and made definitive stipulations. Examples of these were the Crittenden Compromise, the Border States Plan, the Kellogg Plan, and the Adams Plan.

VIII. *Peaceable Separation*—Pleas in defense of peaceful disunion. Repeatedly, northern editors insisted that "we want no conquered provinces"; and as frequently they deplored all thought of "subjugating millions of freemen fighting in defense of their homes." William M. Browne, editor of the Washington *Constitution,* might rejoice that the South had seceded, but the rank and file of Democratic editors felt differently. They might condone secession, but they also lamented it. When they spoke for peaceable separation, as most of them did on occasion, they did so only because they loved peace and self-government more than union, or because they hated disunion, alone, less than they hated disunion with war. There was, however, another set of alternatives: on the one hand was peaceable separation, on the other conciliation. Coercion was outside, unthinkable. Presented in this fashion, the choice of Democrats was conciliation; then, conciliation denied, a harder choice took its place. Then it was that most Democratic editors chose separation in peace.

While peaceable separation was as yet only a possible future course and an alternative to compromise, and while the abrasive concomitants of the separation process were as yet unexperienced, Republicans frequently accepted it; but when it became an immediate issue and the alternative to compulsory union, they rejected it. In the sense in which the Democrats favored peaceable separation when they believed that it was an issue in practical politics, the Republicans never accepted it. It was as an actual, present issue that a separation in peace was discussed in the editorials in this group.

IX. *New Confederacies and a Free City*—Speculations on new political alignments to supersede the old American Union. Some imaginative editors envisaged new confederacies, perhaps empires, rising on the North American continent, for, they insisted, once the constitutional compact was broken, the several states would enter into such new affiliations as promised most for their security and prosperity. Editors dreamed of new nations on the Pacific, in the Southwest, in the Northwest, in the Mississippi Valley, and in New England. Sometimes in these visions Canada, Mexico, and the Caribbean islands played unwitting rôles. Mayor Wood, of New York, perhaps a dreamer but a politician first, spoke to his Common Council of possible future greatness for a Free City of New York.

While editorial empire-building was not widespread—nor perhaps seriously regarded—it was pursued by able editors and powerful journals. It was, moreover, seldom condemned. In a signed letter appearing in the Washington *National Intelligencer* on January 18, General Winfield Scott sketched the boundaries of four confederacies which he believed that Nature had decreed for North America. Not only did the general do this without a word of reproof from any paper of the North, but he remained throughout the crisis the nation's foremost symbol of patriotism and union.

X. *"The Everlasting Negro"*—Editorials dealing with the status, the characteristics, and the future of the Negro. Editors discussed his significance in the culture, the economics, and the politics of the nation. Two widely copied articles, "The Niggerism of the Secession Movement" and "The Everlasting Negro," respectively charged many traits of southern character to association with slaves and pointed out the presence of the Negro in every problem of American life. These editorials were widely reprinted without credit and their authorship is not altogether certain. The New York *Times,* recognizing the problem of "the everlasting Negro" and some of the difficulties of emancipation, proposed measures to modify the harshness of the institution of slavery.

XI. *The Morality of Slavery*—Editorial judgments on the ethics of slaveholding. The most uncompromising northern champions of slavery were the Concord, New Hampshire, *Democratic Standard,* the New York *Evening Day-Book,* and the New York *News.* Other journals, too, defended slavery; far more frequently, however, they merely condoned or extenuated it. The views of Lincoln papers ranged from abolitionism to apology, but they never reached downright defense. Most Douglas organs were evasive or apologetic. Antislavery editors usually assumed the immorality of slavery and only now and then wrote in condemnation of the institution. Its more valiant defenders, on the other hand, accepted the burden of proof and on occasion wrote explicitly and at length. Consequently, this selection of editorials on the morality of slavery is not representative of the numbers of the opponents and defenders of slavery but only of their sentiments.

XII. *The "Chivalry"*—Delineations of southern character as viewed by northern editors, mostly written in the heated days of early 1861. "Chivalry" was a term of contempt applied by unfriendly journalists to the slaveholding aristocracy and the non-slaveholding white men of the South who accepted and sustained the political and social philosophy of the planter class. That philosophy, these writers contended, was undemocratic and antisocial; it encouraged selfishness, brutality, and immorality, and so "sapped the foundations" of the republic. This dark picturing of southern character was long the special province of Republicans, but with the emergence of the war policy in April it was used by editors of all parties to arouse the fighting temper of the North. Provocative as such writing must have been, it had long been a favorite device with many newspapers, including, to list a few, the Boston *Atlas and Bee,* the New York *Tribune,* the Philadelphia *News,* the Philadelphia *North American,* the Chicago *Tribune,* the Toledo *Blade,* the Peoria *Transcript,* and the Quincy *Whig.*

XIII. *The Mississippi*—Discussions of the threatened closing of the great inland waterway by seceded riparian states or by the southern Confederacy. The Chicago *Tribune* alone was voluble on the subject; other journals spoke infrequently but grimly. "The great Northwest," they insisted, could never submit to the control of the mouth of the Mississippi by another power; and they used Vallandigham's words to say that the Northwest, rather than be cut off from the sea, would "cleave its way to the sea-coast with the sword." Eastern editors wrote occasionally on the economic necessity of an open river, and they usually concluded that "the great Northwest"—not the federal government—should and would defend it with might of arms. One or two editors advanced the idea that railroads and canals had altered the course of western trade and that the Mississippi might well be left to shift for itself.

XIV. *The Economics of Union*—Attempts by northern editors to analyze secession, disunion, coercion, and civil war in terms of production, markets, southern indebtedness, commerce, the national debt, and other items. The results are disappointing, for they fail to show objective thinking on the economic aspects of the crisis. Most of these editorials were mere attempts to fashion public thought and action by alarmist pictures of economic changes to come in the event of the rejection of a particular policy. They were usually Republican.

XV. *Inaugurals South and North*—Appraisals of the inaugural address of Jefferson Davis on February 11 and of Abraham Lincoln on March 4. President Davis' address was not widely reviewed in the northern press; Lincoln's inaugural, on the other hand, was eagerly awaited and anxiously studied. Republicans commonly viewed it as meaning the preservation of the Union, peacefully if possible, while Democrats variously regarded it as inflammatory, confused, and evasive. A few Democrats approved.

XVI. *The Emergence of a Policy*—Editorials of late March pleading for a definite stand on secession, and others of early April acclaiming or denouncing the administration's preparations for war.

Soon after Lincoln's inauguration, rumors reached the press that the President proposed to abandon Fort Sumter. Within a few days what had been only rumored was said "with authority." The response of the press to these reports was a demand for action. A policy—any policy— was better than continued uncertainty. Democrats clamored along with Republicans, for they felt that the administration dared not begin civil war; therefore, they believed, the "decisive policy" to issue from Washington would be one of vigorous efforts for compromise, or, failing that, one of peaceable separation. In early April the administration's stand became apparent. Republicans rejoiced, notwithstanding their lack of agreement on the objectives of coercion. Democrats, bewildered, turned savagely on the administration and the Republican party. They were resisting the war policy when the Confederates opened fire on Fort Sumter on Friday, April 12.

XVII. *The Strategy of Sumter*—Editorials purporting to see in the clash at Fort Sumter deeply laid plans of President Lincoln or of President Davis. Some of the expressions of views preceded the event and others followed it. The earlier ones may well have suggested a course of action to President Lincoln. Perhaps the most prophetic of all editorials published during the Secession Winter was that printed in the Providence *Post*, April 13, 1861, with the title, "Why?" Another noteworthy one appeared in the Indianapolis *Journal* on April 11. The one suggested the possible strategy of Lincoln at Sumter, the other that of Davis.

XVIII. *The Sequel to Sumter*—Responses of northern editors to the firing on Fort Sumter and to Lincoln's call for troops. Directly and in itself, the battle in Charleston harbor swung few journals to the support of the administration. Republican papers were already cheering the war policy, and Democratic papers, for the most part, stood for peace through the fight at Sumter and until the President's proclamation of April 15. Then came the storm, and it is this storm that may be regarded as "the sequel to Sumter." Even northern Breckinridge papers, like the Columbus *Capital City Fact,* were ready for the fight. The generally recusant New York *Herald* urged war support on April 16.

XIX. *Post-Sumter Pleas for Peace*—Denials that the attack on Fort Sumter need precipitate civil war and prayers for delayed military action, further efforts at reconciliation, and peaceful separation. Protesting editors, Democratic with few exceptions, were in most instances converted to war support by Lincoln's call for troops. Without enthusiasm and with strong and explicit reservations on the necessity and humanity of the war, they declined to be traitors when the issue became one of loyalty or treason. The decision was a hard one, and they confessed that it was with "hearts filled to overflowing" that they set "trembling hands" to "paper wet with tears." They cried to Heaven and to "impartial history" to witness their protestations against "the unholy war." They would fight for the Union and the flag, but with the coming of peace they would turn grimly to the business of punishing the "authors of the conflict."

By April 20 the North was resolute and substantially united. Only a few of the powerful journals persisted in efforts for peace: the Boston *Courier,* the Brooklyn *Eagle,* and the Cincinnati *Enquirer.* A few lesser ones also protested: the Hartford *Times,* the Jersey City *American Standard,* and the Dubuque *Herald.* Here and there county-seat and village papers likewise dissented.

XX. *Objects of the War*—Views of the purposes of the coercion policy. These are opinions written after the administration's call to arms, and so are discussions of the objectives accepted at a time when war was generally approved in the North. The preservation of geographical integrity, the maintenance of the government's authority, the abolition of slavery, the retention of markets, the relief of southern Unionists, and revenge were variously regarded as war aims during the week following the fall of Sumter, but during the closing days of April agreement developed rapidly on the indefinite objective of "the preservation of the Union."

XXI. *The Border States*—Discussions of the conduct and policy of the Border States, particularly Maryland, Virginia, and Kentucky. The northern press was divided between admiration for the Union-saving efforts of the Border States and scorn for their qualified Unionism. Virginia was roundly applauded and soundly abused for her leadership in reconciliation moves; and Kentucky was both toasted and denounced for her venture in "armed neutrality."

XXII. *Western Virginia*—Speculations and advice on the course of the loyal portion of the Old Dominion. Within western Virginia, editors fought bitterly on the issue of secession from the Richmond government, and loyalty to the Union was frankly subordinated to intra-state issues of taxation and representation. The Wheeling *Intelligencer* vigorously espoused both the division of the state and common action with the North. Outside editors relished the prospect of adding another free state to the Union.

XXIII. *The American Experiment*—Editorials insisting that the experiment of self-government "entrusted to the hands of the American people" was—or was not—in the moment of its supreme trial. Asserting that self-government was in its final issue, editors might interpret success as the maintenance of the Constitution to which all states had explicitly or tacitly subscribed; or they might view success as the preservation of government by consent of the governed. Both of these groups might assert the finality of the test in America. Still other editors scorned all suggestions of trial or test; the Union was at stake, they agreed, but not democratic government, for in the event of disunion democracy would prevail in both nations. Republicans had more to say on the subject than Democrats.

XXIV. *Foreign Relations*—Expressions of hope and fear arising from the problematical attitude of foreign powers, particularly England, toward the threatened disruption of the United States; and speculations on sweeping territorial changes in the New World in response to forces loosed by secession. Throughout the winter editors exchanged guesses on English intervention and they came to no conclusion. Occasionally, they ventured arm-chair conquests of Canada or Mexico to offset the loss of the seceding states. Powerful metropolitan journals were not outdone by village sheets: On December 26 the New York *Times* approved the conquest of Mexico, and on January 27 the New York *Herald* followed suit with Canada. On June 8 the *Herald* proposed the subjugation of the British Empire as a means of ending civil war in America.

XXV. *Personalities*—Character sketches of the leading men of the North and the South. While Buchanan and Lincoln were the most frequent subjects, many others were measured in the public press: Seward, Davis, Wade, Greeley, Scott, Bennett, and Stephens. The man always stood against the background of the current political crisis. Both friendly and unfriendly editors frequently ventured to prophesy final historical judgment.

XXVI. *"Sensationism" and Propaganda*—Opinions on the origin and reliability of the news letters and telegraphic reports that performed the "heavy" rôle in the drama of the secession crisis. Throughout the Secession Winter, northern journals carried a constant stream of news items depicting the "true" state of affairs in the South: cruelty, censorship, contempt for law, persecutions, slave insurrections, hatred of Northerners. True or untrue, these reports must have been incendiary. Although usually vague as to place, time, and authority, they were generally accepted as authentic by northern editors. Now and then a journal charged "sensationism" and protested against their acceptance. These charges and protests, appearing almost invariably in the Douglas press, invite a more serious study of the psychological factors in the evolution of the coercion policy.

XXVII. *Moral and Spiritual Values*—Editorials suggestive of moral and spiritual concepts. They provide the material for a revealing study of the ideology of Northerners on the eve of the great conflict. Many journals, for instance, proclaimed the "salutary" effects of war: the Madison *Patriot* believed blood-letting "a great purifyer"; the Springfield *Republican* termed war "a means of grace"; the Boston *Transcript* called the impending conflict "eminently a Christian war"; the Providence *Journal* declared that rarely had it ever been "so glorious and joyful to have a life to give" and called for more hate and less fraternizing on the battle-field. The Washington, Pennsylvania, *Reporter* demurred at the idea of killing on Sunday; and the Albany *Evening Journal* held that after the war "purer aims and more exalted conceptions of Truth and Justice will animate the People." Other journals, however, declared that war could produce only moral and spiritual loss. The New York *Journal of Commerce* protested that religious and philanthropic standards would be thrown back a quarter of a century.

The general northern support of the coercion policy completed the transition from peace to war. Within ten months, twenty million Northerners had put aside the blessings of peace and taken up the "mission for humanity" or the "unholy war." The vision of a great and powerful nation aroused to the defense of democracy and self-government, of Christianity and God, began to fade. Before the close of June editors no longer wrote of the "sublime spectacle," as many of them had written in mid-April. Instead, they voiced charges of greed and inefficiency: the "soldiers of freedom" were being issued shoddy uniforms, paper shoes, and rotten food; peculators and leeches and profiteers of every kind were everywhere; favoritism and bribery were sending trained men to the ranks and officering the army with incompetents and drunks; the government would not fight the rebels, but preferred to hurl its military might against aged Chief Justice Taney as he stood in defense of constitutional liberty. Meantime, the Lincoln administration prepared for war.

A decade later the Republicans emerged from the ordeal of civil war and reconstruction as the self-styled preservers of the Union, and for services rendered they billed the American people at four-year intervals for a quarter of a century. As for the Democrats, they learned the impregnability of success. They stilled their charges of war guilt, for they could not assail the righteousness of a cause for which countless thousands had given "their last full measure of devotion." Northern coercion, like southern secession, had been transformed from a practical intra-sectional issue into a not altogether academic intersectional issue.

I

THE CAMPAIGN OF 1860

1. Policy of the Political Parties

(Lowell Daily Journal and Courier [Lincoln], September 5, 1860)

Each of the parties having candidates for the Presidency in the field have [*sic*] some way of dealing with the slavery question; for however it may be desired to avoid it, the subject will come up. The Breckinridge party propose a slave code for its protection in the territories, not in every instance perhaps, but in the same meaning and on the same principle that the Republicans are in favor of prohibition. That is to say—they recognize the right of the slave-holder to take his slaves to a territory and hold them as property under the constitution, and his right for additional laws to protect that property, whenever necessary, until the Territory comes to form a State government, when the large majority admit the right of the people then to permit slavery to exist or exclude it, though a few deny the right of a State even to refuse protection to what they call property. The ground thus taken makes all territories slave-holding until they have reached a point where their population will justify their admission into the Union as States. Now, if it be true, that the character of the future man is to a great extent determined by the individual while a child, it is none the less true that the institutions of a State are generally decisively controlled by its action as a Territory. And if slavery is protected until the Territory becomes a State there is little hope for its emancipation when it begins to act for itself. The direct tendency of the Breckinridge policy is therefore to make all future territories of the United States, especially where the climate and soil is congenial, slave-holding ones. Now, such a settlement of the question, so contrary to teachings and legislation of the framers of the constitution and of the statesmen who followed for sixty years, and so repugnant to our sense of moral right, can never be permanent. It cannot be permanent because it is opposed to natural law, to natural and moral right. The nearer, therefore, it comes to a triumph, the more dangerous the consequences. Instinct and impulse, judgment and reason, when running in parallel lines cannot long be prevented. [*sic*] They must assert their supremacy, and any system founded upon violation of natural justice cannot command the assent and secure the support of intelligent and thoughtful men any farther than it is so essentially interwoven with the fabric of society as to render violent measures for its removal dangerous to the peace of the community. When it assumes an aggressive character and winds its folds around new communities, it is to be resisted by all who value national honor, strength and integrity.

The supporters of Mr. Douglas, while recognizing the binding obligation of a decision of the Supreme Court upon this question, and which in the last resort leads directly to the same conclusion arrived at by the friends of Mr. Breckinridge, still contend that the slavery question is a proper question for the territories to settle themselves from the earliest stages of their existence. This is also a novel theory— the product of the last few years of agitation, and born of a political exigency.—Looking to its practical results there is nothing in itself or its operation calculated to commend it to conservative and peace-loving men. Throwing the question into the arena of politics, it is calculated still more to arouse and embitter the passions and set neighbor against neighbor. A sad but pertinent illustration of popular sovereignty will be found in the unhappy history of Kansas. Even when finally settled, as in the case with that territory, amid years of fluctuation, strife and bloodshed, no principle or precedent is established.—The same process may be expected to be repeated whenever a new territory is thrown open. Who desires that this turmoil and agitation should become chronic, as it necessarily must if territories are scrambled for as a prize and by the weapons of war? Even when apparently determined, the institutions of a territory by the oscillations of parties may be so unsettled that no reliance can be placed upon their permanence. There is also another defect about this method which must have been apparent to anybody, and that is the total elimination of the moral element in relation to the question. We do not know whether anybody has ever been able to extract a reply from Senator Douglas to the question whether he regards slavery as a moral wrong or not, though the attempt has been repeatedly tried. He and his party certainly treat the question simply as they would one of finance, wholly without reference to the moral character of the institution. In this respect his party are far behind the Breckinridge party, who acknowledge the force of moral obligations by attempting to prove that slavery is right before they ask for a slave-code. The attempt to take the question of slavery entirely out of the department of morals must necessarily fail in a country which acknowledges its accountability to Divine law. The conscience of the country will not permit this abnegation of the moral element.

The Bell party propose to settle the question by putting it off—a cowardly expedient even if it were possible. But it must be met, it cannot be winked out of sight. Like the ghost of Banquo it will not down at their bidding. It is not only an impracticable way of settling the question but it is a useless one. Quarrels do not mend by being protracted. So long as the question is kept open, with all the irritating causes at work on both sides, the prospects of an amicable settlement are constantly on the wane. This party, respectable in intellect and influence in respect to the question of slavery, adopts the counsels of timidity, of irresolution and of indecision—qualities which of all others are least to be trusted in an emergency.—It is like officers of a vessel losing all presence of mind in a storm. Not only are they in this predicament but they have made no provision for future contingencies. They have no plan of adjustment. North and South they differ and cannot meet on common ground. Here is the inevitable parent of future distrust and dissensions.

The Republican party, realizing the responsibility of the case, and aware that it must be met and settled before peace and quietness can prevail, have resolved to meet it manfully and as becomes good citizens and patriots. They know there is but one course consistent with the principles of justice and the recorded sentiments of the civilized world, and that course they propose to take. It is to arrest its farther extension, leaving it where it is to a gradual extinction through the operation of natural causes and the growth of an enlightened public sentiment. At the same time they do not propose to exercise the power of prohibition in a wanton manner. They will not interfere with any vested rights. Their action will be wholly of a prospective character. To this no just objection can be taken, or will be taken. There may be a little bluster and a few threats, but the Southern people, brave as we know them to be, will never expose themselves to the derision of every civilized community by waging a war, or attempting to dissolve the Union because not permitted to desecrate free soil with the insignia of human bondage.

2. THE DANGER A REALITY

(Washington (D. C.) *Constitution* [Breckinridge], September 6, 1860)

The apprehensions excited in the minds of all conservative, patriotic men by the progress of the black-republican cause must not be confounded with the evanescent misgivings of an ordinary presidential campaign. Still less should the declared alarm felt with regard to the future of the Union be treated as the common-place manœuvre of a zealous partisanship. The peril of the position is now realized as it was never realized before. The issue is no longer between parties entitled more or less to share the really national sentiment, but has assumed a shape in which the friends of the Union and the Constitution find themselves pitted against the enemies of both, openly or covertly intent upon the subjugation of the South under the leadership of Lincoln.

Grant, if you will, that in the republican ranks are men more moderate in their views than the Lovejoys, the Sumners, and the Greeleys of the party. What then? Is not its fundamental principle—the source of its vitality and growth—incompatible with the condition of State equality, on which alone the Union can stand? Take the most conciliatory exposition of the sectional doctrine, and what is it but a declaration that the North shall monopolize the benefits of territorial growth? —that the South shall be excluded from participation in territory acquired and held, in part, with its treasure and its blood?—that, in fact, this Union of sovereign States is to be converted into a compulsory partnership, the honors and profits of which are to inure to the controlling partner, the North? Assume, then, for the moment, that a certain portion of the republicans affect, with Mr. Corwin, great regard for existing local rights, still even they would impose terms to which the South could not, ought not to, submit. For they would rob it of the right to grow, to expand, with the ever-widening civilization of the continent. They would force upon it a construction of the Constitution destructive to the cherished feelings and interests of the Southern people. And so, in the end, they would compel the South to sever an alliance which would thus have been stripped of all semblance of justice.

But the republican party proper are not content to wait for this indirect accomplishment of their purposes. The sapping and mining policy has no charms for them. They spurn the pretence of peace. They will have none of your conciliatory counsels. The cunning which induces Mr. Seward to fence around his "irrepressible conflict" with friendly phrases, suits not their temper or their object. Having enlisted for a war against the slave institution, they insist upon attacking it on its own ground. It is not enough that the owner of slave labor shall be excluded from the Territories; not enough that the South shall be circumscribed within existing States. The conflict must be carried further. Accepting the dogma that slavery is an unmitigated evil and a wrong, they demand its limitation only as a prelude to its destruction. The logic of their fanaticism repudiates the idea of a stopping-place short of the full application of their idea. Abraham Lincoln hits it to a nicety: "This Union cannot stand half slave, half free." Slave labor, he and they declare, must be driven out. Squatter sovereignty will serve well as a beginning; that being enacted, and the emigrant aid societies in full blast, the Wilmot proviso might be dispensed with. Is this all? Are the bulk of the black-republicans prepared to tarry even here? Their candidate, Mr. Lincoln, distinctly tells us, No. "This shall be a Union of free States, or not a Union at all." They are bound, if victorious, to push their aggressive policy to its legitimate conclusion; and it were madness in us to doubt what that conclusion is. Nor are we left in doubt as to the steps contemplated—the measures one after another leading to the logical result of the black-republican doctrine. The hostility to the fugitive slave law manifested wherever that doctrine prevails, leaves no room to question the fate of that enactment should the spirit that nominated Lincoln obtain possession of the Federal authority. The unconstitutional legislation against the right of the South to reclaim fugitive labor, which has disgraced Massachusetts—the elevation of the Jerry rescue into an annual festival at Syracuse—the armed resistance at this moment offered to the United States law in Wisconsin in the case of the outlaw Booth, are so many pledges of the assault that is reserved for this portion of the compromise of 1850, in the event of a black-republican victory. And there are other measures as inimical to the South which the sectionalists are equally resolved to apply. Whatever be the trickery of their leaders, the rank and file at least are consistent. They are sworn to expel slavery from the Union and to thrust their version of constitutional obligations down the throats of the Southern people—if the latter consent, meekly and confidingly, to give them the chance.

It is no answer to say that we are presenting only the view of the extreme wing of the black-republican party. This extreme wing it is which controls the party—which enunciates its opinions in Congress and the press, which dictates its nominations in State conventions, and which is represented by the candidate who carries the party colors in the present canvass. The Sewards and Chases and Corwins of the party occupy back seats in the synagogue, and play second fiddle to Lovejoy and Sumner. The stranger who desired to pick out the prominent, ruling black-republicans in Congress might find them enumerated to his hand in the recommendatory advertisement of Helper's book. The incendiary harangues of the Senator from Massachusetts and the member from Illinois are acknowledged specimens of the oratory most in vogue where the fanatics are dominant. Your "moderate men" are nowhere amongst them. Why has Mr. Seward been unceremoniously set

aside? Think you that Greeley's selfish antipathy sufficed to produce so significant a result? They know little of the disposition that thrives in black-republican quarters who can be induced to accept the puerile explanation. The New York senator had fallen short of the requirements of his party. Aiming at the presidency, he had toned down his expressions considerably. He was no longer avowedly aggressive, no longer defiant. And therefore Mr. Seward was thrown overboard at Chicago, as unsuited to the wants of the party. Bates and Chase and Banks were overslaughed for the same reason. They were not up to the mark. They were too moderate, forsooth, to satisfy the demands of the radical and ruling section. Hence the lot fell upon Lincoln, an obscure lawyer, confessedly lacking the culture and capacity which are requisite to the creditable occupancy of the high office for which he has been nominated; but an anti-slavery zealot, nevertheless—a man who realizes the expectation of his party by proclaiming uncompromising hostility to the distinguishing institution of the South, and who, if permitted to acquire power, will be forced by the sentiment which nominated and sustains him to carry out an aggressive policy by every means at his command.

Nor can it be said that any inclination has been shown since the Chicago nomination to hold the extremists in check. The opposite has been the case. The nomination of Lincoln has invested them with an influence which they are not backward in using in several of the States. True, we hear comparatively little of their stump orators in the East. Mr. Douglas is doing their work too skilfully to allow of their being anxious about accredited orators whilst he is upon the stump. But where they do put in appearances, you meet champions worthy of the candidate and the cause: here a Sumner, there a Lovejoy, there, again, a Giddings —out-and-out creatures, whom the leaders have heretofore chained in the background to save the credit of the party during the progress of a canvass. The Lincoln nomination has reversed matters—how completely the recent gubernatorial nomination in Massachusetts sufficiently attests. Driven from the stage by the preponderance of the radical element, Mr. Banks sees the abolitionist Andrew nominated as his successor; the nomination being heralded forth as a concession to those who hold with Lincoln that "this Union cannot stand half slave, half free," and would act accordingly if once installed at Washington.

We contend, then, that the anxiety, the alarm with which the contest is viewed in the South, and by national men everywhere, is not only defensible, but rational and just. Although four candidates are in the field, the struggle is really between two principles, of which Mr. Breck-

inridge and Mr. Lincoln are the respective champions. Were it limited
personally to these candidates, we should not dread the result. The
patriotic sentiment of the country would rise in its might and crush the
party whose progress must render the maintenance of the Union impossible. The danger springs from the aid and comfort which the black-
republicans are enabled to derive from the apostles of squatter sovereignty on one hand, and the remnants of know-nothingism on the other.

3. Our Historic Developement—Shall It Be Superseded by a War of Races?

(New York Herald [Breckinridge], September 19, 1860)

The political issue that is now before the country is a far more
momentous one than has ever before been presented here, and the consequences flowing from its decision will affect our historic developement
for ages to come, if they do not establish an early period to our existence
as a nation.

Party divisions among us have hitherto been based on questions of
policy in government, but without departing from the great principle of
the rightful preponderance of the white race. Thus, in the first division
of parties after the establishment of the constitution, the lines of the
federal and republican organizations were drawn on the great question
of a stronger or weaker form of federal government, involving the right
of controlling personal liberty, the freedom of the press, and other questions of a similar character, which marked our legislation and political
agitation during the closing years of the last century. This was succeeded
by party divisions on the question of a second war with England in
defence of our rights on the ocean, and the patriotic sacrifices the war
party then led the country to make in the face of the bitter opposition
of "the Massachusetts school" were the foundations of our present commercial glory. After this came the great division under Jackson, on the
questions of bank, tariff and internal improvements by the general
government. All of these questions were discussed with partisan bitterness, but in them the doubt of the right of the white man to rule never
entered.

The only party division that exists to-day, aside from the bickerings
of selfish and unscrupulous leaders, who are each endeavoring, with
their petty cockle boats, to gather the fragments that are floating upon
the tide of party revolution, involves a far deeper and older question
than any that has previously been discussed among us during our national career. The issue that is presented by the black republican party

involves the whole question of our social and national existence. Black republicanism, founded on and animated by the anti-slavery idea, and pursuing an exaggerated notion of individual rights, involves not only an attempt to equalize dissimilar and discordant races in their social and political immunities, but also the most destructive theories in regard to the organization of society. Socialism in its worst form, including the most advanced theories of women's rights, the division of land, free love and the exaltation of the desires of the individual over the rights of the family, and the forced equality of all men in phalansteries, or similar organizations, are a part of the logical chain of ideas that flow from the anti-slavery theory which forms the soul of black republicanism.

This anti-slavery idea aims to establish a new social policy in this country—the policy of an equalization of the white and black races—which has never produced anything but bloodshed in other parts of the world, and which can only result in the subjugation or destruction of the numerically weaker race. There is no possibility of the black and the white existing harmoniously together in social and political equality. Even the blacks and mulattoes cannot do it. We have pregnant examples of this truth in the bloody history of Hayti and the Dominican republic; in the scenes that have been witnessed wherever European colonization has been established in Africa; in the events now passing in every Spanish-American republic within the tropics, and even among ourselves, in the popular feeling in the southern counties of the free States bordering on those holding slaves. It is then the question of a revolution in our social organization that the black republicans present to the people—a revolution that brings with it a perpetual war of races, which must endure, when once inaugurated, until the blacks now on this continent have been swept from the face of the earth. With the abolition of slavery in the Northern States, the negroes that once existed among us in family servitude have been almost exterminated. The paucity of their numbers prevented their presenting any resistance to this social extermination, and the same reason applies to the fact that the loss of their labor was not felt to any great degree by the material interests of the community.

But this does not and cannot apply to the Southern States, where four millions of blacks are now held in a position of social subjection, which contributes to their own moral and material welfare, and to that of the whole community in which they exist. The triumph of the anti-slavery sentiment, through the election of Lincoln to the Presidency, will initiate a social revolution among us which will require generations, and perhaps centuries, for its consummation, if we exist through it so long. Such a war of races will absorb all the powers of our society, diverting them from the prosecution of domestic industry and foreign trade. Above all, it will produce division and conflict among ourselves, as it has divided the whites everywhere that it has prevailed, while the blacks, without other policy or impulses, will be united by the bond of color. There is no escape from these logical conclusions. We are subject to the same laws that rule mankind everywhere. There are thousands of conservatives among the black republicans who believe that they can restrain their party from these extreme results; but they deceive themselves. Their party organization is based on an idea fomented by the abolition societies of the North for the past twenty-five years, and it cannot escape from the rule of that idea. This is clearly seen in the public declarations of Lincoln, the teachings of Spooner, the incendiary instigations of Helper, the approval that followed the bloody acts of John Brown, the outpourings of Sumner and Wilson, the diatribes of Greeley, and the recent speeches of Seward at Boston, Detroit, Lansing and Madison.

The real question, therefore, now presented to the people of the United States is the question of our social developement for generations yet to come, and involving our very existence as a nation. If we once begin the war of races, which will inevitably follow from the triumph of the abolition idea and its control of our government, it cannot cease until the black race has been exterminated or driven from among us. Such a war will involve the cessation of the prosecution of many of the industrial pursuits that now constitute our prosperity and national greatness. It will bring civil and servile war to our now peaceful land. It will consume all the elements that now contribute to our intellectual and material developement. With such certainties before us, involving our posterity for centuries in conflict and ruin, it becomes every man to take heart and do his utmost to defeat the fanatical and revolutionary black republicans, who, blinded by their own zeal, following a fallacy that elsewhere has conduced only to destruction, and obstinately refusing to learn wisdom from the experience and disasters of other lands and nations, are bent on establishing here the most destructive conflict of races that the world has ever witnessed.

4. WHY SHOULD WE QUARREL?

(Cincinnati *Daily Times* [Bell], September 22, 1860)

"Man is prone to evil as the sparks to fly upward;" and one of the greatest of all evils to which he is prone is the indulgence of his "angry passions." What is so beautiful as love? It is earth's paradise, when hearts congenial are brought together and awaken each other's sympathies, to enjoy or mourn or to condole. The kind offices of friendship are made bright spots in memory, and come back after long-passed years, to gladden the heart and thrill the pulse.

Why should we quarrel? Are we not the bond-slaves of reason? Has not the Great Infinite, in his wisdom, implanted in man the duty to obey "inexorable logic," and to discard that which in his heart he believes to be untrue? "Let us reason together," should be the inspiration of every mind, and to the only bias of judgment should we lean; taught by the lesson of experience which the Past has brought, and indulging hopes of the Future which rationality inspires. [*sic*] We are all of one family—we are all of one nation. The wisdom of our fathers, inspired from Heaven, gave us a government, unequaled in the annals of the world for the exquisiteness of its machinery and the sound[ness] of philosophy on which it was based. For two-thirds of a century, nearly, we have thriven under it, and, from a few weak and oppressed colonies, have become a mighty and a prosperous nation, composed of an industrious, enterprising, fast and—would we could say—a happy and contented people.

Why should we quarrel? The written Constitution was broad enough to cover the whole nation, as with a blanket; and for years, although we had our individual imaginary and petty grievances, we still were happy, and grew up in friendship and harmony. We were National, then. Ambition had been busy in moving the springs of action in men's minds, but in the only instance that secession of any part of the Confederacy was contemplated with the view of forming a great Southern empire, it was regarded as treason, and the eminent person whose eloquence and plausible pretext had fomented the so-called conspiracy was regarded as a traitor, narrowly escaped condign punishment, and his name was handed down to posterity blinded with every-thing that was odious and rank in the scale of infamy. We were national then, and patriotic. It was all our country over which the Constitution spread its ægis. The Government was the palladium of liberty, and one State, and the people of one State, thought no more of interfering with the rights of another, than they had of severing the great compact that united them under one banner. And for long years this harmony existed and flourished, and all things went well. As a nation, we were content, we were honest, we were virtuous, we were prosperous, we were happy. Why cannot we be so now? Why should we quarrel?

Yes—why should we quarrel? Why was the great forefather of the human race banished from Paradise? Like the baleful reptile that poured poison into the ear of woman, ambition has filled the hearts of men with its subtle influence, until many another EROSTRATUS would fire the Ephasian [sic] dome, or rend the pillars of the Constitution which support the magnificient [sic] structure of our Government and scatter it into fragments. Patriotism no more rules the American heart. The love of country that was the theme of every tongue in the morning of our lives, no more thrills the pulses of the sons of freedom, as we were proud to call ourselves. It is now, with one-half of this great nation, the pursuit of an abstract notion—a phantom, an *ignis fatuus* that traitorous demagogues flash in the faces of a bewildered and infatuated people, to misguide them to become entangled in difficult mazes and discover their error too late. And now they quarrel, and grow angry in their disputations, challenging the vocabulary for names of reproach with which to assail each other. The *cordiale entente* no more prevails. Brothers cease to be brothers—friends no longer friends. A wide gap is opening and growing wider, wider every day. Why should it be so? Why should we quarrel? Why not emulate each other in our devotion to our country and in attachment to the Union, the sole arbiter of America's great destiny? Why not permit each State, as by the original compact, and it was thought was secured by the great instrument under which we have grown great and prospered, to hew out its own destiny in its own way, and with its own institutions, without interference from its sister States? Why seek to meddle with that which concerns us not? Why not return to the happy days, when we were homogeneous, and undivided in sentiment from Maine to Georgia? Why should we quarrel?

5. SHALL THE UNION STAND UPON A BASIS OF MORAL OBLIGATION OR OF PHYSICAL FORCE?

(*Boston Post* [Breckinridge], September 26, 1860)

If there is any one act of misrepresentation meaner and more disingenuous than another, which Mr. Douglas has been guilty of, during his electioneering tour, it is his repeated insinuations that the supporters of Mr. Breckinridge are not sound and reliable upon the question of the maintenance of the Union and the enforcement of the laws. Although he, and every person of common sense, knows well enough there is no anti-law or anti-Union party in the field, in this canvass, excepting the Black Republican organization, he gratuitously raises this issue with the friends of the latter candidate, in order to prevent a reunion of the Democracy, and to give a color of plausibility to his coalition with the Know-Nothings, who have set up the unfounded claim of being the champions of the Union and Constitution *par excellence.*

As to the enforcement of the laws, Mr. Douglas is well aware that no portion of the Democratic party has ever placed itself in antagonism to existing statutes, except some of his own partisans, who, in the rump Convention which nominated him for the Presidency, argued in favor of reopening the slave trade. And, in assuming this overt position, he himself set them a notable example, in proposing to override the decisions of the Supreme Court, by abolishing slavery in the Territories, through the medium of squatter sovereignty, in spite of Congress and the Judiciary. Indeed, he has been unable to adduce a single plausible fact in support of his assumption that the Breckinridge wing of the Democracy is less devoted to the Union, or regard the *constitutional* laws of the country as less sacred and binding, than the most orthodox of his own supporters. The people, who are familiar with the antecedents of all the Presidential candidates and the characters of the public men who espouse their cause, respectively, are not to be duped by any such blarney.

But when Mr. Douglas declares himself in favor of maintaining the Federal authority and enforcing the laws *"in any contingency,"* what political emergencies in the future does he contemplate? His freesoil friends say, and he himself gives countenance to the idea, that he takes this decided stand in view of any possible complication of our Federal relations which may arise under a Black Republican, higher-law administration of the government. Does he mean to say that if such an administration should frame laws manifestly infringing the constitutional rights of the South, (as its controlling minds, such as Sumner, Hale, Wilson, Seward, Lovejoy, Andrew, &c., would insist upon its doing,) that any non-compliance with or resistance to such laws must be forcibly put down? Does he mean that if such an administration shall repeal the Fugitive Slave law, and ignore the compromises of the Constitution touching the institution of negro servitude, the South, notwithstanding this violation of the compact, shall be compelled to submit, and remain in the Union as a subjugated province, shorn of the attributes of sovereignty? It is in this sense that the Black Republican press and leaders understand him; and hence they applaud his stump performances, and count him as an effective ally, if not a pronounced champion of their cause. When he affirms, boldly and unequivocally, that the laws and the executive supremacy must be enforced "IN ANY CONTINGENCY," they are satisfied that he is of them and with them; that he will give his cordial support to the administration of Abraham Lincoln, and prove a worthy successor to him in the Presidential chair. But in thus catering for Republican success and sympathy, he has evidently forfeited the confidence and support of the National Democracy, whom he vainly essays to sell out and betray into the hands of the Philistines.

It is not to be doubted that Mr. Douglas is in favor of perpetuating the Union; and so are the sectional opponents of the Democracy, upon certain inadmissible terms and conditions. They would compel our Southern fellow-citizens to remain in the Union, contribute to the support of Northern commerce and manufactures, and help to defray the expenses of the General Government, without enjoying that protection and equality which are the fundamental objects and conditions of the Union. The partisans of Lincoln and Hamlin propose to circumscribe the domestic institutions of the South, and, on the hypocritical plea of barbarism, to extirpate, by "unfriendly legislation," her system of labor and the profits of her industry. They would virtually disfranchise her in the national councils, and make the measure of her political rights the concessions of the will of an arbitrary majority. Then, if she refuses to remain in the Union on these humiliating conditions, they are ready to let loose upon her the demon of civil war and imbrue their hands in fraternal blood; and Mr. Douglas proclaims that he is ready to join them in this unhallowed crusade. But will the unprejudiced, liberty-loving masses of the North, in such an emergency, suffer themselves to be led to the slaughter of their own kindred, to carry desolation to the homes, and plunge their hostile steel into the bosoms of the descendants of their common ancestors, of glorious memory, because they dared to assert their equal rights and privileges in the confederacy established by those ancestors? Never!

As Union men, there is this important difference between Mr. Douglas and Mr. Breckinridge: While the former proposes to maintain the Union (in any contingency—no matter what wrong or provocation to the seceding States may be involved in it) by invoking the strong arm of the military power, by employing the brute force wielded by the federal army and navy, the latter desires to maintain it only by the moral power of justice, equity, honor, fidelity to the Constitution and fraternal affection. This is the broad distinction which marks the dividing line between rival candidates for the suffrages of the Democracy, and which every true and reflecting Union man can fully appreciate. Let every such candid and patriotic elector at the North judge for himself what would be the value of this Union, when, no longer enshrined in the hearts of the people, its laws and obligations shall be enforced, upon a reluctant and outraged community, at the mouth of the cannon and the point of the bayonet. If those who love and cherish the sacred bond, which has made of the American people one great and happy family, would avoid the alternative of degrading the Union to a hollow mockery and a curse; if they desire to preserve it in the true spirit of fraternity, and upon a basis of peace and mutual good will, they will not fail to give their votes, their influence, their whole mental and moral energies, in favor of the true Union candidates, BRECKINRIDGE and LANE.

6. THE DIFFERENCE BETWEEN THE TWO PARTIES

(Springfield *Daily Illinois State Register* [Douglas], September 28, 1860)

The great point upon which the political parties of the country are at variance, is that of slavery. Who shall decide whether slavery shall continue to exist in the states where it is now tolerated? Who shall decide whether it shall be tolerated in the territories of the Union? Upon these two questions the policy of the democratic party differs widely from that of the republican party, and to the people of the United States is submitted the choice.

The republican party assert that slavery is an evil of the greatest magnitude; that it is a curse to the state where it is permitted, a curse to the society which tolerates it, and a curse to all men who participate in it as masters and owners. In his letter to the Boston committee, Mr. Lincoln declares that the man who will not emancipate his slaves in this life, must undergo an eternity of bondage and slavery in the life to come; that he must in the great hereafter, expiate in eternal punishment the crime of holding slaves in this world. This evil of slavery is so odious that Lincoln has placed on record, in his famous Chicago speech, that he "hates" it worse than any abolitionist hates it. He says that it is such an offence against laws of right and justice that this Union cannot stand, cannot survive unless the nation take immediate steps to appease divine wrath by legislation for its rapid and ultimate extinction. He proposes remedies for the evil. He lays down as cardinal principles that the negro is entitled to all the rights of white men: that any law which deprives him of his liberty is void: that the negro is entitled to all the products of his own labor, and that the man who, under the pretence of ownership, deprives the negro of the proceeds of his own labor, is a tyrant and an oppressor, whose authority may be lawfully overthrown by the slaves if they have the physical power to do so. He proposes as the policy of the republican party, the immediate recognition by the federal government of the rights of the oppressed African; he proposes to legislate so that slavery must soon be extinguished. As a part of this policy, he insists that the negroes as long as they are slaves must remain within the borders of the present slave states, there to increase until they shall outnumber the white population. He proposes to remodel the supreme court of the United States by adding to it a number of republican judges, who shall be pledged to decide against slavery and slave owners. Having thus possession of the executive, legislative and judicial departments of the government, he proposes to carry out his policy by freeing the negroes and thus ultimately extinguishing slavery. The plan is an effectual one if practicable. It would be practicable if he could only induce the white people of the United States to submit to it. If he could overturn the constitution, extinguish state rights and obliterate private rights he might succeed, but to carry out his policy he must do all these things.

Another serious difficulty which presents itself in the way, is, what shall be done with the negroes? Once emancipated what is to become of them? In many of the southern states they will outnumber the whites. To emancipate them will not give them political privileges. A step further must be taken; they must be admitted to the rights and privileges of citizenship. The Dred Scott decision must be reversed and negroes must be declared the equal of the white race.

To trace the republican policy to its legitimate conclusion, it will be found that it must end in the Africanization of the slave states, and a gradual mingling of the races in the political control of the government.

The democratic party however has a much shorter and more direct policy. It has for its cardinal principle that this nation is a nation of white men, in which negroes have no voice whatever in the regulation of its political affairs. Negroes who are here, are entitled to be treated with all the kindness that humanity and christianity can suggest, but they are not entitled to any of the prerogatives of government. They are the inferior race, and must remain so, politically, forever. The regulation and government of this negro race, whether as free or as slave, has been wisely left by the constitution to the people of each state within their respective jurisdictions. The democratic party propose to leave that question where the constitution has left it, and where it has been regulated with great satisfaction for over seventy years. They propose that the white people of Illinois shall have exclusive control over the question of negro rights in Illinois; and that the people of the other states shall have the same exclusive control over the matter in their respective states. They insist that as the people of Illinois have excluded free negroes and slave negroes, that each other state shall have the same privilege. They propose that the entire question of slavery and negroism shall be left to the people of each state to be decided by themselves in their own good time, in such manner as their interests may dictate. They are opposed to overturning the whole policy of the past, overturning the whole theory of the American government, and are opposed to prostituting the government and destroying the peace and harmony of the Union to gratify the wild, extravagant ambition of abolition demagogues.

The democratic party propose that the great constitutional doctrine of leaving to each people the exclusive privilege of regulating their domestic institutions for themselves, and of having or rejecting African slavery as they may deem best, shall be recognized to the fullest extent in the people of each territory of the United States. Under that policy we will have no nationalization of slavery. We will have the entire subject committed to the exclusive control of the people of each state and territory, to be decided by them for their own weal or woe. The nation will not then be responsible if slavery shall be admitted into new territories, nor if it be excluded, but the people of those territories, who are alone to be affected by the absence or presence of the institution, alone will bear the burden or enjoy the profit of their own choice.

Under this policy there will be no pretext for disunion or strife between states or sections. The negro race will continue as at present. The country will not be overrun with millions of free negroes, but the United States will continue to be a nation of free white people.

That is popular sovereignty, and that is democracy.

7. The Decisive Battle Near at Hand—The Belligerents and the Prospect

(New York Herald [Breckinridge], October 1, 1860)

We have entered the month of October, and Tuesday, the 6th day of November, will be signalized by the most momentous Presidential contest in the history of the United States. One month and one week will bring us face to face with the day and the struggle which will determine, perhaps forever, the issue of Union or disunion, peace or war, between the free labor system of the North and the slave labor system of the South. But how stand the belligerents in regard to this momentous issue, and what is the prospect of the battle?

There are four great parties in the field, represented by the four tickets of Lincoln and Hamlin, Breckinridge and Lane, Bell and Everett, Douglas and Johnson. The party of Lincoln and Hamlin—a progressive, offensive, sectional anti-slavery organization—is practically limited to the Northern States. It will not receive a solitary electoral vote from a slave State, and thus, in the outset, we have positively secured against it 120 electoral votes, requiring the addition of only thirty-two of the 183 electoral votes of the North to defeat Lincoln and his sectional anti-slavery party, by casting the election into Congress.

The official returns of our Northern elections of the last four years also show that in Pennsylvania, New Jersey and New York there is a very large majority of the popular vote arrayed in opposition to the republican party; that this party never has approached anything near a popular majority in either of said States; and yet, singularly enough, these are the very States which the republicans count upon carrying by the heaviest pluralities. We say pluralities, because the common enemy is confident that in these three aforesaid States the overwhelming conservative forces opposed to Lincoln will be frittered away between the Douglas, Bell and Breckinridge organizations.

In support of this anticipation, it must be conceded that the stumping tour of Mr. Douglas, now drawing to a close in the West, has betrayed his object to be not so much the defeat of Lincoln as the prostration of the Breckinridge democracy. Thus, while he has instigated the nomination of independent Douglas electoral tickets in some of the Southern States, the only effect of which, if they have any effect at all, will be to divert the vote of those States from Breckinridge to Bell, we find Mr. Douglas at every point the persistent enemy of any coalition with the Breckinridge democracy in the North, a policy which, if followed up, can only result in the election of Lincoln by the solid electoral vote of the Northern States.

The plea of Mr. Douglas in support of this singular course on his part is, that the Southern Breckinridge democracy are scheming and reckless disunionists, and that the defeat of their candidate, therefore, is as essential to the peace of the country as the defeat of Lincoln. But as Lincoln cannot be defeated except through the assistance of the Northern Breckinridge democracy, Mr. Douglas, in repudiating this assistance, is simply laboring to elect Lincoln. This can hardly be doubted when it is considered that in no possible event can Mr. Douglas, or Mr.

Johnson, in the settlement of this imbroglio, become the next President of the United States.

The Douglas democracy of the North, however, in a choice between half a loaf and no bread at all, are very wisely inclined to take the half a loaf. With Lincoln's election they are at once adrift, and without a local habitation or a name; with Lincoln's defeat they are at once identified with the victorious alliance which will thenceforward become the party in power. Grant that in casting the election into Congress there will be no choice of a President, for want of time, by the House, is it not morally certain that, in the Vice President, who will be elected by the anti-republican Senate, whether Lane or Everett, we shall have a President who will organize his administration upon the Union basis issues and elements of his elevation to the White House? [sic]

Actuated by this idea, and properly estimating the Southern disunionists in this canvass as a negative quantity, the Douglas democracy of this State and of Pennsylvania have shown a proper inclination to come together in behalf of the paramount object of Lincoln's defeat. Here and there, however, a few factious and wrangling Douglas and Breckinridge politicians continue to stand in the way, upon what they call democratic principles, when the only principle at stake is that of the peace of the Union against the disunion "irrepressible conflict" of the republican party.

We apprehend that, from this state of things, we must, for relief, await the issue of the State elections, which come off on Tuesday, the 9th instant, in Pennsylvania, Ohio, Indiana, Iowa and Minnesota. In all these States we anticipate republican majorities, excepting Pennsylvania. She has the materials for a Union victory against the republicans —these materials are combining upon Foster, the democratic Union candidate for Governor, and with the hope of his triumphant election. Thus, in 1860, as in 1856, Pennsylvania may turn the tide of the battle, and settle in October the issue of the November election.

In the meantime the anti-republican factions of New York, laying aside all their paltry personal considerations in reference to Breckinridge or Douglas, or Bell, or in regard to Dean Richmond, Dickinson, Washington Hunt or Booby Brooks, or in relation to squatter sovereignty, or Congressional intervention, or the obsolete heresies of Know Nothingism, should at once choose between Lincoln's election, whereby all the factions opposed to him will be ground to powder, and Lincoln's defeat, whereby all the elements combining to effect it will share in the organization of the new party which will be organized under the new administration. This is the only real issue in this canvass

—Lincoln's election or Lincoln's defeat; and while there can be no hope of his defeat so long as his opponents are divided in the great Central States, it is only necessary that they should be united in Pennsylvania or in New York to dispose of him. They are cordially uniting in Pennsylvania. Let New York follow their example, or let all the odds and ends concerned cease their useless clamor, fold their arms and await the consequences.

8. AN APPEAL TO SOUTHERN HONOR AND TO SOUTHERN COMMON SENSE

(Peoria *Daily Democratic Union* [Douglas], October 5, 1860)

A few words of kindness, spoken in candor, may not be deemed out of place at the present juncture. It is hoped that they may be dispassionately considered by those to whom they are addressed. It is time that reason, not prejudice—patriotism, not fanaticism—should control the actions of men in all sections of this Union.

Who have ever been the defenders of the rights and interests of the South, and this, too, often at their own cost? who, but the Northern Democracy? And who is the acknowledged head of this Northern Democracy? who, but Stephen A. Douglas?

Is it possible that the southern people are lost to every sense of gratitude? Have they no friendly or grateful recollections of the past? Are they prepared to turn their backs upon those who have stood by them in their every conflict, and shielded and saved them from every danger? Do they want no friends in the North? Do they wish to precipitate upon us the Lincoln issue of *"all free States, or all slave States?"* We shall be slow to believe them capable of all or any of these wrongs or follies.

In 1848 they demanded, through Gen. Cass, that the Democracy of the whole country should go to battle upon the doctrine of non-intervention. The demand was complied with—the northern Democracy made a vigorous campaign and gained a glorious victory upon this issue, *Gen. Cass being defeated solely through the defection of Southern Democratic States!*

Still, the northern democracy, *notwithstanding their disappointment in the South,* held on firmly to the doctrine of non-intervention, as they do to-day, BELIEVING IT TO BE RIGHT IN ITSELF—and when the compromise measures of 1850, confirmatory of this doctrine, and embracing the present fugitive slave law, came up for consideration, the whole northern democracy, both in and out of Congress, STILL STOOD FIRMLY BY SOUTHERN RIGHTS, and AT THEIR HEAD STOOD STEPHEN A. DOUGLAS! And at a later period (1854) when the South desired the repeal of the Missouri Compromise, restricting slavery by a geographical line, through whose instrumentality were their wishes gratified?—Through whom but THE NORTHERN DEMOCRACY, LED ON BY STEPHEN A. DOUGLAS? Gen. Pierce was elected upon the strength of the compromise measures, which Douglas aided materially in carrying through Congress. Mr. Buchanan was elected principally upon the same issues, with the Kansas Nebraska bill, of which Douglas was the author, THROWN IN TO HELP HIM AT THE SOUTH. And yet, in the face of all these facts, we find men at the South so lost to reason, or so lost to honor, that they are ready to cut loose from the only friends they have ever had, or can ever hope to have in the northern and western States, and even ready to sacrifice the very man who has been their boldest and best defender in every conflict, and who has done more to establish their rights than any other man now living! Neither Mr. Calhoun, in the glory of his prime, nor Mr. Clay, in the pride of his popularity, ever saw the day when either of them, or both together could have satisfied the entire North and West, so triumphantly as Judge Douglas has, of the just claims and rights of the South under the Constitution! And for this shall he be hunted down by the beneficiaries of his life-long efforts? "O, shame! where is thy blush?"

The pretext upon which certain southern politicians affect to base their hostility to Judge Douglas is that he repudiates the idea of a slave code for the Territories—that is, he refuses to back down from the doctrine of Congressional non-intervention. Did not all these gentlemen vote for the Compromise Measures? Did they not all vote for the Kansas-Nebraska bill, Mr. Breckinridge among them? Did they not all vote for the Foote resolutions declaring the Compromise Measures "a finality on the slavery question?" Did they not all vote for the Nebraska bill as explanatory of those measures so far as they related to slavery? Did those measures, or did the Nebraska bill, contemplate ANYTHING MORE, OR ANYTHING LESS, than the simple but positive doctrine of NON INTERVENTION? We submit these facts to every candid and honorable mind in the South, and ask leave to challenge a fair and reasonable excuse for the UNWARRANTED course of conduct now being pursued by THE POLITICIANS of the South against Judge Douglas—a man to whom they are indebted, more than to any other, for the recognition, in the North, of every right and claim of which they boast to-day!

We shall anticipate an answer—it is, that Judge Douglas will not go the full length of the slave code proposition! There are good and sufficient reasons why he does not and should not fall in with an idea at once

absurd, exacting, of doubtful constitutionality, and glaringly inconsistent with every southern as well as every northern democratic sentiment heretofore advanced, and in the face and eyes of every northern
and every southern democratic vote heretofore cast, on the subject of
slavery in the Territories! Non-intervention, on the part of Congress,
is THE ONLY DOCTRINE which has EVER been established by the democracy,
North and South. Upon this doctrine the northern democracy still
stand, and will stand forever, BUT THEY WILL GO NO FARTHER!

The Slave Code idea was conceived in sin and brought forth in
iniquity. It was gotten up by certain southern gentlemen, who have an
evil eye on the White House, for the express purpose of getting Judge
Douglas into an entanglement with southern prejudices, and thus defeat his election at the hands of the people! Shall the game win? Even
if it should, the South will yet live to learn that Judge Douglas and the
northern democracy *never desert their colors, never desert their friends,
and never change their principles!* He and they will go as far as the
farthest to protect every citizen in his property and in his just rights,
wherever the Constitution may extend, or wherever the flag of the
Union may wave, *but no farther!*

We, the democracy of the North, with Judge Douglas at our head,
have for years and years fought the battles of the South against the
constantly increasing hordes of abolitionists. If, at a time when we still
have the power to serve them and to save them, they shall consent to
be led astray by designing and unprincipled aspirants to the Presidency
and to Cabinet places, so be it! It will not be the first time that Iscariot
has had his imitators, or Peter his disciples, in American politics.

As a dernier resort, the people of the South are made to believe that
a dissolution of the Union, in case of the election of a northern man,
will be an easy process and a very desirable consummation. This is an
old trick—one which has heretofore, time and again, ended in smoke,
and must always result in humiliating defeat. The dissolution of this
Union, however much threatened, or however much desired by unprincipled scoundrels who are unfit to live beneath the protecting folds
of the Star-spangled Banner, is a moral, physical, and financial impossibility. A common language, a common religion, and the ties of
consanguinity, affecting almost every family in the nation, forbid it.
A common interest forbids it. The common indebtedness, North and
South, forbids it. The products of the different sections, needed for exchange, forbids [sic] it. Our inland seas, extending almost from zone to
zone, upon whose bosoms are borne the varied products of our almost
unending vallies [sic], forbid it. Our iron bands, which interlace state

to state from East to West, and from North to South, thus linking the Union together and binding it fast as with hooks of steel, and all owing a common ownership, forbid it. Above all, the affections of our people, who cannot but love one another—the patriotism which they cherish as their proudest birth right—and the pride of nationality which instinctively prompts us all to wish to see "our own, our native land," at the head of all governments upon earth, and the best of all governments upon earth, will forever induce them to frown upon the wickedness, and mock to scorn the folly, of any scheme having for its aim a dissolution of this glorious and truly God-like Union, for love and justice form its basis!

We therefore beseech our southern brethren to discard from their counsels all evil advisers. We shall all be better off in the Union than outside of it. The South, it is true, might, to some extent, be better off than the North—but still, she will ever have a necessity for a North, both to supply her wants and to purchase her products. From our individual standpoint, we can look upon these matters dispassionately. The Mississippi valley, which may be called the neutral ground, can find a market either East or South for its products—and should the North and the South ever come to blows, which Heaven forbid! the Giant West, uncontaminated by fanaticism, uncorrupted by monopolies, and too youthful and vigorous to be terrified by silly boasts or idle clamor, will, as heretofore, with Douglas in the van, boldly step forward and say to the contending sections, "PEACE—BE STILL"!

For a most apparent reason, we shall not stop to discuss the constitutionality of the Union-dissolving idea of a Slave Code—an idea hatched in the midnight of treason, and designed for the double purpose of destroying Douglas and of preparing the southern heart for secession. It is, as any one must clearly see, a palpable invasion of all the democratic platforms, and involves the unconditional abrogation of the doctrine of non-intervention—a doctrine which, though originating in the South, has been generously adopted in the North, and has become canonized in the hearts of the whole American democracy. We warn our southern friends against the dangers of this new dogma, for it is next of kin to Black Republicanism, which claims a similar prerogative for Congress. If Congress has the power to protect slavery in the Territories by means of a Slave Code, it also has the power to prohibit slavery in the Territories by means of a Free Code. There can be no division of this question. If Congress has the power to do the one it certainly has the power to do the other. Are our southern friends prepared to abandon their only shield of safety, *non-intervention,* and, by a blind adherence to the idea of a slave code virtually recognize the Black Republican doctrine of Congressional interference on the subject of slavery in the Territories? We hope not—we trust not—nor shall we believe them capable of such self-destruction until the ides of November shall leave us no alternative but to mourn their folly and to denounce their recreancy! Although the infamy of an "irrepressible conflict" may have been conceived in an unpatriotic mind, it may still behoove those most deeply interested to see to it that prophecy shall not become destiny! We warn you as brothers, and as such we shall stand by you so long as you shall take wisdom for your guide and preserve your principles as you would your honor!

9. NORTHERN DISUNIONISTS

(Pittsburgh Post [Douglas], October 10, 1860)

When Mr. Douglas said that all the Breckinridge men were not Disunionists, but that all the Disunionists were Breckinridge men, he thought more of getting off an epigram[m]atic sentence, than he did about stating an actual fact. To our mind there is as much, if not more, of the rampant spirit of disunion in the Black Republican ranks of the North, as there is in the South. And when Mr. Douglas said the Extremists of the South, who sustain Breckinridge, could better fraternize with the Lincoln men than any body else, he uttered, though in a bantering way, a sober truth.

It is simply absurd to say that Disunionism is confined to Southern fire-eaters.—Northern Sectionalism, as manifested by the Black Republican party, is as hostile to the Union, in fact and in purpose, as Southern Sectionalism is now, or ever has been.—Breckinridge claims larger privileges for the South than any other candidate for President; yet Yancey, Keitt & Co. go far beyond Breckinridge in their sectionalism. On the other hand, Lincoln carries his sectional views as far as the farthest of his dusky supporters. Seward, Giddings, Greeley and the rest, have not gone one whit farther in their Abolition track than Lincoln went in his canvass for Senator against Douglas, and he has boldly declared that he "loves the Abolitionists!"

There is another difference between Northern negro-lovers and Southern nullifiers, which is greatly against the former.—Lincoln and his sectional supporters are not complaining of wrongs done to them at their own homes and firesides, and to their own institutions and property. They do not *now,* as heretofore, complain of the South for refusing a tariff for protection—that measure they have formally abandoned in their Chicago platform—nor do they cry out that any measure of Southern policy is urged to their especial damage and detriment. But, at the imminent risk of dissolving the Union, these precious hypocrites claim the right to make a code of laws for the South, not only in the States, but in the Territories, which shall control or prohibit slavery. Now, Yancey and Keitt and the worst of that class, do not propose any reform in the internal laws of the free States—they do not presume to tell us how we shall treat our apprentices or workmen, or how much we shall pay them for their labor—they do not prescribe for us any new regulations about our property, nor anything of the kind. They are acting purely on the defensive against Lincoln, and Fred Douglass, and Seward, and Giddings, and all the rest who "revere the memory of John Brown, of Ossawatomie [sic]!"

But some simple-minded follower of Lincoln and his managers, will, perhaps, interpose, and tell us that Mr. Lincoln, *if elected,* will not administer the government against the South—that he is a safe man, &c., &c. What, then, O! Mr. Forcible Feeble, becomes of the "irrepressible conflict," the inauguration of which is claimed by both Seward and Lincoln? The Black Republicans do not want the government so that they can raise the tariff—their Chicago manifesto does not allege this— they do not want power so that they can alter the naturalization laws. Carl S[c]hurz settled that for them. And if they do not want possession of the government for any of those themes, they must either desire it for plunder alone, or for the sake of carrying the "irrepressible conflict" into the very heart of the Southern States from the capital itself. If we believe that Mr. Lincoln means to do justice to the South, nothing is left as a motive for his party, but the desire that they have to clutch the treasury. Will this be reason enough to satisfy the people? Is every national calamity to be dared so that Lincoln and Giddings may fill the offices with men who sympathise with their love for John Brown? God forbid!

If Lincoln were President, and if he were to issue a message containing the doctrines uttered in Illinois while he was a candidate for the Senate, the Union would be endangered from that hour. He cannot administer the federal government on the principles he proclaimed two years ago, and it was the utterance of those very sentiments that attracted to him the love of the abolitionists, and nominated him at Chicago. Will he abandon those views, if chosen President? If he does, he will dissolve the Republican party, which will scatter like a band of foiled marauders. If he does not, we verily believe he will dissolve the Union? [sic]

And suppose this terrible catastrophe to happen—in compassing it can he abolish slavery? When he shall have torn these States asunder —and destroyed the internal trade of the country—and provoked a servile war, and flooded the whole North with fugitive blacks—and made all anarchy and blood-shed where peace and prosperity reigned so long—will he, we repeat, will he have abolished slavery? Will he have made the negro the political equal of the white man? We can confidently answer, No!

But if the "irrepressible conflict" is to go on, the disruption of the Union will be no hindrance to its progress. The free States will be bound to carry out their abolition views at the point of the bayonet, and to subjugate the white men of the South, will be the watch-word. The plain duty of those who "revere the memory of John Brown," will be to follow his example and to revenge his death!

All these things must come, if Northern Disunionists shall triumph, and hold fast to their principles when in office. Such is [sic] our solemn and sorrowful beliefs. And while we present to our countrymen these gloomy forebodings of the future, we would ask them whether they are willing to run all these risks, to have all these dangers, *not* to defend their own rights, *not* to advance their own interests—but for the sake of tyran[n]izing over the people of the South, and for the inciting of murder and bloodshed amongst them?

10. The South and a Republican Administration

(Cincinnati Daily Commercial [Lincoln], October 18, 1860)

The article from the Charleston Mercury on the "Terrors of Submission," which will be found in another column, is given as a specimen of Southern fanaticism. It is an attempt to sum up the evils to which the South would be subject in case she submitted to the inauguration of a Republican President; and the special effort is to show those evils to be greater than those which would arise from a dissolution of the Union. Our readers will be surprised at the weakness of the case made out by the Editor of the Mercury, whose ability and sincerity there is no reason to question. We must pronounce the several propositions which he submits, ill-considered, imaginative, illogical, and in great part absurd. Yet this is the only attempt we have seen to place the terrors of submission before the public in definite and intelligible form. The Editor of the Mercury is the only man in the United States, within our knowledge, who has had the temerity to undertake to show how and wherein the "submission" of the South would be more calamitous than dissolution.

The first thing that suggests itself to say to men who are of the persuasion of the Charleston Mercury, is that the South is not called on in any offensive or degrading sense to submit. There can be no dishonor and no terror in acquiescing in the inauguration of a President constitutionally elected, and in his administration, under the Constitution, of the Federal Government. The demand of the Northern or Republican sentiment of the country, is simply that the general government shall not be the propagandist of a sectional institution. The great mass of the people are tired of the preponderance in the affairs of our government of the master class of the slave States. It is clear that the PIERCE and BUCHANAN administrations have been implements in the hands of this class. The people of the Northern States owe it to their sense of patriotism and self-respect, to put a stop to the employment of the government in this way. The Republican party has been produced by the irrationally arrogant demands of the politicians of the South, and systematic aggressions by the use of the Federal power. Its mission is to check those aggressions. This it is competent to do, according to the laws and constitution of the United States and the several States, peaceably, and for the benefit of the whole. This it will do, and the South is brought face to face with the fact.—The politicians of the South assume to distrust the Republican party—to count those who are attached to it as enemies—and to arraign its policy as hostile to their section. Now all this argues lamentable ignorance or more lamentable perversity. There is not an item in the Republican platform indicative of hostility to the South; and there are no utterances by those who would shape the policy of the party, if it should come into possession of power, that would authorize any alarm as to its intentions. It contains, to be sure, rash and extreme men, but not those most rash and extreme on the subject of the abolition of slavery. Undoubtedly, the masses of the party have as friendly a regard for the South, as the masses of any other party in the north. They are opposed to the extension of slavery, and to interference with it. They are for non-intervention by Government with the subject —against any attempted abolition of slavery by Government, as well as against the propagation of slavery by the same agent. The natural forces will be sufficient to accomplish all that is desirable in the restriction of slavery.

The Mercury apprehends, if a Republican President should be inaugurated, "a powerful consolidation of the Abolition party of the North." As the Mercury has from long habit become incapable of

courtesy to those who disagree with it in opinion on the slavery question, the fact that it invariably speaks of Republicans as Abolitionists,
is one which we can afford to overlook. But it is a question yet to be
determined, whether the possession of the Federal Government would
consolidate or destroy the Republican party. If Mr. LINCOLN should
undertake to discriminate against, disparage, and harrass the South—
if he should do those things which his pro-slavery opponents say he
would do—the result would be the destruction of the party placing him
in power. If Mr. LINCOLN should be inaugurated President of the United
States on the fourth of March next, (as we believe he will be,) he would
not have a majority of partizan supporters in either branch of Congress.
Consequently, if he were ever so much of an Abolitionist, there could
not be any offensive legislation. And as for the second Congress of his
term, if his Administration were really *sectional,* he would be condemned by an overwhelming majority of every State in the Union, except, perhaps, two in New England, and two in the extreme Northwest;
and his condemnation would appear in Congress. If, on the other hand,
Mr. LINCOLN should be a National President, in the wide and excellent
sense of the term, and administer the laws faithfully, as all persons who
have had opportunities for appreciating his character believe he would
—and as the Republican sentiment demands that he should—why the
South would have nothing to complain of.—The Southern politicians,
who have ruled the nation by false cries and inordinate assumptions,
will of course be exasperated if they should find their occupation gone.
But the Southern people will see that the tremendous buggaboo [*sic*]
which has been exhibited before them with such ghastly effects, is a
false pretense. And there will be a great calm. The muddy waters in
which the politicians have been dabbling will run clear. There will be
legitimate peace and wholesome progress. It is possible, however, that
the Mercury fears this peace—and would stigmatize it in advance as
Southern lethergy [*sic*]. Indeed it will appear upon close examination of
the Mercury's article, that the great fear is the spread of Republican
sentiment among the people of the South.

So far as that is concerned, it is an eventuality against which no pre-
cautions can avail, and we can not bring ourselves to look with regret
or fear upon a prospect of the enlightenment of the Southern people.

The Mercury says:

"The tenure of slave property will be felt to be weakened; and the
slaves will be sent down to the Cotton States for sale, and the Frontier
States enter on the policy of making themselves Free States."

Are we to understand the Mercury that its policy of disunion is to

prevent the Frontier slave States from entering upon the policy of making themselves free States? If the Frontier slave States wish to send their
slaves South and become free, who shall stand in the way? We are prepared to say that a Republican National Administration would certainly not discourage any such proceeding.

The Mercury continues:

"They will have an Abolition Party in the South, of Southern men.
The contest for Slavery will no longer be one between the North and
the South. It will be in the South, between the people of the South."

Well, that will depend upon the men of the South. And if there is to
be a contest on the subject of slavery anywhere, the South is the place
for it. The Mercury surely manifests very little confidence in the soundness of the people of the South on the slavery question. And when it
speaks of an union organization in the South to support a Republican
Administration, can it mean that a party will be found in the South
countenancing aggressions upon that section and seeking to lay it waste?
Are communities in the habit of making war upon themselves? If a
Republican party would spring up in the South, at the nod of a Republican Administration—if the weight of the Federal Government on
the side of slavery is all that prevents the formation of a Republican
party in the South—it is time the fact were known. The logic of the
Mercury certainly is, that the South is a section under a sort of Federal
martial law. If this were true, what possible remedy would disunion be?
If there would be a Republican party in the South, immediately upon
the inauguration of a Republican President, there would be a Northern
party there if the Confederacy were dissolved, which would be still
more dangerous to the peculiar institution of the South.

The sixth of the Mercury's twelve propositions is well calculated to
produce a panic in the South; and nothing has been printed for years
that will give more comfort to the extreme anti-slavery men of the
North. Is this sensitive, timorous thing of slavery, described as now
quivering with fears, that which has been boastfully proclaimed as the
mud-sill of society—the corner-stone of the Republic—the natural condition of the races, ordained by GOD, and of matchless beneficence? We
would say to the South, beware of these panic-mongers. The real incendiaries, who endanger Southern society, are not those who are
advocating the election of ABRAHAM LINCOLN, and hoping for an administration of the Government at his hands, that will give peace to the
country; but the pro-slavery politicians, those who have obtained place
and conspicuity by demagoguery, in the name of slavery, and who are
now croaking of dire calamities if a President should be constitutionally

elected, who does not bow down before the cotton crop and the laborers who produce it. Those who are bringing Southern society, and all that the South most prizes, into peril, are the fanatical Southerners, who assume that if their local prejudices are not humored, the nation must fall straightway into a condition of unquenchable combustion.

The proposition of the Mercury, that the Southern States withdraw from the Union before the conclusion of Mr. BUCHANAN's Administration, is the one above all others that we would have advanced, if we had been solicitous for the introduction of the irrepressible conflict, in its most dangerous form, into the South. It is a proposition which, if seriously agitated in the South, would rouse the people, and the disunionists would, in the language of the Mercury, be "crushed and cursed as the flagitious cause of the disasters around them." The Mercury, in attempting to set forth the terrors of submission, has surely shown up, with singular vividness, the horrors of disunion, and indicated more unmistakably than ever, that it cannot be a remedy for any evils that may befal the South, but would immeasurably increase and aggravate them all.

11. The Order of the Day—The Presidency

(Columbus *Daily Capital City Fact* [Breckinridge], October 19, 1860)

Having in a preceding issue of the FACT discussed at some length the respective merits of the different candidates who now stand before the people for the highest station in the government, we shall on this occasion resume the subject. We shall have especial regard to LINCOLN and BRECKINRIDGE. It is not our purpose to recommend Mr. BRECKINRIDGE, merely by detracting from the merits of the other three candidates. We have no such scheme before us; nor do we base our preference on any such foundation. Our preference is founded, not upon negative, but upon positive considerations. In a question so important, however, it is proper to bring into consideration, and to make the proper comparison among the Presidential candidates. Of Mr. DOUGLAS and Mr. BELL we have already spoken; and now take occasion to discuss the merits of Mr. LINCOLN. We have already characterized the latter gentleman as a sectional candidate, representing and leading a party in the non-slaveholding States, in opposition to the people of the South, and the institutions *they* have established. The great Republican party of the North has taken its rise upon the question of slavery, and upon that alone it now asserts its pretensions. But for the angry contests in Kansas, we should have scarcely found ourselves involved in a controversy so fierce and so embittered. At least not at so early a date. The contest, however, has been brought on, and it is now impossible to evade it.

It has always been our idea that a candidate for the Presidency should come forward on the broad ground of being the representative and servant of the *whole people interested*. In a government like this, embracing thirty three sovereign States, extending over a vast region of country—and penetrating all the temperate climates of the earth— our discussions should be co-extensive with the subject matter before us, and are not to rest in any narrow minded views and discussions.

When the foundation of the American Constitution was laid, it was upon a fair and equal basis. The thirteen States, then existing, by mutual consent, united to form a general union, for the purpose of a common protection against the dangers of foreign aggression, not less than to establish a government among themselves for the benefit and welfare of the whole.

It is well known that most of the then States, indeed a large majority of them, were *slave-holding*—all content with their own institutions, and not intending, by uniting into a confederated republic, to abolish their own polity and laws, except so far as the constitution enjoined it. It is the opinion of many, that the simple declaration of independence, by asserting the general sentiment that "all men are created equal," virtually overruled the principles of slavery theretofore existing in the several States, and set the enslaved African free, by placing him on a common and equal footing with his master. It is needless to spend time in refuting an idea so groundless and so absurd. When the Declaration of Independence was drawn, it was intended merely in reference to our position as British Colonies, and that we were about to break the tie binding us to the crown. We were not complaining of our *domestic* institutions, nor did the American people intend in any wise to affect them. The subject itself was unthought of. The great purpose was to break off their allegiance to the parent State. With this view— *and with this view alone*—and to justify the step before the world, they proclaimed a general truth, that all communities of men are naturally equal, and may set up a free government for themselves, whenever the opportunity arises, and especially when they could give the best of reasons for so doing. To contend that by making such a declaration that they thereby unwittingly acknowledged the freedom of their own domestics, is the higth [*sic*] of error—or, if we please, the hyperbola [*sic*] of nonsense. No sensible, impartial man in the universe, untrammelled by party spirit, or party-madness could draw so weak and foolish a conclusion. And to "make assurance double sure," when the

Constitution itself was framed, the existence of slavery not only continued to be recognized in the respective States, but is incidentally alluded to in that great instrument in three different places. To contend that either by the Declaration of Independence, or the coming into the union under the constitution, that any State abolished slavery thereby, or intended to abolish it, cannot be maintained for a moment of time on any rational grounds whatever. Then the Declaration of Independence, and the formation of the union, did in no wise whatever affect the institution of slavery. This could be done in one way only, and that was, by each individual State acting with sovereign power on its own institutions. This was the doctrine in the beginning, and if so, must be the doctrine now. Time cannot change the true construction of solemn instruments, especially one so solemn as the American Constitution. The judges on the Supreme Court bench take this view, and with deference we say, could take none other.

We will now again speak of Mr. LINCOLN.—We will not discuss his general fitness to fill the highest place in the government. Each particular man must have his own ideas as to this. We shall merely glance him over as to the principles of himself and his party, on the great constitutional question which now agitates and distracts the public mind. It has already been maintained by us, and for the best of reasons, that Mr. DOUGLAS' Squatter Sovereign ideas were in open conflict with the constitution, as maintained by the great and only authoritative tribunal in the country; and not only so, but in conflict with those principles of justice and of equal right, on which the constitution itself was founded. That his ideas of a complete non-intervention by Congress was equally indefensible to the extent Mr. DOUGLAS proposes. [sic] How is it with Mr. LINCOLN? We find him still more in conflict with the constitution than even Mr. DOUGLAS. Mr. SEWARD, in his last Kansas speech, applauds the people of that territory in the most extravagant terms for their Squatter Sovereign achievements in driving out slavery. The whole tenor and bearing of the speech was the maintainance [sic] of Squatter Sovereign doctrines. Mr. DOUGLAS himself would have made just such a speech.—SEWARD, DOUGLAS and LINCOLN all maintain the Squatter Sovereign creed. But Mr. LINCOLN maintains further, that Congress may not only pass police laws and regulate the internal affairs of the territories, under the Constitution, but may go so far as to prohibit the Southern man from taking his slave property into such territory! It seems, according to this idea, that there is a double power to be set up against the Southern settler. First, Congress may pass laws to keep him out, or to turn him out; or, if Congress does not intervene with the great powers of the government, the people themselves may rise and thrust the slaveholder out! Although the Supreme Court decides it is unwarranted by and is against the constitution. [sic] It is contended that no such man as this should be supported by the American people, setting aside constitutional objections, which cannot be gotten over—from the crown of the head to the sole of his feet he is a sectional candidate, glorying in his favorite idea of the "irrepressible conflict," which is now dividing and maddening the Northern and Southern sections of the people. This alone should exclude him from every chance of being elected. The Southern people merely wish to be let alone, and to be left in the enjoyment of their constitutional rights.—Mr. LINCOLN would not admit them even to such an humble privilege. What man who is a friend to the constitution and to this glorious and even-handed Union, can further pretensions such as these? If such a man is voted for it must be for party purposes merely, and not for the good of the country.

In contrast to the three candidates we have named and discussed, we now present Mr. BRECKINRIDGE—a Union-loving man, of fair and spotless reputation—a faithful supporter of the constitution as interpreted by the Supreme Court—a man of fine talents, and of manly and liberal principles—most beloved and admired by those who know him best. After scanning him well, and weighing his merits with an even hand, we present him as a candidate, not of a sectional party, but as a general candidate, for the whole American people, and in every way worthy of their general support in the coming election.

12. To CANDID DEMOCRATS—A FEW PLAIN SUGGESTIONS

(Hartford Evening Press [Lincoln], October 25 and 26, 1860)

There is many a democrat who is convinced that the party with which he has long been associated is seriously, if not incurably, at fault, and who is half disposed to vote with the republicans at least this once. To such we offer a few plain suggestions, in no offensive spirit, and respectfully ask for them a thoughtful consideration.

1. *A change of administration is necessary.* Parties are mere temporary associations for temporary purposes. It is inevitable that, in the long course of time and by the long possession of power, they should become corrupt. They should then be dissolved and new associations formed. The old issues upon which the democratic party was formed have been disposed of finally. The party which now defends the rights of man and contends against monopolies and aristocratic and federal tendencies is the republican party. The spirit of radical democracy

will always exist and work in the country. That spirit has passed out of the old democracy into the new. To many the republican party looks radical, but it cannot look more so than the old democratic party did twenty five years ago when it had a life, a soul and a purpose. And the time was when the old republican party of 1800 was reproached with the name "democrat," just as the modern republican party is with the term "abolitionist!"

It is quite time that the democratic party should acknowledge itself dead, as it really is. Its corruptions are countless and undeniable. But it is not necessary to the point we are now making to claim that the republican party is better, except in consequence of its being younger; it is better because any young party is better than any old one. The chances are beyond computation and amount to an absolute moral certainty that it will for a time at least, if successful next month, conduct the government, not in an ideally perfect manner, but, comparatively speaking, with honesty, economy and justice.

2. *The chief question at issue is one of conscience, involving high moral obligations.* It is this: Shall human slavery be extended into all the territories? The Slave Power demands that it shall be considered as already legally existing in them all, and entitled to the favor and protection of the Federal Government. It quibbles about the word "property," and assumes that the body and mind of a man can be "property," just as a horse or an ox is property. And they cry out against any discrimination, even in territory that is now free, between an ordinary title to the beasts of the field and an assumed title to another man with an immortal soul. Just as well might a Mormon, if he should establish himself in Hartford with a dozen wives, cry out against a prosecution for bigamy or adultery, as being under oppressive and partial legislation;—as interfering with his "domestic relations and destroying the happiness of his family." Calling a concubine a wife does not make her such, nor does calling a man "property" make him, in the language of slave law, a "chattel, a thing personal."

If the slave states, by their local laws, enforce the practical recognition of a title to human beings, we are not politically responsible and have no right to interfere politically. But we do all own a share in the territories and take part by our congressmen in laying in the west the foundations of states that will yet control a mighty nation. And when the Slave Power, through the democratic party, demands that we shall recognize and protect in those territories a system which our forefathers condemned as cruel, shameful and at war with the obligations of man to man and man to God, and which we see clearly retards the growth

of communities, discourages industry and education and degrades labor
—or when it even only demands that we shall acquiesce in the introduction of that system into those territories, then it does become, directly and emphatically, our business and duty to act with speed and
energy. We must neither enact injustice nor fail to prevent it. We
apologize for slaveholders by saying that they were born and brought
up in the midst of the system: how can we, educated in free society, dare
to establish the institution in boundless territories now free? Jefferson,
a slaveholder, "trembled for his country when he remembered that God
is just," and declared that if the slaves should become numerous and
intelligent and should fight for their freedom, "the Almighty had no
attribute which could take sides with us (the slaveholders) in such a contest!" And you remember with what solemnity and intense indignation
Henry Clay, a slaveholder, declared that he "never, *never*, NEVER,"
would vote to extend slavery into free territories. And yet you, our
democratic friend, born in old Connecticut, would vote (to state it
very mildly) to *permit* the extension of slavery!

There is nothing in the constitution against our policy of slavery restriction. The words "slavery," "slave" and even "servitude" were carefully excluded. If slaves were referred [to] they were spoken of as
"persons" and not as "property." Mr. Madison, in the convention,
"thought it wrong to admit into the constitution the idea that there
could be property in men," and in that spirit was the instrument made.
Slavery was left as they found it, sustained only by local, state legislation,
and a large majority of the framers of the constitution have left on
record, either by votes, speeches or letters, their hostility to slavery
extension. They expected, hoped and prayed that slavery might soon
come to an end.

3. *The national revenues from duties on imports should be raised
in the manner best calculated to promote the interests of the workingmen of the nation.* The duties laid upon goods imported should be so
adjusted as to afford assistance to departments of industry not yet firmly
established among us and to give reasonable encouragement to the introduction of new ones. The history of American industry plainly shows
that the rivalry of foreign manufacturers and artificers can often prevent the introduction of new branches of industry amongst us or can
stifle their first feeble results; for it is well worth their while to sell goods
at a loss during a short period if they can thus ruin competitors here
and retain the monopoly of our market. And it is equally certain that if
protected either by the power of a large capital or by such encouragement as a judicious tariff can easily give, the unrivalled shrewdness,

enterprise, activity, inventiveness and industry of our people will within a reasonable period establish such new branches of industry upon a basis too firm to be disturbed by foreign interference, and which will ensure them the full control of the home market and a full share of the profit of foreign ones. Such for instance has been the case with the cotton manufacture, with many departments of the iron manufacture and others. And it is evidently for the advantage of the nation to have its own trading and manufacturing population consume the products of its own agriculture; it is evidently better for the farmer, the artisan and the operative to save for themselves all the profit of the foreign manufacture and as much as possible of the expense of transporting property to and fro over land or water. The republican party does not claim that any money should be raised expressly for protection, but only that the money which must be raised for the support of the government shall be collected in such a manner as to promote the prosperity of the people.

These principles are just, and nine-tenths of the people of the free states would naturally carry them into legislation. But slavery has altogether different interests: it cannot engage extensively in manufactures; it has not the skill, the inventive faculty nor the energy; it must depend upon a few great staples which it must carry to a distance and exchange for the countless productions of some free people. Therefore the Slave Power has always disliked, opposed, and defeated or embarrassed such tariffs as free labor desired. Now free labor has an immense preponderance of numbers and wealth; why then should it not have such national legislation as it prefers? Why should not Free Labor be the national, and Slave Labor the local, sectional, and exceptional interest? So the Republican party would have it.

4. *A homestead should be granted from the public domain, free of cost—except for surveying—to every poor man who needs it, desires it, and will cultivate it.*

It is true in a certain limited and qualified sense that every man has a right to own a piece of land. That is to say, it was never intended that every man should [not?] possess the means of gaining a fair living and bringing up his family respectably. This means might be either a portion of land or some other property or possession.

Accordingly we find that during the whole history of the world, an instinctive sense of injustice has always been felt whenever an excessive share of land has been accumulated in the hands of any person or class of persons. It was unjust and oppressive, and was felt to be so, when a few proprietors owned almost all the lands of Italy in the days of ancient Rome. An obscure but well founded and instinctive sense of injustice at this day pervades the whole poorer class of the English nation, founded upon the enormous accumulation of the lands of England in the hands of a wealthy and titled aristocracy. Precisely the same sense of injustice arises in every honest and intelligent mind in contemplating the engrossment of government lands in our own western states by unscrupulous speculators or ravenous corporations, who hold it with the express design of extorting an enormous profit from the necessities of the poor.

No scheme could be better calculated to promote the wealth and prosperity of our country than the gift of a piece of land to every one who will live on it and cultivate it. The poor citizen owns his share of the public domain. The homestead policy of the republican party would only measure off by metes and bounds his undivided interest in the national wealth of unoccupied land. The transaction would be almost as strictly legal as the division of the farm of an intestate in Connecticut among his heirs. With this part of the policy of the republicans we believe that the great majority of northern democrats substantially agree. Yet a democratic Senate prevented the passage of a thorough homestead bill which passed the House of Representatives last winter, and a democratic president vetoed even the modified bill which the Senate suffered to pass, and which the House accepted as the best they could get. The explanation is this: the land policy of the Slave Power is one of accumulation in the hands of a few great proprietors; the small landholders who are the bone and sinew of the North, the strength and substance of its prosperity, and the rapid builders of new free states, are the pest and poison of the southern planter. And besides this natural hatred to the class, the settled policy of the southern leaders to prevent, if possible, any increase in the number of free states, naturally leads them to oppose the westward spread of small freeholds.

[Concluded on October 26]

5. *The federal government should at proper times give reasonable aid to a system of river and harbor improvements.*

The oceans, the great lakes, and the rivers of our country, are the chief natural highways of our commerce. The same species of powers which authorizes Congress to expend money for the military defence of rivers and harbors, will authorize it to spend money for their improvement in time of peace. If the development of navigation and commerce, and the facilitation of intercourse, were not sufficient reasons for such expenditure, abundant ones may be found in the direct bearing of such improvements on the federal revenue. The better our rivers and harbors are adapted to the purposes of navigation, the greater our wealth and commerce will be, and the greater the revenue thus accruing to the federal treasury. Such, within reasonable limits, would be the policy of the republican party.

6. *A Pacific Railroad should be built as speedily as possible, with reasonable aid and encouragement from the Federal Government.*

The Chicago platform, and both the democratic platforms, all agree that this road should be built, and on this point nothing more can be necessary than to express the pleasure which every right-minded citizen must naturally feel, at finding that there is one measure which all parties and sections join in recommending. But the Slave Power has stubbornly resisted any preparatory measures which seemed to recognize the necessity of starting it from the centre of population and wealth, and has always schemed to run it far to the southward, where it expected to make slave territory.

7. *The disunion question, if it must be met, had better be met now —the sooner the better.*

It seems almost absurd to lay down definite principles on the subject of disunion. Disunion is a threat, not an argument. When a man begins to threaten, he gives up the argument; he confesses that his reasons are worthless, and that he has no mode left of accomplishing his purpose except brute force. When, therefore, northern democrats tell us that disunion is to be the consequence of the election of a republican president, we need not suppose that they desire or recommend it, but merely that they are afraid that southern politicians will bring it to pass. How much, then, is it best to be frightened?

We say, not at all; the threat is an empty sham; those who make it have not the remotest intention of fulfilling it; or if a few of them have, their enterprise has about as good a chance of succeeding as the lunatics in the Retreat at Hartford would have of capsizing the state of Connecticut into Long Island Sound. They are too few and too crazy.

If the threat is worth regarding; if the purpose is earnest, the meaning of such a state of things is serious indeed. In that case, it means that the great political experiment of these United States is a *great failure;* that the will of a peaceful voting majority can no longer govern the nation; that any minority wicked enough and desperate enough can govern us on the great principle of a pirate in a powder magazine, who will blow the ship to atoms if his orders are not complied with. Now, of all the hateful despotisms in the world, none is so infernally hateful as an oligarchy; even Nero was not so bad as the thirty tyrants; and if an attempt is to be made to subject our thirty millions of people to the arbitrary will of three hundred thousand tyrants—for that is about the number of slave-holders—every independent, honest northern mind must desire that this issue be made NOW, *met promptly,* and decided once for all. We are ready for the decision. And we fully believe that when given, while it would result in the annihilation of the shallow traitorous fools, it would only consolidate more firmly the national power. These men say to us, acquiesce in one wickedness or we will commit another. If the Union has arrived at such a state of moral imbecility that its voters can be frightened into a course of action by such a choice of wickedness as this, it is high time that the fact were fully proved.

But, it may be urged, disunion is threatened in consequence of the unconstitutional measures proposed by the Republicans. We answer that we defy any man to point out any measure proposed by any Republican leader which is not constitutional.

———

To conclude:—pray tell us, democratic friend, what there is wrong or incorrect in anything that we have said. If we are right, how is it possible for you to give your vote honestly for either Breckinridge or Douglas? We have said nothing about the candidates—men of all parties have highly complimented ours for their great integrity and ability; to say the very least, they are equal to any of the others. We claim that their political creed is infinitely better. Come with us then, at least once; let us make the popular voice so overwhelmingly powerful that slavery propagandism and disunion shall forever hide their diminished heads, and Freedom and Free Labor resume their undisputed sway over the destinies of our idolized country.

13. FREE AND SLAVE LABOR—TO WORKINGMEN IN OHIO

(Columbus *Daily Ohio Statesman* [Douglas], November 2, 1860)

The Republicans claim to be in favor of Congressional exclusion of slavery so that, as they allege, free labor and slave labor shall not be brought into competition in the Territories. On this ground they make the most earnest and affecting appeals to workingmen for their votes.

Never was a more transparent humbug invented to deceive and entrap the honest mass of the people. Congressional enactments never did and never will make a fact of free or slave territory. According to locality, climate and production, the system of free or slave labor will prevail. This will be determined by the natural laws governing immigration to and settlement in the Territories. The Republican State organ in this city, not long since, contained articles logically demonstrating that in the natural and necessary course of events our present public domain must all, with perhaps trifling exceptions, be and remain forever free territory. It is perfectly clear that where the people of a Territory want slavery, they will have it in spite of Congressional prohibitions, and where they do not want it, neither legislative enactments or judicial decisions can force it in. It is, therefore, sheer deception to claim votes for LINCOLN in order to keep slavery out of the Territories.

But there is a view of this subject of free and slave labor, to which we invite the serious attention of workingmen in Ohio. It is the habit of the Republicans to represent the two systems as antagonistic, and for this reason to demand, not only the exclusion of slavery from the Territories, but its extermination in the United States.

The two systems of free and slave labor, as they are called, are only so far antagonistic, that the people of a State or Territory will, in the regulation of their domestic policy, adopt the one or the other. If they do not choose the system best suited to their condition and interests, it is their own business, not that of other people. But as respects the different sections of the Union, free and slave labor are not antagonistic, but mutually beneficial to the people of each section.

Leaving out of view the abstract question of the justice or injustice of slavery, it exists, as we all know, under the Constitution of the United States, in the States which have made it legal. These States owe their wealth and the production of their great staples to slave labor. This production—this slave labor is the basis of the commerce, the manufactures and the general prosperity of the North. It is this despised slave labor which gives the working men in the North employment, and affords them better wages than the same labor will command in any other country on the globe.

It requires no deep insight into the intricate principles of political economy to understand why this is so. It is plain and obvious upon the surface. Of the exports of the country, seventy per cent. is from the South. These exports are made almost wholly in Northern ships owned by Northern capitalists, built by Northern workmen, and manned by Northern seamen.

The South is the great consumer of the manufactures and produce of the North. The consumption of Northern manufactures and of the produce of the free States of the West in the South, amounts annually to the immense sum of $240,000,000. It is this great consumption—it is the mutual intercourse and traffic between the two sections, which infuses life and activity into Northern capital and industry, and benefits the workingmen, whether employed in the manufactory, the work-shop, or on the farm.

The Republicans are making war upon the Southern people to depreciate and make them ultimately forego that system of labor which they prefer, and which is so interwoven with their own prosperity and that of the whole country, that its destruction would be disastrous to both North and South.

If the Republican policy should prevail in the administration of the Federal Government, or even if that party becomes dominant in the North, and arrays the free States against the South, as it has already done where it has had the power, the consequence will be, if not an immediate dissolution of the Union, an interruption of that unrestrained intercourse which has heretofore existed between the two sections, and a determination on the part of the South, in self-protection, to depend less upon the North, and more upon its own resources.

This will gradually, and if LINCOLN should be elected it may suddenly, produce a stagnation in Northern trade and productive industry that will repeat, on a broader and more enduring scale, the terrible financial crises of '37–'40, and reduce fearfully both the number of laborers and the wages of labor in the North, while increasing fourfold the cost of many of the necessaries of life.

We have given briefly a few hints to the workingmen of Ohio. But if they follow out these suggestions, they will see clearly the result to them and their families and children of this political antagonism to slave labor in the South, which the Republicans are fomenting, under the pretense of being the friends of free labor. They are really the enemies of free labor, and are doing all in their power to injure it. The election of LINCOLN, if such a disastrous event should take place, will inflict a blow upon every workingman in the North who needs, for the support of himself and family, constant employment and the highest wages he can now obtain.

If, therefore, the laborers in Ohio desire themselves and their fellow-workmen to remain independent and prosperous, they will vote unhesitatingly for that Presidential candidate who is the true friend of free labor, and who can, if they do their duty, defeat LINCOLN in Ohio.

14. Who Shall Rule?

(Daily Pittsburgh Gazette [Lincoln], November 2, 1860)

The great question to be settled by the approaching Presidential election is, Shall the majority rule?

Mr. Douglas started out with the plausible theory that the only way to settle the Slavery question in the territories was to leave it to the people of the territories; but events have shown the unwillingness of the South to submit to *any* decision of that question unfavorable to themselves, and they have now started a still more important question, viz: whether they ought to submit to the decision of a majority of the people, in this Presidential election, constitutionally expressed.

A large party—*how* large we cannot say, but we know it is very noisy —contends that the South should not submit to a President constitutionally chosen by a majority of the people. Nay, more, they contend that the mere choice of a particular man, no matter what he may profess, nor how carefully the constitutional forms may be observed in his election, will of itself be sufficient cause for rebellion against the government. They declare that they will not submit to a President chosen by a party other than their own; and while Gov. Wise proposes to organize an armed resistance to the government so chosen, Roger A. Pryor offers himself as the Brutus to plunge a dagger into the heart of the President to be placed at its head by the American people.

If these men are to be taken at their word and permitted to do as they threaten, the majority does not and cannot rule. So long as the majority chooses to elect a man satisfactory to these blusterers, it is all right; when they choose to do otherwise the government must be overthrown. In this view of the case, we as a people are no longer free. We are mere serfs, subject to the tyrannical caprices of aristocratic masters. We may register their edicts; but we must not dare to do as we please. It was upon this basis that Napoleon conceded universal suffrage; those to whom it was conceded could vote as they pleased; but if they did not vote as they were told they were to be shot down.

We live, nominally, under a Constitutional government. The Constitution guarantees to us certain rights, among which is the right of the majority to choose a President in the way pointed out in that instrument. If that right has any value it consists in the enjoyment of it without hindrance or extraneous restriction. An attempt is now making to cripple the exercise of it; to say that it shall be used only for the elevation of certain men; and that if the majority choose to exercise it in any other way the government shall be rent in twain.

The grand, overshadowing issue of the campaign, therefore is, Will the people submit to this dictation? Will they assert their rights or yield to those who menace them? Will they maintain, intact, the privileges secured to them by the Fathers of the Republic, or will they basely yield them at the bidding of the southern oligarchy—a pitiful minority which has insinuated itself into the control of the government?

These are the questions to be answered on Tuesday next. It is no longer a mere contest between four men, but a struggle for the maintenance of the great majority principle in this Government. Shall the people rule? The oligarchs say no—not if they elect LINCOLN; and it behooves the people to elect LINCOLN, just to show that they *will* rule, in spite of incipient traitors like Wise and volunteer assassins such as Pryor.

The time has come for a firm and resolute assertion of the majority principle. Our government can be maintained upon no other. The majority has the right to rule only within Constitutional limits; but within those limits it *must* rule or yield up the government to a usurping minority. The North has always acted upon this principle. When beaten it has uniformly submitted, although always the sufferer by submission. It has stood firm by the Union under Embargo Acts and low tariffs. It has seen its commerce swept from the ocean by the former; and when it turned its active energies to manufactures it has seen them also swept away by the free trade theories of the southern dictatorship. Beggary and starvation have been endured. Merchants have seen their ships rot at the wharves. Manufacturers have seen their spindles lying idle and their workmen gaunt and famished for food; and yet the North has always been true to the Union of the States, seeking no remedy except within the Union and beneath the Constitution. And now when the hour of the remedy has come, when the twenty millions of the North are reaching out their hands to right themselves in the way provided by the Constitution, seeking only their own rights and not the wrong of any man, they are met with the cry of Secession and Disunion!

If it has come to this; if we have reached that degraded state of serfdom that we dare not vote without the consenting nod of Southern dictation, then let us assign our share in the government to South Carolina, and humbly request that chivalric State to do our thinking for us, and assume the charge of our federal interests. But until it has come to that, let us do our own thinking and acting, and stand prepared to back up our acts with a resolution adequate to the occasion. We have always yielded, when the fate of war was against us, and the South must be taught to follow our example and learn that she does not possess a monopoly of the government.

As to the threats of Revolution so freely indulged in, we do not care whether they are sham or in earnest. We believe them to be mere bravado—empty gasconading, intended merely to alarm; but that is no matter. They are equally disgraceful, whether made for political effect or otherwise; and the people of the North will be false to their rights if they fail to rebuke them. The time to stand by a right is when it is threatened or in danger; and the time for fearlessly asserting the right of the majority to rule, within Constitutional limits, is *now,* when desperate efforts are making to prevent its successful exercise.

15. The Voice of Warning

(Indianapolis *Indiana Daily State Sentinel* [Douglas], November 3, 1860)

The St. Louis *Republican* says that those who heard or have read the speech of Hon. John J. Crittenden, delivered in that city on Monday evening last, will not have failed to observe the apprehensions expressed by that venerable statesman as to the effect upon the Union of the election of Abraham Lincoln to the Presidency. It were well—infinitely well for the country if it could be safely assumed that those apprehensions are groundless. But, as we have before declared, there is, unhappily, too much reason to fear imminent danger from the fiendish designs and efforts of the enemies of the Union. We have endeavored faithfully to do our duty in exposing those designs and efforts ever since they manifested themselves in the disruption of the Charleston Convention. We have shown, again and again, that the influences which produced that disruption, proceeded from those who were intent on destroying the Union, and that their machinations were deliberately directed to the one great object of effecting the election of Lincoln, *in order that they might avail themselves of that result as a ground for* "precipitating the cotton States into a revolution." As we near the period when those machinations appear to be reaching their culmination, let us calmly inquire what is to be the end of all this? Never was a more momentous inquiry presented to any people. He who turns away from it, or treats it lightly, may very soon find that he has committed an error for which there may be no possible remedy.

In the first place, in the language of Mr. Crittenden—"There never

WAS SUCH A FINANCIAL AND PECUNIARY CRISIS IN THIS COUNTRY AS THAT
WOULD BRING." No powers of description can give any adequate impression of the disastrous effects upon all our material interests, if the country should once become involved in the throes of attempted disunion.
We have no disposition to become alarmists unnecessarily, but we can
perceive no hope for the agricultural, manufacturing and commercial
interests of the nation, if that awful extremity should be reached. There
are those who would disregard the prophetic warning; but if the country should be precipitated into disunion, night does not follow day with
more inevitable succession, than will universal bankruptcy soon overwhelm the entire nation. Men who now are counted affluent will see
their wealth drop from their grasp, and themselves and their families
reduced to want. Every branch of industry will be struck with an in-
stantaneous and deadly paralysis. The artisan and laborer will be without employment, because capital will have vanished; and soon the cry
of the strong man for *bread* will be heard in accents of woe and dread,
in every part of the land. A people who have never heard *that cry*, have
but a poor conception of the gloom and terror it will carry to every
heart. And what shall follow it? Can we hope that such a day of tribulation would pass, without bringing with it fire and blood—the torch of
the incendiary, the blow of the assassin, the war of the poor for food,
the struggle of men for life? But we will not follow the gloomy train of
thought which this view of the impending danger begets.

But if we turn from it, shall we find any more cheering prospects in
other directions? Can secession be attempted by any State without inevitable bloodshed? And if the blood of American citizens be shed by
American citizens in such a struggle, when will it cease to flow? Ay,
when will it cease? He who can answer that question with certainty, can
tell when the bad passions of man will cease to hurry them [*sic*] into
crime, when peace shall be universal, when strife shall cease on earth, and
love shall encircle the world with the gentle bonds of universal brotherhood. And when the fatal blow shall be struck, what will be the effect
upon those noble institutions which our fathers bequeathed us, and
which we have been accustomed to regard as resting upon impregnable
foundations, because those foundations were cemented with their blood?
Can they stand? Is it *possible* for them to endure such a shock? We are
constrained to declare that we do not see how they can bear up against
it. They were made for a people linked together as brothers, not for a
divided nation whose several parts are at war with each other. The simple, undisguised, and terrible truth is that if once the fires of civil war
be kindled they will burn until all is consumed that can be, and the

land shall become a waste, over which shall brood the silence of an utter and hopeless desolation.

If this is to be the end of this people and their Government, at whose door lays [sic] the mighty wrong? Can there be any doubt on this point? Can not every man in the Nation see that the fomenters of *sectional discord* are the authors of it? Under no conceivable circumstance would a struggle between any two *National* parties have produced the dangers of the present hour. The Northern Sectionalists, in their insane warfare against an institution which enters into all the interests and all the relations of the South, have been met by the Disunionists with an equally insane demand for the exercise of the power of the Federal Government to protect that institution in a region and under circumstances requiring no such protection. The latter have seized the occasion to exact what they know can not possibly be granted, and to base upon the failure to grant it, the deadly resort to revolution. There was no evil threatened, for which the Constitution and the laws do not afford a peaceful, complete and permanent remedy; but it was no part of the traitorous designs of Southern revolutionists to appeal to the means of Constitutional redress. For years they waited for an opportunity to bring their treasonable purposes into action, and they found or made it in the contest of the present year. They met a willing ally in the present occupant of the Presidential chair; and under the united impulse of hostility to the Union and hatred toward STEPHEN A. DOUGLAS, the traitorous movement was begun, which now threatens to destroy the country.

With renewed energy we invoke every man in the country to bear witness that upon the originators and supporters of the plot which presented JOHN C. BRECKINRIDGE as a candidate before the people, rests the terrible responsibility of the perils which now environ us. But for them the Democratic party would have been united over the whole country, and would have defeated LINCOLN, and overthrown his party with an irretrievable defeat. But for the divisions they produced in that party, the great Union loving element which now ranges itself under the lead of BELL and EVERETT, would have sided and acted with the Democracy in the North and the South, and fanaticism and treason in all their forms would have been at once and finally repulsed. Upon them must forever rest the deathless odium of the overthrow of our institutions, if they fall. Let them, if they can, meet the dire retribution which, sooner or later, must visit those who precipitate the ruin of the noblest fabric of freedom that men have ever reared or looked upon.

16. SHALL WE GOVERN OURSELVES?

(Cincinnati Daily Commercial [Lincoln], November 3, 1860)

In the distribution of powers between the three-fold departments of the Federal Government, it was the aim of the framers of the Constitution to guard against any infringement on each others' functions on the one hand, and any violation of popular rights by either department, on the other. Hence the Constitution was most carefully worded so as to define the power of each of the several branches of the Government, and clauses of reservation were put in, for the purpose of guarding against usurpation on the part of either, of powers not clearly granted.

The greatest jealousy appears to have been felt, by the more democratically inclined members of the Federal convention, of the probable absorption by the Supreme Judicial tribunal of an inordinate and dangerous share of authority. THOMAS JEFFERSON, PATRICK HENRY, GEORGE MASON and BENJ. FRANKLIN, than whom there were no more enlightened or patriotic statesmen in those days, solemnly protested against the investiture of the Judges of the Supreme Court with a life tenure of office. They stated in the most forcible manner, the objections against such a violation of the democratic principle, upon which the government set out. They pointed to the inevitable tendency, on the part of officers unappointed by the people, irresponsible to the people, and irremovable by the people, to enlarge their jurisdiction, and assume powers dangerous to popular liberty. They showed that the privilege of power so unlimited, was almost certain to be abused; and they put on record the most earnest warnings against the manner of appointment, and the tenure of office of these Federal Judges of the Court of last resort.

It is impossible to deny, at this day, that experience has largely justified the apprehensions of these sagacious statesmen. The Supreme Court of the United States, even composed, as it has usually been, of men of high character and attainments, has nevertheless exhibited the inevitable tendency of men in whose hands is lodged a great and irresponsible power. It has undertaken to decide not only legal and constitutional questions, but questions of government and political polity. It has transcended its sphere of arbiter between parties in suits legitimately before it, and undertaken to arbitrate between the views which divide political parties in this nation. It has overruled and reversed the decisions of our State Courts, even on questions of purely local and domestic policy. It has arrogated to itself the power to nullify the legislation of sovereign States. It has stealthily incorporated political *dicta* in its judicial decisions, and pronounced opinions which have acquired a *quasi* judicial sanction on matters wholly beside the case in hand, and entirely beyond the jurisdiction of the Court.

One of the clearest rights of the people of each separate political community would seem to be the right to refuse to the institution of human slavery a place in their governmental polity and social order. A question so vitally associated with the interests of every citizen can only be properly determined by the aggregate voice of the citizens themselves. —Yet the Supreme Court of the United States has indirectly, if not directly denied this right of self-government, in proclaiming that slaves are property under the Constitution, and then it follows that it is the duty of the *Federal* Government to extend protection to that property in the Territories. This monstrous decision cuts off the people from controlling their own institutions. It compels them to submit to the introduction of a system of servile labor, odious in most cases to a majority of the people, and destructive of the interests of the free white man. It strips the people of the right of self-government, and delivers them over, bound hand and foot, to the government of the Supreme Court. It invests nine irresponsible and nearly superannuated Judges with the power to dictate the institutions of a nation yet to be.

Are the people of the United States prepared to submit to so great a perversion of the forms and the substance of free government as this? If they are, they deserve not only to have negro slavery thrust upon them as an institution, but also to be slaves themselves. If the spirit of liberty has so far succumbed, if the manly independence which should characterise freemen, has so far deteriorated, that they are willing to have their laws made over their heads by the royal fiat of a Supreme Court, it is as well to surrender the name, as we have parted with the essence of free government.

For the Supreme Court to undertake to mould the institutions of future States, is to usurp powers, not only undelegated to it in the Constitution, but expressly reserved by that instrument to the people. It is one of the elementary rights of every people to decide such questions for themselves. There is no meaning or relevancy in a democratic form of government, if the democratic principle is to be straightway extracted from it, by nine respectable gentlemen in black gowns, sitting in conclave at Washington. This centralized junta of power, which is to lord it over the people's heritage, and make or unmake institutions at a word, is a singular outcome for a nation which set out to be a republic. We might as well have king and lords at once, or be ruled by an oligarchy of nobles, as to arrive at the same end of surrendering the first principle of a representative government, through the covert but absolute usurpation of the Supreme Court.

17. The Great Battle

(Chicago Daily Democrat [Lincoln], November 5, 1860)

The greatest political battle which has been fought in America since the formation of this Government, is to be decided to-morrow. Issues the most momentous hang upon the result. Let us enumerate them, briefly and simply:

In the first place, if the pro-slavery party triumph to-morrow throughout the Union, one of two things will be inevitable, to wit:

Either the slave power will go on from conquering to conquer, driving every vestige of freedom before it, planting the institution of slavery on every foot of our land, degrading free labor, and erecting an oligarchy of capital and an aristocracy of wealth, the way for all which is already marked out by the decisions of the Supreme Court and the construction of existing laws; or else, driven to desperation, and deprived of the hope of obtaining redress through the ballot-box, the people of the North will rise against the oppressors and sweep them away forever. True, the defeat of Mr. Lincoln to-morrow may not prevent the election of an anti-slavery President four years hence, or eight years hence; but it will be easier and safer to elect one now. Nothing but embarrassment and dangers can arise from any further delays. The irrepressible conflict must be decided sooner or later, and the sooner the better. The Union cannot endure permanently half slave and half free. We do not expect the Union to be dissolved—if a Republican President is elected it cannot be dissolved—but we do expect it will cease to be divided. If Mr. Lincoln is elected, the Administration of which he will be the head, will arrest the further spread of slavery, and place it where the public mind shall rest in the belief of its ultimate extinction. If he is defeated, its advocates will push it forward until it reigns over all the land.

Secondly, If Mr. Lincoln be elected to-morrow we may consider the question of the suppression of the slave trade fully settled. During Mr. Buchanan's Administration the slave trade has flourished to an almost unprecedented extent. Thousands of negroes have been stolen from Africa and landed on our shores. Some of them have been reclaimed and sent back; a far larger number have died; still more are now toiling in the cotton fields and rice swamps of the far South. All this will be put to a sudden and complete stop, under Mr. Lincoln's government.

Thirdly, The pro-slavery interpretations of the Constitution of the United States which have been so freely and continually disseminated and enforced will be reversed, and that glorious instrument will be construed, as its framers intended it should, as a charter of freedom, and not as a bulwark of slavery.

Fourthly, The present infamous Fugitive Slave Law will be repealed, and a law substituted in its place which will give the slave owners only what the Constitution provides, not a jot more. Their pound of flesh they may have, but not a drop of blood.

In a word, the whole policy of the government will be a policy of freedom. The spirit that will actuate all its departments will be a spirit of liberty. The patronage and the influence of the government, at home and abroad, will be exerted on the side of freedom. The rights of all the citizens of the United States will be made as secure in South Carolina as it is in Massachusetts. [sic] The sanctity of the mails will not be invaded, and the postmasters of the southern States will no longer be allowed to decide what newspapers their neighbors may read. Liberty shall be proclaimed through all the land and to all the inhabitants thereof. The slave States will be surrounded by a cordon of free States, and slavery, confined to its present limits—limits, too, speedily to be still further circumscribed by Delaware and Missouri becoming free —will become unprofitable, and a pecuniary, as well as a moral curse. Then emancipation societies will spring up in all the slave States, and the blessed work will go on, until the last slave is free, and America is redeemed from the foul stain that now degrades her in the eyes of all mankind.

Such are the issues depending on the result of the great battle to be fought to-morrow. In view of these, who that loves his country, his race, the rights of man, and the blessings of a free government, will hesitate to do his duty at the polls? The weather to-morrow may be unpleasant; it may be rainy and cold, and very disagreeable. But we had better endure every privation and make every sacrifice, rather than by our failure to do our duty, lose the inestimable blessings which the election of Abraham Lincoln will confer upon us and our posterity.

18. Do It with Your Eyes Open

(Chicago *Daily Times and Herald* [Douglas], November 6, 1860)

The course of the Republican leaders has been to blind the people of the North to the true feelings and position of the Southern States. The efforts to blind them, and keep them blinded, have been unceasing and determined.

It is not only due to the South, but it is a matter of sheer justice to ourselves, that we should act with our eyes wide open in this perilous crisis. He who would suppress the truth, and delude the people in this dangerous hour, is a moral traitor to the country and the enemy of American civilization and liberty.

The *people* of the South have never wronged the North nor felt like doing so. Fire-eating disunionists have insulted us, and committed personal indignity upon some individuals; but the Southern people have never sought nor desired to force their institutions upon us, nor to attack those which we already possess. Under these circumstances, then, the South had a right to expect that her rights under the Constitution would be maintained in good faith and her peace respected. Has this been done so far as the Republican party is concerned? Have the South just reason to believe that it *will* be done, if they win the election? Let facts speak.

For thirty years and more, there has been a continuous war waged upon the institutions, property and constitutional rights of the people of the South. They have the undoubted right to a return of their fugitive slaves. This right is directly overridden by State legislation by more than half of the Northern States, and its practical benefits utterly denied in nearly all of them. They have the undoubted moral and constitutional right to judge of their own institutions, and to the peaceable enjoyment of such as they may adopt. And yet the Northern agitators have, for thirty years, kept them in hot water by their incendiary efforts against their most vital institution; have organized a system of robbery of their property; have already robbed them of millions' worth of that property, and as time progresses have only increased their efforts to render it more insecure and worthless. The people of the South have an undoubted right to peace and repose in the Union, with whatever domestic institutions they may have. And yet these anti-slavery agitators have rendered insecure every home south of Mason & Dixon's line, and by their machinations have induced armed bands of fanatics to invade the peaceful homes of the South; have stirred up servile insur-rections, and have caused bloodshed and crimes of the most atrocious character. These acts of hatred and aggression have grown in number and atrocity, as time has advanced, until the Southern people feel that there is to be no end to them, and that there is no hope of safety for life or property in the present condition of things. Should matters even grow no worse than they have been in the last five years, *they regard* such a state of insecurity and excitement as utterly intolerable and subversive of the very ends for which governments a[re] formed.

But the most terrible feature of this fanatical movement has yet to be told. The enemies of the South, not contented with nullifying the fugitive slave law, the establishment of the underground railroad sys-tem, the bloody raid of John Brown, and the general terror and crimes caused by servile insurrection, have banded together to control the peo-ple of the North, and by getting a majority—not of the votes in the whole country, but a majority of one section only—to seize every branch of the common government, and thus exclude one whole section of the country from all participation in the government of the country. By this unheard of movement, they propose to govern the Union by not over *one third* of its voters,—and those voters all in one section! If this were a mere temporary spite at the South, it would create less alarm. But when the South sees that it is the result of a settled and fierce de-termination to rule over and oppress in defiance of her wishes, safety and rights—when she sees her people systematically and villainously slandered, to bring them into contempt and hatred before the Northern masses,—when they see the Lincolns, the Sewards, the Greeleys, the Wentworths and every moving spirit of this aggressive attack, proclaim-ing boldly to the world that this war upon them is "irrepressible," and never to end until all the States shall be free and until every negro shall have the ballot to vote or the bullet to slay,—when they see a perpetual unrelenting war proclaimed against their property and peace, and the determination of a sectional majority to wield the money, arms and powers of the common government to aid in this monstrous and inhuman war. [*sic*] When they see themselves thus powerless to defend themselves in the Union, they begin to turn, with maddened sorrow and tears, to examine what hope there is for them *out* of the Union.

Such are now the views and feelings of even conservative men of all parties at the South. With these views her people are arming at the cost of millions for their defence, and the spirit of rebellion and dis-union hourly grows more rampant and determined.

Think of these things, patriotic men of the North of all parties; and if there be reason in these complaints of our Southern citizens, redress them at the polls, like honest and patriotic men should do. You have the power—use it, not only justly, but generously and nobly.

19. Victory and Its Consequences

(Philadelphia *North American and United States Gazette* [Lincoln], November 7, 1860)

The people have elected Abraham Lincoln President of the United States. This result was clearly foreshadowed when Pennsylvania decided, by her great majority on the 9th of October, that the Administration in office was unworthy of confidence, and a change was imperatively needed. We have no feelings of exultation to express over a triumph which has long been morally certain; which was rendered inevitable by the crimes and follies of the party which is now doomed and defeated, and which was announced with emphasis by us the morning after our Governor's election. Success involves new and grave responsibilities, which must be met with reason and reflection, and require the exercise of a stern and unselfish patriotism. In this hour of victory especially, when we have conquered not only our old enemy, but discomfited others whom natural sympathy and former fellowship should induce us still to regard as friends, moderation comes commended with more than ordinary propriety. To be worthy of such a victory, is to bear it with becoming dignity for ourselves and with proper respect towards our opponents.

It may be proper at this time to consider what principles and policy are involved in the election of Mr. Lincoln, and the causes which operated to produce it. In the first place, we deny distinctly that it is either a triumph of the north over the south, or of any sectional aspect of the slavery question. No such issue was practically asserted, because the complexion of all the present territories is settled, and the declarations of the Chicago Convention against the extension of slavery, and the power of Congress over the territories, can only be applied when the case shall occur. Southern politicians, and their northern echoes, have attempted to force the issue upon us, and we have accordingly announced our principles calmly and firmly, in case the contingency should arise. There is therefore no reason for agitation, and no danger of any, if the agitators, who constantly agitate, as they say, to prevent agitation, will consent to let slavery alone, as we desire and propose to do.

The great idea settled by this election, and which, perhaps, operated as much as any other on the public mind, was the purpose to change the administration of public affairs at Washington, and to purge and purify the whole political machinery of government. The people were convinced that the long possession of power had demoralized the public service, and introduced practices which were undermining its integrity. They saw examples of corruption and profligacy go not only "unwhipped of justice," but even encouraged and favored by those to whom the guardianship of the public treasury had been confided. They saw power and patronage employed to establish a sectional domination, and the influence of the government openly enlisted in Kansas to force slavery upon an outraged and unwilling people. They saw our material interests neglected and injured, the press subsidized, elections controlled by money extorted from Federal office-holders, unworthy partisans rewarded by jobs and contracts, nepotism spread through the departments, defalcations common and countenanced, the laws evaded or misinterpreted, and abuses audaciously defying opinion everywhere. These and other outrages were seen and remembered, and the people determined they should be punished, and the democracy expelled from power. This general purpose operated more than any other upon the election, and we are free to admit it.

Pennsylvania, particularly, demanded that the principle of protecting American industry should be recognized and avowed. The Chicago Convention asserted it satisfactorily, while all the others either evaded the test or accepted it doubtfully. This question entered largely into our local contest, and was everywhere accepted. The western majorities speak as decisively, as those of the east, and the protective policy is again re-established as a part of the old creed. Economy in the conduct of the government, Homesteads for settlers on the public domain, retrenchment and accountability in the public expenditures, appropriations for rivers and harbors, a Pacific railroad, the admission of Kansas, and a radical reform in the government, all entered into the canvass and contributed to the election of Abraham Lincoln. No one issue controlled it, and any such belief is erroneous and cannot too soon be corrected.

We have thus seen that slavery was not the dominating idea of [the] Presidential contest, as has been assumed, but that various national influences co-operated to produce the result which has been witnessed. But if even the assumption were true, there is a vast difference between the positions of a candidate for the Presidency and the President of the Union. One represents a party and the other the nation in its unity, and without regard to section. Our belief has always been, and is not now for the first time expressed, that the mere fact of going in to the White House nationalizes, so to speak, the elected President, whatever may have been his previous predilections. He is compelled, from the necessity of the case and from personal contact, to mingle with all interests and men of all parties, and therefore to ignore, even if he cherished, all local or sectional jealousy. Mr. Lincoln will enter upon the duties of President as free from bias, and with as national sentiments, as any incumbent of that office ever did. More than that, he will go to Washington disposed not only to conciliate but to convince the south, by fair dealing, that he has no war to wage against it, and is anxious to have peace, happiness and prosperity. It does not belong to us to speak for Mr. Lincoln, but we venture to assert, upon no other evidence than that furnished by his past career, that his inaugural address will do more to restore confidence and to dissipate apprehension than any public paper issued for a quarter of a century. At all events let us give him a fair trial, and at least hear before we strike.

II

THE PROSPECT OF SECESSION

20. "The Folly of Secession"

(Providence Daily Post [Douglas], November 8, 1860)

The Republicans have a great deal to say of the "folly of secession." First, they prove to us it would be very unreasonable. Next, that it would be very unprofitable. And finally, that all that is said on the subject, by the South, is the merest *bosh.* So, what is begun, sometimes, in serious- ness, is sure to end in ridicule; and plain facts, which can be seen by any person not stark blind, elicit only a pooh-pooh or a sneer.

While the election was pending we uttered our own opinion in regard to secession and its prospects—in regard to the temper of the South, more especially—with plainness and with frankness. The Re- publicans treated our statements and cautions with all the appearances of contempt. It was all done, they said, for partisan effect.

There is no election pending just at this moment; and we certainly, in what we now write, have no wish to influence any man's vote. But we nevertheless repeat the utterances which our enemies had the pleas- ure of laughing over one week ago. A few short weeks will witness a formidable effort for a dissolution of the Union by the secession of three or four of the Cotton States; and there will probably result from it such a panic and crash in business circles as has never been witnessed in this country.

This is our belief; and all the sneers of all the Republicans in Christen- dom will not change it. Nothing but time can show to us its unsound- ness, unless these pooh-poohs will open to us some sources of infor- mation, touching Southern temper, to which we do not now have access. That the movement will injure the South, we do not deny. We do not deny that it is unwise, unreasonable—nay, very foolish and very reckless and very criminal. But all this does not reach the fact that it will be made.

And we say, too, that this Southern indignation is not wholly without a cause. The attitude of the Republican party goes far to justify their apprehensions of evil. We do not wonder, that they are apprehensive, or that they are indignant. In our honest opinion, if they knew the Republicans better, they would fear them more and love them still less.

It is undeniable that the Republican creed is based upon *hatred of slavery and hatred of the South.* Their leaders may tell us, fifty times a day, that they have no wish to interfere with slavery *in the States,* and that they stand ready to protect the slave States in all their constitutional rights. But the fact that they insist upon using the federal government to interfere with slavery in the Territories, is sufficient proof that they hate the institution and its supporters, even if no other proof existed. The fact that they have assailed slavery in the District of Columbia, assailed the internal slave trade, assailed the fugitive slave law—that they have charged the Southern people with being thieves and robbers and barbarians; with ignorance and cowardice and hypocrisy; with almost every crime under heaven; have complained of their slave representation in Congress, and of the large expenditure in which they involve the government, especially for the support of the army and navy; and finally, have adopted a course of legislation in the free States which has had no other motive than to virtually and practically trample under foot a plain provision of the Constitution of the country;—all this has had the effect to irritate and exasperate the South. And it seems to us that that man must be blind or insane, who wonders that the South should feel indignant when *such* a party—embracing all the outright abolitionists, all the John Brown sympathizers, all the anti-slavery fanatics in the land—gets hold of the reins of government.

Secession may be foolishness—resistance may be madness; the South may be the most unreasonable community on the footstool of the Creator,—but we tell this Republican party in plain language, that with a feeling of deadly hostility towards an institution which exists, almost as by an act of God, in fifteen States of the American Union, you have no right to expect a peaceful reign. You will not get it. The South will resist. The excuse for resistance may not be a good one, in your estimation; but it will answer the purpose, for the long-harrassed and indignant people of the South. They do not look upon slavery as you do; and much as they may love the Union—greatly as it may be for their interest to remain in it—they will assuredly make an effort to go out, before submitting to the rule of an organization whose very life-blood is hatred of their cherished institutions. Bring the case home. How would you feel, should the government fall into the hands of a party whose great leading principle was based upon bitter hostility to an institution which existed in the New England States—which had existed here two hundred years—which was interwoven with your social as well as your political organizations—which formed the basis of your industrial policy—and to destroy which would be to revolutionize your social condition, and deprive you of your greatest source of wealth? Would you stand it? You threatened secession when Texas was annexed, and when Kansas and Nebraska were organized. What would you do in the case we have supposed?

"But if the South attempts to secede," say our Republican friends, "we will subdue them." Can this be done? How large an army would it take to march into and subdue the four States which are supposed to be foremost in the Disunion work—Mississippi, Georgia, Alabama and South Carolina? Could an army less than one hundred thousand strong, succeed in crossing their lines? And if it got there, and found a people asking only to be let alone, what could it do? Allowing that the ties of kindred and friendship offered no restraint, yet how long could this army employ itself profitably—profitably to the North—on this Southern soil? Nay, suppose it should succeed in *subduing* the South, and its commander should issue his proclamation announcing "It is all right," what would the Union, thus held together, be worth? How long would it last? Have you ever counted the cost of thus preserving it?

We are not now speaking as a politician. We are not after votes. Mr. Lincoln is elected, and there is no help for it. But we deem it right to call the attention of the people to the evils which threaten them. We say that we are standing upon the brink of a fearful precipice. It is too late to avert the danger by a resort to the ballot box. But it is right that the people should understand what the danger is. By and by, we predict, their lips will be red with curses upon the men who have led them on, and laughed and pooh-pooh'd at our warning. Before that time arrives, would it not be well to ask themselves, "What may we best do, when secession is attempted? Will it be better to attempt to subdue the seceding States, than to *let them alone?*" These are questions which will, we fear, have to be discussed; and instead of this everlasting harping upon "the folly of secession," our Republican friends would do well to consider them.

21. WHAT OUGHT THE SOUTH TO DO?

(Albany *Atlas and Argus* [Douglas], November 10, 1860)

In appealing to our citizens, before the election, to render such a verdict in that great contest as we believed would preserve the Union and the Constitution in their integrity, we freely expressed our apprehensions of danger in the event of a different result. The crowning calamity which the South has apprehended—the election of a President upon the issues and devoted to the principles advocated by the Republican party —has fallen upon them and upon the nation. It is yet too early to understand the real sentiments and intentions of the Southern people under this decision. Telegraphic accounts of excited feeling and action in a few States reach us, but it is possible they are to be regarded as the outbursts of the first feeling of indignation at Northern action, rather than as the deliberate declaration of the immediate future policy of the States in question.

We are not at all surprised at the manifestation of feeling at the South. We expected and predicted it, and for so doing, were charged by the Republican press with favoring disunion, while, in fact, we simply correctly appreciated the feeling of that section of the Union. We sympathize with and justify the South, so far as this—their rights have been invaded to the extreme limit possible within the forms of the Constitution, and beyond this limit their feelings have been insulted and their interests and honor assailed by almost every possible form of denunciation and invective; and if we deemed it certain that the real *animus* of the Republican party could be carried into the administration of the Federal Government and become the permanent policy of the nation, we should think that all the instincts of self-preservation and of manhood rightfully impelled them to a resort to revolution and separation from the Union, and we would applaud them and wish them God-speed in the adoption of such a remedy.—But, we desire to say to the few people of the South whom our voice will reach—we do *not* believe that the spirit of sectional Republicanism, as thus far displayed in its struggle for power, can be carried into the administration of the government at Washington—much less that it can become the settled policy of the country, and we will give some of our reasons for this conclusion.

In the first place, the Republicans will only have possession of the Executive Department, with Congress and the Judiciary against them. The majority in both Senate and House will be so decisive as to effectually prevent the passage of any laws giving effect to any offensive theories of Republicanism. The South, therefore, is safe from aggression, so far as offensive legislation is concerned—more strongly fortified even, than under the present Congress. It is also safe against Mr. Seward's threatened re-organization of the Supreme Court against it.—

That body can only be changed, by filling such vacancies as may occur by death or resignation, and the Senate can exercise a check upon filling those improperly.

The only increased danger, therefore, to the South, is from the Executive. What can the President do? How can he invade Southern interests, fenced in as he will be, by opposition in the co-ordinate branches of the government? What power has he to strike a single blow against Southern rights? We know of nothing that he can do or leave undone, materially affecting questions of pending interest to the South, unless it be to refuse to execute faithfully the Fugitive Slave law. We are aware that his party has pandered to the Abolition feeling against obedience to this obligation of the law and the Constitution, and has passed State laws nullifying and arresting it, so far as such laws can.

But Mr. Lincoln in the Presidential chair, clothed with the responsibilities of that position, is in a very different situation from your irrepressible agitators on the stump or in the Legislative Assembly, and he dare not refuse to execute the Fugitive Slave Law. The curses of the present and future generations would brand him as a perjured traitor and the Constitutional process of impeachment would expel him from the Presidential office, should he thus refuse obedience to the law and the Constitution.—Moreover, it is only due to truth to say, that there is no reason to believe that Mr. Lincoln will be disposed to shrink from the performance of that duty—as it is well known that he stands publicly pledged, by his speeches in the Illinois campaign, to the execution of the Fugitive Slave Law.

No—we beg leave to suggest to our Southern brethren, that the accession of Republicanism to the power and responsibilities of the government—*unless rash and violent action at the South shall supply it with vitality*—will be the certain death of it. Its impotency to accomplish a tithe of what it has threatened and promised, will reveal its hypocrisy and false pretences, and disgust its more rabid supporters and they will drop it and turn their backs upon it. Mr. Lincoln, as a matter of absolute necessity, when once in office, must become conservative—must execute the laws and obey the Constitution—and this course will disappoint the fanaticism which has animated his party and elevated him, and Republicanism will be stricken down within a single year, as by paralysis.—*We say this will be the case, if our Southern brethren will look at the matter in the light of philosophy and common sense and wait a little, in quiet and repose, for the progress of events.* If they will do this, we at the North will be able to take care of Republicanism, and in another short year, the crisis will have passed, and fanaticism will have burned out, and a healthful reaction will give renewed life and vigor to the body politic. But if unwise and rash counsels should prevail in some of the Southern States—if premature action for separate State protection should occur, and secession from the Union, or even serious demonstrations in that direction, be attempted, this might furnish sufficient excitement and outward pressure to hold the Republican party together and continue this hated struggle. Its only bond of union is the slavery excitement, which with quiet at the South and Lincoln in the Presidential chair, impotent to accomplish anything which fanaticism has anticipated as the fruits of victory, will prove a rope of sand, and the discordant materials—of which this political organization is composed—will fall to pieces and repel each other.

Such—we, who have sympathized with them and fought for their constitutional rights, say to Southern men—are our dispassionate views of the present crisis and of the action and policy which wisdom and patriotism demand. We ask for them the calm consideration which becomes the occasion. Southern men owe it to themselves and their own honor—saying nothing about courtesy to their hosts of true friends at the North—to act in this emergency with dignity and deliberation.

22. Secession, The Folly of the Hour

(Boston *Daily Atlas and Bee* [Lincoln], November 12, 1860)

The most prominent, and indeed almost the only topic of political interest just now, is the rumored insane attempt of a few hot-headed fanatics, to induce the people of a few slave States to secede from the American Union. There is in this nothing new, unexpected, or alarming. The truth is, the slave States have neither the right, the power, nor the inclination to secede—therefore they will not. Let us consider the matter a little. The right of a sovereign confederated State to withdraw has been often asserted, and is now believed in by many men both South and North; but it has been generally denied, and the arguments in its favor controverted by all the ablest statesmen and patriots of the country. Mr. Webster's argument against the right of secession is, in our judgment, unanswerable, and we suggest to those who think the right of secession defensible, a perusal of that great statesman's opinion. So long as the several States retain, as they now do, sovereign control, within their own domain, of all their local affairs, and are not interfered with by the federal authorities in those State concerns, it is absurd to claim the right of secession. Those concerns that are committed to the exclusive jurisdiction and control of the federal government, were so committed by the original confederated States, with the distinct understanding that the States should not attempt to resume these delegated powers. They have no more right to claim the rendering back to them of these federal prerogatives, than the general government has to claim any control over subjects of special and exclusive State jurisdiction.

In only one conceivable contingency could the right to secede be maintained, and that goes back to the primal right of revolution, of rebellion against an existing government. Should the federal government undertake to take away from a State the control of its State affairs, within its State jurisdiction, then a State might claim the right of revolutionary resistance, on the ground that the federal government had itself violated the compact and rendered it null and void. But no man pretends that any such case as this has arisen, or is likely to arise. The rights of no State have been interfered with by the federal government, nor is there any purpose, declared or supposed, on the part of the present or the incoming administration to give any such provocation to rebellion. If it be said that the rights of some States have been interfered with by other States, acting in their separate capacity of State sovereignty, this although true would not meet the case nor afford any basis for revolution. A law of Massachusetts may be oppressive of a citizen of South Carolina, but even if so, it is operative only within Massachusetts domain and jurisdiction. Exactly so with the laws of South Carolina, which are unjust towards citizens of Massachusetts. Besides, if there are cases of this sort in one section of the country, there are as many and as flagrant in the other, and the only defensible mode of redress or adjustment is through the arbitration of Congress and the judicial tribunals of the country.

If the federal government should attempt to invade the domain of State rights, that would be despotism and cause of resistance—but there is no such cause, and there will be none. Should any State attempt to resume powers expressly yielded to the federal government, that would be treason, and would justify the exercise of forcible means by the federal government to bring back the offending State to its allegiance to the Constitution and the Union. But no such case has arisen—none will arise. There is, therefore, no existing right of secession, and the claim for it is utterly indefensible. Secession ought not to be, and that is one of the strongest reasons why it never will be.

Secondly, the slave States have not the power to secede. Unless permitted by the federal government quietly to withdraw, they cannot go. It is absurd to suppose that a President and a Congress and a Judiciary sworn to maintain the Constitution and the laws will ever permit a State to secede. If they should, they would violate their oaths and become participants in the crime of treason. The only other possible method of secession is by violence, involving the nullification of the federal laws and armed resistance to the federal authority. In such a contest the slave States would be speedily and deservedly crushed by the strong arm of power. They have neither the wealth, the intelligence, the arts, the arms, nor the character, requisite to maintain the struggle.

The preponderance of all these elements of power is so largely with those States that will remain loyal to the confederacy, as to render the idea of the ability of the slave States to secede utterly preposterous. The only results to the rebellious States would be a bloody strife confined entirely to their own territory, the immediate and violent abolition of slavery, the destruction of their commerce, the ruin of all their material interests and finally a forced submission to the authority they had resisted and the government they had defied. This we say in no spirit of unkindness or boasting, but because these are the incontrovertible facts which no appeals of passion or flourishes of rhetoric can remove or change.

Thirdly, the slave States have no inclination to secede. A reckless and passionate minority, a very small minority, of the people of three or four States are preaching disunion. But they are all either intriguing politicians or are adventurers, who are playing upon the fears of the people and raising an uproar in Ephesus because "their craft is in danger." They see in the accession of the Republican party to power the certain end of that reign of terrorism over the expression of public opinion at the South, by means of which they have so long climbed to places of political power and exercised a domination in the federal government.

They are not in the least apprehensive of the abolition of slavery, or of any aggression upon southern rights by the administration of Abraham Lincoln; but they do apprehend and with good reason that their political ascendancy in the South is about to terminate, and that power there will soon pass into the hands of the patriotic, liberty-loving men of that section of the country. This and this alone is the Banquo's ghost that rises to disturb their feast, and foreseeing this they are making use of the temporary excitement and the disappointment consequent upon defeat, to secure to themselves snug places in Congress and in lucrative local offices at home; to illustrate—let South Carolina only elect to the United States Senate Gov. Gist, who is a candidate for the seat, and who has just issued his silly and treasonable disunion proclamation, and Gist will at once subside—he understands the real gist of this business, and, his coveted office secured, he will forthwith "roar you as gently as any sucking dove," and advise the Palmetto secessionists to wait for some overt act!

As for the rest, the great mass of the southern people desire no secession or disunion; they are loyal to the government, patriotic in their feelings, and laugh to scorn the treason and the nonsense of the braggarts and demagogues with whose presence and blatant bellowings they are now afflicted. Nobody in the free States need feel any anxiety about secession. The people of the South will take care of these agitators—if they don't, Old Abe will. If ever any actual attempt is made to subvert the Constitution or destroy the Union, if any assault is made upon the integrity of the Republic by fanatics from any section or party, the law-abiding, loyal and patriotic men of the slave States will stand as a wall of fire against them, and will meet and roll back their turbulent hosts, as the solid cliffs of the ocean shore beat back the angry surges of the sea.

Such is our judgment of the prospect and the probability of secession and disunion; and until philosophy is false, experience vain, reason powerless, facts converted into fiction, self-interest no longer the main-spring of human action, and principle extinct, that judgment will be vindicated and verified by the events of the future.

23. THE DISUNION RANT

(Daily Pittsburgh Gazette [Lincoln], November 14, 1860)

The true way to treat the Disunion bluster now so prevalent at the South, is to leave it alone. The attempt to resist it or put it down by force, would assist instead of repress it, and make that real which is now only a sham.

The Disunion cry has been the bugaboo of the South for thirty years. With it she has always, hitherto, been able to scare the North into submission; and the sole object of resorting to it in the late election was to drive the North into compliance with her wishes. The noisy blusterers of the South had no doubt of their ability to accomplish their end. Failure was never anticipated, not even dreamed of by them.

But they *have* failed. Had they succeeded, the hollowness of their threats would never have been discovered; but having failed, the sole question with them now is, how best to escape from their embarrassing position. They must do *something*, to make their people at home believe them in earnest, and yet so manage it as to prevent the consummation of what they threaten.

This is the explanation of the present attitude of the South. The leaders—Toombs, Yancey, Chesnut, Iverson, Wise and the other noisy fellows, who declared without reservation that the election of Lincoln would be followed by a dissolution of the Union, must either attempt to dissolve it or go into utter disgrace. They are therefore pretending to carry their threats into execution in order to put themselves right at home. They have promised; and they must at least *seem* to perform.

It would be the madness of folly, therefore, to treat these men as being in earnest. To do that would soon make them in earnest. Let them alone and play out their play. When they show signs of being in earnest, and put their necks in a halter, it will be time enough to string them up. They will not do that, if left to themselves. They have been, for years, engaged with the zeal of demagogues in inflaming the public mind of the South with artful misrepresentations of Northern sentiment and designs, and extravagant appeals to Southern peculiarities; and now, when the crisis has come which they have provoked, but not anticipated, they find themselves confronted by a people who have taken them at their word and have not only believed, but profess a willingness to follow, them. How shall the poor devils escape? That is a question for *them* to answer. Let us rather sympathize with them in their dilemma than think of dealing severely with them. They must wriggle out of their trouble; and it will be amusing to stand by and witness their manoeuvres in doing so.

In less than a month this farce will be played out. Within that time the true Union sentiment of the South will develop itself. There is patriotism and good sense enough in the South to manage the whole affair. Let us leave it, then, in the hands of the true men of the South. It does not need our interference. Hands off. The time *may* come when the whole country will have to interfere; but just now all that the North has to do is to leave the Hotspurs alone.

24. THE UNION—ITS DANGER

(Cleveland *Daily National Democrat* [Breckinridge],
November 19, 1860)

That the Republic has fallen upon evil times, the most common observer of passing events must admit. The Union is now in its hour of travail, but whether it will give birth to new hopes, or go the way of all flesh, is the sad problem now about to be solved. If it survives now, it may bid defiance to any future shock, for truly the crisis through which we are now passing, is the most imminently dangerous one the Republic has ever felt. Heaven grant the storm may subside and reason and patriotism again resume their empire.

While many of those who, we trust, without knowing what they were doing, have labored with the fell spirit of Abolitionism to bring about the state of things which has brought the Republic to the verge of dissolution, feel most keenly that they have been guilty of wrong doing, there is another class who "mock at the calamity and laugh when fear cometh," over the patriotic of the nation.

To maudlin philanthropy, the idea of elevating the negro race to terms of social and political equality, commends itself. In it the idea is a fine one, that the sun shall set on no master and rise on no slave, but as this Utopian scheme cannot be realized, it is far better for us to "bear the ills we have than to fly to those we know not of." The Union of these States is a landmark to the struggling of other nations. As long as it exists they will have hope—when it sinks the hopes of the oppressed of other lands now struggling for a recognition of the right of man to govern himself, go down in blackness and in night.

Valuable as are the supposed rights of the negro race to morbid philanthropy—painful as to Abolitionism may appear the enslavement of a race that since tradition exists have ever been "hewers of wood and drawers of water"—whose normal condition here, and whose normal condition in their own land, was slavery, they must indeed be blind to the benefits of the Republic who think that liberty to the black race is worth more than the unnumbered blessings of the Union? [sic]

For our own part, bearing in mind the fact that the negroes of the United States are further progressed in the scale of humanity than in any [other] part of the world—that here they are more christianized, more humanized than anywhere else, and that in comparison to the situation of the blacks of Africa, the most degraded of slaves in the South is far, very far above the best of the masses in Africa, yet, far better would it be for mankind that they all be sent back to their own original barbarism —again made slaves in Africa, with the power of life and death in the hands of the master, as was the case when first, by English and New England cupidity, brought, against the entreaties of the South, to the United States, than that the smallest and most insignificant of the States of the Republic be forced, by oppression and by having their Constitutional rights denied them, from the Union—that a single star which has its place upon our flag be rent therefrom, or its lustre dimmed. Of all the evils which can befal our people, that of disunion—secession, is the greatest. In comparison with it, other evils are of small moment. Rent into factions—formed into small Republics, with a bitter feeling, which must of necessity spring up—torn as they must be by intestine broils and lighted up with the horrors of civil war, Disunion presents an alternative too dreadful to contemplate, and yet to this complexion must we come at last, unless justice and the Constitution is soon made to take the place of the excited and unjust feeling which now pervades the Abolition States.

25. WHAT IS TO BE DONE?

(Chicago *Daily Times and Herald* [Douglas], November 21, 1860)

The question is asked at every street corner, "What is to be done now?" A very grave question, indeed. A question involving very much more than the questioner himself dreams of—involving in fact the manufacturing, commercial and laboring interests of the North to an extent *incalculable;* involving the future destiny of the American continent, politically, socially and in every respect, to a degree inconceivable to the clearest minds. The fall of stocks, the breaking of banks, the ruin of our currency and general bankruptcy are the very smallest of evils that will flow from an unwise answer to this question.

The men who have *caused* all these incalculable evils can never solve the question. The morbid and insane mental action, that has driven them forward on the path of ruin, has become chronic. The judicial blindness which has followed them at every step through their mad and passionate hallucination will still cling to them. They will never believe in a disastrous result to their maniac schemes, until it has happened; and then they will refuse to believe further, and, with the true inspiration of mania, will account for the results by every cause on earth save their own "insane idea." Individuals are known to become deranged by the prolonged concentration of thought upon a single idea, and all the more readily when that idea is a visionary or impracticable one; *perpetual motion* has deranged thousands. To the reader of history nothing can be clearer than that large bodies of people are alike subject to monomania, resulting *always* from a determined, prolonged and passionate concentration of the public mind upon an abstraction. History is full of such instances. The true representatives of the insane idea —those whose fanatical zeal have [*sic*] deluded others—can never heal the disease they have created, because they cannot heal themselves. To confess an error is the most difficult and sublime act of our rational life. To surrender a hallucination is well nigh impossible.

The Abolitionists of the North are utterly given over to a hallucination. The abstract idea of the *equality of races,* and the Utopian dream of a *human level,* have so far engrossed them as to exclude all calculation based upon practical life and common sense. They have lost the power of appropriating rationally the *facts* by which they are surrounded. They force facts to suit their procrustian [*sic*] bed, and will believe all things that strengthen the stimulant which has become a part of their life; they will believe *nothing* that weakens it. But worse still, they have lost the power of correct reason, and take causes for effects and effects for causes. The sunlight of heaven is not more clear than that the Anti-Slavery agitation is the true and only cause of all our woes and trouble. It has been the thermometer that has marked the stages on our road to ruin. As it has mounted in the scale, discord, passion, and misery have followed. As it has subsided peace and happiness have returned, and danger has fled from our doors. It has been the bulletin of the stock market of our hopes. And yet its leaders *will* not see, or seeing will not believe. They hug their bantling with the fervor of a mother for her deformed child. They swear that the *results* of their *own* agitation and mania are the prime cause of the evil. They thrust their thumbs to the knuckles into the eyes of their victim; and when the poor victim screams under their delightful operation of gouging, they exclaim, "confound the EYES, what a muss they are kicking up."

Let the people look for no solution of the present difficulties, or of the future destiny of the Republic, from these will-o-the-wisps who have lured us into the "slough of despond." They are both unwilling and incapable to advise you. For God's sake, for your own sakes and for your country's sake, throw off these miserable nightmares that have so long bestridden you, and once more return to the path of practical common sense, and *think for yourselves.*

But the question recurs, *"What is to be done?"* The remedy is so *simple* that thousands will revolt at it. Nevertheless it must be taken, or the "galloping consumption" will fasten its fangs upon us with renewed force. Our fathers were not Abolitionists. Our fathers executed the fugitive slave law in good faith. Our fathers neither disturbed nor sought to disturb others in the enjoyment of their rights under the law. Our fathers did not abuse or slander or villify [*sic*] the people of the country any where. When differences arose, our fathers got together, like all sensible men would do, and, making allowances for each other's feelings and wishes, compromised and settled their differences in a practical manner, and went on their way rejoicing. Our fathers certainly *did* do these plain, simple, neighborly things. Our fathers somehow got along bravely, and lived and died in a country "half slave and half free," in spite of the "irrepressible conflict;" and we trust in God and believe that a goodly number of these brave old men and women of the past got safely HOME after they *did* die. "GO THOU AND DO LIKEWISE."

Slavery will never be abolished by any thing *we* can do. We may fasten the chains of the poor slave tighter, and render it impossible for him to enjoy his past fat, jolly life any longer. We may delude him into struggles with his master, which may destroy his peace or take away his life. We may harrass his master very much. But we will never free the slave. That is in the hands of ONE higher than you or we—higher than Abolitionists or Fire-eaters,—hands that will deal with it in the great march of humanity as seemeth best to HIM. Time and the moral and physical laws of the world will do their work *well*—rest assured of that. Not fast enough for you, oh, dreamer, but in "HIS own good time," HE will do it, without your help in fact, and without the slightest regard to whether you like the time or not. Consent to believe this, oh, ye sapient "helpers" of the Omnipotent; return to the practical common sense of your fathers; worship God as your fathers worshipped; "love your neighbors" as they loved them, and the watchmen on the watch towers will again cry, *"All is well."*

But what of secession? Will there be secession? Yes—a hundred to one, yes. Oh, you vile Disunionists, how dare you say such ugly things! Simply, our friends, because they are *true*. Because it is a *fact* that the iron pen of time is steadily and diligently writing on the record of the great *present*. Have you so long listened to the soothing lies of the demagogues, that it startles or offends you to hear the truth? Do you wish us, as a public journalist, to tell you a deliberate falsehood—that we know to be a falsehood—to lull you into a single hour of delicious but fatal repose? If the Union is to be dissolved, do you not wish to be warned in advance and be prepared for the emergency? Does our saying that the fact *is* so, *cause* it to be so? We do not *make* the facts, nor does our opinion of them cause or control them. Our duty is to tell you the fact and give you our opinions honestly. If you do not like the facts, it is not *our* fault. Like it or not like, the cotton States *will secede*.

But can this be prevented now? We doubt it. The steps necessary to prevent it will not be taken. The public mind will not act promptly enough to affect this result.

But what then,—is this Government to finally go to pieces? No,—a hundred times, no. When the fiery fury and sense of wrong which has hurried the Gulf States into secession has subsided, their sense of independence and honor will be relieved, and a more dispassioned judgment will have regained its throne. A cold water bath, followed by the depletion of general bankruptcy, will have cured the North of the "negro-mania." Both sections will begin to see that their present good and future hopes are inextricably linked together. Both will learn that they have played the game of "cutting off your nose to spite your face." Both will learn that they have made asses of themselves in the face of the civilized world. Both will again remember that the only way in which they have won their past glory and present greatness was by getting together as *friends,* and in the true spirit of patriots and brothers settling their difficulties.

This course will be again pursued. A NATIONAL CONVENTION will be called. The politicians who have fostered and egged on this unholy family war will be driven into that oblivion which they deserve. The PEOPLE of both sections will again be heard. This negro question will be again settled, and settled in a manner never again to disturb railroad stocks in this world. The nation will again return to loyalty and fraternity, and move forward once more to greatness and glory. This is what *can* be done—what *alone* can be done and what *must* be done. The PEOPLE of both sections will *have* it done. *So mote it be.*

26. WILL THERE BE DISUNION?

(Indianapolis *Indiana American* [Independent], November 21, 1860)

Of course not. The idea of a peaceable secession is too preposterous to be entertained for a moment by any sane mind, and no less absurd is the supposition that a feeble State like South Carolina, with neither men nor money nor credit, could even seriously annoy the nation by an attempt at forceable disunion. It does not mend the matter to combine five or six states of like character. They all have not the means within themselves of keeping their negroes in subjection in such a contest, much less of seriously annoying the nation.

Will there be an effort? We greatly fear there will not be. We speak not for others, but we say that for one we are heartily tired of having this threat stare us in the face evermore. If nothing but blood will prevent it, let it flow. It has been the most mischievous power that has ever been known in our nation. To say nothing of the unequal and unjust concessions it extorted in the formation of the government, it has been a frightful ghost all along our pathway. In 1829 a wholesome tariff was enacted, under which most of our national debt was paid, and the country began to prosper. It was repealed in 1833, and the celebrated *compromise* tariff was substituted, just to please South Carolina, and keep her from secession. We need not remind our older readers of the financial crash which followed.—The industry and business of the country were not half so much paralized [*sic*] by the war with Mexico.

To say nothing of the constant shying off from that supposed danger in every act of national legislation—in the nomination of presidential candidates, and the selection of cabinet officers and foreign ministers, the same ghost frightened our congress in 1850 to the enactment of a law which would be a stain and a blot on any heathen nation—it is an outrage and a disgrace to ours, that should make every christian patriot blush. It was enacted to keep South Carolina from seceding, and the same thing induced good men, who abhorred it, to acquiesce in it.

Nothing but a fruitless effort at rebellion will cure the South—nothing but a successful one to crush it out will assure the North. We never have been better prepared for such a crisis than now. We most ardently desire that it may come. Except a few cowardly sycophants, or sympathizing traitors among us, we are ready. We are the more anxious because we fear some silly iniquitous *compromise* that will disgrace us more and embarrass us worse than ever, will be devised. Even now it is looming up. Leading Republican papers are pleading for it.—Rather than submit to another dishonorable *compromise,* we would prefer to settle the question of equal rights by the sword if need be. If a fear of secession—rebellion, TREASON is to overawe us forever, then are we not freemen.

27. The Union—Its Danger—How Shall It Be Preserved?

(Concord (N. H.) *Democratic Standard* [Breckinridge], November 24, 1860)

Whatever some men may talk, or whatever they may pretend to believe, no one can shut his eyes to the fact, that the great American Union, at this moment, is in imminent danger of dissolution. South Carolina has already taken incipient steps to that end, and Georgia, Alabama, Mississippi and Florida are following fast in the same direction. The people of the other slaveholding States sympathize with the States already moving towards the catastrophe of disunion, and although, perhaps, now reluctant to take the decisive step, they will, in all probability, be ultimately drawn into the movement. Now this is the real, serious, and appalling fact which the people of the North as well as of the South are compelled to recognize and contemplate. Men may talk doubtingly;

those, in some measure, responsible for the great evil that impends over us, may talk sneeringly; but no intelligent man can deny that now there is danger of the disruption of this mighty Confederacy of sovereign States—the pride and the hope of mankind.

What has brought this appalling danger upon our country? It requires no prophet nor philosopher to tell. The school-boy of ordinary intelligence knows the cause, and can give the reply. *It is the war which has been waged by the fanatics and demagogues of the North upon the domestic institutions of the South, culminating at last in the election of a President upon the avowed principle of hostility to the South.* It is the fruits of the crusade of Northern Abolitionism against Southern Slavery, carried on in violation of both the letter and spirit of the Constitutional compact under which both sections have agreed to live: That war has been waged in all forms insulting to the South, and subversive of her rights;—by gross misrepresentation; by insulting invective; by invasions of her rights of property; by a violation of the express provisions of the Constitution in the form of State nullification of the Fugitive Slave Law; by refusing to the South an equal enjoyment of the common domain of the Republic; by actual invasion of the territory of a sovereign State and the murder of its citizens. Of all this has the North been guilty. Without any right so to do, the people of the North, now constituting an actual majority, speaking through the fanatical priest and the political demagogue, have proclaimed their determination to extirpate, ultimately, an institution of the South—her system of organized labor, on which her prosperity depends—and, of course, to change her social system and her present form of civilization,—to effect, indeed, in her institutions a more radical change than was effected between these States and the mother country by the American Revolution. In this war, the people of the North have been the aggressors, and at this very moment Massachusetts, Vermont, New-Hampshire, and every northern State which has nullified the Fugitive Slave Law, are more out of the Union than South Carolina. So far South Carolina has merely talked and passed resolutions, while the States already referred to have actually nullified and infracted the Constitution.

These are the causes of the crisis that has come upon us. Now what is the remedy? Within a few days we have heard that remedy suggested by the authors of the evil, which they think will be adequate, sufficient, and the rightful remedy. The thoughtless and guilty Black Republican imagines that coercion is the true remedy. Nothing but war and bloodshed suggests [sic] themselves to the brood of unthinking religious and political fanatics whose heedless and reckless conduct has brought this impending calamity upon their country. Send down an army and fight the South back into subjection. That is the remedy which they would apply to the portentous and appalling evil which they have brought upon their country.

Have they yet asked themselves, *who* are to do this fighting? *Who* are to make this conquest of our brethren of the South? Will *they* do it? Will the democrats of the North aid them? No, we tell them they will not. If they have courage to undertake the task, they will have to undertake it alone, and when they march down to subdue the South, they will have a fire in the rear which will not add either to the pleasure or the success of their enterprise. If fighting is to be done in this miserable business, we shall all learn from sad experience that it will be done in the North as well as the South. Civil war, if once begun, will overspread the whole country, with its carnage, its conflagrations, its frightful desolation.

No; war and fighting are not the remedies for the evil that is upon us. Justice is the remedy. Concession of the just rights of our Southern brethren is the remedy, and none other will answer. And to that conclusion must the triumphant northern majority come, or disunion is inevitable. It is idle to expect that the people of the South will surrender their just rights which the Constitution secures to them. It is idle to expect that they can be persuaded from the experiment of disunion by any other course than by yielding their just claims under the common compact of union, and by permitting them to enjoy their institutions and their forms of society in peace and tranquillity. If the alternative of submission and degradation, or secession, is forced upon the South, it is idle to expect that she will hesitate at the choice of secession, however great may be its inconveniences, its perils, and its sacrifices. When driven to the point of election between honor and dishonor, between existence and destruction, the instinct of honor and self-preservation prompts both men and nations to dare every danger, and to submit to every privation and sacrifice. And when the people of the South shall have been pushed to the conclusion, that they have no remedy against the insults and aggressions of the fanatics and political demagogues of the North save secession and disunion, their assailants will find that the South will dare the perils of disunion however threatening and formidable their aspect.

In conclusion, we repeat, that the time has come when the conduct of the North, with respect to the institutions of the South, has got to be changed, totally and radically. The North must now cease her warfare upon the institutions of the South; acknowledge the equality of the

South under our common constitution; acknowledge her claim to the equal protection of her property, of whatever nature it may be, in the common domain of the Union; recognize her constitution of society and her forms of civilization, whatever they may be, and respect them; or prepare for a disruption of the Republic. FORBEARANCE and JUSTICE alone can preserve the Union; not force and coercion.

28. THE REMEDY FOR EXISTING EVILS

(New York Journal of Commerce [Breckinridge], November 26, 1860)*

The causes of the present troubles in our political system, and of the threatened disruption of the Federal Union, lie deeper, and wax stronger, upon investigation. It is easy to say that the North should repeal its "personal liberty bills," and that the South should be satisfied with the Congressional majority under the control of Union men, but when we come to look to the origin of our sectional difficulties, and examine into the conduct of the people at large we find that the real cause of alarm is to be found in the mistaken public sentiment which pervades the people of the Northern States. To this we must go for a solution of the questions which now agitate the country, and seriously threaten the existence of the Government.

We are aware of the thanklessness of the undertaking, which sometimes forces itself upon the conscientious journalist, of running counter to public opinion, and of exposing the errors and the follies which have taken root in the public mind. It is easier to go with the current, and to float down the stream of time lazily and sluggishly, without any effort to resist the evils which sometimes fasten upon the minds of communities; but such is not the duty of men in public position, whether of an official or other character, and as we have more than once been compelled, by the stern dictates of duty, to stem the tide of error, so now, it shall not be said that we shrink from the responsibility, in the hour of our country's trials and dangers. To rebuke acknowledged vice and criminal actions is an easy task, since it is but echoing the voice of all good citizens, but to beard the monster, public sentiment, when he appears under the guise of humanity, of morality, and of philanthropy, is quite a different affair.

We assume that the fundamental mistake of the people of the North, the fatal error which has led to most of the troubles now pressing like an incubus upon the country, consists in that meddlesome spirit which prompts them to interfere with the affairs of other communities, and to seek to regulate and control them as they rightfully do their own.

They seem to consider it their mission to dictate to the people of the South what shall be the character of their domestic institutions, what the relations of master and servant, and how all their matters shall be regulated, precisely as they act upon the same questions at home within their own proper jurisdiction. They forget, first, that they have no business with these questions, and that Southern men have a right to complain of their meddlesome interference; and secondly, that conceding their premises that slavery is wrong, it is but a few years since they were themselves involved in the guilt, and would not even now be rid of it except by the concurring circumstances of climate and production, which render it unprofitable in the Northern States. The extraordinary idea appears to have seized upon the public mind, in most of the free States, that it is the mission of the people of those States to correct what they deem the wrongs of other sections of the Union, and hence they have set about the task in a most censorious spirit, and a manner deeply offensive to those whom they seek to influence.

It is not necessary here to discuss the abstract question of the rightfulness or the wrongfulness of slavery. Our mouths are closed upon this point by the folly of Northern men, who have undertaken to correct the assumed errors of the citizens in other portions of the country, and thus have silenced the public voice upon this issue, by raising the more vital one of the right of every community to judge of its own proper course, and of every State of this Confederacy to determine its own policy and the system of social and political economy, which it will legalize and maintain. When we entered the Federal Union and became parties to the Federal compact, we surrendered to the General Government such powers as were essential to provide for the general good, and to give to the United States the strength needful to maintain its rank and position among the powers of the earth, but we reserved to the States respectively the control of their immediate domestic affairs, and especially the control of the whole subject of African slavery within their borders. And we agreed, as a constitutional right between the several States, that "fugitives from service or labor," escaping from one State to another, should be surrendered by the State to which they had fled, on claim being made by their owners. Now if this provision means anything, it certainly means that when slaves from one State escape into another, they shall be freely and honestly surrendered, and all reasonable facilities afforded, for carrying into effect the provision in question. If it does not mean this, then were we guilty, in subscribing to it and ratifying the Constitution in which it is contained, of a fraud and a cheat, unworthy of the character of honest and Christian men.

What is our practice in this respect? How have we discharged this solemn Constitutional obligation? Have we lived up to our deliberate agreement, and fulfilled our engagement toward our sister States? These are questions of self examination, self-inquiry, which every honest man should put to himself in this time of excitement and of national peril. We make no application of our remarks to individuals, but as communities and as States, it is notoriously true that we have failed to abide by the compact made at the formation of the Government, and have placed in the way of its fulfillment all the obstacles which we have been able to throw around it. In many States laws have been passed, expressly designed to prevent its full and complete operation, hedging it about with difficulties and offering inducements to every citizen of such States to practically resist the execution of the laws of Congress designed to carry into effect the obligations imposed upon us by the Constitution. But it is not in these State laws, infamous as some of them are, that we find the most serious obstacles to the full discharge of our Constitutional engagements. The difficulty lies deeper than State legislation. It is to be found imbedded in the public sentiment of the New England and many other Northern States. The people have been educated, through the agency of a sectional press, and a sectional pulpit, to a code of morality which teaches that meddling with the rights and affairs of others is not only a privilege but a Christian duty; that the most solemn and deliberate agreements may be broken when they stand in the way of the modern standard of governmental relations; that to deprive sovereign States of the rights guaranteed to them by the Constitution, and individuals of the possession of property which, by the Federal compact, we have promised to return to them when found within their borders, is an act of philanthropy, fully justified by the standard of religious teachings now recognized by a large proportion of the people.

Instead of inquiring what duties and obligations we owe to others, and how we can most surely and effectually discharge them, we undertake to pronounce upon the question of slavery, in its moral and religious aspects, not as a question of right or wrong for us, but for other communities having separate governments and laws to regulate their conduct in this respect, and then we go to work as law makers— as Executive officers and private citizens, to see how the laws of Congress can be rendered null by our action, and the provisions of the Constitution negatived through our agency.

In common with others, we have recommended and urged the repeal of the State laws in conflict with the statutes of the United States, and the honest fulfillment of all our obligations respecting the return of fugitives, measures of the first importance, if we expect to maintain the Union of the States, and preserve intact our present form of Government. But this is not all. We must go farther, beginning with the people themselves, and demand not only of every public functionary, but of every citizen, that moral support without which no remedy, however powerful the legal pains or penalties, can be of the slightest avail. We must demand from the press and the pulpit the inculcation of lessons of honesty and morality, and we must insist that they shall abandon the new-fangled doctrine, that to rob our neighbor of his slave, or to prevent his return, is a Christian duty, while the repudiation of a deliberate contract between the parties to the confederacy of States, is also considered a compliance with our duty to God and to man. We must return to the golden rule of doing to others as we would that they should do unto us, and thus render unto States and individuals that equal and exact justice which is due from one State or person to another.

Such a reform in the public sentiment of the Northern States will cure the evils now existing, but which, if unchecked, will surely overthrow the Government. We dare not hope for the change, and yet we do not believe that, without it, the Union can last for any considerable time. Great responsibilities rest upon the people of both sections—the North and the South—but the former (as the aggressors) owe it to themselves, to justice, and to public faith and honor, to correct their own errors before demanding of the latter submission to new demands or additional injuries. Let us first pull out the beam from our own eye, before complaining of the mote in our brother's eye.

29. The Progress of Disunion Sentiments—Its Cause

(Washington (D. C.) *National Republican,* November 28, 1860) [1]

There have been secessionists *per se*—men who have been plotting a dissolution of the Union, in some of the Southern States, for more than twenty years past. Until quite recently, however, they have remained in a meagre minority in every State except South Carolina, if, indeed, they ever were in a majority even in that State. Until within some two or three years past, the disunion sentiment at the South was limited to a class of ambitious politicians, who conceived that their chances for political preferment would be better in a new Southern Confederacy, than in the present Federal Union. This has been the ruling cause of

---

[1] The first issue of the *National Republican* appeared on November 26, 1860. Its prospectus of that date declared that it would "advocate and defend the principles of the Republican party."

the disaffection to the Union which has prevailed more or less in some of the Southern States, ever since Mr. Calhoun conceived the idea of attaining, in a Southern Confederacy, to that elevated position which he vainly strove for in the Union made by our fathers. But until recently, men who represented the property and enterprise of the cotton-planting States, and who were seeking to better their condition by other means than political preferment, have been slow to yield their sympathy and support to mere political schemers and agitators, for the advancement of their selfish and ambitious aspirations.

It is manifest, however, that within some two or three years past, the disunionists in the cotton States have been receiving large accessions from a new class of citizens—those who represent the great planting interests of that section. These gentlemen are, as a body, intelligent and enterprising, and act from *motives,* as much as mere politicians do. What new motive, then, has lately brought so many of them *en rapport* with the advocates of disunion? Every one knows that the election of a Republican President is not the *cause* of the great increase of disunion sentiment now so manifest in the cotton States. Every one knows that this has been merely seized upon as a *pretext* for a secession movement which the hearts of the people had been previously prepared for. If some new and powerful motive had not been presented to the people of those States, to induce them to view disunion in some new light, the secession movement of 1860 would have received no more countenance from them, than did those of 1832 and 1850.

Now, what is this new motive, which has wrought so great a change in public sentiment? Every careful observer of the "signs of the times," will recognise the truth of our averment, when we state that the disunion sentiment has been gaining ground in the cotton States, ever since the proposition to reopen the African slave trade began to be agitated, and viewed as a measure possible of attainment; and that it has advanced *pari passu* with the change of opinion in favor of that measure.

The increasing demand for cotton, and the high price of that great staple for some years past, has stimulated its producers to extend its cultivation to the utmost of their ability. The great check upon their enterprise in this direction has been the high and constantly-increasing prices of negro laborers. Slave labor being the principal ingredient in the cost of cotton producing, to cheapen the cost of that labor has of course been a great desideratum with those engaged in its cultivation. The proposition to reopen the African slave trade presented the only possible mode of effecting this desired result; and it was only necessary to inspire some degree of faith in the practicability of that measure, to arouse the wildest enthusiasm in its favor.

A little reflection, however, satisfied every man of ordinary sense, of the utter hopelessness of attaining this object *in the Union*. But in a Southern Confederacy, where the reign of "King Cotton" would be supreme, the measure was conceived to be perfectly feasible. The hope of obtaining negro laborers at one-tenth of their present cost, was a powerful argument addressed to men who were directing all their energies to the extension of cotton planting. The visions of wealth which this prospect opened up to their excited imaginations, did more to shake their loyalty to the Union in one single year, than all the appeals of ambitious politicians had previously done in twenty years. Herein, we think, lies the secret of the great progress of disunion sentiments in the cotton-planting States within the last two or three years.

We sincerely believe that this design of reopening the African slave trade is the most powerful motive now operating upon the Southern mind, in favor of a secession movement. This view of the case affords a solution of the fact, that the Secessionists of the cotton States do not desire the border or grain-growing slave States to join them, at first, in their revolutionary movement. They want the cotton States alone to secede, and set up a new Confederacy, which the border slave States may come into after a while. In other words, they want the cotton States alone to have the framing of the *Constitution* of the new Confederacy. They know that a Constitution made by *all* of the slaveholding States, would contain a prohibition of the slave trade. Hence, such States as Maryland, Virginia, North Carolina, &c., whose interests are directly opposed to the importation of slaves from Africa, are not to be trusted to aid in making the Constitution of the new Confederacy; but when the cotton States shall have made one to suit themselves, and gotten the slave trade fairly under way, they may come into it if they see fit.

The *avowed* motives of the secessionists, for the revolutionary movement now on foot, are so manifestly inadequate, as a justification or even an excuse for that movement, that every reflecting mind must be satisfied that their real motives are kept in the background. The most prominent of these real motives is, unquestionably, an avaricious passion for cheap negroes.

30. THE STRENGTH OF SECESSION

(*New-York Daily Tribune* [Lincoln], November 28, 1860)

The secession strength in the South is overrated. Vociferous, ostentatious and intolerant, it appears greater at the hustings than the polls, much more imposing in the hurly-burly of street-corner harangues than in banking houses where bills of exchange are discounted, or the rural districts where the crops and the men are raised that must ultimately pay them.

What ever South Carolina may threaten, we opine that Rhett, Keitt and their fiery followers, will have hard work to persuade her to go out of the Union alone. They may utter incendiary philippics, and mount Palmetto buttons and blue cockades; she may hold Conventions and pass ordinances, and seem to hang on the very verge of secession; but when the hour comes for her to actually go out of the Confederacy and set up an independent Government, solitary and alone, she will pause. Then we shall look to see Virginia, or a general Convention of the South, tender its counsel; and after much cogitation, we fancy South Carolina will wait for the co-operation of her slaveholding sisters, or even for an overt act of the incoming Administration. We need not say that she will wait in vain for any such act, as an excuse or pretext for breaking up the Union. Will the other Southern States, or even a majority of them, join her in this mad scheme, either before or immediately upon the inauguration of Mr. Lincoln? What is the strength of the secession sentiment in the other slaveholding States?

The large vote for Bell, and the respectable support of Douglas in the South, must, with some exceptions, be counted against secession. Douglas carries Missouri; Bell, Kentucky, Tennessee, and Virginia. He and Douglas and Lincoln have a larger popular vote than Breckinridge in Delaware, Maryland, Georgia, and Louisiana; while they press him hard in North Carolina, Alabama, and some other States. Full returns are not yet received, but it may be safely assumed that a decided majority of the popular vote in the slaveholding States is against Breckinridge. Now, the larger share of this majority is hostile to secession in any form and under any pretext; for, every out and out Secessionist voted for Breckinridge. At the outset, then, one half the South has recorded its emphatic verdict against secession.

Nor can all the Southern supporters of Breckinridge be counted as Secessionists. Many of them are utterly opposed to that mode of redressing alleged grievances. They voted for him for no such reason as this. Others of his advocates, while they may admit the right of a State to secede, yet, ere taking the final step, they would require firmer ground on which to walk out of the Union than the mere election of a Republican President. They would stay for some positive act of Federal aggression to justify a severance of the ties which bind them to sister commonwealths. Others, still, would never consent to secede unless in conjunction with all, or nearly all, the Slaveholding States. They would not dream of leaving Virginia, Maryland, Kentucky and Tennessee behind them. This analysis, it will be perceived, reduces the number of Secessionists *per se* in the South to a comparatively small body.

And even those States which, upon a superficial view, seem eager to leave the Union at the earliest moment, are far from being unanimous in their choice of this insane remedy for imaginary wrongs. Owing to the oligarchic features of her Constitution, and to the death or ostracism of her conservative statesmen, the politics of South Carolina have fallen into the hands of hair-brained fillibusters [*sic*] like Keitt, Rhett and Chesnut. They are now having their day. When the secession movement reaches a point where, if another step be taken, retreat will be impossible, we shall hope to hear calm voices, as we did in the analogous convulsions of 1832, counseling caution and demanding delay. We believe she will not leap into the gulf of Disunion alone, but, when she reaches its brink, will wait for the countenance and co-operation of sister States. Will they join her, and go down with her?

Georgia, upon which South Carolina is chiefly relying for aid and comfort in this crisis, has cast a majority of her votes against Breckinridge. Cobb and Iverson are quarreling about a seat in the Senate. The defeated aspirant will be apt to take the side of this question opposed to that espoused by his successful rival. Alexander H. Stephens, one of the strongest men in the State, and in the South, and Herschel V. Johnson, who has staked his all upon this issue, are both opposed to this treasonable scheme. Other influential citizens act with them. A majority of the people have just repudiated Breckinridge and secession at the polls. Can it be that Georgia, when the culminating point in the exigency is reached, will not advise deliberation? Will she consent to start upon this perilous journey with no other companion than South Carolina?

How is it with the other Calhoun States? The popular sentiment in Alabama, as indicated by the recent election, is not widely different from that of Georgia. The vote for Breckinridge does not largely exceed that of Bell and Douglas combined. Yancey, who heads the Secessionists in that State, though regarded as a man of genius, is held by her considerate people as an erratic declaimer, wholly unfit to lead in a trying crisis; while, on the other hand, many of her most distinguished citizens are utterly averse to this rash plot. As to Mississippi, the Union sentiment of that State has always been strong since it overthrew Davis in the State election which followed the adoption of the compromise measures of 1850. However it may be with her demagogues, the majority of her people will be slow to join in a treasonable conspiracy for destroying the Republic. Only one other State belongs in this category—little Florida. Though she may stand ready to take a leap in the dark with any State that will consent to strike hands with her, we think the proud Palmetto Commonwealth will disdain to make the perilous plunge with so feeble a companion.

These are the five States which originated this Secession Conspiracy. Upon their hearty and prompt coöperation its success depends. In all of them, with the exception of South Carolina, probably a majority of the people are at heart opposed to withdrawing from the Union upon any such pretexts and for any such reasons as have yet been announced. But when madness rules the hour, calculations based upon the reasonableness of men are ofttimes very much at fault. The Secession leaders are bent upon precipitating their scheme ere "the sober second thought" of the rural population can make itself felt in restraining the headlong movement. Impelled to action by a foregone purpose, these leaders do not stop to calculate consequences. They have succeeded in turning the popular current in these five States toward disunion. It may sweep them to a point where retreat is impossible, and thus carry both the willing and the unwilling over the precipice into the chasm.

31. SECESSION

(*Sioux City Register* [Douglas], December 1, 1860)

That man must be blind to passing events who does not, in the widely extended and tumultuous excitement of the Southern people see fearful indications of imminent peril to our institutions. There is in the South a class of radical "fire eaters" whose sole aim for years, has been to inflame and exasperate the masses.—But all their efforts have hitherto been fruitless. The value of the Union has always largely preponderated over all real as well as immaginary [sic] wrongs to which public attention has been directed. The really distinguished statesmen of the South have always avowed their determination to sustain the Union, and their patriotic councils [sic] have been heeded.—It cannot be denied, however, that disaffection and open hostility has [sic] now reached an extent and intensity far beyond any precedent. In many of the States, if there be any reliance in the usual sources of information, the secession party is very largely in the majority, embracing a large share of the talent and influence of these States; and while the border States will for the time being be found sustaining the Union and the Constitution; yet, it is exceedingly questionable whether in the event of a rupture, a common interest would not speedily unite all the Southern States in what would be regarded as an issue upon the question of slavery.

Of the results of such a contest it is hardly possible to form an adequate conception. Under the most favorable circumstances we can calculate upon nothing less than a literal destruction of all our industrial interests; a financial panic such as was never before known; a loss of confidence in all classes of securities; repudiation of indebtedness and universal bankruptcy. We shall have made a happy escape if in addition to all this we are not plunged in a civil war, which must in the nature of things be characterized by scenes of misery and ruin, horrible to contemplate. With such a condition of things it well becomes us calmly to survey the field—to see and acknowledge our errors, and strive by conciliation, and acts of justice, to calm the troubled waters, and avert the impending blow.

We must not expect to find the wrong all on one side, but direct attention to the mote in our own eye, as well as to the beam in that of our neighbors. There are certain land marks that have been lost sight of, and as a consequence our noble vessel has drifted far out of the established channel. Prominent among these is the constitutional requirement for the rendition of fugitives. Stubborn facts, oft repeated, should force from the North the admission that they have come far short of their duty in this regard. Not only has every subterfuge been made use of to evade the plain provisions of law, but in numerous instances its ends have been defeated by the most lawless and revolutionary proceedings. And besides this, States in their sovereign capacity have declared the law null and void, and have made its enforcement a penal offence. For such proceedings we have no excuse, nor have we any reason to expect other than retaliatory measures of like character from those whose rights are thus wantonly disregarded. If we value the Union as we claim to, and deprecate the evils of disunion, we should manifest our feelings by a careful observance of the terms of the compact, by "rendering unto Cæsar the things that are Cæsar's." Were we to exhibit good faith in the discharge of this unquestionable duty, by a repeal of the offensive and unjust State Statutes, and by rendering that prompt and efficient aid in the enforcement of Congressional enactments, which is due from every law abiding citizen, it is probable that there would be no trouble in effecting an amicable adjustment of all other sources of alienation and discord.

It is conceded by all that the question of territorial jurisdiction, so far as slavery is concerned, is a mere abstraction; one which will never effect [sic] the status of a single slave in existance [sic],—and surely such a question is susceptible of settlement were other more important ones satisfactorily disposed of. It is manifest that all these distracting questions in and of themselves are less important than the impression that has grown out of them throughout the South, that there is a wide spread Northern hostility to their people and institutions, such an one too as will admit of no abatement until slavery shall have been overthrown, or the Union dissolved,—and if we would maintain the confederacy we must dispel that illusion. We must satisfy them that we do not seek any interferance [sic] with their domestic or local institutions; that we are willing that they alone should assume the responsibility of slavery within their respective borders, and continue it or not as to them may seem best. This is no less than the South have a right to demand, and no less than justice requires at our hands.

Under the impulse of an intense excitement it is by no means improbable that a step may be taken that will lead to results the most disastrous. The exercise of prudence, wisdom and patriotism, brought to bear at the right time, and in the right direction, may arrest the first step, which if once taken, may never be restored.

Never were the responsibilities of those holding commanding positions greater than in the present crisis. Will the venerable President of the United States acquit himself as becomes a cotemporary and successor of JACKSON? Will he emulate the example of that great man whose administration he so nobly sustained[?] If so, his last official acts will be the most glorious ones of his protracted career as a statesman. DOUGLAS, though smarting under the pangs of a Waterloo defeat has spoken, and has acquitted himself nobly. He invokes his friends to rally as one man around the standard of the Union. There is yet another distinguished statesman, a representative of one of Kentucky's noblest families, who will prove untrue to the name of BRECKINRIDGE if he does not, in this critical hour raise his clarion voice for his country. There are hundreds of others whose council [sic] and influence would tend largely to allay the storm that menaces us. May they all prove themselves worthy the position they hold in the country's esteem.

32. What Can You Do?

(Hartford Evening Press [Lincoln], December 3, 1860)

The dissolution of the Union in any manner or to any extent, even should South Carolina be the only seceding state, would be the just cause of profound sorrow. It would show that the great experiment of self-government for the sake of Liberty had failed, at least temporarily and apparently. It is clear that we can even now have Union, but it is not so clear that we can have Union *and Liberty.* The object of the Union was to secure the blessings of Liberty to ourselves and our posterity, and it must be acknowledged to be true as a general proposition, however much men might differ in its practical application, that the Union might be preserved by measures which would render it wholly false to its original object.

A great many men, actuated by the kindest and best motives, (we except the professional compromisers and born doughfaces) are desirous of offering some olive branch, or making some concession, or giving some assurance, they scarcely know what, that shall induce the cotton states to pause in their mad and destructive career. We should be perfectly willing to join them, standing upon no technicalities, if we could first be satisfied as to the truth and justice of the declarations to be made. But there is the difficulty. There is no use in telling lies to the South, or cheating any faction into delay and submission by pretenses which a brief lapse of time would expose.

We cannot tell Mr. Yancey that we do not believe slavery wrong, for the reverse is the profound conviction of three fourths of the whole North, all parties included. This conviction takes its birth in the best instincts of our nature and is fortified by the principles of Christianity, the teachings of the chief preachers of all ages and countries, by the teachings of legal writers, by the inspirations of poetry, by the laws of civilization. The belief that slavery is wrong is as firmly settled in the minds and hearts of the people as any article of their religious creed. It would be dishonest to say that this conviction will not remain and grow stronger every day.

Nor can we tell Mr. Yancey that we do not believe that at the foundation of our government it was the belief of the leading statesmen that slavery was discordant with our fundamental principles and destined soon to pass away and that this belief influenced them in building the constitution and in their general legislation. Indeed, the South now stigmatizes Washington, Jefferson and their compeers as abolitionists.

We must tell him that we believe that we can constitutionally exclude slavery from all the territories and put a final stop to its extension. We must say that to do this is, to all appearance, the positive, irreversible determination of a majority of the voters of the free states and that very many more wish for this result and are daily coming into the ranks of those who work and vote for it.

We must not, as honest men, refrain from saying to Mr. Yancey that the general sentiment of the civilized world is against slavery. The great fact stares us in the face and southern men have repeatedly acknowledged it. All Europe is practically abolitionized, and America must feel the influence.

And we are compelled to say that the laws of immigration, population and civilization work against slavery. It would be idiotic to assert the contrary in any compromise resolutions, in the face of the crushing contrast made by the census between the slave and free states, as to all that makes intelligent and prosperous states. No man can deny that free white laboring men, whether from Europe or the North, or the South, prefer to immigrate to free territories, nor that the free states are increasing in number more rapidly than the slave states.

We cannot deny, even for the sake of saving Yancey from treason and the gallows, that in Missouri there is a powerful and growing emancipation or abolition party, which casts near 20,000 votes where a short time ago there was not one, and has, besides, numerous adherents who chose this time to vote for Bell. Missouri will soon be a free state, and so will Delaware. We know it and Mr. Yancey knows it.

Nor can we deny that the religious sentiment of the North and portions of the South is strongly anti-slavery, has steadily grown in that direction for many years, and is absolutely certain to continue that growth. Ecclesiastical organizations may be and often are behind the real Christianity of a country, but in this case most of the churches and religious associations are unhesitating in expressing their opposition to slavery.

Have we told the truth? Who can deny it?—Then, if these things are so, to assure the secessionists that slavery shall be protected and made perpetual, and that it shall be extended and recognised as a controlling power in the Union, and that all opposition to it shall cease, would be to tell a base lie, and a very foolish lie. As well promise them that water shall run up hill and two and two shall make five.

Then shall we promise that the fugitive slave law shall never be modified? That were to make it stronger even than the constitution which can be changed at any time if the people so will. Shall we promise that the people will cheerfully catch runaway negroes? They are under some sort of an obligation to do so now but you may promise to all eternity and still the people will think it very mean business and will consider it unfair to throw a man into perpetual slavery without a jury trial. Shall we under the uplifted threat make haste to repeal all personal liberty laws?

Repeal them all and if you leave in force the sentiments, movements, tendencies, principles and moral and economical laws—in short, the facts—that we have referred to, you will have only touched the surface, done nothing at all to satisfy the disunionists. You must promise them a complete revolution in the moral and political convictions and policy of the whole North and of the civilized world. If you tell them that such a revolution is likely, you tell a falsehood. If you tell them that without it slavery can live, you tell another falsehood.

Those men who talk about the repeal of a personal liberty bill as likely to appease men who have plotted disunion for thirty years, grossly misrepresent. Not a single southern paper calls that enough. Their favorite ultimatum is the full recognition and protection of slavery in all the territories. But the real disunionists make no such condition, for they know that such a promise could not be fulfilled.— They have made up their minds that slavery cannot be supreme and perpetual in the federal Union; in that they are right; they think that they can secure that end as independent states; in that they are mistaken. Whatever is wrong will come to an end.

33. A Comparison of Forces

(*Chicago Daily Tribune* [Lincoln], December 13, 1860)

If war should grow out of the present domestic difficulties besetting the Union, the maxim of Louis XIV would be as applicable to the condition of things now as it was to that monarch's long struggle with William of Orange. "The last piece of gold will win." The last piece of gold, of course, meant the last ounce of powder, the last piece of artillery, the last pound of bread and meat, the last blanket, the last pair of shoes—the last everything required in the business of destruction. We may assume that there will be no lack of men and no lack of courage on either side. We cheerfully admit that the Southern people are brave; if they think the Northern people are not brave they have only to put Northern valor to the test. We are of the opinion that Northern *endurance* has considerably the advantage of that quality as it is found in the tropics, but that is a matter of opinion merely, and can only be decided by actual campaign life. We are very clearly of the opinion that the North can carry on war years after the South is utterly exhausted and impoverished. Our reasons for this belief are mainly as follows:

I. In a conflict waged in defense of the Constitution the present armaments of the United States would fall into the hands of its defenders. The officers of the army and navy would owe allegiance to the President and Congress, and they would uniformly yield obedience to them. If their sympathies lay in another direction they would perhaps resign, but they would not dare to commit treason by attempting to transfer any portion of their trusts to an enemy of the United States. Although these armaments are comparatively small, yet they are already in existence and not to be put in motion. If they had to be created anew much valuable time would be lost, and the bill of expense would have a formidable look if required to be footed all at once. This is an item of immense advantage to start with, because

II. It would enable the government to blockade all the Southern ports one month after war should have been determined on. The South has no navy and no sailors, and very small facilities or genius for creating either. Her commerce would at once be cut off. Her productive industry being chiefly agricultural, and her agriculture chiefly of a kind which depends upon commerce for its value, such a blow would come with stunning effect upon her people. Under the most favorable circumstances she could not build and man a navy during the continuance of war, and without a navy she could not raise the blockade nor relieve her crippled industry.

III. The regular revenues of the country would continue to fall into the treasury of the government. All persons would be taxed alike, the willing and the unwilling. The liberality of individuals or of individual States would be a bagatelle in comparison with the giant forces at the command of Congress. If direct taxation should become necessary, (as it probably would not), the tax would be laid and collected from more than double the number of people, and more than treble the number of dollars to be found in the South. It would be simply the melancholy failure of Charles I. fighting his Parliament reenacted, or even a feebler and more melancholy failure than that.

IV. All the principal manufactories of arms and munitions of war are located in the North. Congress, in virtue of its power to regulate commerce between the States would immediately prohibit the exportation of muskets and the various cutlery of war, from one section to the other. The implements of destruction now distributed thro' the South would go only a little way in such a war as the government would be enabled to set on foot.

V. The South is already in distress for food. Her people are buying corn largely in Illinois and the other Northwestern States. It would perhaps be cruel for Congress to prohibit the exportation of bread-stuffs to the revolted section, and thus starve them out, but war is cruel in all its forms, and Congress would certainly have the power to do so. It is yet many months to the harvest. Northern granaries are full to overflowing, and the great markets of Europe are always open to take our surplus. The South is very poorly supplied even for the palmiest days of peace. Once deprived of the means of replenishing her empty flour barrels, her plight would be as desperate as her most vicious enemy could desire.

VI. We will not go into the census tables to demonstrate the superiority of the North in material wealth. Those facts are potent to everybody. A very large portion of Southern capital is invested in negro slaves. This species of property, so far from being an available means of offensive or defensive warfare, is exactly the reverse. If some slaves would fight for their masters, a larger number assuredly would fight against them if the means and the intelligence were supplied them. But we forbear.—We have written thus much for no purpose of provoking our Southern brethren or inflaming our Northern neighbors. We pray fervently that the occasion may never arise which shall test the truth of these statements. War is the last, the very last argument to be resorted to among children of a common parentage. Let it be avoided by every sacrifice short of the legacy which our fathers left us in *the Constitution of the United States.*

34. THE FUTURE OF SLAVERY

(Indianapolis Daily Journal [Lincoln], December 14, 1860)

The dissolution of the American Union seems at last inevitable. Grave and patriotic counsellors who, from their position at the Federal Capital, are able to take wide survey of our vast empire, see as yet not one chance of escape from the impending calamity. Instead of the calm repose of peaceful prosperity that has hitherto marked our country, there now meets the anxious gaze nothing but uproar, confusion and incipient anarchy. It is like the spectacle of a splendid ship, freighted with the world's wealth and packed with human souls, with every inch of canvas set and her flag full high advanced at the mast-head, drifting with a deadly certainty into the mouth of the maelstrom. The comparison is feeble; for the real scene which we may soon have to contemplate is the most awful and tremendous in its consequences of any public event for two thousand years. It will be the death scene of a Government which, during its brief career of seventy years, has astounded the world by its incomparable progress in material prosperity and by the rich fruits, never before so fairly developed, of the truest liberty united with the highest civilization. The passions of men never in any revolution dealt so deadly a blow at human progress, as will be struck in the hour when the States of North America shall fall from their confederated position to the rank of petty empires.

There is one reflection, however, not altogether devoid of satisfaction to those who, like ourselves, believe that slavery is a moral and political evil. The dissolution of the American Union seals the doom of American slavery. As an abstract of philosophical truth, a grander idea never was uttered than that of Seward's "irrepressible conflict."—There *is* an irrepressible conflict; not of States or of armed men—not of John Brown forays or Montgomery incursions; for these are attacks upon slavery where it exists by municipal law and has a right to exist. But there is an irrepressible conflict of *principle,* and in the violation of the divine purposes which are being worked out among men, through the cycles of time, either slavery must go down and freedom prevail, or freedom must expire and slavery reign triumphant and universal.

The strife between freedom and slavery on this continent is most interesting to us certainly; but it is but a fragment of the great conflict of ages, the ever raging war between those things which are just, virtuous, useful and good, and those which are hurtful and vicious and wrong. And every man's judgment as to the final result resolves itself, in the last analysis, simply into a belief or disbelief in a ruler of the universe who is benevolent to devise and Almighty to execute his government of the world. We would protect, and have always advocated the protection of slavery where it exists; believing always, however, that in some way or other it would work its own extinction. But not content to let slavery have a peaceful existence and perhaps, at last, a fearful death, the secessions will precipitate the final result of the irrepressible conflict, they will hurry the plan of Providence and hasten the downfall of American slavery at least one hundred years.

If the Cotton States secede and erect a Southern Confederacy, slavery will be the essence of the government. When they come to form commercial treaties with England, two considerations will influence that great Empire in the slave States. In the first place there is in the English Government a deep-seated hostility to slavery on humanitarian grounds.

They are all Abolitionists, and honest, active ones, from Queen Victoria down to the lowest man in the realm. Further than this, it is the far-sighted policy of England to kill the culture of cotton in this country, and encourage its production in Africa and her own colonies. As a supposed step to this end she will strive to root out American slavery. Thus, then, on both moral and selfish grounds, the resistless diplomacy of that great Empire will be instantly directed against the peculiar institution.

But more than this, the Southern Confederacy will be born a foreign nation. No more protection then, no more fugitive slave laws, no more right of transit, no more surpressing [sic] of slave insurrections by Federal troops. The real Abolitionists of the North (as different from Republicans as night from day) will swarm upon them, and for every one that is hung fifty will take his place. Moreover, they must form commercial treaties with the free Republic of the North, as well as with England; and who can doubt that our policy will co-operate with that of England to grind out slavery? How long would the abnormal institution of slavery, already effete and staggering to its grave, live when brought under the crushing effects of these great influences? The logic of events is a stern and terrible thing. The rigid syllogisms of facts make iron conclusions that must either be avoided, or will crush whoever opposes them, and to the final disappearance of American slavery, when the causes we have spoken of once begin to operate, the terrible vengeance of time points with inexorable certainty.

These are our reasons for saying that the dissolution of the Union is the doom of slavery; and this is the only good to humanity that, so far as we can see, can possibly be evolved from the downfall of our present form of government. The catastrophe may yet be averted, and Heaven grant it may; but, if it come, then it will have happened to those now living to see the ruin of the grandest social fabric of all time. The men may never be born who will rear its like again.

35. THE GREAT QUESTION

(Reading *Berks and Schuylkill Journal* [Lincoln], December 15, 1860)

It is much to be regretted that in the present crisis of our national affairs, the disposition of events will be, to a great extent, in the hands of mere politicians; and that the sentiments of the masses will be scarcely known. The present unfortunate state of public feelings has, to a great extent, been created by ultra men on both sides, while we believe that the great body of the people, North and South, love the Union, and would deplore its dissolution as the greatest of earthly calamities, and a death blow to the cause of freedom throughout the world.

The people of the South have been taught by their leaders that every man who voted for Lincoln is an abolitionist,—hostile to the people of the South, hostile to their institutions, and bent upon their extermination. It would be well that these matters should be understood; that false issues should not be created, and made the pretense for revolutionary acts. In the case of South Carolina, it is not disputed, that it was averse to going into the Union, and while in it, has never been satisfied. That the State has not had its own way in the late election, —that the majority of the people of the United States have voted otherwise than was agreeable to South Carolina, may furnish a convenient excuse and occasion, for Secession, but the politicians of the State cannot pretend that it is a cause. While the border States have lost large numbers of Slaves, from the disinclination of the North to aid in their arrest, South Carolina has lost none, yet South Carolina takes the lead in disunion, and is endeavoring to commit the whole South to the same work.

In so large a party as the Republican, it cannot but be supposed that a great variety of sentiment exists. Voters must act with the party that comes nearest to their individual views in regard to the great questions of the day, and no party can, or should be held responsible for the opinions of the more ultra men, who belong to it, and who are always most solicitous to be heard. There are, no doubt, many who voted for Lincoln, who are entirely indifferent to the subject of Slavery, who have never given it any consideration, and have no particular views in regard to it, while, on the other hand, many genuine abolitionists may have voted the ticket,—though not the more rabid ones, for these refused to vote at all, and denounced Lincoln more bitterly than did any other of his opponents.

The great mass of the Republican party is to be found between these two extremes, and hold the conservative views so often expressed by Lincoln himself. Of these views the South has no right to complain.

There is no desire to interfere with slavery in the South. We recognize to the fullest extent,—and have done so throughout the campaign, —the right of the Southern States to regulate their domestic affairs as they see fit. In this particular every State is sovereign and independent. Pennsylvania has no more right to interfere with slavery in Maryland and Virginia, than she has in Cuba or Brazil. There is no difference of opinion on this point. The recommendations of the President on this point are simply superfluous.

Again, it must be admitted that all laws,—call them "Personal Liberty Bills," or by any other name,—which are hostile to the Constitution of the United States, and in derogation of its provisions, are null and void, and wherever they exist, should be blotted from the statute books. It is a part of the solemn compact between the States, as embodied in the Constitution, that fugitive slaves shall be delivered up to their masters, and any State laws throwing obstructions in the way of their capture, are in direct violation of the Constitution, and should, and no doubt will, be cheerfully repealed, whenever their incompatibility with this instrument is made apparent.

But, while we believe that the North will, willingly, do what is right towards the South, we trust that the *South* will abandon the system of *outrage upon Northern citizens* who happen to be within its border, which has been so disgraceful to its people, and has excited so much just indignation in the North; and above all, that Southern men in Congress will give up a style of talking treason which only makes those who use it ridiculous. The habits of language learned by commanding slaves, is not that which is best adapted to the discussion of great questions among equals. The people of the North are conscious of no wrong to the South in the matter of the late election, and with all regard for the rights of the South, and all desire to be upon terms of brotherhood with its people, would vote as they did, were it to be done over again to-morrow. That they owe to their self respect, and to those Constitutional rights, which they claim, for themselves, as they accord them to others.

It is sad to think that this great Republic, in the first century of its existence, and before the men who periled their lives that she might take her place among the nations of the world, shall have passed away, —sad indeed that our boasted Union should be but a rope of sand, and this great experiment of self government prove but a grief and reproach to the friends of freedom, and a glory to despots throughout the world. If the time has come when the stars and stripes shall no longer float over an united people, when the name of an American citizen shall no longer be a glory and defence throughout the world; if the good and great men of the nation can not heal the difficulties which distract the country,—if the hour of dissolution has come, then in God's name let us separate in peace. There should be no appeal to brute force. That government which does not live in the just consent and in the affection of the governed, is a tyranny. The hand of brother must not be arrayed against brother. In spite of what violent men of the North and South say the *people* of the North love their Southern brethren, and wish them all happiness and prosperity. The people have not forgotten their common brotherhood. If a dissolution there must be, let it be in love and kindness,—with tears rather than curses,—and the recollections of our lost strength, and lost glory, and the suffering of a common peril, may bring us once more together, with a true and lasting sense of the value of that, which in the exuberance of our prosperity, we so unwisely abandoned.

36. THE UNION, IT MUST BE PRESERVED

(Springfield *Daily Illinois State Journal* [Lincoln], December 20, 1860)

There are not a few who seem to think that the Union will be dissolved whenever the South Carolina Secession Convention passes a resolution to that effect. The Union cannot be dissolved by the passage of resolutions. South Carolina may resolve that she is no longer a part of this Union. She may hold secession meetings, mount disunion cockades, plant palmetto trees, make palmetto flags, trample under foot the glorious flag of our country, and proclaim from the housetops her treason and her shame, but all this will not dissolve the Union. She may compel her citizens to resign official place held under the Federal Government—she may close her courts and post offices, and put her own people to a great deal of inconvenience and trouble, but she will still be in the Union, unmolested. She cannot get out of this Union until she conquers this Government. The revenues must and will be collected at her ports, and any resistance on her part will lead to war. At the close of that war we can tell with certainty whether she [is] in or out of the Union. While this Government endures there can be no disunion. If South Carolina does not obstruct the collection of the revenue at her ports nor violate any other Federal law, there will be no trouble, and she will not be out of the Union. If she violates the laws, then comes the tug of war. The President of the United States, in such an emergency, has a plain duty to perform. Buchanan may shirk it, or the emergency may not exist during his administration. If not, then the Union will last through his term of office. If the overt act, on the part of South Carolina takes place on, or after the 1st of March, 1861, then the duty of executing the laws will devolve upon Mr. Lincoln. The laws of the United States must be executed—the President has no discretionary power on the subject—his duty is emphatically pronounced in the Constitution. Mr. Lincoln will perform that duty. Disunion, by armed force, is TREASON, and treason must and will be put down at all hazards. This Union is not, will not, and cannot be dissolved until this Government is overthrown by the traitors who have raised the disunion flag. Can they overthrow it? We think not. 'They may disturb its peace—they may interrupt the course of its prosperity—they may cloud its reputation for stability—but its tranquil[l]ity will be restored, its prosperity will return, and the stain upon its National character will be transferred and remain an eternal blot on the memory of those who caused the disorder.' Let the secessionists understand it—let the press proclaim it—let it fly on the wings of the lightning, and fall like a thunder bolt among those now plotting treason in Convention, that the Republican party, that the great North, aided by hundreds of thousands of patriotic men in the slave States, have determined to preserve the Union—peaceably if they can, forcibly if they must.

37. THE PRACTICAL DIFFICULTIES OF SECESSION

(Philadelphia *Press* [Douglas], December 21, 1860)

The members of the South Carolina Disunion Convention, as they approach the consideration of the practical questions involved in a faithful and thorough-going execution of their secession project, are beginning to realize some of the difficulties they will be compelled to encounter. It is a comparatively easy matter to burn down a house if no one attempts to arrest the flames, but it requires much laborious toil to erect a new one. Even if the efforts of the States which propose to secede should prove successful, they will not soon be able to erect a new Government which will be as useful and beneficent to them as the present Confederacy, notwithstanding their loud complaints against it.

If, by secession, they do not mean anything more than the adoption of empty resolves and pronunciamientos—the passage of ordinances repealing their ratification of the Federal Constitution, the resignation of leading Federal office-holders, and the virtual abolition of the Federal courts, they will certainly do much to alarm and agitate the American people, and to bring discredit upon the nation; but they will still virtually be in the Union. The convenience of the present Post Office system is acknowledged even now in South Carolina. They are not prepared to furnish a sufficient substitute for it. The best plan they have yet devised is to form some sort of an amicable arrangement with the powers that be at Washington, by which the postmasters of the Palmetto State will perform their duties as usual, while they refuse to recognize in any way the authority of the Federal Government, and consider their own local rulers the only ones they are obliged to respect and obey! If Mr. BUCHANAN adheres to the programme laid down in his message and to the doctrines enunciated in the elaborate opinion prepared for him by the late Attorney General BLACK, he cannot well avoid collecting the Federal revenues at all Southern ports, even after the passage of secession ordinances; and if this duty is discharged, any State which assumes a rebellious attitude will still be obliged to contribute revenue to the support of the Federal Government or have her foreign commerce entirely destroyed. There will be no necessity for a collision unless some of the American forts are attacked, or the collection of duties meets with resolute and determined opposition. In either of these events, the National Government of this country will still have full power to vindicate its authority and to enforce compliance and respect, if those who rule its councils shall deem it expedient to avail themselves of the ample resources at its command.

All these obstacles must be entirely overcome, either by force, or by the connivance of the Federal Government, or by the consent of the States which remain in the present Confederacy, before any effort at secession can become completely successful, and before South Carolina or any of her discontented sisters can fully assume, among the Powers of the earth, a free and independent position. Many of the ablest men of our country have ridiculed the idea of "peaceable secession" as preposterous, and although it probably meets now with more favor than at any former period, it will be a singular event if we should fail to settle our existing quarrels within the Union, when we have common tribunals to appeal to, and yet preserve amicable relations during the progress of a dissolution of the Confederacy, and after so dire a calamity was consummated.

But, even supposing that a peaceable secession policy should prevail, and that the Gulf States should have but to declare their desire for independence to secure it, they could not rationally expect to form a new Government which would be more useful and advantageous to them than the present one has, up to this time, proved itself to be. No section of our country has derived greater benefits from the American Union heretofore than the very States in which the secession sentiment is most formidable—South Carolina, Georgia, Florida, Alabama, Mississippi, Louisiana, and Texas. The anxiety of the latter to enter our Confederacy was a striking evidence of her appreciation of the advantages it could confer upon her, and certainly her anticipations must have been more than realized when we consider that we not only assumed and finally disposed of her long-standing quarrel with Mexico, by defeating and humiliating the latter, but that we paid off all her heavy old debts, and that, in wealth and prosperity, she has constantly been increasing, with wonderful rapidity, since her annexation. Louisiana and Florida were purchased outright from foreign Governments, and owe to the power of the American Union not only the freedom they enjoy, but nearly all their prosperity. It required all the energy, and much of the treasure, of the Federal Government to finally subdue in Florida, Georgia, Alabama, and Mississippi, the powerful Indian tribes which once inhabited them. The rich plantations, which now send forth their large annual products of cotton, would probably still be under the control of their aboriginal owners, if the forces of the United States had not driven them from their native haunts, and if the white settlers had not relied upon the support and protection of a great nation. South Carolina has always exercised in the councils of the nation quite as much, if not more, influence than any State of equal population, and has reaped her full proportion of all the benefits it has conferred. She complains that she has been onerously taxed, but she will find it utterly impossible, if her secession ordinance should really sever her connection with the Republic, to secure advantages equal to those she has heretofore enjoyed, without incurring a much larger expenditure than she has heretofore been subjected to. In what new Confederacy, or under what new system, can she be as well protected from foreign invasion and domestic insurrection, and have her rights at home and abroad as well secured, as under the one from which she appears so anxious to escape? The expense of our army and navy, of our diplomatic system, of our whole machinery of National Government, weighs but lightly on thirty-three States, but any new organization which approaches it in efficiency would be exceedingly burdensome to any small Confederacy.

Viewing the secession experiment in the most favorable light that its authors can possibly consider it, it is still full of embarrassments and perils; and while we trust that the Representatives of the North will be ready to do all in their power to remove every just cause of complaint, and to destroy every plausible pretext for a dissolution of the Union, we trust that when the prevailing excitement in the Cotton States subsides, their citizens will coolly and calmly consider this subject, in all its aspects, to ascertain whether it is not even better to bear the ills they have than fly to others that they know not of.

III

BUCHANAN'S MESSAGE TO CONGRESS

38. THE MESSAGE

(Jersey City *Daily Courier and Advertiser* [Lincoln], December 5, 1860)

No President's message was ever so anxiously waited for as that of Mr. Buchanan, just promulgated; none more curiously and attentively read, and none cast aside with such unqualified disappointment, after a vain search for something satisfactory and conclusive upon the most important topic which an American President ever had to treat.

The document is carefully written and will take a respectable rank among literary compositions, and that is about all the commendation it will ever receive. Though not deficient in professions of patriotism and wise suggestions in natural political economy, Mr. Buchanan in no place rises above the Democratic politician, and in no degree improves his position or mends the poor fame he has thoroughly earned, as the mere attorney of a party, and a party which is only a semi-faction at that. He has shewn himself utterly incapable of rising to the altitude of an impartial nationality, and has apparently been careful that no one should for a moment be justified in mistaking him for a great man and an efficient magistrate, capable of comprehending a grave crisis and fully competent to meet and manage it.

On the grand question of the right of secession he might as well have been silent as to utter the neutralising and inefficient doctrine he has propounded. The purport of what he says is simply that secession is revolution; that revolution is wrong; that the constitutional union is at the same time theoretically indestructible and practically transient, being designed and constructed for perpetuity but containing no provisions for its own continuance beyond the limit which any individual state may dictate at its own caprice; that the North are the sole aggressors in the quarrel between the sections which has brought about the present crisis, but the South are solely to blame for proposing to remedy their alleged wrongs by revolution; that disunion is inevitable and may yet be averted by timely concessions which, however, come too late; that having argued the whole matter, he has no suggestion to make, and that Congress must do the best they can under the circumstances and he will assist them to the best of his ability, albeit he is quite helpless and powerless. As a cotemporary pertinently says, he lets "I dare not wait upon I will," and also upon "I ought"—his views are satisfactory to his reason and conscience, but too strong for his stomach. He stands by them theoretically, but runs away from them practically. All that he builds up as right he pulls down as impracticable.

He pleads that he cannot execute certain laws in South Carolina because certain officers have resigned, at the same time assuring the country in respect to other laws which he specifies that he is still able to enforce them and will continue to be, even if the office[r] appointed to execute them should resign, as he can at once appoint a successor: thus a Judge or a Marshal may resign and the vacancy paralyses the Federal government, while if a Customs Collector throws up his appointment another can be forthwith put in his place who will not refuse to act.

To remedy this complex and embarrassing state of things Mr. Buchanan thinks Congress ought to make laws conferring new powers on the President, and immediately after enters into an argument to prove that Congress has no constitutional right to do so, quoting Madison, the "father of the Constitution" to shew that to attempt to coerce a refractory state would be for the Federal Government to make war upon one of its own members, which is not an allowable idea, albeit there is nothing whatever in the way of a state being practically at war with the general government, as Mr. Buchanan thinks.

This sophistication and inconsistency is palpably nothing better than a mere cover of retreat from the sacred responsibilities of his position; an elaborately contrived excuse for pusillanimity; an evasion of confessed obligation, by the plea of official infirmity; an attempt to shift the responsibility of the Executive back upon the inefficiency of the organic law.

In all Mr. Buchanan's argumentation, there is no word or hint that peradventure the Slavery interest may be a trifle too exacting, or in any degree unreasonable. There are suggestions of constitutional amendments which shall secure every thing to the South, and deny every thing to the North, East, and West, which the sections respectively claim; there is complaint of Northern personal liberty laws, and a demand for their repeal, but never a word of Southern violences upon Northerners by banishment and imprisonment, and the kidnapping of free men by Southern ruffians; there is a demand that the Dred Scott opinion shall be incorporated into the Constitution, and that Carolinians and Georgians may be authorised to carry their local slave laws with them into free territories; with much more to the same purport. But there is nothing of liberty—not a word for the rights of man—not an allusion to the final prevalence of the spirit of the Declaration of Independence—no breathings of the aspirations which came from Washington, from Jefferson, and the other fathers, that slavery might finally cease from the land —no admission that the country were better off without it—but the whole document is black—black—with the hue of oppression, and bristling with the spirit of a rabid slaveocracy.

Not to extend our comments on this most deplorable effusion of a most deplorable Executive, let us suggest a thought in connection with this Message which must excite the unhesitating gratification of every reader. It is this: that in all human probability, it is James Buchanan's LAST.

39. THE PRESIDENT'S MESSAGE—THE STATE OF THE UNION

(New York Herald [Breckinridge], December 5, 1860)

The President's annual Message to Congress is before our readers. At this extraordinary and alarming crisis in our political affairs this important State paper will be read with unusual interest by all sections, parties and classes of the American people.

As the closing regular exhibit of Mr. Buchanan's administration, we had expected a good report, and we should have been disappointed had he failed to meet the sectional discords and dangers of the day with such arguments and recommendations for the preservation and perpetuation of the Union of these States as his position, the occasion and the public expectations demanded. So far, however, from being in any degree disappointed upon these essentials, we are delighted with the calm, patriotic, consistent and convincing views thereon of this admirable annual Message. The last from Mr. Buchanan, it is his best, good as its predecessors have been each in its adaptation to the requirements of the time.

The first and absorbing topic discussed in this Message is, of course, the revolutionary crisis in our political affairs, which has followed so quickly the late Presidential triumph of our Northern anti-slavery republican party. While "the country is eminently prosperous in all its material interests," Mr. Buchanan's first inquiry is: why is this Union, the source of all these blessings, threatened with destruction? The cause is at hand. It is "the long continued and intemperate interference of the Northern people with the question of slavery in the Southern States."

But the immediate peril comes from the danger of servile insurrections in the South, from the "vague notions of freedom" which the slaves have imbibed under this incessant Northern anti-slavery agitation. Hence it appears that among our Southern brethren "a sense of security no longer exists around the family altar," but that "many a matron throughout the South retires at night in dread of what may befall herself and her children before the morning." This is the great cause of danger to the Union; and how is it to be removed? This is the question; but it will be presently answered.

The Message takes the just ground that the election of Mr. Lincoln, in itself, involves no provocation for disunion, and that the South, from said election, is in no immediate danger of any Northern aggressions through the action of the general government. But Northern nullification acts and acts of resistance to the Fugitive Slave law are justly complained of, and, if not redressed within the Union, will afford a sufficient cause for "revolutionary resistance to the government of the Union." Secession Mr. Buchanan considers a revolutionary act. He denies the doctrine of constitutional secession. The general government is not a rope of sand, but a great and powerful organization, contemplating no separation of any of its co-partners short of revolution; but this is a right which underlies all constitutions.

Mr. Buchanan next contends that the federal government has no authority to coerce a seceding State into submission, and that coercion, in any event, is utterly impracticable. What, then, is he to do in regard to South Carolina? Her federal law officers having all resigned, he, to the extent of their jurisdiction, is estopped from doing anything. He may still at Charleston secure the collection of the federal revenue from foreign imports; but there are the federal forts, the· property of the United States, placed in his charge. Is he to give them up on demand or hold them at all hazards? He says:—"It is not believed that any attempt will be made to expel the United States from this property by force; but if in this I should prove to be mistaken, the officer in command of the forts has received orders to act strictly on the defensive. In such a contingency the responsibility for consequences would rightfully rest upon the heads of the assailants." But the power to coerce a delinquent State back into the Union was tried and rejected in the Convention forming the constitution, so that the only remedy for secession is reconciliation.

Thus, with this case of secession on the part of South Carolina in the foreground, Mr. Buchanan still thinks that the Union may be saved through an explanatory amendment of the constitution, embracing these concessions to the South, viz.: 1. An express recognition of the rights of property in slaves. 2. The recognition of this right in all the Territories during their territorial condition; and, 3. Universal good faith in the restoration of fugitive slaves. And we fully concur that some such constitutional remedy is demanded by the evil of the day. Let this movement be initiated, and let South Carolina quietly go out, if she will not remain in the Union, and in the event of a new treaty of peace between the North and the South, we may rest assured that, tired of being solitary and alone, outside in the cold, South Carolina will come back to the family table.

Meantime we are admonished that this alternative of an amendment of the constitution, or a break up of the confederacy, will surely bring its troubles upon the country. We may escape dissolution and a civil war; but the processes incident to any change of the constitution will require a period of at least two or three years. In this interval of uncertainty, agitation and reconstruction of parties and Northern opinion, we apprehend such a prostration, in all our monetary, commercial and business affairs, as we have never suffered heretofore. The beginning of this revulsion is now upon us, and during this winter we fear that the suspensions of manufacturing establishments and the general loss of employment will create such masses of destitute and desperate men as may put in peril the peace of many Northern communities. And such are the consequences, upon us and before us, of the "irrepressible conflict," which is only to end with the downfall of slavery.

It appears that this Message of Mr. Buchanan, in Congress, satisfies neither the North nor the South. We suppose this means impracticable Northern republicans and Southern disunionists. But we still hope that the patriotic views and suggestions of the President will create such a reaction for the Union, in Congress, and in the North and in the South, among Union loving men of all parties, as will be sufficient to arrest the work of Southern disunion, to put an end to Northern abolitionism, and to save the country. Mr. Buchanan has laid down the required landmarks for action. Now let our Union men, North and South, come up to the work of a revision of the constitution. After seventy years of wear and tear, can we wonder, all things considered, that it fails to meet the necessities of this day.

Touching the regular operations of the general government in all its departments, and the policy of Mr. Buchanan on the tariff question, the affairs of Mexico, &c., we can only to-day commend to the reader a careful perusal of this eminently satisfactory Message.

40. The Message

(Philadelphia *North American and United States Gazette* [Lincoln],
December 5, 1860)

The President truly says, at the outset, that no great and tangible fact of evil has fallen on the country during the year just closed, that nothing of oppression or of special misfortune has been endured by the south or the north. There is agitation at the south, however—an agitation which he should have declared unnecessary as well as injurious to those who indulge in and promote it. Being injurious to all concerned, and useful by no possibility to any, the President of the United States should have made an effort to allay it for once, and not an effort to stimulate it by again falsely charging on the great body of the northern people an intention to interfere with southern security. This style of arguing that the north meditates aggression, and seeks power only to use it offensively, has planted the very root of the popular discontent now prevailing at the south. We would have been glad to record its omission from the last message of Mr. Buchanan.

The argument which the President puts forth in regard to the right to resist a constitutional election is sound, and his statement that the very position of the chief executive renders him conservative is also sound and just. Apprehensions that Mr. Lincoln will invade the rights of any section are not justified by his past history, and on a mere contingency of such danger it is most unwise to break up the Union and to wreck the fortunes of the south first of all. The President says there is no single act of Congress or law in existence impairing, in the slightest degree, the rights of the south in their peculiar property. There is no probability of the passage of such a law, he says, and were such a law enacted the Supreme Court stands as a barrier strong enough to overthrow any such legislation. The act of the Legislature of Kansas Mr. Buchanan declares will be declared a nullity by the Supreme Court if ever tested. Even the State laws, if any such exist, tending to obstruct the operation of the Fugitive Slave law, are equally harmless before the Supreme Court. Mr. Buchanan does not presume that the incoming President will violate his duty. What stronger argument can be made against the justice of the present position of the south than this? It is satisfactory and complete. It is the truth, and we thank Mr. Buchanan for stating it, as it was his duty to do.

The message argues fairly and justly as to the character of the Union and the nature of the ties and obligations which bind us together. No right of secession exists. It never occurred to any individual that the labors of the founders of this nation could be frustrated by the secession of single States. It is demonstrated by the nature and extent of the powers conferred by the general government that the Union formed was a perpetual Union. "They placed both the sword and the purse under its control—the highest attributes of sovereignty." The President proceeds to set forth the conditions on which this government, intended from the outset to be great and powerful, was founded, stating them forcibly and clearly in the main, and closing by demonstrating that revolution alone can change it, or overthrow it, or sever a State from it. This is the truth, and we proceed to see in what light he regards the revolution now threatened—a revolution which has no justification, by his own showing, in present or past injuries; no footing in the original terms of union, nor in any rights then reserved to the States or the people.

On this branch of the subject the President first declares it his duty solely to execute the laws, an obligation from which no human power has absolved him; but, while this declaration is a fair one, he evades its force, as regards a most important point, by substantially recognizing the extinction of the Federal administration of justice there already. Is not this a great error? The resignation of a judge or marshal is not the extinction of the court. Has the President appointed successors, as it was his duty to do? Has he cared for the preservation of records, and for the important duties that belong to him in the maintaining of this court? We fear he has not, from the wording of the message; yet it is scarcely credible that he, as President, should dare assume so great a responsibility as the recognition and acceptance of an act so grave as the destruction of a branch of the Federal judiciary. The declaration to this effect in the message is an error of the very highest rank.

As to the forts and the revenue the message is clear and in the main correct; they must be preserved against violation by any force whatever. The message is also correct as to the right of the President to consider or to open any question whatever with any single State as an independent authority. We hope the most rigid observance of this separate position will be continued, and that no lapsus of duty, implying discretion of this sort, such as appears to have occurred in regard to the federal judiciary in South Carolina, will again be permitted. The President has, with a fair degree of accuracy and justice, stated his obligation to enforce the laws everywhere, and to recognize no movement as justifiable or legal which attempts to contravene the authority of the general government. Though the mildest possible form in which revolution ever was or ever can be met, there may be cases requiring this degree of mildness, and at present we will not demand more. The country did not expect so much, perhaps, of Mr. Buchanan.

The message proceeds to offer advice to Congress as to the further duty of the aggregate power of the government, and as to the mode in which it shall deal with revolution in this case. On this point we are surprised to find that he has come to views quite at variance with those of the opening of his message. He believes that no power has been delegated to Congress to suppress revolution in a State; this government of so much power becomes powerless in the very crisis which tries its strength. If resistance to the laws is attempted by a State government, such resistance cannot be suppressed because to do so would be making war on a State, in [is?] his argument; and if this position is correct, the legal ties which bind the Union are less than ropes of sand. This part of the message, if it were not extra-judicial, and therefore of no more value than any individual's opinion, would destroy the whole force of the statements of duty which precede it, for if a President can act on principles so loose he can destroy all law and all order when he will. We believe, however, that this part of the message was prepared in a spirit of weak concession to the disunion elements of the Cabinet, and was intended to cater to the prevailing sentiment of the disunion States. We regret this error, not because we advocate coercion, or assume now to say what the duty of the general government may be when the exigency comes, but because we deprecate the loosening of all restraints and the release of all penalties at a time when such release directly incites to the worst acts of treason to the only power which can preserve the nation in peace.

As an alternative through which the Union may still be preserved, the message proceeds to suggest amendment of the Constitution by the addition of an "explanatory amendment" on the subject of slavery. This explanation is in three points—the first declaring a national recognition of the right of property in slaves in the States; the second the duty of protecting this right in all the territories; and the third a recognition of the right of recapture, and a declaration that all obstructive acts of the free States are null and void. We do not wish to pronounce upon measures of conciliation in advance of any declaration of sentiment by the body of the Opposition in Congress, but we have no expectation that the only real point in these propositions would ever be ratified as an amendment to the national Constitution. It is a grave matter to open the Constitution again to alteration, and the attempt to do so would produce much, if not dangerous, discussion. The points

named are all below the rank of constitutional provisions, also, whatever their merit. The case is really an inadequate one, and it would be
as unnecessary as it is inadequate in any other state of the public mind
than the present.

So much for the Presidential message on the gravest event yet known
to our history—a treatment of the case characteristic of the President
we have now. With much soundness of argument, we have singular inadequacy of results, but we hope that in the brief period yet remaining
to the author of this message, we shall have nothing to lament of greater
and graver error.

There is nothing further of importance in the Message except what
relates to the finances and the tariff. It is said that great efforts have
been made to reduce the annual expenditure, and if to exhaust the
public resources by the shortest process be such an effort, the case is a
clear one. Both Mr. Buchanan and Mr. Cobb have accomplished great
results in depleting the Treasury, so that money could not be freely expended. The most the message says on this point is mere stuff. On the
tariff, Mr. Buchanan renews his recommendation of specific duties, this
time calling his policy a free trade policy, and the opposite of protection. A year since he said precisely the reverse. Great Britain is cited as
having a great free trade policy and universal specific duties; and,
though the fact may be unknown to Mr. Buchanan, other people are
well aware that Great Britain is even now far beyond us in recognizing
the protective principle in her revenue policy. It is of little consequence with what words this Administration goes out; we all know it
by its bitter fruits and its incessant contradictions and self stultifications.
On finances it has shamefully and totally failed, sinking the country in
debt some eighty millions of dollars in a time of uninterrupted peace,
and leaving the Treasury in utter confusion, as well as bankruptcy.

41. The Message

(Philadelphia *Morning Pennsylvanian* [Breckinridge], December 5,
1860)

The Message of the President was received in this city yesterday,
soon after noon—read in several public places to large and anxious
crowds, and soon extensively circulated. Never, within our recollection,
was there a more intense desire to know the views of the Chief Magistrate. Calumny for once was mute, and all—foes and friends—awed by
the solemnity of the crisis, united in respectful attention to the farewell utterences [sic] of a wise and experienced statesman. Nor has popu-

lar expectation been disappointed, for what the President has said on
the engrossing topic which the Constitution required him to discuss,
"the state of the Union," is characterized by energy, decision and moderation. There is no abdication of the authority of the Government of
the Union. On the contrary, it is expressly and emphatically but not
offensively asserted. He does not brandish Federal authority in the face
of an excited community. He does not scold. He does not threaten—but
in the single phrase, in which he says that the property of the United
States in South Carolina shall be defended, and that, if in its defence,
human life should be sacrificed, the responsibility will rest on the
hands of the assailants. He comprises the distinct but positive expression of the sense of duty which binds him to execute, at all hazards, the
laws of the United States. He discusses calmly and intelligently the abstract right of secession. He examines it as a question of history as well
as a question of criticism on the Constitution itself, and he comes to the
conclusion that it is, after all, but a question of words and phrases and
equivocation. "In short," says the President, "let us look it fairly in the
face. Secession is neither more nor less than revolution. It may or it may
not be a justifiable revolution, but still it is a revolution."

So considering it, applying this view of the Constitution to the state
of things existing just now in South Carolina, a less tolerant and sagacious man might easily have been betrayed into broad and rash assertions of the coercive powers of the Government, and into an assumption that, because South Carolina has no right to secede, she ought, by
the strong hand, to be forced from her position. It was once wisely said
—if we remember rightly, by Sir ROBERT PEEL—that the omnipotence
of Parliament was too grand and solemn a thing to be paraded and
lightly talked about and threatened—that it ought to be sacredly veiled
in the very recesses of the Constitution. If this be true of that arbitrary
power—the vast sovereignty known as the Imperial Parliament—how
much more true is it of the limited and well-defined power vested in
our Federal Government—limited, too, by the express nature of the
grants which enacted it, and the reserved rights of the States that support and stand around it. And so the President seems to regard it. So
far as the laws of the United States are contravened by her citizens,
whether they live in South Carolina or Massachusetts, he will enforce
them, and he will not recognize any exemption from obedience to those
laws by the authority of a State that claims to have "seceded." But he
won't make war, and he thinks Congress has no right to make war upon
the State itself. "Suppose," says he, "such a war should result in the
conquest of a State, how are we to govern it afterwards? Shall we hold

it as a province, and govern it by despotic power? In the nature of things we could not, by physical force, control the will of the people, and compel them to elect Senators and Representatives to Congress, and to perform all the other duties depending upon their own volition, and required from the free citizens of a free State as a constituent member of the Confederacy."

This is sound, constitutional and conservative doctrine,—and not the less so because it is gentle and merciful; and the moral of it all is, the duty of conciliation and a recognition of the power of public sentiment, as constituting the safeguard of our institutions. To that public sentiment, even as represented in Congress, the President appeals. He asks the South, the irritated and justly exasperated South, to pause—to bear the ills, the confessed ills, they have, rather than rush to others that they know not of. He supplicates the North to retrace its steps, to check the spirit of what may well be called sentimental enthusiasm on the subject of domestic slavery—in plainest English, to mind its own business—and thus appealing to both sides of this heated issue, he suggests a practical remedy in an amendment of the Constitution for the territorial question, and a repeal of offensive local legislation.

He thinks that Congress has the remedy in its power, and recommends that it shall propose an "explanatory amendment" to the Constitution on the subject of slavery. He says, "this might originate with Congress or the State Legislatures, as may be deemed most advisable to attain the object." This explanatory amendment would be intended to settle, finally and forever, the true interpretation of the Constitution on the three following points:—

1. An express recognition of the right of property in slaves in the States where it now exists or may hereafter exist.

2. The duty of protecting this right in all the common Territories throughout their territorial existence, and until they shall be admitted as States into the Union, with or without slavery, as their constitutions may prescribe.

3. A like recognition of the right of the master to have his slave, who has escaped from one State to another, restored and "delivered up" to him, and of the validity of the fugitive slave law enacted for this purpose, together with a declaration that all State laws impairing or defeating this right are violations of the Constitution, and are consequently null and void.

It remains to be seen how these recommendations will be received by the country. Such is the temper of the public mind that no man, however wise, can pronounce upon the effect of any proposed measure. Human judgment, always fallible, is in the present emergency altogether at fault. If patriotism is not extinct, we may hope for a reaction at the North which will be generously responded to at the South, and which will result in that consummation so devoutly to be wished for, the preservation and perpetuation of this great Republic.

It is gratifying to know that our foreign relations are of the most pleasant and friendly character.

The President adheres to his former recommendation in regard to the Tariff, to wit: specific instead of [ad] valorem duties, on all articles that will admit of it.

We, of course, expect in future to notice the recommendations of the Message more in detail. It is a document that will bear searching scrutiny and close reflection. Our columns are so crowded to-day that we have but little room for comment.

42. The Message

(New Haven *Morning Journal and Courier* [Lincoln], December 6, 1860)

Mr. Buchanan's last Annual Message, as President of the United States, will have a more wide and careful reading than is often accorded to such documents. As the chief officer in the government—the man especially entrusted with the enforcement of the laws, and the protection of the Constitution, his opinion and purpose are naturally looked for with intense interest by the whole nation. Very little attention will be bestowed upon those parts of the Message which relate to foreign affairs. Our relations with other nations are generally satisfactory, and excite no comment. Our home affairs are generally in a most depressed condition, but Mr. Buchanan has little to say about them, except to recommend an increase in the tariff. The great subject of interest is the treason plots being hatched at the South—the doctrine of secession, and the right and power of the government to perpetuate its existence. It is about these things that the public is concerned, and it is to see how the President stands in relation to them that his Message will be so widely read. We regret to say that Mr. Buchanan shows a weakness, imbecility and inconsistency which proves him utterly unfit for the emergencies of the times, and that he has no better remedy for preventing a dissolution of the Union, than a concession of all and every thing asked by the disunionists.

Letting pass, as idle misrepresentation, his assertion that the North is an aggressor upon the South, and the originator of all the present agitation, we come to his argument against the right of a State to secede. He argues this point well, and we had a right to expect that having established it, and proved that our government was meant to be perpetual, and had delegated to it all the power necessary to maintain its perpetuity, he would proceed to declare that he, as the head of the government, would see that it was maintained and perpetuated, and advise with Congress as to the proper and most judicious way of doing so. But no, the man turns face upon his own argument, and declares that after all secession is simply rebellion, and then says neither he nor Congress has the right or power to prevent rebellion because no authority is given to "make war upon a State."—This then is the end of his powerful argument against secession—call it by another name, and it becomes another thing. It is a melancholy exhibition of servility and incompetency for Mr. Buchanan to call the enforcement of the laws of Congress and the Constitution of the country as making war against a State. Did any body before discover that the collection of duties at the port of Charleston; the arrest and trial of criminals before the United States Courts, or the transportation of the mails and maintainance [sic] of Post Offices, even if maintained by force, and against the menace of South Carolina, was "making war upon the State?" If Mr. Buchanan is right in this, how can he enforce the Fugitive Slave law in any State which resists its operation? It is a dead letter the moment any State declares it shall not be obeyed within its limits. The fact is that the execution of the laws is the duty of the government, and if resistance is offered, then sufficient force must be used to secure their execution. The resistance comes from the individuals, the State is not known in the transaction. It may legislate as much as it chooses, but its legislation is simply void, because it is inconsistent with the Constitution. But the United States will not make war upon it for its legislation. It will punish the individuals who oppose the law, but it neither knows or cares for the State in the matter.

Mr. Buchanan cannot see this perfectly palpable distinction, and so he surrenders the duty of the President and Congress to enforce the law, because there is nothing in the Constitution authorizing making war against a State. Mr. Buchanan proceeds to avow his inability to execute the law in South Carolina because Judges, Marshals and Post Masters have resigned. It never seems to occur to him that he can appoint successors, and afford them sufficient protection to enable them to discharge their duties. He has a little hope of collecting the revenue because the Collector at Charleston has not yet resigned, and he thinks when he does, he may appoint a successor to *him*. What wretched drivel this is, to come from a President of the United States!

But the worst is yet to come. Mr. Buchanan after having labored hard to prove that the government cannot hold itself together, proposes that the trouble shall be remedied by amendments to the Constitution. Not amendments which will give it that power of self-preservation he thinks now wanting. Not amendments to enable it to do what he thinks it ought to do, but cannot for want of authority. But amendments which shall entice the seceders back again until they, or some other States choose to disorganize the government in the same way. He very coolly proposes to the people of the United States that they shall coax South Carolina back into the Union by *making the Breckinridge platform a part of the Constitution!* The people, by a vote of 3,900,000 to 600,000 have just voted down that platform, and yet Mr. Buchanan proposes that the thirty-nine hundred thousand shall surrender to the six hundred thousand, and fasten their obnoxious platform forever on the country, by incorporating it in the Constitution!

This, Mr. Buchanan thinks, and this only, will restore peace and unity. We never have seen the experiment tried in a free country, of restoring power and unity by the submission of six sevenths of the people to one seventh, but we doubt the feasibility of the scheme. This Message of Mr. Buchanan's removes the last hope of a reliance upon the Chief Executive of the nation. His remaining ninety days of office will be only so much more time given for disunion to augment its forces, and Mr. Lincoln's position will be all the more embarrassed by the encouragement his impotent predecessor has given to the violators of the laws, and the destroyers of the nation. There is far less hope now of the preservation of the Union than there was a week ago. It may be that there is wisdom and sagacity enough in Congress to effect it, without the aid of the President, but we doubt it, and are more than ever prepared to witness, within the next month, the sloughing off of some half dozen of the disaffected States.

43. THE PRESIDENT'S MESSAGE

(Buffalo Daily Courier [Douglas], December 6, 1860)

The message of President Buchanan, which we issued in an extra, yesterday afternoon, in advance of our contemporaries, appears in our regular edition this morning. We shall confine the few remarks we have to make to that portion of the message devoted to secession, reserving other topics for future comment. The President has our full concurrence in all that he says in regard to the palpable violations of constitutional duty by the Legislatures of Northern States. It will always be the duty of the President to execute the Fugitive Slave Law, against the conflicting enactments of State Legislatures, and without regard to the public sentiment which may prevail in any locality. The whole power of the Federal Government should be exercised to enforce this, a part of the Supreme Law of the land. After establishing this point, the President enters upon an elaborate and conclusive argument to prove that there is no such thing as voluntary secession—that secession is neither more nor less than revolution—that the Union was designed by the framers of the Constitution to be perpetual, and that it clothed the General Government with the power to protect itself from foes without and foes within—that the government created by the Constitution, and deriving its authority from the sovereign people of each of the sovereign States, has precisely the same right to exercise its power over the people of the States, in the enumerated cases, that each one of them possesses over subjects not delegated to the United States, but "reserved to the States respectively, or to the people." The President also says that "he is bound by solemn oath before God and the country 'to take care that the laws be faithfully executed,' and from this obligation he cannot be absolved by any human power." Never was a case more complete at every point.

But following this perfect vindication of the Constitutional power of the government, and this statement of the duty of the President, comes an ill-timed confession of weakness. What if the President finds it impracticable to discharge his duty? What if federal officers resign? We ask in response, "What is the federal government good for, if it has no resources in an emergency? Why should the citizens maintain this government, with all its costly machinery and expensive officers, if it is a mere rope of sand?["]

If the federal officers resign, has not the President power to appoint others to the vacancies, and the power to sustain them in the discharge of their duties? Has the President the right to assume that the population of South Carolina "would constitute one solid combination to resist him?" And if this were the fact, does it constitute sufficient reason why he should not execute the laws? There is a deep-seated aversion to the execution of the Fugitive Slave Law in some of the Northern States; but the President congratulates the country that he has performed his whole duty in this regard, "though with great loss and inconvenience to the master, and with considerable expense to the government."

Does he propose to permit secession, which he proves unconstitutional, revolutionary and treasonable, because he is informed that a majority of the people are opposed to the exercise [of] the duty he has, by solemn oath before God and the country, sworn to discharge? State sovereignty has nothing whatever to do with this question. If there is any resistance to law and its processes, it must come from citizens of the United States —men who, with the President have sworn allegiance to the Constitution. Whether they live in Vermont or South Carolina is of no importance, so far as the Federal Government is concerned. The Constitution is the supreme law of the land, the laws of any State or the declarations of any body of men to the contrary notwithstanding, and the President is bound "to take care that the laws be faithfully executed."

We are not advocates of any aggressive movement by the General Government toward the disunionists. The threatening position of some of the Southern people is not too lightly spoken of, nor are they to be frowned or bullied into loyalty to the Union. But the Executive of the Union owes it to the confederacy to put down revolution in South Carolina as he would in Vermont or New York. It is true, as the President says, that if the Union "cannot live in the affections of the people, it must one day perish;" but can it long live in the affections of the people, if they are informed that the Union is powerless, when its integrity and perpetuity is menaced? The present crisis in National affairs requires great prudence and forbearance on the part of the Executive; but it does not demand the virtual abdication of executive power by the President. The government should not have one policy toward the Abolitionists of the North, and another toward the disunionists of the South.—The extremists of both sections would glory in the dissolution of the Union, and they have been agitating the slavery question for years in the hope of accomplishing their treasonable purpose. And now, when the shadow of impending ruin clouds the land, the duty of patriotic citizens is plain. They must insist upon "The Union, the Constitution and the Enforcement of the Laws."

44. PRESIDENT'S MESSAGE—ITS ILLOGICAL AND INCONSISTENT
PROPOSITIONS

(Cincinnati Daily Enquirer [Douglas], December 6, 1860)

The President is right in attributing the present unfortunate political and pecuniary condition of the country to the general Abolition agitation on the subject of slavery, which has been carried on in the free States for so many years. It is that which has put enmity between the North and the South, and which threatens, unless arrested, to bring disunion, universal bankruptcy and civil war. This is indeed now apparent to all men. It is equally patent that the whole agitation has been unnecessary and profitless; nay more, that it has been wicked and incendiary. It was created by crack-brained fanatics, ignorant or care-less of their duty to the Government as citizens of the Union, and it has been augmented immensely by political demagogues for party pur-poses. The plain truth should be spoken—the people of the North must put down this party in their midst, whose only basis is hostility to the institutions of half of the States of this Union, and which has got into power upon that issue, or they will see this Union rent into fragments and utterly destroyed. No man is a good counselor who does not give this advice in the loudest tones from the house-tops. The free States must purge their statute books from all the acts of nullification which disgrace them, and which tend and were intended to defeat the execu-tion of laws providing for the rendition of fugitives from service, if they intend to be fair and honest in their Constitutional relations with the slaveholding States.

On the all-absorbing and exciting question—that of secession from the Union—the President takes two exceedingly contradictory and illogical positions. They are:

1. A State has no Constitutional right to secede from the Union.

2. The Union has no right, under the Constitution, to *compel* a State to remain in it.

We regard this as simply absurd. If a State has no right to leave the Union, the latter must necessarily have the right to coerce her into submission, if she pursue such a course. The framers of the Constitu-tion put no rights in it without remedies of some sort. It would have been the sheerest folly for the framers of that instrument to forbid a State leaving the Union, and yet allow her to commit the wrong, if she was disposed, without question. The President's reasoning that the Constitution and laws of the United States act directly upon individuals, instead of States, leads irresistibly to the conclusion that, if any number of individuals—even although they may compose a State—resist the laws or Constitution, it is the duty of the Executive to treat it as an act of rebellion. It is the most barren and idle abstraction in the world to make a long argument against the right of State secession, if it is not followed up with the corollary of coercion. All that the President says about the Union being a rope of sand, if the secession doctrine is true, applies with equal force, if his own argument is well founded. So con-tradictory are the President's positions, that it looks as if the first one was written to express his own views, and the second contradictory one put in to please Secretary Cobb. Seldom have we known so strong an argument come to such a lame and impotent conclusion.

The President suggests the propriety of Congress recommending to the States as a settlement of the slavery question certain amendments to the Federal Constitution. They are as follows:

"First, an express recognition of the right of slave property in the States where it now exists or may hereafter exist; second, *the duty of protection in this right in all the common Territories throughout their Territorial existence, and until they shall be admitted as States into the Union, with or without slavery, as their constitutions may prescribe;* third, a like recognition of the rights of the master to have his slave, who has escaped from one State to another, restored and delivered up to him; and of the validity of the Fugitive-slave Law, enacted for this purpose, together with a declaration that all State laws impairing or defeating this right are violations of the Constitution, and are consequently null and void."

The second amendment suggested will never be acquiesced in by the free States, and it is useless to talk about it. The free States might agree that slave property could be taken into the common Territories like other property, and be there held subject to the local laws, but further than this they would not go. They would never say that the people of the Territories should protect any particular species of property that they might regard as detrimental to the public interests. The South has an exact equality with the North when it can take its property into the public Territories on a par with other property, and it must take its chances for protection, just as other property takes its chances. The President's proposition, which is substantially that of the slave-code, is utterly inadmissible, and it will not be insisted upon by the discreet men of the South. The other suggestions national men will subscribe to.

45. THE PRESIDENT'S MESSAGE

(Harrisburg *Daily Patriot and Union* [Breckinridge], December 6, 1860)

At no previous period of our national history has the message of the President of the United States been looked for with more solicitude than was the last annual message of Mr. Buchanan; for it was felt that upon his recommendation might depend the future of the country, and that the issues of peace or civil war were, to a great extent, in his hands. The whole tener [sic] of the message is calculated to soothe the asperities now threatening to disrupt the Union. If any man in the country has the right to speak with authority to the South it is JAMES BUCHANAN, as President of the United States and head of the Democratic party; for in his official capacity he has ever been faithful to all his constitutional obligations, and as a party leader has endeavored to bring about those just concessions which, had they been granted, would have saved the country from the perils that now environ it. His position as an officer and a man demand[s] that his counsels should fall with great weight upon the people of the Southern States, now contemplating revolution as the last remedy against real or fancied oppression.

The President traces our present difficulties to their true source when he attributes them to the persistent agitation of years against the system of negro slavery as it exists in the Southern States, and to the alarming sense of insecurity growing out of that agitation. Before the Republican party existed there was a band of organized agitators in the Northern States devoted to running away negroes and inciting servile insurrections at the South—and the evil has been growing and extending, until it culminated in the formation of a sectional Northern party, thoroughly imbued and entirely controlled by hostility to the institutions of the Southern States. It is true that the platforms and creeds of the Republican party profess loyalty to the spirit of the Constitution, and disclaim any intention of interfering with the domestic institutions of the Southern States. But professions weigh nothing when contrasted with facts. While a party exists with the paramount idea of hostility to slavery, it necessarily encourages every form of that hostility, and must be held responsible for every degree of its manifestation. Since the organization of the Republican party the Abolitionists have ceased to exist in this latitude as a seperate [sic] party, because they merged themselves in the Republicans, deeming that the best means of promoting their ultimate objects. Every form and degree of Abolitionism has flourished and developed under the fostering care of this Republican party, which, when confronted with the fruits of its own teaching, meekly points to its platform, and says, "we mean no harm to the Southern States."—Turning from fair words to foul deeds, the Southern people find that the consequences of Republicanism are—the encouragement of Abolitionism, which does not hesitate to avow hostility to slavery wherever it exists; the enactment of unconstitutional laws by Republican Legislatures to nullify the fugitive slave law; the circulation of incendiary publications throughout the South, calculated, if not designed, to encourage servile insurrections, and endanger the lives of the Southern people; the promotion of John Brown raids, and the subjection of the Southern States and people to a position of inferiority. These are unmistakably indicated as the consequences of the existence of the Republican party, which, however moderate its professions, cannot escape direct responsibility for what it promotes or encourages, and is naturally judged by the Southern people from its fruits, and not from its platforms. The fact is apparent that while these things continue the

Union cannot endure. It has sustained the pressure for many years; but we have at last reached a point when the bond of union must be broken, unless the pressure upon it is immediately abated—and the first step to be taken in lightening the cargo which threatens to sink the ship, is to throw overboard the personal liberty acts that now disgrace the statute books of so many Northern States controlled by the Republican party.

The President shows conclusively that secession is not a remedy conferred upon any State by the Constitution against the encroachments of the General Government, but that it would be a revolutionary step, only justifiable "as the last desperate remedy of a despairing people, after every other constitutional means of conciliation has been exhausted."

Notwithstanding that the message takes grounds against the constitutional right of any State to secede from the Union, the position is maintained that the Constitution has delegated to Congress no power to coerce a State into submission; and this doctrine is fortified with powerful arguments. We do not see how they can be controverted. The proceedings of the Convention that framed the Constitution—the very highest authority—show that "Mr. Edmund Randolph's plan, which was the ground work of the Constitution, contained a clause to authorize the coercion of any delinquent State. But this clause was struck out at the suggestion of Madison, who showed that a State could be coerced only by military force; that the use of military force against a State as such would be in the nature of a declaration of war; and that a state of war might be regarded as operating the abrogation or dissolution of all pre-existing ties between the belligerent parties, and it would be of itself the dissolution of the Union." Thus it appears that the idea of coercing disobedient States was proposed in the Constitutional Convention and rejected.

But the President advances one step further in the argument. Suppose a State can be coerced, how are we to govern it afterwards? Shall we invite the people to elect Senators and Representatives after they are subdued and conquered? or shall we hold them as subjects, and not as equals? How can we subdue the unconquerable will? and how can we practically annul the maxim that all governments derive their just powers from the consent of the governed? Such a process would undermine the foundations of the government and destroy the principles upon which it is reared more certainly than to admit the want of coercive power in the general government.

The President concludes that portion of the message relating to our domestic troubles by suggesting that they may be settled by amending the Constitution, in the way provided by that instrument, so as to secure to the South the rights for which she contends.

It would be well for the country, in this the hour of her peril, when embittered sectional feeling has brought us to the very verge of dissolution, and possibly of civil war, if both sections would profit by the patriotic advice of the President of the United States, and agree to perpetuate this Union by mutual forbearance and concession. Let the South pause before striking the last fatal blow at the Union, and await the time when a returning sense of justice shall induce the North to concede all her just demands, and make her continuance in the Union more desirable than a separate Government. Let the North cease its unmanly aggressions—repeal its unconstitutional statutes—stop its reckless agitation against an institution for which it is not responsible and over which it has no control—overthrow any man or party that seeks to perpetuate strife—and the Union may yet be preserved, and even made stronger and more enduring by reason of the shock it has endured. But without this spirit of concession and mutual forbearance, there is nothing to hope for in the immediate future but contention and disunion.

46. [THE PRESIDENT'S MESSAGE]

(Boston Daily Advertiser [Lincoln], December 7, 1860)

The President has found a more excellent way than the common for settling a great family quarrel. Ordinarily when brothers come to hard words by reason of a difference of opinions conscientiously held on both sides, the pacificator does not begin his work by saying to the one, when in the heat of passion, that he is an impertinent meddler and that his conduct has been insulting and atrocious from the outset. Neither does the pacificator say to the other that if his opinions are not accepted throughout, he will be justified in changing the quarrel into an open battle. Common experience shows that there are few quarrels either among individuals or among States, in which either party is wholly right or wholly to be condemned. If Mr. Buchanan's own observation is not enough to satisfy him that such may be the case now, the fact that so many of our best and wisest, and whom he will acknowledge as such, declare it to be so, ought to make him cautious in urging any sweeping charge against either party. But if this could not influence him, still mere policy ought to teach him that at this moment the contending parties must be brought together again, not by one who assumes the position of a partisan, but by a mediator.

Mr. Buchanan starts with the declaration that all our present troubles proceed from the "long continued and intemperate interference of the northern people with the question of slavery in the southern States." Saying this, he knows that he says that which a majority of the northern people conscientiously believe to be untrue. Grant that he is right and they are wrong; the arrogance of the assertion is scarcely calculated to incline them favorably to his subsequent proposition. Mr. Buchanan elsewhere declares that all that the slave States want "is to be let alone and permitted to manage their domestic institutions in their own way," —as if any of the other States desire to interfere with them; he argues that the northern States are not responsible for slavery,—as if any considerable party says that they are so responsible;—and speaks of the candidate for whom those States voted, in terms which carry a strong implication, that the President elect is disposed to invade the constitutional rights of the South and will only be restrained by his position. Such gross perversion of facts which are within the knowledge of all, is little calculated to conciliate the feeling or appeal to the reason of the northern people, while it does feed the excitement of the South. In every respect Mr. Buchanan's statement of the case is conceived in a partisan spirit. As might be expected, this leads him into fatal mistakes as to history. A law prohibiting slavery in a territory, he terms a law "impairing the rights of the South to their property in slaves;" and no such law he says has ever passed Congress "unless we may possibly except the Missouri compromise." He forgets the ordinance of 1787 and its subsequent ratification, and the extension of its prohibition, to territories afterwards organized, as Wisconsin and Oregon. Had he recalled those acts it would have appeared, as was the case with the Missouri compromise, that it was in each case a southern President and a slave-holder who sanctioned what he terms an attack upon the rights of the South.

We need hardly say that if the partizanship of the message were all simple justice, and its error historical truth, still viewed as a matter of policy, it would hardly afford a promising foundation for the scheme which follows. And what is that scheme? The President proposes that the Constitution should be amended; that it should expressly recognize property in slaves in the States; that as there has been great doubt what the court decided in the case of Dred Scott, the view of that decision, most objectionable to the North and a large part of the South, should be made a part of the Constitution; and that the present fugitive slave law should be virtually incorporated into the Constitution. The first proposition touches a matter entirely foreign to the pending controversy; the second proposes an unconditional surrender by one-half of the country of the whole matter which is really in dispute at this time; the third, so far as it recognizes any right on the part of the South or declares void any State legislation impairing that right, is a mere repetition of what the Constitution already provides, and so far as it undertakes to incorporate specific legislation in the organic law, is as much at variance with the lessons of political experience and with a due regard for future changes, as with the feelings of the people in the non-slaveholding States,—a large part of whom it is true, share to some extent that repugnance to particular features of the law in question, which was expressed even by some of the legislators who voted for its enactment. In short, both in his view of the cause and position of the controversy, and in his scheme for its settlement, Mr. Buchanan can see no injustice or mistake on one side, and no prejudice to be overcome or conciliation to be attempted except on the other. This failure on his part argues [augurs?] ill for his success in the work of reconciliation.

We confess that it is with pain as well as indignation, that we see the chief magistrate thus destroy his own influence for good at this crisis. That a plan for reconciliation will be devised and carried out, we have never ceased to hope and believe. Such a plan might have been offered with good effect by a statesman, holding the chief executive place of dignity in the nation, enjoying the light of a long experience, and soon to retire forever from public life. But Mr. Buchanan's disastrous administration began by disappointing the friends of peace, and it was fitting that it should close in like manner. The country must look to some one besides its present President for the means of safety, and it must relinquish its last hope of seeing any act, either of impartiality or of wise policy touching our present disputes, to illustrate the dreary annals of his official career.

47. The President's Message

(Detroit Free Press [Douglas], December 7, 1860)

If in ordinary times there have been people who have been content to gather the substance of the annual message of the President in other ways than by reading it themselves, the number of such is greatly reduced at the present time. Probably no message of a President has been awaited by the whole country with so much interest as that of President Buchanan transmitted to Congress on Tuesday, and none has been so universally read as will have been that.

The President at once goes to the all-absorbing subject. He states correctly the causes of the lamentable condition of affairs, or the cause, rather, for there is really but one,—that is, the continuous, persistent and rapidly growing agitation in the North of the slavery question during the past quarter of a century, and the aggressive form which this agitation has assumed, producing, as its natural consequence, vague conceptions of liberty and discontent among the servile population and stimulating insurrection. The President rightly declares that "no political union, however fraught with blessings and benefits in all other respects, can long continue, if the necessary consequence be to render the homes and the firesides of nearly half the parties to it habitually and hopelessly insecure."

The President wholly denies the constitutional right of a State to secede. If the right existed, he tells us, the Union would be a rope of sand. But, in his opinion, the Federal government has no constitutional right to prevent a State from seceding! His argument against the constitutional right of secession is sound; it is unassailable; and it will seem strange to most people that after he had made it he should himself turn round and attempt to assail it—that he should make the Union a rope of sand at any rate. If a State has not the right to secede, it follows as a logical consequence that the power rests somewhere to prevent it. It is certain that the power exists in the government of the United States to enforce the constitution and laws of the United States, and the exercise of this power is all that is necessary to prevent secession. When the President had so conclusively shown that a State has not the constitutional right to secede, he should have followed up the same line of argument by showing that the Federal government has not the constitutional right to permit a State to secede. It strikes us that the President has surrendered the whole ground of the power of the Federal government to preserve itself, and has opened the way, if his view were the true one, for a State or any number of States to bid good bye to the Union at any time and on any pretence. We are not now arguing as to what should be the particular policy of the Federal government in the present juncture, but against the dangerous and utterly inadmissible doctrine that the Federal government has not the constitutional power to preserve itself. The President says that to coerce a State is to declare war against her. Not so. There is no coercion except to uphold the constitution and laws in every State. If the people of a State do not choose to have postoffices, it is not necessary to the execution of the laws that postoffices should be forced upon them, but they cannot set up postoffices on their own account; and so with regard to the operation of other Federal laws,—they may not be carried out in all their parts, but they cannot be resisted nor subverted. The broad legal proposition may be laid down that a State can only go out of the Union by an amendment of the constitution establishing the right and prescribing the manner of exercising it. But we do not desire to discuss this question now; we only desire to seize the first opportunity to protest against the novel and alarming doctrine which the President has announced.

We are glad that there is room for more general concurrence in the remedy which the President proposes for the existing disorders. This remedy is in the nature of what he calls an "explanatory amendment" of the constitution, embracing three special points, viz;

"1. An express recognition of the right of property in slaves in the States where it now exists or may hereafter exist.

"2. The duty of protecting this right in all the common Territories throughout their Territorial existence, and until they shall be admitted as States into the Union, with or without slavery, as their constitutions may prescribe.

"3. A like recognition of the right of the master to have his slave, who has escaped from one State to another, restored and 'delivered up' to him, and of the validity of the fugitive slave law enacted for this purpose, together with a declaration that all State laws impairing or defeating this right are violations of the constitution, and are consequently null and void."

We can cordially endorse these propositions with the understanding that, as to the second proposition, its meaning is that slaves are property in the common Territories, that they stand upon precisely the same footing as other property, and are entitled to the same protection as other property. We can cordially endorse the propositions with this understanding, and conscientiously declare that there is nothing in them that ought not to command the approval of the whole northern people.

There is no certainty that the Union can be preserved by any action in the direction above indicated, but it is certain that it cannot be preserved without some such action. And this the North cannot understand a moment too soon. The South will not sit down in the future under the same state of things that has prevailed of late. Slavery must be let alone in the States where it exists, the fugitive slave law must be faithfully executed, and whatever rights the Supreme Court adjudges to slavery in the Territories must be insured, or separation of the South from the North, in some form, will speedily ensue. If it shall not be by mutual agreement, it will be by revolution, for it cannot be by secession. Down to this point is the issue narrowed, and it is for the northern people now to make up their minds how they will meet it. It is possible that, with regard to the Territories, the re-establishment of the Missouri compromise line and its extension to the Pacific, by amendment of the constitution, would be an acceptable compromise to the South; if so, perhaps it would be as acceptable to the North as to stand by the constitution as it is.

The President undertakes to justify his Lecompton policy. He had better have omitted that undertaking, for that policy the people of the United States have emphatically condemned and they will never reverse their judgment. It was that policy which gave the republican party the power to bring upon the country the present woes, and the less the President says about it the better for his fame. However, his defence is rather apologetic than otherwise. He says:

"Had I treated the Lecompton constitution as a nullity, and refused to transmit it to Congress, it is not difficult to imagine, whilst recalling the position of the country at that moment, what would have been the disastrous consequences, both in and out of the Territory, from such a dereliction of duty on the part of the Executive."

Nobody ever asked him to treat the Lecompton constitution as a nullity. It was his duty to transmit it to Congress, and there his duty ended. But he went further and made the support of it, in Congress and out, *a test of democracy*. If he had done his simple duty regarding it, and nothing more, the democratic party would not have been split, and LINCOLN would not have been President.

Other parts of the message invite comment, but this we must defer.

48. THE PRESIDENT'S MESSAGE

(Utica Daily Observer [Douglas], December 7, 1860)

Probably no public document issued since the organization of our government was ever read with greater interest than the Annual Message of President Buchanan, which has just been placed before the American people. No such crisis in political affairs as that which now agitates the minds of all men, has ever occurred in our history; never have the people looked more eagerly in every direction for some escape from the calamities which seem impending. No President has ever been called upon to write a Message under more embarrassing circumstances; no officer has ever been expected to adjust difficulties so far beyond his control, or to suggest relief where human wisdom has thus far proved so utterly at fault.

If the Message fails to point out any available mode of speedy relief to the country, its deficiency in this respect is owing to the difficulty of the case with which the President has to deal. The docu-

ment carries upon its face evidences of patriotic spirit and lofty purpose, and a very clear conception of the lamentable difficulties which
beset the country. It displays deep and earnest thought, and abounds in
striking suggestions. If it does not suggest satisfactory means of relief,
it certainly gives to every reader a more realizing sense of the critical
danger of our present condition. Perhaps in doing this, it has done the
greatest service which could have been done the country. The great obstacle in the way of relief has been and is yet, the sturdy obstinacy of
the great majority, in refusing to believe the evidences, which are daily
accumulating, that the continued existence of the Union can hardly
be hoped for.

The picture drawn by the President of the evil effects of the slavery
agitation, and of the violations of the Constitution by Northern legislatures, is too true to be denied or evaded. Whether we may agree with
him or not in all that he says, no one can palliate the bitterly hostile
feeling which has been nursed into existence by designing politicians,
among a large portion of the northern and southern people, against
each other. The results of this feeling, manifested at the North in nullifying legislation and in the election of a President on a strictly sectional
issue, and at the South in direct and deliberate movements towards disunion, are but indications of the sentiments of the sections towards each
other. So long as this feeling exists, so long our institutions are in danger.
Legislative acts and official declarations are of little consequence, unless
this feeling can be changed.

The suggestions of the Message show how completely our form of
government relies upon the confidence and kind feeling of the people for
its continued existence. The employment of force to preserve it is out
of the question. It is shown very clearly that the right of secession does
not exist; yet of what avail is the strongest argument in this behalf, when
States determine to secede, right or wrong, and when it is admitted on
all hands that to retain them in the Union by coercion would be an
absurdity?

The remedy which the President proposes,—an amendment to the
Constitution,—presents perhaps the only available cure for the evils
which exist. Such a remedy would be valuable chiefly as an indication of
a change of sentiment on the part of the Northern people towards those
of the South. Additional constitutional guaranties to slavery would be
of no avail, unless the Northern people are disposed to stand by them
in good faith. Congressional protection of slavery in the territories
would be ineffectual to extend the institution, but would show simply a
willingness on the part of the Northern people to give those of the South

every advantage to which they had a shadow of a claim. In approving or disapproving these recommendations, we must remember that the question is not whether they meet exactly our own views, but whether we are prepared to concede so much for the preservation of the Union. —It must be evident to every candid mind that the Union is on the verge of dissolution, and can be saved, if at all, only by some new compromise, some prompt and decided proof that the North will not invade the rights of the South. The question is not what we regard as sound and correct doctrine in the abstract, but what compromises we are willing to adopt to prevent the result now impending over the country. In other words, what sacrifices of principle are we willing to make, to secure the continued existence of the American Union?

What compromises the North is willing to make, what guaranties she is willing to give, depends [sic] upon the Republican party. That party holds the power in every Northern Legislature, with insignificant exceptions. The Northern Democracy have labored against the popular current for many years to prevent the calamity which is now upon us. Their efforts have been in vain, and their worst forebodings have been realized. They are now powerless, and will remain so until another annual election.—But what is done must be done before that period. It may very gravely be doubted, whether it is not already too late.

49. Last Message of the O. P. F.

(Quincy (Ill.) *Daily Whig and Republican* [Lincoln],
December 10, 1860)

The O. P. F.[1] has had his last "say," for which let Heaven be praised. He may, to be sure, send in a few special messages as the winter progresses, but nobody will care; his last annual message is got rid of, his last wail in behalf of the Cotton Lords is written—and printed; and may a merciful Providence soothe the unhappy old man's pathway to the tomb, and if it *be* possible allow him to live long enough under Republican rule to become ashamed of his own iniquitous course and truckling subserviency to his nigger-driving masters. "So mote it be."

The poor old man learns nothing good, forgets nothing bad. Devotion to slavery has become chronic with him, and had every man at the North voted for Lincoln he would probably have held out his everlasting nigger panacea and nigger compromise to quiet the "agitation" which he and such as he have brought upon the country. There is nobody in the

---

[1] "O. P. F." was occasionally used by unfriendly editors in speaking of President Buchanan. It meant "Old Public Functionary."

nation with any grievances or any wrongs to be righted but his Southern masters. It is nothing to him that seventeen and *four-sevenths* States, by majorities without parallel in our previous history should decree the overthrow of his shameless party; he only whines like a whipped cur and begs of Congress and the people to give the Cotton Lords and incipient traitors not only all, but more than all they have asked, and precisely what the people have said should not be done. His demands are an insult to the country, but *he* does not see it. Politically he is blind; he knows no North, no East, no West—only a South, and his shriveled soul knows no higher manliness, no more genial labor, than to plead for the capture of negroes, and for new constitution[al] props to a demoralizing institution which has brought upon itself not only the condemnation of the nation, but of the enlightened world.

Never till now have the slave Barons asked to have the Constitution opened that new coils might be thrown about the slave. Their interpretation, except in the Dred Scott case, has been accepted by the majority North and South; the Supreme Court is still theirs, and only Death can wrest it from them; the Constitution has been their Shibboleth in all past contests; but now, it no longer serves them—it is not black enough, and must be re-baptised and soaked in *nigger,* or they spurn it! What patriotism, what manliness, what philanthropy is this! What an exemplification of "progress" for a Christian land when its rulers and its mighty men seek, not to lift up the down-trodden and the oppressed, not to re-assert their own doctrine that "all men are endowed by their Creator with certain inalienable rights," but to make the barbarous customs of heathen Africa their model—the buying and selling of their own people the corner stone of their political temple! No wonder that prosperity departs, that gloom settles on the land, and Almighty favor seems to be withdrawn at such a spectacle. No wonder that patriots weep; and angels may well do so at the thought of what America *is* and what she *might* have been to-day but for this foul blot on her escutcheon.

True to all his double-dealing antecedents the President takes two positions on secession. First, secession is unconstitutional, illegal and peaceably impossible; and second, it is unconstitutional, illegal and impossible to stop it! His four solid columns of verbiage amount to that and nothing else. We suppose he means that if the Cotton States resolve themselves out of the Union they cannot be forced to repeal their resolves and send men to Congress as before, and we do not know that anybody proposes any such steps. If they only *do* withdraw their Representatives, Congress will become not only a Republican, but a decent and a harmonious body, making laws which the nigger-drivers cannot repeal when they become hungry and come back to the National crib. But as to seizing the forts and opening Southern ports to free trade he himself says that he has given orders "that the laws be faithfully executed," and there is not *much* reason to expect that his successor will fall behind him in courage.

It is bad enough and humiliating enough to see the Chief Magistrate of a great nation bend all his argumentative powers, such as they are, to the spread and upbuilding of an institution which degrades the country, and which the masses loathe; it is worse to see him start off in the first paragraph of his message with a brazen *lie*. He says "the long continued and intemperate interference of the Northern people with the question of slavery *in the Southern States* has at length produced its natural effects." The Northern people have only sought to keep slavery out of the territories, and never have raised a finger as a people against slavery *in* the Southern States, yet this Pharisaical old hypocrite, probably thanking God each night that he "is not as other men are," dares thus publicly and officially to bear false witness against millions of his countrymen because they do not reverence *his* atrocious sentiments. Let Heaven be praised that his official race is nearly run; and may it be twice ten thousand years before we shall ever see his like again.

50. The President on the Crisis

(Des Moines *Iowa State Register* [Lincoln], December 12, 1860)

The message of the President is before our readers, and will be read with more than usual interest, in consequence of the Secession movements of the extreme Southern States. A feeling of disappointment will follow a perusal of the document. With that fatality and perverseness that has characterized his action throughout, he takes a course that will fail to satisfy either section of the Union.—Hardly had the reading of the document been closed, when Mr. Clingman, the Senator from North Carolina, took occasion to express his dissatisfaction with it. When the President denies the right of secession, and denounces it as revolution, he does what every patriotic citizen will commend. But, what a reflection it is upon the wisdom of the men who formed this government, to say that they have made no provision for resisting and suppressing treason. What is secession but treason, if it destroys the Union and nullifies the action of the General Government? Once let it be understood that there is no remedy for secession; that the Constitution fails to provide for its suppression; that the Union is not an inviolable compact; that one or more States may sunder their connection with it, with impunity, not so much as saying by your leave; and the bond of Union becomes a rope of sand. Any imaginary grievance will be deemed sufficient ground for imitating the example of South Carolina. We are no longer a great nation and a great power in the world, but a collection of States, banded together for temporary convenience and transient purposes, destitute of every element of strength and nationality.

But, worst of all, most pestilent in its character and effects, is the partizan spirit of the message. The arraignment of the North as an aggressor upon the South, is so atrociously inconsistent with the truth of history, as to excite profound indignation in every reflecting mind, not jaundiced by partizan passion. The message, in this respect, is a counterpart of the special message of the President on the Kansas question, delivered in the early part of his administration. Not one State in the Union has denied the right of the Slave States to reclaim fugitives from labor. There cannot be found among the statutes of any State in the North, a single law designed to nullify that provision of the Constitution, which proclaims the right of the slave-holder to his absconding chattels. The personal liberty bills, so much decried, were all designed for the protection of the rights of citizens, and to secure at least a semblance of a hearing to those whose right to themselves is called in question. Some of them go so far as to prohibit State officers from assisting in the reclamation of fugitives. But, such provisions were intended only to proclaim the settled conviction of men of all parties in the Free States, that it is no part of their business to catch the runaways of the South. Where Slavery does not exist, it is no part of the legislator's business to recognise it. When the slave-holder seeks to reclaim a fugitive from the house of bondage, the Free States say to him, "Sir, prove your property; establish your right of property in accordance with the rules of common law, and we ask no more." Is it not meet and proper that as many safe guards be thrown around the rights of the black man, as are given to secure a man's right to his dog? The answer to this is, that fugitives are sometimes taken out of the hands of southern officers, after the right of property has been established according to the forms of law. Admit this to be so, is it not an all sufficient defence, to say, that we cannot cure northern abhorrence of Slavery[?] Regarding Slavery as a great moral and political wrong, we cannot seek to eradicate that abhorrence of it, which is a part of the religious education of a free people; that education which is necessary in order to teach them how to value their own rights and to respect the rights of others. But, the slave-holder has his redress for all such accidents in the reclamation of his chattels. He can bring his action against those who interfere with him; and in many such cases has secured damages to the full value of the property lost. We have in mind now several cases in Ohio. It may hereafter be deemed advisable to make counties responsible for the results of mob-law violence in such cases. A suggestion to that effect has already been made; but it will, unquestionably, meet with strong resistance, growing out of northern repugnance to Slavery.

Had the President seen proper to glance candidly at the history of the country, setting forth the wrong doings of the South, his counsels at this juncture would have great weight. He closes his eyes to the outrages perpetrated upon Kansas by Atchison and the border-ruffians of Missouri. He has no word of rebuke for the cold-blooded butcheries in Texas; the lawlessness in Kentucky and Virginia, carried to the excess of driving out whole families from their homes; the wrongs practiced every day in some of the southern States upon men who are suspected of a want of devotion to Slavery; the deliberate exclusion of northern men from the ports of South Carolina; the shameless espionage over the mails practiced by nearly every P. Master in the Slave States; the tyranny that excludes tens of thousands from a free exercise of the right of suffrage; that strikes down the freedom of speech and of the press, and perpetrates a thousand kindred wrongs, characteristic only of an iron despotism. But, when he ignores such facts, and brings his railing accusations solely against that section of the Union with which it should be his pride to sympathise, he sinks the statesman in the partizan, and brings upon himself the contempt of honest and candid men of all parties.

In vain are the efforts of the President to induce a change in the convictions and policy of the North. In vain will he strive to educate it into new concessions to the arrogant demands of the slave power and a love of the peculiar institution. Slavery will not be admitted into Free Territory. It will not be permitted to throw its black pall over territory that belongs to free labor. The Free North will never sanction the monstrous heresy that the Constitution carries and protects slavery in the territories of the Union. The Constitution does not chattelise human beings, and no system of terrorism that the South can inaugurate will drive the free States into an admission that it does. Freemen will never resolve themselves into blood-hounds, to run down the panting fugitives who are seeking the freedom of Victoria's dominions. If such baseness and humility is the price at which the Union is to be preserved, its dissolution is inevitable; for the price will not be paid. Union, purchased at the expense of liberty, is a boon that the revolutionary patriots would have spurned; and the recent election, if it proves anything, proves that the dictation of the slave power is at an end.—The people of the Union have asserted their rights and purposes, according to the methods prescribed by the Constitution. If the will of the majority is no longer the governing power in this country, free government is at an end. Had the Republican power been overthrown in the late contest, submission would have been regarded as a matter of course.—Shall it be otherwise because the verdict of the ballot-box is in favor of that section of the Union whose rights and interests have so long been disregarded? New concessions, will lead only to new demands and new perils.—The issue may as well be met now. The Union may be dissolved, but it will be by no act of the people of the Free States. They are loyal to the Union formed by the Fathers. They desire its preservation; and will labor and pray for it to the last. They will stand by the Constitution in its purity. They will vindicate all the rights of the States and maintain the Compromises that have been lawfully established. They will not lay the weight of a finger upon the institutions of the Southern States. But they cannot be made to surrender the fruits of the recent victory. They will stand by their platform and the men of their choice, and thus fulfil the glorious destiny of the Union, whether the cotton States are inside or out of it.

With the threats of secession ringing in his ears, and an admission that he is powerless to prevent it, still upon his lips, he counsels still the purchase of Cuba. He would tax the people of these States hundreds of millions, to purchase Territory that may secede with the Gulf States before the ink used in drawing up the bill of sale is dry upon the paper. He knows that Old Bullion declared only the sober truth, when he maintained, years since, that there was treason in the heart of the cotton States—that a Southern Confederacy has long been a darling project of ambitious men in and out of South Carolina. Yet he stands ready to further all their schemes of aggrandisement at the expense of the North, even while they are plotting their treason daily under his own eye.

IV

SECESSION: RIGHT OR REVOLUTION?

51. CAN A STATE CONSTITUTIONALLY SECEDE?

(Dubuque Herald [Douglas], November 11, 1860)

This is one of the questions of the day, and it appears to be no longer a mere abstract or theoretical question. The Constitution makes no provision for secession. A Government is not a corporation whose existence is limited by a fixed period of time, nor does it provide a means for its own dissolution. The Constitution of the United States provides that it may be amended, and prescribes how this may be done, but it does not, as it exists now, contemplate its own destruction, nor a dissolution of the Government of which it is the living evidence. Constitutionally, there can be no such thing as secession of a State from the Union.

But it does not follow that because a State cannot secede constitutionally, it is obliged under all circumstances to remain in the Union. There is a natural right, which is reserved by all men, and which cannot be given to any Government, and no Government can take it away. It is the natural right of a people to form a Government for their mutual protection, for the promotion of their mutual welfare, and for such other purposes as they may deem most conducive to their mutual happiness and prosperity; but if for any cause the Government so formed should become inimical to the rights and interests of the people, instead of affording protection to their persons and property, and securing the happiness and prosperity, to attain which it was established, it is the natural right of the people to change the Government regardless of Constitutions. For be it borne in mind, the Constitution is an agreement made among the people that the Government formed by it is to be just such a Government as it prescribes; that when it recognizes a right to exist, it must protect the person in the enjoyment of that right, and when it imposes a reciprocal duty upon a portion of the people, the performance of that duty it will have enforced. When a government fails in any of these essential respects, it is not the Government the people intended it to be, and it is their right to modify or abolish it.

So, if the rights of the people of the United States as recognized by the Constitution, are not secured to them by the Government, and the people of any State have no other means to redress their grievances except by separating themselves from their oppressors, it is their undoubted natural right to do so. Now it is unquestionable that one of the rights recognized to belong to the Southern people by the Constitution, and pledged to be respected by the other States, and secured to them by the Government, has nevertheless been violated, wilfully and intentionally by twelve Northern States; and this course towards the South has been virtually approved of by a large majority of the Northern people at the recent election.

What then is the South to do[?] Suffer the compact which brought them into the Union to be violated with impunity, and without means of redress; submit to incursions into their territory and trespass upon their property by northern abolitionists[?] Look on submissively upon every aggression upon their domestic institutions[?] Who expects, who desires the South to submit to all this? The South will not do it. The South ought not to do it.

Let the Northern States repeal their Personal Liberty Bills, and pass laws recognizing the rights of the Southern people to their property. Let Southern people be permitted to enjoy their rights unmolested and undisturbed. Let them, if they desire it, carry with them in their tours of business or pleasure their domestic servants. Let the Southern people be treated as friends and neighbors, not as aliens and enemies. If this be done, no Southern man will think of secession, much less desire it. If this be not done, there is but one course left for the South by which its people can enjoy the rights which they believe to be theirs by nature and by the Constitution of the United States.

52. Peaceable Secession an Absurdity

(New York *Evening Post* [Lincoln], November 12, 1860)

In behalf of the treachery and imbecility of the Administration at Washington the new doctrine is invoked that each state has a right peacefully to secede—that nullification of any particular law of Congress is to be resisted and punished by the government, but that secession, *i. e.,* the absolute nullification and defiance of all such laws, and of the Constitution and of the Union, is perfectly right and within the power, at all times, of each and every state. The faithless members of the cabinet seek thus to shelter themselves and their partisans in disunion from resistance by the general government, while the imbeciles aim in the same way to find an excuse from [sic] shrinking from their duty of affirmative and energetic action for which they lack courage if not principle.

A more monstrous and absurd doctrine than that of the right of any state at its pleasure to secede from the Union has never been put forth. The government in such case would indeed be a mere rope of sand. According to this dogma, Cuba, after we shall have paid $200,000,000 for her purchase, as a state may at once secede, and leave the United States Treasury to place that small item to the account of "profit and loss." Texas, when she came into the Union after we had paid many millions to discharge her debts, and other millions to go into her coffers, was and is entirely at liberty to secede with the booty. Each and all the states carved out of the Louisiana purchase, for which we also paid such an immense sum, may do the like.

So, too, states in which the largest amounts of the public property may be situated may at any time secede with that property. When the Pacific Railroad shall be constructed, at an expense of countless millions, paid from the common treasure, the two or three states through which it will run may decamp with the plunder and plant a customhouse on the site of our storehouses. Vermont, New Hampshire, Indiana, Illinois, Ohio, Kentucky, Tennessee, and the other inland states, which will have contributed to these great disbursements, and in which states hardly a dollar of the public treasure is even [ever?] expended, are to look quietly and approvingly on the exodus of those which have been thus purchased and enriched at their expense, and to recognise the right of each of them to secede and take the property with them.

Again, if this right exists it exists at all times, until no two states remain united. What, then, would become of the national debt and the national credit? To whom would the creditors of the government look for payment? Should the government be, as it may at any time be, indebted on its stocks hundreds of millions of dollars, its creditors could look, in case of secession, only to the states which should remain united. Those which should have seceded and established independent governments could not be reached. The creditor could claim of them no percentage of liability. They would plead that they had never contracted, and that they had been only stockholders in a corporation in which there was no individual liability.

Nor could the continuing government of the United States compel the payment by the seceding state of a portion of the public debt. There would be no data from which a definite percentage could be assigned to it, nor would it have the ability to pay. If South Carolina finds it

SECESSION: RIGHT OR REVOLUTION? 161

necessary to repudiate at the outset by suspending specie payments, and (as already foreshadowed) by annulling even private debts due by its citizens to those of other states, it is plain that both ability and principle will be lacking for payment of her share (if it could be allotted) of the public debt. There is no court by which any fixed amount could be established as due from her on account of that debt, or which could issue execution for its payment. It results therefore that the seceding state could only be compelled to pay any share of the national debt (contracted on her account, as well as that of the other states) by war and reprisals by the general government. This puts an end to the idea of peaceable secession and the right of secession.

But can any of the democratic book-keepers tell us how (if payment could be compelled) they could make out the account current between the seceding state and the government, so as to strike a balance between the debit and the credit sides? Large amounts have been expended by the government on her account and within her borders. Forts for her harbors, light-houses, court-houses, coast-surveys, custom-houses, nonpaying postoffices and post routes, and salaries of the swarms of officers and leeches attendant upon all these, in addition to her undefinable share of the public debt, have all been paid. But then she has a credit side of the account also, which it will be impossible to adjust. How are we to ascertain the values and the proportions thereof to which she is entitled of the public arms and ammunitions of war, arsenals, ceded places, public edifices, ships of war, and of the public lands? Is there any court, or is there any form of action by which partition can be made of the territories? This last item is a very material one, for the only point of principle on which the secessionists take issue with the Republicans as to the platform of the latter (adopted at Chicago) is that of carrying slavery into the territories. What foothold or property in the territories will the seceders retain on leaving the Union? They will be foreign states, and we believe it has not yet been claimed, even by Judge Taney, that the laws of foreign states extend *proprio vigore* over the territories.

Another difficulty in making up the account with *South Carolina* would result from her claiming an almost incalculable credit for the disproportion of the public burdens which she fancies she has borne in the confederacy, by reason of what she considered the unequal operation of the various revenue laws.

Now, this right of secession, if it exist at all, is an absolute one, and a state has as much right to exercise it at one time as at another. If she may secede at will, she may do so in anticipation of war, or in time of war. If she can secede when she chooses, she owes no allegiance to the government an hour after she decides to secede, but will then be just as independent of the government as she is of any other nation. In the midst of war, then, it will be the right of any state not only to desert our own government, but at the same time to ally herself to the enemy. The *Hartford Convention* complained that New England was heavily taxed, but not defended by the general government, and merely proposed to ask the consent of the government to expend in the defence of New England the taxes raised in New England. This was not claimed as a right, but the consent of the government was to be sought. This was hardly an approach to secession, but the democracy of that day did not tolerate even the proposition, and the Hartford Convention was execrated.

But the absurdity of this new doctrine of the right of secession is too palpable for serious argument. The government under such a principle could not have twenty-four hours of assured existence. Neither other nations, nor its own citizens, could have confidence in its permanence. It would lack the vital principle of existence, because it would wholly lack credit. Nobody would lend it a dollar, for nobody could be sure that it would hold together long enough to pay a six months' loan, to say nothing of loans for long terms of years. The *public faith,* on which alone all who deal with governments can repose, would be utterly lacking. Business could have no security or stability, for men would not embark either their industry or their capital, unless under the shelter of laws and institutions not liable to change.

No—if a state secedes it is revolution, and the seceders are traitors. Those who are charged with the executive branch of the government are recreant to their oaths if they fail to use all lawful means to put down such rebellion. The people of no party base any confidence either in the fidelity or nerve of the Administration at Washington, but fear they will prove, some of them from inclination and others from timidity, practical allies of the revolutionists. They and their partisans have done all in their power to inflame and mislead the South, by charging upon the northern states the design of interfering with the rights of the people of the South, and the mercenaries here have co-operated in this false clamor and deception. The Administration, in relinquishing the government will endeavor to leave all possible embarrassments in the way of its successors, but we much mistake if those of its partisans here who have been foremost in the false work, will not be the first with whom the consequent mischief will come home to roost.

·   ·   ·   ·   ·   ·   ·   ·   ·   ·   ·   ·

53. Secession

(Bangor Daily Union [Breckinridge], November 13, 1860)

The government of a State is but the *agent* of the people. Its powers, limitations and instructions are all contained in a written constitution. The people are the principal, and they alone possess the power "to alter, reform, or totally change" that constitution. In any controversy between the sovereign people, and their agent, the government, the people alone can be the final arbiter of differences. The simple statement of these propositions is sufficient to command for them the assent of all reflecting men. If the government of our State, then, shall undertake the usurpation of powers not delegated, and that usurpation shall be sanctioned by every department of the government, including the *judiciary,* we know where to look for our own remedy. We know where the *principal,* the creating and controlling power, is. When the sovereign people speak through convention, or otherwise, the government must hear and *obey.*

The government of the United States is but an *agent,* and as such, is likewise a creation, and the subject, of some controlling power. What and where is that power? The power that created this agent must be the power to control it. To suppose a government not answerable to any power, and the final judge of what powers it may or may not exercise under its constitution, is to suppose an irresponsible despotism.

We are not obliged to resort to speculations or theories to ascertain the origin of our National Government. We read it in history authenticated by public records and living witnesses. A convention of the thirteen original States met in Philadelphia in May, 1787, and on the 17th of September, in the same year, completed and published the present Constitution of the United States. According to the terms of the instrument itself, it was to remain a dead letter, a mere form of power without any vitality, until it should be adopted by the sovereign people of *each* of nine States, and was then to be the constitution of those States only which had adopted it. Each State was perfectly free to adopt or reject it at the will of the sovereign people of that State. On the 26th of July, 1788, it had been adopted by eleven States, and the government went into operation in April following; but it still had no force in Rhode Island and North Carolina, which had not then adopted it. Its adoption by *eleven* States gave it no force in the *two* States which had not adopted it. It could only become a vital force in those States by the sovereign act of their people acting separately and independently of each other and all others. Indeed, the government had been in full operation more than one year in the States which had adopted it before Rhode Island ratified it; still during that year the government had no more right and made no more attempt to exercise its powers in that smallest of the States, than it did in France.

The people of Virginia, by a sovereign act, made the Constitution of the United States *their* constitution in precisely the same sense and same manner in which they had previously made their State constitution their fundamental law. It became binding on the people of that State *solely* because of their own act, and not because of the act of New York, or of all the rest of the States. As we have already shown, the unanimous voice of the other twelve States could and did give the Constitution *no* authority in little Rhode Island.

The foregoing remarks contain an answer to the question who or what are the *principal* of which the Government of the United States is the *agent*. That principal is the sovereign people of *each* State, and *not* the people of *all* the States taken in the aggregate. That sovereign power in Maine, which makes and unmakes, alters, amends, and totally changes our State constitution, resides in a majority of the people of Maine, irrespective of their geographical position. Our State is divided into sixteen counties, and though every person in Penobscot, Piscataquis, Aroostook and Hancock counties, should vote in the negative on a constitutional question, whilst a majority of the people of the whole State, taken in the aggregate, should vote in the affirmative, yet the action of the majority would be binding on the people of the negative counties. Not so, however, in regard to the United States. Twenty of the largest States cannot impose a single constitutional obligation on any one, or all, of the remaining thirteen. *No power can impose any obligations or restraints upon the citizens of a State save a government instituted and ordained by the sovereign people of that State.* The citizen of a State is bound to obey a law passed in pursuance of the Constitution of the United States, *not* because it is a law of Congress, signed by the President, and sanctioned by the judiciary, but because the sovereign people of *his* State ordained and established that Constitution, and thereby commanded him to obey such law.

We say then that the creating, controlling power of the Government of the United States is the sovereign people of *each* State. The People of *each* State are the *principal* of which the Government of the United States is the *agent*. But as one principal may have many agents, so many principals may have one agent. The Government of the United States to-day is the agent of thirty-three principals, and the State of Maine has ordained two agents, the government of Maine and the Government of the United States.—In any controversy between an agent and his principal about the extent of the powers delegated to the agent, the difference must be decided in the manner prescribed by the principal. In any controversy between the sovereignty of a State and its agent, the Government of the United States, no department of the Government can be the final arbiter, but the difference must be settled in the manner prescribed by the sovereign people of the State, *or they have their remedy in resuming their delegated powers.* The sovereign people of South Carolina have prescribed in *their* United States Constitution that in any controversy between them and their agent, the General Government, the difference may be settled by the Conventions or Legislatures of *three-fourths* of all the States, and this mode of settlement is authoritative and binding on South Carolina only because *her* sovereign people have prescribed and ordained it.

And now for the practical conclusion of the whole matter.

A controversy has arisen between each one of the Southern States and the Government of the United States. That Government, in the hands of the Republican party, is about to claim to exercise a power, which the Southern States declare they have never delegated it, to wit, the power to abolish slavery in the territories. Let, then, a Convention of all the States be called at once in the manner prescribed in the fifth article of the Constitution. Let Congress do this instantly on its reassembling. Let there be no delay, else our glorious Union is gone, and gone *forever.* It is to be regretted that many of the Southern States have no confidence in this mode of settling the difference, and are about exercising the sovereign right of *resuming* their delegated powers. It may yet be in the power of the North, which has most wickedly and unjustifiably provoked this unhappy controversy, to save the Union. Let it at once and instantly abandon its proposed usurpation of powers not delegated.

The Union of Maine with South Carolina rests and depends for its continuance on the free consent and will of the sovereign people of each. When that consent and will is withdrawn on either part, their Union is gone, and no power exterior to the withdrawing can ever restore it. A sovereign State may be conquered and held as a subject province; but no aggregation of power can ever force or compel it to be a co-sovereign and co-equal member of the American Union.

54. The Commotion at the South

(Brooklyn Daily Eagle [Breckinridge], November 13, 1860)

The question of the abstract right of secession is one which has never been thoroughly discussed. The framers of the Constitution made no provision for it and no provision against it. As the Grecian legislators refused to attach penalties to certain crimes, or even to mention them in their statutes, because they were deemed such as human nature in its normal condition would never perpetrate, and their mention might suggest them to the morally depraved, so the founders of the Republic thought it unnecessary to stipulate pro or con with reference to a contingency which they could hardly contemplate as even among the remote possibilities of the far-distant future. Scarcely has a generation passed away, when the question comes up for practical solution, certain States claiming the right to withdraw, and threatening to put it into execution. Putting aside the abstract right of secession, the present aspect of the South demands attention, as it is fraught with immediate and important consequences to the country at large.

There can be no question that the intention of the statesmen who framed the present Constitution, and arranged the terms of Union was to establish a permanent government capable of protecting and perpetuating itself. Still it must be remembered that the Federal Government is the result of a voluntary compact between sovereign States, based upon a written agreement, and the real existence of the union must depend upon the faithful performance of the terms of that agreement. Whether the right to secede be admitted or denied there can be no two opinions on the fact that any violation of the constitution by the general government, deliberately persisted in would relieve the state or states injured by such violation from all legal and moral obligation to remain in the union or yield obedience to the federal government. But who is to judge of this violation? The constitution itself provides a judge. It provides that "this constitution and the laws of the United States which shall be made in pursuance thereof shall be the supreme law of the land." The very letter of the constitution is law and other enactments framed in harmony with it. Consequently any law not in strict accordance with the constitution is null and void. And if a question arises as to whether any particular piece of legislation is in conflict with the constitution or with the reserved right of any State it is not the state or states to be affected by the law, nor the Congress that passes the law that is to judge whether the law is just and operative or unjust and void, but an impartial tribunal erected for the purpose. The federal government consists of a judicial, as well as a legislative and executive branch; and to that authority all disputed questions are to be referred. Should a state feel aggrieved, this is where her appeal properly lies. Until every branch of the government conspires to violate the compact by virtue of which it exists, the last resort of secession or revolution should not be invoked. The South will therefore be clearly in the wrong in seceding under present circumstances.

At the same time it is well to remember that there is a logic above that of facts which sometimes precipitates revolutions. The South believes that she has received provocation sufficient to justify her in refusing to place any further confidence in the justice or friendly feeling of her sister States, and most of all because the future is pregnant with signs of danger and aggression far beyond anything attempted. It must be confessed that a large number of Northern States have, by their legislatures, nullified a plain provision of the Constitution, as regards the return of fugitive slaves. That constitutional provision is unpleasant to the feelings of northern people, therefore they have set it at nought. Is not such action as rank nullification as ever South Carolina attempted? Yet we hear nothing but denunciation of Carolinian nullification from the very lips of those who voted for or sanctioned northern nullification. But the action of separate States can afford no valid plea for secession to other States. The general government has not only not sanctioned nullification in either case, but met it with equal promptness when necessary, and the Burns slave case in Boston, in the very heart of abolitionism, was a vindication of the guarantees of the Constitution which ought to satisfy those who complain on this point. We doubt not but Mr. Lincoln will faithfully execute the provisions of the Constitution which apply to his office, and whether or not, it is time enough to condemn him when he proves recreant.

While we see no real cause for secession on the part of the South, should any states attempt it there is nothing to be done but let them go. To hold any state by force of arms and compel it to remain attached to a confederacy it ceased to respect or trust in and obey a government it despised, would be to convert our government into a sanguinary and odious despotism. The difficulties which must beset any state or states that choose to secede will be naturally so great, the advantages so few and the disadvantages so many, that even South Carolina, when brought face to face with the reality, may yet reflect and draw back. But whatever may be the result of the present excitement there can be no hope entertained of the permanence of the union if the present acerbity of tone and bitterness of feeling shall continue to prevail in the respective sections. Already we have ceased to remember that we are one people, the inheritors of a common patrimony and the joint heirs to the proud memories of the revolution and the most magnificent achievements ever accomplished. Instead of brotherly feeling and kindly consideration for each other[']s diversity of sentiment, we criticise each other with merciless severity and in a spirit of malice and all uncharitableness. If we think the Union worth preserving we must curb our insolent pride and pharisaical assumption of superiority. The white men of the South are of our own blood and race. The haughty feelings of Caucasian manhood, and the spirit of freemen that will acknowledge no superior, animates their souls, and we may accept them as brothers and equals, or drive them into the position of terrible and unnatural enemies. Many believe that the apprehensions expressed with regard to Lincoln's election were insincere; and many fail to see the significance of the commotion that has followed that event. But that there is danger ahead, few can fail to comprehend, and that danger may be averted by conciliation, or it may be precipitated and rendered irremediable.

55. The Right of Secession

(Cincinnati Daily Commercial [Lincoln], November 14, 1860)

Has a State the right to secede from the Union? is a question just now discussed with much interest, and decided in a manner indicative of anything but unanimity in the public sentiment. Although the question itself is not a new one, the present attitude of a portion of the South is rapidly rendering it a practical one. What was once held to be the gasconade of orator Yancey, about "precipitating the cotton States into a revolution," has now reached the length of State secession Conventions, resignations of United States Senators, provisions for arming States for offence and defense, and a general excitement and tumult in the public mind of several States, strongly significant of a purpose to make secession from the Union an established fact.

The doctrine of secession is based upon the extreme idea of State Rights, as held by Mr. Calhoun and his school of political theorists. According to this, the Federal Union is not a government of the people of the nation, acting in their aggregate capacity, but a Federal compact between States, acting in their State capacity. The States are sovereign and independent political communities, and surrender, in entering the Union, none of the attributes of sovereignty which they have not a right to resume, when they consider that their rights and interests will be promoted in so doing.—Hence the CALHOUN theory of government logically implies not only the right of nullification within the Union, but the right of secession from it. A State which deems its rights invaded by any action of the Federal Government, may resist or nullify the execution of the obnoxious act, or, failing in doing this effectually, may secede from the Union, and resume her independent sovereignty.

This extreme doctrine of Mr. CALHOUN has hitherto found little favor among American statesmen or parties. The test to which it came near being subjected, in 1832, rather served to strengthen the opposite doctrine of Federal supremacy, than to give weight to the nullification side. Under the influence of a vigorous and defiant attitude on the part of Gen. JACKSON's Administration, seconded by Congress in the passage of a Force Bill—giving all needful power to enforce obedience to the Federal laws—the claims of South Carolina,—then, as now, the leader in revolt, were held in abeyance until the threatened conflict was evaded by a compromise.

Yet the doctrine of State Rights, shorn of its more odious features of secession and nullification, has always found a powerful support in this nation. The principle of local self-government—the right of every State to make all laws pertaining to its internal and domestic polity— to exercise sovereignty over all matters not expressly reserved to the Federal Government in the Constitution, is accepted as sound doctrine by many of the strongest opponents of Mr. CALHOUN. Precisely where to draw the line between the doctrine of State sovereignty, and the doctrine of nullification—would doubtless puzzle many of the adherents to the former. It might also give them some trouble to show how even a secession from the Union, on repeated and persistent infringements upon State sovereignty by the Federal government, would be inconsistent with the strict doctrine of State Rights.

The opponents of the right of secession base their argument upon the principle that the Federal government is not a confederacy of States, but a consolidated government of the people of the whole country. They set out with showing historically, that the first United States government, under the Articles of Confederation, was a mere confederacy, which experience proved ineffectual to secure the ends of power and stability, which are necessary to the permanence of all government. Under this confederation, the power to enforce obedience, on the part of the United States, was wholly wanting. The present Constitution was framed expressly to obviate the evils connected with so loose and disjointed a government. It sets out, in the very preamble, with declaring that the Union then formed was a government of "the *people* of the United States." It confers upon the three branches of the general government, large specific and general powers, which are thereby taken away from the States. It declares, in terms, that "this Constitution and the laws made in pursuance thereof, shall be the Supreme law of the land—anything in *the Constitution or laws of any State to the contrary, notwithstanding.*"

Hence it is inferred that the intention of those who founded the federal government was to make a government, not of States, but of the people; to found, not a league—but a nation; and it is also maintained, that as the Constitution contains no word or hint of any right of secession, the States are bound to adhere together, in all contingencies, and to abide by the action of the majority. It is denied that a State has any more right to secede from the Union, than a single county has to secede from the State of which it forms a part. And this analogy is pushed farther—to the extent of declaring that the Federal Government is necessarily the sole judge and exponent of the extent of its own powers, and of the proper construction of the Constitution—just as a State government, under a State Constitution, must be the arbiter of its powers as against the lesser local governments subsisting within its jurisdiction.

It is alleged further that an admission of the right of secession leads to monstrous absurdities and injustice. If one State has the right to secede, and dissolve the Union, clearly every other State has the same right. If South Carolina can be suffered to secede and set up for herself, then New York may do the same, which would cut off at one blow, two-thirds of the Federal revenue, arising from customs; then Louisiana may do the same—which cost the Federal Government fifteen millions to purchase; then California may do the same—which cost us the war with Mexico, and a hundred million of dollars; then Florida, which we bought from Spain, could steal herself from the government which purchased and paid for her, and sell herself to Spain again; Texas could do the same by Mexico, and Louisiana by France. Each State may at its mere whim and caprice, break up the Confederacy, and withdraw without even reimbursing the Federal Government for the "blood and treasure" invested in its acquisition. While three-fourths of the States are required to amend the Constitution in the smallest particular, the government which it founds may be dissolved, and the Constitution in effect abolished by the act of the smallest member. The right of secession, like the right of nullification, implies that each State has a veto upon all the others. What kind of a confederacy is that, in which a single member rules the majority, under penalty of dissolving the concern? How can treaties made with foreign powers be valid, if each State has the right to reject, or refuse to be bound by them? On this hypothesis, foreign governments would have to negotiate with each of the United States separately. In short, the doctrine of secession not only violates the majority principle, on which our whole institutions rest, but it is incompatible with the existence of any national government whatever. If the right of secession exists, a federal government having any of the attributes of sovereignty, does not exist, and *vice versa*.

A multitude of authorities, from among the great men of the nation, are brought forward in support of this view, but as authorities prove nothing but the opinions of individuals, we need not consume space in citing them.

But, however clear in theory the denial of the right of secession may be, it must be admitted that, in practice, great abatement from its rigor would probably be made. Practically, the American people are largely impregnated with the idea of local self-government, or the sovereignty of each separate political community. When it comes to Federal coercion of sovereign States, the stoutest opponents of nullification and secession are apt to pause. Even in the former crisis of South Carolina nullification, after all the lofty proclamation that was made of Federal power—not a finger was laid upon a citizen of South Carolina, to enforce the Federal laws. The rugged issue was avoided by a subterfuge in the shape of a compromise tariff, which satisfied the belligerent Palmetto State, while it salved the public consciousness of the strength of the Union and the supremacy of the national power. So, now, we find a majority of our people, however strongly they may reject all idea of the right of secession, are perhaps willing to concede the privilege. Seeing that most, if not all the evils of secession would be sure to fall upon the heads of the seceding States, there is a very general disposition to say, "Let them try it." However clear and indisputable the right of coercion may be, there would be a strong party in the North against compelling States to continue in the Union against their will.

We have sometimes heard the question argued with some animation, "Whether an individual has the right to go to the devil, if he pleases?" A somewhat similar problem is before us with regard to our seceding brethren of the South. No sane man doubts that they would lose infinitely more than they would gain by a separation. But the question recurs whether it is not better to let them work out their salvation or destruction in their own way, than to attempt, by forcible coercion, to save them in spite of themselves?

56. The Right of Secession

(*Daily Boston Traveller* [Lincoln], November 16, 1860)

Boston, Nov. 13, 1860

Editors of the Traveller:—Gentlemen: I hear the question asked almost every hour, how can a State *get out* of the Union, or become independent of the other States? This question has doubtless been suggested by the course the Southern States are taking. Will you please state in your valuable paper this P. M., what the process is by which a State can become free and independent of the other States, and you will much oblige many of your subscribers.

No State can legally leave the Union. What is called "the *right* of secession" has no existence. It means the *right of revolution*, which belongs to every people, and which may be called an appeal to that "higher law" concerning which so much nonsense has been written ever since Mr. Seward uttered a truism on the subject. Any community which is seriously aggrieved, and which cannot legally remove the grievances under which it suffers, can resort to revolution, which is a right over, and above, and beyond all law, and which depends for its character and justification upon the degree of success that shall attend the movement made. If the revolutionists succeed, history justifies them; if they fail, it condemns them, even while not condemning their motives of action. William III. placed himself at the head of the men who were discontented with James II.'s rule, and succeeded; and we call the movement the English Revolution of 1688. James II.'s grandson, Charles Edward, placed himself at the head of the Scotch Jacobites, and because he failed we call what was then done the Rebellion of 1745. History tells us of the American Revolution, but if George III. had been victorious instead of George Washington, history would call the war of 1775–'83 the American Rebellion. If the "Cotton States" should set up the standard of revolt, they would act illegally, no matter what might be their grievances, and supposing them to be really aggrieved. Their action would be revolutionary, and could be maintained only by an appeal to arms. They have no *right,* in any legal sense, to withdraw from the Union, no more right so to do than the counties of Suffolk, Essex, and Norfolk have to withdraw from the State of Massachusetts. To suppose that such a right exists, is to suppose that the men who made the Constitution were fools, and that they provided the means for the destruction of their own work. A fine opinion that would be of such men as Washington, Franklin, Hamilton, and the rest of the statesmen of 1787! We cannot now cite the many facts from the history of the Constitution which prove that its makers never intended that any State should have the right to leave the Union, but one consideration is decisive on the point: no government was ever yet deliberately provided with the means for its own destruction by its framers, and to have allowed the right of secession would have been to provide such means for our government. Instead of organizing a polity, the statesmen of that day, had they provided for peaceable secession, would have organized anarchy. It might, perhaps, be judicious conduct in our government and people to allow a State to leave the Union, under certain circumstances, but their forbearance would be illegal, and subversive of the Constitution. They might be morally right, but in a legal sense they would be entirely wrong. As to the present business, South Carolina has no more right to secede because Mr. Lincoln has been chosen President, than Massachusetts had to secede because Mr. Buchanan was chosen President in 1856. If the right of secession existed in full force, in a legal sense, she has had no cause for falling back upon it. If she had, there could not be an election held in this country without bringing on some act of secession. We should be in a worse condition than are any of the Spanish American countries, the irregular action of whose people has made them spectacles at once laughable and melancholy. If South Carolina should rebel,—and secession is rebellion,—and if other States should join her, it would be the duty of the general government to compel them to observe the law: and that is precisely what the Lincoln administration will do, and in doing which it will be supported by the people, and by the people of the South as well as by the people of the North. The Constitution not only does not provide for secession, but it absolutely forbids it, by prohibiting the doing of various things that would have to be done to render secession effective. It is forbidden to a State to enter into any treaty, alliance, or *confederation,* or to pass any law impairing the obligations of contracts; or to lay duties on imports or exports, or to levy tonnage duties, or to keep up an army or a navy in time of peace; or to make a compact with another State, or with a foreign power; or to lay taxes on articles from other States, or to give preference in its ports to the vessels of one State over those of other States. The secessionists would have to do these things, and many others of an illegal character, were they to attempt to carry out their designs; and it would then be the business of the General Government to force them to submit to the law. That business the Republican administration will perform, firmly but moderately, and to the nation's satisfaction, should the secessionists act as well as talk.

57. THE RIGHT OF STATES TO SECEDE

(*New York Daily News* [Breckinridge], November 16, 1860)

The people often act without reflection. Statesmen and politicians, either contracting the sentiment of the populace or influenced by ambitious motives, encourage the action of the people upon an erroneous and often fatal idea. The present agitation at the South is of this nature. If it is not quieted it will bring evils upon this Confederacy, the number and extent of which it is painful to think of, and the termination of which it is impossible to foretell. The Herald and The Tribune both tell us that a State has a right to secede; but can we believe them? Let the reflecting men study the formation of this Government, the only true source of information, and learn for themselves whether a State has such a right or not.

On the Fourth day of July, 1776, thirteen American colonies declared themselves free and independent States. Throwing off their allegiance to the British Crown and the Governments, which at that time consisted of the Provincial, Proprietary and Charter Governments, they established one of their own. In 1774 the first Congress passed the Bill of Rights, which is as dear to us as the Bill of Rights passed during the reign of Charles the First is to Englishmen. The affairs of the Government were conducted by Congress until near the close of the Revolution, without any substantial form of government.

In March, 1781, the last State acceded to the Articles of Confederation, and the Thirteen Independent States became a confederacy called The United States of America. The object of the States in establishing a confederacy under the Articles of Confederation was to form a *permanent union* for the mutual support and protection of each other. The intention of parties in forming a contract should always be considered. Knowing the intention of our forefathers, can we violate their contract? Each State, in accepting the Articles of Confederation, was bound by them. It was a contract and was binding. Secessionists ask who would enforce it? We answer, the majority. The Articles commenced thus: "Articles of Confederation and PERPETUAL UNION, between the States of," &c. Then came the articles defining the powers granted by the States to Congress, and the rights reserved to themselves. In Article 13 it says: "And the Articles of this Confederation shall be *inviolably* observed by *every* State, and the Union shall be *perpetual.*" At the close of the last Section in the same Article and immediately preceding the signing of the Articles—that there might be no mistake in the duration of the Union—the language is nearly repeated, viz.: "And that the Articles thereof shall be inviolably observed by the States we respectively represent, and that the Union shall be *perpetual*."

One of the main arguments used by persons believing that States have a right to secede is this, that there is no *definite* time fixed for the duration of the Confederacy. Can anything be more plain than the language used that it is to be *perpetual, to endure forever*? They will say to this that under the Constitution, which is substituted for the Articles of Confederation, no such language is used. Not until they had signed the Articles of Confederation did they become United States, and in that contract they declared themselves to be United States, and to remain united forever. They, as United States, adopted the Constitution. It reads thus: "Constitution of the United States of America. We, the people of the United States, in order to form a *more perfect Union*, &c." Not to limit the Union, but to make it more perfect! They became United States, and *forever* under the Articles of Confederation, and neither was abrogated or annulled by the Constitution! In the words of the preamble, both were affirmed. Where does the power lie to alter the compact? In the highest power of the land. In the States themselves and with the Government, as with all corporate bodies, the majority must rule. No decree of a Court can dissolve the States as it can a Corporation. The only power is with the States themselves, and a State once a member of the Confederacy cannot secede without the consent of the others—the majority must rule. If there was any other power to decree the dissolution of the Union, it should be left to that power; but there is none. The General Government cannot coerce a Territory to become a member of the Confederacy. But once having signed the compact and become a member of the Union, it cannot withdraw without the consent of the other members.

If one State has a right to withdraw, all may withdraw; and we should have loss of name, loss of national existence, civil war, servile war, loss of liberty, and, ultimately, the subjugation and overthrow of the most glorious Republic which ever existed. Could Pennsylvania withdraw from the Union if Congress did not impose a high protective tariff on iron, what would be the result? She would have to support a Government at great expense; maintain an army and navy; the tariff she might impose would not benefit her at all; on the contrary, it would prove a detriment; there being no greater comity between her and other countries, the other States would purchase iron where they could buy the cheapest. Bankruptcy of the State would follow, and, consequently, poverty of her citizens. The same rule would apply, in a greater or less degree, to every other State. The whole country, and every individual, would necessarily feel the effects of secession; but it would be most injurious to the seceding States. History tells us that States cannot exist disunited. The compact of these States is binding upon all, and the man who attempts to violate it will be responsible to future generations for the misery which his acts may produce.

58. The Right to Secede

(Davenport Democrat and News [Douglas], November 17, 1860)

The position has been assumed and boldly argued by several of the leading and most influential papers of the Union that any State of the Union has a right to secede from the United Confederacy at its own pleasure, and that there is no power in our government to coerce them [*sic*] back again.

President Buchanan, it is said, assumes the ground that he cannot interfere to save the Union from overthrow, unless he is authorized to do so by a special act of Congress. Col. Forney, in the *Press,* takes issue with the rest, which admits the right of secession, and also with the President himself, and very truly declares that if any State in this Union may secede at pleasure, and with impunity set up a standard of revolt, *there is an end to our Federal compact, and therefore an end to the Republican experiment in this hemisphere.*

The ground upon which the President assumes that he has no power to compel the return of seceding States to the Union, is that because the "first and fifth sections of the force bill of 1834,—which authorizes the President to employ the army and the navy in executing obedience to the law—expired within the year 1834, therefore the law conferring such authority must be revived, in order that full efficiency may be given to the Executive arm."

If such is the case; if within our government there is no control[l]ing power by which it is held together and preserved by which States can be compelled to recognize the united compact, then it is clear beyond cavil that the laws of the United States are subject to nullification any day, or upon any pretense by any State which may take a notion to slide out. This doctrine may be right—but we cannot see it in that light. There should be in every government some control[l]ing instinct for self preservation, and we have yet to believe that there is none in this republic of ours, though after all, it may be that Congress will have to convene and pass an act similar to the force bill of '34 [*sic*], before any step can be taken by the Executive. If such is the case, we would humbly recommend that such an act be kept in force for future use, not that it is advisable to make use of force only as a *dernier resort*. The first movements should be calm and conciliating—avoiding force of any kind if possible, attempting to convince the stubborn child of the errors of its way, and use force only when nullification becomes too flagrant to be endured. [*sic*]

We are yet of the opinion that there will be secession on the part of some of the Southern States, but we cannot yet clearly discover how that "peaceable se[ce]ssion" which is so much talked of, can be accomplished. It will be difficult to secede without nullification, and with it civil war must ensue. Others view the matter differently, but we can see nothing but union or fight, and we fear the latter will be the ruinous alternative.

59. STATE RIGHTS AND THE CONSTITUTION

(Providence Evening Press [Independent], November 17, 1860)

The character of the present ominous movements at the South naturally and properly directs the popular mind not only to the circumstances under which they take place, and to their consequences, but also to the consideration of "the right of secession" in certain cases. This question has such an intimate connection with the subject so unhappily thrust upon the public, that we need not apologize for resuming its examination. It may be an unpopular proceeding to maintain that right, at a time when it is invoked to support a grievous wrong; but this shall not deter us from upholding the principle at the moment that its attempted perversion, by withdrawing it from its abstract position, gives it especial interest. We conceive that by manifesting our loyalty to the right so far as it exists, we give emphasis to our condemnation of the gross offences committed under its cloak. It is for similar reasons that true religion derives new interest from attempts to commit actual crimes in its name, while its advocates enforce their censure of such wicked conduct, by demonstrating the existence of pure religion.

We must keep constantly in view the purposes for which the Constitution was formed. Hence we must not forget that it was formed by *Sovereign States*. None of them—not even our own little Commonwealth, the smallest of all,—desired to lose its own individuality, but was anxious to preserve it; else their boundaries would immediately have undergone that complete revision which would have been better suited to the requirements of a consolidated government having its territory divided into departments for merely administrative reasons. Each State assumed to be capable of governing itself. But with the double object of better protection against invasion, and to secure proper relations to each other, the several States were mutually desirous of coming to a solemn arrangement between themselves, which should give them jointly all the advantages of a great nation, without an unnecessary sacrifice of their respective pre-existing rights as Independent Sovereignties. There was entire unanimity in this respect, while the mode in which this common desire could be most surely realized, was, as is well known, a subject which taxed the powers of the ablest statesmen to the utmost. So numerous and serious were the difficulties which presented themselves, that many persons thought the task hopeless; and it was not until some time after all the other States had acceded to the Constitution finally submitted to them, that Rhode Island consented to accept it—so jealous was she lest her sovereign privileges should be in some way overwhelmed by the operation of the new system.

The result of such profound, prolonged and patriotic deliberations, was an instrument which its framers admitted to be not without those imperfections which must pertain to whatever is of human contrivance. Nevertheless, they believed—as well they might—that they had provided so far as was in their power, for all contingencies that could be anticipated so long as the great body of the people should remain true to the patriotism imputed to them, and without which no Constitution could endure. Sensible, however, that the product of their labors was not faultless in every specification, and aware that while experience might reveal defects, the boundless future would almost certainly require changes in the Constitution to adapt it to changes which no man could foretell, they inserted a provision whereby the Constitution might be amended. A bare majority of the States was wisely deemed of inadequate authority to alter the fundamental law, and a three-fourths vote was made requisite for that purpose. It is a significant fact, that although the sovereignty of the States was already rigidly guarded, especially by the institution of the Senate, and although the history of the country proved, and the course of legislation admitted reserved rights on the part of the States, one of the first uses of the amendment clause was to declare, in express terms, that "The powers not delegated to the United States by the Constitution, or prohibited by it to the States, are reserved to the States respectively, or to the people."

The importance of strict adhesion to the truth thus impressively declared, cannot be over-estimated. It lies at the very bottom of the Union and its manifold blessings. If we ignore it in practice, the Constitution will be prostituted even under its own forms, to its own sub-version by the resulting dissolution of the Union. Consider a moment. What if, as is likely to happen, by the admission of new States or otherwise, three-fourths of the States should be what we call "Free States?" They would then have the "constitutional" power to engraft upon the Constitution any amendment that they might choose. They could, in fact, reconstruct the Constitution to suit themselves. They could abolish slavery by constitutional provision, against all remon-strances on the part of the hopeless minority. They could obliterate all State lines and form a solid government, as the States might have done but did not choose to do in the first instance.

We say that they might do all this under the Constitution, if we once admit any right to disregard those historical antecedents which forbid it. Who does not perceive that even a single State may thus become the sole remaining example of the government ordained by our fathers? and may thus claim the original, undelegated rights of which she can-not be deprived; sovereign rights, which may thus concern her very existence; sovereign rights, by virtue of which she may with dignity gather her full robes of majesty about her and leave the confederacy which would already have left *her;* sovereign rights, by whose warrant she would be free to pursue the old path so far as might be practicable to her.

Within its own sphere, as recognized by the Constitution, this sov-ereignty is as perfect as is that of the Federal government in *its* sphere. It necessarily includes what we call the "right of secession," but which is really the right to keep itself intact from encroachment or an-nihilation. And this right must be maintained. It must never be sur-rendered, unless we would establish upon its ruins the reign of anarchy, or of that colossal despotism which the men who achieved our liberties religiously shunned, and against which they uttered their solemn warn-ings.

60. THE SECESSION THEORY

(Madison *Wisconsin Daily State Journal* [Lincoln], November 17, 1860)

The present ebullition of disunion feeling at the South is reviving the old discussions, so general during nullification times when General Jackson issued his famous proclamation against the nullifiers of South Carolina, respecting the limits of State and federal authority under the Constitution.

Such discussions can only result in good. They lead to a study both of the fundamental law, and of the early history of the Republic, too much neglected by a people who are themselves the source of all political power, and who, under the Constitution, are "the rightful masters of both Congresses and courts."

Our whole system of Government is founded upon the supposition that the majority of the people are not only just and honest, but intelligent. Yet it must be conceded there are too many who exercise the right of suffrage without that knowledge of the government and its history essential to enable them to cast an intelligent vote.

Whatever tends therefore to turn the attention of the reading public in the direction of the Constitution and its history, must produce, in this respect at least, beneficial results.

The particular point which is now most discussed, is the right of a State to withdraw from the Union without the consent of the other States, and to set up as an independent nation. It might in some cases be just and politic to permit such a secession. But this is not the question.—It is whether, upon some alleged grievance, or on account of some fancied good to be obtained, a State has the *right* to dissolve the bonds of the Union.

The great majority of the Northern press take ground against this right. Madison, who was better entitled, perhaps, to the name of the Father of the Constitution than any other man, denied it in the most explicit language. Such was Webster's interpretation. Such is the view taken by President Jackson in his proclamation already alluded to. That document contains an admirable summary of the argument against the alleged right. It is yet more fully argued in Webster's celebrated speech in reply to Hayne. The other side of the question is presented most fully and ably by the writings of John C. Calhoun.

The whole question depends for its solution upon the manner in which we understand the character of the Union. If it be a mere loose league of confederated sovereignties, the right to secede undoubtedly exists. If it be more than that, if it be a government, if the states are not complete sovereignties but have given up a portion of their sovereignty to a national government for the sake of mutual protection and benefit, then that right must be denied, although it would still remain a question of policy whether, in a particular case, force should be employed to restrain a state attempting to cut loose from the Union.

Some of the disadvantages which would result from the right of secession, if granted, will readily suggest themselves:

1. The people of the United States have bought and paid for Florida, Louisiana, and other states. Under the secession theory these may step

out of the Union to-morrow without any obligation to refund the money they have cost us.

2. Texas was an independent sovereignty. But she was overwhelmed with debt. She asked and was admitted into the Union. The Union has paid her debts; it has defended her territory at the sacrifice of both blood and treasure. Wisconsin contributed of her means and men; so did New York, Massachusetts, and every State in the Union. Having got rid of her debts, upon this theory of secession, Texas has the right, at any time, to cut loose and set up for herself again.

3. The Union may buy Cuba to-morrow, at a cost of $200,000,000, of the common treasure of the States. The next day she may assert her right of secession. Spain will have the $200,000,000. We shall have nothing but an illustration of the beautiful results of the Calhoun construction of the Constitution.

4. The Atlantic States may, under this doctrine, secede, and set up an independent confederacy, or confederacies, compelling the interior States to pay to them, for their sole benefit, a duty upon all their imports and exports, while Wisconsin, Illinois, Ohio, Pennsylvania, and the other interior States, now prone to suspect that they have some little interest in the Atlantic ports, must quietly submit.

5. If the Union is involved in war with some foreign power, and becomes plunged in debt by a heroic struggle for her existence—no matter how just her cause—any craven and selfish state, under the doctrine of the right of secession, may abandon the Union at the beginning and thus avoid the dangers which the others meet, or, at the close of the struggle, and thus avoid the payment of her proportion of the debt incurred.

These are but a few of the evil consequences which attend this theory. We believe it is alike without foundation in the Constitution or in common sense and we have no doubt but it will find in ABRAHAM LINCOLN as prompt and as decided an opponent as it found in ANDREW JACKSON.

61. THE PEOPLE, THE STATES AND THE UNION

(Providence Daily Post [Douglas], November 19, 1860)

When the people of the thirteen Colonies felt the necessity of a government which should direct the operations of a general war and provide for the welfare of the whole country, the several States formed "a league of friendship," and adopted the Articles of Confederation. The war of the Revolution tested the value of those Articles as a rule for the government of the States, and the defects discovered were sought to be remedied by the adoption of the Constitution of the United States. A new principle was then adopted; and the new government formed, emanated from the people of the United States and not from the States themselves. That this was clearly the intention of the framers of the Constitution appears from the words of the preamble to that instrument: "We the people of the United States." The Constitution was not adopted by the Legislatures of the respective States as it would have been had it been intended to form a new league, but by conventions composed of delegates elected for the purpose by the people. It has already been fully shown what were the sentiments of the early statesmen of the country as to the right of the people of each State to adopt the Constitution in such a manner as to reserve to themselves the power of seceding from the Union. But we have also the authoritative language of the Supreme Court of the United States to point out the true meaning of our Constitution. In the case of Martin vs. Hunter, reported in the first of Wheaton's Reports, Judge Story says: "The Constitution of the United States was ordained and established, not by the States in their sovereign capacity, but emphatically as the preamble declares, 'by the people of the United States.' The people had a right to prohibit to the States the exercise of any powers which were, in their judgment, incompatible with the objects of the general compact; to make the powers of the State governments in given cases, subordinate to those of the nation; or to reserve to themselves those sovereign authorities which they might not choose to delegate to either. The Constitution was not therefore necessarily carved out of existing State sovereignties, nor a surrender of powers, already existing in State institutions. *The instrument was not intended to provide merely for the exigencies of a few years, but was to endure through a long lapse of ages,* the events of which were locked up in the inscrutable purposes of Providence."

The complete subordination of the States to the general government, in cases where there is concurrent authority, on the same subjects given or reserved by the constitution to the States and general government, was clearly pointed out by the Supreme Court in the case of Houston vs. Moore, reported in the 5th of Wheaton. Judge Story delivering the opinion of the Court, then said: "Where the laws of the States and of the Union are in direct and manifest collision on the same subject, those of the Union being 'the supreme law of the land' are of paramount authority, and the State laws, so far and so far only, as such incompatibly [*sic*] exists, must necessarily yield."

The illegality of any laws passed by any State Legislature with a view of abrogating the authority of the United States within the limits of such State, is perspicuously pointed out by Chief Justice Marshall in his opinion delivered in the case of Cohen vs. Virginia, 6th of Wheaton, in which he says: "That the United States forms, for many and for most important purposes, a single nation has not yet been denied. In war we are one people. In making peace we are one people. In all commercial regulations we are one and the same people. In many other respects, the American people are one; and the government which is alone capable of controlling and managing their interests, in all these respects, is the Government of the Union. It is their government, and in that character they have no other. America has chosen to be in many respects and to many purposes a nation; and for these purposes, her government is complete; to all these powers it is competent. The people have declared, that in the exercise of all powers given for these objects, it is supreme. *It can, then, in effecting these objects, legitimately control all individuals or governments within the American territory.* The constitution and laws of a State, so far as they are repugnant to the constitution and laws of the United States, are absolutely void. Mere States are constituent parts of the United States. They are members of our great empire—for some purposes sovereign, for some purposes subordinate."

Such being the relation which the States bear to the Union, what utter folly is it to talk of the right of any State to secede! No one State has even the right of revolution. That right belongs to the people of the whole nation. A State or the people of a State may rebel against the government of the United States, but when such rebellion takes place, it will be the duty of the general government to crush such rebellion with all the power given to it by the Constitution. It is to be hoped that no attempt at rebellion will be made by any considerable portion of the people of this country; but there can be no doubt in the mind of any intelligent person as to the manner in which any such attempt should be treated. Our fathers declared their purpose to be "to form a more perfect union." If any State can secede at pleasure, our government is but a rope of sand. A successful rebellion or secession by a few States now, will be followed by a new rebellion or secession a few years hence, when the States remaining after the first secession shall adopt a line of policy towards some portion of the country, which shall be deemed a cause or made a pretext for a new declaration of independence or an alliance with some foreign power. It is the duty of the North to pursue a mild but firm policy towards the people of the South. If this can be done, all will yet be well. Repeal our obnoxious laws, which make our citizens believe their duties as citizens of the State and citizens of the United States, are conflicting. We have not much hope that this will be done; for the effort to accomplish it, will be met by the rabid and fanatical men of the Republican party, with the cry that we are yielding or succumbing to the threats of the South. Let the conservative, the Union men of the North, of Rhode Island, heed not the ravings of such men, but demand of their servants in the Legislature, that they remove from our statutes every cause of complaint that we are unfaithful in letter or in spirit to the national compact. Such action is demanded of us as patriots and statesmen. Do this, and insist that the Union shall be maintained by all the powers conferred upon the general government by the Constitution.

62. The Indissoluble Union

(Philadelphia *North American and United States Gazette* [Lincoln], November 20, 1860)

No one, up to the hour of the present outbreak, would have credited the statement that at this late day the principles on which the union of these States was formed would require defence or elucidation. It was not more the act of the States than the irresistible impulse of the whole body of the people that originally formed the Union. The laws which draw them together can never become inoperative or inapplicable, because the same ties of nationality, the same geographical association, and the same primary interests forever remain. This is not a loose federation of States of diverse races, and having such diverse interests that they are not bound to remain together longer than the whim lasts them. It is an indissoluble political union, because there is nothing powerful enough to part a country in the middle, separating families and kindred, and substituting for the insensible lines of States the barriers that distinct nations set up.

In the doubt which prevailed as to the political future at the time of separation from England, the loose federation system was tried, and was deliberately repudiated after a very short trial. The Union then formed was a wholly different thing, the States were asked to adopt it for all time, and were denied the option of choosing it for a few years only. An indissoluble Union was inevitable, one which, while it would cement us in a body having no thought of boundary lines in our business or social intercourse, would still preserve those distinctions of local legislation which would conform to whatever diversity of local interests and local opinions should exist. It is marvellous that any considerable number should now undertake to deny the great facts of that historical time, and to overturn the majestic structure which the advancing civilization of the age erected.

It is impossible to overturn our political system. It is impossible to break up the Union and revert to the colonial federative system. National barriers, with custom houses, police, and armed men, can not be stretched across this country anywhere, for there is not a line in it intended by nature for a boundary. What idea have we of public property that is not in common? We cannot entertain the idea of dividing the public buildings, of distributing their value among retiring States, or of holding them after a portion of the original Union has gone out. There is no basis or precedent for the negotiations which it is said that some commissioner from South Carolina intends to undertake in a mission to the foreign city—to him—of Washington.

The utter absurdity of the entire schedule of foolish intentions respecting "separate State action" becomes apparent when the very first step in negotiation between the respective powers is undertaken. The very proposition to negotiate is inadmissible. Neither the President nor Congress can utter a word in such a case, because neither has authority to consider such a case except as rebellion, or internal resistance to law. The people must meet in general convention to say whether the old basis of this national Union can be reconstructed, and Congress be empowered to legislate and the Executive to treat, with a part of our own body which has set up for itself.

The principle with which the secessionists open their case is thus an impossibility while this government stands. To admit their first claim is to upset the whole body of our national theory of government. Complaint on the part of any State is, or may be reasonable, and remonstrance, urgent representation by deputation, and possibly in extreme cases temporary resistance to oppressive laws, may be tolerable and necessary. But all this is conformable to the principles of our system, as well as according to reason and to law. Secession is the very antithesis of this, and almost as much a burlesque of legality as it is absurd in respect of sense. It is revolution against the authority set up originally by the very revolutionists. It is like the declaration of independence on the part of a county against a State, or by a township against a county. Perhaps the parish of St. John's, Berkeley, or of St. James', Goose Creek, may declare that the rule of South Carolina State is no longer endurable, and instead of undertaking to obtain justice in regular legislation, may secede, and arm its population for resistance. The upper counties of most of the southern States have a decidedly different opinion from the lower counties as to many questions of public policy, local and general. Shall the mountain counties secede because of the strain of differing interests which annually agitates North Carolina and Virginia? Shall the Pan Handle, a spirited if not a large section of our common country, and now attached to the State of Virginia, fly off in dudgeon because of taxes levied to pay for Gov. Wise's military expeditions? We have heard of no such intention, yet we are compelled to say that a dozen instances of injured counties and oppressed parts of States exist, far more deserving sympathy and assistance than anything in the relation of South Carolina to the Union.

The inadequacy, the painful inadequacy, of conception of their case on the part of those who threaten secession scarcely permits the grave refutation which might have been made in the early years of our history. They attack the massive and colossal strength of the political systems under which they live in the spirit of a township feud. They would subvert the institutions which are the pride and glory of the age, not in a deliberate and dignified manner, as becomes so great an act, but with passion, with enthusiasm of the small and local sort, and with merely childish accessories of means and of men. It is difficult, under these circumstances, to bring ourselves to the great work of declaring anew the character of the most imposing, powerful, as well as the most beneficent, form of government devised since the world began, and we earnestly hope the necessity to do so may not be forced upon us by any greater gravity of the case that now pains and mortifies us.

63. The Right of Peaceable Secession

(Cincinnati Daily Press [Independent], November 21, 1860)

The thing that politicians in their haste, are most likely to overlook in [is?] the organic principle of their own government, perhaps it might be said that this is the thing of which, in general, they have the least practical conception. We all admit that the organic principle of our form of polity is the right of self-government—the will of the people constantly active in the frame-work and administration. We hold that the right of self-government is a native right, inherent in humanity, and vested, for its own purposes, in every body of people; and yet we are prone to forget that, as a corollary from this idea, we have no title to impose any species of constraint upon the self-governing power of other communities.

So it has been in all ages of the world. The Grecian Republics saw nothing inconsistent in their claim to exercise despotic authority over their provinces. The Republics of Switzerland had their subject cantons, which they taxed and governed regardless of the principle upon which they founded their own title to independence; and the people of the thirty odd Republics of the United States find it impossible to get over the notion that their brethren in the Territories need some sort of outside permission before they can attain to the right to govern themselves.

South Carolina—we employ the name of a single State to indicate the whole of those be they more or less, who assume a similar position— South Carolina *talks* of seceding from the Confederacy of North American States; and the question—urgent in proportion to the probability that she will carry her talk into effect—is, What then? We suspect that the question is purely a fancy one; like thousands of others which the people will, and therefore the journals are obliged to discuss: but it is up; and we should be, as the orators say, "recreant to our duty," if we should fail to meet it with a solemnity commensurate with its possible importance.

We believe that the right of any member of this Confederacy to dissolve its political relations with the others and assume an independent position is *absolute*—that, in other words, if South Carolina wants to go out of the Union, she has the right to do so, and no party or power may justly say her nay. This we suppose to be the doctrine of the Declaration of Independence when it affirms that governments are instituted for the protection of men in their lives, liberties, and the pursuit of happiness; and that "whenever any form of government becomes destructive of these ends, it is the right of the people to alter or abolish it, and to institute new government, laying its foundation on such principles, and organizing its powers in such form, as to them shall seem most likely to effect their safety and happiness."

Whether the Government of the United States is such an one as is best calculated to protect the lives, liberties and so forth, of the people of South Carolina, is a question which they alone are legally qualified to decide. We may have our opinions; but our opinions, whatever they may be, are not, and can not be made, binding upon them. When the people of the British Colonies declared the Government of the Mother Country intolerable, they did it as the result of their own reflection and experience: nor did they deem it necessary to inquire whether King George, his counsellors or his home subjects, concurred in their convictions. They thought it wrong and a burden, and therefore they threw it off. The world has pronounced a clear verdict in favor of their right to choose, and of the correctness of their conclusions.

If this view of the legal aspects of the case is correct, it goes to settle the entire question. What is to be done? Simply nothing. Will we go to imitate the conduct of the "British tyrant," which we have in so many thousand forms condemned, and send armies and navies to South Carolina to reduce her to subjection? The idea of forcing men to belong to and carry on their share of the machinery of a government—of which the very essence is the free will of the constituent parts to act as they please, or not to act if they prefer, is to the last degree preposterous. Let South Carolina, in God's name, go if she wants to. The fact that she does want to, constitutes all the title that is necessary. Let her go in peace; and the States of the North would be violators of the fundamental doctrine of the Declaration of American Independence, if they should take any forcible measures to prevent her departure.

If our opinion were asked upon the point, we should say that South Carolina has no good reason to offer for leaving the Union, nor any substantial cause of complaint against it, and that her conduct at the present time is as unjust in its professed aims as it is ridiculous in its demonstrations. But this misjudgment and folly works no disfranchisement. She has still the right to judge, and to act upon her judgment; and the only party to which she is responsible for the correctness of her decision is herself. It is a curious circumstance, however, that it is in the South we find the advocates both of the right of secession and of the right of coercion. The general voice of the North is, we believe, in favor of permitting South Carolina to go out of the Union, or not to go out of it, as she prefers. It is otherwise with the South, where the doctrine of the right of coercion pretty generally obtains. The South may, therefore, be quite safely left to itself; nor is it improbable that upon this very point of the right of peaceable secession there will be an almost irrepressible conflict.

64. Secession

(*Circleville* (Ohio) *Watchman* [Douglas], November 23, 1860)

This country is just now agitated from center to circumference on the subject of secession—the right of one or more of the States peaceably to withdraw from the federal Union. The press and the politicians are discussing the merits of the question, generally confining it, however, to the constitutional and legal points involved therein. The conservative portion of the Republican leaders generally assume the position that no State has a right to withdraw, while the more radical portion of that party do not affirm or deny the right of peaceable secession, but are willing—indeed some of them are anxious—that the South shall secede from the Union, leaving the North in full possession and control of the present federal government, including the army and navy, the revenues of the country, and also, we presume, the national debt. Such we understand to be the position of the New York TRIBUNE, the leading and most influential paper of the Republican party. The ultra abolition portion of that party go still further, and insist that the South shall not only be permitted to secede, but that she shall be expelled from the Union.—This latter class is made up of the disunionists of the North, the bigoted and fanatical portion of the Republican party—the negro-thieving, higher-law portion, which is the control[l]ing wing of that party in all the New England States.

Many Democrats, both North and South, especially those who pretend to venerate the principles and policy of ANDREW JACKSON; and to follow in his footsteps also deny the right of a single State to withdraw from the Union and declare herself an independent Sovereignty, at least without the consent of the balance of the States. Many we opine arrive at this conclusion, through their love and veneration for the Union and the constitution, and the recollection of the manifold blessings which all of us have enjoyed in the Union as it is. To this class of our party we accord due mede of praise, for they are true patriots and trusty friends of their country and of mankind, and the rights and interests of the people, and the equal rights of the States, would be safe in their hands. But still we think they do not consider the whole question in that broad and comprehensive sense which true Democracy would prompt. As to the legal points involved in the question of secession, we shall not now attempt a discussion of them. But we are quite free to say that, our ideas of true Democracy, of the natural and inalienable rights of man, lead us to the opinion that any State of the confederation has, or at least ought to have, a perfect and undoubted right to withdraw from the Union and to change her form of government whenever a majority of her people shall be of opinion that their rights are being enchroached [sic] upon and impaired by the other States. The Constitution of the United States declares in plain and emphatic language the objects which the people had in view in the adoption of that instrument. Those objects were "to form a more PERFECT UNION, establish JUSTICE, insure DOMESTIC TRANQUIL[L]ITY, provide for the COMMON DEFENSE, promote the GENERAL WELFARE, and secure the BLESSINGS OF LIBERTY." Worthy and glorious objects, and beautifully expressed. But we hold that whenever the acts of the people of one portion or section of the Union are such as to be destructive of those worthy objects, and to disregard and encroach upon the constitutional rights of the people of the other section, it is the privilege of those whose rights are impaired to withdraw and absolve [sic] their political union with their imposters. We believe, too, that the people of each sovereign State are capable of being their own judges as to when and how their rights may be violated and trampled upon. In short, we believe the right of secession to be one of the "reserved rights" of the States. If it were not so, our government would not be deserving of the name of Republic —it would be a despotism—as tyrannical as any political confederation of States in despotic Europe.

But while we thus concede the right of secession to both the North and the South, and also acknowledge that the constitutional and personal rights of the latter have been shamefully and ruthlessly violated by the former, we are not willing to admit that the present is a proper time to exercise that right by seceding from the Union. The South should take into consideration the fact that, notwithstanding the recent triumph of the sectional Republican party of the North in the election of a President, that party is in the minority and powerless in both branches of the legislative department of the government. It will only have the power to appropriate and distribute the spoils of office. It will be compelled to bear great responsibilities without the power to do much evil or even to do itself justice; and it will be within the power of the opponents of that party to increase and multiply those responsibilities.—Whenever the President shall fail to discharge his duties in accordance with the Constitution, and to enforce the laws of Congress, it will be within the power of a Democratic Senate to arraign him before that body upon charges of impeachment. Those Southern Senators who talk about resigning their places in the Senate while that body is composed of a majority of Democrats, act an extremely foolish and inconsiderate part. They should esteem it an important part of their duty to remain there, and see that the laws are executed.

There are many other reasons which might be urged against the policy of secession at this time. They are too numerous to specify. Amongst those reasons we believe we may properly urge that the race of fanaticism is nearly run out in the North—the people are alarmed and many already seem to be returning to their sober senses. At any rate, the people of the South may be assured that the Democracy of the North—that Democracy which has ever defended and maintained the equal rights of all the States, and which can poll one million and a quarter of votes—will continue to defend and support the constitution and the Union as they are, and will battle for the old and time-honored principles of the party, the perfect equality of the States, and that the people of each State and of each Territory shall be permitted to govern themselves—that is, to regulate their own domestic institutions in their own way, subject only to the constitution of the United States.

65. SECESSION—HOW CAN IT BE ACCOMPLISHED?

(Washington (D. C.) *National Republican*, November 26, 1860) [1]

The present indications are, that South Carolina will, through her Convention, which is to meet on the 17th of December, formally declare herself out of the Union. A few other extreme Southern States may follow her example.

We often hear expressions to the effect, that "if South Carolina is determined to secede, let her go—we hope no attempt will be made to detain her," &c. This idea has been thrown out, in various forms, by some of our leading Republican journals. Yet we very much doubt whether many who indulge in such expressions have any very clear ideas, as to their meaning.

No Republicans, we presume, and very few Northern men of any party, are ready to concede the *right* of a State to separate from the Union, and thus bring about its dissolution, at pleasure. How, then, do they suppose that the Federal Government can "let" a State "go," which may resolve to secede? A vague idea seems to be entertained by some, that the Federal Government may, through the action of some of its departments, *agree* to the secession of a State, without conceding the absolute *right* of secession. This, however, is a gross fallacy. What department of the Federal Government does any one suppose possesses the power to *consent* to a dissolution of the Union? Is it the Executive? Let us examine.

Whenever a State shall assume to secede from the Union, she must necessarily repudiate and set at defiance all Federal laws and Federal authority within her jurisdiction. The Federal Executive, therefore, must either abstain from any attempt to execute the Federal laws within the jurisdiction of such State, or must attempt to overcome resistance by the powers vested in him by the Constitution and laws. To abstain from any attempt to execute the Federal laws, would be simply to *admit* the absolute right of a State to secede at pleasure, and to *acquiesce* in the exercise of that right. And this he could not do ex-

[1] See p. 104 n. The hiatus (seven lines) in this editorial is due to a defect in the only extant copy (Library of Congress).

cept in flagrant violation of that clause of the Constitution which enjoins upon him the duty to "take care that the laws be faithfully executed."

Is it supposed that the President and Senate, through the treaty-making power conferred by the Constitution, can consent to the secession of a State? This cannot be, for the plain reason that a treaty can only be made with a *foreign* Power. So long as a State is *in* the Union, she cannot be a party to a treaty with a Government of which she is an integral member. She must first get *out* of the Union, before she can be in a condition to enter into a treaty with the Federal Government.

Can a State be turned out of the Confederacy, and absolved from her allegiance to the Constitution, by an act of Congress? Surely not. Congress, like all other departments of the Federal Government, derives its powers from the Constitution. . . .

In short, it is sheer nonsense to talk about *permitting* a State to secede from the Union. So long as the present Constitution stands, no State can get out of the Union, except by a forcible and successful *revolution*. The Federal Government is as powerless to *consent* to the secession of a State as it is to *expel* a State from the Union without her consent. However desirable it may seem, therefore, that a State whose people are desirous of dissolving their connection with the Federal Union should be permitted to "go in peace," the thing is constitutionally impossible.

We do not deny the power to *amend* the Constitution, in the mode pointed out by that instrument, so as to provide for the secession of a State or States. But no one who talks about permitting restive States to "go out" proposes to prepare the way by an amendment of the Constitution. In fact, it would be an anomaly in history for the organic law of a Government to provide the means of its own dissolution. Nevertheless, those who think it would be wise to incorporate such a provision into our Constitution may advocate its amendment to that effect without talking sheer nonsense, which is more than we can say of those who, while denying the absolute right of secession, talk of permitting a State to secede under the Constitution as it now stands.

We do not think it wise or prudent to irritate public sentiment at the South by unnecessary threats of coercion. But we may as well look this matter of secession fairly in the face, and see in what it must result, if persisted in. To talk about acquiescing in it, or consenting to it, is only to encourage, with false hopes, the spirit of disloyalty now unhappily rife in certain States of the Union.

66. THE RIGHT OF SECESSION

(Trenton *Daily State Gazette and Republican* [Lincoln], December 6, 1860)

The recent threat of South Carolina to secede from the Confederacy has called forth considerable discussion among the journals of the country as to whether a State has, or has not, a right to secede—some contending for, and others against, the right of secession. Those who contend for the right say, that each State is an independent sovereignty, and, as such, has a perfect right to do its own sovereign will and pleasure without regard to the wishes of any other State or sovereignty; while those who contend against the right of secession take the position, that, though each State is a sovereignty, yet it is not absolutely, but only conditionally, so—that is to say, it is sovereign so far as relates to its *State* regulations, but not sovereign as to any powers confided to the General Government by the Constitution of the country.

We are of those who believe that no State has the right to secede; nor do we believe in submitting to any measures of mere expediency, when the basis for such measures must be founded upon a wrong. South Carolina may secede, so far as words and paper resolutions go; but when ABRAHAM LINCOLN takes his seat on the 4th of March next, he will tell them in a language not to be misunderstood, that secession can not be, and will not be, permitted.

The nature of the American government is in many respects, different from any that has ever existed. It is a government of checks and balances; the federal government has its limits, and the States have their sovereign rights. The questions upon which our political parties have divided have generally been such as involved the consideration of these respective sovereignties—national and State.

When the thirteen provinces—all of them having less than three millions of people—fell like unripe fruit from the parent stem they had no permanent connection with each other; they were united only by consanguinity of race, common interests, and most of all, a common cause. They were independent States, in league through their congress, as the nations of Europe may be to-day, for mutual protection. That congress proposed a convention to form a confederation, but it was not till more than a year after the Declaration of Independence that the articles of confederation were agreed to and submitted to the several States; and it was not till 1781, or nearly five years after the Declaration, that Maryland, the last to accede, came into the league, and the confederation was perfected. The object of that confederation was declared to be a "PERPETUAL UNION," but it was soon found that the States had not conceded sufficient powers for the general government properly to regulate the revenues and the public credit, and in 1787 congress adopted a proposition for a convention at Philadelphia, for the purpose of "REVISING" the articles of confederation, to render the federal constitution adequate to the exigencies of the government and the preservation of the Union.

The convention of 1787, instead of revising the old confederation, formed and submitted the constitution—which did not abrogate the "PERPETUAL UNION" already existing, but proposed a "MORE PERFECT UNION,"—a union that should consolidate the States for specific purposes. This constitution did not provide for its own destruction, any more than God has provided man with the right and powers of suicide.

We may see the absurdity of peaceful secession, by examining its practical operations. We see Virginia, for instance, ceding to the National Government her vast interests in the Northwest, and even agreeing, with a generosity that it would be well for the North to remember and reciprocate, that it should be free forever, and formed into other States. Who believes that Virginia would thus have acted, if she had not thought the government permanent? Would she have said, here, take these lands and make of them five free States, if those States one and all of them, the day after their organization, would have the liberty of seceding from the Union, and become rivals of herself? Then we purchased Louis[i]ana and Florida, and paid large sums of money for Texas and California—for what?—that they might secede the next day? Preposterous proposition! What a fine idea it would be to pay a hundred millions of dollars for Cuba, as Mr. Buchanan proposed, and give to Cuba the right of becoming independent immediately, and that without a why or wherefore from us! And what wisdom we should show, to expend millions to clear the rivers and harbors of Michigan, or to build the Pacific railroad through Kansas, when to-morrow Michigan by her own will and against our wishes might be united to Canada, and Kansas set up independent under some military dictator! How could we ever declare war, or make peace, or have national revenue or credit under such an arrangement?

The right of secession, as the South term it, is a sham of shams, a humbug of humbugs, as gross a delusion as political insanity ever conjured up. We are one nation from many States; and for better or worse are we to remain so for ever, or till treason and revolution blot the stars from our banner; and God grant that they may not fall as long as supernal powers hold the stars in the heavens.

67. SECESSION

(Burlington (Vt.) *Weekly Sentinel* [Douglas], December 14, 1860)

There are many words in use in our country which have different meanings in different parts of our land. The meaning of words moreover changes from time to time, and once in a while the change seems to be controlled by the parallels of latitude on the earth's surface. An instance of this is the word *secession*—at the head of this article—what does it mean, this word *secession,* which is in everybody[']s mouth nowa-days? Without any attempt at a pedantic display of the original signification, as deduced from the original *root* of the word in ages past, we are content to take it as a word "of modern acceptation," in our modern political vocabulary. In the North [we mean thereby the States having voted for Lincoln in the late election,] it means, if we are to judge from the republican press, just nothing at all. At best, with the republicans, it means an attempt on the part of the South, to scare the North by a threat of disunion, or *secession,* which the republicans think, speak of, and treat as mere gasconade; a fitting theme for ridicule, jeers and sneers, on the part of a large majority of the republican press. On the other hand, the southern States, all south of Mason and Dixon's line, the press there, the politicians there, the *men* and the *women* there, give a deep, and we may say with propriety, an *awful* significance to the word. There, it means no more or less than a dismemberment of the United States of North America, peaceable if soon yielded, forcible if not; at any rate, and at any cost, dismemberment of the country.

The entire republican press of the North, with one or two exceptions, is criminally listless and careless about the matter, treating it lightly, as a thing of no importance, whether the great problem of self-government be solved by self-destruction or not. Without formally admitting the right of a State to secede, the republicans say, "let South Carolina go, if she wants to go, she will ask to come back soon, and then we will make terms with her as we please!" And there they leave the matter. It is the careless folly of an unthinking boy to speak so.

If South Carolina alone, or in company with other States, fails to maintain her relations, *as a State,* to the general government, one or two results must take place. Either she remains in the Union as a territory, and therefore subject to the regulations which Congress may make, or she goes out entirely, and the government of the United States is destroyed. From the position which South Carolina assumes, and the feeling which is there rife, it is certain that she will not as a territory peaceably submit to the jurisdiction of the general government. But the government must cause its laws to be enforced, if it is to live as a government. What then but the presence of the foulest minister of God's wrath, *civil war!*

Suppose South Carolina does goes [*sic*] out of the Union, under cover of that silly subterfuge, "the consent of parties," that establishes the *right of secession,* and this the republicans really yield. Without stopping to inquire what the result will be within and to the seceding State, let us look in another direction. One of the integral portions of the nation; one of the parts, which in their sum, make the Union, has gone, and the Union with all its glory, with all its high hopes, with all its power, with all its interests has gone, and stands in history as another monument of the inability of man to govern himself, under the forms of constitutional law.

If one State has a right to go out from the Union, and thus to destroy the unity and integrity of the government, what State may not go out? And what portion within any State may not secede from the State? Why may not a man declare that his farm or his house, or his shop, in Burlington, is no longer under the constitution and laws of Vermont; that he will pay no taxes, obey no process, &c., in a word, inform the world in general, and the State of Vermont in particular, that he had *seceded?* The right of secession exists in and under a government, as the right of suicide exists in the individual, and in no other way or manner.

Let every lover of this country, every patriot, every one who believes in the security of government, every one who has hope for the future, an interest of to-day, a recollection of the past, stop and think, and seek for light and wisdom in the sound principles of political science set forth in the writings of our earlier statesmen, and in contemplation of the vast interests wrapped up and enfolded in the glorious Union of the States of North America.

68. How to Secede

(New York *World* [Independent], December 15, 1860)

The country is in one of those great epochs which make a landmark in history. We are drifting steadily, rapidly, irresistibly, into the horrors of civil war, and our wisest counselors point out no way of escape.

But is the condition of the country really so hopeless? Is our national

Constitution—the theme of so much eulogy, the source of so much prosperity—not merely inadequate to the exigency, but incapable of being so modified as to meet it? Has it, not merely shut and locked the door against the peaceful secession of aggrieved and hopelessly disaffected states, but supplied us with no key by which it can possibly be unlocked? Those who think so do injustice to the great statesmen who framed it. We believe, on the contrary, that it is susceptible of being adapted to any emergency that can ever arise in the history of the country.

What is the condition of things that causes all this apprehension and alarm? Why, that one state certainly, and probably four or five states of this Union, have determined to withdraw, and yet, that there is no power in the federal government to allow them to do so, till they have established their independence by a contest of arms. If this is really so, the progress of events has disclosed a grave defect in the fundamental law.

Let us dismiss from view the sufficiency or insufficiency of the reasons alleged by the South for secession. Let us inquire what ought to be done in case a state, with grievances which really made the Union intolerable, should insist on going. In other words, what remedy is there against the tyranny of a majority of the states over the minority? The Supreme court is not a sufficient barrier; for a compact majority of the states would, in the long run, control the organization of the court, by appointing all the judges. A compact majority of the states would ultimately mould all the departments of the government into subserviency to its will. But the tyranny of majorities is the most intolerable of all tyranny. One of the chief duties of government is the protection of minorities. If the federal compact does not already afford them adequate security; if, in the progress of events, we have reached a point where a defect is disclosed in the guarantees of that instrument, a way is still opened out of the difficulty in the provision the Constitution makes for its own amendment.

We know enough of the public sentiment of the country to pronounce, with certainty, that any amendment is impracticable which would make greater concessions to the slaveholding interest, than are made by the compact as it stands. If, then, the South will not be satisfied with a frank concession of all the rights granted by the Constitution, the continuance of the Union is impossible. When this long dreaded conclusion shall be reached, a case is presented which was not in the contemplation of the founders of the Constitution, and for which, therefore, they made no *direct* provision. But they were too well versed in human affairs not to know that unanticipated events would occur; and they *indirectly* provided for them in the fifth article, which authorizes amendments, whenever two-thirds of both Houses of Congress, and three-fourths of the states shall deem them necessary.

We therefore submit to the consideration of the country whether the time has not come for an amendment to the Constitution providing for the peaceable secession of states. These threats of dissolving the Union have been held over us about long enough. They have had great influence on the political action of the country, not because the naked fact of separation is anything very formidable, but because secession, as the Constitution now stands, would be the certain forerunner of civil war. If Texas had *staid* out of the Union, we should get on very well without her; if South Carolina and Georgia had *never ratified* the Constitution; if Florida had never been purchased from Spain, and Alabama and Mississippi had never been admitted into the Union, we should, nevertheless, have been a prosperous nation. It is not the mere fact that one or two states, more or less, are in the Union or out of the Union, that makes such a mighty difference; but the dangers which must attend a breaking of the compact when it is once formed. It is by compelling us to face the appalling horrors that would accompany separation that the South has been enabled, for the last quarter of a century, to wield an undue influence over the political action of the country. If the present controversy should be patched up it would be only a temporary truce. Like ulcers driven in, it would reappear in another spot with increased virulence.

We can't afford to have this thing constantly recurring. We can't afford to carry along this disease in our political system. Almost any purge is preferable, so it be thorough. Let us have some medicament that will reach the seat of the malady. No matter whether it is emetic or cathartic, the lancet or the cauterizing iron. The tortures of the most "heroic" practitioner are preferable to the disease, if he will only achieve a permanent cure. It is inconsistent with manliness, and it is therefore intolerable, for the majority of the states to be coerced into the abandonment or modification of a policy, which it deems wise, by threats of disunion on the part of the minority. It is inconsistent, also, with a just regard for the rights of the minority to compel them to remain in the Union against their settled conviction that the Union is not for their advantage.

We therefore appeal to the South in a spirit of kindness, of conciliation, and of just regard for their interests and opinions, to unite with us in the adoption of a remedy. It is so simple, so easy, and, if adopted, it would be so surely efficacious that it ought to be regarded as a grand specific for this chronic, national inflammation. It should meet the views of the South, because it would enable any disaffected state to retire, constitutionally, honorably, peaceably, and with the full consent of her sister states, whenever her citizens, after having the question fairly submitted to them, should decide it to be for their interest to go. It ought also to satisfy the North, because it would extract the fangs from this disunion monster, and render its bite harmless. The provision should, of course, be so guarded as to prevent a state from acting on a sudden, hasty impulse, which it would soon repent of. The mode adopted for ascertaining the will of its people should be such as would make it evident that secession is their deliberate judgment and choice.

The South is now acting on its apprehensions, and not on its experience of actual evils. It refuses to wait for overt acts, but it does not allege that the federal government has yet committed any overt acts against it. We appeal to our southern brethren, therefore, to wait till the feasibility of this *constitutional* remedy which we now propose can be fairly tested. We believe that it would be alike for the advantage of both sections, and hope to find many colaborers in urging it on northern acceptance.

69. THE RIGHT OF SECESSION

(New-York Daily Tribune [Lincoln], December 17, 1860)

The Albany Evening Journal courteously controverts our views on the subject of Secession. Here is the gist of its argument:

"Seven or eight States" have "pretty unanimously made up their minds" to leave the Union. Mr. Buchanan, in reply, says that "ours is a Government of popular opinion," and hence, if States rebel, there is no power residing either with the Executive or in Congress, to resist or punish. Why, then, is not this the end of the controversy? Those "seven or eight States" are going out. The Government remonstrates, but acquiesces. And THE TRIBUNE regards it *"unwise to undertake to resist such Secession by Federal force."*

If an individual, or "a single State," commits Treason, the same act in two or more individuals, or two or more States, is alike treasonable. And how is Treason against the Federal Government to be resisted, except by "Federal force?"

Precisely the same question was involved in the South Carolina Secession of 1833. But neither President Jackson, nor Congress, nor the People, took this view of it. The President issued a Proclamation declaring Secession Treason. Congress passed a Force Law; and South Carolina, instead of "madly shooting from its sphere," returned, if not to her senses, back into line.

—Does *The Journal* mean to say that if *all* the States and their People should become tired of the Union, it would be treason on their part to seek its dissolution?

—We have repeatedly asked those who dissent from our view of this matter to tell us frankly whether they do or do not assent to Mr. Jefferson's statement in the Declaration of Independence that governments "derive their *just* powers from *the consent of the governed;* and that, whenever any form of government becomes destructive of these ends, *it is the right of the people to alter or abolish it,* and to institute a new government," &c., &c. We *do* heartily accept this doctrine, believing it intrinsically sound, beneficent, and one that, universally accepted, is calculated to prevent the shedding of seas of human blood. And, if it justified the secession from the British Empire of Three Millions of colonists in 1776, we do not see why it would not justify the secession of Five Millions of Southrons from the Federal Union in 1861. If we are mistaken on this point, why does not some one attempt to show wherein and why? For our own part, while we deny the right of slaveholders to hold slaves against the will of the latter, we cannot see how Twenty Millions of people can rightfully hold Ten or even Five in a detested union with them, by military force.

Of course, we understand that the principle of Jefferson, like any other broad generalization, may be pushed to extreme and baleful consequences. We can see why Governor's Island should not be at liberty to secede from the State and Nation and allow herself to be covered with French or British batteries commanding and threatening our City. There is hardly a great principle which may not be thus "run into the ground." But if seven or eight contiguous States shall present themselves authentically at Washington, saying, "We hate the Federal Union; we have withdrawn from it; we give you the choice between acquiescing in our secession and arranging amicably all incidental questions on the one hand, and attempting to subdue us on the other" —we could not stand up for coercion, for subjugation, for we do not think it would be just. We hold the right of Self-Government sacred, even when invoked in behalf of those who deny it to others. So much for the question of Principle.

Now as to the matter of Policy:

South Carolina will certainly secede. Several other Cotton States will probably follow her example. The Border States are evidently reluctant to do likewise. South Carolina has grossly insulted them by her dictatorial, reckless course. What she expects and desires is a clash of arms with the Federal Government, which will at once commend her to the sympathy and coöperation of every Slave State, and to the sympathy (at least) of the Pro-Slavery minority in the Free States. It is not difficult to see that this would speedily work a political revolution, which would restore to Slavery all, and more than all, it has lost by the canvass of 1860. We want to obviate this. We would expose the seceders to odium as disunionists, not commend them to pity as the gallant though mistaken upholders of the rights of their section in an unequal military conflict.

We fully realize that the dilemma of the incoming Administration will be a critical one. It must endeavor to uphold and enforce the laws, as well against rebellious slaveholders as fugitive slaves. The new President must fulfill the obligations assumed in his inauguration oath, no matter how shamefully his predecessor may have defied them. We fear that Southern madness may precipitate a bloody collision that all must deplore. But if ever "seven or eight States" send agents to Washington to say "We want to get out of the Union," we shall feel constrained by our devotion to Human Liberty to say, Let them go! And we do not see how we could take the other side without coming in direct conflict with those Rights of Man which we hold paramount to all political arrangements, however convenient and advantageous.

V

"THE ENFORCEMENT OF THE LAWS"

70. Let the People Arm

(Daily Pittsburgh Gazette [Lincoln], December 27, 1860)

We give this advice reluctantly. We have been loth to believe it necessary. But events are crowding on us so rapidly and rendering it so necessary, that we can no longer refrain. The time has come when it would
be criminal to withhold it.

Our advice, therefore, to every Northern man is, Arm yourself at
once. If you have a gun, get it ready for instant use; if you do not own
one, get one as soon as possible. For it will take time to get one. The
North is, to-day, almost bare of arms, and he who orders one to be made
will have to wait some time before his order can be filled.

Look at the facts. The Northern Arsenals belonging to the United
States have been denuded, within the last three months, every available
arm within them having been shipped South. The State Arsenals are
empty. The rifle and pistol manufactories have all been emptied by the
Southern demand, and have orders far ahead of their ability to supply.
The government has ordered all the U. S. troops to the Pacific Coast,
out of the way; and all the available force of the Navy has been sent
to distant stations, where orders of recall cannot reach them under a
month's time. All these facts demonstrate that while the South is fully
armed and ready for war, the North is defenceless.

The military spirit, besides, has not been active for some years past,
and the number of volunteer companies is smaller than it was. The
number of arms in the hands of the volunteer soldiers, therefore, is
comparatively trifling. Hence our chief reliance must be on the arms
in the hands of individuals; and no Republican should now feel himself
secure without one.

We are not alarmists; but it would be criminal to hide from the
people the fact that they are in danger. They have been betrayed by
their government into the hands of their enemies. There is a well settled purpose on the part of the Southern hot-heads to take possession
of Washington City and prevent the inauguration of Lincoln. When

that conspiracy develops itself, as it will, in what position will the North be to resist or prevent it? Can she do it in her present unarmed condition? She has numbers; but she has not the weapons, and she will be false to herself if she does not supply the lack, at once.

When, however, we advise the people to arm, we do *not* advise them to put themselves in an attitude of resistance or hostility to the government. It is as a precautionary measure, simply, that arming is necessary. An ounce of prevention is worth a pound of cure. Let us take no steps toward resistance; but let us be in a position to defend ourselves and sustain the government of Lincoln, when the time for its inauguration comes, should that be necessary.

71. The First Act of Illegal Violence

(Daily Chicago Post, December 29, 1860) [1]

The telegraph brings us the news that yesterday the State authorities of South Carolina took armed possession of Fort Moultrie and Castle Pinckney. This act is the initial point of aggression, and it becomes one of serious consideration for the people. The Constitution of the United States, when adopted, contained a provision, giving to Congress exclusive legislative authority over the seat of government and over all places, which, by the consent of the several states should be occupied by the nation for forts, dock yards, arsenals or other needful public buildings. Under this clause the general government has purchased the sites, and erected public buildings, forts, dock yards, navy yards, custom houses, light houses, post offices, hospitals, and perhaps other public buildings. In each case, however, the United States, demanded and required, preliminary to any purchase or expenditure, that the State, by solemn act of the legislature, should cede absolutely to the United States the privilege of exclusive jurisdiction over the site, and in the building erected thereon. Such has been the action of the States and the federal government, since the formation of the government. The State of South Carolina, however, has recently passed an ordinance, repealing all former acts of that State by which the Constitution and its amendments were ratified and by which the sovereignty of the Union was admitted.

[1] The first issue of the *Post* appeared on December 23, 1860. The chief proprietor and editor, James W. Sheahan, had some months earlier sold the *Chicago Daily Times* to Cyrus H. McCormick; and Sheahan at that time had contracted not to associate himself with the publication of any political newspaper in six states of the Middle West. Consequently, as in the present editorial, he felt called upon to deny the "political" character of his political editorials. He was an ardent champion of Douglas and popular-sovereignty.

In other words, so far as South Carolina has the power, South Carolina has abolished her union with the other States, and put an end to all her compacts and obligations unto her sister States. So long as the acts of South Carolina were confined to mere declarations on paper, her abjurations and her secessionizing amounted to nothing. But when South Carolina invades the property of the United States, seizes upon the public treasure and the public mail, when she sends troops into a fort of the United States and captures or expels the force left there to maintain it for the Union, then South Carolina goes beyond empty paper declaration, and puts the individuals who may do her bidding in these acts, in the position of "levying war against" the United States. That act is by the Constitution declared to be treason.

We do not discuss this matter as a political one—this is not a political paper—but we discuss it purely as a legal question, involving, as it does, the grave question whether we have any government at all that has the power of protecting the property of the people. If we have no government invested with such power, then the fathers of this Republic instead of being revered for their wisdom and sanctified for their patriotism, should be execrated for having palmed off upon the world a solemn fraud, and for having handed down to their posterity a miserable cheat.

We remember that some years ago, a mob of wild fanatics attacked the federal court house in the city of Boston, where the officers of the United States held a miserable negro a captive. It was then asked, had the federal government the power and authority to protect its own officers in its own buildings, where by constitution and law, the federal government had exclusive jurisdiction? That question was promptly answered by the President of the United States, under whose orders the United States marines were marched from the Charlestown navy yard to the court house in Boston, and there, behind glittering bayonets, with iron chains stretched across all approaches to the temple of justice, the judicial officers maintained their position, defied the lawless, and executed their duty. For a while, abolition madmen shrieked of State sovereignty and of the tyranny of the federal government, but the American people, from their innate loyalty to law and order thanked the Executive for his promptness and for the fidelity with which he preserved the national power and authority.

Yesterday another armed mob, not in Boston, but in Charleston, suddenly seized upon one of the national buildings. They have seized not upon a peaceful court-room, but upon one of the national forts, one of the buildings provided by the nation for the national defence. What is to be done? What has been done? Instead of imitating the example set him by Pierce, the unhappy old man who is at the head of national affairs, is wringing his hands and exclaiming that to send troops to Charleston would but excite the mob to greater madness.

What has his forbearance accomplished? A gallant and experienced officer was in command; that officer was charged with the responsibility of protecting these forts. As commander he advised the President that his force was not sufficient. The President refused him succor, and directly informed the leaders of the mob that he would not re-inforce Anderson's garrison. The President will not perform his duty; he violates the law, he stands shivering before the men who in pompous language bid the government defiance. Such a ruler is worse than the despot whose dominion was overthrown by the American revolution. The government which will not protect its people from an armed mob, is as criminal as the government which opens the ports to an external enemy. Gen. Hull surrendered Fort Detroit to the enemies of his country, without firing a gun, and the act has been blazoned with all its infamy upon the history of the world. Is it possible for Buchanan's surrender of Fort Moultrie to escape an equally infamous memory[?]

The State of South Carolina claims the right to secede, to withdraw from her contracts. We do not intend to discuss her right to do so, but we think that according to every principle of law, justice and equity a State cannot, any more than individuals, throw off contracts and obligations to which other States are parties, without the consent of those other States. By the express terms of the contract, exclusive jurisdiction was vested in the United States. While South Carolina may desire to resume her jurisdiction, her deed of cession stands in the way, and she is as effectually barred from so doing, until the United States shall relinquish their authority and yield their consent, as if the government had actually moved the Forts from her harbor and placed them in the waters of New York. Contracts are mutual, and one party cannot impair or destroy them without the consent of the other. Having therefore, taken possession of Fort Moultrie, without the consent of the Congress of the United States, South Carolina has, through her agents, committed an act of unlawful violence, which in the individuals perpetrating it, is rank treason.

It is the duty of the President to employ the powers of the government to put down that treason. The miserable Mormons, the negroes of Boston, the vagabond gang of Montgomery in Kansas, have all felt the prompt severity of the federal power. Is insurrection less insurrection because it is approved by the traitorous resolutions of a convention in

Charleston? If the President will not do his duty, then Congress owes it to the Union, to impeach him, and hurl him from the seat which he has disgraced by his cowardice, if not by his complicity with open and avowed traitors.

72. Northern Blood Begins to Warm

(Buffalo Morning Express [Lincoln], January 5, 1861)

The people of the Northern States are slow to anger. Their blood moves tardily, but we begin to see indications that it is warming up under the influence of Southern depredations upon the Constitution and the integrity of the Union. The course pursued by South Carolina against the flag of the United States, the seizing of the forts—the running up of piratical colors in place of the stars and stripes—the assuming of federal powers over the port by the rebels—the obstruction of the harbor—the erection of fortifications to be brought to bear upon the federal troops and forts—the imbecility of the President, and a sense of deep wrong to the Constitution and the Union, all conspire to awaken the people of the North to a sense of duty and danger. We have no hope left of any conciliatory measures which will avert the impending calamities. South Carolina has gone too far to recede. She rushes madly into the vortex of her own destruction. She defies the federal power—insults the federal flag—seizes the federal forts—turns their guns upon federal troops,—and is guilty of acts which are alike injurious and insulting to the United States. This the people of the North, who are devoted to the Constitution and the laws, and have lived for the Union in the midst of evil as well as good report, have borne, until forbearance has ceased to be a virtue. These insults to the flag of our country will not be brooked for any length of time. These defiant threats of haughty Southrons against Northern prowess, begin to take effect upon Northern blood. The North—the Northeast—and the Northwest have stood calmly and witnessed these assaults upon the integrity of the Nation, until the fires of '76 begin to be relighted in New England hearts, and the love of country and pride of nation excites men of the North and Northwest to stern determinations and a desire for action in rebuke and punishment of these overt acts of treason. Not one man in fifty now will stop to reflect upon a plan of compromise or pacification. Almost every man feels that his country and its institutions have been wronged—that treason is abroad, and that no alternative remains, but for men of courage and patriotism to meet force with force until this question shall be settled effectually, and in a manner that shall leave the bond of union in the States unbroken.

Men may talk and bluster of breaking up this Union, but it cannot be done. South Carolina may pass ordinances of secession, and assume a hostile attitude towards the federal government—her ragged battalions may erect fortifications, and the General QUATTLEBUMS of the South, covered with gold lace and feathers, may inveigh against the federal power, but all these things must be answered for to the people of the North who stand inflexibly by the Union. There is no escaping condign punishment in the end. The time will come when bluster will be of little avail and menaces will be laughed at. Then the mighty hosts of the far North will sweep over the region of Slavery with a power that cannot be resisted. We have the resources, physical and financial, to preserve this government, and under the blessings of a just God it will be preserved against treason and rebellion. When this blow is struck, and blood is shed, we can place the date of the beginning of the end of slavery on this continent. That institution can never survive a collision of States. It must fall as assuredly as that God is just. Its friends and defenders should know and consider this well, before they push the issue to extremity.

The present attitude of affairs in South Carolina has a warlike tendency at the North. No war has ever yet broken out on this continent in which Northern blood has not mingled, and when we find our troops menaced with danger from rebels, there is a strong feeling here which looks to their relief. In this connection we expect daily to see recruiting stations opened in our city, under the stripes and stars, for volunteers to defend the government against treason. The men are ready—and twenty days may find a regiment of one thousand men ready to march from this city southward in defence of the Constitution and the Union.

73. THE AGE OF BRASS

(Saint Paul Daily Press, January 9, 1861) [2]

We admire impudence. Downright effrontery we respect. A patronizing manner always awes us into submission. How can we, then, fail to regard with due veneration the present condition of the Southern mal-

[2] The first number of the *Press* was issued on January 1, 1861. In that number the editors announced their support of the Republican party.

contents and their Northern allies towards the Republican party? In it, impudence the most sublime, effrontery hitherto unequalled, and the patronizing airs of a thousand Howards are commingled.

The whole motely [*sic*] of our opponents unite in demanding something from us—agree in threatening something, if these demands are not granted.

What has the Republican party done—what left undone—to warrant demands of any kind? It has never been in power in the nation; it cannot, therefore, be held responsible for any one of the numberless misdeeds which have stained the administration of government these late years. It proposes, no violation of the Constitution, the fundamental law of the land. It has never, in any instance, sanctioned any such violation. Indeed it is just coming into power because people are determined that the government shall be taken from those who have shamefully violated that Constitution. It proposes administering the government in consonance with the principles which led to its establishment. This is the extent of its offence. If the Republicans insisted upon a bond from the adherents of the present administration that they would not turn traitors when out of power, there might be some propriety in the demand, though we question whether such a bond would afford any security; but for them to demand stipulations from us, under the circumstances, is the height of impudence.

But what demands are made upon the Republican party? It is difficult to tell. Scarcely any two notes are pitched upon the same key. The most mutter and mumble something about a compromise—intangible, vague, indefinite—yet the nearest approximation to an idea, seemingly, which our opponents can grasp. Now, a compromise presupposes two parties with conflicting claims. Republicans recognize no such parties under the Constitution.—They are content with the charter as it is. They ask no alteration. They mean that its principles shall be faithfully and impartially carried out. If there are those who demand more, or expect anything essentially different, they are outside of the Constitution, and therefore not entitled to a hearing.

Granting, however, that a hearing is to be afforded—what are we to accede, we ask again? "An express admission that slaves are recognized in the Constitution as property, and that such property is to be protected in the Territories, to the same extent as all other property is protected?"—say some. It cannot be done. We deny that slavery is recognized under the Constitution in any other light than as an artificial system of labor existing at the time of its adoption in certain States. To that extent—the constitutional extent—we go; but no further. If we are told that the Supreme court has so decided, we deny that a legal decision to that effect has been made. When it is made, if ever, we shall not cease agitating until the correct construction is put upon it.

"The incorporation of the Missouri Compromise principle in the Constitution," say others. We cannot do it. We contend that the normal condition of the Territories of the United States is freedom. We deny the right of any body of men to legalize the institution of slavery therein. Besides, supposing such a concession were made, we are dependent upon the Supreme Court for the construction of such an amendment. From past experience, it is impossible for us to be certain what that tribunal might choose to decide that we had admitted by such an amendment. *Obsta principus,* is the safest maxims here. [*sic*] We had no idea when we hurrahed over the compromise of 1850 that we had thereby abolished the Missouri Compromise. As it has since been strenuously claimed that we did, we prefer henceforth being upon the safe side. We are content to "let well enough alone."

"The repeal of the 'Personal Liberty Bills' of various States," say still others. That is none of our business. Each State must judge for itself, in the first instance, of the propriety of its legislative acts. If the unconstitutionality of any enactment is established, it goes at once by the board.

"Put down the anti-slavery feeling of the North," cry others. As well might we be asked to suspend thought, to waive judgment, to stifle reason. It cannot be done. The convictions of the mass of the inhabitants of the Free States, of all parties, relative to that institution are not of such a nature that they can be whistled down the wind at bidding. A breath did not make them, nor can a breath unmake them. We have trained ourselves to discharge our duties under the Constitution relative to the system. Thus far we can pledge ourselves. Thus far we have, over and over again, shown ourselves ready to go. Beyond it we cannot move—not one inch.

This is the sum and substance of the whole matter. Any one can see how senseless is all the clamor of those who spend their days in charging Republicans with the responsibility for the present disordered state of affairs. That clamor, however, will not cease just yet. "Those tuneful peals will still ring on" while there is the slightest ground for expecting that a concession of principles can be extorted from us. All that we have to do, is to stand firm. We have embarked in this struggle, conscious that it would be no holiday play. Those who have long enjoyed the sweets of power do not relinquish them without an effort. Dry husks do not hold out an enticing prospect for them. We purpose seeing the contest out. If there are any bearing our name who have not enlisted heartily with us, let them leave us at once. We have no room for such. If there are any in our ranks who cannot endorse decisive words, they have mistaken their place. "Men in earnest have no time to waste in patching fig-leaves for the naked truth." If there are any who in this age of brass are frightened by the jangling and clanging and clashing around, we beg them to fill their ears with cotton and retire from the busy scenes of active life as speedily as possible.

We propose understanding, once for all, of what Chinese thunder is made.

74. Law or No Law

(New Haven *Daily Palladium* [Lincoln], January 11, 1861)

The cotton States have drawn the sword against the Union, the Constitution and the Law. They cut short all consultation; they strike the first blow; they seize the property of the Union, garrison its forts against the officers of law, take possession of its revenue-cutters, rifle its arsenals to arm their forces against its authority, gather armies to seize the Federal capitol[,] its public buildings and its archives, and fire upon the national troops while peacefully obeying orders. This is not secession; it is not dissolution; *it is rebellion and aggressive war!*

Men of Connecticut! look this thing squarely in the face! All past differences of opinion, all interests or ties of party dwindle into nothingness; all political questions, all proposals of compromise or schemes of settlement are swept aside by armed rebellion making war upon the nation. A new and appal[l]ing issue confronts us—have we a government, or are we to be delivered over to Parisian mob-law and Mexican anarchy? It is no longer how shall we be governed, but shall we have any government at all? It is no longer what laws shall be made, but shall we have any laws?

Compromise with armed rebellion is impossible. When the constitutional election of Abraham Lincoln was followed by mutterings of discontent and threats of secession, the first impulse of the Northern people was for conciliation. They knew how grossly they had been belied, and were willing to do and endure much to remove an honest mistake. Even those Republican papers and speakers that believed no further compromise could be made with safety or honor were as conciliatory in tone as possible, and carefully avoided anything that might exasperate the Southern people. Our Senators spoke the language of conciliation and forbearance. To remove misapprehension Senator

Seward proposed a resolution disavowing the purpose and disclaiming the right to interfere with slavery in the States. Other Republican authorities proposed measures of compromise and schemes for removing the vexed questions forever. Some advocated the restoration of the Missouri line; others the admission of all territories as states; others the repeal of any laws that gave pretext for complaint. No pains was [*sic*] spared to assure the South that three months['] trial of Mr. Lincoln's administration would satisfy them that they were safe in all their rights under the new rule.

To all these overtures the Gulf states have been deaf. The men who have for twenty years been plotting the destruction of the confederacy had succeeded only too well in propagating their treasonable spirit. Their deliberate purpose to seize the Government by force is at last unmasked, and they have swept the cotton states into open, armed, aggressive rebellion.

All the old questions of slavery in territories, admission of States or return of fugitives vanish with the smoke of the first gun fired at Charleston. One issue confronts us: Shall the majority of Law and the authority of government be vindicated, or have we mob-law and anarchy? Compromise with treason is treason itself. Nothing can be done until the sword of rebellion is sheathed and the sanctity of law acknowledged. Are rebels to seize the United States arsenals and forts with impunity? Then what protects the country against a rebellion every month? Is there no power in all the land to enforce the laws and quell treason? Then what power is there to carry into execution any scheme of conciliation? If any faction or State or section may remedy a defeat at the ballot-box by an appeal to force, and beat down the authority of law by arms, any other may do the same. No other question can even be considered until we know whether we are to have a government. If the Constitution has no competent defenders, no amendment of the Constitution is worth a straw. If the laws have no power, any change of laws is folly. *Law or no law* is the only question now.

On that question the people of the mighty North are a unit. Party lines are obliterated until it is settled. Democrats, Unionists, Republicans, alike love the Union, stand by the Constitution, demand the enforcement of the laws at all hazards, and recognize the supreme necessity of a government that can protect the country, put down rebellion and execute the will of the people. Let the laws be obeyed, let order reign, and then the people of the North will attend to all complaints and listen with patient ear to all requests.

With rebel armies making war upon the United States it is no time to be talking about fugitive slave laws or personal liberty bills, party platforms or constitutional amendments. The very government is on trial for life. The new issue is not of our making. The people of the North, of whatever party, were anxious to settle all differences in a peaceful and law-abiding way, and were willing to submit quietly to the lawful decision. The traitors of the cotton States have precipitated the new issue upon us. So long as they presented requests, however intemperately, and passed resolutions, however passionately, so long as they talked of peaceable secession and sent commissioners to arrange and arbitrate, we could consult with calmness and offer the olive branch with dignity. But when they take arms to inaugurate in this country a Mexican revolution, when they make war upon the United States, and organize forces to seize upon the Federal Capital, they leave us no alternative, and every honest freeman of the North will answer: The Constitution shall be obeyed! the flag of our country shall be respected! the laws shall be enforced!

75. The Duty of the Government and People

(Philadelphia *Daily Evening Bulletin* [Lincoln], January 14, 1861)

It will not do to underrate this tremendous question which the American people have to settle. That we are upon the very edge of the most fearful civil war that the world has yet seen, we fully believe. *On the edge,* we say. It is the earnest hope of every patriot that the nation may yet step back. But how can this be accomplished?

Three plans only have been proposed as embodying the duty of the Government and people of the United States at this juncture. The first is to allow peaceable secession. "Let them go," it is said. "The South can never be coerced," say others. To this view of the case there are two or three sufficient answers. The first is, that there can be no peaceable secession. It cannot be, as we see in the events now transpiring in the South. The first movement of each seceding State is to seize upon the Government forts and provoke war. The Union is openly insulted by the feeblest of these States.

It cannot be, because the result of secession would be a war upon the borders over fugitive slaves. The line must be run somewhere, and wherever it is, there will be an immense frontier over which fugitives will pass, and wherever it is, there will be a bloody and prolonged conflict.

It cannot be, because to allow secession once or any where, is to give up the very idea of the Union. There is no law without penalty; there is no government without power. If every fragment of this nation can secede whenever passion or faction dictates, then indeed we have a miserable imbecility of a country, that will fall to pieces, because it is not worth preserving. A monarchy, anything with strength in it, is better than the anarchy that would follow the establishment of the principle (!) that the Union contains in it its own dissolution, whenever any body becomes tired of it. Treason is then a mere name, and loyalty, by parity of reason, becomes also a mere name. Who could live under the flag of such a Union without shame, or who would be willing to die for such a miserable abortion of a Government? This weak idea, then, of "let them go," must be abandoned, at once and forever.

The next plan is to effect a compromise. If any conciliation, which did not violate essential principles, would avail, it is certain that the great mass of the North would cordially consent to it. It seems, however, to show the intensity of the difficulty which is around us, that compromise has been tried in every shape, and hitherto without success. Committees of thirteen and of thirty-three; Northern men; Southern men; border State men; caucuses of Pennsylvanians; of Democrats; of Republicans—every form of proposition and consultation and debate has been tried. The votes both in the Senate and the House on the Crittenden resolutions, which embody substantially the border State proposition, though those votes were not direct, yet seem decisive against them.

Mr. Hunter's proposition seems to have taken every one by surprise. It is strange that any sensible man could suppose that a dual government would not contain in it, from the very beginning, the elements of strife and dissolution.

We have already spoken of Mr. Seward's speech, the most eagerly looked for of the whole session, as embodying the views of the new *premier*. It is exceedingly patriotic in sentiment and kindly in tone. But will it satisfy the South? Brim-full as it is of conciliatory feeling, and appealing to all that we have been most accustomed to regard as Americans, will the South yet consider it as placing them in that commanding position which they have hitherto occupied in the Union? And if not, will they be content with its assurances, so unquestionably true, that the vast body of the North do not desire to deprive them of any constitutional right?

Mr. Seward's desire is to refrain himself, and restrain the North from irritating the South. He knows well that ours is a government of opinion. He sees the difficulty of attempting force within the lines of a Republic. All good citizens must sympathize with this patriotic effort.

So long as there is a lingering hope that these strange steps of the South may be retraced, let us welcome them in the Union.

But if this effort of Mr. Seward, like all other efforts of reconciliation should fail, then there seems to be but one ultimatum. Mr. Seward himself cautiously alluded to it. The great States of New York and Pennsylvania, by overwhelming majorities, offer their whole resources to the President, to be used in sustaining the laws. The whole power of the Government must be brought to bear against any form of opposition to its sovereignty. Our very salvation lies in it. It is not merely a question about keeping South Carolina or Florida in the Union. *The question concerns the very possibility of the existence of a Republic.* If we dare not shed the blood of a citizen of South Carolina, then Massachusetts may rebel if Congress pass a free trade bill, and California may secede if we refuse to pass the Pacific Railroad bill, and the feeble imbecility called a government, at Washington, could only give advice to these States.

All men agree that some things are dearer than life. A man's religion is: else the blood of the martyrs could never have been the seed of the Church. Liberty, in the noblest part of history, was so regarded. But law, sovereignty, is more essential than all things else. "It springs," says Hooker, "from the bosom of God." It is the very atmosphere of the universe. Without it all things gasp and die. It is the very power that upholds all things. Religion, liberty, commerce, art, science, all fall together into a heap of ruins, without a sovereign power whose strength is the law. Hence the Roman Lictors, in the purest age of that great nation, bore the axe and rods which have become the very emblems of the Republic—swift strength to enforce the law. Hence, in great emergencies, a Dictator was appointed with absolute authority, because the sovereign power must make itself efficient against anarchy at all hazards.

We say, with great seriousness, to our fellow-citizens, that the very essence and idea of a nation tremble now in the balance. If, all conciliation failing, every olive branch spurned, there is not power in this Union to descend upon treason like God's lightning and consume it, then there is nothing to fill the pages of our future history but despotism. For that is the logical end of anarchy.

76. Forbearance Has Ceased to Be a Virtue

(Columbus *Daily Ohio State Journal* [Lincoln], January 15, 1861)

The flippant talk against coercion is worn threadbare. Likewise the pathetic sniveling about shedding fraternal blood. If a mob was at your door, threatening your property with destruction, and panting to slay yourself and family, would you hesitate to enforce one of the first laws of nature—that of self-defence—because in so doing you might possibly shed "fraternal blood"?

The United States Government is assailed by a horde of disunion traitors, and is, or soon will be, compelled to act on the defensive, or surrender at discretion. Which shall we do? If a man attempt to take your life and you kill him, who is responsible for the act? If traitors attempt to destroy the Government, and the Government turn and overwhelm them, can the Government be held responsible for the civil war involved, and the pouring out of blood?

That the General Government cannot coerce a State is the specious doctrine by which the leaders of secession delude their followers into a frenzy of treason. How often must this trick be exposed ere the infatuated mass of seceders become disillusioned? If the whole, or a part of the people of a State, resist United States law and authority, the penalty for the offense must be suffered in an individual, not a corporate, capacity. So, likewise, if the same persons make war against the General Government, the punishment for their treason must be administered to each offender as in cases of other crimes. It is true that a *State* cannot be coerced as it is a mere creature of law—an immaterial existence. Neither can a railroad company be made to expiate an offense through capital punishment. Yet the law reaches its agents—through whose instrumentality murders have been committed—with the death penalty.

However much is to be deplored the want of vigor and promptness in the present administration of the Government, all persons actuated with the sentiments of humanity must rejoice that actual hostilities have been delayed, that every possible opportunity might be given the misguided and frenzied people of the extreme South to retrace their erring steps and become once more loyal, peaceful and law-abiding citizens of our common country. Although we deprecate the evident complicity of our national rulers in the treason of the Cotton States, we sincerely believe that it will yet redound to the advantage of the patriots; for should the latter be compelled to take up arms to save the country from fatal dissolution, the moral strength of their cause will be augmented in the fact that aggression has been wholly on the rebel side.— Had the Administration been thoroughly loyal and patriotic, the danger of impulsive, precipitate action would have naturally been imminent.

But beyond certain limits forbearance ceases to be a virtue. We believe those limits have been reached in the present crisis. The rebels have seized United States fortifications; they have appropriated to their own treasonable use, by force, United States arms and other property; and more daring and criminal than all, they have fired into a vessel bearing the ensign of the Republic! What other nation on the face of the earth, civilized or savage, would permit such high-handed treason to go unpunished? The time is now upon us to test whether we have a government or not; whether a nation of thirty millions of people is at the mercy of a few thousand restless, desperate traitors. Shall we still delay action until there is no government to act, and anarchy reigns supreme? What if duty is hedged about with trying difficulties, and its path lead through blood, should we hesitate at its performance? Though the responsibility be fearful, should a people who boast greatness and power, energy and courage, shrink from meeting it? The government is the recognized power in this land; treason against it has not grown out of oppression; and the government must be sustained, the consequences falling on the heads of the traitors who would pull it down. Now is no time for temporizing or dodging. The State coercion trick will not win. The people understand that the secession action of the cotton States is simple treason, and will treat it accordingly. They fear not to test the strength of the Union. The majority believe it superior to treason[,] superior to slavery. They believe it will have a flourishing existence when all traitors have been subdued, and when the abomination of African slavery will have passed into history. The gleam of sunshine penetrating the thick gloom enveloping the country is the irresistible fact, that the neck of the slave power is broken.

77. Secession and the Revenue Laws

(Philadelphia *Press* [Douglas], January 15, 1861)

There is great danger, at this moment, of some portion of the Northern and Southern minds being led astray by the false use of words. Men will agree that the Union should be preserved at all hazards, but will instantly disagree when they come to discuss the mode of its preservation. The touchstone of this mere logomachy is just this—shall the laws of the United States be enforced, say in South Carolina? It is not a question about *coercing that State*, but about *enforcing the United States laws* in it, so far as those laws need to be enforced.

Can South Carolina, upon any constitutional ground, say that those laws shall not be enforced within her limits? If that be admitted, then the old exploded heresy of nullification of Mr. Calhoun is right, and it follows that General Jackson, and Henry Clay, and Daniel Web-

STER, and EDWARD LIVINGSTON, and all that class of great statesmen, were wrong.

But if they were right (and who will deny that they were?), South Carolina cannot say, upon any constitutional grounds, that the United States law shall not be enforced within her limits. Knowing, right well, how false her old position was, that State to-day takes the new one of her right to secede from the Union, and declares herself to have done so, and that, therefore, the United States laws are inoperative within her limits. The whole North, with a few inconsiderable exceptions, and, we believe, a great majority of the honest people of the Southern States, do not believe in this new-fangled right of secession in any other form than as that ultimate right of rebellion against tyranny, of which man cannot divest himself by any constitutional or social compact.

That is the belief of the people, and the interpretation which they put upon the Constitution of the United States. It is the interpretation, as well, of the whole line of Presidents and of American statesmen from WASHINGTON down to these days. South Carolina denies and defies that interpretation, and proceeds to act on the line of that denial and defiance.

Can we coerce South Carolina to alter her views and opinions? By no means. Let her entertain them if she pleases, so long as she entertains them as mere political abstractions. If it pleases her to think herself out of the Union, let her think so. But she cannot legally resist the execution of the United States laws, or seize the United States property within her limits.

If her citizens will not serve as United States postmasters, the United States cannot compel them to do so. But they must not resist the passage of the United States mail on the post-roads in South Carolina. No law of South Carolina can make such resistance lawful.

If her citizens will not serve as United States judges, or marshals, or jurors, the United States cannot compel them to do so. But they cannot lawfully resist such persons as please to serve in those capacities, nor can any of her laws make such resistance lawful, or such service unlawful.

If her citizens will not serve as collectors of the United States revenue, and in the other fiscal offices, the United States cannot compel them to serve. But they cannot legally resist such persons as do serve. No law of South Carolina can make such resistance lawful.

If she does not choose to send members to Congress or to vote for President, she cannot be compelled to do either thing.

If the forts of the United States upon her sea coast displease her, and she covets the possession of them, she can only lawfully obtain them by an act of Congress ceding them to her. To seize them when ungarrisoned or by force, and to maintain them forcibly against the Federal Government, is levying war upon the United States, and that is high treason by the Constitution.

Now, these are the main points of resistance by South Carolina, and of collision between her and the Union. They are powers of sovereignty, that she has once yielded up, and now claims the right to resume at her own will and pleasure. The United States say that she cannot so resume them. And that is the issue.

It is not the policy of our Government to settle any such questions as these by war. It is not the wish of any considerable body of the people to do it, and that is proved by the intense repose of the North and West and East at this very moment. The idea of marching armies into the South, and subjugating States, has not been seriously entertained. At a time and under circumstances like the present, the central authority of the nation acts purely on the *defensive*. Its object is simply to hold its own, not to grasp at anything beyond. Conquest, subjugation, coercion, war with views of either, are objects of an *offensive* policy. Why should South Carolina be conquered, or subjugated, or coerced? She is not a foreign Power, however much she may think she is. She is still a sister State, and it is still hoped that the land of MARION, and SUMPTER, and PINCKNEY will remain a sister State "to the last syllable of recorded time."

It is not necessary to quarrel with her about the post-roads. If there are obstructions and difficulties placed by her in the way, we can withdraw the United States post-contracts and mail-service, so far as they are within her limits, and let her try, in her sovereign capacity, to furnish postal facilities to her citizens as best she may, while we refuse to recognize her arrangements, or to allow any connection of them with the United States mail-service. The pressure *upon* her own people, and *of* her own people, as well as that from neighboring States, would soon settle that difficulty if the secession mania does not meanwhile spread over nearly the whole South.

We would not enforce the administration of justice just now in the United States Courts in South Carolina. The Judge has resigned. There need be no haste to fill the vacancy. There would be a necessary suspension of business until a successor was appointed, at any rate, and it can make no difference whether that is a suspension of a couple of months, or of as many years. There is no use of seeking collisions at this precise moment of time.

With regard to the customs revenues in South Carolina, it may be

questionable whether the best plan is to send a new collector or to
repeal the acts creating the several ports of entry on the coast of
South Carolina. This latter arrangement would avoid the collision of
two sets of officers, and would prevent trade with foreign countries.
It would be proper, we suppose, to prohibit coast-wise trade to and
from the ports of South Carolina, whilst she is in her present attitude
of armed defiance of the United States. In the enforcement of the
revenue laws, the forts become of primary importance. *Their guns
cover just so much ground as is necessary to enable the United States
to enforce their laws.* The ground on which they stand has been
bought from its private owners and paid for by the United States,
and South Carolina has assented to the cession. Those forts the United
States must maintain. It is not a question of *coercing* South Carolina,
but of *enforcing* the revenue laws. We cannot allow a sovereign State
to nullify the revenue laws—to which point the whole question reverts,
whether the process by which she undertakes to accomplish that end
is called nullification or secession. The practical point, either way, is
—whether the revenue laws of the United States shall or shall not be
enforced at those three ports, Charleston, Beaufort, and Georgetown,
or whether they shall or shall not be made free ports, open to the commerce of the world, with no other restrictions upon it than South
Carolina shall see proper to impose.

If the forts are not maintained by the United States, then the revenue laws can only be enforced by blockade, and that upon a dangerous, nay, an almost impossible cruising ground. It would be a monstrous mistake to allow those forts, that command those ports, to pass
into or remain in the hands of South Carolina. They are the only point
around which there need be any fighting, if the people of South Carolina will fight. And fighting for the possession of those forts, they are
fighting directly against the United States, and are guilty of rebellion
and treason.

Maintaining or retaking those forts, then, is not *coercing* South Carolina. It is but retaining in the hands of the United States, or recapturing,
rightfully, what belongs to them. They are a convenient means of enforcing the revenue laws of the United States, and of protecting South
Carolina and other States from foreign invasion, both of which are high
sovereign duties of the United States. They are, also, a convenient means
of restraining treason and rebellion, which is also a high sovereign
duty.

No one dreams of *coercing South Carolina;* but, on the other hand,
no one dreams of letting her coerce the Union. The forts are to be held

to *enforce the revenue laws,* not to conquer that State. The talk about *coercing a sovereign State* is got up by desperate demagogues to lead the people astray, and divide them upon false issues, whilst treason stalks boldly on to do its hellish work. It is a mere mask of treason.

We would not have a soldier to march upon South Carolina, hardly under any conceivable circumstances. If she chooses to rush upon their forts, upon her own head be the blood of her gallant sons. She must neither be allowed to hold or to take them. That battle can be fought in and around them. That is all of her soil that the United States claims. That belongs to the United States; is essential to their sovereignty, and must be maintained, come what may.

It is *the enforcement of the revenue laws,* NOT *the coercion of the State,* that is the question of the hour. If those laws cannot be enforced, the Union is clearly gone; if they can, it is safe.

78. The Carolina War

(Worcester Palladium [Lincoln], January 16, 1861)

The war has begun between South Carolina and the other states of the Union; and as it has been customary to give every war some peculiar designation we call this the Carolina war; for she was the first to rebel against the common government, and the first to deal the fratricidal blow.

"Quem deus perdit, prius dementat;" whom the gods would destroy, they first make mad. Such was the adage of the Romans; and whatever truth there is in it, will apply as well to the moderns as to the ancients —to states as to individuals. It means nothing more than that men, in the exercise of their free-agency, suffer their passions to pervert and mislead their judgments to such an extent that they hurry themselves on to ruin. That is the point to which South Carolina is running with railroad speed. How far she is conscious of it, we, at this distance, can not decide. It is possible, though by no means probable, that she does not know that she stands to-day like a man upon the crust of a volcano that is boiling and seething beneath his feet, and ready in a moment to belch forth fire and death.

South Carolina has fired the first gun at the Union of the states. The details of this portion of her rebellion may be found in another column of this paper. The record has one redeeming feature; and that is the wisdom as well as bravery of Major Anderson. And it forces upon us the conviction that if, two months ago, the government at Washington had displayed a tithe of Anderson's patriotism and high resolve, South

Carolina, in all probability, would have been checked in this her career of unmitigated madness and folly. But Mr. Buchanan's cabinet has been a nest of nullifiers, who have been quietly giving events this direction while they have kept his attention engrossed with the minor details of government.

The crisis has at last come. It must be met. A trial is now to be made, *whether there is any strength in our national government.* Now is the time in which the government is to be maintained in all the vigor of its supremacy, or fall in weakness and contempt. And the first thing to be done is for *South Carolina to humble herself, or be humbled!* If she will do it herself, she will save herself from many a scalding tear and many a sharp anguish. There is no other alternative. The Union must maintain its supremacy, or be forever contemptible in the sight of all other nations—to be jeered at by all, and insulted with impunity. Bitter, therefore, as is the necessity, South Carolina must be brought back to her loyalty to the Union.

1. There are many reasons why the other states should exercise the virtue of forbearance. Of all wars, *civil war* is most to be avoided. It is full of evils, full of embarrassments, and fraught with consequences which every sane man must deprecate. These Carolinians have been up to this time our brothers and friends. Innumerable have been the ties, the relations, that have existed between us of the north and them of the south;—ties of blood relation, of early and long-continued patriotism, of historic associations, cemented on the battle-fields of the revolution, as well as the many ties which bind together peoples who live in different climes, and have with each other the connections which commerce creates. These relations have subsisted too long between Carolina and the northern states to be broken for any slight or trivial causes.

If South Carolina wished to go out of the Union, she had no occasion to insult that Union until she had given ample opportunity to determine the question, whether *peaceable secession* is a possibility. She has precluded us from that consideration. She has precipitated us into this rash collision of two governments, with an apparent recklessness of consequences to herself; thus rendering it a matter of grave doubt whether forbearance upon the part of the other states can be further extended.

2. South Carolina is governed by a mobocracy, notwithstanding there are, among the men who give direction to events there, some who have been prominent at Washington and elsewhere. We have the best of reasons for believing that there is a conservative spirit among the excited elements of South Carolina, that is chained down by the turbulence of

the mob;—families who adopt the Napoleonic creed that "peace is the first of necessities," but whose pacific sentiments find no room for utterance. Then there is the *negro element;* and God only knows what that element would accomplish, should it sweep over the land in the form of an ungovernable insurrection. It might annihilate family after family, and desolate many a plantation.

3. South Carolina has committed herself to this rebellion against the national government upon a mere bundle of abstractions, and without provocation or apology. We call her REASONS for her course the merest *abstractions* that ever converted sane men into lunatics. What is it to the people of South Carolina, as the people of a state, whether slavery goes, or does not go, into the territories of the Union? Everything it may possibly be to her *politicians,* but nothing, absolutely nothing, to her planters, her poor whites, and her enslaved blacks. She has no negroes to sell; and, if she had, the sending them out to cultivate other lands, and raise crops like her own in other localities, would add nothing to her wealth.

We doubt not that there are multitudes who believe themselves right, and have not much chance to outgrow the idea that *they are all right, and we of the free states are all wrong.* They have grown up in the midst of slavery, and have never yet reached the conclusion that there is anything wrong in its nature. It gives them the lands they cultivate—the houses they live in—the cotton, rice, &c. their lands produce—the clothes they wear—the luxuries, the leisure, the abstinence from toil, and the means of cultivation and refinement they enjoy; and those are ideas which are not readily touched by the hand of reform.

4. The Carolinians do not comprehend northern institutions, sentiment, and life; if they did they would have seen that there is too great a disparity between their condition and ours to warrant the course they are taking. They have been *beaten in an election;* and that is all that the iron pen of impartial history can record as their justification. Had the south gone in for *Douglas,* and given him the entire vote of the slave states, she would have stood an equal chance to have beaten the republicans. So that history must record also the truth, that possibly the south was beaten in the election *because she could not dictate the nomination.*

5. The republican party is not yet in power. It has not done the first thing in the way of government; and the South Carolinians have assailed the government while there is *a president of her own choice at the head of it.* Her Declaration of Independence must announce to the world that fact, or it will be a falsehood. It must announce also that

she begun [sic] this rebellion without waiting for the inauguration of a new president—without waiting to see what would be his appointments, whether they would be from both sections of the Union, or only from one section—and without waiting for the first act of his administration, or any authoritative exposition of the policy he intends to pursue.

6. South Carolina has rushed into this war upon false representations of the people of the northern states. They have been made to believe that republicanism is but abolitionism in the blow, and just ready to run up to seed; that John Brown was an exponent of the ideas of the great body of the republican party of the free states; and that his raid into Virginia was by the instigation of leading republicans, and carried forward by their money. They have been made to believe also that we live less by our own industry than by the profits we derive from their products; and that our thrift is all a deduction from their prosperity.

They ask of us what we can not give. They ask us to surrender our convictions of what is right, and of the duties we owe to ourselves and to the race, here and elsewhere, now and hereafter. If they had the disposition to know, they might learn, what they do not know, and seem to care not to learn, that republicanism is not abolitionism; that the republicans, as a party, do not go a step beyond the verge of their platform; and that where their principles halt, their organization halts likewise.

7. But the leaders in this rebellion manifestly care nothing for the republican party, its principles, or its policy. Disunion is no new idea or project with them. For many years they have been waiting a pretext for cutting adrift from the free states, and they have found it in the republican victory, which takes the control of the government from the hands of the minority, and gives it to the majority of the people. Evidently they have become dissatisfied with republican institutions, and believe in the necessity for new restraints upon the tendencies of the popular mind and heart; restraints which they can not put in force while they are in affiliation with the free north, nor until they have the power alone to shape their destinies.

This war they have entered upon for the realization of some chimerical dream. As we have already said, in this article, *the trial has got to be made now of the strength of our government.* Carolina is in rebellion, and has insulted our national flag and our national honor. What we have, we shall keep. What she wants, she will not get. But, instead thereof, she will get the stern hardships, the keen sufferings, the bitter deprivations, the fire and blood of civil war, and, it may be, of a servile war the recital of which will make the ears of unborn generations tingle with horror. South Carolina and other states that are rushing madly into a career of insane opposition to the national government, have only to *stop where they are,* to save themselves from the awful abyss into which they are plunging; for he must be blind to the power there is in the free states who can not foresee that Mr. LINCOLN, if he lives, is sure to be inaugurated, and that the supremacy of the Union will be maintained at whatever cost.

79. THE ANTI-COERCION DELUSION

(Springfield (Mass.) *Daily Republican* [Lincoln], February 9, 1861)

That portion of the northern democratic leaders who are attempting to make an "anti-coercion" issue with the republicans are only repeating in a more flagitious form the mischief they did during the presidential campaign. The strength and virulence of the disunion movement is due in no small degree, as all now see, to their perverse misrepresentations of the principles and designs of the republican party. The great mass of the southern people undoubtedly believe that the incoming administration intend to assail slavery in the slave states, and it is this belief that has caused the intense feeling and precipitate action for secession. We speak of the people of the South; the leaders know how utterly false is this opinion. The northern leaders of the democratic and Union parties are responsible for this mischief, for they have had the ear of the South, and have filled it continually with these malign falsehoods. Now they are doing still worse. While pretending to be patriotically anxious to save the Union, and calling lustily on the republicans to sacrifice party to country, they are repeating the same game of falsehood and fraud in an infinitely more injurious form. They now accuse the republicans of a design to coerce the South, to invade and subdue the seceding states, to desolate them with the horrors of civil war; and the most frightful pictures are drawn of the punishments the republicans are preparing for the southern people. What is the natural effect of these falsehoods? There can be no question on this point. Their effect is already seen in the increased determination of the seceding states to resist to the last, and in the avowed purpose of the other southern states to defend them against "coercion." It avails nothing that coercion is disavowed; democratic papers and conventions and sham Union meetings continue to repeat the alarming outcry. They seem bent upon exasperating the South to uncontrollable phrensy, as if to precipitate the terrible evils they profess to deprecate. Their eager-

ness to break down the republican party by any available means completely overrides their patriotism, and under pretense of a desire for
peace and Union they are pursuing the very course to destroy both. It
is no injustice to these men to say that they are in effect the worst
enemies of the Union and of the South, and that they are doing more
by their false appeals for peace and conciliation to prevent reconciliation and to bring war than any class of men in the South have power
to do.

The fact is, and those who assume to be especial friends of the South
in the free states should assure the South of it, that what they mean by
"coercion" is proposed by nobody and would be sustained by nobody
at the North. The idea that the free states intend to march armies into
the seceding states to force their return to loyalty seems too monstrous
for serious denial, and yet this is precisely the thing now declared by the
partizan Unionists and the democratic leaders to be the purpose of the
republicans and of the incoming administration. What is the plain
truth in the matter? The republicans deny the right of a state to secede
from the Union, and do not admit that the declaration of a majority
of the people of any state can separate it from the Union, and there are
so few of any party holding the opposite doctrine that this may be
set down as the unanimous opinion of all parties in the free states while
it is equally the opinion of the most conservative and patriotic portion
of the South, as the late bold and admirable speeches of southern members of Congress plainly indicate. On this basis there can be little room
for difference of opinion as to the duty of the general government. While
it cannot for a moment admit that any state is out of the Union, it cannot compel any state to accept the advantages offered to it by the Union.
A state may refuse to be represented in Congress, may prevent the administration of justice by the federal courts, and may give up its mail
facilities, or so obstruct them that the government will be compelled
to discontinue them. If the state goes further and refuses to let the
government collect the revenue on imports, as prescribed by law, then
the collections may be made by government vessels stationed at the
ports, or the ports may be closed altogether. And this is all the government can do. It involves not a single act of war, or even an indication
of hostility, and there never can be war while the government adheres
rigidly to this policy, to which it is constitutionally bound. If the rebels
attack the government officers while peaceably fulfilling their duties,
they must be resisted. But resistance to attack is not "coercion;" much
less is it invasion or civil war. If the rebels invade Washington and Gen.
Scott repels them, it will not be coercion but defense. Whatever co-

ercion there is will be on the part of the rebels themselves, as it has been thus far in the unhappy controversy. And this is absolutely the whole matter—the defense of the government against warlike assault by armed rebels—over which the South and its pretended friends at the North are raising so great a clamor.

Now what do these enemies of coercion propose to do? Let us have their plan. Would they let the seceding states collect the revenue? But the constitution forbids that; and besides the revenue laws must be enforced in all the states, or they are of value nowhere. Would they have Gen. Scott surrender Washington and the national archives, if Gov. Wise brings up his regiment of Minute Men to bombard it, rather than shed "fraternal blood" in its defense? But it is useless to discuss this subject. Every man of sense must see, and every honest man of whatever party will admit, that there is no course for the general government but to defend itself from attack, and to keep the Union unbroken. We are compelled to doubt both the honesty and the patriotism of the men who are now attempting to get up the false and fallacious anti-coercion issue. It is impossible to believe that they are so stupid as not to see that they are giving direct aid and comfort to treason and counteracting the efforts made to preserve the Union. Besides, it seems to be forgotten, when talking of secession and the South, that there is still a party at the South loyal to the Union. The president has been appealed to by Union men in the seceding states, asking him if no protection can be hoped for by those who still wish to remain citizens of the United States. There is in all the seceding states, except South Carolina, a large and respectable minority, in some of them possibly a majority, who desire still to remain in the Union. The general government has most sacred duties to perform towards these loyal citizens, and though it cannot enter the disaffected states to repress rebellion by force, it is bound to hold the Union together until the popular phrensy and delusion, which constitute the power of secession, subside, and the loyalty and good sense of the southern people have an opportunity to make themselves manifest. It will be time enough to talk about permitting peaceable secession when it is demonstrated that the South cannot recover itself. And if separation must come at last, let it not be by war of the seceding states upon the Union, such as the secessionists have already inaugurated, but by the consent of the states represented in general convention, and by deliberate and solemn act of the whole people, so that the two confederacies may begin at peace and with mutual guarantees for its preservation.

80. [The Right of Coercion]

(Hartford Daily Courant [Lincoln], February 11, 1861)

One of the bug-bears that the Secessionists have created for the purpose of frightening the timid, is that of Coercion. It is a magic word, but unfortunately its magic applies only to the Federal Government. You cannot *coerce* a Sovereign State, say these State Right Abstractionists. Is that so? Is our Government so powerless against domestic traitors? Are its hands so tied that it cannot protect its own property against the lawless seizures of State authority? If so, it is a glaring, gross defect in our Constitution. It is worth nothing as a Government, unless there is some idea of *force* in its very construction. To "govern" means to "coerce." It is involved in the very idea of Government. If such things have been done in South Carolina, under the false but specious plea of State Sovereignty, and the General Government must sit idly and tamely by without reaching out its powerful hand to protect or to punish, what is the Government worth? Its authority is a mere farce, not worth the paper on which the Constitution was engrossed.

Before the formation of the Constitution, each State was an independent community, subject only to its own laws. When Great Britain signed the declaration of our independence and dissolved the colonial condition, it left every State a distinct sovereignty. By assenting to the Constitution of 1788, *each State gave up that sovereignty.* She surrendered by that vote, absolutely and forever, that right. Whatever was not thus formally given up by the acceptance of the Constitution was retained by the State, such as the internal management of her domestic affairs. The vote to accept the Constitution was a final renunciation of independent sovereignty, which of course involves the right of secession, and the rights of separate action involved in secession. By this Constitution the Federal Government became The Sovereign with all the rights of restraint and coercion which all Governments necessarily possess.

How idle then this talk about Coercion. If a State rebels, there must be a *right* in Government to punish the individuals engaged in that rebellion. Without that power, federal authority is a farce, and the existing government will soon terminate in anarchy. The liberty of anarchy cannot be allowed in any community. Better, far better, would it be to live under a despotism.

But you cannot *coerce* a State. To be sure, a State is but an abstraction. It has no real existence, beyond the tangible, *accountable* existence of the individuals that compose it. The individual rebel is the accountable being which requires the coercion, and on whom we hope to see it exercised. We prefer the tyrannical exercise of the authority of Government, to the anarchy which the exercised right of secession would produce. GOVERNMENT MUST HAVE POWER. There must be "power" lodged somewhere. The sovereign States now composing this Union, by their solemn votes, voluntarily and deliberately gave this power to the Federal authority. They and their descendants are bound by this contract forever. Nothing but the unanimous consent of all the contracting parties can release any one from this binding obligation.

81. THE INCOMING ADMINISTRATION

(Springfield *Daily Illinois State Journal* [Lincoln], February 13, 1861)

We are not ignorant of the fact that we occupy a responsible position. Living in the town where Mr. LINCOLN has resided for a quarter of a century—having been in almost daily contact with him for years past —sympathising with him and supporting him politically, it is but natural that the country should conclude that we know something of, and reflect his sentiments in our columns. We have no disposition to deny that we are familiar with the views of the President elect, but we solemnly affirm that he has not dictated a line that has appeared in this paper since his election, touching political affairs. He is not responsible for what we say, but when we assert anything positively respecting him or his intentions we know whereof we affirm. We should be false to duty did we not urge Republicans to stand unflinchingly by the principles on which they elected Mr. Lincoln to the Presidency. We *know* that HE will stand by them to the last. We can afford to be just and generous, but we cannot afford to surrender the highest and holiest principle that ever animated man in political or martial contest. Mr. LINCOLN is now speeding on his way to Washington—in a few days, if he lives, his sentiments, his policy and his objects will be known to the world. They will command the admiration and support of all good men, in this and in other lands. His heart takes in his whole country— for that country he will speak, act, and, if necessary, lay down his life. Let no friend of humanity, Freedom, the Union, the Constitution and all the high interests of our country even doubt, for one moment, the firmness of ABRAHAM LINCOLN in support of them all. He regards the Republican cause as a just one, and he will never desert it. Before the blast of treason a few party leaders may bend and be swept away, but such will not be the act or the fate of the brave, true, liberty-loving President of our choice. Broken by the power of slavery and the treachery of friends, he may be, but he will never bow to either. From our knowledge of the man, we boldly assert that Mr. Lincoln will plainly declare, in his inaugural address, his unfaultering devotion to Republican principles. He will take pains, we doubt not, in an address likely to have general publication, to explain just what Republican principles are. When he does this, the South will at once see how outrageously he and the Republican party have been belied. They will see that no aggression upon their rights is contemplated, but that every constitutional right of every section will be protected to the full extent of the power of the Administration. Mr. Lincoln believes that the People of the United States can alter or abolish their present system of Government if they desire to do so. He will not stand in their way. If the people desire to amend the Constitution, he will interpose no obstacle in the way of a consummation of their wishes. But while the Constitution stands as it is, the supreme law of the land, he will regard it as such, and will enforce the laws made in pursuance of it, in obedience of his oath of office. He cannot do less, nor is it his disposition to do less. He will have an oath registered in Heaven to perform the duties assigned him by the Constitution of his country. HE WILL PERFORM THOSE DUTIES AT EVERY HAZARD. He will insist upon the restoration to the Government [of] all forts, arsenals, custom houses, post-offices, mints, revenue cutters and other national property wrongfully withheld, AND HE WILL HAVE THEM, unless, in some constitutional way, the title of the United States Government in such property shall be vested in another party or parties. He will use all the power vested in him by the Constitution to enforce the laws of Congress. *This is his plain constitutional duty,* and every man who loves our Government, will stand by him in the discharge of it, regardless of section or party.

We have asked Republicans to stand firmly by their principles. Loving our country—the only free land on earth—we could not do less. We have asked that those principles should not be deserted—not to subserve partisan ends, not to humble political foes, but because we believe that upon the triumph of those principles depends everything that is dear to freemen in this land and throughout the world.

> "Nothing great is lightly won,
> Nothing won is lost. "

We have no idea that Freedom is to assert her sway in our country without a struggle, but we are prepared and willing to make that struggle. We never have, nor do we now, despair of the Republic. Influenced by the madness that rules the hour, men may desert the holiest cause of earth—States may resolve themselves out of a Union that their people, with rare exceptions, love—but reason will return, and, returning, will lead misguided States and men back to the fold of duty. Through the thick gloom that enshrouds the present hour our faith beholds the glorious sunlight of the future.—We believe that ABRAHAM LINCOLN, whatever may be the troubles that beset his pathway now, will perform his whole duty to his country and the cause of which he is the representative, and, in 1864, deliver up to his successor the reins of Government over a people reunited, prosperous and happy.

82. WHAT IS COERCION?

(Cincinnati *Daily Times* [Bell], February 14, 1861)

The penalty is the strength of the law, and there can be, of course, no government without the power to coerce. The only question, indeed, relates to the mode and extent of the exercise of this power. Absolute sovereignty is one of the attributes of God Himself, and of Him alone, but even this has been sacreligiously [*sic*] stolen by Kings, and Emperors, and Presidents. In a mere human sense, an essential element of *all* government is tyranny. The patriarchal system was based upon absolute despotism. The Egyptian and Assyrian governments were of the same nature. The aristocracies were only systems which contemplated ten or twenty despots, instead of one. A pure democracy never existed, except in the imaginations of impracticable men.

Governments, then, have their origin in the necessities of the world; they are instituted for the good of mankind, and ought not to exist an hour longer than they fulfill the ends for which they are designed. To talk of their being "imprescriptible," is simply absurd; the whole doctrine of "vested rights" has been exploded by the common sense of the world and the march of intelligence. The Government instituted by the Almighty Himself was adapted to the age of its enunciation, from the Mount of Sinai, but even *this* failed to meet the wants of later centuries. From age to age the world has progressed; the synthetic philosophy of the olden time disappeared as a cloud before the clear sunlight of experience.

It is the first duty of human legislators to accommodate their systems to a world which is undergoing an uninterrupted change. MOSES, and LYCURGUS, and SOLON, did, perhaps, the best they could for the eras in which they lived, but they could not look down the stream of time, and provide for the necessities of communities more capable of self-government than their own.

The true theory, then, is to establish, if possible, a government not subject to be overthrown by sudden political shocks, but which will change and adapt itself to the gradual progress of enlightenment and the general elevation of humanity. Our fathers, who formed the Constitution of the United States were only human beings, it is true, but then they were incomparably above the average of mankind; they were the prophets and seers to whom

> "The sunset of life gave mystical lore,
> And coming events cast their shadows before."

With eyes like those which enabled DANIEL to behold the golden, silver, brazen and iron systems in their regular order, they lifted the veil of futurity, and though they could not see all the way down to a political Millennium, they grasped the essential requirements of long ages which were to succeed them.

They established, not a mere confederation of independent communities, but one great, indivisable [sic] nation. Their clear vision embraced the tremendous fact that, from the necessity of the case, there could not be, at least for many centuries, more than one great power whose headquarters should be on this continent, and they, therefore, contemplated, in the beginning, and as the necessary basis, A GOVERNMENT COMPOSED OF STATES WHICH SHOULD SURRENDER EACH THE ESSENTIAL ELEMENTS OF A COMPLETE NATIONALITY.

Not one step could be taken until Virginia, South Carolina, and each of the other States that had fought the battles of the Revolution, consented to part with the chief incidents of absolute sovereignty. The power to contract alliances, enter into treaties for peace, declare war, coin money, maintain armies and navies, etc., was absolutely yielded by each member of the old Confederation to the Government of the United States.

In pursuance of the plan adopted by the framers of the Constitution, Congress proceeded at once to establish forts, lighthouses, arsenals, mints, vessels of war, etc., for the protection of the lives, the liberty, and the property of the people of the United States. Where land and materials were not furnished gratuitously by the States or by individuals, *it was* [sic] *purchased and paid for by Congress, and, in* every instance became the *absolute property* of the General Government. Such was the case with Forts Sumter and Pensacola, and the mint at New Orleans.

A vast amount of this property has been seized by bands of armed men, acting under the direction of temporary political juntos which profess to represent the "sovereign nations" of South Carolina, Florida, Georgia, Alabama and Louisiana. What we have insisted is, that the property which has been taken shall be returned to its legitimate owners, and that the forts, custom-houses, mints, which we still retain shall be held by force and arms [sic]. For recommending this policy, we are termed by shallow-brained men "coercionists." How few that use this word know what they are talking about!

The same principle would deny a man the privilege of defending his house, and barn, and furniture against highwaymen! The same principle would deny him the right to raise his rifle in defense of his wife and children! The same principle would not permit him to resist the assaults of armed men in a lonely alley, at midnight! The idea is too ridiculous and too cowardly to be entertained for a moment.

What is it to "coerce?" The dictionary defines it to be to assault, to attack, to employ a positive or outward agency, whether that agency be of a moral or physical character. Who, then, are the "coercionists?" Charleston "coerced" Castle Pinckney, Fort Moultrie, the Custom House, and the "Star of the West;" she only refrained from "coercing" Fort Sumter, because she was not able to assault that water-bound Gibraltar. Florida, Georgia, Alabama and Louisiana, followed in the illustrious steps of Charleston.

It matters little that the Cotton States propose to *buy* the property they have illegitimately grasped. Civilized men are not accustomed to take forcible possession of their neighbors' stores and dwelling houses —whether they be occupied, as in Pensacola fortress, or empty, as was Fort Moultrie—and then commence negotiations for purchasing, or renting.

Our esteemed friends, SHERLOCK and VATTIER, would be rather surprised if we were to attack their private dwellings, yet they would not be an iota *less* surprised if we were to assist a body of armed men, under the direction of Gov. DENNISON, in assault upon the Custom House and Post Office of Cincinnati.

In both cases we should be called *coercionists;* yet, we would be doing precisely what Charleston did when she *demanded* money of her citizens; and what New Orleans did when she seized the United States Mint.

If to defend, by the use of the army and navy, the property of the General Government, and the honor of the American flag, on the sea and on the land, be to *"coerce,"* we acknowledge we are coercionists.

83. THE SECESSION LABYRINTH

(Peoria Daily Transcript [Lincoln], February 22, 1861)

When men get into a difficulty the great question is to get out. The people of the United States are in the midst of a great national difficulty. Let us cast aside the question how we came in it, who is to blame in the matter, and address ourselves to the question how we shall get out. If our dwelling were on fire we would not spend our time running about to ascertain through whose culpability or carelessness it occurred, but we would go at once to work to quell the conflagration.

Several methods have been proposed for the settlement of our national troubles, which we propose now to consider. They are, 1st. Compromise, 2d, Peaceable Separation, 3d, Masterly Inactivity, 4th, Enforcement of the Laws.

The first method, that of compromise in the manner proposed in Congress (amendment to the Constitution of the United States) is, in the present condition of the country, wholly out of the question. We need not discuss whether such a course is proper or improper. It is sufficient that it is impossible. The Constitution of the United States requires the concurrence of three-fourths of the States to give force and vitality to any amendment. To do this, twenty-six States must concur. Seven have left the Union and will not vote. At least a half dozen of the remaining States will vote down any amendment that may be proposed. The border States will vote them down if they do not concede their demands, and certain Northern States will vote them down if they do. Any compromise not incorporated into the Constitution will not be accepted by the South. Any compromise not incorporated into the Constitution in the manner proposed by that instrument will not be accepted by the North. To incorporate amendments in the manner provided we have shown to be impossible, and that puts an end to the first method.

Peaceable separation is proposed by those who perceive that compromise is impolitic or impossible, and who hope by it to avoid war. But peaceable separation leads as surely to war as night follows day. The United States would not allow Great Britain, France, Russia, nor all Europe combined, to maltreat citizens as our citizens are maltreated daily at the South, without war.—Maritime and border disputes would arise which would plunge us into strife before six months had passed over the heads of the two confederacies. Escape of slaves and attempted recapture and reprisals would bring the people to blows without any action of the two governments. We fought Great Britain in 1812 for one half the provocation that would be given us. No dread of civil war would stay our hands. The Southern Confederacy would be a foreign nation. We would not have to fight it for once only, but unless we absolutely conquored [*sic*] it, we should have to fight it forever. It would be hostile in interests, hostile in institutions, hostile in everything.

The third method is that of "masterly inactivity," the policy inaugurated by our present imbecile executive. Such a course leads to national debasement, anarchy and ruin. It is a confession that no power exists in the government for the enforcement of the laws, or that we are too cowardly to enforce them. Our revenue would be cut off, for if the South refuse to pay duties the North will refuse likewise. We could not raise money by taxation, for we can no more collect taxes than we can collect revenue.

The fourth method is enforcement of the laws. This is the only method that indicates the least chance of success. People say we have no right to coerce a State. We say a State has no right to contravene the Constitution. The Constitution of the United States, is in certain particulars supreme, and is clothed with full power to enforce those particulars. Every law passed by a State or the people of a State, in contravention of the Constitution is null and void. Any attempt to enforce those pretended laws is without legal sanction, and in as much a crime to be punished as counterfeiting, smuggling, and piracy. The question is,—Is secession right or wrong, lawful or unlawful? If not right and lawful, it ought to be put down. If we attempt to put it down, what are the chances of success? It will be the government against a faction. It will be a nation of seventy years['] growth, fighting for the supremacy of the principles which brought it into being, against a wicked combination to defeat those principles. It will be might and right against weakness and wickedness. It will be the memory of the heroes of the revolution, against the dogmas of Calhoun, the thievings of Floyd, and perjuries of those who plotted to overturn the Constitution while their oaths to support it were yet warm on their lips. It will be a people with a navy against a people without a navy. It will be a people with the sympathy of the civilized world in its favor, against a people without that sympathy. It will be a people connected by treaties with other governments, against a people cut off from all communication with the rest of mankind. It will be numbers against numbers as four to one, and that one hampered by a servile population ready, it knows not how soon, to rise and cut its throat. It will be wealth ready to be poured into the lap of the Government, against oppressive taxation and forced loans. It will be all the holy traditions[,] treasured songs, brave speeches and glories of the past, the Declaration of Independence, the love of freedom, the hopes of the future, the preservation of free speech and a free press, against the eruption of a plague spot, and the rebellion of a petty oligarchy who would "rather reign in hell than serve in Heaven." Under these circumstances who doubts our success? We have the right and the might, and there is no such word as fail.

84. A Firm Position

(Miners' Journal, and Pottsville (Pa.) *General Advertiser* [Lincoln], February 23, 1861)

Notwithstanding the changes in the aspect of the Southern rebellion have been since its commencement, as numerous as those of the kaleidoscope, rendering any definite opinion of the result, almost impossible; yet it now seems conclusive that secession in word though it be, is confined to the States that have rushed into it, rashly and inconsiderately. The votes of the people of the Border States, decide that they will have nothing to do with the perilous business in which South Carolina and the other seceding States are engaged. One of the greatest evils which has arisen from this difficulty, and [from] the attendant want of firmness on the part of Mr. Buchanan's Administration, is the estimation placed upon our Government by Foreign Powers. Had he acted with firmness in the first place, and discharged his duty, rebellion would have been crushed, and our strength been assured.

In glancing at the present position of the country, and the means which must be adopted to bring it back to the position from which it receded through want of firmness on the part of the President, it is manifest that the only plan to adopt is the one which unfortunately, was neglected at the outset. Certain States are found in open rebellion, and proclaiming that they will not submit to the laws until they have received all they demand.—Many Unionists and Democrats say that what all these States demand should be yielded. They say that everything should be conceded ere the Union should be dissolved. On the other hand, the Republicans take a bolder and a better course. They say that as none of the just rights of any State have been infringed, those States who are in open rebellion have no right to dictate the terms upon which they will resume their allegiance. They say that this Government is not one depending for its existence upon the will of any one State, and that when a State thinks her rights invaded she must seek redress by lawful means. They say that this Government must be preserved, and that the way to preserve it is to be firm—to show rebels that they must return to their duty, and that no sacrifice of principle will be made to them. The idea of sacrificing any principle to preserve a Government, which is to be broken up whenever a State cho[o]ses to think that she is aggrieved, is simply ridiculous. If this Government be what the Secessionists claim that it is, then the sooner we change it the better. The Republicans believe, however, that our Government is all that is needed, and that whatever it has seemed to lack in strength, has been only an apparent weakness, resulting from a want of firmness in those who administered it. They propose to restore it to its normal condition, merely by enforcing the Constitution and the laws. Such a course is evidently the only one by which rebellion can be put down, and our Government proved to be what its founders intended it should be.

It seems that the views of the Republicans are somewhat similar to those entertained by those abroad who are interested in this country. In a letter to a gentleman in Boston, Mr. Peabody, the London banker, says that the credit of this Government is now on trial in Europe, and that concessions to rebels, in the purchasing of the permission to peacefully inaugurate the President-elect, would give that credit a fearful blow—that people there will not trust a Government which, when its foundations are attacked, instead of upholding law and order, treats with the traitors.

Now, the London *Times* may proclaim that this Federation has been shipwrecked, and the President of the so-called Southern Confederacy may add one hundred speeches to the twenty-five he has already made, declaring that the time for all compromise has passed, that Southern independence must be preserved, and that no propositions for reconstructing the Union be entertained; but notwithstanding all this, rebels will be brought to their senses, and our Government, proved to be full as strong as is necessary. Every day only gives proof that the vaunted vigor of the new Confederation is rapidly declining. Time effects wonderful cures, and in the present case of Secession, it is already doing its work. Sober, second thought is very apt to lead to a business view of affairs. Secession, theoretically, is no doubt very promising. It leads to thoughts of future greatness, and of the acquisition of immense territory. Secession, practically, is evidently very unprofitable, so much so that the seceding States are yet unwilling to yield up the practical benefits of Union. Facts show, too, that secession is not the desire of the majority of the South, and when the madness of the Secessionists is fully spent, the voice of the Unionists will be fairly heard. Had Mr.

Buchanan dealt promptly and firmly with that miserable little piece of territory denominated South Carolina, the conservative portion of the South would have been able to exert its influence. The people of that State need strait-jackets in the shape of blockaded ports and the stoppage of the mails. They already kick in their new harness. Nothing but firmness on the part of the Federal Government can restore their reason. This firmness may be looked for after the fourth of next month. When the people of the Southern Confederacy find that there is still some firmness and some strength in the Federal Government, they will not be long in discovering how silly a game they have played.—Mr. Davis will then be compelled to seek something more profitable than making treasonable speeches, and constructing Cabinets.

VI

CONCILIATION AND COMPROMISE

85. COERCION OR CONCILIATION?

(New York Herald [Breckinridge], December 24, 1860)

The republican journals of the North are daily becoming more and more bitter in the tone of their belligerent manifesto[e]s, and in their vituperative advocacy of the extremest measures, to reduce the slave States to submission to the doctrines laid down in the Chicago platform. Appeal to the inexorable logic of grooved cannon, Sharpe's rifles and the bayonet takes the place of reflection and argument now, just as rant, abuse, calumny and diatribe did that of truth and facts while they were arousing their readers to that pitch of anti-slavery excitement which has produced the present crisis. They demand that Mr. Lincoln shall inaugurate his administration with blockades, bombardments and invasion, as flippantly and impudently as though the welfare of the country could be promoted by conformity to such diabolical fancies. They decree that the South shall be "put down," as glibly as if fifteen States were a vagrant to be arrested by the first policeman. With quasi-authoritative language, they pretend to foreshadow the policy of the incoming administration, as substituting the blood red flag of civil war for the stars and stripes which float over the Capitol, and confidently predict that the "irrepressible conflict" will be carried out with a ruthless barbarity which John Brown himself would have hesitated to sanction.

The transparent motive of so much furious clamor on the part of the republican press is to drive Mr. Buchanan into initiating aggressive measures against South Carolina, and any other States that may secede, in order that he and his government may hereafter be chargeable with a responsibility which they are afraid Mr. Lincoln may have sense enough to shrink from incurring. One day the President is called an "idiot;" another we are assured that he is "insane," and, again, that he is a "traitor," "sold out to the South," because he will neither send more troops to Fort Moultrie nor encircle Charleston harbor with a naval cordon of steamships and revenue cutters. The choicest billingsgate is resorted to, with most refreshing disregard of truth, knowledge and propriety, in denouncing his repugnance to bloodshed and endeavoring to hound him on to acts of violence. It would harmonize with abolitionist plans to the letter were Mr. Buchanan to suffer himself to be moved or intimidated by such scurrilous boistering. Were he to yield one jot to the suggestions of his adversaries, they would be the first to turn upon him the full vials of popular indignation, and to represent the calamities which would thenceforth befal the country as an unwelcome legacy bequeathed by him to a successor, willing but unable to evade or avert them.

The forbearance which marks the course of the administration in the peculiar and trying emergency to which abolitionist fanaticism has reduced it is eminently wise and prudent. Its pacific attitude has involved the sacrifice of no principle, and its patriotism has been equally displayed in what it has done and in what it has left undone. It has refused to recognise the right of a State to secede, though it has not denied its revolutionary power to do so. While maintaining, what is undeniable, that no power to coerce a State is delegated by the constitution to either the President or to Congress, it has as strenuously asserted that individual delinquents may, if expedient, be reached and punished by the strong arm of the central government, through its federal courts. The attempt to coerce a State by military force would, as declared by Mr. Madison, be an act of war—a virtual recognition of its separate independence, and tantamount to a dissolution of the Union. Such an act of folly will never be committed by Mr. Buchanan. The States belong together. Their reserved rights, individual constitutions, and different social institutions, are, each and all, a part of a common bond, sheltered by the constitution, entitled, in their divergencies, to mutual respect and protection, and he will not complete the work of destruction which fanaticism and sectionalism have begun. With the treason of individuals, if it should ever come to any overt act, he might be strictly entitled, perhaps, to pursue a more rigorous method; but even then it will be his duty to consider the circumstances of the case, and to weigh, in the merciful side of the scale, the injuries and provocations which have wrought up the Southern masses into their present state of frenzy. Goaded to insanity by the persevering aggressions of over a quarter of a century, which have culminated in the election of a chief magistrate of the confederation upon the avowed hostile, sectional principle of an "irrepressible conflict between opposing and enduring forces, through which the United States must become entirely a slaveholding nation or entirely a free labor nation," the insane effervescences of feeling which are beheld in the slave States should be regarded with paternal and affectionate concern, and not with the stern and severe front of inexorable justice. The skill of the physician and the kindness of the nurse are the appliances through which the South must be redeemed from its present extravagances. The administration is acting faithfully to its duty, faithfully to the law, in accordance with the soundest principles of policy and the wishes of the vast majority of conservative minds in the country, in holding in abhorrence the harsh and outrageous recommendations of the organs of republican opinion in the North.

Ten weeks will bring us to the time when Mr. Buchanan will resign his incumbency of the Presidential chair to his successor. In the meanwhile, all that can be accomplished by peaceful, persuasive and constitutional means will be done to rescue the country from impending evil, and pilot the ship of State from the midst of the breakers that surround it. After that period the responsibility of the future will pass into the hands of Mr. Lincoln. It is to be hoped that he, too, will comprehend the signification of the portentous events which are hurrying the nation with headlong speed towards a precipice, and employ the influence which timely concession may have in staying the progress of destruction. We have frequently had occasion to show of late that the position he occupies is more enviably free from ties and embarrassments than that of any President who has ever preceded him. The sentiment of three-fourths of the people is conservative, and but a small minority at the North are in favor of those violent measures for checking excitement and disorder at the South which most of the republican organs demand. It will be a day of sorrow and misery for America if he should be guided by the counsels of these latter. Civil war, marshalled by fire, famine and slaughter, will thereafter take possession of the land; property will lose its value; commerce and trade be cut off, and agriculture abandoned; "the rye fields and wheat fields of Massachusetts and New York," and "the cotton and rice fields of South Carolina, and the sugar plantations of Louisiana," will be trampled under foot by armed men, and the future of the Union, which we have been accustomed to contemplate so proudly, be dimmed by a terrible vista of anarchy and blood. We cannot believe that Mr. Lincoln will be willing to inaugurate a period of disaster before which the imagination quails in dismay. The policy which true wisdom would point out to him is unmistakeably [sic] clear. He has but to plant himself upon the rock which afforded a sure and safe foothold for his illustrious predecessors of the early days of the republic; to soar above party weaknesses, and emulate the greatness of statesmen like Washington, Jefferson and Madison, in times of difficulty for the republic; with a firm hand to guide the country back to its pristine condition, recommending for both South and North such amendments to the constitution as shall define and maintain forever hereafter the rights of each; to repudiate every tendency opposed to conciliation, forbearance and the largest amount of toleration of their respective social institutions by different sections of the country; and he will carve out for himself a name which shall stand among the highest in the history of great and patriotic benefactors of the human race.

86. What Is to Be Done?

(Philadelphia *Press* [Douglas], December 27, 1860)

In an article on our first page, we present "the matters in issue" between the South and North, under such general heads as we suppose fairly embrace all the grounds of complaint which the South has or can have against the free States, their people, and the Federal Administration in their hands. Our answers to them are made briefly, too briefly, perhaps, to satisfy the reader on all the points considered. But it is not our purpose either to discuss those matters with the disaffected of the South, or to make the defence of the North against them. We have too little hope of good to come from any argument we can offer to the Seceders to undertake it. It is not the time to waste words by addressing them to those who are not likely to listen. It may be more to the purpose to address ourselves to the other party—our own readers, the people of the North. If they have any duties to perform in this exigency they will listen, and we will not lose our labor.

There are fifteen slave States in the Union, embracing eight hundred and fifty-one thousand square miles—within fifty-six thousand miles of half the area of all the States at present in the Union. These slave States hold near four millions of slaves, worth to them about two thousand millions of dollars, at the market price. Eight of them depend for all their staple products upon slave labor. The interest of all of them in this property, and its profits, is beyond calculation. Here, in mere money-worth, there is an immense interest. The people who hold it are alarmed for its security. Their whole industrial and social policy is involved in the system. They profess to have serious apprehensions for the safety of the whole frame-work of their society, and for the peace and the lives of their people. They complain of an active and dangerously hostile sentiment in the North, which threatens them with perpetual disturbance and possible destruction. Of all this they must be taken to be the judges, for their own opinions, not ours, will rule their conduct. They are looking about for such remedies as they can find, or for such defences as they can interpose. Can we, as a party involved in all this trouble and apprehension of evil, do anything to help them? We have given them the assurances which the Federal Constitution pledges for us, but they say these are not sufficient; that, in practice, it fails them, and that they must seek other securities, outside of that instrument, and more satisfactory than our action is under it. Right or wrong, this is the attitude in which they stand to us now, and we have something to do about it. The compromises of the Constitution were made to meet these wants of theirs at the time it was formed; but it did not settle their beneficial interest in the Territories, and it has failed to preserve their equality in both branches of Congress, and in the Executive department of the Union. Their only security now, under that compact, is in our justice, forbearance, or generosity, upon which they believe they can no longer rely. Ever since the adoption of the Constitution the power of the free-labor States has been growing upon them, and, more than once, efforts have been made to redress the in-jury and reassure them. Lou[i]siana was purchased from France, and out of it they got the States of Arkansas, Louisiana, and Missouri; afterwards Florida was purchased from Spain; then Texas was annexed; and, finally, a large domain was secured by conquest and purchase from Mexico, of which, however, they have no certainty of receiving any share. All these acquisitions of territory were made at their instance, and, in the main, in their behalf, to meet the ever-growing necessities of their condition. California disappointed them; New Mexico and Utah give them no present aid, and promise them very little in the fu-ture; and the immense domain of Kansas and Nebraska is gone from their power. They have lost the balance that the compromises in-tended; their power in the Union is gone; and they are at the mercy of a force of numbers which they believe to be desperately hostile to them. On these terms they will not stay in the Union if they can get out. They have no faith in the letter of the agreement as a protection. The promised fidelity of the President elect in the discharge of his official duties is no guaranty of their special interests; for the questions open to legislation may be constitutionally settled against them, and the legality of an injury is neither compensation nor consolation to the sufferer. They say that, while we insist upon what is "nominated in the bond," employing our preponderance of power to give it an injurious force against them, they will be suffering penalties, not enjoying expected benefits. Is there anything in all this that rightly demands our consideration and claims our help?

Surely the Territorial question can be adjusted. There can be no difficulty, even in point of policy, in conceding anything in this matter which we never can by any means acquire. A compromise that accords accurately with the inevitable issue of this dispute, however conducted, involves no forfeiture of either honor, conscience, or interest to either party. We know now very well where such an adjustment would touch the subject. Let us either agree upon the principle which will leave the matter to the natural law that rules it under our system of self-government; or, by a safe anticipation, fix the line of demarcation, and so put this radical source of discontent at rest forever.

This root difficulty of Territorial distribution is one for which the Constitution made no certain provision. It cannot be settled under it by legislation or by judicial construction. It is a question outside of the compact; and we must meet it as our fathers met those which troubled them. We must exercise our best discretion in settling it, and that can be done honorably and rightfully. Get that once out of the way, and what would be left?

The exponents of the Southern sentiment tell us that it is not the election of LINCOLN that disturbs them, but the sentiment which that election manifests, which they take to be a determined hostility to their system of slavery. And against this danger they seek security. They are clearly right in distinguishing between the election of a sectional candidate, who will doubtless be a good Union President, and a sectional spirit, which lies in wait to spring upon them at every turn where injury can be inflicted. They are right in their understanding that LINCOLN was elected rather by the demoralization of the opposing political party than by sheer force of anti-slavery sentiment in the North. The enormous majority of Pennsylvania, the most conservative State in the Union, is full proof of this. They know, as we know, that in other circumstances Pennsylvania, New Jersey, Indiana, and Illinois would have gone, as they did in 1856, for the candidate of a compact, conservative Democratic party. But, have they not, also, some ground for believing that the anti-slavery feeling in the North was immensely cultivated and emboldened by the Republican canvass—that one side of the "irrepressible conflict" felt encouraged to believe itself an irresistible force, and is inclined to exercise it? We know better. We know that there is a power in the North that will never allow its extremists to invade the rights of the South, or endanger its peace and prosperity. Mr. WIGFALL tells us that we must repeal our public sentiment, as well as the personal-liberty bills; that we must check the assault of tongue and press, and the tide of popular hatred against their system. He would be right in finding his true danger there, if it in fact existed, as he imagines. The situation of the South would be intolerable if the North really stood menacing it, as he supposes. But he and all the Secession declaimers are mistaken in this apprehension. It is only while there is a real, substantial matter of political agitation open between the sections that the moral sentiment gets opportunity for troublesome expression and action. Strike the bone of contention out of our political platforms, and the anti-slavery sentiment among us would instantly fall into the category of moral suasion enterprises. Slavery, like intemperance, and sin in general, would be handed over to moral and religious missionaries, and would disturb the system about as much as tracts and preaching interfere with horse-racing and mint-juleps in Virginia. To meet Mr. WIGFALL's demand upon us, as far as we can and should, therefore, we call upon the North to adjust the Territorial question definitively, and then we will say to them, "our moral war upon your system is tempered to your own handling; it no longer uses the ballot-box for your conviction, but appeals to your conscience for your conversion, and if you can't manage it in that form, you will, at least, not blame us with the difficulty."

To our own side of the controversy, then, we say, this we can do, and ought to do, frankly, and effectually, and promptly.

The matter of fugitive slaves is a trifle, when it stands alone. It was only a point on which to fight out other and deeper issues. And these are the troubles which lurk out of sight under cover of a more presentable and more feasible pretence of quarrel. It would be awkward to put a popular sentiment forward as the ground of secession. The Senate laughed at Mr. WIGFALL when he exposed it, and this is just the reason that nobody can tell exactly what the South demands. To bring it to the surface and find its roots is the way to find the remedy for it. Our exposition of the matter seems to us the true one, and we submit it for the action of those who have the responsibility.

But the North has a vital interest in the preservation of the Union on its own account. The well being of our millions of men and women is not to be endangered or thrown away upon a sentiment of doubtful philanthropy, to result in a state of things which can do no good in any way to the objects for which the sacrifice is made. Our trade with the slave-holding States is much greater than is commonly thought. Every man in business, and every laborer depending upon full employment for his daily bread, now feels the mischief which a temporary suspension of trade and credit between the sections has the power to inflict upon him. A rough approximate estimate of the amount of this trade serves to explain the extent of the business revulsions produced by our political embroilment, and the consequent interruption of home commerce which we are now enduring.

In 1855, Mr. GUTHRIE, Secretary of the Treasury, put the manufacturing, mechanic, and mining products of the whole Union at sixteen hundred millions nearly, obtaining this result by adding fifty per cent. to the report of the census for the year 1850; and the head of the Census Department estimated the agricultural products for the year 1854 at sixteen hundred millions. Allowing for the increase of both these departments of productive industry since that time, we may state them at two thousand millions each for 1860. In 1850, the census credited the South and Southwestern States with one-tenth of the manufactures of the nation, and the Eastern and Middle States (embracing only Maryland and Delaware belonging to the slave section) with nine-tenths. In 1859 we exported to foreign countries thirty-four millions worth of manufactured commodities, which would leave nineteen hundred and sixty-six millions worth that must find a home market and home consumption. If the South supplies herself with only one-tenth of this amount, and consumes only one-fourth of them, she gives the Northern States a market for two hundred and ninety-six millions of their manufactures. We do not stop to inquire now how the balance of agricultural exchanges stands between the sections. The Northern farmer has his share of this trade in manufactures of which we are now speaking, and participates largely in its profits, and as largely in its losses and suspensions. It is enough that, without pretending to statistical accuracy, we show a market for our surplus manufactures in the South nine times larger than all the world besides affords us. The foreign exports of all the free States, of every kind, do not average more than one hundred and twenty millions a year; their sales to the Southern States are more than twice that amount. The slave State trade is of as great value annually to the free States as that of the Union is to all Europe, Asia, and South America.

Is it any wonder that our property and our labor decline twenty-five per cent. in present value, when so large a commerce as this is interrupted, and the commercial confidence of the parties is shaken?

We present the claims of trade as a motive to conciliation, without shrinking from the answer that sentiment, opinion, party spirit, or philanthropy may offer. There is another style of sentiment, opinion, and philanthropy which warrants us in this appeal; the men who do the work and conduct the business of the North have such claims upon just consideration that they may be safely confronted with any feeling or speculation which would push us upon so immense a sacrifice as persistent hostility between the slave and free States must occasion.

It is true, that trade will find its natural channels at last, and it is just as true that the tide forced into the shallowest and most round-about may dig them deeper and broader than the more direct, which have been abandoned under compulsion.

For such reasons as these we second the appeal of Wall street, Pearl street, and Third and Market streets, because they represent every street, alley, highway, and byeway; every factory and field; every house and hovel in the land.

87. The Question of the Day

(Philadelphia *Public Ledger* [Independent], January 1, 1861)

In the present temper of the public mind North and South, it seems to have been lost sight of that the only means by which this excitement can be allayed, the authority of the government restored, and the country saved from civil war, is by conciliation and concession. The public mind is fast drifting into the idea that a collision is inevitable between the two sections of the country, the North and the South; and as this idea seizes it more strongly, there is defiant language, bitter taunts, a disposition to shut out all compromise, and preparation for war. It is an easy thing to rush into a conflict—ill-temper can bring us to blows at any time. But after blows are exchanged between equals, and war has desolated the land, and the belligerents cease from mere exhaustion to do each other mischief, they have to come back again to reason and compromise to settle the original cause of quarrel.

The question then occurs, is it not wiser to begin with reason and compromise, and avert the dreadful catastrophe of war? Is the object sought by such contention so much greater in its benefits as to out-weigh all the evils of conflict, and make men talk of going to war with their fellow men as if it were some pastime or exercise of rivalry where skill, activity and courage were to be exhibited? Few of us can realize the destruction to life and property a war would cause among a people as intelligent and as skilful in arms as the people of the United States —so resolute, courageous and self-willed. The most atrocious crime against humanity would be to array such a people in hostility to each other. And yet we are drawn so near the extreme verge of this catastrophe by the fanaticisms of the day, that at any moment we may hear the terrible announcement that war has begun. Passion seems to rule the hour. The Government is defied on one hand by rebellion, and on the other subjected to the most unsparing and acrimonious censure and abuse. Half the pains that men take to work themselves into a fury over every seeming insult or circumstance they do not understand, would serve, in a calmer mood, to judge correctly of the value of that which has produced all this contention, and to suggest whether they are not fighting more for an idea than for any practical reality.

What is there about this question of slavery in the Territories which at this time forces it upon us as one of such a momentous issue? And supposing that there were no restrictions now or at any time upon the spread of slavery in any Territory of the United States, how small a part of it would ever have that as one of its social institutions? One by one the States now free have abolished slavery as one of their domestic institutions, till the free States outnumber the slave. One by one the Territories have entered the Union, and the vast majority of them as free States, till free territory extends from the Pacific to the Atlantic. These things occurred when the influences were less adverse to slavery than they now are, and if freedom could grow to such formidable dimensions then, why may it not be left to take care of itself now that it has everything, population, emigration, the peculiarity of soil and climate in the Territories, to help its growth?

Questions like these, we think, would be better discipline for the mind at the present time, than all the talk of war which indiscretion and recklessness may utter. Wars are sanctified only when they are undertaken for a nation's salvation. But when they are commenced for the destruction of a free people, enjoying themselves all the blessings which good government, unexampled prosperity and a future of freedom and happiness can present, they are the result of criminal and reckless infatuation. Instead, therefore, of inflaming our passions against each other, or giving more than their due importance to the acts and speeches of people in a state of excitement and revolution, as in South Carolina, let us endeavor to satisfy the other portion of the South, which remains true to the Union and the Constitution, that we mean to be just in our action and friendly in our spirit, and, while regarding the Union as the greatest blessing to the people of the North, will make it equally a blessing and security to those of the South.

88. Fearful and Perilous Times

(Allentown Democrat [Douglas], January 9, 1861)

Thoughtful people upon every side are concerned about the future, for it is shrouded in darkness and doubt. It seems that every day involves the country into new and dangerous issues. At first it was not considered in much danger, but things have grown worse rapidly. The Union is in danger. It never was in a greater one. The action of South Carolina has produced the effect we sadly anticipated, and three or four other southern states seem inclined to defend the seceding one by following her example. In this delicate moment—a moment demanding the exercise of all the forbearance, public spirit, and patient endurance of which a Christian people ought to be capable—what do we witness? Northern journals discuss the propriety of resorting to arms; northern legislators calmly suggest an immediate call of the militia of northern states; southern presses and politicians indulge in the most exciting displays of local independence, and southern executives take possession of United States property. Do any of these things suggest an amicable adjustment of existing difficulties? Do they not, on the contrary, aggravate the original disorder, and render it still more difficult for the wisest statesmen to arrive at a compromise calculated to meet the necessities of the case and at the same time the conflicting sentiments of the people?

Yes, the Union is in imminent danger.—Both of the parties in this sectional struggle are in earnest, and both have been so assiduously incensed against each other, both so mutually misrepresented by sinister parties, that neither is in a condition promising to the views of conservatism, and neither sees the frightful consequences of continued ultraism in the only light favorable to ultimate harmony. Separation appears to be the aim of both extremes, and as General Wool has truthfully remarked in his letter to General Cass: "If a separation should take place, you may rest assured that blood would flow in torrents, followed by pestilence, famine, and desolation; and Senator Seward's irrepressible conflict will be brought to a conclusion much sooner than he could possibly have anticipated."

But what is to be done in this emergency? We still repeat our confidence in an appeal to the people. The people constitute the fountain of all rightful government. The popular will is peculiarly the basis of all governmental change in this country. A vast majority of the people of the United States are hostile to disunion in any shape and under any circumstances. They are prepared, we firmly believe[,] to do justice between the north and the south, to discard all feelings of sectional discontent, all geographical prejudices, and unite upon any equitable common-sense compromise.—The politicians are perfectly aware of this popular proclivity, but they are opposed to it as incompatible with their own interests. They desire agitation, for they thrive by it. They labor, therefore, to keep the popular sentiment in abeyance—to crush the popular conservatism out of sight—to irritate, by artful misrepresentation, the popular petulance into an implacable disaffection. Shall they succeed? Shall they, to compass their selfish purposes, plunge this hitherto peaceful nation into a civil war which cannot but end in its political destruction? Or shall the *people* of the United States take in hand a matter so deeply affecting their public and private interests, and utter their will in tones which shall be authoritatively heard from the St. Lawrence to the Rio Grande?

Out of the five millions of voters in the United States, we doubt not that at least four and a half are, in heart and soul, warm Unionists. Those among the republicans of the north are intimidated by a sense of policy, at present, from expressing openly the nature of their loyality [*sic*], and those among the extremists of the south are dismayed into silence by the enthusiasm of their opponents. But, let the bold, the fearless, the untrammeled friends of the Union call forth conventions of the people, in both sections of the confederacy, to consider the most feasible means of peacefully terminating this heart-rending difficulty, and then behold the result. For we emphatically deny (as we have denied before) that the late presidential election decided the will of the people in regard to slavery in the territories; and even if it were so considered, surely the anti-Lincoln majority of nearly a million of votes in the thirty-three states would demonstrate that three-fifths of all the votes in the Union were opposed to the views announced in the Chicago platform on this subject. The politicians *dare not* leave this question distinctly to the ballot-box. They should be compelled to do it. They should be forced by the pressure of public opinion to submit to the popular vote Crittenden's or some other set of acceptable resolutions, and the demagogues would stand aghast at the rebuke their time-serving course had elicited. We place our trust, to use the language of the Cincinnati platform, "in the intelligence, the patriotism, and the discriminating justice of the American people." We insist upon it that the people alone erected, and the people alone have a right to demolish, this great fabric of liberty. We protest against any conclusive settlement by any less authority; and if left to them, we have no fear for the preservation of the republic.

Even though we have the fearful ordeal before us, no efforts whatever are made by the Republicans in Congress to pour oil upon the troubled waters. Why not make the effort at least to do something to stop the progress of a catastrophe which must end in horrid scenes of suffering and blood? Instead of engaging to bring about measures of peace, they urge coercion and force, and are in favor of driving back at the mouth of the cannon and the point of the bayonet, the seceders, even though all the Slave States should eventually go out. But, God be thanked, these "leaders" of a sectional party are not the People. When the irrepressible conflict ceases to be waged on paper or in legislative halls, or in Wide Awake assemblies, and comes in the true spirit of a blood thirsty fanaticism to court the arbitrament of the sword, then the voice of that People will be heard, as with the voice of God, for PEACE! Brothers are not going to imbue their hands in brother's blood to oblige Mr. Lincoln, Mr. Sumner nor Mr. Wade. If these gentlemen have a stomach for civil war, let them throw away their lives, if they choose, but they must not expect us to follow their foolish example. Mr. Seward is rolling in wealth, and most other of the Republican politicians, who will not "budge an inch to save the Union," probably have enough of the good things of this world to enable them and their families to live on through this "conflict" without visions of almshouses or starvation to haunt them. The laboring millions, who constitute the real bone and sinew of our Northern population, however, are otherwise situated, and being otherwise situated they are not going to starve that they may FIGHT,—and they are not going to fight, in order to make great men of small demagogues.

89. WHAT IT ALL MEANS

(St. Paul *Daily Minnesotian* [Lincoln], January 19, 1861)

The present clamor on the surface seems to mean, "Union;" at heart it is nothing but the old contest for political supremacy.

The two parties were arrayed against each other prior to the election. It was then attempted to deter the American people from asserting their views by threats of the consequences. We did not heed them. It is now attempted to overwhelm the Republican party in one grand burst of Union-loving indignation. It will fail as the threats did.

What men love the Union better than we do? Who else have sought to make it worth perpetuating by retaining in its development the great principal [*sic*] of *freedom* out of which it arose? Who else have sought to preserve it from the universal spread of that institution which would have made the name of our country in a few years a jeer and a mockery?

It is said that our institutions are to sink in a sea of blood. We do not believe it. We have faith in the educated good sense of the American people. But be it so. We prefer the wildest delirium of which a nation can be capable, to that slow, gradual obliteration of liberty under the "sum of all villainies"[,] slavery, a doom that but, for the resistance of the Republican party would be the inevitable fate of the Republic.

Other nations have fallen upon revolutions, desperate and deadly ones, but they have arisen from them renovated and with new life. But what nation in the world's history, has ever voluntarily assumed the shackles of slavery, has voluntarily submitted to the domination of a caste, and yet lived? A people may survive convulsions, but never self-degradation.

If, then, we are right in our principles the question comes down to one of two things, resistance or submission. We have chosen resistance to the encroachment of the slave-power. We have made it the vital essence of our party. We have resisted it in Congress, we have resisted it by the press, we have resisted it at the polls, and if needs be, we are ready to resist it at the mouth of the cannon. A RIGHT does not take its shape and nature from surrounding circumstances, but has the same claims upon our hearts and minds in the smoke of battle as in the calm of peace.

What Republican believes the principles enunciated in the Chicago platform to be a violation of the rights of the South? None. What, then, have we done of which we need be ashamed, or from which we should recede? Nothing. Then, as we have supported those principles with our voices and our votes, let us, if necessary, support them with our arms and our hands. As we have withstood threats and sophistry, let us withstand clamors and violence.

But, we are asked,—will you do nothing to preserve the Union? Yes; we will strictly adhere to all the terms and conditions of the Constitution; we will do no wrong to the people of any section of our common country. Nay, more, where the South misapprehend our purposes and views we will do all we can to disabuse them. Hence, as they suppose us about to inaugurate an armed crusade against their institutions, we offer Mr. SEWARD's proposed amendment to the Constitution, declaring that Congress shall never interfere with Slavery in the States.

But when the South ask us to abandon our principles—to apologize for our own existence as a party—to give up what we have gained in the last great campaign—we say emphatically, *never!* And if they madly abandon the argument and rush to the arbitration of the sword, *they will find the Northern people ready to meet them.* We will argue and reason to the uttermost limits of time, but when it comes to the question of being kicked, we will put a period to discussion and drop our logic.

90. WHERE THERE'S A WILL THERE'S A WAY

(Newark (N. J.) Daily Advertiser [Lincoln], January 22, 1861)

The homely old adage, "Where there's a will there's a way," applies as well to the settlement of our political difficulties as ever it did to the countless little incidents that have demonstrated its truth in the past. It is now clearly apparent that if the political disputants who can quiet the troubled elements, feel any honest desire to do so, they may effect the object without any serious sacrifice to their own interests or honor. While patriotic hearts all over the country are prayerfully yearning for a restoration of the lost peace and quiet, they are misrepresented by the designing schemers who will not permit such a result till their own selfish purposes are accomplished. These are unconsciously sustained by a more honest, but equally impracticable set, who, mistaking policy for principle, are kept up to an inflexible purpose, of refusing any compromise that does not fully realize their extremest ideas, and completely humiliate those who oppose them. So long as this spirit prevails there cannot be any satisfactory settlement. Like all true business transactions, the bargain must be on such terms that both the parties will feel the benefit of it. It is a real misfortune that the men who now control our destinies appear to have completely ignored the experiences of their whole lives. Their business transactions, as well as their domestic relations, have required a daily and hourly yielding of some personal object for a more general good—the sacrifice of some immediate interest for the prospect of greater ultimate advantage. Concessions are constantly made to feminine caprice or juvenile folly for the peace of the family; and even our stern courts of law often find it expedient to yield something from their extreme judgments through mitigating circumstances. This experience seems to have been completely forgotten by a large body of well-meaning people in one section, while another very dangerous set in the other secretly appreciate the truth, but play upon their firmness for the promotion of their selfish schemes [f]or the prostration of the Union with their own fall.

If we had more patriots than partizans in the National Councils the difficulties which now perplex the public mind and paralyses its industry would have been settled long ago, in a manner perfectly satisfactory to just minded men of all sections,—and without serious violence to any right principle or policy. While the great mass of the people are anxious for some such settlement, every proposition for that purpose in Congress is met by some insurmountable objection, or some amendment is offered which involves a direct and humiliating abandonment of principle on one side or the other. Hence there is no compromise in the leading projects which bear that name, the efforts are wasted, and the great interests of the people crushed, while they—the original source of all political power—are not permitted by their mere agents to decide the question for themselves.—Thus far no real progress has been made by the contracting parties in Washington. The South are divided into many classes, with so many objects, that no one of them is yet sufficiently prepared to accept any reasonable terms of settlement that may be offered, and many of our desponding people of the North are just as much mistaken in grasping at every proposition to appease them, as the invalid who swallows all the nostrums of the drug shops, without any definite knowledge that they will even approach the seat of the disease.—Though many propositions have been made, touching almost every point in controversy, there is no indication that any of them will satisfy the extreme ideas of the section opposed to that from which they came. Those of the South have too inflexibly involved a radical abandonment of the popular principle of the North; while those from the latter have not gone far enough for the advancing demands of the former—meanwhile, as time rolls on, the breach appears to widen. If the South could now agree upon almost any plan not absolutely inconsistent with the spirit of the Constitution, and pledge themselves to abide by it, it would greatly simplify the controversy, and they would doubtless receive an overwhelming response from the North in its favor.

The Crittenden amendments, which sprung from a truly patriotic purpose, will probably fail to realize their object, because they make the constitution, which does not now mention the subject, declare that slavery shall be *protected* in territories south of 36° 30', and the mover has since consented to an amendment extending the provision to all territory hereafter to be acquired. This strikes so squarely at the lead-ing principle of the Republicans that they refuse to go to that length —especially as they foresee that the acquisition of Mexico, Central America, and the islands, would place the slave power forever in the ascendant. This consideration will doubtless account for the recent votes of our Senator, Mr. Ten Eyck, on this subject, and also induces a vast body of conservative men, who are really in favor of a com-promise, from endorsing Mr. Crittenden's proposition.

If it could be divested of the protective clause—so as to merely re-store the Missouri line, and extend it to the Pacific—leaving slavery to its own fate, as the Constitution leaves that and other property—for local laws to manage—it would doubtless receive a hearty support from our own members, and, their whole constituency. Mr. Rice's plan, to get rid of the whole territorial question, by admitting the territories as States at once, would be equally agreeable. But before any compromise can be made, there must be a more earnest and honest desire for it than has been thus far manifested. The extremes of the two sections must con-sent to meet each other half way, and whatever agreement may be made in that spirit will command the applause of the people. Such a hoped for result is not yet impossible.

91. Should There Be Any Further Compromise with Slavery?

(Akron *Summit County Beacon* [Lincoln], January 24, 1861)

There has been, and is yet, a great degree of nervousness among the Republicans, and indeed people of all parties, in the North, lest our Senators and Representatives in Congress should, through menace, fear of a dissolution of the Union, or from some other cause, again yield to the clamorous demands of slavery, and consent to a further sacrifice of principle, in the compromise measures sought to be agreed upon, in adjusting the unhappy difficulties existing in our country, at the present time.

The truth is, the people have become heartily tired and sick of compromises, and this interminable talk about them; and, after all the abuses to which they have given countenance—the enormities that have been perpetrated under them, and the utter want of fidelity, that has hitherto attended the observance of their most sacred provisions, the people would experience great relief, if the very word "compromise" could be expunged from the English language and the sound thereof never again heard—at least upon the American continent.

Freedom, the stronger, has for the sake of harmony, been compromising with slavery, the weaker, ever since the formation of our Government. "The Compromises of the Constitution,"—"The Missouri Compromise of 1820," and the "Compromise measures of 1850," are household words and familiar to every ear, to say nothing of the thousand and one concessions and unwritten compromises, between those high in authority, who have mal-administered the government, and the propagandists of the accursed institution.

And yet, notwithstanding Freedom, has ever, thus, been ready to make concessions to slavery, to secure peace, and having made them, has, in every instance, religiously observed them, we find that the moment the latter, either through numerical strength, or intrigue, or even the most gross corruption, finds itself in a condition to enhance its own interests and trench upon the rights of the former, by so doing, never scruples to disregard and annul the most sacred compacts, as is evidenced by its wanton abrogation of the Missouri Compromise line, and the unheard of atrocities, which, under that same influence were perpetrated upon the people of the then new territory, but now populous State of Kansas.

We believe, therefore, that we speak the sentiment of every man in Summit County—we know we do our own—when we say that there should be no further compromise of principle, with slavery, whatever may be the result of the present contest.

While, as an order-loving and law-abiding people, we are ready and willing to stand by and faithfully fulfill any contracts that we may enter into, we are emphatically opposed to the renewal of any such contract, after its most vital principles have been annulled and trampled in the dust by the adverse party thereto—much less are we willing to consent to such a renewal as shall give said adverse party infinitely greater advantages under the new, than they were entitled to under the old.

Who desires the restoration of the Missouri Compromise line? Nobody! The South does not desire it, for the reason that she had appropriated, previous to its repeal, all that she was entitled to, or could expect, under that compact. Hence the repeal. The North does not desire it, for the reason that she has a method, quite as effectual and far more honorable, of saying to that accursed blotch upon the escutcheon of our beloved country, "thus far shalt thou come, but no farther"—in her enterprising and industrious population, which constantly and rapidly, like the "Star of Empire, westward takes its way."

Indeed, the North desires no compromise, whatever, and if one is entered into it must be for the benefit of the South alone. And what kind of a Compromise, pray, will satisfy the South? The old line of 36° 30', extended to the Pacific, with slavery forever prohibited North, and the territory South of it left open to competition between free and slave labor? Not a bit of it! They will never be satisfied with anything, short of having the whole of that territory given over, bodily, to slavery; not merely to be admitted as slave States, when sufficiently populous, but to be constituted slave territory, and protected as such, by solemn act of Congress, or Constitutional amendment, if, perchance, they will abate any of their late pretensions, that the Constitution carries, and should protect slavery everywhere.

No! No! The day for concessions and unholy alliances between Freedom and slavery has passed by. As things are now situated, there is but one form of Compromise that the North will consent to enter into, with the South, the terms of which, must be speedily accepted and complied with, or even that proposition will be withdrawn.

That compromise is simply this. Let the traitors of the South, who, by their hot-head[ed] and criminal tom-foolery, have brought the Nation to the verge of civil war, as far as possible, retrace their steps—restore to the Government the property they have stolen—return to their allegiance—and swear, upon the Constitution, that from now, henceforth and forever, they will remain loyal to the Union, and the North will consent to the issuing of a general amnesty—and that the leaders in that rebellion, and their aiders and abettors may be permitted to "go unwhipt of justice" and unhung.

This is our ultimatum!

92. THE TRUE POLICY

(Boston Daily Courier [Bell], January 25, 1861)

Multitudes of persons, in various parts of the country, taking counsel of natural fears, instead of the hopes which seldom abandon a noble mind, are almost disposed to give up the cause of the country, as beyond any rational prospect of redemption. The indulgence of this despondent temper is, of all others, the most likely means of making their apprehensions confirmed by the issue. For our own part, long since foreseeing to what consequences the sectionalization of the country must lead, we have still felt a reasonable confidence, that as events became more and more developed, the public mind would become awakened to the dangers and necessities of the case, and that the great body of the people, freed at last from the grapple of self-seeking political managers, would express themselves in such a way, as to check our national progress to the point of final extremity. Undoubtedly now, could the sense of the people be reached in any legitimate manner, we should find a spontane-

ous expression of sentiment, leaving no doubt whatever of their preference for a settlement, even upon terms not particularly agreeable to
them, to the surrender of their fair and glorious inheritance to the full
possession of the demon of discord, and all the countless ills of anarchy
and civil war. This manifestation of popular feeling is now reaching
Congress from all those quarters of the country, which are not already
deeply implicated in the actual process of secession, and we doubt not
will be attended to. The question then will be— Will they avail to effect
the grand aim of saving the Union from final dissolution?

The progress of startling and momentous events has been so rapid,
within the two last months, the effect of movements at the South and
the North have both so tended to aggravate the originally existing causes
of the controversy—that at times it has seemed almost impossible to
distinguish even the promise of a ray of light out of the superincumbent
gloom. At such times, one would be more than mortal, not to experience
some despondent emotions. Reason might be invoked to assure us, that
no madness, on the one side or the other, could be equal to the contemplation of the ruin of a country, at the very point of attaining unparalleled supremacy and prosperity—when that ruin would be incurred chiefly from a misunderstanding merely between its different
sections, and by them of each other, and not from any irresistible or
"irrepressible" cause. But, on the other hand, the ungovernable passions of men, resolutely bent upon suffering the penalty of their folly,
and on making whatever causes they could not find for the common
destruction, might in the end disappoint every deduction drawn from a
rational analysis of the case.

Still, upon the whole, we have never lost confidence in one guiding
principle, which seemed to us to render a final solution of all our troubles, if not easy, at least inevitable, except for an alternative, never to
be thought of, so long as reason or Christian feeling exercised any control in this not altogether unreasonable and still Christian land. In a
word, effectual secession we hold to be impracticable, in the very nature
of things. A State, or half a dozen States, may declare themselves out of
the Union—but, besides material ties still holding them by an indissoluble bond, any active and united struggle of the South to dissever these,
and other bonds still stronger than these, inwrought into the very frame-
work of our civil organization, would of itself be war,—and a war from
which all men capable of realizing its horrors, and not mere desperadoes
in spirit, must shrink away.

To talk about "reconstruction," after such a dire experience as that,
appears to us little better than mere raving—and, therefore, every mo-

tive and feeling and intelligent principle serve to lead, during the period of formal "secession," to the negotiations of peace. If we look upon the seceding States as enemies, and act accordingly, we may have war—if we treat them as alienated friends, with whom reconciliation is to be desired and sought, the restoration of friendly relations is within our power, however late, and however difficult to be brought round. We are far from asserting that reconstruction would be impossible. The country of our ancestors, after its last civil war, fell into a settled government, in the course of about a century and a half. What a prospect for us! And with us, there would be impediments which did not exist there. We should be divided into independent sovereignties, and the cause of the quarrel, it is probable, would still remain. We talk now of concessions by the North—which really mean nothing more than the sacrifice of Northern opinion and pride in it, and the control of hostile sentiment and action—since there is no substantial and insurmountable cause of difference—but in case of a separation completed between the North and the South, and an effort at reconstruction, even if the North yielded all that was required upon the slavery question—as it must to effect any settlement,—on the part of the South there would be unavoidable a self-humiliating retrocession from its assumed independence, and an implied confession of weakness, as well as wrong, which make any concessions asked of us now seem incomparably trivial and insignificant in comparison.

All talk about coercion is, therefore, not only useless, but in the highest degree unwise, on the part of those who sincerely desire the preservation of the Union. The fatal day may indeed come, when a resort to arms may be unavoidable, in order to maintain the government, and any semblance of the once glorious Republic. As yet, patience under outrages very hard to endure, and in themselves, full of peril to the highest interest of the country, is the only policy, in the pursuit of which we can hope for any probable adjustment. The grand object with every patriot will be, to prevent secession *becoming fixed,* by converting it from a formality into a position identified with irretrievable deeds. Our point is, to break up the quarrel, not to aggravate it. To this end, Congress may agree upon a basis of settlement, which may lead to a final return of all the seceding States, if the terms of it are fairly adapted to that end. It can do no more than this. For the rest, the people must determine the question for themselves. If this is done, we shall not despair of the restoration of the Republic to more than its former strength—and perhaps the blot which will still rest upon its fame, may not permanently tarnish it. It will probably take years to restore all things to their former channels. But our best hopes here rest upon the fact, that substantial good feeling is not now disturbed between moderate people in the several sections of the country. In every seceding State there are plenty of Union men and Union women and of Christian men and women, whose unceasing efforts will be devoted to this greatest and noblest cause of the age. When political sclf-seekers and disturbers of the public peace have accomplished their evil work, they will go down and their influence be no more felt. The true friends of the Union may then work effectually and together, and they must be in the end triumphant.

93. "No Compromise!"

(Syracuse Daily Courier and Union [Breckinridge], January 28, 1861)

Every proposition for a settlement of existing difficulties is persistently and steadily voted down by Republican leaders. No compromise on the question which has already dissevered the confederacy—no compromise out of the many proposed, with a view to remedy[ing] subsisting business embarrassments has met their approval. No compromise to avert civil war with our own white brethren and fellow citizens, is the cry of the partizans who have always opposed every war with foreign nations and shown themselves ready to compromise, with foreign powers, every American claim and unfrequently unquestioned rights!

The line of 36° 30' as a compromise line by congressional action, was, it is true, without and beyond the constitution, and of no obligatory effect except as a matter of mutual agreement. Such was the doctrine of the Democratic party in times past; and such is now the decision of the Supreme Court. That line, or the line of 37°, is not therefore NOW proposed as a mere law to be established by Congress; but as an amendment to the constitution. As such, it would unquestionably have a positive, permanent and unchanging validity!

If the adoption of that line does injustice to any section, it is not to the North. It was originally an encroachment on the equal rights of the South, reluctantly yielded for the sake of peace, and in the hope that it might prove a lasting settlement of a dangerous question. If unsatisfactory to any portion of the people, it is the southern and slaveholding citizen, who under the decisions of the Supreme Court, would alone have the right to complain. And yet we find Republican legislators and Congressmen voting nearly in a body against any practicable compromise of that character, and persistently initiating and advocating every war measure,—war *the last* and desperate resort of injured nations!

What would the proposed line effect? It would secure an honorable peace. It would guarantee more than two thirds of the national domain against slavery; while slavery might gain a slight foothold and maintain a brief and sickly existence in the other third. It would exclude slaves from a territory the whole of which as a portion of the Louisiana purchase, was a slaveholding territory, in which slave property equally with every other was protected by the treaty for its acquisition, and the existing law. It would exclude the South from common territory into which the supreme federal tribunal has declared its right to go with its slave property. And yet such vast concessions and advantages are repudiated by northern representatives!

Are the republican leaders the self-constituted-avengers of the North, crazed enough to be fit for the lunatic Asylum? Are the Northern people gone stark mad with the frenzies of Abolitionism? Is it to-day true, that "whom the Gods would destroy they first make mad?" Can there come but one of two issues from this crisis, a peaceful settlement of difficulties or mutual slaughter and devastation? Do the signs and portents of the day really indicate an avenging Nemesis; the wrath of an offended Deity blinding the people; and an utter abnegation of all reason, judgment, and discretion to the citizens of the Republic? Is the fair fabric of this government to be annihilated? Are its cherished Constitution, its Judicial tribunals and its boasted liberties to be drenched in fraternal blood, or consumed in the fires of civil conflict? Shall the impracticables of the day stand defiantly upon a boasted principle, which is denied, in practice at least, by the whole world; denied in substance by even the anti-slavery nations of the old world, who are again importing slaves under the more fashionable name of coolies; denied in practice by the founders of the government, (all slave holders, acquiring and organizing slave territories and slave States without a question,) and repudiated by the Constitution, if the constitutional tribunals of the land are to be the judges? Shall these impeachables, by a sullen adherence to such an abstraction, be permitted to deluge the land with fraternal gore, and cause the sun of National liberty, which had begun to illumine at least, the white races of the world, to go down in eternal gloom alike for them and for all others? God forbid! We cannot believe that the hand of Deity is in this madness! We shall not believe until the conviction is forced upon us, that the great mass of quiet, law-abiding, peaceable citizens of the North, constitutionally brave as they are, are ready for such ends, to precipitate such results, and enter upon a bloody career of desolation at home, so widely in contrast with the peace and prosperity of the past!

It may be that some portion of the Republican party and some of the Republican leaders, are anti-slavery or abolition mad! But the patriotic citizen will still hope and trust that God and the people will save us from such a terrible future!

Let the people demand an opportunity to act and be heard for or against these propositions! Let them demand a submission of amendments to the Constitution, and, if need be, of counter-amendments in case of disagreement, to them for their decision. Let not the men now clothed in a little brief authority dare to withhold from them this question NOW while we are yet at peace.

"*Quo[u]sque tandem abutere patientia nostra, Catalina?*" How long, ye political Catalines, will ye abuse the patience of the people? How long trespass upon their good nature and trifle with their best interests and their highest and purest hopes? How long shall the people bear with the insane ravings of Abolitionism? How long shall they be compelled to listen calmly to the worn-out platitudes of so-called Republican dogmas? How long to be vexed by the quibblers who set their own imaginations and illegal technicalities in array against the solemn decisions of legal tribunals delivered after a full and exhaustive argument? While our merchant princes are bankrupted in every direction; while prudent capitalists, in reasonable fear of coming convulsions, hoard their funds; while laborers are deprived of ordinary employment and mechanics fund diminished [*sic*]; while the wheels of business generally are blocked; while States are arrayed against States, and commotions grow by what they feed on—how long shall partisans mock at the public calamity? How long will the people be content with their Fabian policy of delay?—Will they willingly permit this condition to continue one, two or three years? Let the people answer.

94. [INDIANA WANTS PEACE]

(*Cannelton* (Ind.) *Reporter* [Douglas], January 31, 1861)

WHO dares to do right just now is a brave man. We have had too much partisan idolatry for the good of the country. He who sees the right, and hesitates to act until he consults a party leader, or because it is in conflict with partisan platforms, is simply a craven and a coward; he is a pitiable serf, unutterably beneath a freeman—dead to patriotic emotions, blind to the condition of his country, and deaf to her urgent calls upon him as her son. Has it come to this, that to be true to our country we are to favor civil war? is a man no longer a patriot unless he blinks the errors of his own section of the country, and expends all his breath in denouncing the people of another section? Is coercion the only term to be used to entitle a Northern man to the respect and confidence of Northern men? Are we to fling out the starry folds of our national banner and march with it to bloody strife against our Southern brethren; is the march of freedom to be tracked in blood and desolation; are the institutions of this country to be upheld by bayonets; is the salutation of brothers to be drowned in the belching thunder of cannon and the clash of arms; are we to forget God, gospel, religion and humanity, and make the Union one great human slaughter-pen? If not, in God's name we ask, why the Senate of Indiana passes a series of resolutions which are cowardly in that they are calculated to bring this state of things about, while there is unmistakably an effort to conceal the mad design; they are malicious and cowardly; no brave man voted for them, or can sustain them. They place Indiana in a false position. Indiana will not contribute her power to subdue the South. It is a bald and infamous libel upon her sons for the Legislature to so enact, inferentially or otherwise. We may question the right of secession; we may believe Southern States have acted prematurely, but we won[']t go to war with them. Our past, our present, and our future forbids it. But the Senate resolutions are not only an infamous slander upon Indiana, but they were uncalled for. Compromise is what we want just now. Any act which tends to lessen the chances for compromise is a parricidal blow aimed at the Union and at peace—and such we regard the Senate resolutions. That Republicans should vote for them is strange enough, but that a Democrat should do so is passing strange. Indiana is panting for an opportunity to tell the Union, North and South, that she is in favor of the Crittenden compromise. In Perry County we honestly believe that ninety out of every hundred voters would vote for them. An honorable settlement of the difficulties is what they want; not war or coercion, or anything that is calculated to bring it about. If the mad fanatics can press us into a war, it is us of the border who will have to give and receive the blows; it is our trade and commerce that is to be ruined; it is our towns that are to be sacked and pillaged; our wives and children who are to starve and suffer; our fields which are to yield briars, and our blood that is to purple the Ohio and its tributaries. We tell the Senate that we of Perry County are not the enemies of Kentucky. You may write strings of coercion resolutions upon all the foolscap of the nation, and pass them too, and we will be friends still. Before the election we believed if the Republicans were successful that troubles would come, and we boldly proclaimed it.—They have come; and now we do not intend, by any word of ours, to express the slightest sympathy with the party which hopes to escape the just odium of its principles by such resolutions as were passed in the Indiana Senate. We are determined that the Republican party shall have the full benefit of their record from the Chicago platform to the day of the final fall of the "divided house."—Let the ghost of a once great and powerful, peaceful and happy country stalk before them. Let their President, Governors, Senators, orators, and the rank and file of the party, look at it and contemplate the ruin they have wrought, until they shall be made to feel their loss, and be ready to make such compromises as are demanded by the constitution and by the equal rights of white men.

95. DISUNION AND COMPROMISE

(Boston *Daily Atlas and Bee* [Lincoln], February 1, 1861)

We are a commercial people. We are devoted to making money. Every gold dollar that comes into our possession is submitted to the alchemy of commerce with the intent to transmute it into four silver half dollars. Everything that tends to draw our attention from this permutation of the precious metals is considered a nuisance, and everything tending to reduce the net results of the transmutation to or towards four silver half dimes is considered an atrocity. And whenever the operation of mercantile schemes is interrupted, from any cause, the mercantile mind naturally seeks to remove the clog so that the machinery may run on as before, or change the gearing so that the power may be applied to other objects and produce other results.

Just at present the commercial interests of the United States are threatened. There is a disturbance in the workings of the machine. The cause is well known to be political, and to remove that cause is of course the object of everybody. We all know that a determination to withdraw from the Union, to break up the government, and action upon that resolve, have given rise to the trouble. And we are asked to compromise the difficulty.

But, before we compromise, we want to know whether by any compromise, any concession, any submission, we can remove that determination, annul that action? Before we concede, we want to calculate the "value received."

It is certain that South Carolina, Florida and Mississippi will not be satisfied to remain in the Union on any conditions. But we are told we may save the border States. It is, then, simply a question of value there.

The demand is made to secure and protect slavery in New Mexico, in Chihuahua, Sonora, Sinaloa and the northern departments of Mexico, when we shall have acquired them; to secure the right of slave transit in the free States; to pay for rescued fugitives. This is the very lowest price the country has to pay for the exercise of its privilege in electing a President.

It is generally agreed that the individuals who are concerned in the demonstrations consequent on the secession movement are guilty of treason. It is also generally agreed that of all the States which have passed ordinances of secession, but two, Georgia and South Carolina, and of these there is some doubt, have any right to be considered, if there be any vitality in the ordinances of secession, *States*. They were Territories of the Union before they were States. They became States of the Union. They are not States out of it. They never were, and except by conquest of their soil from the United States, and forcing an acknowledgment of their independence, they cannot desert the right of eminent domain which the federal government has over them. They have stolen the personal property of the government, they have proposed to seize their forts, to destroy the right of eminent domain, the reversionary right, in the real estate, and we are now asked to give them and all others more privileges than the most blatent [sic] platform of a pro-slavery party ten years ago, ever asserted as an attraction to the ignorant vote. The results of secession are clear. Commerce is at once stopped.

The only trade in ships that can be carried on must be the coastwise. No ship from a seceded port can get a clearance to be respected by the meanest gun-boat of the smallest power. With harbors closed, an embargo on the shipping, trade languishing, expense increasing, taxes heavy and business light, no end of debts to pay and no beginning of resource to pay with, is not the likelihood of retraction on the side of the rebels? If so, what is the cost? Does it compare with the cost of passing Crittenden's bill? What is the expenditure for a blockade, compared with the value of self-respect, settled principle, consciousness of honor, knowledge of well settled regulations? But the result. If any further guarantees are wanted, just let some State resolve itself out of the Union, and anything may be extorted, from a constitutional amendment that the President shall invariably be chosen from Florida, down to a repudiation of government bonds after the example of Mississippi. This is part of the cost of concession at this time.

With a government thus incompetently abject to the will of a State, does anybody suppose that American credit will be good? No future war could ever hereafter be carried on; no loan could be contracted at a less ruinous rate than that of Turkey or Austria. This is a part of the cost of concession.

The people decided, three months ago, that slavery should be excluded from the Territories. The proposition is now to override the people *forever* in this matter. We are told that anything is better than disunion; but we deny the alternative. We assert that the government has power to preserve itself; we want that power tried. And, at any rate, we are not disposed to give up anything that is our right without an equivalent—value received.

Abolish slave representation, and we will then consider about the establishment of slavery in Mexico and New Mexico. There is no dilemna [*sic*] now. A plain duty is before every patriot. The issue is not disunion or concession, it is the triumph of treason or the triumph of law. Do not despair of the Republic. If the strong arm raised the sword against its sacred life, let the strong arm oppose to the descending blade the defense of another blade, ready alike to shield or strike, and let the assassin be punished by the attacked. In our opinion if we desire the flag which braved the cannon of Algiers in the cause of freedom to the slave, which flaunted proudly on the battle breeze above St. George's cross for the rights of oppressed seamen, which waved over the National Palace in Mexico, proclaiming order in that turbulent city, to flutter as the emblem of a mighty nation on land and sea, we shall proclaim as our policy, the Union first, submission to traitors NEVER.

96. The Policy of Republicans

(Milwaukee Daily Sentinel [Lincoln], February 4, 1861)

To our apprehension, never was there [a] simpler matter, and one more easily comprehended, than the cause of the difficulty now existing in the country. Palpable facts, as well as the uniform and oft repeated assertions of Southern men, who are at the bottom of the difficulty, put it beyond question. The cause is, the fact, as manifested by the recent election of the dominance of a sentiment in the country, which does not regard the principle, or system, or policy of African slavery, as the chief good and chief interest of the country, to be protected and preserved at all hazards, even at the expense of any and all other interests.

It is not claimed that the party which is successful has ever done anything to the detriment of Slavery. It could not be claimed, with the least show of even common sense, for the reason that the party never before having been in power, could, by no possibility, have harmed it in any manner. Nor is it claimed that the party, when it comes into power,

266   NORTHERN EDITORIALS ON SECESSION

proposes any particular thing to the detriment of Slavery, where it has
any shadow of a constitutional right to exist.—It is not claimed, because
search would be vain for any evidence to base such an assertion on.

It is simply claimed that the late election has revealed the dominance
of a sentiment in the country which, as we said, does not regard Slavery
as a thing to be fostered by the hand of the General Government. It is
not enough that this sentiment does not propose to meddle with Slavery—that it is a sentiment, in fact, which so far as Slavery is concerned,
is really more of a sentiment to let it alone, than to interfere with it in
any manner. Indeed, that is the main complaint against it—that it *does*
propose to let Slavery alone; the South understanding well that nothing
can make the institution strong or even respectable, except the undivided energies of the General Government, and that, if left to itself, it
must pass into the course of ultimate extinction.

Such being, beyond peradventure, the grievance of the South, there
is no occasion whatever for becoming confused as to the remedy. The
remedy is as simple as the disease.

It is only to abandon the sentiment which the late election manifested. Simply to have LINCOLN come into power—to do precisely what
BRECKINRIDGE would have done had he come into power—maintain
Slavery as the corner stone of our Republican Institutions—and the
difficulty is at once at an end and the Union saved. Nor is there any
other remedy for it; and it is folly to talk of any other. To propose any
other concession or compromise to the South is to insult it by denying
the honesty and candor of its own assertions as to its grievances. We
speak, of course, of the remedies which negotiation or legislation involves. And our remarks are just as applicable to the Border States, as
to those further South. The Constitution now stands just as far in support and protection of Slavery, as the People of this Nation are willing
to go in that direction. The Republican party won power on a platform
quite as moderate, in that respect, as the temper of the People would
tolerate. There is, then, no concession we can make in that direction
without sacrificing everything. One backward step and the Republican
party tumbles from its platform into an unfathomable gulf. The Virginia Resolutions probably indicate as mild a concession as the Border
States—that is, those which demand any concession at all—will submit
to. Can we accede to those demands? Do not they sacrifice everything just
as fully as the demands of the most ultra Cotton States?

What the necessity, then, of becoming confused or disordered or disorganized? What the object of moving toward concessions, if we are not
prepared to sacrifice everything? Who can tell what possible good can

arise from sending delegates to the Border State Convention, or any other Convention, unless those delegates have authority to make an unconditional surrender of all the principles, purposes and objects of the Republican party? What the use, then, of denying our master, of seeking to escape from, or to deny the legitimate deductions of our own triumph, or of our own labors? If that triumph was not the triumph of the free sentiment in the Nation, and if our labors were not directed to that end, for heaven's sake, will some one tell us for what we have been struggling? Timid Republicans, pursued by the Pro-Slavery power, may, like the hunted ostrich, thrust their heads in the sand, but will they hide the purposes and objects of the Republican party thereby?

Never was the policy of the party plainer—never had it less to confuse it. The manifest facts of the nature of the opposition to it should make it as one man.

It has won power under the Constitution, precisely as the Pro-Slavery party has heretofore won power. It is entitled under the Constitution to that power. It is not called on to amend the Constitution, or in any manner to buy the right to that power. It is cowardly—it is a wrong to the Constitution and the Government to talk of it even. We should turn our ear as deaf as a stone, to any and every proposition which looked to even a consideration of compromise or constitution-mending, as a condition precedent to its peaceable possession of the Government, and obedience to the Government by all the members thereof.

From the action of the Illinois Republicans, and from other sources, we have reason to believe such is the position of President LINCOLN. It is the only position which contemplates saving the Government without first destroying it—and that in the hands of Mr. LINCOLN it is the policy which will save the Constitution and Union, and restore the country to peace, we do not doubt. Will not the Republicans everywhere stand by this policy?

97. LETTER TO HON. ABRAHAM LINCOLN

(Cincinnati Daily Enquirer [Douglas], February 10, 1861)

DEAR SIR: Early in the present week we understand that you will pass through this city, on your way to Washington, to take upon yourself the duties and assume the tremendous responsibilities of President of the United States. Notwithstanding the fact that you have expressed yourself highly indignant that any person who did not vote for you should have the hardihood to offer you any suggestions touching your future policy and course, we propose, in the best spirit, to address you upon that point. You ought not to take offense at any counsel that may be tendered you in the present exigency of our public affairs, even if it comes from a political opponent. You ought to recollect, although you were elected by a party, that you are now the President of the United States, and that you will require something more than the support of a party organization (which, upon the popular vote, was in a minority of a million of the people of the whole country,) to carry you successfully, and with credit and honor, through the arduous trial (from which the boldest might shrink) that lies before you.

No person was ever inaugurated President under such circumstances as will signalize your advent into power. In ten States of this Union having a population of *seven millions* not a single person cast his suffrage for you. In four others your vote was but a meager handful of a few hundreds in a population of millions. You were elected entirely by one section of the Union upon a platform of principles hostile to the rights and interests of the other, and you see to what calamities it has led. *Seven States,* with extraordinary unanimity, have passed ordinances declaring themselves out of the Federal Union, and eight more are preparing to follow if you and the party which elected you do not offer them some guarantee for their constitutional rights.

As the news of your election flashed over the lightning wires it had all the effect of a terrible national calamity. Contrast the condition of the country, political and pecuniary, now with what it was on that eventful 6th of November that saw you elected to the office of President. Not the loss of a dozen battles in a war with a first-class power—not the partial destruction of the crops by an affliction of nature—not the ravages of terrible disease and pestilence—would have produced that great public gloom and distress which have settled upon the country in consequence of your election to the Presidency. The objection, my dear sir, is not to your personal character, for of that the country has but little knowledge; but it is a fear, an apprehension of the policy of the organization which elected you, and to which it is understood you are committed. You, therefore, journey to Washington under peculiar and extraordinary circumstances; and such is the distressing condition of the country that you can hardly expect to receive those *fetes* and be met by the people with that joy and homage that they have always hitherto displayed in welcoming the President of the United States.

Hilarity and pleasure are out of character with the grave and solemn aspect of our political and business affairs, which have caused the most patriotic and sagacious to shake their heads with dismay and despondency. Dark and lowering as are the clouds of the future, you can do much to dispel them, and bring that peace and prosperity to the country which existed before you were elected. The influence you possess as the incoming President, with an immense patronage of millions at your disposal, gives you a position that is potent for weal or woe—for the preservation or destruction of the country, as you may see fit to use it. A year ago you were an humble private citizen in Springfield, Illinois, with no prospect whatever of greatness; but circumstances, in twelve months, have placed entirely in your hands the future destiny of the greatest Republic the world ever saw. The question is, can you rise above and throw off the shackles of party, trample under your feet all platforms but the Constitution of the Union, to which you will look with an eye single to the welfare of the whole people. It is said that you are wedded to the Chicago Platform; that you are opposed to any concessions or deviations from the path there laid down; that you will carry it out, whatever may be the consequences. We devoutly hope that such is not your intention; or if it is, that wiser counsels will prevail when you shall reach the Federal Capitol.

If you shall display that uncompromising spirit, then indeed are the days of the Union numbered, and we can bid farewell to all hopes of peace and prosperity. We may then close with the name of the present incumbent the catalogue of American Presidents! Your name will never be enrolled upon that glorious list, although for a period you may direct the affairs of a fragment of the Confederacy. Have you not, sir, an honorable and laudable ambition to fill the seat of a WASHINGTON, JEFFERSON, and JACKSON, and are you not willing to sacrifice even the dearest party ties in order to save your country from ruin? Patriotism, honor and the national good are in one direction, while party interests and personal prejudices call you to another. In a few weeks we shall see which of these paths you will take. The people are looking forward to your choice with breathless impatience. You have forborne to give, since your election, any official sign of what your intentions were, but the private signals we have had from Springfield from your immediate friends, have been of an ominous and unpleasant character. Your silence and those interpretations have been such as, thus far, to defeat the compromises which are pending in Congress. Do not take counsel, sir, of indiscreet pride, which says, "No compromise with States which have assumed a hostile attitude to the General Government." Personal punctillo [sic] and imagined honor can not be brought into a great question when the fate and fortunes of millions are involved in the issue. National prosperity against national destruction, peace against war, can not be allowed when thrown into the scale to kick the beam because punctillo [sic] and pride so decree.

Such was not the spirit which JACKSON and CLAY manifested when they compromised with the single State of South Carolina, when she stood in the menacing attitude of nullification and secession, in 1833. It is not the spirit which a statesman or a patriot displays when dealing with interesting and delicate questions, upon which hangs [sic] the fortunes and fate of their country. Do not say inauguration first and compromise afterward; for, believe us, if you do, and act upon it, the terrible words "too late" will be thundered in your ears after the ceremony is over —if you begin to move in the path of concession after Congress (which alone can afford relief) has adjourned, not to meet in many months, in the regular order of events. What is done must be done speedily—before the 4th of March—if we would save the country from ruin. In this conflict of passions and prejudices which has been invoked, the time for compromise and concession is rapidly passing away; and the golden opportunity that now presents itself, to restore peace and concord before Congress adjourns, will, if not improved, be lost forever.

By identifying your name and throwing the weight of your Administration upon the side of compromise and concession, you can cement again the bonds of the Union that have been rudely broken; you can achieve a fame that will be immortal in history. But if you stand out against compromise, you will fill a most dark and unenviable place in American annals, and it will be universally admitted that you have inflicted the fatal stab that destroyed the finest Government the world ever saw, and buried the brightest hopes of freemen in the gloom of an unparalleled disaster and ruin.

98. Is All Hope Lost[?]

(Madison *Wisconsin Daily Patriot* [Douglas], February 11, 1861)

If the saying, "it is darkest just before day," has any meaning in it, as applied to the present storm, then we think it must be nearly day— for we must confess the horizon is so dark that not a ray of light can be seen, and this darkness has become more and more intensified for the past two weeks, until it surpasses, in impenetrable gloom, the fabled Egyptian darkness, or the darkness which is said to have accompanied the crucifixion of Christ, and does it not portend the crucifixion of our Government and our liberties? Every electric flash from the South, announces some new and rash act, and these begin to quicken into culminating clouds, as portentitous [sic] and frightful as the dark, gloomy and impenetrable vapors that oft have been suspended over Mt. Vesuvius as a signal of destruction to beholders of the dreadful phenomenon.

First we heard of the peaceable secession (on paper) of a State—then another, and another, &c. Then the seizure of forts, arsenals, munitions of war and Government vessels—and even the Government funds—the common property of all. These, together with the lawless and brutal indignities offered to unprotected citizens, whose birth-right vouchsafed to them personal immunities from insults and degredations [sic]—these were enough to paralyze the faith of our people in the virtue of law, and the stability of Government, and to chill every hope by a fatal paralysis of disloyalty; but now we learn that not only Government property is seized but reprisals have been made of [on?] merchant vessels, the property of individuals, and the next flash may electrify the people with the dreadful, though not unexpected intelligence that blood has been drawn, and that sanguinary war, with all its horrors, has belched forth its sulphorus [sic] fire and smoke to shut out forever the last ray of hope, that this glorious Union may be spared the awful death of that sentence pronounced by fanatical politicians and demagogues. Reader, we arrogate no prophetic inspiration, but it is our firm belief, based on the madness that rules the hour, that we are on the threshhold [sic] of one of the most gorey [sic] struggles that ever deluged this fair earth with blood. We can see it in the electric flash—we can hear it in every gale that sweeps from the South—we can *feel* it in the unreasonable demands of the two extreme factions, that for the time rule the two dissevered sections, and in the utter refusal to yield an inch on either side.

This Government is no longer in the hands of the people. Factions, cormorants, and a banditti of unyielding, greedy demagogues have wrested it from the people, and like demons in conclave, are holding high carnival over the prospect of its downfall. True patriots try in vain to soothe the irritations, and to pour oil on the troubled waters. Philanthropists in vain appeal to the suicides to stay their hands. Christianity lifts its pleading voice to the God of nations in one ardent petition, that we and ours may be saved the dreadful shock of National annihilation. Old men, with gray hairs, and young men in the vigorous blood of youth—mothers—daughters—all ages, sexes, and conditions, save the ruthless pirates that bow down to the ephemereal [sic] idol of platform, or throw the blood of revenge on their altar of sacrifice—cry out in one voice—spare our country from the threatened desolation.

Civil war is staring us in the face. Its horrors already menace our peace and safety.—The Southern fire-eaters will not yield—the Northern fire-eaters are inexorable. Without a reconciliation, War is inevitable. We have seen that for months. We have warned the people of it. We have preached it to the people through the columns of the *Patriot* and from the stump—everywhere we could wield our pen or lift our voice, have we sounded the alarm, and in our humble way, endeavored to convince the people that the first attempt to carry out the Republican platform, would be met by resistance—that resistance was secession—secession revolution, and revolution would be nothing milder than a bloody, internecine war, that would enfeeble the people—eat out their substance—paralyze their energies—break up their commerce —ruin their prosperity—and slaughter their fathers and sons. We have urged these things, in the sincerity of our heart, because we believed them; and now, that these fears are taking shape, these warnings are being fulfilled, and the evils predicted are already upon us, it staggers our credulity in human intelligence to see men, either on the street or in the forum, exclaim "there is no danger."—Before the election, when party interests were at stake, we expected such responses, but now, in the hour of fatal realization, it amounts to one of those idiosancrasies [sic], of which political ambition and personal pride are the parents, and bodes the most fearful consequences.

The Union *is* in *imminent* peril. Unless something is done within the next ten days, to satisfy the Border States, this Union, and all its blessings are lost forever. This is no frantic delusion, but is the sum and substanse [sic] of reality. The Southern mind is inflamed, and it is a useless waste of time and breath to stop now to enquire whether they are unreasonable or not. The dilemma presents but too [sic] horns. We must either take the Crittenden proposition or disunion and war. That proposition covers an area of territory embracing twenty-four slaves, which Mr. Seward says are already slaves for ever, by existing laws. If the Union is dissolved that territory goes with the South, and slavery for ever fastened upon it, by laws and customs that no power this side can control. If the Union remains as it is, slavery is nominally there. The whole question is then a mere *abstraction*—a *theory*, with no power to practically change it. Now, we may take the "abstraction" horn—treat that as settled by the 1,800,000 who voted for the Chicago platform for President, and welcome war with all its blighting ravages; or we may take the other horn, and yield that abstraction to the South, and receive peace, amity and prosperity in exchange. Which will you take? Tell us, ye self righteous platform worshippers, which choose ye?

Remember, that if you force the country into a war, by your hair splitting theories, you must expect to fight the battles of your own choice. How many battallions [sic] of Wide Awakes can you rely on to penetrate the cane breaks [sic] of Mississippi, or the rice swamps of South Carolina, during the approaching dog days, to force your abstraction down the throats of the seceders? How can you expect the power of the Conservative element of the North to assist you, when you utterly refuse to listen to their friendly appeals—beseeching you, in God's name, to cease splitting hairs with swords, and to yield a little of your stubborn[n]ess for the general good and quiet. If you will do *nothing*, save to saintify [sic], your "great principle," and threaten the South with open war, we advise you now to send out recruiting officers, and an army roll, to be filled with valiant Wide Awakes as soon as possible, you will need them soon—very soon. And then, suspend the rules—pass your "war footing" bill, and have it enrolled and signed before midnight —issue bonds for $2,000,000—send out agents to negotiate, and put the interest in your tax roll—pass joint resolutions commiserating the hardships of the people, in the fall of 30 cents a bushel on wheat since the election, and the general paralysis that has overtaken trade and commerce, on account of your "great principle," then adjourn for six weeks, go home and tell the "dear people" how much you love them, and how well you have fathered their interests, and ask them to give you a *carte blanc* for another election.

99. WHAT OF THE NIGHT?

(Wilkes-Barre *Luzerne Union* [Douglas], February 13, 1861)

We are constantly asked our opinion of what will be the result of the present disturbed state of the country; but we know not that our opinion is worth more than that of any other intelligent man. Not long since we fancied we saw a ray of hope for a settlement that should at least prove satisfactory to the border States. If such could be brought about, we should then have great faith that the seceding States would finally, after having staid out in the cold awhile—after finding that the government will deal firmly in never receding from the collecting of the revenue, the protection of its property and the enforcement of its laws —after the "sober second thought" should have returned, and reason resumed its sway—that then those States would retrace their steps, and resume their place and their duties in the confederacy. But however ardent these hopes have been, we confess we see little to hope for now. The retiring of Southern members of Congress has given the Republicans a majority in both branches of that body; and it is painfully evident that the controlling forces of that party are in no temper for conciliation. Only last Thursday, Mr. Kellogg, of Illinois, made a speech in the House urging his Republican friends to accede in substance to the border State proposition. He was met with the jeers and the rebuke of nearly his whole party. The cry of that party, from the conscience-keepers of Lincoln down to Miner, is "no concession or compromise with armed traitors"—"first bring them in subjection and compromise afterwards." We regard this as a wicked trifling with the only hopes to save the country, for it requires little sagacity to see, that only by satisfying the border slave States, and attaching them to the fortunes of the North and the Union, can the Union be saved. And those border States are not traitors with arms in their hands. They are loyal to the Union and the government; and, at this moment stand, as they have all the while stood, discountenancing secession, and with outstretched arms imploring the North to meet them half way, give them solid ground upon which to stand, and they will give every guarantee that through good and ill they will stand by the country—survive or perish with it. But they are met with sullen indifference or absolute denial. For their fair and just propositions for conciliation and compromise, they are answered only, "we stand upon the Chicago platform, and we cannot sacrifice principle!" What principle of the Chicago platform, Messrs. Republicans, are you asked to yield? Is not its main plank, as regards slavery, a simple declaration against its introduction into free territory? Certainly it is. Now is there a single foot of the territories the character of which, for freedom or slavery, is not already determined? Certainly not. Then where do you stand? Are you not manifesting a disposition to permit the dissolution of the Union—to plunge, it may be, the country into civil war—to drench the whole land with fraternal blood, rather than yield what is a mere abstraction—rather than yield what after all would make no man a slave nor a single acre of the common domain slave territory? You cannot escape this conclusion, for your conduct and your words place you in just this position—we mean the radical portion of the party. Now we appeal to the conservative men of that party and ask, are you willing to take the fearful responsibility of refusing to meet the patriotic men of the border States, and thus precipitate this unnatural strife till it can be determined only on the field of blood and carnage? Is the Chicago platform so sacred—a mere platform of a political party, like other platforms passing away with the occasion that created it—is it so sacred that it must be held to though the very Republic shall crumble in ruins? Is such the part of patriotic men to act? No, no! Before God and the world, the men who bring such disasters upon the country as are now gathering thick and fast around us, for such reasons, will merit and receive the execrations of humanity in all eyes to come. Better ten thousand political platforms be overthrown than that the Union of these States for one hour be dissolved.—For us, rather all the negroes in Ethiopia be enslaved, and all that ever will be there, than that the great hopes of humanity and the race go down amid the ruins of the American Republic!

Could the people have an opportunity to speak, we should have high and exciting hopes yet for the welfare of the government. But their voice is smothered. The danger is imminent—cannot long be averted, and the avenues of public sentiment, as embodied in the people, are closed up. Even the voice of Pennsylvania can be heard in the Peace Congress at Washington, only through such fanatics as Wilmot and others of his ilk, who no more represent the sentiment of her people in this crisis than they do the sentiment of French Jacobins. Congress is inactive, the States North cannot be heard, for the forces of their government are stifled by partizan zealots and by a blind and unreasoning fanaticism; and therefore it is that we see no hope of reconciliation. It cannot be long before events will transpire, that must inevitably bring every slaveholding State in concert with the others—the line of separation will be drawn, and the Union irrevocably dissevered; for we have little hope indeed, that when once the bonds shall be broken they can again be united. Fraternal feeling once supplanted by the terrible hate and animosity of sectional determination and revenge, will never again be restored. If a Union in name, it would be but a union of discordant and belligerent elements, bringing back none of the glories of the past, nor the affections of a united people for their common country and a common government.

Looking at the matter in this light, we see but one hope left for the preservation of the Union, and that is this: Let the conservative men of the North, for the sake of the Union, discard party names and party platforms, and come together on the broad platform of the Union. Indications are developing every day that a large class of the Republicans are ripe for such an object. In Pennsylvania they would be marshalled by Cameron, Morris and others; in Illinois by Kellogg and his friends; and in other States by those who have already spoken, whose names we do not now recollect, embracing several in New England; and after Lincoln shall have been inaugurated, and the cohesive power of public plunder shall begin to weaken, thousands all over the country will take their places in the ranks. Such a party will be irresistible, and then as the elections are held and the issue of conciliation and Union, or no conciliation and disunion, shall be passed upon by the people, that verdict may be made so emphatic and overwhelming as to arrest the border States and save them from being driven into the ranks of secession. This is about the only hope we have left, and we shall hail a movement in that direction as a harbinger of peace and promise. Will not the Convention at Harrisburg, on the 21st, inaugurate it? It seems to us if it would do so, it would strengthen the hands and the hearts of the border States, and that there might yet be hopes of salvation.

100. COMPROMISES WITH SLAVERY

(Daily Milwaukee Press and News,[2] February 15, 1861)

He who says he will make no compromises with slavery is no friend of the Union, for the Union could never have existed, but for compromises with slavery.—Milwaukee News.

Does it follow that because some compromises with slavery were made in forming the Union, that we are to be eternally compromising with it? The people of the free States are willing to abide by all the compromises of the constitution, but are not willing to go on compromising and conceding forever.—Madison Journal.

That is the very question at issue—the matter of difference which is now threatening the destruction of the Union. It is not because the compromises of the constitution were not sufficient for the protection of the rights of the South, but because they have been disputed and denied, that new guarantees are now demanded. The South has never asked, and does not now ask, a single concession which it does not believe that the constitution, as it now exists, guarantees to it. Had the institutions of the South never been assailed by the North; had the compromises of the constitution been faithfully adhered to; had no attempt been made to pervert or evade the letter and spirit of that constitution, there would have been no irrepressible conflict; no demands for new guarantees; no compromise or concessions required; no secession attempted, for there would have been no ground for complaint. The Union would have remained as our fathers framed it; each section regulating its own domestic institutions in their [sic] own way, without let or hinderance [sic] from the other.

---

[2] The Press and News was not in existence during the presidential campaign of 1860. It was formed on December 15, 1860, by the merger of the People's Press and the News, both of which, however, had supported Douglas.

In presenting this question, our opponents assume that they are entirely on the defensive; that they are simply resisting the aggressions of the South. This position is utterly false. From the beginning of the slavery agitation, the aggression has been entirely and exclusively from the North, except slight retaliatory demonstrations from the South. Every compromise made has been at the expense of the South. The Republicans, or anti-slavery portion of them, start upon false premises, not justified by law or fact. In the first place, it is not true "that the normal condition of all the territory of the United States is that of freedom." The rule applies to just that condition in which the government found the territories. The normal condition of *all the territories* of the United States was that of *slavery*. The North West territory belonged to Virginia and was subject to her laws until she conceded them to freedom. The South Western territories were left to slavery, just where the laws of North Carolina and Georgia had held it. When Louisiana was acquired, its normal condition was that of a slave territory, and the treaty guaranteed to the people of that territory all their rights of property, and it remained a slave territory until the people of the South conceded all that portion lying north of 36 degrees 30 minutes to freedom. On the formation of our government slavery was the rule, *norma,* and free territory the exception. All the concessions since, have come from the slave states. These are the simple, historical facts and cannot be controverted. Now all the concessions demanded by the people of the South are the right of common use in the territories to the whole of which they had a legal and equitable claim. When compromise was demanded by the North, the South compromised; when an equal division of the common territory was asked for, they conceded it; shall the North now say, "We will make no further concessions and compromises, because we have the power to take the whole?"

We are not now arguing the moral right or wrong of slavery, but simply its political and legal *status* in our government. The legal right of slavery in the states is acknowledged by the Republicans; they deny, most emphatically, any intention of meddling with the institution where it exists by local laws. It being then an admitted right in the states; it being recognized and protected by the constitution of the United States; when we say it shall have no rights in the common territories of the United States in which it was the normal condition, we nullify by the strong hand of power, constitutional guarantees, treaty stipulations and the equality of States. Can the minority States accept this ultimatum without degredation [sic]! No matter what we may think about slavery; each State is to decide that question for itself, and we have no more right to prescribe freedom to them than they have to prescribe slavery to us. Under our form of government their rights are as sacred to them as are ours to us; and we assert without the fear of contradiction, that there is not a Northern State which would remain in the Union had the South the power and used it as unscrupulously towards us as the anti-slavery party of the North propose to use their power towards them. When the attempt was made to force slavery into Kansas, did the people of the North content themselves with waiting for legal and peaceful remedies? No! public meetings were held all over the North; men were enlisted for war, and arms placed in their hands; State legislatures voted supplies, and the authority of the federal government was scouted and defied.

Can we, ought we, to expect the people of the South to be less jealous of their rights or less ready to resent wrongs which they regard degrading and humiliating to them as a people?

Regarding the question of slavery simply as a political question—and beyond this we have no more right to meddle with it than we have to meddle with the religious sentiments of our neighbors—can we ask the South to accept less than is proposed by the Crittenden plan of settlement—a right to take their slaves with them to only a small portion of a common territory, in the whole of which slavery was the normal condition and confirmed by treaty?

Had these just rights of the South been half respected, there would have been now no demand for concessions and compromise. But these are not their only ground of complaint, as the editor of the *Journal* well knows. The old compromises guaranteed to the South, by constitutional provision, the rendition of their fugitive slaves; a majority of the free States have, by legislative enactments, evaded, avoided, or openly and squarely nullified that provision. This same editor of the *Journal*, only two years ago, signed an address to the voters of Wisconsin, urging the election of a candidate for Supreme Court Judge solely upon the ground of nullifying the fugitive slave law in this State; and one of his colleagues, no more guilty than himself, is now in prison suffering the penalty of a violation of that law, after having been once discharged from the custody of the United States Court by our State Court, and after having been rescued by a mob, protected by our State authorities. In view of these facts, is the South not justified in demanding additional securities, or refusing longer to be bound by a compact which the North openly disregard and violate at will?

101. The Reaction—The Union

(Boston Post [Breckinridge], February 16, 1861)

The talented Senator Green, of Missouri, has just made the remark in the Senate, that there must be a reaction in the public mind of the North, or else the Crittenden amendments, would be good for nothing. Certainly, the remark is a sound one. Law, to be efficient, must be based on public opinion. Now, the most favorable sign of a re-construction of the old Union, or to speak more precisely, of a return to the normal form of our national life, one Congress, is the substantial reaction that is going on in the North. All that is now asked is for the time that is necessary in order to clothe this reaction in the shape of authentic evidence.

Our Federal Government is emphatically the offspring of public opinion, and is the first instance of such in the modern civilized world. It may be accurately said that American nationality never appeared as a great central power conferring local rights, but as a popular sentiment dictating successive forms of law devised to protect the rights of the primordial elements of the nation, the States, and defending the common flag. This feeling always regarded the people of the several States, so far as the *sentiment* of nationality is concerned—as one people, with common rights, common interests, and a common destiny—as brethren of one family. Such unity as this made our country.

Nothing during the past ninety days has been more depressing to discriminating observers here at the North, to all indeed who see and deplore the mischief of abolitionism, than the extent to which the existence of this old feeling of fraternity has been kept out of sight at the South. Especially in the secession States, the great fact has been mostly ignored, that there is a majority of the people of the thirty-four States of more than a million by the November vote, and which has been vastly increased since, holding precisely to the vital unity of the Fathers; the same unity that joined together the patriots of the South and of the North in the revolution; the same unity that gave birth to the early Congress, and that culminated in that matchless result—the Federal Constitution.

Those who make this feeling the paramount rule of their political action cannot but shrink back with horror at the bare idea of shedding the blood of brethren in a civil war. This is the sentiment that is astir now; it is making itself felt North and South with effect, and will march on as certainly as the sun shines, with a conquerer's [*sic*] mighty strength. It is not for civil war, but for the Union of the Fathers. At present Tennessee, as though the spirit of the Hermitage felt itself insulted, bears the palm at the South; Rhode Island and New Jersey at the North. It is assuredly here in Massachusetts. The evidences of it are as many as circumstances have permitted to be exhibited, and all that a patriot could wish. Go among the people, in the mechanics' shops, and the merchants' stores, and in the village centres, and see how patriots of all parties, Lincoln men as well as others, are rasping down the whole brood of Abolition, civil war men. This feeling is finding vent in petitions for conciliation. It is seen in the fourteen thousand petition[s] from Boston alone; it is seen more precisely in the petitioning for the Crittenden pacification. Charles Sumner feels this. To be sure, he has a short, crisp, fanatic sort of a mode of explaining this away, namely, by telling the people they do not know what they are about, as though reading hadn't been taught in the common schools for a whole generation! This won't do. The people know what they are about, and see with indignation what he is about. They know that such Abolitionism as he has flooded the Senate with, has well nigh destroyed the fairest nation which the sun shines upon. As soon as the people can get at him they will tumble him from the seat of power which he has abused, and fill his place with a man with heart and mind enough for the whole Union.

We repeat: there is nothing more certain than the fact of reaction here. It is seen in the last municipal elections in nearly all the large cities, where the Republicans of the Andrew and Phillips stripe were beaten horse and foot. Sumner would explain this by saying the people didn't know what they were about! Then, too, there is the tremendous feeling not only here in Massachusetts, but all through the North, against those pests, Abolition demagogues, which will not respect the sex. Even Susan Anthony can't get a hall to speak in, far or near; or if this noted Abolitionist does get one, to the regret of all friends of free speech, people won[']t listen to her. All this cannot be justified, but such is the fact; and it seems at least to show the drifting of the current.

In truth, the Union of the fathers is *not* dissolved. Between the men who have just voted for the Union in Tennessee and the like men all through the South—the six Cotton States not excepted—and the conservatism of the North, as represented among Republicans, in the West by Kellogg and Douglas, in the East by Adams, and in the Middle States by Cameron, there is the old Union feeling, the vital spark of a true National Unity. It is to such hands that the country looks to see the dark curtain of the present lifted. Then will appear the blue sky of peace and future glory for our country.

102. THE SACRIFICE DEMANDED

(Sandusky *Daily Commercial Register* [Lincoln], February 23, 1861)

The basis [*sic*] principle of popular government is that the will of the majority, within the prescribed limits of the Constitution and the law, shall rule. There is no such thing as popular government without this rule. That popular will may not always be right in matter of principle, and may also be wrong in matter of bare expediency or policy. But in our form of Government, the frequency of popular elections admits of the speedy application of a corrective by the people, after the sober second thought. The nicest care and the rarest wisdom were displayed in the arrangement of the machinery of our government to avoid all the evils of popular excess or error, by the checks and balances which are interposed. The election of Representatives every two years, infuses the freshness of popular life into that branch of the Legislature, while the less frequent election of Senators, holds in check the people so that, except in case of misrepresentation or actual corruption, when a concurrence in sentiment of the two branches of Congress is reached, the will of the people will necessarily be prudently and dispassionately expressed. Back of these being the Executive and Judiciary, the one still farther removed from the people and the other altogether removed from them, to hold in check the Representatives; surely the will of the people is sufficiently restrained.

Resting beneath the whole structure, and giving life to it all and animating it, is the will of the people as the governing power.—Subject that will to any restraint other than that imposed by the Constitution and the laws and you destroy the Government. You rob it of the one grand animating element. No matter what you consent to interpose it would be equally fatal. It may be an armed and organized mob, or it may be military despotism; no matter what it is, the moment the will of the people within the safe limits prescribed is deliberately defeated and purposely denied, that moment a fatal blow is struck at popular Government. That denial of the popular will may come in open and armed rebellion, may come in the shape of restraints upon free discussion, may come in the pretended form of resistance to oppression—no matter how it comes—if it succeed, popular government is destroyed in so far and so long as the popular will is denied.

It is at this very point that the great sacrifice, the fatal sacrifice is demanded of Republicans and all Union men, as it is said, to save the Union by concessions. The first step is the most fatal step of all, and that once taken, it scarcely matters what others follow. The people, the whole people, on the 6th of November last elected the executive officers of the nation, in full and complete conformity to the Constitution and the laws. In that election they indicated the policy which they wished their chosen officers to pursue. If they acted unwisely either in the choice of their officers or the approval of the principles on which they elected them, the wise forethought of the framers of our Constitution prevented any evils from flowing from their action, before the people themselves could again reconsider their verdict. Congress, in both branches, was against the new officers and the new policy, and a new election would have to be held before either branch would contain a majority of those friendly to them.

In advance of carrying out the will of the people as expressed by their votes, men band themselves together to destroy the Government, dissolve the Union and defeat the expressed will of the people. Outside of them are a multitude more who say, though in a different form of words, for fear of war, for fear of bloodshed, for fear of strife, the verdict of the people must be qualified by concessions and Compromises. The gist of the whole matter is, that the voice of the people must be denied, the fundamental principle of our Government must be set aside. The vital principle of a popular Government must be destroyed. No matter that it is claimed that the people have changed their views and would decide differently in the view of threatened war and armed rebellion than they did on the 6th of November last. That does not change the result, for at any time, threats of war, the forms of rebellion and the phantom of bloody battle fields may be evoked for a like purpose. The very engagement to concede, would make a sacrifice more fearful than all other sacrifices combined. Of course misapprehensions, perversions and misrepresentations may be corrected, but nothing more, without doing the most grievous hurt imaginable to the cause of human liberty.

We ask Republicans, we ask Democrats, we ask all men who love liberty and would jealously guard the rights of freemen as guaranteed in the Constitution framed and perfected by the wisdom of our fathers, to calmly consider this view of the present trouble. It is vastly easy to talk about compromises and concession [and] to mouth conciliation and thunder anathemas against those who refuse, but it is another thing deliberately and with premeditation, to consent to the destruction of popular government. It is one thing to breathe sentiments of peace and Union and promise concession for the sake of temporary and short-lived repose and a false and treacherous harmony, and quite another thing to carry out those pleasant words and promises, when by so doing the strong foundations of our free institutions are sapped, and a worse than the Trojan Horse is introduced to capture the citadel of freedom. If that were possible, the incipient step of a compromise of essential principles, is worse than guaranteeing the extension and spread of slavery itself. Even now, when a "Peace Congress," so called, is in session, and so many are clamoring for the perversion and denial of the will of the people, we thrust these thoughts before our readers, and ask for them the most serious attention.

103. Adjustment, Compromise, Concession

(*Philadelphia Inquirer* [Independent], February 23, 1861)

Intending things right and expedient—things just, honorable, and proper, we do not hesitate or stumble at words. Things are wrong, alarmingly wrong, just now, and we labor for their rectification. Just as far as the cry of the ultraist for "The Union, the Constitution, and the Enforcement of the Laws," has any practicable and proper meaning, we yield to none in our devotion to them. But the *Union* arose from, and rests on, the consent of the people of every section of the country; the *Constitution* is a bundle of compromises; and the *enforcement of the laws* does not fairly contemplate civil war. The Union is not a consolidated Republic; the Constitution is not a system of pure democracy, conferring omnipotence upon a simple majority of the federal citizens; and the Federal laws have ends to be secured as well as obligations to be enforced.

It is plain as reason can make it, that the States did not intend to surrender or even imperil their essential differences of interests and pursuits by entering the Union. They did not intend to be forced, by majorities of votes in Congress, or in the Electoral College, into conformity and uniformity of industrial and civil enterprizes and institutions. The provisions of the Constitution show that the individuality of every State is carefully guarded. The amendments pressed upon the first Congress, as conditions subsequent to the adoption, serve hardly any other purpose than to show the jealousy, and emphasise the caution, with which the Slave States yielded to the Union. Everything that could be done was done to equilibrate the jarring interests of the Confederacy. The States were made equal in the Senate, without regard to population, to check the power of numerical majorities in legislation, and, as far as that element goes, equal in the election of the National Executive. Even a three-fifths representation of slaves in the lower House was conceded to the South, to bring its power as near as possible to a balance. This apportionment did come within eight votes of equalizing the Slave and Free States after the first census was taken. But the race for power between the sections had scarcely begun when the South was found relatively weaker. Louisiana for this, as well and as much as for other reasons, was brought in to restore the balance. Soon after, Florida contributed her mite as a make-weight; then Texas, and finally the acquisition, by conquest and purchase from Mexico, was added in the same spirit of compromise or equilibration that ruled the Convention of 1787. "No compromise" at the beginning would have meant no union, and at every epoch in its history which tried its force, would have meant disunion. Our Federal Union has no precedent in the world's history. It was an experiment at the beginning—it has been an experiment, demanding expedients, in every crisis since; and it is an experiment still. Seventy years of current success, secured by concurrent concessions, have not given it permanence independent of the concessions, compromises and adjustments which are the very essence of its character.

We are told that nothing has happened to create the present crisis; that no wrong has been done; no injury inflicted; none threatened; and that all is Constitutional in the action of the party now virtually in power—that the protection of Government, which draws with it the allegiance of the people, has not been withdrawn, and will not be stretched to usurpation or abuse. In the logic of law and civil polity, this is true, to the letter and in the spirit. Neither jurist nor publicist can have any doubt of all this. But something else has happened, which, while it in no way justifies secession, may be entitled to consideration as matter and ground for new concession, adjustment or compromise, in the spirit of the Constitution and the several virtual amendments made at the intervals which required them.

Any time before the year 1800, the Slave States had an equal representation in the Senate, and were only eight votes in minority in the House of Representatives, and in the Electoral College. Now they are eight votes behind the Free States in the Senate, and about sixty-two in the lower House, under the next apportionment, and consequently in a minority of seventy in the election of the President. This, so far as political power in the Union depends upon mere representative force, puts them at our mercy, or our justice or magnanimity—a dependency that we would be as slow to accept as they are to rely upon. Moreover, the North has just now made a fearful demonstration of its power. It has elected a President without the help or consent of a Southern electoral vote. The North has been provoked and driven into sectionalism; the South is beaten, punished and humbled for its many transgressions, and both parties are angry. The "Union, and the Constitution as it is" are without the harmony of union, and without the proper force of a supreme law; and the enforcement of the laws asks the destructive coercion of the sword, in the place of that salutary coercion by the magistracy which the Constitution intended.

It does seem to us to be the time for a new adjustment, or for new assurances to the party menaced by the present condition of things.

But we propose no surrender of right; we do not propose to cement or reconstruct the Union with wrong. We would offer the South the securities and assurances that should satisfy their just claims and well founded apprehensions from the Federal power which has passed out of their hands, never to return again until peace is restored, confidence renewed, and that aggressive spirit which their fears inspired is laid aside. For, not until the recklessness of slavery extension, slavery intrusion, and slavery propagandism is wholly abandoned, can the South again have a party in the North to work with them and for them to any purpose.

The Constitutional election of a President by a sectional vote is no ground of complaint under the Constitution, and it is, therefore, no ground for secession; but it may be a reason for giving renewed assurances. An Executive, like an Executor, may be fairly asked to give additional securities, when additional power and additional trusts are vested in him, beyond those contemplated in the original bond. The Constitution took care to prevent both President and Vice President from being citizens of the same State. If the present exigency had been in contemplation, ten to one but the fathers would have provided that the chances of the Executive office should have been balanced over MASON and DIXON, so as to prevent that sectionalism on a grand scale, which they ruled out on a smaller and less dangerous one.

But the concessions which we propose are not gifts or favors—not sacrifices of the North, or helps for the extension of the institutions of the South. We believe that climate and the natural course of things rule the matter of slavery absolutely; and that no interference by Congress can ultimately affect it. Believing this, we would anticipate such ultimate settlement, agree to it now, put it out of debate, out of Congress, and out of party politics; and so give the Union peace, quiet its fears and its struggles; and while giving the question time to settle itself according to the necessities of things and the will of Providence, turn the attention of the people, the parties, and their representatives, upon the proper business of the nation, and so secure its real welfare.

The crisis is, in the language of Mr. LINCOLN, an artificial one, though not the less fearful and severe on that account. It is artificial, so far as it lacks present substantive cause, and even as it is employed or engaged with a subject which it can in no wise manage or control. The extremists of the North are quite sure that the Secessionists can do nothing for the benefit or the security of their pet scheme of extending or defending slavery, by withdrawing from the Union. The extremists of the South risk all the chances and changes of revolution and dissolution, hostile legislation and civil war, in the expectation of equivalent benefits. But who shall convince either party that it is wrong in apprehension or conduct?

The Unionist can answer both without an argument with either. He can agree with both and dissent from both at the same time, upon the issues which they have raised, and reconcile both without convincing either of them, by proposing the concessions which give away nothing that the one party can in any event withhold, and at the same time bestows [sic] nothing which the other is in any danger of losing. He only ascertains the inevitable, and compromises a quarrel which can no way influence it, but may destroy the belligerents, and must do much damage while the final issue is settling itself by its own proper forces and tendencies.

Everybody knows that slavery cannot live above 36 deg. 30 min. Let us agree upon that now, and pledge ourselves to settle it without further dispute. It is just as clear to us, that all the existing territory South of that line is destined to free labor, and is just as unfit for slave occupation. But the point of honor, or abstract right, or equal right or chance comes in, and the South insists. Very well; we will submit New Mexico to its chances by any fair arrangement which will give us peace, and then await the issue. If Northern and foreign immigration cannot take that region from the slave colonizers, it is because it does not invite the free laborer and his free institutions, as Kansas and California did, and for its unfitness is to be abandoned to the slow occupation of the people encumbered with a system which can scarcely get a foothold in any but semi-tropical regions, and cannot long hold its place except in the most favorable conditions. New Mexico is below the geographical line of compromise, but it is above the line of climate favorable to slavery. It is an idle quarrel, indeed, or an artificial one, if the phrase has more authority, but the bloodiest wars have had as little cause. It is as capable of mischief as if it were worth all the sacrifice it may cost. We would therefore treat it gravely, and do what in us lies to avoid and avert the evil. Woe to the men upon whom the responsibility rests, if they fail their country and the world's hopes in this crisis. Platforms must give way to the Constitution, party to the Union, and the laws must be executed—not made incapable of execution.

104. Shall We Have a Federal Union?

(New-York Daily Tribune [Lincoln], February 27, 1861)

The border Slave States make certain enormous demands of the American People, as the condition of their future allegiance to the General Government. Many well-meaning, but short-sighted persons clamor for these concessions, in the hope of thereby preserving the Union. They forget that the nature of the concessions demanded, as well as the fact of making them at all, under existing circumstances, will involve the destruction of the Central Power, and must result, if granted, in a dissolution of the Federal Government altogether.

The border Slave States are said to be desirous to maintain the Union. We wish it were so, but unhappily they have, at the outset, assumed a fatal position. They say that the enforcement of the United States laws in any seceding community will be considered "coercion," and that, if it be attempted, they will go with the South. What, then, do they propose to us? A Government which cannot be enforced! Laws which inflict no penalty in case of their violation! But can any human authority be respectable without the means to make itself respected? Can the body politic survive in a state of permanent paralysis?

Now, what are the concessions demanded? The resignation of the very principles and measures on which an overwhelming majority of the People have just instructed the Federal Administration to insist; the establishment of the very policy which the popular verdict has so emphatically condemned; the incorporation into the Constitution of the very Breckinridge Platform which even the corrupt Democratic party was compelled to repudiate!

Suppose we succumb to the will of the minority. Suppose we stifle our convictions, desert our principles, stultify ourselves in our own eyes and in those of our antagonists, and guarantee the perpetuation and extension of Slavery over all present and future territory south of 36° 30'. Suppose, also, that the seceding States are thereby pacified, and induced to resume the outward forms of Union. What then? All this will not preserve nor restore our national unity. On the contrary, it will have destroyed it forever; for we shall have established a new and fatal precedent. Henceforth, the bare majority of any single State can nullify our Government at its pleasure. To-day it is Carolina, to-morrow it may be Rhode Island or Delaware which assumes to dissolve the Confederacy. The will of the majority of the American people constitutionally expressed can no longer decide anything. We have established anarchy and inaugurated chronic civil war. Hereafter, Congress will no longer be a legislature, but a debating society. Its enactments will not be laws, but mere empty expressions of sentiment. The judicial functions of the Supreme Court of the United States will be superseded. The supreme power will be vested solely in the Legislatures of the States, and the forms of national unity will henceforth be an idle mockery. The only real alternative, therefore, is between the enforcement of Federal authority upon every citizen of the United States who resists it, or an actual dissolution of the Federal Government.

If, in our effort to enforce the Federal laws, we find it necessary, or expedient, to slough off the fifteen Slave States, we shall at least have left us a Federal Union of nineteen homogeneous States, free, populous and powerful, with an efficient central organization and a continent for its developement. The Southern Confederacy, on the contrary, vitiated by the suicidal principle of State Secession, will be only an aggregated disintegration, a rope of sand, a tossing, incoherent chaos of petty nationalities. There can be no question as to the result. Rent by internal discords and jealousies, the seceding States will, one by one, abolish Slavery and return, under the irresistible force of social gravitation, to the peaceful haven of national unity, under the Constitution handed down to us by our fathers.

The vital question, then, for our consideration is not whether Freedom or Slavery is to be the future guide of the Federal Government, but whether we shall have a Federal Government at all. If so, it must be by prompt, decisive action. We must either treat the fact of Southern Secession as a revolution, and recognize the independence of the seceding States; or we must confront it as treason, and put it down by the military forces of the loyal States. Either course will be frank, honorable and comprehensible. Either mode of action will result in a permanent Federal nationality. Any other proceedings involve a logical fallacy, and must result in imbecility and failure. Shall we maintain a national existence? Shall we have a Federal Union?

VII

MEASURES FOR PEACE

105. Party Policy

(Muncie *Eastern Indiana Courant* [Lincoln], January 3, 1861) [1]

In these times of secession and compromise, it is well for the people of the North to look about and determine upon some course of policy, and in so doing it is of vital importance that we should let that policy conform strictly with right and justice to all portions of the country. In view of the fact that a number of propositions are now offered to the country for the settlement of existing difficulties, it is necessary that they should be carefully examined before we commit ourselves to them. In the first place we would warn the members of the Republican party of the danger to which the party is exposed through the operation of a class of men styling themselves the conservatives.—They, with Tom. Corwin at their head are engaged in a movement which is calculated to utterly destroy the Republican party, unless we nip the thing in the bud. Under the pretext of compromise, they are attempting to commit the Republican party to a truckling pro-slavery policy, which they are offering to the people under the specious title of *Conservatism.* This plan is embodied in the following propositions:

The first is, a division of Territory with the South, prohibiting slavery North of a certain line, and leaving the question open South of it.

Who cannot see that this is a total backing down from the principle of opposition to the extension of slavery into Territories, which was sanctioned by every Northern State, by the election of Abraham Lincoln to the Presidency? This policy is advocated upon the ground that it will operate against the extension of slavery. It is contended that we would secure a certain amount of Territory to freedom, and the balance would be made free by the over-powering influence of freedom in populating them. It is the old doctrine of the Missouri Compromise, and is sustained by the same argument. The question to be decided by the people

[1] Taken from the Centreville *Indiana True Republican*. The date given is that of the appearance of the editorial in the *Republican*. There is no *Courant* (Muncie, Indiana) listed in Gregory, *Union List of Newspapers*.

is whether they are willing that we shall be sold out to this slave-driving policy. Every man is acquainted with the history of the Missouri Compromise. That was declared unconstitutional by the Democratic party, and it repealed it. Shall we take up the same measure, and commit the country to the re-enactment of the same policy? Shall we make another sacrifice of freedom, by another compromise, to be broken at the will of the South? The history of the Missouri Compromise teaches every intelligent man that compromise is useless. The interests of freedom have been sacrificed to slavery for the last forty years, for the purpose of preserving the Union. The slave power has controlled the entire administration of the Government during all that period. It demanded the Missouri Compromise for its benefit, and it destroyed it for the purpose of advancing its interests. The advancement of the institution of slavery has been, during all that time, the policy of the general Government; while the interests of freedom have been totally disregarded. The people have lately repudiated this policy. Shall we return to it for the sake of the Union? Shall we bow our necks, and humiliate our selves before the slave oligarchy of the South? Shall we allow the slave drivers to dictate to us the only terms upon which the Union can be perpetuated, when it assumes that the Government shall be administered solely and exclusively for the advancement of slavery? Shall the majority succumb to the minority and allow it to constitute itself a supreme dictator in the Government, or shall we adhere to the doctrine that the majority shall rule, and that its will, when constitutionally expressed, shall be the supreme law of the land?

The first proposition, if we can understand it, is designed to prevent the extension of territory in a southern direction, thus checking the opportunity of the slave States to extend their institution in that direction.

The second proposition is simply abandoning the doctrines of the Republican party, and endorsing the Popular Sovereignty doctrine of Stephen A. Douglas. It is supported by the same argument used in defence of the Compromise measure. It is predicated upon the hypothesis that the North will populate the territories, and convert them into Free States. It throws down the gauntlet to a perpetual strife in the Territories, between the free and slave interest[s]. It leaves all the territories subject to all the evils which Kansas has suffered by the conflict of opposing interests. The doctrine has been repudiated by every Free State, and the attempt to commit the Republican Party to its heresies will meet with universal condemnation.—Some weak-kneed & cowardly politicians may be intimidated into this policy by the threats of the

South to dissolve the Union, but the majority of the people will never consent to it.

We predict that the Republican Party will not permit itself to be [s]old out to the Douglas party, by any such movement. Let the Republican party even countenance this truckling policy, and before the next five years it will be totally annihilated in every State in the Union, and upon its ruins the pro-slavery dynasty will be re-established and the reign of slavery will again be inflicted upon the country. The only safe course for the Republican party to pursue, is in the line marked out by the Chicago Platform, and any divitation [deviation?] from that course will be its death knell. We again warn the Republican Party. Those are traitors in our ranks, who are plotting against its principles and who are attempting to betray it into the hands of the enemy. Be firm: stand by the fixed principles of the party—forsake them, and all is lost. Beware of the specious coloring of conversatism [sic]. It conceals the essence of treason to our principles, and aims to strike down the anti-slavery element of the Republican Party. It is conceived by sore-headed politicians—men who are disloyal to the Republican Party, and if it is not scrup[ul]ously guarded against it will totally annihilate the Republican Party. The leaders expect to rally around the standard, the Douglasites, Bellites, and water gruel Republicans. They anticipate the erection of a great *conservative* party, basing its principles, upon a milk and water policy upon the question of slavery. They expect to drag together the odds and ends of all parties, but the chief strength will come from the Democratic party.—Routed and defeated upon its false pretenses, it will seek the most congenial home offered by the other parties. In this conservative party they can find comfortable quarters. *Conservatism* was its rallying cry during the late campaigns and it will readily find a place of action in the ranks of the *conservatives*. The future strength of such a party is easily seen. It will carry with it no moral force, having no fixed principle of action, save that of party triumph. It can never stand against the combined forces of that great party which is based upon the great principle of freedom, justice and equality.

The third proposition, in reference to the Fugitive Slave Law, in part, will meet with the approbation of all parties. It is generally conceded that the South is entitled to an efficient Fugitive law, and a law of that description, allowing the right of trial by jury, the right of appeal to the higher courts, and a fair and impartial trial of the Fugitive, would be executed in good faith by every Northern citizen. The "personal liberty bills" [of] some of the States, which are the result of the odious features of present law would be instantly repealed. The punishment of persons for obstructing the execution of the law, would be just, but the policy of making a State pecuniar[i]ly responsible for the acts of any of its citizens, would never be consented to. He will find men to meet him, and assist him to gain his freedom, however wrong it may be in the eyes of legal enactment. If there are persons so indiscreet as to disobey the law they should be amendable [*sic*], but there is no justice in requiring a State to pay for the illegal acts of its citizens.

106. The Attitude of the North

(New-York Daily Tribune [Lincoln], January 7, 1861)

To the Hon. John J. Crittenden, *U. S. Senate:*

Dear Sir: The People of the Free States observe and appreciate your efforts to reconcile what are improperly termed "sectional" differences and maintain the integrity of the Union. They do not doubt your sincerity nor your patriotism. They realize that, even when you most wronged yourself in upholding the policy embodied in the Nebraska bill and the consequent dragooning of the free settlers of Kansas with intent to bend their necks to the yoke of Slavery, you yielded to a local ignorance and prejudice which you could not control, and which, because you would not minister unreservedly to its wild exactions, has consigned you to private life after the 4th of March next. They make due allowance for the ferocity of the Pro-Slavery fanaticism which has thus ostracised you, and leniently judge that, though a bolder man might have done better, an average man would have done worse; and they are not ungrateful for your honest and earnest efforts to save the Union from disruption and the country from the horrors of civil war. They feel sure that, were the People of the Slave States in the average as enlightened and as just as you are, the dangers now impending might be dispelled or averted. Nevertheless, they do not and will not assent to the Compromise proposed by you—that is a fixed fact. Here and there one who never shared their convictions, but only affected them in order to get himself elected to some high office, or who owns real estate in Washington City and feels that it is likely to be ruined by Disunion, or who has a great Railroad contract in Missouri or some other Slave State, and may be broken by the depreciation of that State's bonds, or who is a lame duck in the Stock Market and hopes to win back all he has lost and more with it if a Compromise can be fixed up, may accede to your project or to something equivalent; but ninety-nine of every hundred Republicans are opposed to any such bargain, and will not be concluded by it if made. Moreover, thousands of Democrats and of

11

1

Conservatives who stood with you on the platform of "The Union, the Constitution, and the enforcement of the Laws," are also opposed to any such arrangement while the Federal authority is defied and the Union threatened with subversion. Let me briefly set forth the reasons which unite the North in resistance to any Compromise at present:

I. One State to-day is in open rebellion against the Federal authority; others are preparing to follow her immediately. Federal arsenals and forts, containing great numbers of cannon, many thousand stand of arms, and great quantities of military stores, have been seized and are now held by the insurgents, not in South Carolina only, but in Georgia, Alabama, and I believe other Slave States which have not yet declared themselves out of the Union. The slender Federal garrison of the forts in Charleston harbor is this hour in peril of destruction by an overwhelming rebel force, and not only its commander, but the President of the United States is railed at and defamed because that commander has concentrated his three or four score soldiers in that fortress where they can hold out longest and sell their lives most dearly. The Federal Custom-House at Charleston has been turned over to the state and the late U.S. Collector assumes to clear vessels on the authority of the nation of South Carolina. That pseudo nation assumes to be out of the Union, withdraws her Members from Congress, and sends Embassadors to Washington as to a foreign capital. In view of these high-handed proceedings, and the scarcely dissembled menaces that all the Federal forts in the South will soon be seized by the Disunionists, and the inauguration of Lincoln at Washington on the 4th of March next prevented by an insurgent force, the People of the Free States very naturally repel any Compromise that will enable these rebels to boast that they have frightened or backed down the North. We are *not* frightened hereabouts; we do not feel a bit sorry for what we have done; and we do not capitulate to traitors. If, then, what you propose were inherently admissible, we could not assent to it now.

II. I need not tell you that what you propose (the line of 36° 30′, with free course to Slavery below it) has been thrice offered to and thrice rejected by the Free States. We deem it unfair on many grounds, but conspicuously because, when Louisiana, Florida, and Texas were successively acquired, the fact that they were previously slaveholding was relied on to bar any demand that they should henceforth be even half Free; and we insist that the rule which gave them to Slavery now consecrates New-Mexico and Arizona to Freedom. You would not expect Republicans to vote for your project if there were no threats and no danger of Disunion or violent resistance to Mr. Lincoln's rule; and you must not hope to extort from our fears what you could not expect us to concede from a sense of justice. You do not mean to degrade us; but your proposition, if accepted, would have that effect; and you must allow us to judge what is due to our own honor.

III. Your friends in the Slave States do not talk right. Take the following samples from the resolves of a *Union* meeting held on the 1st inst., in your own city of Frankfort, Ky., and addressed by your friend, Gen. Combs:

"8th. That the resolutions of compromise submitted by Mr. Crittenden in the U. S. Senate, should have met with prompt acceptance by the people of all the States, and by their constituted representatives, and while we ask for nothing more, *we will submit to nothing less.*

"9th. That we condemn all hasty and precipitate action by individuals or States; but, being under like condemnation, we cordially sympathize with the people of the other Slave States, and if all other redress shall fail, *we will cordially and promptly appeal with them to the God of Battles,* in defense of our common rights, and in redress for our common wrongs."

Is this conciliation? Your friends propose to decide the matter in issue between themselves and us, and then to enforce their decision by a prompt appeal to "the God of Battles." Is not yours a God of ballot-boxes as well as of battles? You claim to have a majority of the People on your side: why not appeal to votes rather than to bullets? Nay: You have already (it is said) secured a majority in both Houses of the next Congress: why not appeal to that? You have the Supreme Court fast against us for at least the full term of Mr. Lincoln: why not appeal to the tribunals? We have passed no act of Congress whereof you complain: you do not fear that we shall have power to pass any: You have three departments of the Federal Government out of four, and say you would have had the fourth had you not quarreled among yourselves; then why should you appeal to "the God of Battles?" If you have the People, as you surely have Congress and the Judiciary on your side, what need have you to threaten rebellion because we have the President?

IV. I am not forgetting that you propose a submission of your proposition to the judgment of the People, each Congressional District to have one vote upon it. But this would not be fair, for many reasons. In the first place, the Slave States would have a dozen more, the Free States a dozen less, than their present population entitles them to respectively. But, beyond this, you know, as I know, that there can be no fair submission to a popular vote. In every district of the Free States, your side of the question could and would be fully and fairly argued; it could not on our side be argued, nor could votes be polled in the

Slave States. You, for example, need not be told that you will be heard with polite attention by large audiences in any Republican State; but I assure you that Gov. Wise and Mr. Yancey may speak as freely and will be heard as patiently in Worcester, in Auburn, in St. Lawrence, in Wilmot's district, as any Republican. But would I be allowed to set forth to the non-slaveholding whites of the Slave States my reasons for wishing Slavery excluded from the Territories? Could I even be allowed freely to distribute throughout the Slave States journals and documents setting forth my view of the question? You know that we could not be allowed to present our side to the people of the Slave States, though you may not know the fact that not one-third of those citizens of Slave States who wanted Mr. Lincoln elected dared vote for him. It was so in your own State; so in others; it would be so if a vote were taken on your proposition. We would not be allowed to present our case to your people; and even those who, without such presentation, are with us, would not be free to vote as they think. Have you forgotten the destruction of more than one Anti-Slavery press by Kentucky mobs? do you not recall the expulsion of the leading families from Berea in your State for no pretense of fault but their hostility to Slavery? You are a lawyer and a good one: would you like to submit a great case to a jury one-half of whom were not allowed to hear your argument, and could only give you a verdict at the peril of their lives?

V. The People of the Slave, and especially of the Cotton States, have for thirty years been taught that the Union taxes and impoverishes them for the benefit of the North. Believing this, they are frequently impelled to menace us with Disunion, presuming that we will do or say anything to avert that calamity to our section. It is high time that mischievous delusion were dispelled, since the North can have neither equality nor peace in the Union until it shall be. The issue having been fairly made up—Let the North recede from its principles or bid adieu to the Union—I do not see how we can make *any* concession of principle without dishonor. We regard it as a dictate of conscience—so Mr. Webster taught us—that we should never consent to an extension of the area of Slavery. We mean to be faithful to that conviction.

—Mr. Crittenden! the People of the Free States, with every respect for you, propose to stand by the Constitution as it is; to respect the rightful authorities, State and Federal; to let Congress enact such laws as to the majority shall seem good; and to back the Executive in enforcing those laws and maintaining the integrity of the Union. For whatever troubles may impend or arise, those who conspire and rebel are justly responsible; if they would submit when beaten, as we do, there would be unbroken peace and prosperity. If the system established by our fathers is to give place to one of South-American *pronunciamientos* and revolts by the defeated in each election, let us know it now, and be prepared to act accordingly. In any case, allow me with deference to suggest that *your* proper place is with those who, whether in or out of power, defer to rightfully-constituted Government and uphold the majesty of Law.

Yours,   HORACE GREELEY

New-York, Jan. 7, 1861.

107. The Missouri Compromise Line

(*Utica Daily Observer* [Douglas], January 7, 1861)

Is it not possible to prevail on the North to consent to the Missouri Compromise line, extended to the Pacific? That is now about the only plan that can be adopted with any hope of permanent success. And is there really any serious objection to it? We do not believe it would make any material difference with the institution of slavery whether that line is agreed upon or not.—For, after all [is] said and done upon this vexed question, we must come back to this simple, practical, common sense truth,—that where the people *desire* to have slavery, *there* they will have it; if not while a territory, they will have it when they become a State; and where they do *not* desire to have it, *there* they will not have it, and no power can force it upon them. No! not if we had at command for that purpose, all the powers of the general government. And where the location, climate, soil and productions, are such as to render slave labor less profitable than free labor, *there* there would be no desire for the institution; and even where it would be nearly an even thing between free and slave labor, the latter would disappear before the former. It could not stand the competition. The laws of nature and self-interest are all-controlling in a matter of this kind. They are of more real force than all the legislative enactments in the world.

It would by no means follow that because the constitution recognized the right to hold slaves in any particular territory, that slavery would of necessity go there and exist there. Certainly not. It would depend essentially upon something else.—Not upon the law, nor upon any conventional arrangement, but upon the wish and the interest of the people to be affected by it. The law might permit it, but still, it would not exist to any considerable extent, where free labor would be more profitable.

Under the present order of things, slavery can go into any territory, north as well as south, where the people thereof, when they come to form a constitution as a State, resolve to have it. There is now no legal or constitutional difficulty in the way.—Nothing of man's invention exists to prevent the spread of slavery in all directions, if the people will it.

What would the North lose, then, by this Compromise line? Nothing. What would the South gain by it? We answer again, nothing; for the simple reason, that south of the line, the question, would not in point of fact, be determined by the line, or by any written law or constitution. It would rest entirely in the hearts and consciences of the people, who might prefer to have it, or not to have it, just as they pleased; and who would, at all hazards, decide just as they believed would best promote their own interest, whether others agreed with them or not.

If any advantage would accrue to either party by the adoption of this line, it would be manifestly to the North. For, by it, slavery would be forever prohibited north of the line. The provision being a constitutional one, it could not be overcome by legislation, local or general, and it would not be disregarded. No State formed out of such territory could come into the Union with slavery. The prohibition would be absolute and irrevocable, and however much the people might desire to have it, they could not have it *there.* They would be compelled to go elsewhere to possess and enjoy it. The territory north would be lost to the South beyond the possibility or even desire of recovery. The question would be absolutely and unalterably settled. So much, at least, of the territory would be constitutionally secure against slavery, forever. While the territory south of the line would be just as open to free state men, and just as accessible to free labor influence as it now is. [*sic*] The climate, the soil, and the laws of nature and of self-interest, would remain the same, and they would be just as free as ever to work out their own legitimate results of freedom or slavery, as the people, unrestrained by any constitutional provision, might deem best, they being themselves the judges.

So far, then, as there would be any gain at all, it would be all for the North. Let us state the case in a few words. There is nothing in the present constitution of the United States, prohibiting slavery anywhere. By the proposed amendment, slavery would be forever prohibited north of the line. While south of the line, *there would be no prohibition of free States.* It is true, slavery could be established there if the people desired it. *So it can be now.* But it could not be established north of the line, as it can be now. The North, therefore, could lose nothing by this line, nor would the South gain anything by it, except, perhaps, domestic peace, prosperity and happiness.

The only real difference is of little practical importance. The quarrel, after all, is about an unsubstantial right—a mere abstraction. The question in dispute covers only the comparatively brief period of territorial existence, for all concede that when the people come to make a constitution preparatory to admission as a State, they may determine the question of slavery for themselves, and they may come into the Union with or without it, as they please.

Let the question, then, be constitutionally settled on the basis of this line, and that will end the controversy. It will bring joy and prosperity to the whole country. It will give to the world additional evidence of the strength and durability of republican institutions, and of man's capacity for self-government.

Let us, by all means, be admonished by the fate of our neighbors, the Mexican and South American Republics. Do not let us imitate their wretched example. Ours is the best and freest government on earth. —We inherited it from our fathers, and it is our duty to preserve it for those who come after us. We should not madly destroy it, because we cannot do with slavery just what we may happen to think ought to be done with it. If we are thus wickedly reckless of our great trust, all history will condemn our sacrilegious conduct, posterity will execrate our memory, and the very bones of our ancestors will cry out against us.

108. "No Compromise"

(New York Daily News [Breckinridge], January 9, 1861)

The "no compromise" policy of the Republican party, which at first had only a few ultramontane advocates, is now the watchword of that entire organization. Senator Crittenden and the border States are scoffed at for their milk and water recommendations. "We won the battle fairly and we will have the spoils;" "let the worst come now while we expect it;" "slavery must be settled this time or never," are the cries which echo from every Republican journal, from all Republican speakers, and from, we regret to say, those whose Republican sentiments have hitherto been avowed in sensible terms. In short, Senator Seward's dogma that slavery cannot coexist with union in these States is the sole platform on which "Northern policy" stands to-day. All the subterfuges used by it to conceal its nature, all its publicly promulgated doctrines have been met, discussed, and are abandoned one by one, until its whole faith, the vital evidence of its life, the prompter of "no

compromise," looms out clearly as the irrepressible conflict. Horace
Greeley is now more than ever the mouthpiece of Republicanism. More
timid men have sunk into oblivion in the storm of Northern bigotry;
and he only, who spits compromise in the face, and stands boldly up
for all or nothing, is made the exponent of Republican ideas. If any
one imagines, for a moment, that the South's rashness has had no
mitigating, no justifying cause, let him take an impartial look at the
aspect of Republicans, and his erroneous impressions will be removed.
There is no mental telescope required to see behind the glittering
proclamation of no compromise—the Abolition mania hourly rising
into importance. The liberation of the negro is the sole object of
Greeley, Seward and the party which put the reins of power into Lincoln's hands. Further concealment is impossible; there can be no peace,
as the North will hear of no concessions until the South is either conquered by fire and sword, or driven out of the Union. The fanatics,
who are hourly gaining such influence among us, actually fear that the
Southern States on any terms will remain in the Union, or be quieted
in it by peaceable means. Either of these contingencies would defeat,
to a certain extent, the speedy accomplishment of anti-slavery intentions. If the South be forced to secede, then slaves may escape—be
cajoled and coaxed into the North, where no owner could hope to recover them. If, on the other hand, matters are precipitated, war must
come on, and the army and navy be employed to crush our Southern
brethren, whose servants would be kidnapped, excited and roused into
rebellion by the crowd of dangerous miscreants who would follow
the incendiary forces below Mason and Dixon's line. Thus, everything
seems to make Abolition interests depend on war. Hence, "no compromise." Peace would now be more fatal than ever to the preachers
of so called liberty, and they appeal to the God of War, to extreme
issues, to the last argument of madmen.

It is to be feared that they will attain their ends. Things look like
it at present. The army and navy are gradually being brought within
arm's reach of Washington. The pressure of rabid abuse has been too
great on the President, whose heart is in the right place, and he has,
unwisely in our opinion, concluded to use the military and naval
strength to devastate a part of the country that always contributed its
mite to the common weal. These soldiers, these ships and these guns
that are to be brought into the field against the South, were and are
paid for by Southern as well as Northern money. Eight millions of
people, in a nation of less than thirty, could not, in any case, properly be called rebels, much less so when their lawfully designated prop-

erty is threatened and their legalized institutions are in danger. "Woe be to that ruler," says Macaulay, "who cannot distinguish the cry of a people from the indignation of a mob." If, before November, there were any doubts as to the determination of Republicans to interfere with slavery, they can hardly exist in the mind of any observing man now. The whole system is violently inveighed against, in every form, by the same individuals, who, a few weeks since, denied having any idea to interfere with it.

As "no compromise" will be listened to by the Lincoln party, why does it advocate coercion? Why not tell the South to go quietly out of the Union? Why oppose all and every measure brought forward to relieve the Southern States from their embarrassing position? The South has declared its fears and asks formal proofs that they are unfounded. By opposing all attempts to furnish these, the North bears evidence to the well founded apprehensions of the Secessionists. The truth is that coercion and abolition are the direct ends aimed at by the incoming power, and embodied in the motto "no compromise." The apparent desire of The Tribune to oppose coercion while it evidently works for it, is too shallow not to be seen through by a schoolboy. It proclaimed Mr. Buchanan crazy, because he refused to fight, and then made a weak attempt to imitate his madness by opposing hostile action. Was there ever a more inconsistent position for a paper to be placed in?

Self-protection is now the only security left the South and other portions of the country which do not choose to be domineered over by a Republican mob. Since the sentiment of the nation cannot again be heard at the ballot box, let it be known otherwise. The South has need of all its young men to fight for their homes. It is not wonderful that they should flock to arms unanimously. The question next to be solved is, whether Lincoln will be the authorized President of the millions of Northern men who opposed him at the polls. New Jersey ought to have a say in this matter, and other places likewise.

109. The Only Possible Compromise

(New-York Daily Tribune [Lincoln], January 19, 1861)

The proposition discussed in The Tribune a few days ago, that Congress should purchase and emancipate the slaves in the Border Slave States has already attracted considerable attention, and meets with much favor from all but the fanatical devotees of Slavery in the North, who, like Charles O'Conor, consider the institution a divine blessing, and would be glad to re-introduce it into the Free States. A resolution in favor of gradual compensated emancipation in the Border States and of colonizing the negroes in Liberia, was yesterday offered in the New-York Assembly, and referred to the Committee on Federal Relations.

The facts are briefly these: In the States of Delaware, Maryland, Missouri, Arkansas, Texas, and Louisiana there are about 600,000 slaves, and more than four times as many whites. Last week a gang of twenty-four cotton and plantation negroes were sold at auction in Charleston for an average of $437. The price of slaves, it is well known, is not so high in most of the States we have named as in South Carolina. Taking into account the old, and the feeble, the women and the children, it is evident that the average worth of negroes cannot be more than $400, and is probably much less. The sum of $240,000,000 would, therefore, be an ample compensation for the liberation of all the slaves in the States we have named.

It is not necessary, however, to contemplate their immediate, unconditional emancipation. Whatever scheme may be adopted, should conform in a measure to the wishes of the States immediately concerned; that is to say, such of them as may see fit to accept an offer by Congress to pay for the slaves. Delaware, for instance, which has already upward of 18,000 free blacks, could have no serious objection to allowing her two thousand slaves to remain after emancipation as free laborers. Louisiana, on the other hand, with more slaves than whites, might prefer to have them gradually emancipated and removed to Central America, or to Hayti or Jamaica, where they would be gladly welcomed. By an organized system of transportation their removal to those countries could be effected with comparatively little difficulty or expense. Some definite period, not very remote, say 1876, the Centennial Anniversary of the Declaration of Independence, could be fixed upon as the date of final emancipation; Congress, in the meantime, buying and removing those whom their owners were willing to emancipate at once for a compensation fixed by capable and impartial Commissioners.

The arguments in favor of this scheme are that it offers a peaceful solution of the troubles which now agitate the country; that it would check the increase of Slavery, and in time rid us of an odious and formidable evil, the ultimate result of which, if some remedy be not soon applied, will be to Africanize one-half of the continent; and lastly, that it would add largely to the general wealth and prosperity of the nation by the immense rise in value and in profitableness of real estate in the South. For Delaware, Maryland, Missouri, and Texas, emancipation, with the aid of the Federal Government, is not nearly so great an undertaking as was the abolition of Slavery in New-York,

New-Jersey, and Pennsylvania, which was effected by those States without any assistance from any quarter.

To the nation at large, and especially to the Free States, the money this project would cost would be no objection. One year of war would cost as much or more. The purchase of Cuba, on the terms proposed by Mr. Buchanan, would have required as large a sum. The nation has at hand an obvious and available resource to carry out the financial part of the measure in the public lands, whose value at the lowest estimate cannot fail to be more by several hundreds of millions of dollars than that of all the slaves in the States north of the Potomac and west of the Mississippi.

110. [THE COMMITTEE OF THIRTY-THREE]

(Boston Daily Advertiser [Lincoln], January 21, 1861)

The failure of the "committee of thirty-three" to agree upon any scheme for adjusting the political difficulties referred to it for solution, appears to have created an impression that the committee was a failure, and that its deliberations were fruitless. We cannot see the matter in this light, however. If the committee had [sic] done nothing else, it has performed a very essential public service and one which, as affairs go, may be of more importance than we now see, in enabling the House to transact the regular routine business of the session, which has to be finished to keep the wheels of government in motion. With political topics of such absorbing interest in every one's mind at a session which must close peremptorily on the fourth of March, and leave the country with its new House of Representatives yet to be completed at the summer elections in several States, it is a matter of no trifling moment that this committee has kept the topic of the day in a measure out of the House of Representatives, until the other business of the country is in such condition that the House can safely launch out upon that boundless sea of discussion.

This is an incidental service, however—originally designed, we suppose, by those who have led in the business of the session, but still apart from that field of usefulness in which the public have looked for the return for the labors of the committee. But in spite of this acknowledged failure to agree upon any scheme of settlement, it appears to us that the committee has rendered very essential service in exposing the real purposes of the secessionists, and in showing what can be done to check the further spread of their treasonable movements. Without reviewing minutely proceedings yet fresh in the minds of all, we may state, as a fact

within the recollection of any reader, that the committee drew from the
representatives of seceding States the confession, that they do not hold
themselves bound to stand by the result of a fair and constitutional
election, that they are not embarking in treason because of unfriendly
legislation on the part of northern States, because of any apprehended
dangers from northern aggression, or because of any rights withheld in
the territory of the United States, but that they have undertaken disunion for the sole reason that they have resolved to extend slavery into
territory not yet owned by the United States.

That we do not exaggerate when we thus state the result of the committee's labor is plain, we think, from the character of those measures
to which a majority of the committee would have agreed, had the representatives of disaffected States consented to them. The committee
were ready to advise the repeal of the personal liberty acts, to insert in
the Constitution a denial of all rights in Congress to interfere with
slavery in the States except with the consent of every State in the Union,
and to close up now and forever, on unobjectionable terms, the question of slavery in all territories now within our limits. The committee
were thus ready by an exhaustive process to settle the slavery question
in all its necessary relations, to bring the North forward as far as concession can go without palpable sacrifice of principle, and to offer a
really just and practicable middle ground for accommodating the differences of the two sections. This failed to pacify the advocates of secession,
and the failure was a plain demonstration of the real object for which
they have taken their present dangerous stand.

It is gaining a great point, we think, that the committee has thus
served to bring our real difficulty so plainly before the country. The
record has thus been made up against the party of secession in the most
effective manner, and should convince every one that as for that party
no plan of action which can be offered can satisfy their demands. It appears to us, however, that the committee has also served to disclose a
basis of action, on which much may be done to strengthen the Union
party in other Southern States, which are not yet openly the prey of
treason. The committee has shown that the majority of the Republican
party as represented in Congress is ready to make a fair and reasonable
settlement of all questions now open, in the spirit of conciliation and
equity. Even a gentleman of such tenacity of opinion and purpose as
Mr. Adams of this State only asks to be satisfied that some good result
is attainable, in order to give his active support to such a plan, some
leading features of which have been suggested by himself. And it for-
tunately happens that at this juncture the country has assurances to

the same effect from the lips of the leading cabinet officer of the future administration. We feel that substantial ground is thus pointed out on which the North and a large part of the South can unite for the preservation of the Constitution and the Union. We shall not yet admit that love of country is so far lost in either section, that this great purpose will be sacrificed, either for a punctilio, or from sympathy with a wide-spread frenzy, nourished by the most unholy passions and leading to political and social ruin.

111. ANOTHER MODE OF SETTLING THE SOUTH CAROLINA DIFFICULTY

(Augusta *Kennebec Journal* [Lincoln], January 25, 1861)

It is quite obvious to any one who has observed the present secession movement, to say nothing of the progress of treason in the South for the past thirty years, that the whole trouble springs from the factious, disloyal, rebellious and mischievous people of South Carolina. All the other States that are now in the attitude of insurgents, have been coaxed, driven or bullied into it by the example and evil teachings of the Palmetto State. The very origin and heart of the disease that now infects the Body politic are to be found on her soil, and unless a remedy, speedy and radical, is applied there, the consequences may prove more direful than the most evil forebodings now conjecture. Were the exciting cause removed, we have no doubt that the evil already done would soon be corrected, and that the other States, however gangrened they may now seem with secession and nullification, would very soon be restored to their wonted soundness of loyalty to the Union and allegiance to the Government. But there is no hope of infusing into the South Carolina rebels any feeling of true devotion to the Confederacy. Their veins are filled with Tory blood, and with some honorable exceptions that shone out with splendor in the earlier days of the Republic, their leading men have been at all times secretly or openly hostile to the Federal Government. Under this condition of affairs it is idle to expect that they will ever become good and loyal citizens of the Union, and their own happiness as well as the peace and prosperity of all, seem to demand a separation.

We cannot afford, however, to have them exist as a distinct nation where they now are, for no disintegration of the Confederacy can be permitted under any circumstances—"The Union—it must be preserved." A middle ground of fair compromise may, however, be found on the proposition which we have now to make—and that is to purchase at a fair valuation the *territory* of South Carolina and remove the present inhabitants—just as thirty years ago the Federal Government removed the Creeks and Cherokees from Georgia and Alabama and at a later day the Seminoles from Florida. We could supply them a new home in Sonora, or Chihuahua, or some of the adjoining Mexican States, where they could peacefully work out the great problems of Palmetto statesmanship and theorize and grow poor *ad infinitum* without any outside interference from any quarter whatever. We should be willing to bind our Government by Constitutional obligations and Treaty stipulations to protect the Utopians in their new realm and guaranty unto them the sublime right of making fools of themselves so long as the experiment should prove pleasing.

And then with the fair soil of Carolina, rid of its burden of impracticable malcontents, a great State would at once be built up. It might be opened for settlement by Congress under the provisions of the Homestead Act, and at once be filled with an intelligent, industrious, thrifty and loyal population. Its product[ion] of Cotton and Rice and Indigo would be immensely stimulated by the new order of things, agriculture would flourish as never before, and the demands of commerce would then make Charleston an Emporium indeed, instead of the decayed city wherein pride and poverty and treason now find a joint and congenial habitation. The other States of the South then, with the inciting cause taken away, would bound back to loyalty and love, and we should have as of old a Union wherein "peace and good fellowship" should find their homes. Let Congress take this proposition into consideration. It has every characteristic to recommend it to all sections and all classes. It is pacific; it is reasonable; it is practicable; and if adopted, would secure to us an "era of good feeling" till the generations should forget or fail to know the evils wherewith we are now beset.

112. The Propositions of Virginia

(Springfield *Daily Illinois State Journal* [Lincoln], January 30, 1861)

The question, as to the duty of Illinois, to send Commissioners to consult with Virginia upon the troubles of the hour, is one that ought not to be passed over without some consideration. It is due to Virginia, not less than to ourselves, that the position of Illinois Republicans should be clearly defined, and being defined, should not be departed from without some higher motive than that of fearing a dissolution of the Union. If the propositions of the Democratic Legislature of the State of Virginia were simply to ask at the hands of those who differ with her a free and frank consultation upon our present difficulties, it would doubtless be our duty to listen to them with some degree of consideration. What is this proposition of Virginia? She does not ask us to come to her, cherishing the principles and policy of the Republican party, but she insists that before she meets us upon terms of equality, we must give up every thing that is dear to us as Republicans. We are not permitted to talk over these difficulties unless we can do so upon the terms prescribed to us by Virginia. She prescribes to us terms, and seems to make those terms the condition of her continuance as a member of the Confederacy. She says to us, "unless you see fit to comply with our terms, we will lead our people to the commission of treason, and compel you to coerce us to obedience to the laws." She proposes to us that we should adopt the Breckinridge platform as a basis of settlement. Not only this; but she insists that in all territory that may hereafter be acquired, slavery shall be protected by constitutional amendment. That is the proposition. And we can scarcely consider it with that degree of patience its importance would seem to demand. The character of the proposition can find a parallel only in the demand, that Mr. Lincoln having been constitutionally elected, shall resign, and allow tra[i]tors and rebels to fill the offices, which the people have decided, shall be filled by Republicans the next four years.

We would not be understood as having any objections to a consultation with Virgin[i]a, if she will come to us with clean hands, proclaiming her determination to stand by the Union in every emergency. But when she asks us to meet her, upon terms so dishonorable as those we have indicated, we feel that we but utter the sentiment of Illinois Republicans, when we say that they will not give up either principle or honor, for the purpose of inducing even Virginia to remain in the Union. We insist that all national troubles shall be settled IN THE UNION, that those States that have rebelled and those that threaten to do so, shall convince us by their *acts* that they are again devoted to the Union —having done that we will meet them in a spirit of fraternal kindness, and pledge ourselves to secure to them every right to which they are entitled under *the Constitution as it is.* The Democratic Legislature of Virginia asks Republicans, Douglas men, and Bell men to give up every principle that they struggled for in the last election, and accept in place of them the Breckinridge doctrine of a Slave Code for the Territories. The modesty of this demand will doubtless be appreciated by those who but a few months since were saying that the platform of Non-Intervention, or of "the Union, the Constitution and the Enforcement of the Laws," was sufficient for all national purposes. There is something more to be taken into consideration, in deciding what disposition shall be made of this proposition of Virginia. The Commissioners she has authorized to represent her at Washington, on the 4th of February, come clothed with no power to make any adjustment of present difficulties.—They come to present Virginia's *ultimatum,* and to report back what they have done, to the Legislature of that State. Their action will be repudiated by Virginia if they shall make any departure from her propositions as indicated by her Legislature. We are rejoiced to know that Illinois Republicans look with no favor upon propositions for concession or compromise, which demand such base surrender of principle, as is demanded by the propositions of Virginia. We do not like the idea of *buying* the right to control the offices which the people have given the Republicans a Constitutional right to hold for the coming four years. We do not like to have those who did not contribute to that result, prescribe to us the *terms* upon which Republicans shall administer this Government. We say to Virginia, and to all other States, that are asking us to *"compromise"* and *"concede"* something, that we are not aware of having done any wrong to them or their people. That we propose to do no wrong either to her or them—or to any of the States of the South. That being our position, we do not propose to make either concession or compromise—if in doing so we are required to yield up any essential principle of Republican faith.

113. The Virginia Proposition—A Rampant Majority

(Springfield *Daily Illinois State Register* [Douglas], February 2, 1861)

For several days past the close corporation of republicanism in and about the legislature has been in a snarl. The friendly proposition of the state of Virginia for the several states to appoint commissioners to meet in convention at Washington on the 4th instant, has been the subject of animated strife. The ultras, those who reflect, right or wrong, the extreme views of the president elect, have opposed any response to the Virginia proposition. They were for treating it with contempt, and Gov. Yates was loth even to lay it before the legislature. But so frank and fair a proposition—one so in keeping with the spirit of our institutions, based as they are on compromise and concession, could not fail to find favor even with the members of the party assembled at the Mecca of its faith. The subject was caucussed [sic], canvassed, debated and finally the senate committee, after much tribulation, compromised the matter, by excluding all propositions of the democratic members thereof, and agreeing to recommend the appointment of a set of *party* commissioners, bound by provisos and instructions, to the effect that nothing of the party platform could or should be conceded, and that the appointment of commissioners is only conceded as matter of form, Illinois republicanism having nothing to concede or ask in the premises. Our senate report shows the animus of the party immediately surrounding the president elect. The party is the ruling idea—the Union a secondary consideration.

The democrats of the legislature insisted upon the appointment of commissioners. They asked their appointment by the joint resolution of the two houses. They asked that the 160,000 democrats of Illinois might be represented (though by a minority) in that commission. In the senate the veteran Richmond appealed to the patriotism of the majority—to their professed desire to heal our national troubles—to their professed love of the Union—to give the Illinois democracy some voice in the proposed commission. Messrs. Kuykendall, Underwood and Higbee also eloquently urged this, in a spirit of amity and national and state brotherhood. The rampant and overbearing senate majority told them, no! You, the representatives of 160,000 freemen, we have ten thousand more than you in the state. You have no rights. It is for you to acquiesce and approve what we do. We, rampant black republicans, will represent Illinois at the Washington convention, as we are forced by weak brothers to go there, and you democrats can make the most of it. We heard Mr. Oglesby's speech, and this was the spirit of it.

And this is Mr. Lincoln's state's mode of meeting the friendly offerings of Virginia for amicable conference! A party representation to settle a dispute involving the unity of the republic! Conceding nothing at home, even the courtesies which should exist among party opponents, they go instructed to yield nothing, hear nothing, consent to nothing, that does not square with their party platform. True, there is nothing binding upon their constituency to require them to assent to the convention's action. True, nothing can be done by that convention but to recommend some plan of adjustment for the people's approval. True, the convention is only called that the representatives of the several states may confer, and, if possible, devise some suggestion to the people for their approval or rejection. But Mr. Lincoln's henchmen will not risk this. First, by his instruction, they were advised to refuse all conference, but they now reluctantly consent to send an instructed party delegation, with an ultimatum, denying half the people of the state a voice in the conference, telling them, through their agents in the state senate, that, as a conquered minority, they cannot be heard, even in so

MEASURES FOR PEACE 309

good a work as advising and counselling as to the best means of preserving the national Union.

On ordinary questions we might concede that the majority should speak for the state, but in the troublous times which are upon us, is it the part of wisdom, is it the part of safety at home, in the event of ultimate blows, that such a spirit should be evinced? Rather, is it not our duty, when untold trouble besets us, that a spirit should be cultivated which will render our noble state a unit, come weal, come woe[?] We submit that the dominant party in Illinois, if its state senators represent it, are not pursuing a course to compass so desirable an end.

The majority report of the committee to whom was referred the various communications relative to the appointment of commissioners, directs the governor to appoint the commission, and the remarks of republican senators inform us that it is to be composed exclusively of republicans. The eloquent and telling report of the minority, and the forcible remarks of Messrs. Kuykendall, Richmond, Underwood and Higbee expose to the people of the state the spirit which animates the legislative majority.

Gov. Yates may be more wise than those who have delegated to him the appointment of this commission. Neither he nor they were for any appointment, but the popular pressure compelled some sort of acquiescence. We trust that the executive may feel that, as a commission is to be appointed, the state should not be represented in the Washington convention by a strictly party delegation.

These antics of a flushed majority cannot be without their lesson—to the democracy of Illinois at least. In other states, where the republican party have a majority, a greater degree of tact, if not a higher sense of justice, is evinced by the ruling powers. But it may be that those who live under "the droppings of the sanctuary" are better representatives of the chosen of the party than are those who are more remote, and hence less blessed.

Yesterday's proceedings in the senate will show to the country the spirit which animates the leaders of the party in Mr. Lincoln's state. They will further show the stand of her democracy. The former assume to have all the rights. The time may come when they may not be so willing to assume all the responsibility.

114. Affairs at Washington—The Subject of Compromises

(*Newark* (N. J.) *Daily Mercury* [Lincoln], February 11, 1861)

The condition of the country, the probabilities of the secession of the border Slave States, and the subject of compromises, are discussed at Washington with a constancy and eagerness which is to be accounted for by the magnitude of the interests at stake. *There* are assembled many of the leading minds of the country, strong representatives of its immense manufacturing, commercial and banking interests, and keen and far-sighted politicians who look beyond the turmoil of the present into the sober second thought of the tranquil future. To one who scans the various elements which are there gathered with coolness, who is neither carried away by timid fears or unmindful of the serious consequences of a decision, who feels alike the responsibilities of the Present and of the Future, the whole scene is an impressive one.

A short stay in Washington has convinced us that there is but little hope of a satisfactory adjustment of existing difficulties, and we presume our readers will agree with us that any other is entirely useless. There are those who think otherwise, but we shall state our opinions, and the reasons we have for entertaining them. The substantial propositions, urged by the Breckinridge and Fusion parties of the country, (those of Mr. Crittenden) are entirely inadmissible, and yet they have been sustained with such pertinacity and earnestness that they are continually present in the minds of the Southern border men as the necessary basis for a settlement. A more moderate solution of the difficulty, and one freed from the insuperable objections which cling to those propositions, is regarded coldly by the great mass of Southern men, and yet we have the assurances of our moderate Representatives in Congress that there is not a single Republican in either branch who will support them.

The Border State propositions meet with but little more favor from the Republicans than they do from the Southern men. The Republicans will not support five amendments of the Constitution in the interest of slavery, with a territorial compromise of a doubtful character, while the Southern members of Congress say that these propositions are no protection to their people and will not be satisfactory to them. The Union men of the border States regard them with favor, but do not pretend that they can carry their States upon them. Like the Crittenden propositions too they require to carry them two-thirds of Congress, and the ratification of twenty-five out of twenty-seven States, a practical impossibility. Thus these two plans, which are urged by the greater number of people, have no real and substantial prospect of success, and we are thrown upon the report of the Committee of Thirty-three to see whether that presents any greater strength. It was the result of the initiative movement, and it was reached after a full discussion of all the difficulties involved.

Had this result been welcomed by the country and sustained by its business interests with earnestness and determination, it would have been adopted by Congress. It presents a feasible, if not an unobjectionable, scheme for adjusting the points of difference, and we have felt disposed from the first to favor its suggestions. But it met on its presentation with no substantial support from any quarter. While none have opposed the masterly argument of Mr. Adams in its support, few have seconded the effort, and yet it is, in our opinion, the only plan possible of adoption. There are very many Republicans who favor it, but the Democracy stand aloof, and the Southern Representatives regard it with disfavor. It is approaching a vote without the strength necessary to secure its adoption. Mr. Corwin has delayed the vote with the hope that the Conference, called at the request of Virginia, may endorse it or adopt some practicable substitute.

But will the Peace Conference be better able to present a plan of settlement than Congress? We think not, and if it does it will have but little weight upon Congress. There are grave doubts as to the Constitutional character of such an assemblage, and at the best its views are only entitled to the weight of so many individuals. It will not be able, we think, to agree upon any distinct propositions, while it is possible that it may unite in the recommendation of a National Convention, in accordance with the requirements of the Constitution. Public opinion, North and South, is tending towards this solution of our difficulties. It would, at least, give us the opportunity of so framing the fundamental law, as to give power to the general government to put down rebellion and treason, and to decentralize the appointing power.

The project of a National Convention has been broached by the Kentucky Legislature, and is endorsed by the *National Intelligencer,* and many Union men of the South. It is supported by Messrs. Lincoln and Seward, and would, we think, be favored by the Republicans. The great advantage of such a recommendation is that it would give time for the country to rise above the unreasonable panic which prevails. The judgment and statesmanship of the country, the unwavering convictions of the people, the true interests of capital and labor, the real elements of National growth and prosperity would have time to recover from the shock of rebellion and the panic of want, and the result would be such as all men might approve. It is not for the true and better influences of the age to oppose such changes in our organic law, as the progress of the country may render necessary.

But what will be the effect on the Border States of this policy of "the Inauguration first and Adjustment afterwards?" It will depend entirely upon the Union sentiment of the people, and upon their decision as to where their true interests lie. Nothing is more clearly settled than that the Gulf States will not be swayed or controlled by their action. They have determined their course, and it remains for the Central Slave States to decide whether they will cast in their lot with those who are trying the scheme of revolution, or remain in the Union, and trust to the national rule of the Republican party. Upon this subject we have no clear opinion, for recent events have shown that it is impossible to tell what madness may be committed when reason and judgment are lost. The hopeful are confident that all will be right, and the desponding bid us to prepare for the worst.

There is nothing which is cheering on the part of the Border Slave States in their official utterances. They deny the right of the General Government to maintain its power and enforce the laws in the seceding States. They regard the patriotic declarations of Northern States that they will adhere to the Union and sustain its authority with men and money as threats directed towards them. They avow that they will take part with the rebels and traitors, unless certain concessions are made. They stand apart sullenly when the national flag is insulted, and quibble when the Union is endangered by revolt. It is true that there are brave and worthy men standing up with fearless courage for the right, but we fear that they do not represent their States. Let us still hope however, that the fanaticism of the hour may give way to juster ideas of State policy, and that they will remain faithful to the Union and the Constitution which their fathers framed.

There is very little doubt but that the new administration will favor a most decided policy. It will reinforce Forts Sumter and Pickens, and it will collect the revenue. It will take away the postal facilities of the revolted States, and it will maintain and enforce the laws. Such is the uniform opinion of the Republicans in Congress, and of those who are familiar with the views of Mr. Lincoln. This policy will call out the union sentiment of the whole country.—There will be no longer division in our ranks or discord in our counsels. A determination to maintain the Union and the Constitution is to be the grand doctrine of the incoming administration.

115. The Crittenden Compromise—An Argument for a Territorial Division

(Rochester Daily Union and Advertiser [Douglas], February 11, 1861)

Free institutions and Slave institutions have come to be regarded as two Opposites or Antagonistic Facts, which cannot coëxist in the same State or Territory. A State is classed as a Free State or a Slave State. As these terms are understood, it is simply impossible that a State can be a Free State and a Slave State at the same time—though it may be composed of Slaveholders and non-Slaveholders. It will be universally admitted that the same proposition applies to *Territories* precisely as it does to States—a Territory cannot in the sense in which we use these terms, be at the same time a Slave Territory and a Free Territory.

Now let us proceed one step further: The South claim that under the Federal Constitution they have a right to hold Slaves as property in *all the Territories* of the United States; and however unreasonable or unjust we may regard that claim, it has unquestionably been sanctioned by the Supreme Court of the United States. An acquiescence in or the assertion of this claim or pretension, would exclude Northern or Free institutions from all the Territories of the United States.

On the other hand, the North (as represented by the dominant party in November last,) claim that under the Federal Constitution Congress possesses and should unhesitatingly exercise the power to prevent the establishment of any other than Free institutions in any and all the Territories of the United States. An acquiescence in or the assertion of this claim or pretension, would exclude Southern or Slave institutions from all the Territories of the United States.

—Thus we see that the assertion of the extreme claims or pretensions of either the North or the South, *would effectually exclude the other* from the enjoyment of its "equal rights" in the common Territories— using the terms which occur in this article in the sense in which they are used by the respective parties to this great controversy.

It necessarily follows then, from what precedes—that whereas both parties have common rights in the Territories; and whereas the institutions of either necessarily excludes [*sic*] the institutions of the other, *so as to render it utterly impossible that both should occupy, possess, or enjoy the same Territory:*—we say it necessarily follows from these premises that *the only practicable mode* of reconciling their conflicting claims, *is to agree upon a division of the Territories* between the two parties contestant. To state these several propositions thus briefly—and we trust with sufficient clearness to render them easily understood by every class of readers—is to PROVE them. At least we should find it extremely difficult to make them clearer to any class of minds by additional arguments.—But we may properly say here, that it is a matter of no consequence whatever that we and many others dissent more or less from the theories of both the parties above represented. The position of the parties whose disagreements must be compromised or reconciled if Disunion and Civil War are to be averted, is here fairly set forth; but not *our* position nor the position of thousands of others who, agreeing with *neither* of the contending parties, are endeavoring to seek out a basis of adjustment between them, which, by mutual concessions dishonorable to neither, shall compose our sectional strifes and reëstablish the Union as it came to us from our Fathers.

—Well then, if we approach this great question in the proper spirit; if we admit that each of the contending parties sincerely believes in the justice of its own pretensions; if we reach the conclusion (as we necessarily must) that to grant to EITHER *all* its claims, is to grant *nothing* to its ANTAGONIST; if we recognize the fact that the only practicable Compromise consists in a DIVISION OF THE TERRITORIES of which each claims the whole, the only question which remains to be considered is this: *is the proposed division on the line of 36° 30' a fair and equitable one?* Or rather, is it a division to which two parties—*each* of whom claims THE WHOLE *as its right*—may consent without dishonor and without humiliation?

We beseech every Northern man to *look at the map of his country* before he answers this question. He will see that the Territory North of 36° 30' is several times larger than the Territory South of that line. Yet the Moderate, Conservative, Union-loving men of the South, notwithstanding they claim the right to hold their Slaves in all the Territories, and the Supreme Court has said that they possess that right, are willing to divide on that line. They are as firmly convinced of their rights as we are of ours; and their "conscience" affirms the righteousness of their claim not less authoritatively than our "conscience" affirms the righteousness of ours. Shall we then, in view of the apparent impossibility of any other adjustment or reconciliation than one based on a division of Territory—shall we in a spirit of magnanimity, of expansive patriotism, of true Christian brotherhood, give in our adhesion to this plan of settlement? Or shall we 'stiffen our backs,' and harden our hearts, and endeavor to persuade ourselves that our duty to our fellow men and our duty to God, bid us say, 'let our fields be saturated with fraternal blood—let our wives be widows and our children orphans, rather than consent to this thing?' Of those who heard Dr. Robinson's able discourse yesterday afternoon, we would like to inquire—*is not this fanaticism?* And yet it is the voice of perhaps a million of Northern men to-day, whose honesty and patriotism we would not impugn; but whose error of judgment we profoundly deplore.

—We shall doubtless be met with the objection to the Crittenden Compromise, that it applies to *future* Territory. That is an objection in our estimation as well as others'; and we should indulge a strong hope, in case the North should approach this vexed question in a proper spirit, that its appeal to the South to strike out this feature, and to leave the status of future Territorial acquisitions to be fixed by those who make them, would not be made in vain. But even though in the present excited state of the Southern mind—when a fierce "fanaticism" bewilders the judgments of Statesmen and renders the masses deaf to the voice of patriotism and reason—even though under these circumstances it should be deemed expedient *not* to strike it out lest the measure thus modified should prove ineffectual to stay the tide of Revolution, we should counsel its acceptance by the North. Under the new census nearly two-thirds of the House and a decided majority of the Senate will be of the North. Henceforward it must wield the power of this country. The question for us to decide is whether our country shall consist of *the North alone;* or whether it shall embrace all that vast Empire which hitherto all Americans have been proud to call their own. We may with safety to all interests—to the interests of Freedom and Free States and Free institutions as well as all others—leave the question of acquiring more Territory to our children, or to ourselves when the present excitement shall have subsided. If such Territory when acquired must be appropriated by the South exclusively, it will remain for the North to decide whether any Territory shall be acquired. And surely the North will not be afraid to trust itself to determine whether it will or will not acquire Territory for a given purpose.

But should this great and free and enlightened and hitherto happy confederated nation, be torn into fragments, and become the theatre of never-ending wars between people of the same lineage, the same language, the same religion and the same general views of Civil Government, merely because we cannot agree whether one feature of a Compromise or Peace measure shall or shall not contingently apply to Territory, which we do not own and may never acquire, what will other nations say of us?—what will History say of us?—what will our own Posterity say [of] us?—what, speaking through His providences—what will the Sovereign Ruler of Nations *say to us?*

116. Crittenden Compromise vs. Popular Sovereignty

(*Evansville* (Ind.) *Daily Journal* [Lincoln], February 12, 1861)

A great number of memorials have been presented to Congress and State Legislatures favoring the adoption of the "Crittenden Compromise," as it is called. It is no compromise at all, but a total surrender of every principle for which the Republicans and Douglas Democrats contended, in connexion with the subject of slavery, during the last Presidential canvass. The Republicans contended that Congress *had the power* to legislate so as to exclude slavery from the territories, or delegate it to the territorial legislature at its option. The Douglas Democrats contended that Congress had not the power to legislate on the subject, but that the people had the sole right to admit or exclude slavery as they chose; and the Yancey-Breckinridge Democracy contended that the Constitution of itself carried slavery into the territories, and fixed it there beyond the control of Congress or the people. The Crittenden Compromise is nothing more nor less than the Breckinridge platform. —The Yanceyites in the Charleston and Baltimore Conventions contended for the doctrine that the Constitution, *as it is,* recognizes and protects slavery in the territories.

They know that this doctrine can be sustained judicially so long only as a majority of the Judges of the Supreme Court of the United States are capable, from imbecility or corrupt motives, of lending themselves to the purposes of a set of party leaders who are traitors at heart, and who belong to that class of accursed miscreants who would rather rule in hell than serve in heaven. Hence, they want to ingraft upon the Constitution, by way of amendment, the Crittenden Compromise and thus fasten slavery upon all territory now possessed and hereafter to be acquired south of 36° 30' in spite of the people inhabiting such territory. And now, Douglas Democrats are just as busy as the Yanc[e]yites in circulating, and procuring signatures to, memorials favoring this Crittenden Compromise. Among them we find brigadier generals, who adhered to the doctrine of popular sovereignty in the Charleston and Baltimore Conventions even after it was demonstrated, that if they continued to do so, it would result in the destruction of the Democratic party. They knew that if they yielded, their power in the North was at an end, and hoped that by standing firm to the end, in favor of popular sovereignty, they might yet sustain themselves in the North notwithstanding the loss of five or six Southern States. It was a matter of life and death. If they abandoned popular sovereignty death was certain; and they could only die by maintaining it to the end.

Democracy is now dead, and the leaders—even Douglas men who were members of the Charleston and Baltimore Conventions, and are now brigadier generals, colonels &c.—abandon popular sovereignty and favor the Yancey platform, as expressed in the Crittenden Compromise, and exert themselves to delude republicans, union men, and popular sovereignty democrats, into the abandonment of their principles. They have no desire that any compromise shall be made. They are determined to force the republicans to abandon their principles and humbly sue for peace and to this end they are willing to bring the republic to the verge of utter and eternal ruin if necessary. The object is not the welfare of the country but to place the Republican party apparently in the wrong, in the hope that thereby democracy will be enabled again to triumph in 1864.

If the adoption or rejection of the Crittenden Compromise depended upon the votes of the mass of the Douglas Democrats alone, they would unhesitatingly reject it, and it is hoped that they will, ere long, with as little hesitation, discard and consign to deserved infamy, as enemies of their country, the unprincipled political gamblers who would induce them to assume an attitude which would justly subject them to the imputation of yielding, like dastardly cravens, to the insolent and unreasonable demands of the imperious slave-holders of the South; who, having been accustomed from infancy to secure implicit obedience from negroes by force, seem to have persuaded themselves that by the same means the freemen of the north can be made to ignore their honor and their manhood and lick the hand that smites them. If the Douglas Democrats and Republicans do not in this crisis firmly, and regardless of consequences, resist every attempt to fasten slavery upon the territories by constitutional provisions placing it beyond the control of Congress or the people, they are cravens and fit only for slaves.

117. A Prospect for Peace

(*Morning Courier and New-York Enquirer* [Lincoln], March 1, 1861)

When the Peace Congress assembled, it was not generally supposed that its deliberations would be attended with any practical results. It was, nevertheless, expected that it would decide upon some measures which might be taken as a basis of settlement, and it was believed that the discussions which would take place in it would have a good effect.

To observing men, however, it was evident that the only settlement of the present difficulties that could be made was to be made by Congress, and that body had regarded, with no little jealousy, the assembling of a Convention to which was to be entrusted a work which it believed to be within its own province.

The deliberations of the Peace Congress have not been ineffectual. Time at least has been gained by its session, and the excited passions of the people have had an opportunity to cool. But while many will rejoice that it has at last arrived at a basis for the settlement of the difficulties now before the country, a greater number will rejoice over the passage of the resolutions of the Committee of Thirty-three. These resolutions are drawn in the most admirable spirit, and, excepting the territorial question, they meet all the issues which have been presented as causes of vexation. They give to the slave-holder every assurance that he can reasonably desire, and if there has been any doubt as to the disposition of the Republicans to do what was right, it is now most decidedly removed. There remains not the slightest ground for accusing them of a want of right spirit, of a want of nationality. The resolutions to which they have given their approval prove that they are not the mere sectional men that their opponents have accused them of being, and that so far from being opposed to conciliation, they are willing to do almost anything, but sacrifice their principles, to preserve an attachment to the Union.

The passage of these resolutions will be received by all but ultra men, with the greatest satisfaction; and they are the beginning of a good work which, it is to be hoped, will soon be completed. But little time is left the session of the present Congress, but this time can now be most profitably employed. It is in the power of this Congress to confer upon the country a greater blessing than perhaps any of its predecessors ever has. It is in its province to do what will remove the remaining causes of disagreement, to calm excited passions, and to pave the way for the Administration of Mr. LINCOLN to commence its labors freed from great embarrassment. If this Congress can settle at once and forever the question regarding the Territories, then surely its duty is manifest, and it cannot discharge it too quickly. The Territorial question is, after all, *the* question, for the others were only secondary. As to the settlement of these, there has never been any real difficulty, but the Territorial question has been the rock against which the waves of passion have been dashing. To remove this has been the aim of every so-called compromise measure. Each of these, with but one exception, has been objectionable to a great body of our people. Some have involved the conceding of more than was before demanded, and others have demanded sacrifices which could not consistently be made. The only proposition which could fully meet the question, and which proposed a settlement definite and final, involving no sacrifice of principle on the part of those who were opposed to the extension of Slavery, was that of Mr. ADAMS. By ultra men on both sides that proposition met with coldness, but by the reasonable and the conservative it was regarded as a ground upon which all Union men might meet. While the extension of the Missouri Compromise line, even as agreed to by the Peace Convention, might find opposers, the proposition of Mr. ADAMS can be objected to only by those who are determined to do nothing, rather choosing to let the country remain unquiet than offer anything savoring of conciliation to the Unionists of the Border and Slave States. The more this proposition has been discussed, the more satisfactory has it appeared. Those who at first doubted the wisdom of it, and who deemed that it involved a sacrifice that could not be made, have been led to a different conclusion. Daily has the number of its advocates increased. It is such a simple, yet such a satisfactory method of putting an end to a question pregnant with evil, that it now seems strange that it should ever have been opposed by sensible men. The readers of this journal know that it has urged repeatedly the passage of this proposition or one similar to it. It has constantly asserted that, while the Constitution should be abided by and the laws enforced, something should be yielded to the Unionists in the South, since it might be yielded without a sacrifice of principle.

Congress having had laid before it various propositions, and having thus far taken no action affecting the Territorial question, and there being no prospect of its being presented with any proposition the basis of which will be more acceptable than that of Mr. ADAMS, a more opportune time than the present for action upon this one could not be found. The adoption of the CORWIN resolutions has paved the way for this action, and the passage of an enabling act for New Mexico, will at once dispel the cloud which has lowered over our country. That Territory can never become a slave-holding one. Climate, soil, every thing, in fact, makes it a region to which the slaveholder cannot profitably emigrate. Make, then, this territory a State, and the vexatious question of Slavery is forever removed from the province of Federal legislation, and the two great sections of our country will have no further cause for difference. This done, the new Administration will enter upon its duties with all cause of opposition to it removed. Its position in regard to Slavery will be well understood, but the assurances the slaveholders have received will forbid their harboring any feelings of distrust. If then, so great benefits can result from the ADAMS proposition, surely Congress should lose no time in passing it.

118. THE PROPOSITIONS OF THE WASHINGTON CONVENTION

(Providence Daily Journal [Lincoln], March 1, 1861)

THE PROPOSITIONS OF THE WASHINGTON CONVENTION appear in another column. It was for a long time doubtful whether the commissioners would agree upon any report. More than once those who desired an agreement have despaired of seeing one reached. But at last a series of propositions, based on those which Mr. Guthrie presented some days ago, yet differing from them in several respects, received the votes of a majority of the States represented in the body. These propositions are now before Congress, accompanied by the request of the convention that the people of the various States be permitted to say whether they desire to adopt the amendments to the constitution therein suggested.

Though we have never cherished very high hopes that any, except indirect benefits, would result from the labors of the convention, we are not of those who would look with the least prejudice upon any commendable plan of settlement because it came from the convention rather than from Congress. If our judgment approved it we would advocate it, whether suggested by one body of men or by another.

But we have grave doubts whether an adjustment of the present difficulties will be directly reached through the path indicated by the convention. Let us notice a few of the obstacles which their scheme must encounter. We will say nothing about any prejudice which may exist in Congress against the convention; though we can readily understand that some of the members of Congress may look with no friendly eye upon a body of men who undertake, however respectfully, to suggest to them what they should do. But, waiving this point, there are many men who are opposed on principle to making any important change of the constitution, and particularly in times of excitement like the present. It is necessary too to have the vote not merely of a majority, but of two-thirds of each House. But still, suppose that this vote should be secured. Suppose that a number of members who do not approve of the propositions, are willing to lay them before the people, and that thus the question is sent out to the various States.

The close vote by which they were adopted in convention does not inspire very sanguine hopes of their receiving the approval of three-fourths of the States. They will have to undergo a thorough examination and sifting. At the very outset we want to know what is the real feeling of the border States about them. It is of no use for the northern States to proceed unless the border slave States desire this change. The amendments are offered to satisfy a discontent on their part and not to appease us. We are abundantly satisfied with the constitution as it is. Now we are confronted at once with the fact that Virginia, North Carolina and Maryland voted against these propositions in convention. Did the commissioners from those States fairly represent the public sentiment of their constituents? If they did, if these three great States really will not be satisfied with the proposed amendments, why should they be made? Our opinion is that the States are more loyal to the Union than the vote of their commissioners would indicate. But the northern States will want some conclusive evidence on that point.

Of course there will be a great diversity of opinions respecting the propositions themselves. As we understand the first section, neither Congress nor the territorial legislature of New Mexico will have power to prevent a Mississippian from taking his negro slaves into that territory and keeping them there, unless a federal court decides that he has no right to keep them there. It will be said, however, that no Mississippian or other slaveholder will take his slaves there, any more than he will to Colorado, where slavery is not forbidden, and for the same reason, that he cannot make it profitable. We shall be reminded that while for the last ten years slavery has had full liberty to plant itself there, it has succeeded in carrying only twenty-four slaves into the territory, and that, therefore, neither under this law nor any other, will slavery, as a matter of fact, gain a foothold there. Of all this people must judge for themselves. For our part we are free to say that we think the project to admit New Mexico as a State is decidedly preferable to this, and should be very glad to see it substituted for this first section.

The second section is open to objections. It smacks of Calhoun's old system of dual government.

The third section will be opposed by all those who insist on the right and the power of Congress to abolish slavery, if it pleases, on soil under the exclusive jurisdiction of the United States. Nor do we see clearly how the right to touch at ports with slaves, which is recognized, is practically to be distinguished from the right of transit, which is forbidden. May a Virginian take fifty slaves to New York on his way with them to Texas? May he stop at New York? If so, how long?

The sixth section we are opposed to. We think that the consent of all the States ought not to be required for any amendment to the constitution.

We hope it is not heterodox in these days of secession, to say that we should have been pleased to hear from the convention some explicit condemnation of the doctrine of secession. It has become a question whether we do not need in the constitution some express declaration on this point. At all events, when guarantees are asked on other points, we should like to have some definite understanding with our friends in the south upon this disputed question. Mr. Doolittle, we observe, offers a proviso as an amendment to the first section, touching this matter. We cannot comprehend how our government can ever be stable and strong, if any State has a right to secede when she pleases. We may settle all other questions as often and as satisfactorily as we please; but if this one remains open, if the doctrines of Mason and Toombs are correct, and those of Andrew Johnson wrong, if the border States do not agree with us in denying *in toto* the doctrine of secession, we do not well see how our Union can be compact and permanent.

But, at all events, there can be no rash action on the propositions of the convention. If Congress decides by a two-thirds vote to-day to send them to the States, there must necessarily be a long delay before the States can pass upon them. It requires, too, the approval of three-fourths of the States to give them the force of amendments to the constitution. We shall all have ample time to consider the subject. We shall be glad if, by the aid of this convention, or by any other means, we find the initial step towards an honorable adjustment of our national difficulties.

119. A Basis of Settlement—The Montgomery Constitution

(Philadelphia *Morning Pennsylvanian* [Breckinridge], March 21, 1861)

The position of the border States is such as to awaken the solicitude of every man who values the perpetuity of the Union. They are in a position of extraordinary precariousness, which they cannot possibly long maintain. It is anomalous and unnatural, and must speedily have a determinate character. States must have a fixed settled status and policy.

Nominally in a Confederacy which is controlled by a party hostile to their best interests, they are in immediate juxtaposition and contact with a Confederacy of seven States, whose sentiments, sympathies and interests are identical with their own. These two Confederacies are rivals for their favor. Both boast of having the Constitution of our fathers. In one that Constitution has been misconstrued, perverted, abused by the dominant Anti-Slavery party, and converted into an instrument of oppression and injury. The men appointed to administer that Constitution and the laws passed in pursuance of it, are pledged to a line of policy which threatens inequality, degradation, injury, ruin to the predominant interest of the Border States.

In the new Confederacy, on the contrary, that Constitution in itself, its letter and spirit protective of slavery, has been so amended as to remove all possibility of abuse, perversion and misconstruction on the subject of slavery; to limit its financial policy to the rigorous rules of revenue without protection; to forbid the African slave trade; to extend the Presidential term to six years, and make him thereafter ineligible; to authorize the Congress to provide by law that the heads of Departments may have a seat upon the floor of either House of Congress, with the privilege of discussing any measures appertaining to their Departments.

They provide for the acquisition of new territory, and for the recognition and protection of slave property throughout such territory, and for the admission of new States. One amendment is particularly noticeable. It is as follows:—

"The principal officer in each of the Executive Departments, and all persons connected with the Diplomatic service, may be removed from office at the pleasure of the President. All other civil officers of the Executive Department may be removed at any time by the President, or other appointing power, *when their services are unnecessary, or for dishonesty, incapacity, inefficiency, misconduct or neglect of duty, and when so removed, the removal shall be reported to the Senate, together with the reasons therefor.*" This effectually destroys that distracting, corrupting and dangerous evil which now prevails at Washington—"the wild hunt after office."

The amendments made at Montgomery on the subject of slavery are precisely such as the Border States desire, while the amendments on other subjects are just those on which the public mind, at both the North and the South, have settled down. The amendments on the subject of slavery embody the very guarantees which the Border States demand, and which the Democrats throughout the entire free States—a large majority of the masses—are perfectly willing, and have all along been willing, to grant to the South.

The Border States have before them three alternatives—to remain in the Union without guarantees—to cast in their fortunes with the new Confederacy, in which they are offered all they require—or to set up for themselves and make such a Constitution as they shall choose. Should they do the last, and carry with them the present Constitution, then would we have the eccentric spectacle of three adjoining confederacies with the same Constitution, varied only in a few particulars.

When we contemplate so unnecessary and so unnatural a division —unnecessary and unnatural, geographically, socially, commercially, in respect of race and in respect of national policy, how revolting appears that insensate, intolerant and wretched fanaticism which criminally wrecks an empire because it cannot control it, and divides and enfeebles the white race because they cannot be forced to accept the negroes as their equals.

The Republicans who have up to this time availed themselves of every conceivable pretext, make-shift and subterfuge, have sought to justify their failure to offer suitable terms to the Southern States by saying that they are ignorant as to the nature and extent of their demands, can no longer plead that doubtful plea. The Montgomery Constitution indicates to them plainly, precisely and fully both the nature and extent of those demands. They cannot henceforward plead ignorance either as to the demands of the Cotton States or of the Border States. They are both the same.

There stands that Montgomery Constitution, containing our old, venerated compact, with such additions and amendments as experience, the conflict of interest and prejudice, and the lapse of time have shown to be necessary. There it stands quietly, proudly, without menace to any, but with promise and hope to all, offering itself as a basis of universal reconstruction. It invites the Border States, the Middle States, the States of the East, and the States of the Northwest.

There is nothing in that Constitution that can repel any man, any party, any State, not fatally bent on disunion and Abolitionism.

Were the Montgomery Constitution submitted to the people of the North, they would accept it with joy and with unexampled unanimity.

120. A NATIONAL CONVENTION

(Philadelphia *Press* [Douglas], March 25, 1861)

The wisdom and necessity of some such measure as Mr. SEWARD proposed in his last speech in the United States Senate, and Mr. LINCOLN endorsed in his Inaugural—the assemblage of a National Convention— is daily becoming more and more apparent. Our country is in an anomalous condition for which no precedent can be found in its past history, and none in the history of other nations, whose institutions and modes of government are decidedly different from our own. It is not at all strange that a constitutional chart, devised seventy years ago, as the binding, fundamental law of a great Confederacy like this, should be found, in some respects, defective, or not sufficiently explicit upon subjects of vital importance and of universal interest. There is scarcely a State Constitution in the Union which has not undergone numerous, and in some cases radical and thorough changes. There is scarcely a Government in the world, except our own, where any degree of enlightenment and civilization prevails, which has not been remodelled and changed during the last seventy years in regard to such subjects as are provided for in the Constitution of the United States, and therefore unchangeable by the ordinary processes of American legislation. One important amendment has already received the sanction of two-thirds of the members of both branches of Congress, and preparations are being made to submit it to the action of the Legislatures of the different States, so that, when ratified by three-fourths of them, it may become a part of the fundamental law of the land. The Peace Conference, which assembled at Washington last winter, only embodied the wishes of a large portion of the American people, when it prepared and submitted for the consideration of Congress a number of propositions, which are by the citizens of the Border Slave States considered essential to their protection, and which a majority of the people of a number of the free States would, no doubt, cheerfully endorse, if they were submitted to a popular vote for ratification or rejection. The people of the Cotton States have flatly refused to comply with the plain injunctions of the present Constitution, and, after seceding separately from the Union, they have formed a new Confederacy, which has adopted our present Constitution, after incorporating into it a number of important amendments.

Thus, directly or indirectly, quite a general expression of a desire for a modification of our Government has been made. Yet the plans suggested for its change have been so numerous, the propositions presented so diverse in their character, and the difference of opinion in regard to them is so great, that it is probable the nation will never be entirely restored to its wonted state of peaceful tranquillity and harmonious political action until its fundamental law has been thoroughly revised, and a new basis of common agreement arranged. The experiment is not altogether free from danger, it is true, and the assemblage of a National Convention would doubtless bring into contact many antagonistic and explosive theories and opinions; but, after all, this is an inevitable incident of all republican governments, which cannot be effectually administered unless they rest upon the broad basis of a cheerful and willing obedience of the masses of the whole people over whom they assume to rule.

At this particular juncture, there appear to be two especially im-

portant reasons for convening such a body, or in some other way changing the Constitution. The prevailing sentiment of the Border Slave
States, as far as we are enabled to understand it, undoubtedly is that
their safety requires new constitutional guarantees, while the revolutionary condition of the Cotton States is so completely apparent that
few can doubt that, if they are to be restored to the Union, its Government must, in some respects, be changed, and if their assumed state
of complete independence is to be acknowledged, it should only be
done by the same high and solemn authority that formed the nation
they propose to dissolve. The executive, with the consent of the Senate,
may, it is true, negotiate treaties; but only with foreign nations and Indian tribes, and not with associate commonwealths. Congress has specific
power to admit new States into the Union, but not to authorize or
formally permit their departure from it, so that even if it should become
apparent that the revolting States were determined to persist in their
rash experiment, and all the faithful Union States were perfectly willing to allow them to depart in peace, and to recognize their new Confederacy, the Government, as at present constructed, would have no
constitutional right to give full validity to such a movement.

Essential changes of some kind, therefore, appear to be important in
any probable event; and until the waves of public opinion, which have
been stirred to their profoundest depths by the course of affairs during
the last six months, quietly subside into some well-defined and unmistakable channel, constant difficulties, doubts, and uncertainties will
probably continue to cast a cloud over the whole destiny of our nation.

121. [RECONSTRUCTION BY GENERAL SECESSION]

(Boston Daily Advertiser [Lincoln], April 1, 1861)

The idea of reconstructing the Union by a sort of general secession
and agreement to the Montgomery Constitution, when first proposed,
strikes the mind of every one as too monstrous to be seriously entertained. It appears to us in the same light, we may add, after a tolerably
careful consideration, and we have therefore been slow to believe that
it could recommend itself to anybody not an actual confederate with
the secessionists. We are forced to conclude, however, by a variety of indications, that the way is being prepared for some movement which
shall make the Montgomery instrument the basis of adjustment, and
that the friends of the present Constitution will have to meet this issue
at last. We apprehend that it will be presented by an active if not a
strong party, and enforced by appeals to the general love of Union, and

by assurances that the Constitution of 1787 is now lost, and that the substitute is the only possible basis on which we can expect to secure the substantial blessings of peace and regulated liberty.

It is hardly necessary for us to argue how complete an abandonment of honor and of hope for future harmony is implied in this scheme, whatever artful disguises may be used to conceal its real nature. We now wish to point out that for those who can make up their minds to forget honor and right and our duty to those who come after us, the scheme is not after all so very unnatural. Especially for those who gave their adhesion to the plan wrongly called Mr. Crittenden's, this new step in abasement does not appear to present any very great difficulties, for the reason that, after all, the Montgomery Convention went no farther in providing for slavery than that plan went. Indeed, that Convention placed the prohibition of the slave trade in the Constitution itself, while the Crittenden compromise was satisfied with a mere resolution by Congress,—in addition to which the latter undertook to deprive the African race of the right of suffrage or of holding office, while the former did not.

The Montgomery Constitution, however, in its general treatment of the subject of slavery differs but little from the Crittenden compromise. It makes slavery the normal characteristic of all territory now possessed or hereafter to be acquired, and imposes upon Congress the duty of protecting it; it secures the right of transit and sojourn with slave property, and rejects the euphemism by which direct reference to slavery was excluded from our present Constitution. In all this the Montgomery schemers have not gone a whit beyond the framers of last winter's plan, but have merely undertaken to make the Constitution more homogeneous and more clear, than the adoption of that plan would have made it. It is hardly necessary even to have recourse to the adage, that "it is as well to be hanged for an old sheep as a lamb." The Montgomery Constitution, wherein it differs from the Crittenden compromise on the matter of slavery, is not the worse for the difference, and requires no more violent effort to make it acceptable.

The changes proposed at Montgomery in the ordinary working of our government, the change of the President's term to a single term of six years, and other alterations, would not be likely to be the subject of serious difference at any time. The prohibition of protective legislation and of appropriations for facilitating commerce, simply express long standing democratic doctrines. There remain then simply two objections to the Montgomery Constitution, for those who regard a complete surrender to treason as honorable, or an entire abandonment of principle as right. The new instrument expressly rests upon the action, not of the people, but of State sovereignties, and reduces the general government to a mere league. In this, however, it simply conforms to the doctrine practically approved in the present crisis by the democratic party. It also makes slavery the corner-stone of the institutions established by it, as was distinctly explained by Hon. A. H. Stephens to the satisfaction of every one. But as it does this simply by adopting the construction which the democratic party has already placed upon the Constitution, and which was expressed in the Crittenden compromise, we confess that it does not seem altogether strange to us that those who have swallowed the one should make no wry face at the other. "It is the first step that costs." One wing of our democratic friends and some who do not call themselves democrats took that first step some time since. We need not wonder, therefore, if before long they set forward with some vigor upon the path to Montgomery.

122. A National Convention

(Grand Rapids Daily Enquirer [Douglas], April 6, 1861)

It is now very evident that nothing can be done, in the way of adjusting our national troubles, except through a National Convention. A National Convention has been spoken of, and favored by the President. None would more gladly favor this suggestion than we, did we believe that it could be possibly carried out, in its design and intent, and with any good to the country. But the manifold difficulties which must inevitably attend its successful formation, are so great as almost to preclude the possibility of that formation. In the first place Congress can call such a convention only upon the demand of the Legislatures of two-thirds of the States.—Therefore under the present enumeration, twenty-two States are necessary to this end. There are thirty-four, of whom eight have *practically* withdrawn from the Union. It is not likely that the abolition element in Michigan, Wisconsin, Massachusetts and Vermont, would even permit any demand from those States.—It is claimed by that wing of the Republican party, that any amendment less restrictive of slavery than the present provisions of the Constitution cannot be submitted to. So that any Convention for such a purpose, would never command their support. They also claim that the South have no justification of withdrawal, that the concession of such a right would be in violation of every principle of governmental law, and therefore inadmissible. So that, a Convention for the purpose of proposing any amendment whereby the disaffected States could withdraw, would be opposed by them, to the end. And we confess that there is much reason in this last proposition. We are not sure but what it is sound doctrine. We are far more willing to recognize secession as an *accomplished fact*, than to recognize the right, by constitutional amendment. And again, many months must of necessity elapse before the Legislatures of the several States could convene. Then Congress must be assembled, and endless time consumed in unnecessary discussions. One or two years must elapse before a Convention could by any means be assembled. During all this time however, some policy in regard to seceded States *must* be adopted. If coercive, it at once neutralizes any benefit that might result from the action of the Convention. If *peaceful*, it must involve a recognition of the *de facto* government. The Montgomery Cabinet will go on, consolidating its power, extending its resources, receiving from other nations their congratulations and hearty support for the free traffic system, holding out to the Border States the benefits and protection which their Constitutions gives [*sic*] the slaveholding system, founding an immovable and formidable power.—And it cannot be disputed that should the present state of things continue six months longer, the remaining moi[e]ty of the slaveholding States will have joined those already withdrawn. Every question of interest, of self-preservation, affords them that solution, and we really cannot see how they could do otherwise. Still it should be prevented if possible.

It is easy to perceive that a National Convention would be of a strongly Republican character, unless a tremendous revulsion in the political status of the North should take place. If Republican, any amendment such as they demand would not be accorded, for the Republican party would oppose any recognition of the right to extend slavery. Verily, what will they do? Under present aspects, a National Convention would be a mere mockery. Even should the Convention settle upon some proposed amendment or amendments, they must be ratified by a vote of three-fourths of the States. Any *two* States could therefore under the present condition of things, prevent their adoption. How slender the chance thus of receiving the adoption of such amendments as would be settled upon. As regards those States already out of the Union it could do nothing except in paving the way for re-construction, and that it would not do, so long as Republicanism is a political power. No, we must accept what has befallen us. And when one thinks of the unhappy condition of our country, when one remembers that it was once peaceful and prosperous, he cannot but in his heart, demand from history the perpetuation of the infamy of that party which was too sectional, too selfish, too grasping, too fanatical, to preserve the integrity of the Union. The chronicles of the present will be a sad narration of national disintegration through folly and wickedness.

VIII

PEACEABLE SEPARATION

123. Done at Last—What Shall We Do?

(Indianapolis Daily Journal [Lincoln], December 22, 1860)

South Carolina has seceded. The mysterious operation was performed on Thursday at half past one post meridian. It appears to have been done "as easy as rolling off a log." If anybody has an idea of the facility implied in that phrase he can judge how easily South Carolina broke the Union. It may not be unworthy of remark that the sun rose on Friday morning very much as usual, and, either in joy or curiosity, made a decided effort to get through the clouds far enough to see the hole Carolina had left. The world moved on with no perceptible indication that it felt the "rent" the "envious" State had made in its integrity. Somebody announced it in Congress, and somebody cheered over it in Charleston, and secession was accomplished, and its terrors fairly encountered. Well, we are a severed nation. We are a divided house. And we are none the worse for it. All the mischief that the apprehension of disunion could do has been done, and disunion itself can do nothing if we do not force it to. We are well rid of South Carolina, if we are only wise enough to count it a riddance, and nothing worse. She can do far less harm out of the Union if we let her go out quietly, than she has always done in it, and can now do in double measure if she is forcibly kept in. We insist that she shall go out, and we shall thank God that we have had a good riddance of bad rubbish. South Carolina has always been a nuisance, only lacking the importance which an attempt at "coercion" would give her to be magnified into a pestilence, and we think we owe her so much gratitude for trying to leave us that we should help her on the way. If other States follow her, let them. If all the South follows her, let it. If they can't endure an association with us except on terms which ignore the vital principle of the original compact between us, and impose on *us* the support of slavery, we should be ashamed to ask them to stay. In God's name, and for humanity's sake, let them go in peace, live with their cherished institution while they can, prosper if it be Heaven's purpose, or within man's power, and if they

331

ever learn that a great wrong can never be made the foundation of a great government, they may be willing, in the ruin of their hopes, to seek a refuge in the abandoned old Government, and abide there peacefully forever.

But this policy, the dictate of humanity and wisdom, as we conceive it to be, is not in favor with many warm Republicans. They insist, and quote Gov. Morton for it, that it is the duty of the nation to preserve itself, and they quote Gen. Jackson and the Chicago Platform for the necessity of preserving the Union at all hazards. They argue, and nobody ever denied it, that secession is not permitted by the Constitution, and if one State may go out all may go, and then where will the nation be? True, but oh! sagacious patriots tell us where will the nation be if you attempt to keep it together by instituting a war between its members?—How will *that* process save the Union? "The Union shall be preserved," you say. So say we. But we insist that it shan't be ruined in the act of preservation. We don't believe in pickling a putrifaction [*sic*]. The Union *preserved* is worth any effort, except the surrender of its vital principle. But a civil war is not preservation. It is sure, speedy, overwhelming ruin. War, instead of preserving the Union, must rend it first, and ruin the fragments afterwards. Is any man so blind as not to see that? Is any man so devoted to the idea of "enforcing the laws" and "maintaining our glorious Constitution," as not to see that maintaining it by civil war is the surest way to destroy it? The *right* to demand obedience of the seceding States to the Constitution they have adopted, and the laws they have themselves enacted, is indisputable. But if they can only be made to obey by fighting them the process is too expensive for the result. We can afford to do without their obedience, and without them, better than we can afford to ruin ourselves to retain either. Therefore, inconsistent, as it may appear, while we hold that the Constitution requires the chastisement of rebellious States, we hold that humanity, our own interests, and the demands of this enlightened age, require us to stay our hands. There is a higher consideration than the Constitution, and it is the good which the Constitution was intended to effect. That instrument is only a means to secure an end, a law to preserve liberty, property and happiness to all under it. If its enforcement cannot secure those objects, then it is our *duty* to secure them without the Constitution. Now will any man say that a war between the North and South, to enforce the obedience of the latter to the Constitution, will preserve liberty, or property, or promote human happiness? We presume not. Every man can see that it is the most direct way to destroy all three.

Freedom will not be more firmly established in the North by it, and if it be established in the South it can only be by a servile war promoted by the civil war, and *that* is a dear price to pay for emancipation anywhere. We eagerly proclaim now that we never would encourage it, and its character will not be changed, though our feelings may be, by a civil war. There is nothing to gain for liberty then by war. And it is an insult to common sense to prove that it cannot benefit property or personal happiness. War, therefore, would enforce the Constitution, which was intended to promote these great objects, at the expense of defeating the very objects it was intended to secure. A strong government is not worth so much as peace between brethren. If the Federal Government were as strong as the Russian autocracy it would be a poor compensation for the blood, and money, and opportunities for good, lost in making it so.

The world is going to climb to a higher philosophy of government than that which underlies monarchies and grew out of "the Divine right of kings." That philosophy claims the preservation of a government as its highest duty. The nobler philosophy demands that the objects of a government shall not be sacrificed to the government; that the end shall not be lost to save the means.—And if blood is to be spilled in maintaining one government over a people, when the people want another that they believe will benefit them as much, it is blood needlessly and cruelly spilled. The statesman can always see where to draw the line between the demand of a people for a change of government and the resistance of outlaws to wholesome restraints. Kossuth gave the world a higher and nobler idea of international law, in his plea for the aid of other nations to those struggling against oppression, than it ever had before, and the United States, by wisely applying the law avowed in her own Declaration of Independence, in the present crisis, may give the world a higher idea of the duties of governments than has yet been taught by man or nation.

This view of the duty of governments, which we are only confirmed in by each new examination, shows us the course to be pursued towards South Carolina. It is to let her go freely and entirely, let loose all revenue chains and postal cords, and push her out into a separate national existence, if not with good wishes at least without resistance. Henry Stanbery, the celebrated Ohio lawyer, in his speech at the Cincinnati Union meeting last Wednesday, contended that it was easy to coerce South Carolina without bloodshed, by simply blockading her ports. He opposed coercion if it involved war, but he was in favor of bloodless coercion. This is the position of a lawyer, not of a statesman. It is not a wise policy, but a quibble. We must do one of two things with South Carolina. We must either compel her obedience, or let her pass away from our control into her own. Mr. Stanbery's plan is to enforce the laws, without enforcing obedience, to collect the duties at Fort Moultrie, or out at sea, so as to keep the South Carolinians subject to our laws, and yet keep ourselves out of their reach. This is manifestly impossible. If South Carolina pretends to be an independent government, she *must* control her own ports, and if we blockade them she must drive us out. It is as absolutely necessary to her national existence as the air is to individual existence. By blockading their ports, therefore, we only resort to a trick to bring the first attack from South Carolina, instead of making it ourselves.—And that trick is unworthy of a great nation. If we are right we can begin the attack, without seeking pretexts. If we are not right, we are only showing cowardice as well as cruelty, in resorting to such a trick. There is, therefore, no escape from a war, if we refuse to admit the independence of South Carolina.—Mr. Stanbery does not avoid it. He only changes the first blow from one to the other. We must, then, determine either to fight openly and at once, or openly and freely permit South Carolina to depart. If we fight her, we shall fight every State in the South.—It is idle to blink this fact. Sooner or later, by sympathy, by relationship, by business connections, by volunteers from the States above leaving fathers, mothers, and brothers at home to grow more and more indifferent to the Union as their relatives are more and more bloodily mixed up with disunion, by a thousand influences, the border States, will be drawn gradually into the fight, and before it is over the whole South will be fighting the whole North. This we regard as the inevitable result of a war with South Carolina. And a war, we believe, is a thousand times worse evil than the loss of a State, or a dozen States, that hate us, and will not stay with us without ruling us. We don't believe in standing on trifles or technical difficulties. Let us consider South Carolina a foreign nation the hour she gives the Federal Government notice of her secession, and in spite of all obstructions and questions of propriety, treat with her for an adjustment of our common debts and common property, and for the arrangement of treaties for the continuance of business. If we do so disunion will soon kill itself. If we attempt to kill it with bayonet and ball it will wound us fearfully before we can succeed, and when we have succeeded, its dead body will be as pestilent as its living body. We shall be burthened as badly to carry the corpse as to bear the restive and struggling live carcass.

124. Dissolution

(Kenosha (Wis.) *Democrat* [Douglas], January 11, 1861)

In all human probability James Buchanan will be the last President of the United States. One of the sovereign states of the Union has already declared the compact broken, and her allegiance dissolved. There can be no longer any doubt that several other states are ready to-day to follow her example. All the balance of the slaveholding states are hastily preparing to do so. No greater mistake can be made by any one, than to suppose a people accustomed to political free agency, can be chained together with an iron fatalism, in the bonds of an unwilling confederacy. The very freedom claimed by every individual citizen, precludes the idea of compulsory association, as individuals, as communities, or as States. The very germ of liberty is the right of forming our own governments, enacting our own laws, and choosing our own political associates. The most valuable gift has lost its worth, if we are not free to reject it; and governmental protection is another name for tyrannical *surveillance* when forced on an unwilling people. The right of secession inheres to the people of every sovereign state. Governments were made by them, and can be unmade. Constitutions are adopted and repealed, by every free people. What any state by act or compact, has done; if it violate no vested right she may undo. The laws of one legislature, are repealable by the next with this single limitation. It has ever been the doctrine of the Democratic party that no generation can take from its successors by any act of legislation, the power to amend or repeal. This should be obvious to all. Without this right of each generation to pass on the question of its own rights and interests, there could be no progress in legislation, or in civilization. Deny this principle, and we are to-day the subjects of laws enacted a thousand years ago. The power to make laws, and establish governments, implies the power to unmake them; as the major proposition contains the minor. By this test the right of secession is maintained. South Carolina voted herself into the Union; she can vote herself out. *The Constitution of the United States was ratified by several of the states, with this express understanding.* This alone, would determine the right of secession. If eight of ten men agree to terms of partnership, and the other two state at the time of *their* agreement what they consider its terms and requirements are; if assented to by the others, this interpretation becomes a part of the compact. This right was ably vindicated by Mr. Nicholson of Virginia at the time of its ratification by that state. Many delegates were opposed to voting for the

Constitution until all the other states had assented to this view of it. Mr. Nicholson contended this delay was unnecessary, for if Virginia adopted it on this condition, a refusal to recognize this interpretation would absolve her from all obligation to it. South Carolina took then precisely the same stand she does to-day for the rights of States. The celebrated Virginia and Kentucky resolutions do but embody the same principle.

The framers of the constitution hoped, and no doubt expected the Union to be perpetual; but they confessed it could only be perpetuated by the cheerful obedience of a willing people. They expected a time to come when one or more of the States should determine to secede. The[y] refused to incorporate a clause in the constitution enabling Congress or the President to use force against a seceding state. They declared any state had an inherent right to secede at pleasure, and a forcible union would be an invasion of that right. Mr. Madison expressly stated that he was opposed to the use of any force to unite the states, or to keep them united. He said any attempt to use force would involve the country in civil war, and forever separate the states. This accounts for the lack of constitutional prohibition of secession.

It is a common maxim of law, that every right has a means of enforcement; and every wrong a remedy. By this rule the right of secession is undoubted. *The Constitution provides no means of coercing a state in the Union; nor any punishment for secession.* The postal and revenue laws of the United States cannot be practically enforced in South Carolina by means of *her* courts, or the District Court of the United States for *that District.* The constitution expressly provides that all trials for crime shall be *by jury, and in the district where the offense was committed.* How then can any prosecution be sustained against a citizen of South Carolina? Collection of customs is impossible also. If the people of any state are united in their opposition to the revenue laws of the government, they can successfully nullify such law in defiance of the United States authorities. This may be startling to many readers, but is unqualifiedly true. Every master of a vessel can demand the privilege of discharging his cargo in the port of Charleston. The United States cannot enforce the collection of customs there, nor inflict a penalty on those who resist it. Art. 9th, sec. 5th of the constitution expressly says:

"No preference shall be given by any regulation of commerce or revenue, to the ports of one state over those of another; nor shall vessels bound to or from one state, be obliged to enter, clear, or pay duties in another."

The founders of our government were constant secessionists. They not only claimed the right for themselves, but conceded it to others. They were not only secessionists in theory, but in practice. The old confederation between the states was especially declared perpetual by the instrument itself. Yet Jefferson, Madison, Monroe and the hosts of heroes and statesmen of that day seced'd from it. In the constitutional convention the delegates from dissatisfied states used this "binding clause" in the articles of confederation, as a threat to secure still greater admissions from other states; just as the republican party of the north now hold the "perpetual obligation" of our constitution over the heads of the south, as a means of intimidation. They were speedily disenchanted then; they will soon be so now. Brave men claimed the God-given right to govern themselves then; their sons will not be slow to demand it now. The men who *threatened* in that hour of national peril, were deemed no true friends to our country's welfare; and those who do so now, deserve a deeper measure of condemnation.

125. THE GREAT ISSUE AND THE CHOICE—SEPARATION OR WAR

(Albany *Atlas and Argus* [Douglas], January 12, 1861)

The sectional doctrines of the Republican party have—as thinking men have foreseen—at last brought us to the verge of civil war. Indeed, war has already commenced. Four States have formally separated from the Confederacy and declared themselves independent of the Federal Union and are in the attitude of supporting their position by arms. The Republican leaders adhere to their partisan and sectional dogmas and utterly refuse to do anything to arrest this impending danger and restore peace to the country. The present Congress will do nothing and before its term expires on the 4th of March, thirteen or fourteen of the slave States will have established a separate government, which they will sustain at the hazard of fortune and life. We shall be confronted with the stern issue of peaceable, voluntary separation, or of civil war. We shall be compelled to bid a sad farewell to the brethren with whom we have so long dwelt in liberty and happiness and divide with them the inheritance of our fathers—or to undertake, by all the terrors and horrors of war, to compel them to continue in union with us. We must separate from them peaceably, and each seek happiness and prosperity in our own way—or we must conquer them and hold them as subjugated provinces. Fellow citizens, of all parties and of whatever past views, which course do you prefer? Shall it be peaceable separation or civil war?

If such be the issue—and none can now deny it—before choosing war, it will be well to reflect whether it will effect the desired object of preserving the Union of these States? With thirteen or fourteen States banded together and fighting with as much pertinacity, as our fathers of the Thirteen Colonies, for what *they* deem their rights and liberties, the war must be a deadly and protracted one. We do not doubt that the superior numbers and resources of the Northern States might prevail. We might defeat them in battle, overrun their country, and capture and sack and burn their cities, and carry terror and desolation, by fire and sword, over their several States. We might ruin the commerce and industry of the country, North and South, sweep the whole land with the besom of war, and cause the nation to resound with the groans of widows and orphans; all this we might do, and through it all, possibly, be able to boast of the triumph of the Federal arms, and to see the stars and stripes waive [*sic*] over every battle field and every smoking city.

But would peace thereby be restored? Would the Union be thus preserved? Would these conquered States quietly assume their old places in the Confederacy? Would they send Representatives to Congress, take part in the Presidential elections, and perform their functions as loyal members of the Union? Would they be anything but conquered States, held in subjection by military restraint? No—peace and concord between these States cannot be reached through the medium of war. The probable result of a long and deadly struggle would be a treaty of peace, agreeing to a division. War is necessarily disunion and division, and we prefer division without war—if it must come. By a peac[e]able separation the enmities of the two sections will not be inflamed beyond all possible hope of reconciliation and reconstruction, but war will be eternal hostility and division. Let the people of this country pause before they draw the sword and plunge into a fratricidal strife.

We say emphatically, let the great State of New York not be foremost in kindling a flame, which never will be quenched except in the blood of our kindred. The public passions are easily aroused and the great danger at this moment is that the war spirit will take possession of the populace and hurry us and the country on to ruin. The press, influential citizens, legislators and other public men—instead of inflaming this feeling and seeking ephemeral popularity by ministering to it, should seek to restrain it and lead the people of this State to act with moderation. New York should not forget her position, as the most powerful State of the Union and should put forth her influence, in this emergency, in favor of peace, and if she cannot stay the mad torrent of disunion, should hold herself in condition to be able, when the passions of men shall have cooled, to engage in the work of reconstruction and of re-uniting States now dissevered, for causes so trivial that time and reflection—if we escape war—may be expected to remove them.

We repeat—if disunion must come, let it come without war. Peaceable separation is a great calamity—but dissolution, with the superadded horrors of internal war, including the ruin of business, the destruction of property, oppressive debt, grinding taxation and sacrifice of millions of lives, is a scourge from which, let us pray, that a merciful Providence may protect us.

If the present Congress, and the political leaders in it, who have brought the country into this danger, have not the patriotism to adopt measures for the restoration of peace, better than plunge the nation into civil war, let them propose Constitutional amendments, which will enable the people to pass upon the question of a voluntary and peaceful separation. Then, at least the hope will remain that the people may in good time discard their fanatical political leaders and apply themselves to the reconstruction and renovation of the Constitution and the Union.

126. LET US REASON TOGETHER

(New York Journal of Commerce [Breckinridge], January 12, 1861)

We suppose the most incredulous of the people of the Northern States, including possibly the New York Board of Currency, who as late as November were of opinion that our political troubles "would soon blow over," are by this time convinced that the difficulties which agitate the country are of a serious character, and that all plans of pacification, thus far suggested, have proved and are likely to prove fruitless and unavailing. We suppose further, that every intelligent and sensible man, fully and clearly understands that the Union is already broken up, and that it is as idle to appeal to the Southern States to continue their political connection with the free States, under the present system, as it would be to speak to the winds in order to stop the devastation of the hurricane. That power which controls all things, can alone allay the storm and save our beloved country from dissolution.

The time has come when we may as well stop discussing the question of responsibility for existing evils, and address ourselves to the *facts*, as they appear upon the theatre of events. We have all had our say about the causes of the dissaffection [*sic*] in the slaveholding States, and we have also pretty generally freed our minds on the next point in issue, viz., whether the seceding States were or were not pursuing the path of wisdom, in thus hastily withdrawing from the Union, before the conservative men of the North could have a chance to make a last and solemn appeal to the patriotism and judgment of the people in the free States, on behalf of their injured brethren in the South. Upon these points the press and the people of the country have spoken with characteristic freedom.

There is another topic also, upon which there has been no lack of discussion, and no withholding of opinions: we mean, The duty of the Federal Government in the crisis impending. Upon this question, as upon others involved in this unhappy controversy, there have been wide differences of opinion, and, we may add, some very intemperate expressions, both against the South and the Administration. Madness would be a soft term to apply to the language of a large portion of the press, including two or three of the leading papers in this city, upon the duty of the Government in this hour of dissolution. Our own opinions have not been withheld—are never withheld—from our readers, but events have followed each other in such rapid succession that what may seem wise and imperatively called for to-day, becomes impracticable, inoperative or unwise to-morrow. Consistency in opinions and policy is always commendable, and with a fair-minded man always a point of honor, but when startling announcements follow each other in quick succession, as well might the persons who had taken shelter under a tree from an approaching storm persist in remaining there when the lightning is seen coursing down its trunk, as for man to insist upon sticking to a preconceived policy when he sees State after State going out, and the Union in fact already dissolved.

Such is the present case. We have fondly hoped to arrest the progress of the disunion movement, and to this end thousands of our citizens have raised their voices and employed their pens, in support of this or that plan of pacification. But the only body to which we could turn for action—the Congress of the United States—has proved entirely powerless and imbecile, while the country has looked to the President to preserve the peace, and to stay the tide of disunion, without for one moment reflecting that the powers of that officer were too limited, and our Government altogether too much on the voluntary system, to admit of any such remedy becoming effective.

It is but nine weeks since the election, and already three (and perhaps before this goes to press four) States have left the Union, with the certainty that several others will immediately follow. It is too late to say these States have done wrong—that they have acted without cause, and ought to return to their position in the Union. It is too late to talk of using force to cause them to return or prevent others from following them out. Such a policy, never right or capable of justification under our system, would be madness at the present stage of the controversy.

It is a part of wisdom, as well [as] a prompting of necessity, to look at the facts as they now exist. The condition of things a year, a month, a week or even a day since, belongs now to the past. A day in revolutionary times, stands for years and perhaps for ages, in periods of profound peace and quiet. *Let us then take up the question of to-day.* How do we find it? What is the condition of the country at this moment? Just this—the Union broken up, several States already formally withdrawn, others on the point of withdrawing, and the probability reduced to a moral certainty that a majority if not all of the slave States, will within a few short weeks declare themselves out of the Union, and refuse to acknowledge all or any obligations or allegiance to the Federal Government. This is the sober reality—what *ought* to be the state of the case is quite immaterial. The practical question then is how are we to deal with these facts—not how ought the facts to be? Will any one furnish an answer to this question? Is any man, any statesman, in or out of Congress, prepared to lay down a rule of action which he can assure us will be the wisest and best which can be adopted?

Perhaps it may be answered that the seceding States must be compelled to submit, that their treason must be met by force. This is the language of thousands of people throughout the North, but we are not aware that any statesman worthy of the name, has yet seriously proposed to make war upon the South, to force her to remain in the Union. There has been a great amount of bluster of that sort, but no public man has thus far ventured upon such stern reality, in the form of a distinct proposition in Congress to raise men and arm them for the bloody work of butchering their friends in the Southern States. There are enough ready to abuse and denounce the President for not doing this, but they prefer to avoid the responsibility for themselves. But suppose this policy were adopted, will it be successful? Are the ten or twelve millions of people, the seven or eight millions of freemen in the Southern States to be thus subdued? It was found impossible for Great Britain, in the war of the Revolution, to subjugate three millions, with resources vastly inferior. Assuming, however, that in a war between the North and the South, the latter are subjugated—what then? Are they thus to be made brothers and friends,—to return to a willing and fraternal Union upon the voluntary plan of our political system? No, never, while the spirit of brave men animates them, and the blood of freemen courses in their veins. Subjugated they possibly may be, but willing members of a

Union like the present never, except upon terms of equality, such as *they* deem honorable and just.

What then is to be done? Shall we make war upon the South, and reduce them—if we can, which is more than doubtful—to slavery? We denounce African slavery, shall we then make slaves of white men, our equals and our brothers? Shall we, by such a policy, change our government from a voluntary one, in which the people are sovereigns, to a despotism where one part of the people are slaves? Such is the logical deduction from the policy of the advocates of force.

The most difficult question to be determined by the statesmen of to-day, is, what shall be done now? The President has declared that until some new action of Congress, he has "no alternative, as the chief executive officer under the Constitution of the United States, but to collect the public revenue and protect the public property, so far as this may be practicable under existing laws." At the same time, he urges upon Congress the necessity of immediate action, whereby may be secured "a peaceful solution of the questions at issue between the North and the South." We think the President is wise in thus committing the subject to Congress, who alone have power to conform the action of the Government to the existing state of things. The exercise of this discretionary power on the part of Congress, is the more needful because events of a startling character follow each other so quickly that what seemed wise and practicable a week since, might be unwise and impracticable at this time. Then South Carolina alone had passed the ordinance of secession, and the public property and revenue service there only was threatened. Now, several States are out of the Union, and nearly all the fortifications from North Carolina to Texas, are in the hands of the secessionists. To recover, and to hold them, will be to deluge the country with blood; and for what? Simply to be able to say we have subdued an unwilling people. When subdued they will not and cannot be compelled to discharge the functions of government under our system, and we cannot inaugurate a new system—a system of force—without departing from the great principle of self-government upon which our institutions are based. Is it not better to let them go,— go in peace and with our benediction,—relying upon their good sense and our justice to reconstruct a Government which has failed to perform all the functions expected of it, and which therefore must be reviewed and revised to adapt it to the times and the altered condition of our population? We throw out these suggestions for the consideration of statesmen and official persons, no less than for the people. We wish the facts were different. We grieve over the fallen spirit of our people, but as practical men, we meet practical questions in a practical way. It is for Congress to act, and we must be permitted to say, that action cannot be a moment too soon.

If the separation which must take place is to be peaceful, let the fact be proclaimed before we shall have imbrued our hands in each other[']s blood. Not a week should elapse,—nor a day, if that were long enough for the purpose,—before Congress determines the policy, and gives the President authority to carry it into execution.

127. The State of the Case Now

(Indianapolis Daily Journal [Lincoln], January 17, 1861)

There was a time before South Carolina had placed herself in open hostility to the Union, when we, and we believe a large majority of the North, would have consented to part with her, if she had consulted the other States, and requested permission to try a peaceful experiment as a separate nation. Her turbulence, and avowed maintenance of doctrines at war with the existence of the nation, made her, at the best, a useless member of the confederacy, and very many would have been glad to give her a chance to test the wisdom of her theories in a solitary existence. So with those States that sympathized with her, and were preparing to follow in her lead. But the case *now* is widely and fearfully changed. These States do not ask, or care to consult their associates, and learn whether it may not be possible to arrange our difficulties so as to move on in harmony as heretofore. They have put it out of our power to *consent* to anything.—They have met us, not with a request for peaceful consultation, but with war. If we concede their demands now it is the surrender of a nation *conquered* by rebel members. If we make no effort to resist the wrong we submit at once to disunion and national degradation. There is no course left, either for honor or patriotism, but to reclaim by the strong hand, if it must be so, all that the seceding States have taken, enforce the laws, and learn the traitors the wisdom of the maxim that it takes two to make a bargain.—All questions of expediency were thrust out of reach by the act which took Fort Moultrie as a hostile fortress, and hauled down the national flag as a sign of the conquest.—They have all been decided without our help. We have had no opportunity to say a word.—The seceding States have raised the issue, argued it to their own satisfaction, and decided it by war. We have been left no alternative but to resist or submit. We deplore this state of things. We had earnestly hoped that the Gulf States would give all shades of sentiment a fair opportunity of expression in the election of their Conventions, discuss their grievances calmly, request a consultation with the nation, and if they firmly and deliberately refused to abide in the Union as it is, we were willing to let them drop out, still holding our government unchanged over ourselves. In this way it *was* possible to get rid of the rebellious States, by simply diminishing, instead of dissolving the Union, which the London *Times* says is impossible. It is now, but it was not, and need not have been, if the seceding States had been willing to meet the Union fairly and come to an understanding.—Such a course would have been in accordance with the enlightenment of the age, the dictates of Christianity, and the best interests of both sections. But the hope of such an adjustment is all past, at least till the seceding States restore the government property, submits [*sic*] to the laws, and return to their former position of peaceful members of the Union. *There can be no conciliation with them till they do.* The government must be preserved. It is ours as well as theirs, and when they attempt to overturn it by force, we must preserve it by force. A government kicked aside at the will of any State, is nothing. The right of secession would make the government a mere accident, subsisting because thirty or forty members happened to agree in regard to it. We insist that our government is neither an accident or a trifle. It is the best yet devised by the wit of man, and is worth a dozen wars to keep. And we mean to keep it. To allow a State to rebel against it, and give way to the rebellion, is to consent to its destruction. We cannot claim that it exists even for those still remaining in it, when it is set at naught and defied by any other member. It must be whole or it cannot be at all. The people may let a member out of it, but no member can break it down to get out without breaking it to pieces. We are therefore for the most determined measures of resistance to the rebellion in the Gulf States. We insist that the Union shall be preserved till those who made it shall consent to change it. No refractory State or combination of traitors must be permitted to peril it in the pursuit of insane vengeance or impracticable theories. And if their madness leads them to open war let them suffer the doom of traitors.

128. TO THE READERS OF THE CONSTITUTION

(Washington (D. C.) *Constitution* [Breckinridge], January 30, 1861)

Circumstances of recent occurrence, both of a public and private nature, have made it expedient for me to suspend for a short time the publication of the *Constitution*, until I can complete arrangements, now in progress, for its reissue elsewhere under better and more favorable auspices.

To-morrow's paper will be the last which I shall issue in Washington City.

On the first of July last, immediately after the adjournment of the Baltimore Convention, I assumed the proprietorship and editorial control of the *Constitution*. During the exciting and momentous Presidential canvass that ensued, I used my best efforts to secure the election of JOHN C. BRECKINRIDGE and JOSEPH LANE, not merely because I was convinced that those distinguished men possessed, in an eminent degree, all the qualities requisite for the proper discharge of the duties of the high offices for which the national democracy had nominated them, but because I was firmly persuaded that their election, by entrusting the power of the Executive to men who would truly and faithfully administer the Government for the benefit of the whole nation, with an equal regard for the rights of all sections, and a stern devotion to the letter and spirit of the Constitution, was the only means of saving the Union from the dissolution which is now an accomplished fact. I believed that if the republicans succeeded in electing their candidate by a purely sectional vote, on a sectional platform of principles directly antagonistic to the rights, interests, safety, and honor of the Southern States, the Union must perish, because I knew that those States would neither submit to oppression nor degradation, and I felt that they ought not to do so.

When the result of the election was made known, and it was ascertained that Abraham Lincoln of Illinois was elected President of the United States from the 4th of next March, in compliance, it is true, with the *forms* of the Constitution, but in palpable contempt of the spirit of that sacred instrument, I hesitated not to defend the South, thus assailed in all her vital interests, and to commend and applaud the courage, the dignity, the patriotism, and the wisdom which she displayed in her prompt resolution not to submit to the degrading rule of a sectional majority banded together for the sole purpose of oppressing her, and animated by no other feeling than deadly hate of her and her institutions. I felt that the South ought to insist on perfect equality *in* the Union, or on independence *out* of it. When it became evident to all that she could not obtain the former, I hoped that she would promptly secure the latter, and I have faithfully used every exertion of which I was capable to aid her in striking the blow which was to free her from a partnership which had been diverted from the pious purposes of its founders, and made an instrument of oppression and insult.

Whether the right of secession were considered a right legitimately exercisable under the Constitution as belonging to the residuary mass of powers reserved to the people of the several States, and not delegated to the Federal agency, or whether it were considered as the right of revolution, did not appear to me to be a matter of much practical importance. I believed that the right of secession was specially reserved to the States by the framers of the Constitution, and the history of the formation of that compact distinctly justified the belief. But, even as a right of revolution, secession was, in my mind, not merely justifiable, but essential to the security of the Southern States, from the moment that the Chicago platform was declared by the dominant party to be the fundamental law of the land in place of the Constitution of the United States. On no day since the sixth of November would I have counselled a single Southern State to abate one jot or one tittle of her just rights, or to submit for one hour to the practical execution of the doctrines of the republican party.

I advocated secession. I hoped, and still hope, that all the Southern States will secede. I thought that an attempt to coerce a State to remain in the Union after she has solemnly declared by a vote of her people in sovereign convention that she will secede, would be the extreme of wickedness and the acme of folly. To "enforce the laws" within the limits of a State which had so seceded without collision with the people who had abjured those laws, was clearly an impossibility. It must lead to war,—a war the most calamitous, the most unholy, the most infamous that was ever declared since the world began.

The stealthy despatch of the Star of the West to carry Federal soldiers to reinforce Fort Sumter, and thus in all human probability bring on a conflict with the South Carolina troops, devised by General Scott and executed by Mr. Holt, I denounced as it deserved. It is not to the foresight of the Commanding General or the Secretary of War that we are to attribute our escape from a conflict which, had their plans been carried out, was inevitable.

By condemning the coercive policy of these officials, by a fearless avowal of my honest convictions, by an outspoken declaration of what I believe to be the duty which the South owes to herself, I necessarily incurred the increased enmity of my enemies; the displeasure, and, I may say, the hostility of those whose private interests are affected by secession, and who are, therefore, for the Union no matter at what sacrifice of principle or consistency; and I have been visited with the most vindictive animosity of certain members of the President's Cabinet, who never held an office of popular trust, and know nothing of the popular heart, because I did not permit their irresponsible and unwarranted conduct, exposing the country to war, and implicating the honor of their chief, to pass unrebuked. Having deceived the President,—informing him of orders issued when it was too late for him to recall them, and knowing that those orders were opposed to the President's policy and in violation of his assurances to others,—these men, elevated by chance, and to the country's misfortune, to the high offices they now hold, are the fit originators and executors of the petty vengeance which, in the abused name of the President, they have wreaked upon me. I regret that the President did not punish their treachery; but my knowledge of his character will never suffer me, to believe otherwise than that his kindness yielded what his judgment condemned, and that if he had been previously consulted as to General Scott's and Mr. Holt's strategical dodges, he would never have permitted the Star of the West to have been chartered and sent to Fort Sumter. It was very unfortunate that the President should have permitted such men to complicate [sic] him by acting in the most vital matters without previous consultation with him, since he must know that the world and posterity will hold him responsible for their proceedings.

I do not allude to the official persecution with which I have been visited for the purpose of complaint or remonstrance. Had the punishment been heavier than the withdrawal of the patronage of the Executive, I could have borne it cheerfully as the most signal tribute to my consistency, and fidelity to the principles I have always advocated. Secession being now a great, a glorious fact, which only pert Post Office clerks can affect to ignore; a Southern Confederacy on the eve of formation, with all the elements of power, prosperity, and greatness in its possession; most of the friends with whom I have associated and acted in political concert having followed the fortunes of their respective States and having withdrawn or being about to withdraw from this city; the approaching advent of an administration not only foreign, but hostile to those with whom I am bound by every tie of sympathy, I have resolved to adopt the counsel of those in whom I place most confidence, and to publish my paper within the limits of the Southern Confederacy as at present constituted, hoping, as I do most fervently, that in a short time, Washington, and the State to which she belongs, may be included within those limits. Within four weeks my arrangements will be complete, and the publication of the *Constitution* will be resumed. I trust that my friends and patrons will pardon the temporary suspension, and continue to me in the more genial atmosphere of the Southern Republic that generous support which they gave me in the capital of the late United States. To those of them who have paid their subscriptions in advance, and are unwilling to hear from me in my new locality, I shall promptly repay the sum in which I am indebted to them on their notifying me of their wishes. The Publishers who have sent me their journals in exchange will, I trust, continue to do so. I shall notify them promptly when my arrangements are complete.

I go hence with well-grounded hope of success; but not without regrets. I am indebted to friends whom I leave behind for many acts of courtesy and kindness. To all such I bid a respectful and cordial farewell.

WILLIAM M. BROWNE

WASHINGTON, January 29, 1861

129. WILL THE PEOPLE OF THE NORTH PERMIT COERCION?

(New York Herald [Breckinridge], February 5, 1861)

It was clearly evolved from the discussion between Senators Seward and Mason, on Thursday last, that the future premier under Mr. Lincoln, has calculated civil war as among the probabilities of the future, and as an inevitable consequence of persistence on the part of the South in its resistance of Northern aggression. The arguments of the tyrant —force, compulsion and power, as a last resort—were employed by him without stint, and he declared his readiness to "stand or perish," with arms in his hands, if upon that condition alone the Union may be preserved. "Everybody," he said, "who shall resist, oppose or stand in the way of the preservation of this Union, will appear as moths upon a summer's eve," when the whirlwind arises which shall sweep them away. Vaunting that the issues between North and South were founded upon a mere abstraction, in behalf of "twenty-four African slaves, one slave for each forty-four thousand square miles of territory;" acknowledging that "slavery has ceased to be a practical question," he could yet declare that "battle was the measure to be resorted to last, for the salvation of the confederacy." Mr. Mason, in reply, deprecated "measuring swords" to settle such a controversy. "I trust," he exclaimed, "that we may avoid the *ultima ratio* of the Senator from New York. I trust the good sense, the wisdom, the civilization, the humanity of the age, will rescue the country from the effect of any such counsels. I trust that in the free States there is a body of good sense, an enlightened basis of patriotism, sufficiently free from the shackles of party obligations, to see the folly of such advice. What! war to restore this Union or preserve it? And that men of sense shall be deluded into war under the pretence of only enforcing the laws of the nation? I appeal to the free States to repudiate the counsels of the Senator from New York, and disown them; and if, in the Providence of God, it is to result that we are to separate in two confederacies, then let the counsels of peace prevail, and not the counsels of the Senator from New York. Let the counsels of peace prevail, as the only counsels which can avert that greatest of all calamities—war between brother and brother—a war between races, which could conquer peace only through oceans of blood and countless millions of treasure."

Nine out of ten of the people of the Northern States are prepared to re-echo the patriotic sentiments of Mr. Mason. The citizens of the free States are not prepared for civil war, nor will they consent to imbrue their hands in the blood of their brethren at the South. The views promulgated by Mr. Seward have excited the deepest feeling of distrust and alarm, and it is the common utterance of men's mouths, that any attempt on the part of the incoming administration to carry out his coercion theory, will meet with no less resistance in the non-slaveholding than in the slaveholding States. It is true that the bitter end so long foreseen is approaching, and that the period has arrived for the country to pay for the treat of elevating anti-slavery republicanism to power; yet the catastrophe has not come upon us so suddenly, or without such premonitory signs, that citizens of the States north of Mason and Dixon's line, can be hurried into a course so suicidal, atrocious and wicked as a portion of our republican leaders would mark out for them. We have drifted to a point where the problem has ceased to be, whether the Union can be saved; and, in answer to the still more important question, shall the South be permitted to go out peaceably? every conservative, right minded man at the North has already given, in his heart, an affirmative response. "Irrepressible conflict" has succeeded in developing the outlines of a fearful shadow over the land; but sober minded, patriotic citizens will never permit it to acquire a bloody substance. In the annals of history, there would be no parallel of a nation, from a similar height of prosperity; surrounded by every external and rejoicing in every internal essential of happiness; having plunged its future destiny, its wealth, fair fame, and the hopes resting upon it, into such an abyss of ruin, desolation and irrecoverable hopelessness of misery, as would be the consequence, if successful, of Mr. Seward's appeal to "battle." Far better that the Union should be dismembered forever, than that fraternal hands should be turned against one another to deluge the land in blood.

The masses of our population, in all of the States, are unquestionably peace loving and conservative. Five-sixths of those who are entitled to vote, in the North, deplore the agitation which is kept alive by the demagogueism [sic] of their representatives. They see the gigantic footsteps with which anarchy has been lately progressing; but they have found it impossible, as yet, to make their voices heard. They have witnessed the culpable inactivity of Congress, and have seen discretion, judgment and patriotism sacrificed before ambition and venality, without having it in their power to remedy the evil. But if in addition to what is past, they see civil discord about to be inaugurated, they will arise as one man and cry out—No! They loathe the thought of internecine strife upon a paltry issue, created by despotism and fanaticism, and they have already issued the fiat that, if the States of the Union must separate they shall do so in amity, and they will hold Mr. Seward and the administration of which he is to form a part responsible, if he exerts his influence to force them into it.

130. "MEN CHANGE—PRINCIPLES NEVER"

(Columbus *Daily Capital City Fact* [Breckinridge], February 9, 1861)

If the principle on which our Government is founded be not incorrect, it should be carried out at all hazards. There is and can be but one RIGHT in the premises—all else is wrong. It is not maintained by others [sic] than reckless men that States in open rebellion should be coerced into measures which are averse to their feelings and their sense of justice. But the fact should not be lost sight of, that the United States Government still exists, notwithstanding a portion of it has rebelled, seceded, or by popular consent dissolved its governmental connection with the parent Confederacy. Such being the case, it is the duty of those having the power to see that all laws enacted for the protection and regulation of the Government be promptly enforced. The conciliatory spirit in which the refractory section has been indulged in her wild and reckless degeneracy and treachery, has been that dictated by reason and sound judgment, and its propriety is acknowledged by all sound-thinking and well-meaning men. It is not to be supposed, however, that calm and righteous conciliation and forbearance are to be taken as inactive submission in all regards to the whims and caprices of the turbulent disorganizers. On this question there is no great diversity of opinion among the intelligent Northern people. When the point is attained at which forbearance ceases to be a virtue, it is found that many who would fain have smothered their indignation for the sake of peaceable adjustment, are constrained to cast off the conciliatory mask and appear in a bold front of determined resolve that the Constitution and the laws shall be maintained.

"Men change," for deceitfulness is a component part of human nature, and, to a limited extent, a virtue. Forbearance is nothing but a commendable exemplification of deceit, but it has its extent, and must end when driven to the wall, for then the first law of nature, self-preservation, assumes its prerogative. Here we find *principle,* which never changes. It speaks, and there is no appeal, except to arms. It is a principle of the United States that they will protect their citizens, their flag, their commerce, and their honor.

In the House of Representatives on Tuesday last, Mr. SICKLES, of New York, made a speech in which he expressed conclusions upon the subject of secession, to which men of all parties in the North are rapidly coming. He said that the secession movement was at first peaceable, and that he was then disposed to let the disaffected States go; but within the last month it had become violent and aggressive, had led to the seizure of United States forts and vessels, to the firing on the United States flag, and to the plunder of the United States Mint and Treasuries, and had consequently lost his sympathies and that of his associates. In concluding his remarks, Mr. SICKLES said: "Armies are raised under the guns of forts belonging to the United States, the jurisdiction of which has been ceded to us by the solemn acts of the seceding States. Measures of open war yielded to Mexican spoliations, and I say, in the presence of this new and last phase of the secession movement, that it can have no friends in the North, but there will soon be no exception to the general denunciation which it must meet with from the loyal and patriotic citizens of this country."

Mr. SICKLES took the position, on the question of coercion, which is taken by the Constitution and the laws of the land, that it is needless and impolitic to invade or injure the seceding States, but that the United States must hold and defend the forts, arsenals, navy yards and territories over which they have jurisdiction, and must enforce the collection of revenues. If the seceding States tamper with the mails, postal communication must be cut off. These measures will be amply sufficient to maintain the authority of the Union unimpaired and its empire unbroken. No suffering or bloodshed need result from them, or will result, except by the act of the States in rebellion. It is no particular respect we entertain for DANIEL E. SICKLES that prompts us in giving prominence to his remarks, but a high regard we have for patriotic principle whencesoever emanating.

We would rejoice at the consummation of any honorable compromise by which the recreant States could be reclaimed to loyalty; but we protest against the Government much further humbling itself through pacific dread of consequences. South Carolina was long since spoiled by the attention paid her; by the forbearance with which she has been treated in all her periodic tantrums and spiteful ways. She is a black sheep, and has spotted the whole cotton flock. Her sister conspirators are no less determined in their treason than she. Let them go, if they will, where they will. But let us protect our flag, our commerce and our honor, though the heavens fall. It is time to dismiss the delusion that the recreant States are essential to our prosperity. Facts and figures teach the contrary—they are a burden upon us, and always have been. It is more through compassion than otherwise that we would retain and protect them—more for ornament than utility that we covet their association. If they are determined to venture the experiment of a separate confederacy, and we believe they are, let us assist them rather than throw stumbling-blocks in the way of their egress and settlement. But while discharging those acts of kindness to the disaffected of the household, we should and must be mindful of our own honor and our own good name in the eyes of the civilized world, which are upon us in steady, jealous gaze.

131. Peaceable Secession

(Greenfield (Mass.) *Gazette and Courier* [Lincoln], February 11, 1861)

It is plain that there is no *constitutional* right for the secession of states from the Union. They have the right recognized in the Declaration of Independence to change their form of government, but that is in fact a revolutionary right. This right,—of revolution—every lover of popular freedom must acknowledge. It is the only protection often which the masses have against the tyranny of men in power. It is this right which justified our rebellion against Great Britain in the Revolutionary War. The Constitution seems designed to curb this right somewhat, lest it should be resorted to on trivial occasions and to secure personal ends, as in Mexico and South America. Under the old confederacy, a state had a right to secede and act as an independent nation. Foreseeing that this right might sometime be abused, and states without just cause withdraw from their connection with the others, and thus cause disturbance, the Constitution was adopted, one object of which was, (see preamble) "to insure domestic tranquil[l]ity,"—that is, subdue fractious states or citizens to obedience by "coercion": "to secure the blessings of liberty to ourselves and our posterity,"—that is, to make the liberty secured by the Constitution perpetual—"for our posterity" —till posterity should cease: and then the Constitution would not be wanted longer.

If the seceding states have thrown themselves on this revolutionary right, for causes to themselves satisfactory, and if it *is* a right, then, to be just and consistent, we ought to let them go, unless their constitutional obligations override their right to secede. They have by adopting the Constitution deposited with the faithful states the right of coercion; and if these states should exercise it, the seceders would really have no cause to complain. Yet, it is not probable that such an event as the secession of half a dozen states was contemplated, and hence it may be said there is no clause in the Constitution adapted to such a condition of things, and at all events it would be proper for the General Government to consider whether it would not be better to regard the right of revolution and allow the discontents to go off, than to exercise the constitutional right of coercion to keep them in an unwilling and sullen subjection. It may seem to us that it would be better to preserve the Union intact; but we are not omniscient. It is conceivable that it *might* be for the general benefit of the people that a separation should take place. It does not look more certain to us that our highest prosperity and happiness would be promoted by the perpetuity of the Union, than it did to our British forefathers that the continued dependence of the old thirteen colonies on the mother country was essential to the highest prosperity of that mother. Yet, what Briton will not tell you now, that his country is vastly better off with us an independent nation than she would have been had we remained colonies to this time? Man cannot see far into the future. The disruption of the Union *may* be a benefit to both sections; and in our opinion, it would be preferable to a civil war by which we should conquer the South and hold her as an enemy in our bosom,—or as a prisoner in his cell. A compulsory connection must be a very unpleasant one, and could hardly be maintained except by a large army, which might lead to an ultimate military dictatorship.

The question arises then, whether it is not best to let them go peaceably: to receive their commissioners and treat with them on terms and conditions. Let them take what public property is in their limits and see if they can do better without than with us. We have no doubt that a treaty of trade and commerce could be made with every one, and in six months southern trade would be just as good and abundant as it ever was. Even the navigation of the Mississippi, which is perhaps the most difficult matter of all to settle satisfactorily, would probably be arranged for the mutual benefit of both confederacies, for it is quite as much for the interest of the slave states on the river to keep the navigation free as it is for the western states. The only other source of real difficulty would be the city of Washington and that would be settled easily if Maryland remains in the Union. If she should wish to secede, it might be necessary to have a conflict: for the possession of Washington is of such importance that the North will not hear one word about giving it up. It has been built chiefly with her money, and its possession would have such an effect upon the army and navy, that nobody could think of giving it up. Now, does it belong to Maryland[?] Its territory once did, but it does not now; nor has it been built by her. It is wholly and exclusively a city of the Union, and the Union must and will keep it. Present indications are that Maryland will resist the arts and seductions of the seceders and remain in the Union, in which case there would be no trouble.

If the above views suggested are correct, the government made a mistake in treating so cavalierly the commissioners sent by South Carolina. But this error might be retrieved, and the course of peace inaugurated if any disposition for such a settlement should be indicated.

Meantime, [the] government should be energetic in defending its property and maintaining its rights everywhere, until they shall be honorably surrendered agreeably to contract. Firmness in defense of rights while they exist, with willingness to adjust difficulties peaceably, will be most likely to produce an amicable and beneficial settlement.

While suggesting the above views, we are by no means disunionists. It seems to us clear that it is best for all parties to go on as we have done. But if part of the people will not; if they so hate the Union that they will fight to get out of it, and we must force them into an unwilling subjugation, holding them as captives rather than as associates; then it may be a question whether all parties would not be benefitted [sic] more by a separation than by such a Union. The matter should be thought of.

132. The Southern Confederacy—Its Recognition or Non-Recognition

(*Detroit Free Press* [Douglas], February 19, 1861)

Why should not the government of the United States recognize the government formed by the States that have seceded? It is, beyond dispute, a government *de facto*, and it has always been a feature of our foreign policy to recognize governments *de facto*. No matter how they may have been formed,—whether by the people displacing a despot, or by a despot overcoming a people; no matter whether established in peace or in war,—we have always been ready to acknowledge their legality, and to institute amicable relations with them. Why should this practice be departed from in the case of the Southern Confederacy? The States composing this Confederacy, it is true, were recently a portion of our own territory; but they now occupy a position of complete independence. Three or four fortresses, garrisoned by mere handsful of men, constitute the sole foothold of our government within their limits. The people of these States, driven to desperation by the incessant warfare of abolitionism upon their most cherished rights, have withdrawn themselves from among us, and resolved henceforth to lead a separate national existence. It would be highly desirable to secure their voluntary return to their old allegiance; but, so long as anti-slaveryism rules the North, such a consummation is impossible. There are but two alternatives left: we must conquer them, or we must recognize their independence.

It is possible—though highly improbable—that we might be able to subjugate the seceded States. We might regain possession of their fortifications, occupy their towns and cities with military forces, and hold their territory by the power of arms. But this could only be accomplished—if accomplished at all—by the expenditure of a vast amount of life and treasure—by the destruction of an immense amount of property —by the annihilation to a great extent of trade and commerce. During the progress of our attempt at conquest, bloodshed, rapine, and conflagration would hold a Saturnalia; brother would strike the sword at the heart of brother, and father would speed the bullet to the brain of son. A scene of horror would be presented which we shrink from contemplating. And, supposing our attempt at conquest to be successful, what then? We should, certainly, have prevented a diminution of the extent of our public domain; but would such a result compensate us for the evils that had been done? And the people of the conquered territory, would they entertain for their conquerors that feeling which all citizens should entertain for their government, and without which feeling any government should at once cease to have existence? Would they not be exasperated to the highest degree, and, if that exasperation were not permitted to be openly manifested, would they not hug it to their souls in secret, and, upon every opportunity, give vent to it by the means of bloody insurrections? Would it be possible, for any great length of time, to keep a people so feeling in subjection? And, besides, what benefit to us would be a people so held? Would they add to our strength governmentally, or to our position morally, or to our ability pecuniarily? Would they not, most decidedly, be to us, in every way, a terrible detriment?

There is but one reply to these interrogatories, and that reply demonstrates most conclusively that an attempt to subjugate the seceded States, even if successful, could produce nothing but evil,—evil unmitigated in character and appalling in extent.

Now for the other alternative. By recognizing the independence of the Southern Confederacy, we should, to a considerable degree, disarm its people of the hostility they naturally feel towards the people of the North, and, in this improved state of feeling, the details of a peaceable separation could easily be arranged. The public property could be distributed, and the public debt apportioned, in an equitable and satisfactory manner; commerce between the two sections could be rendered entirely free of restrictions; in every respect, with the single exception of government, we could be as one people; and, in case of assaults by foreign Powers upon the rights of either, defence should and would be made the common cause of both. Enterprise would develop the resources so lavishly bestowed by nature, industry would reap the rewards of its labors, and tranquillity would pervade the land. And, in the course of time,—when the fanaticism which now sways the North shall have disappeared, and the names of its apostles be held in universal execration,—the South and the North might again unite their political destinies, and, re-united, march forward, hand in hand, in that glorious career which the Almighty, it would seem, has marked out for our race.

Shall we not recognize the government of the seceded States? The administration soon to be inaugurated at Washington will have this interrogatory to answer at the very outset of its existence, and upon its answer will depend the weal or woe of thirty millions of people. A reply in the negative will be pregnant with disaster; and a reply in the affirmative we scarcely dare to anticipate. But let us hope for the best; and, if the worst shall come, let the world be made aware that the responsibility therefor should rest entirely upon the shoulders of the republican party. What the verdict of posterity will be upon the calamities resulting from the carrying out of the atrocious doctrines of that party, it requires no prophet to predict. Far be it from the democracy to have the slightest participation in the disgrace of that verdict.

133. The Possible Alternative

(Springfield (Mass.) *Daily Republican* [Lincoln], February 23, 1861)

The democratic members of Congress from the free states, by their manifest disposition to deny to the general government the means of protecting itself and enforcing the laws, show that they wholly mistake the direction which popular opinion is taking. The anti-coercion issue they attempt to make is false because it is premature. That question has not been raised, and is not likely to be at present. The only point yet made, and in it the people of all parties in the free states are agreed, is that secession is not to be recognized either as a right or as a fact. Consequently the states that have declared themselves out of the Union are to be considered as still in the Union, and their independent governments to be ignored. Therefore must the public mails be carried and distributed in these states as usual, unless obstructed, and the United States troops must continue to protect the exposed borders of these states as usual. It is still more indispensable that the government should persist in collecting the revenue at southern ports, or effectually close the ports where this cannot be done to advantage. Those who pretend to oppose secession and to stand by the government, and yet deny to it the right to do these things, or would withhold from it the essential means, are false to themselves, as well as the country. To refuse to the government the power to maintain itself is to pronounce its destruction. This matter is so clear that all attempts to mislead the people utterly fail, and bring contempt upon those that make them. The people distrust the men who can talk only anti-coercion, when traitors are boldly attempting to subvert and destroy the government.

But notwithstanding that the path of loyalty and patriotism is so plain that no honest man can mistake his duty, it is not to be concealed that there is an ultimate alternative, which events may bring, and another line of policy and duty which the future may force upon us. If it should appear, after suitable time and opportunity for ascertaining public sentiment in the slave states, that a majority of the people of any of those states have a fixed determination to leave the present Union, and that their connection with the Union can only be one of constraint if it is maintained, then the question will present itself in a new aspect. Then the alternative will be to coerce these states and hold them in their present partial connection with the Union, or to allow them to withdraw peaceably and go on with their independent government. Either course involves many and obvious evils to both sections. But if such an exigency comes upon the country the decision of the people will be for peace and acquiescence in disunion, and this not from cowardly fear of the consequences of war, but from a sincere conviction that a Union that can only be maintained by force is not worth the cost. The public mind already inclines strongly to this conclusion. "Let them go, if they will," is the common talk of the people; "we can live without them if they insist upon it."

Suppose there is a peaceful separation by general consent, the terms of which are fixed by a national convention, since Congress has no power under the constitution to provide for so anomalous a state of things; suppose that all the slave states that are really attached to the institution by prejudice or interest go with the cotton confederacy, leaving only Delaware, Kentucky and Missouri, and perhaps a new state formed from western Virginia, in the present Union. In wealth, resources, moral and physical strength, more than two-thirds of the Union will remain. All connection with slavery and all responsibility for it will almost immediately be removed by purging the adhering slave states of the last remains of the institution. The constitution may then be relieved of all recognition and support of slavery, and we shall have a republic in reality as well as in name. It is the sheerest folly to suppose that we cannot go on as strongly and prosperously without the slave states as with them. And, except in the mere matter of extent of territory, we should have lost almost no element of power and national influence, while we should be relieved of a source of weakness and fear growing out of a servile and dangerous population of four millions, which would compensate for many items of loss.

A peaceful separation involves no material loss in commerce and trade. The South can never be commercial to any great extent, and her manufacturing experiments, which have thus far proved costly failures, will be no more likely to succeed under another government. It is a matter of necessity that the southern states should remain agricultural. It is equally [a] matter of necessity that they should trade with the North, whether under the same government or not. The only reason for apprehension on this point is that under the burdens of a new government, and the disorder and confusion that must naturally prevail at the South under the changed state of things, its planters and capitalists, who generally object to secession, will be distrustful, and production and consequently trade will be materially diminished. Suppose then, the southern republic to be peacefully organized and the old Union to go on as it is, minus the seceding states. The free republic of the United States would then be upon a permanent basis, and there would be no place for the secession theory. But the slave confederacy would, still be Secessia, and as Virginia, Maryland and the other northern slave states should be gradually depleted of their black population, and their interests and sympathies become more and more homogeneous with those of the free states, what is to prevent their seceding one by one from the South and coming back again to the Union they have left? It would be the natural and almost inevitable course of things. Separation by war, or after a war, would leave less prospect of such re-union, and this is the reason why the ultra secessionists have all along endeavored to bring on a collision.

Do we go for peaceable secession, then? Not at all. Not for secession of any sort. Not for permitting secession in any shape, as things now stand. We merely speculate as to future circumstances in which events may place us. The Union must be maintained, while we have it; the constitution must be obeyed and the laws enforced. But if it shall be demonstrated hereafter that the Union is dissolved in fact, and that if maintained by force it will be only a Union in form and not in substance, then the unanimous decision will be for peaceable dissolution. Of this we have not the slightest doubt. Equally plain is the duty and necessity of the present hour, and if these are met firmly and hopefully the alternative we have considered may never come.

134. SELF-GOVERNMENT

(New-York Daily Tribune [Lincoln], February 23, 1861)

We have repeatedly said, and we once more insist, that the great principle embodied by Jefferson in the Declaration of American Independence, that governments derive their just power from the consent of the governed, is sound and just; and that, if the Slave States, the Cotton States, or the Gulf States only, choose to form an independent nation, they have a clear moral right to do so. We have never said, nor intimated, that this is a right to be claimed in a freak or a pet, and exercised with the levity of a beau choosing his partner for a dance. We do not believe—we have never maintained—that a State might break out of the Union like a bull from a pasture—that one State, or ten States, might take themselves off in a huff—much less make a feint of going in order to be bribed to stay; but we have said, and still maintain that, provided the Cotton States have fully and definitively made up their minds to go by themselves, there is no need of fighting about it; for they have only to exercise reasonable patience, and they will be let off in peace and good will. Whenever it shall be clear that the great body of the Southern People have become conclusively alienated from the Union and anxious to escape from it, we will do our best to forward their views.

There is no treason in believing that your section can do better out of the Union than in it; it is not culpable to act upon this conviction and seek to diffuse it. But robbing arsenals, seizing forts and armories, stealing the contents of mints and sub-treasuries, and firing on vessels bearing the flag and doing the work of the Union, are very different matters. If these may be done with impunity, then Government is a farce and treason impossible.

We beg the leaders of opinion to keep in view the distinction here indicated. We must not, in behalf either of the Union or of Freedom, trample down the great truth that "governments derive their just power from the consent of the governed." This was the fathers' doctrine, elucidated by their practice. Between their resistance to the Stamp Act and their Declaration of Independence, there intervened twelve years of earnest, patient, emphatic remonstrance and entreaty. They did not draw the sword until their last hope of a peaceful redress of grievances had perished. They did not even declare themselves independent until the cannon of Bunker Hill, the smoking ruins of Charlestown and Falmouth, the dogged determination of their British rulers to crush them under a red-handed despotism, had rendered further forbearance pusillanimous. If the South really wants to go alone, she need not be half so long securing that end by peaceful means as our Revolutionary Fathers were in reaching the point at which they made their choice between resistance unto blood and an abject submission.

As yet, there is no evidence that even South Carolina really wants the Union dissolved, while there is pretty clear evidence that every other State does not. The precipitation wherewith the Cotton States have been forced into a treasonable attitude; the violence, terrorism, and eagerness for bloodshed which have marked the whole course of the Secession movement; the uniform repugnance of the conspirators to submit the question of Union or Disunion to a direct vote of the People; and the emphatic majorities cast against Secession wherever the People have been allowed to pass upon its merits—all these combine to prove the hollowness and emptiness of the pretense of Southern unanimity for Disunion. Let us have a free canvass and a fair poll throughout the South, and Secession will be overwhelmingly defeated. And, until it shall have accorded such a canvass and vote, it is a foul conspiracy, and no more entitled to be respected and deferred to than the pirate captain who has invaded and overawed the timorous savages of some tropical island is to be treated as the rightful Governor of such island.

None are so blind as those who will not see. These may confuse the right of Self-Government asserted by THE TRIBUNE with the right of Secession claimed and exercised by the Gulf States. The majority, however, are more discerning.

135. THE QUESTION OF COERCION

(Trenton *Daily True American* [Douglas], March 11, 1861)

In the course of the animated discussion to which the secession movement has given rise, the question as to the propriety of the employment of the coercive powers of the Government against the seceded States, with a view of exacting from them allegiance to the laws of a Union which they have solemnly abjured, has formed the leading topic, and has been argued with much more ill temper and vehemence than is conducive to a rational solution of the important problem. Followed through all its various phases, and stripped of all side-issues and unimportant points, the argument finally resolves itself into the momentous question, whether the Government at Washington shall acknowledge the independence of the Southern Confederacy, or whether, refusing to do so, it shall embark in the mad and Quixotic attempt of conquering and holding the seceded States in subjection. Strange to say, the latter policy, opposed as it is to the dictates of reason, of principle and of prudence, is not without its clamorous advocates. These are confined with few, if any, exceptions, to the so-called Republican party. Having succeeded by a persistent course of intolerance and invective, pursued in the name of the North, in alienating the affections of the Southern people, and thus destroying the most sacred and only permanent tie which linked the States in one common brotherhood, and finally by a gross and unjust perversion of the Constitution driving them to the terrible alternative of secession in preference to inequality, they now insist that force shall be employed against them, pretending to believe that by such means the Union can be preserved. The ambiguity of Mr. LINCOLN's inaugural renders it impossible to determine to what extent he shares in these sentiments. True, he speaks of executing the laws, &c., but this is only to be done, he says, "as far as practicable"—a reservation which admits of a wide scope of interpretation. Beyond the certainty that the government at Washington will refuse to recognize the Southern Confederacy, we are at a loss as to what the exact policy towards it will be.

Whatever that policy may be, however, it is to be hoped that the administration will not fall into the egregious error of applying the remedies usually applied to mobs. This is not a question whether mob-rule shall be allowed to prevail over law. The people of seven States acting in concert, and under an organized government, cannot be confounded with a turbulent mob swayed by the impulse or passion of the hour. The party or the government which would so confound it, is unable to appreciate the magnitude of the crisis through which we are passing, and would make a most fatal mistake. MACAULAY says:—"It is all very well to talk of confronting sedition boldly, and enforcing the law against those who would disturb the public peace. No doubt a tumult caused by a local and temporary irritation ought to be suppressed with promptitude and vigor. . . . . . But woe to the government which cannot distinguish between a nation and a mob! Woe to the government which thinks that a great, a steady, a long-continued movement of the public mind is to be stopped like a street riot! This error has been twice fatal to the great house of BOURBON." These admonitions of the great statesman and historian apply with obvious force to the case under consideration. And we would add to them the wise and patriotic words of ANDREW JACKSON's farewell address, in which, alluding to a war of sections, he said:—"If such a struggle is once begun, and the citizens of one section of the country arrayed in arms against those of another in doubtful conflict, *let the battle result as it may, there will be an end to the Union,* and with it an end to the hopes of freedom. . . . . . . But the Constitution cannot be maintained, *nor the Union preserved, in opposition to the public feeling, by the mere exertion of the coercive powers* confided to the general government." These are not the opinions of a timid, vacillating mind, but of a man whose public career afforded conclusive evidence that he possessed in an eminent degree the will to confront and the temerity to grapple with any emergency.—Let those who invoke coercion in the name of JACKSON ponder them carefully.

But the advocates of a war policy insist that "the laws must be enforced at all hazards" and the "government vindicated." They desire to test "whether we have a government or not" and urge that if the government fails to assert its power "it will be humiliated in the eyes of the world." These are not new arguments; they are such as prevailed with Lord NORTH and the other minions of GEORGE III in their futile efforts to "crush out" American Independence. Tyrannical and unjust as was the cause in which those efforts were put forth, there was, at least, a certain degree of consistency in their advocacy by the opponents of

Republican institutions and the friends and defenders of a monarchial form of government. But the American government is founded on an idea, and the world does not expect to see it maintained by force against the will of any considerable portion of its citizens. The British government was humiliated much more by its failure to vindicate its authority in the American Colonies, than it would have been had it yielded to their just demands. Our government would incur no humiliation whatever, nor would American institutions suffer any detriment, if, in view of the extraordinary magnitude of the secession movement, and the number of States combined in its support, it were to refrain from an appeal to arms, as inconsistent with the genius of the government, and leave a solution of the difficulty to time. Prudence, principle and sound expediency all conspire in dictating this policy. We are no advocates of a Southern Confederacy *per se.*—We deplore the act of secession as a great political wrong, and as a greater political misfortune. Could we have made our feeble voice heard, we would have persuaded our Southern brothers against withdrawing from the great family of States.— We would have done this because they were our friends,—not our enemies.—But they have left us in anger, and we would not force them back, because in making the attempt we should not only have to deal with them as enemies, but we would blot out the last vestige of friendly feeling and make them our foes forever hereafter. And if we had the will and the power to force them back, we could only hold them as a conquered people at the forfeiture of that equality which forms the essential element of our Republic. A Union maintained by such means would be worse than a mockery. Let not history record that the American government was ever guilty of the stupendous folly of risking the real blessings we enjoy in pursuit of what JACKSON in his parting words pronounced, and what a moment's calm reflection must convince us is a chimera.

136. THE PAST, THE PRESENT, AND THE FUTURE

(Washington (D. C.) *Daily National Intelligencer* [Bell], March 21, 1861)

. . . .

In view of the difficulties which surround an adjustment of the questions raised by the dismemberment of the Union, we have come to the conclusion that no authority less final and comprehensive than a General Convention of the States still remaining loyal to their Federal allegiance can be successfully invoked in the premises. We take it for granted that if the separation of the Seceded States is to be permanent, the questions now outstanding between them and the Federal Government are to be settled in some authoritative manner, and we know of no way in which this can be done so appropriately and effectively as by the arbitration of a National Conference. It would be the duty of such Convention to revise the Constitution of the United States, and this might be done in such a way as to bring about a reconstruction of the Union; or, if this should be found impracticable, provision might be made for contracting the limits of the Union so as to comprise only the States acceding to the project of a Constitution submitted as the fruits of its labors. In the propositions of the late Peace Conference we have already the basis of constitutional amendments, which, in substance if not in form, might be taken as the general rallying cry of conservative men in proceeding to the election of delegates to such Convention from all the States. The work of the Peace Conference, so far from falling to the ground, might thus be made the means of assuring the return of a majority of the delegates committed to its general principles, and thus the proceedings of the National Convention would be restrained within just limits, without diverging into the contrarieties of opinion springing from the predominance of sectional antagonisms over the spirit of concession and compromise.

As no one proposes the subjugation of the Seceded States, it follows that the adjustment of their relations to the Federal Government can be arranged only by their voluntary return to the Union or by the definite recognition of their independence out of it. As soon as it shall be made apparent that the people of the Seceded States desire a permanent separation from their former confederates, it would seem to be the part of wisdom and sound policy for the people of the United States to acquiesce in that desire. Nothing can be gained in the interest of peace or dignity, or good neighborhood or reciprocal trade, by a *persistent* refusal to ascertain and fix disputed relations which must be adjusted in the end, and which can be more satisfactorily adjusted by negotiations before war than by negotiations after war.

And this leads us to remark that the people of the loyal States have an interest in the adjustment of this question at an early day, so soon as it shall be satisfactorily ascertained (if it should be so ascertained) that the secession of the Confederate States is definitive; for, in the interval, a vacancy exists in the representation of the Seceding States in Congress, but as the new apportionment of Federal representation, consequent on the late census, proceeds on the assumption that these States still form a part of the Union, it follows that the people of the adhering

States are *pro tanto* deprived of the additional representation they would receive in case the ratio of representation should be fixed with exclusive reference to the population, which acknowledges fealty to the Constitution and laws of the United States.

There is also another consideration which pleads strongly in favor of adjusting this question according to the accomplished facts of our political situation, as soon as all the indications shall infallibly point to a permanent dissolution of the Union. We allude to the adoption of amendments to the Constitution of the United States. One such, having been proposed by Congress at its late session, is already pending before the several States, and if a National Convention is called others will be submitted. By the terms of the Constitution it is required that such amendments shall be ratified by three-fourths of all the States. The secession of seven States has reduced to twenty-seven the number of States still adhering to the Constitution, and if the former are to be regarded, in spite of their alleged secession, as integral members of the Union, it will be in the power of any two States to defeat the ratification of amendments to the Constitution; for the ratification of twenty-six out of the thirty-four States will be necessary to procure the requisite majority of three-fourths. In the presence of such facts it is obvious that there is a point beyond which it would be absurd to push the exactions of theory in opposition to the dictates of political prudence.

If, then, the developments of the ensuing year shall leave no doubt respecting the determination of the people in the Seceded States to maintain their present attitude towards the United States, we shall advocate the policy of their recognition by our Government, and this, among other questions, might be referred to the arbitrament of a National Convention, which would be called to make arrangements with especial reference to this matter. In the mean time, and equally in behalf of both Governments, we shall not cease to inculcate the duty of patience and the arts of peace.

137. THE FUTURE OF SECESSION

(*New-York Times* [Lincoln], March 21, 1861)

It cannot be denied that there is a growing sentiment throughout the North in favor of *letting the Gulf States go*. The Abolitionists everywhere have been in favor of a dissolution of the Union from the beginning. They have been hoping that the border States would join the secession movement, and that we should then have two Confederacies,—one free and the other slave. In this way they think we should rid ourselves of all responsibility for the existence of Slavery,—deprive it of the protection which it now enjoys under the Federal Constitution, and prepare the way for open warfare upon it. The course of events has led very many persons to concur in the wish for a peaceful separation, who do not at all sympathise with these views of the Abolitionists. The dread of war, the apprehension that collisions may occur between the Federal authorities and the seceding States,—has, perhaps, more to do with this desire than any other motive. Let us separate in peace, —let us dissolve the partnership and let the Slave States take care of themselves, rather than run the risks of a civil war,—is the sentiment and language of thousands who have no sympathy with the ultraists on either side.

We regard this sentiment as unsound and dangerous. It ignores entirely the nature and sanctions of government, and involves perils to the country far greater than those it seeks to avert. The danger of War would, in our opinion, be far greater after separation than it is now. Differences which may arise between the two sections, which now both take the greatest pains to settle, would then be contested with heated hatred, and would end in open conflict. Questions of commerce, of the rights of navigation, of extradition,—cases of insult or maltreatment of citizens,—a thousand sources of hostility would be created by the very fact of separation,—and all the restraints which now prevent war, would be removed. We might remain at peace for a year or two, but War would inevitably follow a dissolution. It would be impossible for two nations, so hostile to each other in the basis and ground-work of their society,—separated under circumstances of mutual distrust and dislike, lying side by side, with only an invisible boundary, touching each other upon a long frontier, and having a thousand sensitive points of dissension and discord, to avoid hostilities for any considerable length of time.

While we remain united, even nominally, there will be on both sides the utmost aversion to a hostile collision. All in both sections who desire the restoration of the Union, will do everything in their power to prevent a conflict. The Federal Government will avoid a resort to force until absolutely compelled to use it in self-defence,—and with every day of reflection the people of the South will become more and more unwilling to precipitate such an issue.

The true policy of the Government is unquestionably that of *masterly inactivity*. The object to be aimed at is, the conversion of the Southern people from their Secessionism. The appeal of the Government must be to the minds of the people,—to their judgment, their political sagacity, their common sense. Force, as a means of restoring the Union, or of permanently preserving it, is out of the question. It has its place in our system of Government as in every other. It may and must be used to repel aggression,—to hold public property and to enforce obedience to the laws, in every case where temporary disobedience would not be a less evil than the attempt to compel assent: and of this the Government itself must be the judge. But no war,—no force can ever restore the Union. *That* work must be done by other means. The people of the South must *come* back,—not be *driven* back: and they will do it whenever they are convinced that their safety will permit, and that their interests require, it. It must be the aim of the Government to *convince them of this fact,*—and to avoid everything which will change the issue and prevent the people from exercising their calm judgment upon the subject. It must not dissolve the Union, nor recognize its dissolution—nor permit any of the bonds of Union which still remain to be severed. Let it hold its forts, its arsenals, and all its public property—not menacingly, but as a matter of right and of duty,—and let it make no attack, and repel none for any other purpose than strict defence and self-preservation.

This, in our judgment, is the policy by which the Union may be preserved, and must be, if it is preserved at all. It should be adopted and carried out vigorously by the Government,—by active efforts as well as by passive avoidance of everything which would interfere with its effective prosecution. The efforts of Union men in every Southern State should be recognized and encouraged. Documents, setting forth the true position of the Administration upon every question involving Southern rights, should be placed in the hands of every Southern man. The patronage, the influence and the power of the Government should be used to build up the Union party in every Southern State, and to enable it to contend vigorously and successfully with the party of Disunion.

This may seem a long process,—but it is the only one which contains the slightest promise of success. It would be easier and more expeditious, doubtless, to sever the Union at once, and thus end the strife. But that would only begin it. The Union is worth an effort for its preservation, both on account of its positive benefits, and because it is the only guarantee for peace, freedom and prosperity. We believe the President will make its restoration the leading aim of his efforts and that he will adopt a policy which will prevent war, satisfy the South of his determination to respect their rights, and eventually bring back every Southern State.

138. The Great Issue, and How to Meet It

(*Philadelphia Inquirer* [Independent], March 21, 1861)

On the morning after the inauguration of President Lincoln, we pointed out an unpretending little paragraph in his Address that "appears to contemplate some action of a National Convention, by which civil war may be averted, through a recognition of the independence of the separated States, by the people acting in their highest sovereign capacity." This paragraph is in these words:—"The Chief Magistrate derives all his authority from the people, and they have conferred none upon him *to fix lines for the separation of the States*. The people themselves can do this if they choose." In this lies the clue to what must eventually be the policy of the Administration towards the seceded States, and the sooner that policy is shaped into action the better.

While our lively and spicy contemporaries of the "Metropolis" are making the most out of their daily discussions about the probable evacuation of Fort Sumter—as if that was the great question of the day—we are of the opinion that the President and his Cabinet regard it as of very small importance, compared with the grave trouble which lies behind it. That trouble is, how to receive, and what answer to make to the Commissioners from the Confederate States. The decision of this comprehensive question includes the settlement of all collateral matters, such as the maintenance of the forts, the collection of the revenue, the enforcement of the laws, and all others. More than this, it embraces the momentous issue of peace or war. The course to be pursued with these Commissioners, with all its train of serious consequences, is, moreover, the immediate issue, and we have not the slightest doubt that the feasibility of some sort of recognition of them or their Government is now engaging the earnest attention of the Executive. If their presence and their business were not to be acknowledged in some fashion, that determination would have been pronounced in some way long before this.

What, then, may be said to the Confederate Commissioners consistent with the dignity and honor of the country and the official declaration of the Executive that he has no power "to fix lines for the separation of the States," and which, at the same time, will not close the door to peace. We have heard this suggested. When the Commissioners present themselves to the Executive, he might say to them:—

"Gentlemen, you come here as the representatives of a Government which I do not know and cannot yet acknowledge. It claims to have been established by a portion of the people of the United States, who wish to separate from the present Union. I have no proof that *the people* have established your Government, or have the desire to separate their States from the United States. On the contrary, I have abundant evidence that large numbers of the people of the States for which you assume to speak are against the whole secession movement. They may be the minority, or they may be the majority; but, in either case, this Government is in duty bound to consult their wishes and protect their rights until the undoubted sentiment of the people is ascertained. I must, therefore, say to you, go back to your principals, and inform them that after they have submitted the work of their Conventions and their Congress to a vote of the people, and it shall have been approved by them, I will so far recognize the *de facto* character of their Government as to call the Congress of the United States together immediately, with a recommendation to that body to take the steps necessary to a proper and peaceful acknowledgment of the independence of the separated States."

How could the Commissioners dispose of such a response as this but by admitting its reason and force? It is pacific, it is just, it is consistent with the dignity and honor of a free Republic, and would disarm the Montgomery Government of all its pretexts looking towards collision. It is an appeal to the judgment of the people of the Seceded States. If they really wish disunion, let them say so in a manner so unmistakable as to release the General Government from its obligations to those who may not favor Secession. If the Disunion sentiment is so unanimous in the Cotton States as the Secessionists declare, there can be no risk to them in submitting the question to the only true test. Should it so result that the people deliberately decide upon separation, who would wish to retain them in the Union against their will? They could only be held by force of arms, and there is no place in our scheme of government for conquered provinces. It rests on the *consent* of the governed.

We have an abiding faith, that if the settlement of this Secession controversy shall be thus cast upon the people of the States that have been carried out of the Union by Conventions, it will be promptly and emphatically settled in favor of the Union by at least four of the seven States of the new Confederacy. If, on the contrary, they shall, at a full and free election, decide otherwise, there is no practicable alternative but to acknowledge their separate independence. In such an event, it would be the duty of the Executive to take such steps as would enable the people of the United States "to fix the line for the separation of the States," as indicated in his Inaugural Address.

139. THE INDEPENDENCE OF THE CONFEDERATE STATES

(Washington (D. C.) *States and Union* [Douglas], March 22, 1861)

We insisted in our issue of yesterday, and we shall continue the same thread to-day, that "a Republican government has no power whatever to protect itself, where the people, for whose benefit it was formed, choose to alter, amend, or even annihilate it." In so far as the *people* are concerned, it is an absolute monarchy, they being sole dictator. Their will is law, their wish the potent voice of majesty. The Constitution is a rope of sand, the government a system of courtesy. Vermont, New York, and Virginia, upon entering the Union, were wise enough to distinctly enunciate this principle in setting forth the independent sovereignty of a State, when they reserved the right to "resume the powers delegated to the federal government" whenever they were found to be used in an oppressive manner—a right which is as pure and as sacred as any political heretage [*sic*] under heaven, and whose forfeiture can never be obtained from the smallest portion of even the Border Slave States.

In the exercise of this right—call it the right of revolution, if you please—the people of the Cotton States have considered themselves capable to judge and act. As independent States they have concluded to resume the powers delegated to the federal government. Having resumed them, they have further found it to their interest to unite in a new government of their own creation, which suits them better than the old Union from which they separated, because a portion of the Northern people had virtually declared war upon them by the election of a President pledged to deadly hostility to a vital institution of theirs. However hasty, impolitic and ill-advised such a precipitate action may have been, it being an accomplished fact, all argument upon its merits ceases to be of moment in the grave issue which presents itself, Shall the government of the United States recognise the independence of the Confederate States?

Up to a very recent period, the single independence of one of these States was denied by nobody. The doctrine of State-rights was as dear to the people of Massachusetts as to the people of South Carolina. So long as Alabama put her portion in the public pot, New York was ready to concede her perfect freedom of thought and deed; but as soon as these States, which have been so wonderfully free, take a notion to employ a little of their much-talked-of liberty, and try independence upon their own hook, State-rights becomes a terrible crime, and secession the vilest treason. Whilst coercion, because on the same principle that secession is admitted to be revolution, an enforcement of the laws must be admitted to be coercion, becomes a duty of the Federal government, no matter at what cost, according to the bloody code prescribed by the radical Republicans.

The laws cannot be enforced. No State can be coerced. The little hamlet of Delaware, should it take it into its head to go out of the Union, could not be whipped back, if its people did not want to come back, by all the other States put together. You might subjugate her, destroy her people and power, but you could never restore her to that love and duty, without whose blessed influence no community is worth a button to any government. State sovereignty, like a woman's chastity, when once invaded, can never be restored to that purity which once made it a priceless jewel to the federal government. Pollute one of those fair stripes with a breath of oppression, and you may as well tear its attendant star from the field of blue forever. Once assail the people of one of those independent sovereignties, thereby uniting all, and never on earth shall you be able to persuade them back to the roof-tree of home, the protecting threshold of the Union. But, just as the father did with his prodigal son, give them their portion, and with it a blessing, and let them go, whither it pleases them, in peace and good will, ready, should their fate still further assimilate with the Biblical illustration, to receive them back, whenever adversity overtakes them, and they come home for shelter and rest, bone of our bone and flesh of our flesh.

140. THE STATE OF THE COUNTRY

(Cincinnati Daily Commercial [Lincoln], March 23, 1861)

Senator DOUGLAS said in his recent speech:

In my opinion, we must choose, and that promptly, between one of three lines of policy:

1. THE RESTORATION AND PRESERVATION OF THE UNION by such amendments to the Constitution as will insure the domestic tranquil[l]ity, safety, and equality of all the States, and thus restore peace, unity, and fraternity, to the whole country.

2. A PEACEFUL DISSOLUTION of the Union by recognizing the independence of such States as refuse to remain in the Union without such constitutional amendments, and the establishment of a liberal system of commercial and social intercourse with them by treaties of commerce and amity.

3. WAR, with a view to the subjugation and military occupation of those States which have seceded or may secede from the Union.

Mr. DOUGLAS does not state the case as we would do, but there is an approximation to the truth, in what he says. Considering the first line of policy which he indicates, and which is the one that he maintains should be adopted, there are no constitutional amendments that would at once restore the whole country to peace, unity and fraternity. If the old Constitution would not unite us in peace and fraternity, a new one would not—for that which would satisfy the Cotton States, could not, in self-respect and honor, be conceded or submitted to by the North. Mr. DOUGLAS's first proposition is simply for the friends of the Government to submit to its enemies.—Whenever, if ever, the Cotton States return to the Union, it must be over the politically dead bodies of the Secessionists. This result is a question of time. We must wait patiently for the operation of the laws that are self-enforcing. War, for the subjugation of the seceders would be unwise and deplorable. There is no province in the world conquered and held by military force, that is not a weakness to its master. Many of the English colonies have drained England of her wealth. The English people are now eaten up with taxation to hold distant possessions in military subjection, and carry on her world-wide system of filibustering which has for centuries been a national passion. The wars, which are visited upon her in her monstrous national debt, were occasioned by the pride of her aristocracy and the intrigues of her politicians, and were not, with an exception or two, in the interest of her people. India, upon which she has lavished her strength, and which is the most magnificent trophy of wars of conquest held by any nation, is an encumbrance to her to-day. Algiers is a costly and unprofitable appendage of France. Venetia is the weak spot of Austria, and the life's blood of the Empire is drained to hold that territory which is absolutely worthless to the Austrians, and fetters her armies in the quadrilateral. The history of the world certainly proves that it is not profitable to govern a people without their consent.

The logical lesson of this fact in this country, is that if there are two nations here who have been living in an unnatural Union, they should, for the benefit of one or both, be separated. We do not entertain the opinion that a forced alliance between antagonistic nationalities has existed in the Union which our fathers made. We believe, whatever the difference in domestic institutions, in temperament, in soil and climate, and in ideas of local government, to be found within the limits of the land, that each interest was secure within the Union, and that all sections were more prosperous and happy within than they can be without the Union.

But, the control[l]ing class of one section have chosen to repudiate the great blessings of the common Government, and have precipitated and almost consummated a revolution. Seven States, by the action of Conventions called and elected in a season of excitement, have adopted Ordinances of Secession, discarding and destroying the Federal authority within their limits, and have established a *de facto* Government.—This Government has no legal existence in the contemplation of the Constitution of the United States. But there it is—a fact extending from the Atlantic to the Rio Grande. Its officers are collecting customs on a thousand miles of sea coast, and on the Mississippi river. Its agents are on the way to Europe, demanding that the Confederate States be recognized among the nations of the earth. A permanent Constitution has just been published, and is submitted to the several Confederates for ratification, which it will certainly receive, in form that it will recognize as authoritative, from at least five States, and probably from the whole seven.—However great the usurpation of the Conventions, and however oppressive the exertion of their power, we cannot expect that the people, though suffering and dissatisfied, will revolt immediately.

What is to be done? The people are recognizing the Government of the Confederates. Our business men trading with the South are constrained to observe its commercial regulations. And eventually the Federal Government must become conscious of its existence, in form as well as in fact. The *statu[s] quo* cannot be preserved. Certainly it will be impossible for the country to remain in the prevailing condition of suspense much longer. There must be an end of the paralysis and stupor, arising from the dark uncertainties of the future.

The confession that the Union is disrupted is bitterly humiliating, but it might as well be made. The fact of disruption and of the incompetency of the Government could not be more forcibly illustrated than in the surrender of Fort Sumter. If the acknowledgment of the military necessity of giving up that post, is not recognition of the existence of the government of the Confederates, we should like to know what would be called a recognition. Whether it would be worth while, after *that* for us to be very sensitive, as to whether Mr. SEWARD has a few conversations with JOHN FORSYTH at the State Department, the common sense of the people may determine.

The news of the surrender of Fort Sumter—the significance of which will seem even greater in Foreign than in home circles—will reach Europe about the time the Southern Commissioners make their appearance at London and Paris; and England and France, and the other great commercial nations, will perhaps, not immediately, but speedily, recognize the Government of the Confederate States. We must consider that European nations—"the despotisms of the old world"—are not particularly sentimental sticklers for the rights of men, and that they care a great deal more about commerce than liberty. Those engaged in the coolie trade are hardly in a position to refuse communications with a slaveholding confederacy. The nations of Europe are not much addicted to making sacrifices for the sake of liberal ideas, and they are not likely to feel any remarkable degree of solicitude for the preservation of the unity of the American Republic, the citizens of which have been so boastful of its superiority to them. When our own Government acquiesces in the revolution so far as to suspend its authority and surrender its property, what can European governments do but acknowledge the power that has asserted and sustained itself?

The experiment of an independent Government, will be tried by the seceded States. There is no doubt remaining on that subject. The Government which has been inaugurated in the Cotton States, is that of the minority of the people over which it is proclaimed—it is, and while it exists will be, a Government where the few rule the many. It is not, however, the province of the General Government, to maintain the rights of the majorities that armed with Constitutional power to govern, abjectly permit themselves to be governed. The people of the South have been basely deceived and terribly wronged by the secessionists. We must trust them in good time to avenge themselves and the nation. Vengeance belongs to them, and they will in due season perform the work that will vindicate their manhood, and make the account even. When the Union men have their feet upon the necks of the disunionists, and returning to the principles of the fathers of the Republic, engage in the good work of rebuilding the Union and making it stronger and more beneficent than ever, the world will learn that the vital idea of the capacity of the people for self-government, did not perish when the fanatics of a few States committed political suicide; and that idea will shine forth over the nations, in hopeful beauty, like the morning star telling of the coming glory of the sun.

The Southern people have to make their election in the issues that have been thrust upon the country in the name of their section. They have slavery, and have now the unqualified responsibility of their own destiny. It is conceded they can go out of the Union if they want to do so. The border slave States are in a position that they cannot long maintain, indeed that cannot long be tolerable. They must speedily joint the secessionists—pass under the yoke set up at Montgomery, and commit themselves to the keeping of the tyran[n]ous plantocracy of the

Cotton States—or they must unequivocally and unconditionally remain in and stand by the Union. They can have all its guarantees in good faith and liberal measure, but in return they must abide by its obligations, maintain its dignity, defend its honor, obey and enforce its laws, and identify themselves with it unreservedly. Otherwise they are not for the Union. Their contingent disunion policy is an endorsement of anarchy, and is insulting, as well as injurious, to the real friends of Union.

It is obvious that the Government is at present, owing to the treachery of the late Administration, and the unworthy caution of the late Congress, almost powerless. Mr. LINCOLN found, in entering upon the duties of his office, a hard complication of strange and humiliating necessities, both civil and military. He found the Union disrupted,—in fact, if not according to constitutional law. Congress had refused to grant additional powers to meet the emergency. The treasury was empty, the navy inefficient, the army insignificant. He had to take the Government and the country as he found them, disorganized and disintegrated. It is much easier to name the things that he can not do, than the things that he can do. But it would be the weakness of cowardice, or a want of understanding, for him or for the country, to flinch from the consideration of all the facts. The "current events and experience" by which he promised to be guided, must, we are convinced, soon lead him to lend the whole influence of his Administration to the accomplishment of the peaceful separation of the disaffected from the adhering States of the Union; and in doing this, it may be necessary not only to mortify exceedingly the national pride, which as a people we have cultivated to an extraordinary degree, but to sacrifice some of the formalities by which the action of the Government is hedged about. The dream of an ocean-bound republic, which has been so grateful to Young America, we yet hope to see realized; but in the meantime there is room for several flourishing nations on this continent; and the sun will shine as brightly and the rivers run as clear—the cotton fields will be as white and the wheat fields as golden—when we acknowledge the Southern Confederacy as before. We would not undervalue the Union. It has ministered to our national pride, as well as to the prosperity of the whole country. But when it is gone, we will still have our fruitful and inviting soil and clime—our seats and channels of commerce—and the unequaled capacity of the people for productive labor.

141. Disunion Triumphant in St. Louis—The Prospect Ahead

(Springfield *Daily Illinois State Journal* [Lincoln], April 3, 1861)

We are grieved to announce that the disunion ticket has achieved a signal triumph at the St. Louis charter election. That city, which heretofore has borne off the palm for its uncompromising devotion to the Union and the principles of the Republican party, now trails the Star Spangled Banner in the dust, and proclaims to the world its sympathy and fellowship with the traitors of the cotton States. Only the opportunity is wanting to make the disloyalty and treasonable schemes of St. Louis plain and manifest to all. We shall not be surprised at the present progress of events, if Missouri, in less than six months, is clean out of the Union, and joined to the cotton Confederacy of Jeff Davis. Matters seem rapidly tending to this conclusion. Not because the State of Missouri has any just complaint to make at the treatment she has received at the hands of the General Government. Not because she has been injured or wronged in the least, by the action of the Federal authorities, or by any of her sister States. In all her gabble about "conditions" to her longer stay in the Union, nothing of this has been suggested. Indeed, that State, so far from having suffered wrongs, is indebted to the Federal Government for all she is and all she possesses. And St. Louis, which now votes in favor of a disunion ticket, owes a full share of her present greatness to the trade she has so freely enjoyed with the people of the free States of Illinois and Iowa. But a mania, a madness has seized upon the Southern mind, and we see whole States, for the mere matter of mistaken pride and a bad spirit which refuses to acquiesce in the will of the majority, busily engaged in destroying the common inheritance of our fathers, and blotting out the hallowed memories which cluster around us as a great nation. We had supposed there was yet leaven enough remaining in the border slave States to preserve the country from the calamity which Jeff. Davis and his fellow-traitors have been threatening. We had indulged in the hope that there was in the Southern heart a stern and unflinching patriotism, which would yet make itself understood and felt all through the disaffected States. But it seems we were mistaken. The election at St. Louis, where we had most reason to place implicit confidence, proves that there is no longer the least love in any of the Southern States for the Union, and that the mad counsels of secession and revolt now have full and uninterrupted sway all through the South. Be it so. If the authority of the Government is to be thus spit upon and outraged, and no move is to be made to vindicate the supremacy of the Constitution and the laws; if even those who call themselves *Union* men at the South are to turn traitors and rise up in arms, should the Administration take a single step towards preserving the integrity of that Union,—as much as we regret the alternative, the sooner we cut loose from the disaffected States, the better it may be for all parties and for the nation. Our self-respect and honor will thus remain uninjured and unsullied; and the disgrace of destroying the best Government upon the earth will fall, where it belongs, alone upon the people of the Southern States. The material or political interests of the North, we are sure, will not be injured by the sad and wholly unjustifiable separation. The South, we are equally certain, will not be better off or happier, however much bad men may now persuade them to believe otherwise.

142. THE NEW CONFEDERACY

(Hartford Daily Courant [Lincoln], April 12, 1861)

Public opinion in the North seems to be gradually settling down in favor of the recognition of the New Confederacy by the Federal Government. The thought of a bloody and protracted civil war, except as a matter of absolute necessity, is abhorrent to all; and its issues may be as perilous to the victors as to the vanquished. To subjugate the Seceded States by force of arms and to compel them to remain in the Union, if it be possible, must involve great expenditure of treasure and life, and can result only in changing the present alienation into deadly hostility and incurable hate. If they remain in the Union, they must do so as peers of the other States, and not as conquered provinces.

But here a new peril meets us. Do we not by the recognition of the Southern Confederacy recognize the principle of secession? No. This principle affirms that any State of the Union has a constitutional right to withdraw from it whenever it pleases. Such a right can never be admitted. It destroys the very foundations of the Government, and would speedily reduce us to a state of political discord and weakness, in which we should admire the wretched Republics of South America, and look with envy upon the stability and good order of Mexico. The recognition of this principle is out of the question. We are not yet ready for such ghastly national suicide. But the problem remains: how shall we admit the independence of the Seceded States without, at the same time, admitting the validity of the act of secession? The difficulty is rather theoretical than practical. Secession, indeed, is to be regarded and treated as revolution, and those engaged in it as subject to all the penalties of treason. Every man who leads in such a movement should know that he puts his life within the power of the law. But here, as always among nations, considerations of public interest come in to modify, or to set aside for a time the execution of an acknowledged right. It may be best under certain circumstances to let a political criminal go free, when under others he would be summarily hung or shot. In every emergency the general welfare must determine how strictly the law shall be enforced.

Seven States have seceded from the Union. The act is revolutionary, and may justly be punished with all the severity which the crime of unprovoked revolution demands. But the movement was not checked as it might easily have been, at the beginning. The cabinet of Mr. Buchanan, if not Mr. Buchanan himself, helped on the treason. The present Administration must deal with the matter as it stands; not simply as a question of constitutional law, but, also as a question of practical politics. The forcible subjugation of these States, under existing circumstances, is not to be thought of. But it is quite another thing for the Federal Government to say to them that their act is revolutionary, and has, and can have, no validity till the other States of the Union have, in a regular and constitutional way, given their assent. Till this has been done, they stand in the attitude of rebels. Their confederacy is treasonable; their constitution, and all laws passed under it, are waste paper. They can have no real political existence till, by a solemn act, the bonds that now bind them to the Union have been legally sundered.

This we understand to be the position of the present administration. The Seceded States are, and must be, a part of this Union until an act of separation has been formally ratified. So soon as they are willing to acknowledge this, all trouble will cease. So soon as they shall recognize that there are two parties to a compact, and that they cannot with lawless violence break their constitutional obligations, there will be peace. But if they hold that a State can, by its own act, set aside all its oaths of allegiance; that it can step out of the Union as easily as a man steps out of his door; that it can any day vote itself into the legal ownership of all the federal property that lies within its limits, and take immediate possession; that it can with perfect impunity fire upon vessels, and bombard forts belonging to the Union, there will be no peace.

We believe that when it can be constitutionally done, the Northern States will be wholly willing to recognize the Southern Confederacy. But there are several preliminary steps to be taken. It must be known that those States wish to secede. Of two or three of them, at least, their willingness to leave the Union is a matter of doubt. There has been there no fair expression of public sentiment. Unscrupulous and violent men have managed to get possession of power, and have forced or beguiled many to follow them: but whether the majority of citizens recognize them as clothed with any legal authority is yet uncertain. They have not dared to permit the people to vote whether they will have the new constitution or prefer the old. Now this matter must be fairly determined. If a majority of the citizens of any of the Seceded States shall declare their desire to remain in the Union, they are not to be intimidated or forced into secession. And the Federal Government is bound to see that each of the Seceded States gives to its citizens this privilege. It is not to recognize the fact that any one of them wishes to leave the Union till its people have so declared.

Another preliminary step is, the assertion and enforcement of all constitutional laws. Till separated from the Union, they must be subject to it. They are entitled to all its privileges, and they must also share its responsibilities. They have postal facilities, they must also pay revenue duties. When once recognized as sovereign, they can arrange their affairs at their pleasure; but till then, all the States have common interests and must have a common policy.

Will the Seceded States acknowledge the righteousness of these so obvious principles, and act upon them? Upon their answer it will depend how long the civil war, which they have begun, shall continue. If they wish peaceably to secede, the way is open before them. Let them only take the proper measures; let them cease to strive to force, with grape shot and sword, the other States of the Union into a recognition of the odious and deadly principle of secession; let them act in that spirit of moderation and wisdom that should rule in those who aspire to be the founders of great States, and all will be well. We are willing that they should go their own way, and solve by experiment the problem whether a Republic built on slavery as its corner stone, can thrive and hold an honorable place among the nations.

143. [Peaceable Separation Rejected by the Confederate States]

(Boston Daily Advertiser [Lincoln], May 10, 1861)

The one point which Mr. Jefferson Davis labors most earnestly to impress upon the world is that he wants peace, and that all he asks is to be let alone. In this he is imitated by all those public men engaged in his scheme who are able to rise at all above the course [sic] and vulgar strain in which men of less sense and craft endeavor to excite the war spirit. History will record, however, as an offset to these repeated asseverations that peace was the constant aim of the Confederate States, that they might have had this had they chosen. History will set down these protestations of reluctance to enter upon hostilities as one of the tricks by which each party in a great struggle uniformly tries to make the right appear on its own side, and setting these public declarations at their true value will find them absolutely controverted by facts which must be patent to every observer of the course of opinion in the Northern States.

When we say that the Confederate States might have had peace, we do not mean merely that they might have been freed from all molestation by abandoning their ambitious designs, nor do we go back to the familiar question as to the attack on Fort Sumter. We mean that beyond these alternatives between peace and war, when the Confederate States made the wrong choice, they might also, if they had chosen, have secured their independence peacefully. We mean that as public opinion stood last winter, the seven original Confederate States, upon satisfactory proof that their people were generally in favor of a permanent separation, might have obtained the consent of the others to such a measure, by bringing the subject up in a peaceable way for amicable settlement by a National Convention, or by such other authority as might have been agreed upon. Even the New York Tribune, a paper which now eagerly advocates the strongest measures for crushing the whole southern movement, then committed itself openly in favor of allowing them to depart quietly and in peace. How far this idea was entertained by republicans generally, we do not pretend to say; but it is certain that of the other parties then before the public, a very large proportion would have adopted it,—enough at any rate to have effectually prevented the government from pursuing any other plan, had the issue been fairly presented by the South, as a question to be settled without blows.

We do not undertake to reconcile the principle assumed in a plan of peaceful separation, either with the nature or with the permanency of our institutions. We simply say that the Confederate States might have secured such a separation had they chosen, by undertaking it amicably instead of making an arrogant demand with arms in their hands and with a claim of inadmissible conditions. And our opinion is confirmed by the course of events down to a very late date, for it is certain that down to the first of April the country was gradually preparing for a practical abandonment of all claim of authority over the seven seceded states, and that even under extreme provocation the pacific policy was not only strong in itself, but if once fairly undertaken promised to find support very extensively and in most unexpected quarters. Indeed we have a fresh illustration of our position, in the declaration made by Mr. Everett at Roxbury night before last, that he was willing, "while this ill-starred movement was confined to the States of the extreme South, and they abstained from further aggression, that they should go in peace." When this declaration is compared with Mr. Everett's entire support of the government in the issue which has been forced, it will show his late supporters at the South that a fearful mistake has been committed by their leaders, if those leaders did in fact wish for peace.

But those leaders could not let the revolution continue in the course described by Mr. Everett,—they could not suffer it to be confined to the seven original States; nor could they abstain from aggression. Had they sought for peace, that course was open to them, and, as we have seen, it unquestionably led towards the successful establishment of their independence. This did not suit their purposes, however. Other States must be dragged into a compliance with their scheme. The seven States which "only desired to be let alone," laid their hands upon seven others, and still demanded to be let alone. They cried out for peace, and yet kept steadily at work moving for the dismemberment of the Union by the withdrawal of States which had testified in the most emphatic manner their disposition to remain under the Constitution. They undertook the reduction of federal fortresses, which, being claimed by both parties as of right, might well enough have been left as they were found, until some final adjustment by competent authority. The seceded States may have wished to be let alone, but they refused to practice the forbearance which they claimed, or to leave other States to determine their own federal relations for themselves.

The course actually pursued then gives the lie to the unblushing assertion of Jefferson Davis and his supporters, that war has been forced upon them. Peace and independence were within their reach, but not only did they at the last open hostilities, but their whole course was such as to force the government finally to defend itself in arms. They had their choice between the quiet separation of seven States, or more extensive movements with the danger of war, and they deliberately chose the latter. It avails nothing now to say that they still ask only for peace. They have chosen to throw the firebrand into other States, and they cannot now complain if in stopping the ravages of the conflagration the government also proceeds to quench the original flame. They took all the risks of an attack upon the very life of the government, from which they affect to desire merely a peaceable release. The world would be lost in wonder, if those risks were not found to involve the very independence which was for a time almost within their grasp.

IX

NEW CONFEDERACIES AND A FREE CITY

144. The Impending Crisis

(Indianapolis *Indiana Daily State Sentinel* [Douglas],
November 20, 1860)

But a few years ago a proposition even looking towards disunion was regarded as treasonable, and a petition presented to Congress asking the consideration of the question met with the prompt and indignant rebuke of the whole country. How great the change. The value of the Union and the voluntary secession of States are now calmly and almost indifferently considered by the Nation generally. What was deemed at one time the greatest of evils which could possibly occur, an event which would probably unfavorably solve the problem of the capacity of the people for self-government, no longer intimidates the public mind. It is painfully evident that the people of the several States have ceased to feel that they are or should be united in a common sympathy and a common destiny. That fraternal feeling which heretofore has been a strong bond of union, is rapidly weakening, if it has not ceased to exist. We are a divided people with diverse interests. In politics the two sections of the country are in direct antagonism; most of the leading Christian sects have divided upon a geographical line; the social relations, North and South, are fast becoming dissevered, and even the ties and interests of commerce, the most selfish of all, are rapidly weakening.

The dissolution of the Union and the reorganization of its parts into separate confederacies, are fruitful themes of speculation in every portion of the country. The cotton States dream of a powerful Southern Republic, with Cuba, Mexico and Central America annexed. Oregon, Washington Territory, California and Utah, with the contiguous Territories, are to become the Republic of the Pacific. And the States North-west of the river Ohio are set off as the Republic of the North-west. Rich in agricultural resources, this portion of the Union will become the granary of the other American States. With no need of a navy, a standing army or restrictions upon trade, she would be blessed with a cheap government, and, therefore, would rapidly increase in wealth, population and power. New York, New Jersey and Pennsylvania, the great Middle States, would probably combine. And the Yankee States proper, which have been fattening off the balance since the formation of the Union, are to be left out in the cold. No matter into how many separate confederacies the other States of the Union may divide, not one would have any desire to unite its destiny with New England.

It seems a dream, a fatal delusion, that even one person can be found who can forget what our Constitution and the Union has cost, the glories it has achieved and the proud destiny which awaits us if we remain an united Nation. We can not yet believe it possible that loyalty to the Union has ceased, that the spirit of nationality has become extinct and that the people of this great Republic no longer glory in the proud title of American citizen. Yet day by day we read that such is the fact. In one portion of the Union arrangements are being made, calmly and deliberately, for a separate confederacy, and in the other the people are awaiting the result with apparent indifference, and express their willingness to consent to a peaceful secession. The Government is thus crumbling to pieces and no hand is raised to save the beautiful edifice which is the wonder and admiration of the world.

Have we become degenerate? Has the spirit of patriotism which animated the Fathers of the Republic become extinct? Is no effort to be made to stay the fell spirit of disunion which pervades the land? Is there no pilot who can safely guide the ship of State through the dangers which surround her, and land her in a secure haven?

145. WHAT IS TO BE OUR DESTINY?

(New Albany (Ind.) *Daily Ledger* [Douglas], November 21, 1860)

Everybody nowadays is talking about Disunion, Secession, a Southern Confederacy, a Northern Confederacy, and similar subjects, and we do not know why we should form an exception. It is true it is a disagreeable subject for newspaper discussion, and one on which the patriot can only speak with regret. But the question is upon us; it will not down at our bidding, and we ought to look it square in the face. Indeed, the people of the North ought to have done that before they elected Lincoln. But they did not; they shirked it; they avoided it; and when it was presented to them, they turned their ears and their eyes away. This will answer the purpose no longer, however. Turn their eyes and ears whichever way they may the Disunion monster is ever present.

Men talk of a Northern and a Southern Confederacy—the one embracing all the "free" and the other all the "slave" States. There may be Disunion, but if that unhappy day should ever come, it would not see the country divided into two but a half dozen Confederacies. We do not believe all the slave States would agree upon terms of union satisfactory to all: most certainly all the free States would not join in a common Confederacy. In the event of a breaking up of the Union, it is not at all probable that the Pacific States would link their destinies to either of the fragments. Beyond all question the States of California and Oregon, with the Territories of New Mexico, Utah, and Washington, with the Arizona region, would soon set up for themselves, believing that they possessed within themselves all the elements of national greatness, with room for expansion both to the North and the South.

Coming to our own section of the country, what would be our destiny? If, through the madness of fanaticism, the present Union, which has brought to us and to all so many blessings, is dismembered, is it probable that we of Indiana would unite with those who have brought about the great disaster? We certainly could not unite with South Carolina, Georgia, and Alabama; *neither could we unite with the fanatical, abolitionized, canting, hypocritical New England States,* the authors of nearly all the evils which have befallen the country since the year 1837, when her people began to pour their abolition petitions in upon Congress, in order that they might be read, printed, referred, reported upon, discussed, and the subject thus be kept constantly before the country—fanning the flames of fanaticism in one section and producing uneasiness and irritation in the other. We do not believe the people of the West would consent for a moment to be tied on to New England, to be taxed to death with protective tariffs for the benefit of Eastern manufacturers, who would thus hope to find here that market for their goods which they had lost in the South. We think we may safely say that if, through the madness of the abolition fanatics of New England, the present Union is broken up, the people of the Southern half of Indiana (and we hope the Northern half also) would protest most vigorously and most earnestly before they would consent to the aggrandizement of the authors of our ills, by entering into a union with, and being compelled to pay tribute to, them.

There is a great and fertile and prosperous region of country, embracing Kentucky, Missouri, and a large portion of Ohio, Indiana, and Illinois, whose people are not to any considerable extent affected by the ultraism of either of the extremes, who would, in the event of the convulsion of the Republic, be drawn together by the ties of commerce, neighborhood, and general coincidence of views and interests. Whose friendship is worth most to the people of Southern Ohio, Indiana, and

Illinois—that of our neighbors, between whom and us there is a community of interest and of feeling, or that of far-off, puritanical New England, whose citizens regard the West and the South as a fair field for the exercise of their Yankee trickery and cunning?

This is a painful and a most disagreeable subject, and one from which we would gladly turn. But we cannot. It is forced upon us, and it is time that we should look around and ascertain where we stand or where we are to fall. If the Union remains as it is—and heaven grant that it may!—it will only be, we are convinced, after some definite understanding is arrived at as to the relative rights and duties of the two sections. If only calm and considerate and conservative men were to be consulted on either side, we think there would be little difficulty in arranging the preliminaries of such an understanding. But if the matter is given over to the keeping of such men as Seward and Hale and Giddings and Julian on the one side, and Yancey and Rhett and Davis and Toombs on the other, for what can we hope? Is there any reasonable ground for hope? Alas! we fear not.

146. DIVISION IS DISSOLUTION

(Albany *Atlas and Argus* [Douglas], November 22, 1860)

A portion of the Abolition press, recognising the seriousness, if not the gravity of the Southern movement for secession, proposes that the discontented States shall go in peace, and speculates upon the comparative resources of a Northern and [a] Southern Confederacy. They draw the assumed line of division to suit their fancies, and assume that the future of the North is to be the combination of that unrivalled prosperity, which, for a century, has blessed it with wealth and advancement beyond all other portions of the world. They forget first, how much the prosperity of the North has been gathered in Southern markets, and how necessary to it has been the unrestrained freedom of trade between the States of the Confederacy.

But they are blind to the fact that the secession of any considerable number of Southern States, is not merely a Division, but the Dissolution of the Confederacy. A single geographical line will not be run East and West, so as to form those two Confederacies of mutual hate, which philanthropists dream of as the successors of our present system. So sure as a Confederacy of the Cotton States is formed and maintained, the border States of the South will be drawn into it. The Pacific States will secede. California, Washington and Oregon will have every motive of interest to establish free trade with the world, and will feel no obligation of loyalty to a broken and dishonored Confederacy sufficient to make them tributaries to those Northern Atlantic States, which, under our present system, enjoy the monopoly of their markets. The gold of California will open all the ports of the world and is even a greater Potentate than Cotton, which is proclaimed King. Geographical position, independence of resources, character of population, interest and feeling will all combine to withdraw the Pacific States from an alliance with either a Northern or a Southern Confederacy. They will set up for themselves—throw open their markets to a competition that will virtually exclude our commerce and manufactures, and commence a career which will draw to them the emigration [sic] and capital that now enrich us.

The Northern Confederacy will then embrace only the States on this side of the great Plains; but its form and policy will have to undergo essential modifications, before it can even commence its new career. New York and the producing States of the West will not consent to live under a tariff devised for the benefit of New England and Pennsylvania. Such a tariff, spread over a wide Confederacy, and embracing millions of consumers, may be little felt in the midst of prosperity such as ours, and it is, besides, compensated by other advantages; but with the South and the West, not only cut off, but erected into rival sovereignties under the banner of free trade, it would be fatally oppressive. You might as well place the Neversink Highland across its harbor, as permit the barrier of a tariff like the present, under such circumstances, to block up the port of New York. That restrictive system, under which commerce would be paralysed, would not last a year, and no Northern Confederacy, though it were unanimous, could enforce it against the people of New York city, even if they stood alone. But they would not stand alone. The Western States would unite in demanding freedom of trade; and the day this voice prevailed would be that of the bankruptcy and industrial desolation of New England and Pennsylvania.

The iron and the coal of the latter State would find no market; the mills and manufactories of New England would stop, and the cold and hardened egotism of her people would have to find support from the granite and ice which alone are her natural exports.

We invite no such results. We have labored to avert them. But if the catastrophe of a Separation of the Union is to take place, the Dissolution that will follow will be a matter of self-preservation for our own State. We owe no allegiance to a Northern Confederacy—can take no pride in one, have no interest in one. We cannot hang crucified between New England and Pennsylvania. Our future will be apart from them, in rivalry to them. Our alliances will be with the producing States of the West. If we can force a system of free trade between the seperated [*sic*] Confederacies and States, as well as with Europe, we will maintain, in part at least, the supremacy of New York. So far as we fail in this, will we recede in position and prospects.

Those who are calculating the value of a Northern Confederacy, must take these considerations and consequences into the calculation. They must consider also whether New York will consent to an equality of representation in the Senate (if there is to be a Senate,) with the petty New England States. Will these States which talk so much about freedom and equality, ask for such a disproportionate representation? If they do, we shall tell them that the motive for once granting it, when it was necessary to secure the blessings of Union, has ceased, now that their egotism and intolerance have brought about the curse of disunion.

In bringing about this competition of rival Confederacies, each finding its final interest and necessity in breaking the chains of Commercial restriction, the party of Freedom will unconsciously have achieved something for Freedom. They will have struck off the chains from trade, and united us in a brotherhood of mutual dependency with each other and with the world. They will not have extinguished Southern Slavery in the blood of insurrection; but they will have emancipated Northern labor and business in the ruin and destruction of Northern capital and manufactures. True, the destruction of all political interest, the repudiation of state debts, the depreciation of paper currency, the extinction of capital will mark the change and constitute the penalty of our folly and the price of such liberty as we may rescue out of our ruin. But others have paid the same penalty before us, and we have shut our eyes blindly to the instruction which they have left in history. We must open them to the experiences of stern reality.

The picture is a gloomy one; but we give it in these colors, that the wicked and besotted speculators, who propose to build a Northern Confederacy upon the ruins of our present government, may realize its true character. There can be no such thing as a Northern and a Southern Confederacy. The moment the Union is broken, Allegiance ceases to be a duty; patriotism centres in the obligation of the community to the State in which it lives. The Constitution which was framed for the Carolinas and Virginia as well as New York and Massachusetts, and adjusted to their conflicting interests, becomes so much waste paper. Not one of the fragments of the Confederation would adopt a system of Union, which in the midst of peace, prosperity and civilization was turned into an instrument of disunion.

We hope we may be spared the calamities which will follow this final catastrophe, by the postponement of the day of evil, or by escape through some avenue which is not yet revealed to us. We pray for such an escape, not because merely of the material evils that would befal our people, but on account of the shame and humiliation that would rest upon our name; on account of the disillusion of patriotism, the despair of the expectant people of other lands, the triumph of the enemies of liberty and the Apostle of Absolutism, pointing to our failure and fall.

We repeat, in answer to those whose delusive speculations about a Northern Confederacy have forced us to confront them with these painful truths, that the separation of the States is the dissolution of the Confederacy, and the obliteration of the Constitution. It is the end of this government; and the beginning of an Era, the character of which no human eye can discern, but of which, we know with certainty, that a long period of Chaos must precede the Construction of Order.

147. A Pacific Confederacy

(Milwaukee *Daily People's Press* [Douglas], November 30, 1860)

Since Senator LATHAM arrived from California, it is announced that an address will be put forth by the members of Congress from the Pacific slope recommending to their constituents the formation of an independent Confederacy by the Pacific States and Territories.—The isolated position of that section of the Union; its completeness in all national material and resources, make the project apparently feasible, but there seems to be one little objection. That territory was purchased by the common blood and treasure of the whole people of the United States; if they choose to relinquish it it is all right, but if they do not, we do not know of any way by which the present inhabitants can throw off their allegiance to the general government and acquire an independent position among the nations of the earth, but by treaty, conquest or purchase.—The same objection lies to the secession of all those States comprised in the Territory acquired by the several purchases from Spain, Mexico, France and Texas, and those acquired by cession from the original thirteen States. If Louisiana, Texas, Arkansas, Mississippi, Florida, Tennessee, Kentucky and Missouri may secede from the Union at will, what becomes of the rights acquired by the whole United States in the purchase of these several territories for which a valid and substantial consideration was paid out of the general treasury? The South has constantly clamored for their equal rights in the common territory of the United States—upon what principle of equal rights then do they claim the peaceable secession of those States from the Union? It was proposed a short time since by Senator SLIDELL, to appropriate $30,000,000 for the purchase of Cuba—did the Senator then hold to the doctrine which he now advocates of the right of Cuba to declare her independence of the United States the day after this money had been paid? The thing is lawless and piratical. These advocates of the right of secession deny the right of the people of the several organized territories of the United States to govern themselves in the Union and within the purview of the Constitution of the United States, because territories purchased by the common blood and treasure of the whole people belong of right to all the States in common; but insist at the same time upon the right of repudiating all these obligations by secession. Who can understand such doctrine?

148. A GLANCE AT THE FUTURE

(Portland (Maine) *Eastern Argus* [Douglas], December 12, 1860)

Many speak of the withdrawal of four or five States from the Union as comparatively a trifling matter. "If they want to go, let them go; we can do well enough without them." Such persons do not appear at all to realize the tremendous import of the proceeding of which they thus flippantly speak. Such a separation of five or more cotton States, will be but the first step in the certain downfall of the Republic. It will be a blow, the inevitable effect of which will be destruction to the national government.

Slavery will form so strong a bond of union, that all the slave States, save perhaps Delaware and Missouri, will soon be drawn into one confederacy, bound together in self-defense for the protection of their peculiar institution. Instead of a tariff upon imports, they will have a tariff upon exports,—will buy their manufactures in the cheapest market, and compel those who purchase cotton and other staples of which they would have nearly a monopoly, to pay duties on them for the support of their government.

The Northwest will have interests of its own. It is the granery [sic] of the continent. Those States will combine, insist upon free trade by the Mississippi and the St. Lawrence; will refuse to be taxed for the support of a navy; for forts and lighthouses on the Atlantic coast—will not agree to navigation laws, but will give their freights to those who carry cheapest; will buy their goods of those who can sell at lowest prices; will refuse to give bounties to fishermen—in a word, will object in all respects to become the servants or dependents of those whom they feed. New England, New York and Pennsylvania[,] which have derived more direct benefit from the Union than any other section, will suffer most in the breaking up and rearrangement of elements. Their interests would be too antagonistic for union and harmony in one confederacy. The article which we copy from the Albany (N. Y.) Atlas & Argus in another column, shows what the interests of New York would demand, and indicates the course she would probably pursue. States can well afford to make sacrifices to belong to a great confederacy like the United States. The importance it gives them among nations, the security against invasion by foreign armies, the protection of its flag to commerce, the advantages of internal free trade over so great a territory abounding in almost every variety of production, the scope it affords to manly ambition and far-reaching enterprise—all these and many other considerations make membership in the great Republic of incalculable advantage. —The burdens and sacrifices imposed for its support are relatively but trifling, and are in inverse ratio to its greatness. But divide up and each curtailment reduces advantages, while it increases burdens until it will often occur that a State can stand alone better than in association with a few neighbors.

Such would be the condition of Maine with reference to the rest of New England. She would be far better alone than as a member of a New England confederacy. She is not largely engaged in the manufacture of cotton, but what she has would probably be destroyed by dissolution of the Union and the withdrawal of that protection which the present tariff affords. Her coasting trade would, of course, be damaged to the extent of the protection now afforded by navigations [sic] laws—perhaps destroyed. Her ships could not compete for foreign freights with those of powerful nations, for lack of a flag to protect them. Without a navy and unable to support one, Maine merchants would see their ships a prey to every free booter. But in the construction of vessels she could, with iron and cordage free of duty, still compete with the world, and might find a profitable business in the sale of first class ships to other nations. Her position is favorable for trade with the British Provinces; and, with her ports free, no small part of the trade of the great West would come to them. With unrestricted free trade, many of the Montreal merchants would establish themselves here for the more favorable transaction of their business. It would be by such a course that Maine could in small part offset the irreparable losses of disunion. To be tied to a New England confederacy, with tariff and other legislation to suit the interests of the other States would be ruin. She would then be but the poor tail to a very small kite. Alone, however, protected by the rigor of her climate, the sterility of her soil and the bravery of her people from being the prey of free booters, she might like Switzerland in modern Europe or like Attica in ancient Greece, maintain a noble independence and secure some degree of prosperity.

We have thus glanced at the future, not from any relish for such painful speculations, but because the probabilities are that we shall ere long have to meet these contingencies as stubborn facts. If the North could have been made to see whither she was drifting prior to the late election, she would have accepted the principles and candidates of the regular Democracy, and all would now have been peace and prosperity. If Pennsylvania, Ohio and Indiana, had declared emphatically for Mr. Douglas in October, the majority of both Northern and Southern States would, in November, have ratified the doctrines of which he was the representative, and a settlement of all serious difficulties would have been secured. But so it was *not*, and what is past is beyond recall. Whether there can be any adjustment now is doubtful. It is certain that none better than that which the Democracy presented can now be secured. And if no adjustment, what then? Disunion, with all its humiliation, with all its disastrous consequences! No one can see the path to peace. The future is a labyrinth to the wisest, through which he cannot see his way. Let us trust in God that a way *may* be found. It does seem impossible that a nation, the equal of any on earth, in all the elements of material greatness, the superior of all others in the education and intelligence of the masses of its people—it does seem impossible that such a nation can be guilty of the stupendous folly, madness and crime of political suicide! We cannot believe it, even while we cannot see the least prospect of its being avoided. What would it be for? What good cause could, by possibility, be advantaged? Can you tell us, ye who have led on this "irrepressible conflict," and who seem now ready to plunge us into the very jaws of destruction? If you cannot,—if you cannot give good reason for the terrible sacrifice, why not even now at the eleventh hour, awake from the blindness of infatuation, recall the dogs of war and proclaim peace and good will[?] Did not our fathers throw everything, even to life itself, upon the alter [sic] of their country? And are their sons unwilling to sacrifice mere petty prejudices, and petulant tempers to save the grandest heritage of any people so dearly purchased for us (not themselves) by the fathers, and which hitherto we have enjoyed? Can there be such ingrates—degenerate sons of patriot sires? God forbid! Our country forbid! Humanity forbid it!

149. SECESSION IN A NEW SPOT

(Bucyrus (Ohio) *Weekly Journal* [Lincoln], December 13, 1860) [1]

Secession is the order of the day, and as soon as South Carolina goes out of the Union, ripping up the Confederacy, there will be an admirable opportunity to redress grievances. Crawford County will at once secede from Ohio, establish a Government of her own, and proudly take her place among the nations of the earth. We have too long submitted to the imperious dictates of a tyran[n]ical government, and gladly will our chivalrous high-minded, high-toned, hi-falutin citizens seize this glorious opportunity of rending the chains from their limbs, hurling them in the face of their foes, and renouncing all allegiance to a government they hate, and a people they despise. Our whole history has been one of aggression on the part of the State.

It refused to locate the Capitol at Bucyrus, to the great detriment of our real estate owners.

It refused to gravel the streets of Bucyrus, or even re-lay the plank road.

It refused to locate the Penitentiary at Bucyrus, notwithstanding we do as much towards filling it as any other county.

It refused to locate the State Fair at Bucyrus, thus blighting the hopes of our free, independent and patriotic pea-nut venders.

It located the Ohio Canal one hundred miles east of Bucyrus.

We have never had a Governor, notwithstanding we have any number of men as much superior to the hoary old dotard * who now fills that post, as the bright, refulgent sun is to a tallow candle.

ditto ditto ditto, as to U. S. Senator.

It has enticed our citizens away, by making them Supreme Judges as soon as they get out of the county.†

It has compelled us to pay, year after year, our share of the state taxes.

It put us in the same Congressional district with Ottowa [*sic*] County.

No citizen of the county has ever been appointed to any place where theft is possible, thus wilfully keeping capital out of the county.

It selected Seneca County men for two terms, for State Treasurer, thus making sure of having the Treasury cleaned out.

It has stigmatised our county as the "mud county."

It refused to pay our railroad subscription, and has never offered to slackwater the Sandusky river.

[1] The *Journal* was at this time edited by David R. Locke, better known as Petroleum V. Nasby. Later, when a national figure, Locke spoke of this editorial as one of his first efforts in newspaper humor.

These are but a very few of the grievances we have submitted to. We could stretch out the list indefinitely, but these are sufficient. We will not longer submit. The storm is rising. Companies of two-forty men are being organized in every township. Our representatives have agreed to resign—next March. The independent flag—musk-rat rampant, weasel couchant, on a field d'egg shell—floats from poles on every corner. Cut off from the state, direct trade with Indiana follows—released from indebtedness to Cincinnati and Cleveland, our merchants will again lift their heads. We are in earnest. Armed with justice and shawl-pins, we bid the hireling tools of a despotic government, defiance.

P. S.—The feeling is intense, extending even to the children. A boy just passed our office, displaying the secession flag. It waved from behind. Disdaining concealment the noble, lion-hearted boy wore a roundabout. We are firm.

N. B.—We are still firm.

N. B. 2d.—We are calm, firm, unyielding.

LATER.—A farmer from the western part of the county came in to-day to get his gun fixed. Tremble, ye Columbusers. We are firm.

* Dennison is neither old nor grey, but will be when he hears from Crawford.
† Judge Scott.

150. NEW YORK AS A NATION

(Troy Daily Arena [Independent], December 18, 1860)

If secession be revolution, and if revolution throws each State back upon independent sovereignty, it may not be too early to glance prospectively at New York as a Nation. If after all the efforts of conservative men, both North and South, to prevent it, the Union must be dissolved, and each State set up on its own account as a separate nation, we shall endeavor to reconcile ourselves to the new state of things, with a great deal of christian fortitude and philosophy. For the great State and city of New York, we have not the least fear. In such a state of affairs, we should unavoidably labor under some temporary difficulties and embarrassments; but our industry, energy, capital and other resources, would soon lift us out of all trouble and place us on our feet, as one of the most independent, enterprising and thriving nationalities of the world. We would be larger in extent of territory than England, and number one third more inhabitants than all the New England States together. Our four million of population is more than several European countries have possessed when they had dominion over the whole ocean, and by their commercial enterprise made their power felt and their name respected on every portion of the globe. The city of New York has the lead of all its competitors on this continent, in population and all that constitutes metropolitan greatness and prosperity, which, added to its vast natural advantages, will always constitute it the great central city of North America. No matter what political revolutions and changes may take place, that will be the great centre of commerce, manufactures and finance. She, also, will be the home of art and science, fashion, literature and refinement. Her commercial relations will embrace all nations —her vessels will plow the waves of every sea, and introduce into every port where there is a market for them, the products and manufactures of our whole North American continent. New York, with or without the Union, is bound to be prosperous, opulent and great.

151. CENTRAL CONFEDERACY

(Troy Daily Times [Lincoln], December 19, 1860)

Among the numerous plans proposed for changing the character of our institutions by a dissolution of the Union, is one for the organization of a central confederacy, to be composed of the border slave, and the border free States, united upon the basis of mutual benefit. If the present Government should ever be dissolved, such an one would eventually grow out of the necessities of the communities named. The danger of servile insurrection and emancipation by force, would be one of the greatest hazards of a Southern Republic. It would be but a step across the border from Illinois, Indiana, Ohio or Pennsylvania, for abolition emissaries who might provoke conspiracies or invite escapes, and returning back into the State whence they emanated, they would be under a foreign government, and beyond reach of punishment. When Slavery dissolves the Union, free States will be unlikely to make laws for the protection of slave property. On the other hand commercial considerations would disincline the border free States to severance from their Southern neighbors.—Pennsylvania is particularly and vitally interested in the Virginia trade;—Ohio, and Indiana, by their great water and railroad routes, have built up important traffic with Kentucky and Tennessee. By means of the Missouri and Mississippi the vast seaboard interests of the Gulf are to be reached, and these would all be involved. The Southern Republic would undoubtedly be free trade. The interests of the Northwest are in the same direction. They would naturally, therefore, prefer affiliation with the States from which they would obtain their goods at least duty.—These and various other considerations of interest, might bring about an organization on the plan proposed. The strong points of repulsion presented by the differences on the question of Slavery, would become matters of arbitration, diminishing in strength as other features of interest attracted attention. As between the border States, free and slave, these questions are less controlling than in reference to those more remote. If the day ever comes when our Union is dissolved, and Governments of rival and conflicting characters and interests established in its stead, we may look forward to an organization of numerous petty confederacies, based upon mercenary considerations, and coalesced by sordid impulses—re-producing in their careers the history of the Mexican and South American Republics. Therefore it is the duty of every patriot, by all considerations of love to his country, to stand firmly and irrevocably opposed to such a radical change of its institutions.

152. The Separation of New York City from the State

(New York Daily News [Breckinridge], December 22, 1860)

If a division of the Union shall unhappily take place, and a Northern and [a] Southern Confederacy be formed, the independence of New York City will be an object exceedingly desirable, not only to the interests of its citizens, but also to those of the State and the whole of the North. New York must preserve, as far as possible, its condition as the center of a free and neutral commerce. It will thus be a bond of peace and continued commercial relations between the two separated Confederacies. Is it not better for the North, that New York should be the market for the South than Liverpool or Havre, and that the trade of the Gulf States should bind them in American rather than European alliances? This must be conceded, and our views on this subject, we submit, are approved by the large majority of the substantial and wealthy men of the city, as well as by the equally patriotic masses of her population.

The strictures of The Herald and The Journal of Commerce with reference to the spirit and objects of the views expressed in this paper on the subject of a separation from the State are not well founded. We did, indeed, characterize the past action of the party that holds the majority in the State as unjust, tyrannical and oppressive. We denounce them as ravening wolves and robbers, and no language can describe the infamy and injustice that we have suffered. We did, however, counsel armed resistance or violence in order to effect the revolution in our political relations to the State. There is a mode pointed out in the Constitution to effect the formation or erection of new States out of the territory of a State; and in case of the establishment of two or more confederacies it will render the division of New York politically expedient, if not necessary, to secure a proper balance in the Confederacy to which she may belong. As for coercion and physical force, we turn from them with horror and disgust. We shall never cease using all our efforts to prevent such a hateful result, with reference to the seceding States of the South, if that policy is adopted, and we are equally opposed to render New York the scene of excesses similar to those which have taken place in the capital and cities of unhappy Mexico. But the unanimous demand of the people of this city, high and low, rich and poor, which will inevitably follow the continuance of the outrages of the last five years could not be disregarded by the rest of the State. A moral and political revolution will ensue that must eventuate in the creation of an independent State, and the first anti-fanatical Legislature will consent to the emancipation of the city and its vicinity from further control. All then required will be the sanction of Congress, and thus the proper authorities will legally and orderly ratify the popular movement.

The position of Hamburg and the free cities of Germany has not been mean, nor has their influence been other than beneficial to German nationality and prosperity. If these seats of commercial freedom were tolerated in the midst of feudalism for the blessings they diffused, and the rights of the burghers respected by robber barons and ambitious princes, New York will surely be allowed to occupy a similar relation here to the agricultural and manufacturing populations of the interior —the channel of their trade with the rest of the world. Nature has made New York what she is, and no jealous legislation could force the current of trade in any other direction, any more than it could turn the tide of the noble Hudson backward, and dry up the Bay that forms our harbor.

The movement which may be made, and will be agitated in the event either of continued aggression on New York City or the dissolution of the existing political fabric, should be fairly discussed on its merits, and not be linked with personal appeals against its assumed author. The taunts of The Journal are unjust. It is not agrarianism to feed the famine struck inhabitants of a great city by extending assistance through the agency of the public authorities. The plenteous harvest just garnered may be sealed from thousands in our city if business is suspended and public confidence destroyed. If it be agrarianism to seek means of affording employment and providing bread for these sufferers, then we are not ashamed of the opprobrious title.

We do not fear the patriotism and intelligence of the honest and hard working masses of New York; they do not form the material for mobs or a revolution of force and terrorism. Witness the order with which our population enjoys the recreations in the Central Park, and how the poor man and his family participate in those innocent pleasures with his richer fellow-citizen. Rapacious politicians may carry on schemes of plunder and be indifferent to the rights and interests of our property owners, but the peace and prosperity of New York will find no truer defenders than her mechanics and laborers. They will not destroy the beauty of Washington Heights or diminish the security of the capital which forms the basis of the trade by which they live.

We earnestly protest against the evil effects of the partial and unjust legislation of the last few years. It has been robbery under color of law. It is only paralleled by the aggressions which are drifting the South into secession, and we cannot help it if like causes produce like effects. The desire of separation is general, and if realized it must prove most advantageous to our city. It is neither unreasonable nor impracticable, and its attainment by peaceful and legal means is worthy of the attention of every New Yorker.

153. AFTER SECESSION

(Boston Daily Journal [Lincoln], December 28, 1860)

In anomalous times like the present, we may be justified in considering some of the results of the great contingency on which the crisis is made to turn. Mr. Webster declared he would not look beyond the veil which separated the country from disunion. But now there are prominent men—there are whole States, we are told—that say this veil must be torn away within a month, or a few months, at most. We may well, therefore, be casting our thoughts beyond, with the understanding that all such considerations are to be taken as speculative or practical, just according to the purpose and work of those who are proclaiming their determination to break up this Union.

Let us, then, for the consideration of a particular point, suppose that not only South Carolina, but the five leading cotton States, including South Carolina, Georgia, Florida, Alabama and Mississippi, should secede from the Union; in what condition would it leave the bonds uniting the rest of the States? Would the latter stand firm, or would the different sections become disintegrated—the border slave States flying off, then the Pacific States setting up for themselves, then the Western States seceding from the Middle and New England States, or even the two latter sections withdrawing from each other?

To begin with dividing the question, we think it may be safely assumed that unless the border slave States should go off with the Gulf

States at first, they would not go at all. They would see their Southern neighbors advantaged in no particular, while burdened with an immense expense of keeping up a separate government, which would eat out their substance, and cripple them in the race of competition. The cotton of North Carolina, Tennessee, Louisiana, Arkansas and Texas, would yield a great per centage of profit over the tax-laden cotton of the new confederacy; and so of other products. As to the position of slavery, inasmuch as nine-tenths of all existing difficulty has been created by the Gulf States, if they should be cut off, the institution in the remaining States would drop out of general politics into all the security which the local laws could give it. Besides, in virtue of the loyalty of the slave States in standing by the Union, every guaranty consistent with our institutions would be given to them. So well has this matter been considered by the leading secessionists, that they disclaim any desire to have the company of the border slave States in going out of the Union.

But how will the Pacific States remain affected? [sic] Senator Latham has already told us. They will cling to the North and West, he says, until the last chance of a connecting railroad shall be extinguished. Such a result is perfectly obvious from the nature of things. What can California and Oregon do as a separate government, situated, as they are, at the long end of every lever which can operate upon "the rest of mankind." Their very mail privileges are now drawing out of the United States Treasury $905,000 per annum, over and above the receipts. Is any cotton confederacy going to supply this? It will neither have the commercial interest nor the funds to do it. But California wants—and lives on the hope of getting—infinitely more than this, to wit: the building of a Pacific Railroad. The Cotton States have thrown every obstruction in the way of this enterprise—the rest of the country is in favor of it. The distinction is becoming well understood among the people of the Pacific States. If, therefore, South Carolina and her extreme proslavery confederates should retire, it would not weaken a single tie between the communities bordering on the two oceans, and having like institutions and a common interest.

But the fear has been expressed that, let the example of secession once be set, the Western States might refuse to stay in the Union with New England. But on what ground? The people of the West are mainly the children of New England, and if their interests are not identical, they are reciprocal and inter-dependent. Create a panic in Boston to-day, and it is felt in Chicago to-morrow; while a bad season in the West tells all along the Atlantic coast. But New England, it is said, is radically anti-slavery. And what, pray, is the land of Giddings and Wade, of Schurz, Lovejoy, and the Washburns? Where are there heavier anti-slavery majorities rolled up than around the Lakes? What Eastern State has taken such a stand against the fugitive slave law as Wisconsin? What section of the country has had Congressional delegations more uniformly firm against all the schemes of the slavery propagandists than the Northwest? Even their Democrats have sometimes been better than the free-soilers of other sections. Surely, if the East and the West were to quarrel, it would be because they were too much alike, rather than from the opposite reason.

But if the West had views or interests seriously clashing with those of the East, there is one very good reason why, as between the two, the seceding party should not be the West—and that is the latter's superior growth in power. Why, look at such a State as Iowa, going up from a population of 192,000 in 1850, to 676,000 in 1860. Look at New England's Congressional delegation of 41, which must lose three or four by the next apportionment, and then contrast it with the force of about 75 which will watch over the interests of the West. With the Union intact, the West is consciously entering upon a career of controlling power in the Republic; but let the cotton States take away their ten Senators and their twenty-seven Representatives, and it is easy enough to see whither the course of empire would take its way. Under such a condition of things, we might as well expect to see a State secede from a country [county?], as the Great West retiring from New England, and voluntarily cutting itself off from the seaboard.

As to other possible dissolutions, as of the Middle and the Eastern States, and of the city and State of New York, (a transcendental notion never rivaled by the philosopher Emerson,) we do not care to speculate. We have gone far enough, and we can only rest our justification on the extraordinary features of the times and the impressions they make on others. For our own part, we do not believe in *one* permanent secession. As we were born, we expect to live and die in the United States of America. But if the worst fears should be realized, and a portion, or even all the Southern States should separate themselves from the North, let us cultivate in these remaining States sentiments of nationality and patriotism. So may we avert the evils which will surely overwhelm the South if they carry out their mad schemes of a confederacy based upon slavery. There is no good reason why property should seriously depreciate at the North, in case of a dissolution of the Union. Its occupations are varied, and its resources enormous. Civil war here is out of the question, and if the South should provoke a contest, it would not be waged upon our soil. We might have our tories now, as in the revolution, but they would give us no serious trouble. Let us then cultivate a spirit of fraternity at home, and thus avoid some of the most alarming of the evils which might result from disunion.

154. The Commercial Interests of the West

(Cincinnati Daily Enquirer [Douglas], December 28, 1860)

It may be well for Western States bordering on the Ohio and Mississippi Rivers to carefully scrutinize the conduct of those who have an interest in throwing obstructions in the way of navigating these natural highways. The North-eastern States, it is well known, have lavished their treasures for the purpose of drawing trade from these channels, and, in a great measure, have succeeded in accomplishing their object. They, to a very large extent, are the proprietors of the main railroads running East and West, which now carry the bulk of Western produce. Their charges of transportation rise and fall with the ebb and flow of water in the rivers.

Such being the case, it is submitted whether, under these circumstances, this conduct of these North-eastern States in the present critical condition of our Union is entirely above suspicion, and whether it is not based upon and controlled by a desire of bringing about a separation of the States! This done, the West, if joined to the North, will be entirely dependent upon artificial channels for her connection with the seaboard. It may be replied that, in case of a separation of the States, the mouth of the Mississippi will not be obstructed, and that we can use it as now; this may be so, and it may not be. Who knows? Who is willing to risk the great interests of the producing States to a may-be-so? All over the commercial world, without exception, national lines offer more or less obstructions to trade. Such would be the inevitable result if the Mississippi should become part of a Southern Confederacy; in that event Western commerce would of course seek an unobstructed channel, even at a greater cost.

The shrewd men of the North are fully aware of the above result, and no doubt have already made a calculation of the profit and loss which will inure to them by a dissolution of the Union. They can not but foresee a very large diminution, if not an entire loss, of their Southern trade; but they flatter themselves that this loss will be more than repaired by the large addition expected to come from the Great West. They know that should the West adhere North (as they anticipated) her entire manufacturing interest would be broken up, because with the loss of her Southern customers the West would be so crippled that she would be compelled to stop manufacturing.

The gain and loss to the North-east may, then, be summed up thus, to-wit:

Loss of Southern trade.

Gain, the residue of Western trade, now enjoyed by the South, to which add all her manufacturing.

There is another item which may or may not be potential in causing the North-east to assume her present threatening attitude, and that is the stock in the railroads before referred to; these stocks are held by her leading citizens, whose influence may now be lent to hastening a separation, for the purpose of giving an additional value to their stock certificates.

We do not desire to attribute selfish motives as being the controlling principle of New England; but we can not believe that so shrewd (not to say so selfish) a people would adopt any course which, in their minds, would not lead to *pecuniary* gain.

As an evidence that the foregoing deductions are properly drawn, we submit whether any man conversant with New England character would for a moment believe that her people would, for *principle,* do any thing injuriously affecting her pecuniary interest; and whether, if our railroads were not constructed, she would be willing to hurry off the South, and thus yield up her Western trade *via* New Orleans?

There is another topic growing out of a separation of our beloved Union, which it may be premature to refer to, but the signs of the times give little to hope, but that ere long the Great West will be called to decide "where she will go:" whether she will ally herself to a kindred people, whose very interest[s], social and pecuniary, are common, or whether she will, on a question concerning the negro, with which, as States, we have nothing to do, will [sic] join herself with the North-east, a people with whom we have very little sympathy, and whose interests are antagonistic.

155. Mayor Wood's Message—Proposal to Separate the City from the State

(New York Journal of Commerce [Breckinridge], January 8, 1861)

The message of Mayor Wood to the Common Council of this city, will be read with attention, not only here but throughout the State. It treats exclusively of the relations of the City to the State at large, and presents, with much clearness and force, the invasions which the latter, acting through its Legislature, has made upon our rights.

With many, perhaps we should say with most of the complaints made by Mayor Wood, we fully agree. The policy pursued by the Legislature of the State towards the City has been an infamous one, subversive of the plainest principles of local government, and of the rights and privileges of the people of this locality. It is no sufficient excuse for this invasion of local rights, that corruption has sometimes obtained ascendancy in our administration, or that the interests of the people could be more effectually guarded, in some particulars, under State than under City management. The *right* to manage their own local affairs in their own way, is inherent; and the Legislature can only deprive us of it by violent and unwarranted usurpation, such as has been resorted to in numerous instances in past years.

It is peculiarly appropriate for the Chief Magistrate of New York, on occasions like the present, to point out the abuses which have grown up, the usurpations which have been practised, and the inroads upon vested rights which have been made by the Legislature. These abuses, usurpations and inroads, can never be justified, even upon the plea that they are designed to promote the welfare of the people of the city; but when notoriously if not avowedly designed to promote partizan ends, and to subject the independent citizens of this city to the domination of a central power, whose strength is to be perpetuated and success promoted by the control of the great amount of patronage thus placed at its disposal, they become simply oppressions, which may be resisted in every lawful and appropriate form until redress is obtained.

The Mayor seems to anticipate, in the disturbed state of the country, and the disintegration going on about us, the approach of the period when the people of the city of New York may throw off the burdens which oppress them, and assume independent existence as a "free city." That there is every probability of a disruption of the Union, and the separation of section from section, is indeed apparent. That such a breaking up of the confederacy may introduce new elements into our system, lead to new complications, and inaugurate with reference to ourselves a new policy, is not at all improbable. Deprecating as we should such a calamity, and hoping to the last for some method of averting it, we cannot, in the present condition of public affairs, refuse to recognize impending dangers, nor do we wonder that the thoughts and minds of our citizens are turned towards measures of self-protection and future security. If the Union shall indeed be broken up, it is not within the compass of man's wisdom to say where the work of disruption shall end. We have already seen its beginning, but its termination can no man understand, until the problem shall have been worked out before his eyes.

The vast commercial relations and the important position of the city of New York, render the present threatening aspect of political affairs a subject of great moment to her citizens, and they may stand justified before the world, for giving it their earnest attention. If the Union is to be broken up, it is by no means certain that the division is to be strictly between the free and the slave States, or that sub-divisions may not follow, dictated by ideas of commercial supremacy or political economy. In any such changes the city and State of New York must play an important part, and her citizens will be prepared, first, to save the Union if that be possible—and next, to protect their own position, interests and rights. Our views of the attitude which the city of New York should assume in so grave an emergency, do not fully coincide with the opinions of Mayor Wood. While we agree with him mainly respecting the wrongs which the city has suffered at the hands of the State Legislature under partisan promptings, we still think that we have a more important part to play on the theatre of events, than to reduce ourselves to a "free city," confined to Manhattan Island. Our position is one of great local and commercial advantages, and we have no idea of surrendering these to any spirit of indignation, however justly entertained, against the party tyrants at Albany, who have lately managed to control our government, and cripple us in our privileges. We have no idea of imitating the hasty action of South Carolina, by separating ourselves summarily from our oppressors, but rather let our policy be, to stick by until we conquer them, and not only teach them to let us alone, but compel them, under the inexorable laws of trade, to contribute to our prosperity and promote our material interests. We have not the most remote idea of allowing "a foreign power" to obtrude itself between our "free city" and the great West, or of placing in the hands of *any civil power whatever,* the ability to cut us off from communication with the granary of the world—the fertile and productive prairies and plains of the Western States. Make the city of New York as *free* as the air which is wafted to us from the ocean, repudiate all authority on the part of the Legislature of the State to interfere with our local privileges and rights, but never must the commercial supremacy which nature has given us, be placed within reach of the cupidity or caprice of any human power. No; if any political changes must occur— if the Federal Union is to be broken into fragments—New York will take care of herself and of her position; but rather would we submit to all the *commissions* and *taxes* which the cupidity of the Albany tyrants can inflict upon us, than narrow our influence and our territory, to the limits suggested by the Mayor, in the message just delivered.

But we will not willingly submit to the exactions to which Mayor Wood so properly takes exception. We will resist them, and continue to resist them; and appealing to the justice of the people of the State, we will overthrow our oppressors, and secure our just rights. In this connection, however, we may proffer a word of advice to the people of this city. The best way to secure our rights and emancipate our city from the unjust burdens cast upon it, is, by inaugurating a respectable, an honorable, and an honest government. Let us prove ourselves alive to our own interests, and competent to manage them, and then let us say to the Legislature, "hands off,"—we prefer to take care of our own business.

156. A DISRUPTED UNION

(Canton *Stark County Democrat* [Breckinridge], January 9, 1861)

Since we have observed the treasonable inaction of the Republican members of Congress, we have concluded that disunion is quite possible if not probable. The Seward and Giddings leaders of the Republican party in Congress are remaining perfectly indifferent, or praying for the secession of all the slave States. At all events, they will lend no helping hand to stay the blow!

> *"Oh for a tongue to curse the slave*
> *Whose treason, like a deadly blight*
> *Comes o'er the councils of the brave,*
> *And blasts them in their hour of might.*["]

We doubt not these Greeley leaders have padlocked Mr. Lincoln, otherwise something might have been heard from him, which would have had an excellent effect. A patriotic statement from "Old Abe," a few weeks ago, would have worked wonders! We fear it may now be too late!

Well, if the Cotton States go, we want blue light New England also to go. Let her go and consume her own manufactures, her own codfish, wooden nutmegs, &c. The other States could get along well when the crazy descendants of Plymouth Rock (whose hearts are frequently as bloodless as the Rock) were got rid of. We would immediately favor a prohibitory tariff on all New England manufactures, such as schoolmarms, poor preachers, Lecturers on Women's Rights, and "the nigger in the woodpile," codfish, and whale ile, brass and wooden clocks, skim-milk and wooden cheeses; to say nothing of calico, shirting and sheet-ing, and ice. After thus getting rid of blood-sucking-blue-light-burning New England, we would either unite with the Cotton States, or form a friendly treaty. Then Pennsylvania and Ohio, having plenty of coal, could go into the weaving and manufacturing business generally, and find a ready market South. Under this state of things, Canton might become a Manchester, and the hills for miles around be ransacked to furnish coal to drive her millions of spindles and thousands of looms.

This is our mode of paying off New England for her fanaticism and treason, and if, by her abolition folly, this Union is to be severed, she will suffer—as indeed she ought.

157. Whither Shall Pennsylvania Go?

(Norristown (Pa.) Register and Montgomery Democrat and Watchman [Breckinridge], January 22, 1861)

Five States are already out of the Union, several others are about going, and in as much as the Republican leaders and politicians at Washington and elsewhere, manifest no disposition towards a compro-mise of the difficulties at present surrounding the country, it is almost cer-tain that on the fourth of March next, fifteen states will be outside of the Federal Union, or in other words that the Union will be com-pletely broken up. States will then assume an independent position. Under these circumstances what will Pennsylvania do, and whither will she go[?]—Should there be no re-construction of our once glorious union of States, will she link her destinies with a northern Republic including the New England States; or will she join her fortunes with the Southern States? This is a question that may present itself for profitable considera-tion. The majority of her people and her tendencies are conservative. They can have little sympathy with that portion of the country—which in turn has hung the Quakers and burned old women for witches, and which in later times has brought forth among its productions, wooden nutmegs and other notions.—With the land of such heresies and hum-bugs, sober, conservative, Pennsylvania can have no sympathy and no desire to come into close communion. On the other hand, the South is the natural market of Pennsylvania's products and resources. The manu-facturing towns, (ours among the number) until the present disturbances, have found a ready market for their articles of manufacture. Whither

then shall Pennsylvania go? In the event of a disruption of the Union
and the resumption of her seperate [sic] independent, position, shall she
link herself with the fanaticism and heresies of the New England States;
or shall she join her fortunes to that part of the country, which has
throughout the whole period of our national existence, whatever its
faults, always proved a bold and fearless advocate of the rights of the
people?—Pennsylvanians may soon be called upon to decide this question.

158. A Glance at the Probable Future

(Easton (Pa.) *Argus* [Douglas], January 31, 1861)

We certainly are on the eve of great events in this country. The
people of Pennsylvania cannot be indifferent spectators; their interests
and commercial relations will force them to look realities in the face,
and act like men. The right or wrong of secession may shortly be no
longer a practical issue. The *fact* of a southern confederacy may be
presented for our consideration.

Under any circumstances, we in this State must suffer very much,
perhaps more than any other.

Suppose a Southern Confederacy under the old Constitution, slightly
modified, and none but slave States admitted, carrying out the idea
of a great southern Confederacy based on slave labor, having possession
of the great cotton zone of the world, and a great Northern Confederacy
based upon free labor, how are our manufacturers (of iron for instance,)
to get along?

At present we have free trade with all the Southern States. Most
of the Southern States do not make a pound of iron. They purchase three
times as much of us as we purchase of them. Nearly all the southern
States get their manufactured iron directly or indirectly, such as wire,
nails, ploughs, castings for cotton gins, saw-mills, sugar mills, &c., from
us. When a cargo of iron goes into a Southern port it pays no duty.
But when a cargo comes in from Liverpool, it pays twenty-four per
cent duty; that is, for every hundred dollars['] worth of iron they pay
our government twenty four dollars duty, and yet we complain of
ruinous [sic] competition. Indeed our iron men say they can hardly
compete with the English manufacturer in the ports of New York and
Philadelphia. How will it be when a Southern Confederacy admits English iron and manufactures of iron duty free? They may say we want
to purchase in the cheap markets of Europe when we sell the bulk of

our cotton, and thus have a return cargo. Does it not deprive us of a market in fifteen Southern States having near ten millions of people and who are comparatively non producers of iron?

But it may be said "we will increase the duty in the Northern Confederacy, and thus keep the English article out altogether;" how much good will that do us in Pennsylvania? They manufacture iron now on the Hudson nearly as cheap as we do. They manufacture iron in Ohio and Missouri for the north west; so that with the Southern States cut off, our market would be a very limited one. But how long would the New England States agree to pay a high tax on iron when they produce none? The New England States now have twelve Senators and Pennsylvania two, so that they could and would prevent a high tariff.—The North-west is always for free trade, besides the Allegheny mountain is a sufficient tariff for them, and they would go with New England to whom they now sell bread-stuffs.

The truth is, that the Southern people can get what they want in the markets of the world. We *must* obtain our supply of cotton from them. We now take in the Northern States thirty millions of dollars['] worth per annum of raw cotton. There are large cotton manufacturing establishments in the neighborhood of Philadelphia, to say nothing of those at Norristown, Reading, Lancaster, Harrisburg, South Easton, &c. Where do they sell their manufactured articles? Not in New England for New England manufacturers have sales rooms in Philadelphia and New York. The truth is New England is our rival. She would never agree to a duty on coal because the coal of the British Provinces is too near. New England merchants never come to make purchases in Philadelphia; the merchants of the Southern States do. It therefore may yet become a great question in this State, whether it will not be sound policy as well as true duty for us to seek political relations with those with whom we have heretofore, and may hereafter have profitable commercial relations.

159. THE FREE CONFEDERACY OF THE NORTH

(New York Herald [Breckinridge], February 1, 1861)

We publish three articles from the Toronto papers on the great question of a Northern confederation, embracing the free communities of the late United States, the two Canadas and all the British provinces of North America. The question arises from the determination of all the republican leaders to resist those measures which can alone reconcile the South to the North, their object being to prevent the seceding States from returning to the Union, and to force the rest of the slave States out of it. This is done advisedly, with a view of annexing the British colonies, which would have nothing to do with the confederacy so long as slavery was tolerated within its borders, but which, with that insuperable objection removed, will be glad to unite their destiny with their Anglo-Saxon brothers in a great free soil homogeneous nation, extending from the Ohio to the North Pole. "For every State that goes out one must come in," says Mr. Seward; "and so I look upon Rupert's Land and Canada, and I am able to say 'It is very well; you are building excellent States to be hereafter admitted into the American Union.' " Mr. Lincoln and Mr. Seward have both declared that this government cannot exist with two kinds of civilization; that it cannot continue half slave and half free; it must be all either one thing or the other. As the Southern States decline to surrender their institution, and prefer to cut adrift rather than submit to Northern domination, there is nothing left but to repair the loss by the annexation of the free States lying to the north of us.

It has been said that the Prince of Wales was well received throughout the British Provinces, and that therefore they will not join us. That is a weak and flimsy argument; for his Royal Highness was received with greater *eclat* on this side the line. The disturbances in Canada during the Prince's visit were very considerable; and the Duke of Newcastle is reported to have taken home to England the intelligence of a desire on the part of the British Provinces to form a confederacy under one British viceroy. But this is a mistake. What they want is to unite with the free States of the North; and they cannot do it too soon, for revolution and war are now rife in Europe, and the chances are that Great Britain will be broken down in the irrepressible conflict. Canada ought therefore immediately to provide for its future. England has not the power to prevent the annexation of the British provinces, and, besides, peaceable secession is the principle of the age. What is good doctrine in Italy ought to be good in America. Canada, from her history and geographical position, belongs to the Northern States, just as much as "the kingdom of the Two Sicilies" belongs to Sardinia and a united Italy. The unity of the Italian States, and the unity of North American free States, are the problems of the time, to be worked out by "manifest destiny."

The Toronto *Leader*, it will be seen, does not object to the new combination, but rather objects to our phraseology of "annexing British America," and says "the annexation will be in the other direction." We are practical. We do not dispute about words if our ideas are carried out. "A rose will smell as sweet by any other name." The Canadians may call the new Union what they like—our annexation of them, or their annexation of the Yankees—so that both are only united under one government. But there is one thing in the arrangement against which we will strenuously object, and that is the annexation of the British islands. They have too many paupers, and are too heavily burthened with debt.

Our contemporary anticipates "a new territorial arrangement" from the fragments of our dismembered confederacy, and says that so far from overtures for a union with Canada being repulsed, he promises there is "every likelihood that they will receive a fair and candid consideration." This is all that we could expect him to say just now, but it is a decided step in advance. The London *Post*—the home organ of the British government—says Canada will henceforth hold the balance of power on this continent. The government organ in Canada gives further elucidation to the idea by showing how it is to be done, even by union with our Northern States.

The *Leader* of the 30th January says:—"There is a feeling abroad in these provinces that we should derive from a union many advantages that we do not now possess. There is an indefinite yearning after a higher *status*—a larger share of nationality." How else can that yearning be gratified, or that *status* attained, but by union with the Northern States? Forever must these provinces be dragged at the tail of Great Britain till they assert their independence. The manner in which the Judiciary of Canada is now treated is an illustration of their degradation. But already one province wants to come in. "The largest vote," says the *Leader*, "in favor of the project would come from the peninsula of Upper Canada, where there is a feeling that *the connection with New York is the natural one, and that it is more profitable than any other that could be formed.*" We are satisfied to take the provinces by instalments—one at a time. But we are told that Lower Canada has a horror of democratic institutions, and changes slowly, while she fears her religion would be in danger at our hands. Can any greater protection be desired than the French Catholic population of Louisiana have always enjoyed under this government? The religious liberty of all is fully guaranteed in our constitution. As to the opposition of the old French noblesse to republicanism, it would avail nothing in revolution. A little gentle outside pressure would quicken the action of the province, and soon make it all right. Now that the South is rent from us, our destined expansion is northward, and nothing can arrest our progress. We are more than twenty millions.

So much for one of our Canadian contemporaries. What says the other? The *Globe* assumes the same tone, and says, before the 4th of

March eight or ten seceding States "will have organized a large military force, capable of defending themselves against any attack from federal troops." But supposing the new administration to attempt the conquest of the South—what then? Our contemporary replies by asking some sensible questions:—"Will such a contest pay? Will victory or defeat bring the greater trouble? Will not the present constitution be destroyed in either case? The ancient Greek republic fell when one or two of the States conquered the rest." The reason is plain: "Though the federal power might be continued, the independence of the States, their freedom of action as separate sovereignties, would be at an end. The central government, having conquered by force of arms, must maintain its ascendancy by the same means. Here, then, is a great military power, centralized and consolidated, the very evil that the wisest American statesmen have foreseen and dreaded and warned their countrymen to resist to the last." This is common sense and sound philosophy, and our contemporary turns the argument to practical account by showing from it the necessity of "two confederacies—a Northern and a Southern—peaceably established, each pursuing its own policy and enjoying its own peculiar institutions, without the let or hindrance of the other."

This is a very suggestive hint that when the Canadians take possession by surprise of impregnable Quebec and other fortresses they must be allowed to quietly secede on paying the mother country for the property. It is significant in another point of view. The people of Canada have now an interest in the Northern States, and do not desire to see them enter upon the suicidal game of Southern conquest, but rather to "pursue a career of annexation and aggrandizement northward and westward, Canada and the Lower Provinces being supposed rife for admission into the free confederacy of the North."

These are cheering sentiments for the people of the free States, in view of their loss of the South, which now seems inevitable. Unlike the proud patricians of the Roman republic, who saved the country by liberal concessions and guarantees to the plebeians when they seceded from the city to Mons Sacer and commenced founding a new empire; and unlike the still prouder aristocracy of England, who saved the British empire from the horrors of civil war by concessions to Ireland in 1829, the republicans, suddenly elevated to power, like all upstarts, are puffed up with a sense of their own importance, and will not bend before the storm which is sure to break them in the end. One of the leaders in Congress—Mr. Stevens, of Pennsylvania—on Tuesday last declared that "rather than give concessions he would see the government shattered into ten thousand atoms;" and this sentiment was not rebuked, but acquiesced in by all the republican members of Congress, following the latest authoritative programme received from Springfield, to the effect that "Mr. Lincoln is not committed to the border State compromise, nor to any other; he stands immovably on the Chicago platform, and he will neither acquiesce in, nor advise his friends to acquiesce in, any compromise that surrenders an iota of it."

There is every prospect, therefore, of the absorption by the new free State confederacy of the North American British provinces, to wit:—

	Square Miles.	Population by last Census.
Canada East	291,980	890,261
Canada West	147,332	952,004
New Brunswick	27,700	193,800
Nova Scotia and Cape Breton	18,746	276,117
Prince Edward Island	2,134	62,678
Newfoundland	35,913	101,606
Labrador	5,000	100,000
Vancouver Island	8,000	2,000
Hudson Bay Territory	2,480,000	180,000
Total	3,014,805	2,758,466

Here is a vast empire, whose area is far greater than that of the free States, and is nearly equal to all the States and Territories of our confederacy, North and South, and with a population which ten years ago was more than two millions and three-quarters, and is now fully four millions. The immigration to the Hudson Bay territory, stimulated by the gold discovery, is immense, and the Canadian population alone is estimated at upwards of three millions. It is hardy and thrifty, and homogeneous with our own Anglo-Saxon and Anglo-Celtic population —the very flower of the Caucasian race. In 1850 there were 56,214 natives of the United States in Canada; and the blood which prevails in our free States is now in a ratio of three to one in the provinces. This we say without disparagement of the French, who in arts and arms and vitality stand to-day at the head of European nations.

In language, religion and institutions British North America is almost identical with our free States. What, then, is to prevent its union with the North? Out of its vast domain eight States, equal on an average to those of the South, might be constructed at once, leaving abundant territory for the erection of eight more at no distant day. There can be no doubt that the whole population of the provinces, with those of the free States of the North, would not at this moment fall short of twenty-five millions. If united in one government, the accessions of population from Europe would be immense, and Yankee activity would soon develope the dormant resources of the new empire. It would constitute a vast naval power, ruling triumphant in two oceans and controlling the commerce of the world. Mr. Seward, flattering alike the Northwest and Canada, has fixed the capital of the new northern confederacy at or near St. Paul, Minnesota, not far from the British line. But it is evident that the seat of empire will be New York, with the federal district of New Washington ten miles round it—New York, which, in spite of all governmental or territorial changes, will maintain its position as the great free city of the New World—the centre and the entrepot of the commerce of three continents. Let Canada and the other British provinces prepare for their mighty destiny.

160. RELATIONS OF THE WEST TO THE SOUTHERN CONFEDERACY

(Dubuque Herald [Douglas], February 20, 1861)

The consideration of the commercial, if not the political relations which it will become the interest of the West to hold to the Southern Confederacy is one which cannot be long defer[r]ed in view of the rapid progress made in the organization of the seceded States into a separate Government and of the probable commercial policy which the Government of the Southern Confederacy will find it to be [to] its interest to adopt.

The policy of the adhering States of the Union under the new regime will be enunciated in the Tariff Bill now before Congress, and which in all probability will become a law. This policy will impose onerous restrictions upon commerce, and burdens in the shape of indirect taxation upon many of the necessaries of life and implements used by husbandmen and mechanics, in their respective avocations, under the pretext of encouraging and protecting home industry, while the Government of the Southern Confederation will either open the ports of the seceded States free to the commerce of the world, or at most impose no greater burdens on it than to raise a sufficient revenue to pay the expenses of the Government of the new Confederation. It is estimated that an average duty of ten per cent. upon imports will be sufficient for revenue purposes in the Southern Confederacy, while the tariff upon similar commodities imported into the adhering States will average not less than fifty per cent.

The question which will soon present itself to the West for its consideration is, whether it prefers to pay a dollar and a half for a commodity at Boston, New York, Philadelphia, or other ports in the adhering States of the Union to purchasing similar goods at New Orleans or one of the Ports of the seceded States at a dollar, should these ports be open to free trade, or at a dollar and ten cents, should a revenue duty be imposed upon foreign commodities.

This question is not simply a speculative one; it will soon become practical in its operations, and as such, the West must soon consider it, and determine what relations this section of the country will hold towards the North and South.

The imposition of restrictions upon commerce is a favorite theory of New England and Pennsylvania politicians and political economists, for the very good reason that by means of duties upon imports all the rest of the country is made tributary to the manufacturing interests of these States; but the moment that the advantages, either of free trade, or of a tariff imposed for the mere purpose of raising revenue, becomes manifest to the West, as it will should the seceded States persist in their apparent determination to establish an independent Government, is it to be presumed that the States of the Mississippi valley will consent to remain tributary to the interests of New England and Pennsylvania at the enormous expense and disadvantage to which a political connection with those interests would subject these Western States[?]

The President elect having suggested in his tour to the Capital the interrogative form of eliciting information, we follow his illustrious example in putting questions to our readers and through them to the people of the whole West.

The world seems to have reached that stage of enlightenment in political affairs which recognizes both the right and propriety of political communities in taking the best care they can of their own interests, provided they do so without infringing upon the rights of others. It is in pursuance of this principle that Northern sentiment in these United States, disregarding and ignoring the constitutional compact made in other times and under different circumstances, arrays itself in hostility to the exercise of rights which it regards as inimical to its interests and well-being; and it is in accordance with the same principle that those communities in the South which have seceded from the United States, have taken a course which to them seems best for the promotion of their own interests and the protection of their rights.

This disruption of the United States changes the relations of the West materially to its late confederates, and there are but few alternatives left it to choose from in the new relation it may think it best for its interests to adopt. Will it for the sake of a mere Political connection with eastern Manufacturing States, consent to pay forty or fifty per cent more for commodities, the manufacture of these States, than it can purchase similar commodities for by forming a Political alliance with those States through whose Ports commerce will be comparatively unrestricted, and where western productions will find a better market than they will at Ports where commerce will be practically inhibited[?] In the language of Mr. Lincoln "we are only asking questions" but we confess that they are questions which embrace considerations for Western thought which will soon have to be determined on, and on the decision of which will depend in a large degree the future happiness and prosperity of the West.

We are not unaware of the effect it may have upon certain minds to put these questions at the present time. There are still left many of a class of persons who perceive evil intent in every foreshadowing of future events which may be repugnant to their wishes. The business of a journalist, to be worth anything beyond the mere publication of transpiring events, is to anticipate, if it can, what is likely to be the effect of certain causes, and to warn the reader in advance of what it thinks likely to occur. [sic] Such has been, under our direction, the course of the HERALD, and although the conclusions we have drawn from time to time from transpiring events have not been such as was [sic] the most desirable to be experienced, and which in several instances it would have been much more desirable to avoid, yet it was not for us to lull into a false security those who depended upon us for a candid opinion, or to remain an indifferent spectator of popular movements which we plainly perceived would revolutionize the country and lead to the establishment of new political relations among the States of the Union. All this was foreseen and anticipated, yet there are those among the community, perhaps among the readers of the HERALD, to whom it is a mortal offense to draw legitimate conclusions from causes which inevitably produce anticipated results. To such persons especially we commend the consideration of the questions suggested by the dismemberment of the Union and the establishment by some of its fragments of a new Confederacy.

The time for mere Partisanship is past, and it is not in the light of Party Politics, nor by means of Party organizations that the future course of the West must be guided. Democrats, Republicans or whatever else we may have been in politics, concerns our future relations to the existing and probable future condition of the rest of the country but little. The PEOPLE of the West must act for themselves as other sections of the Union act for their own peculiar advantage, and in doing so, it is not as partisans but as Patriots and Statesmen that conscience should approve our course.

161. THE BORDER STATES

(New-York Daily Tribune [Lincoln], March 9, 1861)

Whatever else the Border Slave States may do, the plan referred to by our correspondent at Richmond in this morning's paper, of a Central Confederacy, is altogether the most impracticable and most mischievous. It is barely possible, though not probable, that the United States, divided into two Confederacies, a Northern and a Southern, might maintain separate Governments, at least for a period, and preserve amicable relations; but to attempt to divide the country into three Confederacies, would certainly lead to the worst consequences of disunion that have ever been predicted. Disunion, pure and simple, would be an alternative much to be preferred by all parties, and particularly by the Border States themselves. For the formation of such a Central Confederacy must necessarily be preceded by civil war, undertaken by these Border States on behalf of those further South in resistance of the Federal Government; and who can foretell what may be the result of a war so begun, not for the purpose of saving the Union, but because it is destroyed already? Better would it be that these States should go at once with a Southern Confederacy, if such be the will of their people, than that they should step in as armed mediators, without the hope of influence enough to keep the peace on either side, because on the important point of lending their strength to either in a permanent Government, they abandon both. If by a popular vote the Border States unequivocally declare their intention of going with the Confederate States—supposing that they shall not come back—then the revolution is formidable and respectable enough to appeal, with some reason, to the North to recognize the existence of a Southern Confederacy to be met with treaties rather than with arms. But if these States choose to remain faithful to the Union, they preserve their influence over both parties; over the South to return to their allegiance, and over the North to exercise forbearance in any event, whether the union between them shall be preserved or not. While, should they withdraw and form a Central Confederacy, though they may be the allies for a time of their neighbors on the South, they sacrifice, by refusing to go with them altogether, as they do by leaving the North, all influence whatever, and will find themselves, at last, the antagonist of parties on both sides of them, and the debateable ground of their contests.

The interests of the Border Slave States are unquestionably Northern, and Northern they must be, if we are to divide into two. Any attempt on their part to avert that destiny is futile, and is only to condemn them to a long struggle. There is no real reason why there should be civil war between the United States and the South, and should one arise it can be only of very short duration, unless the Border States complicate the question by separate secession. Then will arise a conflict within their own limits between the Northern and Southern interests—the interests of Slavery and Freedom—which will inevitably involve the whole country. When such civil war as this arises among us, it will be complicated by one still more difficult to manage—a servile war. Both undoubtedly are inevitable after a due lapse of time in any purely slaveholding government on this continent. Where they are prevented at all, it will be by the Free State element within the same Confederacy. If the Border States sacrifice now this redeeming element their destiny will be very soon accomplished, because the antagonisms necessary to its accomplishment are already vigorous and well organized within their limits. But as an integral part of a Free Confederacy these antagonisms are subdued and kept in check, and that result is worked out by natural laws and careful treatment which, in the other case, comes through speedy violence. There are, it is to be hoped, quiet, conservative, and reasonable people enough in those States to understand this, and to see that disaster must inevitably overwhelm them if any such movement shall be for a little while—as it could only be for a little while—successful.

162. The Position of Pennsylvania

(Harrisburg *Pennsylvania Daily Telegraph* [Lincoln], April 4, 1861)

In the great revolution which is now threatening the peace and prosperity of this Union, and which has already accomplished its partial dismemberment, the position of Pennsylvania must be both peculiar and important. In the Union of the States as first formed, that position was very important, both in its geographical boundaries and political aspects. Occupying, politically, the position of an arbiter by reason of her conservative influences, the Keystone State has always been regarded with the most friendly feelings by the extremists of both sections. In this particular, the influence of this State has been directed to the peaceable adjustment of more than one vexed question, and in all the compromises which have been asked and conceded by the people of one section to those of another, Pennsylvania has played a most important part. Her people are distinguished not alone for the genius which has made them renowned in their pursuits of the mechanic arts and sciences, or the development and cultivation of the soil, but for a comprehension of and devotion to principle, which the people of few of the other Commonwealths evince or practice. Already in this crisis, through her Representatives in the Peace Congress, the voice of Pennsylvania was potential in proposing and passing a measure of adjustment that has at least temporarily arrested revolution in one section, while it gave to the people of another section time to deliberate and prepare themselves for any emergency which might arise in the future.

If, in the progress of secession and rebellion, the States of the Union should be permanently dissolved, and all hope of reconstruction removed, the position which Pennsylvania will then occupy will give a different aspect to her interests and a different direction to her energies. Geographically, Pennsylvania is located immediately between the great west and the States in the east which depend most on the trade and production of the west to support their manufacturers. The dependency between the east and the west is in fact reciprocal, while the means of supplying this dependency must pass through Pennsylvania, thus constituting her the great highway of trade between the most useful, wealthy and powerful sections of the Union as it once existed. The direct shipment of goods from either Boston or New York for the west, would of course be the safest and cheapest by rail, while a continued transit by railroad necessarily carries such goods through Pennsylvania, over our own great lines of travel. The transit by the lakes or any other route, renders trans-shipment necessary, involving a cost and delay to which the trade between the two sections would not submit.

The advantages to be derived from such a position are not now easily to be calculated, nor can we at once perceive all the benefits which would flow from such advantages. This trade and travel, passing through Pennsylvania, would constantly keep her own resources and skill in labor employed, while she would loose [sic] none of her ancient importance as the keystone of the Federal Arch, by becoming the keystone of an arch stretching from the Atlantic ocean to the banks of the Mississippi. As trade increased, her iron and coal would be in demand beyond her eastern and western borders—while the old industry which heretofore made her capable of contending with foreign and domestic competition, will gather new vigor when she is placed in a position where her strength will be aroused to new energies. If the worst comes to the worst, Pennsylvania will not be the worst State in any Union that may be formed of which she is a member. She has too many of the elements of greatness within her territory to suffer materially by separation—too much energy to be dismayed by opposition from abroad, and has only to fear the political chicanery in her own midst, that has oftener humbled her independence and pride, than it has affected her energy and prudence. No State has been less cared for by federal legislation than Pennsylvania. No State thrown more upon her resources—and no people compelled to contend against more obstacles in trade and commerce, than the citizens of the State of Pennsylvania. [sic] While the material interests of other States were constantly mixed up with legislation—while the west was exhausting enormous grants of lands, and the South was drawing from the inexhaustible treasury of the nation the means of preserving their position in the nationality of States, and fostering and protecting their peculiar institution—while all these advantages were being derived from the Federal Government—the great State of Pennsylvania was compelled to behold English iron on its way for the erection of western railroads, and at the same time keep pace with the strongest of her rivals, and excel even those States in development and progress, which were deriving all the aid and power of the Federal Government to accelerate their improvement. [sic] Surely, however gloomy the future may appear, and whatever the changes may be that now threaten the destinies of the States of this once glorious Union, Pennsylvania has only to buckle on her armor to be ready to battle for and conquer any good she may desire.

163. What Shall New Jersey Do?

(Camden Democrat [Douglas], April 13, 1861)

The Hon. Rodman M. Price has published a long letter in reply to one from L. W. Burnet of Newark, proposing the following questions:

"Will there eventually be two permanent Confederacies—a Northern and a Southern—the Southern comprising all the fifteen slave States? Secondly: In this event, what position for New Jersey will best accord with her interest, her honor, and the patriotic instincts of her people?"

The first question is certainly a poser, and at this time baffles the speculations of all statesmen, and the second is one which would demand the serious consideration of the people of the State, the answer to which would depend very much upon circumstances.

In reply to the first question Mr. Price says, "I believe the Southern Confederacy permanent, and in my opinion, every slave State will in a very short time be found united in one confederacy."

This, to our view, is rather a hasty conclusion, which if accepted, would close the door to all present and future negociation, and render nugatory the efforts of the friends of the Union throughout the South to maintain their position, and enable the PEOPLE to be heard upon the secession movement of the usurpers of the Southern Confederacy. If the permanency of that Confederation is a foregone conclusion, the irrevocable nucleus of a new Union, why do the Border States hesitate to accept their fate? Why do they still strive to persuade the Administration to abstain from force, and prevent the inauguration of a Civil War? Why do they still persist in petitioning the North to recognize Southern rights, to adopt amendments to the Constitution, to assemble in convention to reconstruct the Union? No! The Southern Confederacy is not a permanency, and can only be made so by Administrative aggression. Let Mr. Lincoln withdraw the troops from forts Sumpter and Pickens to prevent collision, and in less than six months, the Union men of the Gulf States will be in the ascendant, the PEOPLE who have not heretofore been consulted in the formation of the Confederacy, will demand a settlement from the traitors who have usurped their power, assumed control of their destiny, and speaking for *themselves,* will accept any fair adjustment of our differences that may again render us a united, prosperous, and happy people.

This the secession leaders know full well, and we therefore are not surprised to learn by a despatch from GEO. N. SANDERS, that "in Cabinet Council, Jefferson Davis strongly urged an aggressive policy towards the United States, and that the Cabinet decided if the ultimatum of their Commissioners to Washington were not accepted, war should be declared." In further corroboration of our views, the Mobile *Mercury,* a Secession organ, says:

"The country is sinking into a fatal apathy, and the spirit, and even the patriotism of the people is oozing out under this do-nothing policy. If something is not done pretty soon decisive [sic], either evacuation or expulsion, the whole country will become so disgusted with the sham of Southern independence, that *they will turn the whole movement topsy turvy so bad that it never on earth can be righted again.*"

Even that fire-eating organ of Charleston, the *Mercury* says:

"Fighting immediately and obviously destroys the Union party in the Border slaveholding States, and brings them into the Southern Confederacy; it destroys, likewise, all hopes of reestablishing the broken Union which the Black Republicans are all loth to give up, and expect yet to mend; and it will raise a powerful anti-coercion party in every Northern State, who will clog and cripple the Government."

Thus we see the secessionists do not consider themselves safe without a rupture, which may give them a pretext for establishing a military despotism, and we only fear that "Old Abe," in his insane efforts to carry out the Chicago Platform, inaugurate the "irrepressible conflict," and prove himself a "second Jackson," will help them to their wish, and render a reconstruction of the Union impossible.

In reply to the second question, Mr. Price says "emphatically she should *go with the South,* from every wise, prudential and patriotic motive," and then proceeds to give his reasons at length.

We are not prepared to agree, or disagree with this hasty conclusion, and while we confess our sympathies are for the South, we dislike even the contemplation of such a possibility as the permanent dissolution of the old Union, and prefer to direct our efforts rather to its reconstruction, than to the future formation of new confederacies. Yet one thing we can say with safety, that even in the event of the withdrawal of the whole Southern States, it would require a material alteration of the Southern Constitution to induce us to accept it as the Supreme law of the land. For instance, how would our politicians like the provision that no one, except a native born citizen, or a resident of the Gulf States, at the time the Constitution was adopted, can hold any *office* in the Confederacy?

But, aside from any objections to their Constitution (as we have neither space nor inclination to particularize its defects), New Jersey might find it very disadvantageous to join a Southern Confederacy, unless New York and Pennsylvania should accompany her. To be sure, we owe them no particular liking, as, while New York has twice robbed us of portions of our territory, they have both constantly infringed upon our jurisdiction, and systematically abused us. Yet, however much glory we may boast for the heroic sufferings of our fathers in the Revolution, (when the Colonies *seceded* from the government of England,) we have no desire to again become the *fighting ground* of the country, especially during a civil war—as would inevitably be the case, from the peculiarity of our geographical position, if we were the most northern extremity of a Southern Confederacy. In the event of a conflict, (which could not be avoided,) it would be the interest of our powerful neighbors to secure our extensive sea-board, and the command of the entrances to the Delaware and Hudson rivers, which, also, it would be of the utmost importance to the South to retain. Who can doubt our gallant little State would be crushed and trampled to death between the two contending forces?

No! Governor, let us drop the consideration of such a future for New Jersey. If you will adopt Com. STOCKTON's line, of "the Hudson and the Lakes, rather than the Potomac and the Ohio," as the northern boundary of the Confederacy, then, indeed, our objection would be removed; but we cannot consent to be the extreme border State of either a Northern or Southern Confederacy. Let us rather pursue the course we have heretofore marked out, and in a conservative spirit, plead for peace, and a reconstruction of the Union, based upon the most ample recognition of the rights of all the States, and whatever fair guaranties may be required to secure them.

New Jersey has no prejudices against Southern institutions to overcome—she has no sympathy with fanaticism of any kind—but her people dearly love the old Union which our fathers established, and will submit to almost any sacrifice to maintain it.

164. Utopian Dreams of the Secessionists of the South West

(Charlestown (Mass.) Advertiser [Lincoln], June 8, 1861)

In Missouri, the present plans of the traitors have been frustrated by the energetic action of Gens. Harney and Lyon. For the present, they have given way to superior force, yet among the professed friends of the government will eventually be found some of its bitterest enemies. The plan of separating the South from the North is not wholly the result of the agitation of the Slavery question, and, in some of the disaffected States, this question does not at all enter into consideration. In Missouri, for instance, Slavery has ceased, for a long time, to be a material and leading interest, hence some other hobby must be started to inflame the minds of the people. Throughout this State the tariff passed by the last Congress, and generally known as the "Morrill tariff" has been seized upon by the traitors to accomplish what could not be done by crying "Abolitionist." They claim that this tariff is unfair to the South, and, a direct blow to the interests of Missouri. However, they are snubbed for the day, but still cherish their traitorous and insane purpose—that of destroying the Union. The traitors assert openly that they will carry out their hellish designs sooner or later. Their enmity to the Administration, and to the North especially, is bitter in the extreme, and nothing but blood will satisfy them. The love of power, position and rule is so strong in the negro-driver that it is with great bitterness of spirit he submits to be ruled. They say the interests of the States of the Mississippi valley are identical, and at the same time, separate and distinct from those of the Atlantic border. They would form a "Mississippi Valley Confederacy," which could control the vast productions of the West, and even make the East a tributary to its greatness. These ideas are now being industriously circulated among the people of Missouri, Kansas and Iowa, and wherever else, in that region, they dare promulgate them. In such manner do these traitors seek to alienate the affections of the loyal people from the general government. Some of them, in their more insane moments, even think that Illinois may be induced to participate in their grand scheme of fraud, rascality and treason.

The traitors of Missouri have all along, in a specious manner, argued that her interest[s] were with the South, but have never committed themselves to the Southern Confederacy, except so far as was necessary, by united efforts, to throw off their allegience [sic] to the general Government. They have ever professed to love and cherish the Union, and have wailed hypocritically over the probable destruction of the Country. But the mask which they have worn so long has fallen from their faces, and the brand of treason can be seen written upon their foreheads. This scheme will fail. Its projectors made the same fatal mistake which was made by the originators of the Confederacy of the South, that of expecting sympathy and co-operation at the North. Whether the argument that the interests of the States bordering on the Mississippi are identical, and separate from those of their sisters be valid or otherwise, is quite immaterial in arriving at a satisfactory conclusion as to the success of the scheme at the present time. So long as the people of the North West retain their present loyal sentiments towards the Constitution and the Union, its success is impossible. That the patriotism of this people is far beyond the reach of the influence of the plausible and insidious emissaries of the South, has been proved in too many instances to be at all doubted. Approaches were undoubtedly made to the chief executive officers of Kansas and Nebraska, during the last Administration, with a view to forwarding this grand piece of villa[i]ny, and though the *people* of those Territories were devoted to the Constitution, the Washington appointees, who ruled them, were looked upon with distrust.

Whatever may have been the views of the traitors of South Carolina and Virginia, the South Western Secessionists never intended to affiliate with and join a Confederacy whose policy should be controlled by the leaders of the movement in those two old States. On the contrary, they were with them most heartily until the Union should be broken, and the power of the United States crushed, then they were for themselves and an independent government. Their scheme comprised Missouri, Arkansas, Louisiana, Texas and the Indian Territory, in the first instance, and secondly, in conjunction with the Southern Confederacy, having secured the control of the navigation of the Mississippi, to dictate terms of intercourse to the great grain producing States of the North

West, and, either by flattery or threats or [of?] conquest, unite with them such other States as the exigencies of the time might demand.

But owing to unlooked for opposition and disaffection at home, and the immense and unexpected uprising and consequent energetic action at the North, their plans were so imperfectly and irregularly carried out, that instead of two grand Confederacies, one controlling the East and the other the West of the United States, the force of circumstances compelled such as had gone too far to turn backward to form that improm[p]tu Republic, the "Confederated States of America." This Southern Confederacy was a mistake, an accident—and a sad one also to the parties concerned.

Pleasing, indeed, to the fancy were the prospects pictured by the orators and newspaper writers of the South West. Compared with their prospective empire, the glory of the Roman Republic faded from the sight, and its historic fame was eclipsed by the imagined greatness of the Republic of the South West. Irrational and absurd as these ideas may seem they found advocates and believers. Their opposers were to be welcomed with "bloody hands to hospitable graves," and, imitating the policy of the great nations of history, they were going forth for conquest and to conquer. The sparsely settled and half civilized Territories of New Mexico and Arizona would fall an easy prey to their invading hosts.

Their disordered vision saw no impediment to its extension but the Pacific Ocean. Now, all these bright visions of honor, prosperity and empire are vanished—treason and rebellion are being crushed—and these traitorous people *know* themselves to be what they really are, a comparatively insignificant part of a great nation which can, not only protect its friends, but annihilate its enemies.

X

"THE EVERLASTING NEGRO"

165. NEGRO EMIGRATION—HAYTI

(Philadelphia Daily News [Lincoln], November 22, 1860)

What to do with our free colored population is a subject that has excited anxious consideration among statesmen and philanthropists. The question is one which deserves attention and action. Negroes are a very prolific race, and their numbers in this country are increasing to such an extent as to excite serious apprehension for the future.

It is unfortunate that any subject connected with our colored population in this country is generally connected in some way with the slavery question. Those humanitarians who have most interested themselves in the negro have generally been Abolitionists, and the public odium attaching to their political views has brought discredit upon their schemes. Yet, there is no subject more worthy the attention of statesmen and public spirited citizens than the disposal of our free Africans.

It is neither for the good of the colored race nor of our own that they should continue to dwell among us to any considerable extent. The two races can never exist in conjunction except as superior and inferior. True, the African is naturally the inferior race, and no injustice is done by keeping it in a subordinate condition. Yet, evident facts demonstrate that the negro population among us is already much too large for our requirements, as regards their menial servitude. A large proportion of them are unemployed, and live by any means, honest or dishonest, while others, through inclination or necessity, engage in occupations more suitable for whites in a country inhabited by white men. Thus a large share of the negro population usurp the business and the living of poor whites.

This state of things cannot properly continue. The two races cannot assimilate on account of natural prejudices. The consequence is that the negroes form a separate society, distinct from that of the whites, and with little sympathy between the two. Negroes may acquire wealth by industry or business talent, but they can never obtain station except

425

among their own people. To whites, however poor, they will always be negroes.

Colonization in Africa has been a favorite scheme with many humanitarians. The societies for this purpose have doubtless effected much good, but there are difficulties in the way of making their benefits sufficiently extensive. Of course, any such emigration of the negro population must be voluntary, and the distance of the African shores from this country, and the uncertainty of finding what they seek there deters many of our free negroes from making the important change. This is natural, and when we consider the actual condition of affairs in Africa, we can scarcely blame even blacks who have been reared in our civilized climate, for not caring to venture so long a journey for a residence in that to them *terra incognita*.

The design of those who favor Liberian colonization is to build up on that distant shore a Republic of enlightened Africans, which shall exercise a civilized effect on the barbarous inhabitants around. The scheme is a grand one, and may in time succeed; but its progress so far has not been in proportion to the hopes of its originators, and doubtless for the reasons we have given. Negroes are not good pioneers nor are they well calculated for missionaries. They rather require to be instructed and upheld than to civilize others.

The Island of Hayti offers great inducements to colored people to emigrate to that Empire. Hayti possesses a soil and climate admirably adapted to the negro, while the Island is really one of the fairest in the world. The inhabitants can live with very little labor, for many indigenous fruits grow there almost spontaneously. This is really a paradise for negroes who are traditionally not over fond of exercise. The mineral resources are said to be surpassingly rich.

Under Geffrard, Hayti is said to be making amazing progress towards as enlightened a condition as could be expected under the circumstances. Geffrard doubtless possesses many qualities of the wise and patriotic ruler. He is developing the resources of the island, and instituting reforms in the government that command surprise and admiration. He is establishing schools and encouraging agriculture and manufactures. He is said to have instituted four colleges and one hundred and seventy schools of lower grades. He has built railroads and public edifices, and established steamship lines.

Yet he finds that he cannot succeed in making Hayti what he desires without increased emigration [*sic*]. The free blacks of the United States, he thinks would make the best inhabitants he can get. He therefore offers flattering inducements to our colored people to emigrate to Hayti.

He will give to every family desiring to make Hayti their home five acres of good land, and to every single person two acres. Land in that quarter it must be understood is much more valuable than here. Five acres in Hayti with very little labor would suffice for the support of a considerable family. He also confers many civil benefits, and perfect freedom of conscience.

No better opportunity could be asked by the free negroes in our country, to obtain the privileges they naturally crave. They will be in a nation composed of persons of their own color, and governed by one of their blood. It is not surprising that emigration to Hayti has become a mania among our free negroes in certain localities. At New Orleans a regular steamship line has been established to Port au Prince for the conveyance of colored emigrants. We hope that the negroes here will, many of them, avail themselves of this excellent opportunity.

166. The Southern Grievance

(New-York Daily Tribune [Lincoln], November 28, 1860)

Whoever wades through the columns of Southern diatribes against the North which we daily publish, and the still denser columns thereof furnished by some of our cotemporaries, must perceive that the master grievance therein heaped upon us is our deficient alacrity in catching and returning runaway slaves. Of course, the especial target of malediction is Northern legislation against kidnapping; but that is merely a casual exhibition, under the spur of the Fugitive Slave act and of the Nebraska bill, of the invincible Northern repugnance to playing the part of bloodhound on the track of a frightened and flying woman, who, having had three or four of her children torn from her and sold to Mississippi or Texas, is flying to save the last of her brood from a fate more abhorred than death. We repeat that the *gravamen* of the offense is Northern repugnance to slave-catching, the particular manifestation given to that repugnance being accidental and inconsequent. The vital, honest, naked truth is, that the mass of the people of the Free States never did heartily coöperate in negro-catching, and never will. Had they been inclined to do so, the original Fugitive law of 1793 would have answered every purpose; since they were not and are not, the act of 1850, savage as it is, amounts practically to very little. Of the fugitive slaves who manage to cross Mason and Dixon's line, nine-tenths get safely to Canada if they really try, as they always did and always will. All the State anti-kidnapping laws have not added a dozen to the number who have thus made good their flights; and if they were all repealed to-morrow, the South would not be profited one stiver. If a fugitive chooses to hang about our cities from month to month, his master, if he earnestly tries, can often hear of him and recover him; but if he makes a straight pull for Canada, he is almost certain to get away; because nearly or quite all of us are anxious that he should. Now and then some poor tool of a Rynders or De Angelis will embark heartily in the work of slave-catching for the sake of the money to be made by it; but there is no man reared in a Free State and gaining his livelihood by any form of honest industry, who does not feel an intense loathing of the whole business of slave-catching, and say of it, with Hazael, "Is thy servant a dog that he should do this thing?" The very dry goods jobber who declaims against Personal Liberty acts would loathe himself if he were to join in hunting a fugitive, and would feel a sense of relief and gladness if that fugitive were to get safely off to Canada.

Southern politicians do not comprehend this—at least, they persist in talking as though they did not. They recognize no difference between hunting a fugacious negro and hunting a strayed or stolen horse, and fancy that all repugnance to slave-catching is impelled by hatred or envy of the South, or some moral obliquity, when in fact it springs directly from reverence to that Divine law, alike of Nature and of Revelation, which says, "Remember those in bonds as bound with them;" (St. Paul.) "Break every yoke, and let the oppressed go free;" (Isaiah.) "Thou shalt not deliver unto his master the servant who has escaped from his master unto thee; he shall dwell with thee; even among you, in that place which he shall choose in one of thy gates, where it liketh him best; thou shalt not oppress him;" (Deut. xxiii. 15, 16.)

Hence we say to those intent on daubing the cracks in the Union with the untempered mortar of a new Compromise, You must not ignore Human Nature. You must pay some respect to the law of gravitation, moral as well as physical. All the Personal Liberty acts may be repealed forthwith—that is a small matter—and you may make ever so solemn a new bargain for the capture and restoration of fugitive slaves; but the up-shot will be that not one in ten will be caught, and after a few years, not one in a hundred. Hence will result reproaches and criminations, charges of broken compacts and bad faith; and the South will be more excited and alienated because of the bargain of Northern politicians to do what in the nature of things is impossible.

If any new compact were now to be made, we should prefer one that stipulated the payment annually of a gross sum by the Free States to the Slave in lieu of all obligations to return fugitive negroes. Let it be agreed that there shall be no more slave-hunting on free soil, and we will gladly consent to a payment by the Free States for the exemption of four times the cash value of the slaves annually recovered. But all stipulations for greater alacrity and efficiency in slave-hunting on the part of the Free States will prove an illusion and a sham, and so tend to greater exasperation and alienation, rather than to union and harmony. Hence we are opposed [to] any such undertakings.

167. THE UNION MUST BE SAVED

(*Daily Chicago Times* [Douglas], December 7, 1860)

It is the custom of late to quote old Jackson's declaration that "by the Eternal, the Union must and shall be preserved!" Heart and soul we join in this devoted love of the Union. Heart and soul will we unite in preserving this glorious home of freedom erected by our fathers. But how is this work of love to be achieved? By reviling the South still more? by renewed falsehoods as to her course and purposes? by taunting her with her alleged weakness? by sustaining the unconstitutional State laws made to rob her of her rights? by denouncing her citizens who seek their fugitive slave property as "kidnappers?" by apologizing for, or applauding the villains, who seek to disturb her repose and peace? by demanding the right to agitate, to subvert her institutions in spite of her wishes? by denying her equality, while prating of fairness, or overriding the very plainest principles of the Constitution, while bleating about our Constitutional majority? Shall we win her into the Union by depriving her, by means of a sectional party, of all participation in the destiny and interests of the Union, and excluding her from all control over her own most vital interests? Shall we woo her into the Union by making her powerless in the common government, through our sectional numbers, and waging a war upon her dearest rights and greatest interests when she *is* in? Are these the means which the great Jackson would have employed? No, people of the Northwest! The sword of the old Hero of New Orleans might have leaped from its scabbard in this conflict, but it would never have glittered in the ranks of the Abolitionists.

The union of these States must be preserved—but by what means? There is but *one way under heaven in which it can be saved*. Either the negro or the South must be given up. The Union cannot and will not stand under this intermeddling with slavery by the North. The issue is made up: we must either let go the everlasting negro, or let go all hope of the Union. The great question now to be solved, before the American people, is whether the party pride of a dominant majority will stand proof against the calls of patriotism, the claims of self-interest, the warnings of their dead fathers, and the pleadings of their unborn children whose inheritance they are despoiling; whether the miserable desire to dictate laws, morals and religion to those who are their equals, shall override every consideration of law, interest, humanity and national prosperity.

The problem of this age, we again repeat, is not the capacity of the negro for liberty, but the capacity of the white man for self-government. Blinded by an utterly impracticable theory of universal equality, certain fanatical minds years ago commenced this war upon the Southern States. Their agitation has bred a horde of isms and driven thousands into infidelity and atheism. It has desecrated the pulpits of our churches and made many of them dens of malice, falsehood, fanatical politics, and unchristian hate. It has severed the churches of God asunder, and left them warring, infuriated and malignant. It has retarded the progress of our legislation for the public welfare, and made the halls of Congress a disgrace to the civilized world, and a burning reproach to freedom and popular government. It has fostered and nourished vile incendiaries to instigate slaughter and crime in one whole half of our country. It has overthrown the only humane and practical movement ever made to liberate and colonize the poor negro. It has forced additional restrictions and harsher laws for the poor slave, and re-tightened and double-riveted his chains. It has driven the country upon the only rock upon which it could ever be wrecked, and formed the nation into sectional and geographical lines. It has sundered all the ties of affection that made us once a united, peaceful and fraternal people.—It now marches to the last act of the fiendish drama which it has been playing for the last thirty years, and it is about to tear asunder the Union and Government of our fathers. Like some huge ploughshare of ruin, it has moved forward with diabolical obstinacy and blind fatuity, bearing down the rights of the White, crushing the hopes of the Black, and tearing asunder every tie that bound governments, societies, religions and social life.

When—oh, when, our countrymen! will you awake from this dread delusion, and throw off this horrid nightmare from the national soul! Evil, and nothing but evil, has ever followed in the track of this hideous monster, Abolition. It has been, and is now, the source of *all* your woes. Look back over the pages of American history, and ask yourselves what was at the bottom of every great distraction, trouble and difficulty through which we have passed. Strike the history and effects of Northern anti-slavery agitation from our records, and the annals of our great

Republic would be all covered over with sunshine and glory. Think of it, oh people of this once happy land, and trample the monster into the earth forever with an iron heel and a remorseless tread! Hurl its dead and loathsome carcass from you, as if it were some poisonous upas, whose very dead ashes would breed pestilence, war, discord and famine! Awake from your fatal lethargy and be *men* again. You have untold interests clustering around this Union, and uncounted hopes must perish with it. Will you allow the brightest American hopes and prospects to be dashed to earth by this vile struggle, not to elevate the negro, but to degrade the white man to the negro's level. The negro! the negro!! the negro!!! What in the name of all that is holy and sacred, *have you got to do with the negro?* Let him alone—send him back to his master where he belongs. You would never know there *was* a negro if your ears were not eternally deafened by the cries of demagogues, prating about their neighbors' business. Let slavery alone! If it is a sin, it is not on your shoulders. Let the South and the new States act for themselves, and bear their own sins; you have enough to bear of your own. If slavery makes the South poor, it makes you rich. If it drives away population and the mechanic arts, it drives them into our own ranks, and gives us wealth and greatness. What is the South's loss is our gain. Every motive on earth, either of humanity, self-interest, patriotism or love of liberty, demands that we should forever close this strife. It has been wrong from the beginning—it is madness now. It was [an] apple of discord from the first—it is destruction at this moment. Let the South have her negroes to her heart's content, and in her *own way*—and let us go on getting rich and powerful by feeding and clothing them. Let the negroes *alone!*—let them ALONE! Your intermeddling is not only not helping the negroes, but it is ruining *yourselves*. Let the whole anti-slavery agitation in the North perish. Let the South take the responsibility for her own sins, and let her have full protection for the maintenance of her property and rights, and let her KNOW that you MEAN to maintain them. This is the way to save the Union, and the ONLY way. Kill the vile CAUSE of disunion, and disunion itself will perish for *lack of food*. ABOLITION IS DISUNION. It is the "vile cause and most cursed effect." It is the Alpha and Omega of our National woes. STRANGLE IT!

168. Practically, The Question of Slavery in the Territories

(Boston Daily Courier [Bell], December 11, 1860)

It does not lie in the power of Congress and the President to plant slavery in a single square mile of those Territories. Grant the right to do so, constitutionally, by unanimous act of both branches of Congress, with the consent of all the people,—give slavery every possible guaranty there for its protection and perpetuation—and yet not a slave would go there. It would require the act of a higher power—by change of climate—to make the conditions by which alone slaves can be taken and kept there. The reason simply is, because "it would not pay." *What will not pay will not be done.*

There are more than 30 million acres of good fertile land, in a state of nature, unimproved and untouched by labor, within the bounds of the Cotton growing slave States—capable of producing twenty million bales of cotton, or about four times the present crop of that staple, or an equivalent in sugar, rice and tobacco; and this over and above a reservation of land enough to supply food for all the laboring force required for its cultivation and its employers. The labor for such a production would require three or four times the present number of field slaves now employed in these crops in all the United States. With the world at peace, trade and manufactures prosperous, and the markets for these productions extending in a ratio like that of the last twenty years, the value of labor—that is, the price of slaves,—must increase in all that region. They have lately been profitably worked at a value of $1500 or $1800 for each able-bodied "field hand." Calculate the time required to supply this labor, and occupy this land *with slaves,* under the powerful stimulus of great profits. Not even the reopening of the slave trade under protection of the United States flag, aiding the natural increase of this class of labor, could supply it fast enough to prevent the five-fold greater stream of free labor pouring down from the Northwest, overflowing and possessing the country down to central Texas.

To talk of removing them from locations of such profitable use as this, and the still greater prospective profits, to a locality where they cannot be profitably used at any price—where they would be a tax and burthen to their owners to feed and clothe them, in comparison with the cost of hired labor, for any crops to which the soil and climate of the Territories are suited—is as absurd as to propose the reversal of the laws of matter, or the laws of trade. Slave labor, like all other purchasable values, must follow economical laws.[1] Its prolonged stay after it has ceased to be profitable, in localities where it has long been established, is exceptional in appearance, because feeling and habit and domestic ties made the change difficult and slow, but not the less sure.

Look at Missouri. Slavery is there established by law, and amply protected by the irritation of opposition, by prejudice, by alliance with other slave States. Yet it has wasted and faded with an accelerating rate before free labor—*because* slave labor was more profitable elsewhere, hired labor cheaper and more profitable in Missouri. It is now virtually and to all intents and purposes a free State. How futile then the attempt to plant slavery in any Territory of the same latitude and climate.

Look at Texas, a slave State with rights guarantied of subdividing it into three more States. Southern Texas has soil and climate admirably adapted for slave labor, suitable for the slave grown crops. Land is cheap, immigration invited and urged. Yet such is the demand for and value of this labor in the other cotton States, that it is doubtful if Southern Texas will have population enough for two States, before Northern Texas will be occupied by a non-slaveholding population.

Practically, then, there is no earthly power can plant any more slave States, and the North and the South are guilty alike of the supremest folly. The one is denying what she cannot give if she would, the other demanding what she cannot accept, and each is ready to rush upon the destruction of itself and the other, for this empty privilege of being insanely obstinate, the victims of the political demagogues who play upon these jarring chords to work their own selfish ends.

169. What Is It All About?

(Daily Chicago Post, December 30, 1860) [2]

The American Union is about to be dissolved; the flag which is recognized the world over as the emblem of a happy nation, where liberty and peace have produced a prosperity unequalled in the history of man, is to be torn in twain, and for what? South Carolina has seceded! The whole South wants to go out! The administration will not move hand or foot to put down rebellion, or enforce the laws! All this is true, but that does not answer the question, what is all this trouble about?

There are thirty-three States numbering thirty millions of free white inhabitants. These inhabitants have come hither from all parts of the

---

[1] In the original the comma follows rather than precedes "like."
[2] See p. 203 n.

civilized globe. The population is made up of the immediate and more remote descendants of all the nations of the world. These have mingled, and though derived from so many sources, it may be said that we are a homogeneous people. These people are engaged in all the pursuits of life,—they have carried commerce into all seas where commerce was ever known; they have penetrated the sealed walls of Japanese exclusiveness; they have visited every accessible tribe residing upon every accessible spot of the earth. They have covered their land with railroads, and connected every point with telegraphs. They have brought the sciences to their utmost perfection, and made learning universal instead of exceptional. They have within their own limits every necessary. Inexhaustible mines—gold, iron, copper, lead, coal, salt. They have immense rivers, extended lakes, hills that are fertile, and plains that are spontaneous in their flowers. They have soils adapted to the growth of every article of domestic food. Every description of grain and of vegetable; every description of fruit can be successfully raised by them. Cotton and silk are naturally produced, while the great staple of wool is supplied by the almost countless flocks that roam over the land. Agriculture has been improved until it is as well understood as the most ordinary occupation. Beef and pork are supplied from the most thorough-bred stocks, and the poorest man in the land dines upon hogs whose pedigree can be traced back to the middle ages; upon beef that is descended from herds that were reared by loyal hands at the time of the conquest, and upon mutton that has come down in regular order from the flocks kept for sacrificial purposes in the days of Agamemnon!

These thirty millions of educated free white people are about to break up the Union, to destroy the Constitution and laws which have linked them together, and under whose mild and loving chains they have reaped such unbounded prosperity. And we ask, for what? Why should not these people live together any longer in harmony and good feeling? We can tell you, it is the negro. Thirty millions [of] white men, women and children are about to break up the government, and rush into civil war, upon the abstract question of the prospective status of the negro, who all admit is, and must be, a slave until death, unless his owner emancipates him. The negro in the United States is either a bondman or a freeman. The condition of the free negro is not a question of controversy between the north and the south. The slave is a slave, held and owned as property by laws which both north and south admit are beyond the jurisdiction of the federal government, and of all other states, save those in which the negro resides. Nobody at the north proposes any federal action having in view the emancipation of the negro. Nobody at the south expects any interference by the federal government with slavery in the states. The north abandons the slave to endless servitude, and the south possesses and enjoys that servitude with all the security that law can afford, and all the severe discipline that their own jealous care can suggest.

We are not discussing a political question; we do not write as partisans; we are stating history as we find it. What, we ask, is there in those facts that should set the people of this land at enmity, should induce them to abandon their present boundless prosperity and all the blessings of peace, to put on the sword and engage in a civil war, which will outrival in horror the bloodiest pages of history. The law of self preservation is the first law of nature. Why should the hopes, the property, the business, the social and commercial prosperity of the thirty millions of white people be wantonly sacrificed about the negro? We are not for giving up, nor for holding on. We are for taking care of the white people first, and then let the negro be considered. We are for putting an end to the wrangle—how we do not care much, so it is settled honorably and forever.

170. The Union and Slavery—Suggestions for a Southern Policy

(New-York Times [Lincoln], January 22, 1861)

The *Tribune,* a day or two since, suggested a compromise of the Slavery controversy quite unique in its character, to say the least. It had the merit of being quite certain to exasperate the South, and to encounter the stern hostility of the North,—and thus was in perfect harmony with the *Tribune's* position, that no compromise on this subject can ever be made. Our neighbor proposes the purchase of the slaves in Delaware and Maryland, together with those of the States west of the Mississippi, including Louisiana, by the Federal Government. It is supposed that these States now contain about 600,000 slaves, and that the owners would do well to sell them for $100,000,000. We think that our cotemporary underrates both the number of the slaves and the price the owners would be willing to take for them. But supposing these points adjusted, why select these particular States as the objects of Federal bounty? Does the *Tribune* contemplate the secession of the remaining States? Nothing could be more abhorrent to them than this policy of surrounding them with a cordon of emancipated slaves. The South cries aloud against being inclosed by States filled with free white men, and the impression which must be made upon them by the proposition to hem them in by emancipated slaves, may be more easily imagined than described.

If Virginia, Kentucky and the States South of them shall follow the example of South Carolina, it may then become a question worthy of consideration, whether the retention of the States north of the Federal capital, and west of the Mississippi, on the terms suggested by the *Tribune,* may not be preferable to embarking in a civil war; but as an original proposition of compromise and conciliation it strikes us as being admirably calculated to defeat the end proposed.

We do not believe that it is either just or wise to introduce into the discussions of the day any schemes for the abolition of Slavery. It must be distinctly understood that we of the North have nothing to do with that subject,—that we propose no Congressional action upon it,—but that we regard it as exclusively under the jurisdiction and control of the Slaveholding States. We have a right, doubtless, to suggest for their consideration measures which we think would renew their loyalty, promote their interests and secure their safety; but even this should be done in a friendly spirit and without needlessly disturbing their fears or their pride.

In the exercise of this right, we have more than once called attention to the obvious duty and policy of the South in regard to Slavery. We have admitted the impossibility and the folly of the immediate abolition of Slavery, and pointed out the ruin certain to flow from the sudden release of four millions of ignorant slaves from the dependence and control of masters, to whose care they have been accustomed for generations to look for the means of subsistence. We believe that the negro is susceptible of civilization, and capable of self-support; but time will be necessary to prepare him for these responsibilities. Slavery, by compelling him to labor, has ingrained into him the seeds and roots of civilization; but that arbitrary system, as it has heretofore existed in this country, by denying mental culture, and every other right, is utterly inconsistent with the development of the germ which compulsory labor has thus planted.

The South cannot hold itself guiltless, nor be at peace with the world, nor rest secure in its position, while Slavery remains what it is. *The great need of the South is a modification and amelioration of her system of Slavery.* We believe that there is not a people under the sun, enlightened, civilized, barbarous or savage, except the slaves of the South, among whom matrimony is not a lawful institution. But with a majority of the people of South Carolina and Mississippi, and with a third of the aggregate population of the Northern Slave States, this fundamental basis of all Christian as well as heathen society, has no existence. There is no law for the marriage of slaves. The union of the sexes, whether long or short, may be severed at any time at the will of the master. This state of things is simply monstrous. It would be a compliment to style it barbarous or even savage; since the comparison would imply that it was no worse than what prevails in other parts of the world. Southern men have admitted the enormity of the evil, and that a remedy should be applied; but from year to year the monstrosity is tolerated, and no one proposes a remedy. Families are separated and their members sold on the auction block, without mercy and without shame.

Here, then, is a great reform needed, which, if adopted, would go far to soften the just indignation of the world against a people who tolerate such a crime against human nature. The marriage of slaves should be put on the same footing with that of white people; and it should be made a high crime to separate husband and wife, or parents and young children. This regulation would not interfere with the leading purpose of Slavery, which is compulsory labor. Neither would it prevent, though it might regulate, the transfer or sale of slaves from one proprietor to another; which would seem to be an essential part of the system.

Slaves should be allowed to learn to read, and for this purpose they should have the whole of Sunday guaranteed to them, and encouraged to go to Sunday Schools, subject to efficient police regulation.

They should be allowed to hold property, and be encouraged to invest their earnings in Savings Banks or otherwise, with the privilege of purchasing their freedom, if proved or judged capable of improving it, at a fair valuation. No State would suffer by tolerating such self-emancipated slaves on its soil, but if prejudices should remain invincible on this subject, emigration to Liberia, or to some tropical colony, might be made a condition of emancipation.

Now we have nothing to propose on this subject. It is one with which the Federal Government has no right to interfere,—nor would we advise or countenance any interference with it except on the application of the States interested, or with the sole intent of aiding them in such steps as they might volunteer to take in this direction. But if the Federal Government is to spend money at all in this matter, it should be done to *ameliorate,* rather than to *abolish,* the Slavery of the Southern States. Suppose the Government were to pay *twenty-five dollars* per slave in stocks of the National Government, to the authorities of each Slaveholding State which should inaugurate a system embodying the reforms to which we have referred,—not for distribution among the slaveholders, but as an Educational and Reform Fund, to be invested in internal improvements, including under that head the drainage of swamp-lands, as well as the construction of railroads and canals. The slaveholders, as the proprietors of the soil, would be enriched by the improvements, while all classes would reap benefits from them and from the unsurpassed educational advantages which so large a fund would secure.

The slave population of the South, by the census of last year, will not exceed four millions; and twenty-five dollars per head would amount to one hundred millions or thereabouts. To this sum might be added ten or twenty millions, by way of facilitating the collection of slaves into families, if that should be thought feasible, as it certainly is desirable. In many cases the husband and wife are owned by different parties, neither of whom would be able to purchase the slave of the other; and where this occurs the Government of the State might interfere with a loan or a small gratuity, by way of effecting a sale from one to another, or from each to a third party. Every Southern man is aware of the multiplicity of these cases, and the evils they entail upon Slavery. Thousands of families are thus separated by distances of three to twenty miles, in all parts of the South. In general, the father sees his family, if not more than seven or ten miles from his master's house, once a week; at greater distances his visits are on[c]e or twice a month; and there are cases in which the family union takes place only once or twice a year. Then the removal of either master to another State or district entirely breaks the family tie of the slave. These scattered families might be brought together, when the law should interpose to prevent the formation of others like them. The owners of female slaves are interested in their early marriage, and it should be made a condition that the parties united should have a common owner and a common home.

Slavery thus modified and ameliorated would become a very tolerable system, and would deserve the title of *patriarchal* which its friends claim for it. We think the Government of this great country could well afford to pay one hundred and thirty or forty millions of dollars for the sake of effecting reforms which are as essential to its good name abroad as to the cause of peace, justice and humanity at home.

We repeat that we have no thought of pressing these, or any other measures of interference with Slavery, upon the Federal Government. We make these suggestions merely to show that there are ways out of the Slavery troubles very different from those urged either by Abolitionists or by Pro-Slavery zealots. And if the time should ever come when the great mass of reflecting men in both sections can take up this question as one of practical statesmanship, instead of sectional controversy, there will be very little difficulty in adjusting it upon such a basis as shall command general assent at home and the respect of the world abroad. If the South should at once enter frankly and cordially upon the grand career of amelioration and reform, instead of finding foes at the North, they would find the whole country much more ready to grant encouragement, aid and support than they would be to ask it.

171. Disunion Is Death to Slavery

(Des Moines *Iowa State Register* [Lincoln], January 23, 1861)

Dispatches from the South bring us the intelligence that the States which consider themselves outside of Federal authority, number *four*. The revolution, inaugurated by the frenzied traitors of South Carolina, has been communicated to the Gulf States; and Mississippi, Alabama and Florida have declared themselves beyond the limits of the Federal Union. The specious reason, assigned in the secession ordinances, for the treasonable course pursued by certain States, is that the Constitutional rights of the South have been invaded by the election of an anti-slavery President. This is the specious reason; the true reason is found in the circumstance that the extreme States of the South, to whom the conservation of slavery is preferred to the blessings of Union, have, for many years, meditated the establishment of a slave-holding empire on the ruins of the present government. Dissolution was menaced long before Abraham Lincoln was thought of for the Presidency. To Toombs, Iverson, Rhett & Co., the reflection has been sweet that, among the contingencies of the future, a formidable empire might be organized whose central ideas would be the original righteousness of slavery, the re-opening of the African slave trade, and the unlimited expansion of the institution.

But will secession, or a dissolution of the Union, subserve the grand purpose of these traitors? Suppose that revolution has accomplished its work—suppose that this grand confederacy of ours has gone down to the grave of nations—suppose that a slave-holding Empire or Republic has been created by the confederated Gulf States,—will these events contribute to the permanency and expansion of slavery? To our mind, a dissolution of the Union will more certainly "place slavery in a course of ultimate extinction" than any other experiment that could be devised. A nation whose central ideas are confined to slavery, and whose very commerce is made up of an abhorrent traffic in the "souls and bodies of men," will meet with neither sympathy nor encouragement from the civilized world. A nation like this will not be permitted to outrage the moral sense of Christendom. At the threshold of its existence, as a slave-trading confederacy, it will meet with determined hostility from every enlightened Republic and Monarchy in the world; and with such formidable opposition, moving directly against it from every quarter of the globe, it is not likely that its efforts to make piracy legitimate and man-stealing a virtue, will meet with any thing like marvellous success. It is too late in the history of the world for any profitable investments to be made by *nations* in the Slave trade.

In the Union, the Southern States are comparatively secure against any disastrous insurrections among slaves. In exigencies of this character, the General government is committed to the preservation of the public peace; and the United States troops, and the militia even of the Free States, would be constrained to march to the assistance of our Southern neighbors at the bidding of the proper authorities. Outside of the Union, no such assistance would be rendered. The new confederacy, encumbered with all the embarrassments incident to new governments, would be compelled to fight its own battles. It would be thrown on its own feeble resources in every emergency; and would be liable at any moment to be invaded and destroyed by servile and hereditary foes.

The most effectual way to bring about the enfranchisement of every slave on this continent, is to dissolve this Union. Slavery outflowing from a Southern nation, and seeking to diffuse itself over the Territories, will be repulsed on every hand. The formidable confederacy of the North which would spring up, full armed, from the ruins of the present Republic, would have much to say and more to do in moulding the character of infant Territories. The North—now loyal and true to the Union, and devoted to the Federal Constitution—is willing to allow to slavery all the protection that the Constitution even by implication requires; but when the severance comes—if come it must—the States of the North that have submitted for the sake of Union to requirements which bound the consciences of their people, will take hold of the moral bearings of the great question, and they will see to it, that the curse of human bondage shall not pass beyond its present limits. They will be more jealously watchful than now of the encroachments of the Slave Power. They will show their fealty to the cause of freedom and their respect for the enlightened convictions of Christendom, by arresting the expansion of slavery, and by stopping the piratical commerce in the bones and muscles of men. The "irrepressible conflict" will not be disturbed by the destruction of the Union; but it will gather fierceness and energy, and will continue until the last chain forged for the enslavement of men on this continent, will fall from the limbs of the bondman.

It is obvious then to every man who is neither a fool nor a fanatic, that the secessionists are as surely working for the extinction of slavery, as they are for the dismemberment of the Government. While they seem to know it not, they are doing infinitely more to liberate their slaves, than all the abolitionists of the country; and it is very possible that God Almighty has stricken them with judicial blindness, that, in their hot zeal for the dominance of slavery, and in their fierce lust for the wages of unhallowed ambition, HIS own right arm might be bared in the liberation of every captive.

172. THE EVERLASTING NEGRO

(Providence Daily Post [Douglas], February 2, 1861)

The negro question has been warmly discussed (one side of it, at least,) in this country for upwards of thirty years. What has come of it? Is the negro any better off? Has he attained to a higher civilization? Are fewer of the race in bondage? Are those in bondage better fed and clothed, or enjoying more privileges? Has social life throughout the country been improved? Are men better husbands, fathers, brothers, neighbors, citizens, christians? Are the churches in better condition? Is the moral standard of the people any higher? Has anybody or anything been made better by this negro question?

Two questions—both of them long since lost sight of by the abolitionists—were originally presented in this negro discussion. First: Is the negro capable of self-government? Can he take care of himself, in a civilized community, without harm to anybody? If he cannot, then he must be taken care of. And to take care of him, involves the necessity of controlling him. If he cannot take care of himself, he is not wise enough to submit voluntarily to the direction of others; and indeed, the white man would not consent to direct his labor, make laws for him, protect him, and be his guardian in all respects, as though he were a minor child, without receiving the profits of his labor, or without the right to enforce, on his part, implicit obedience. We do not consent to feed the hungry—the unfortunate men and women amongst us—upon any other terms. The man who loses all his property, and cannot labor, is taken to the poor house, and submits to the will of the town. He cannot leave his domicile without permission. Even if a man can labor, and is willing to labor, and is not suffering; yet if he has no visible means of

support, the town takes it for granted that he is a dangerous member
of [the] community, and sends him to the poor house or jail. And this,
no matter what may be the color of his skin.

Is the negro in need of this guardianship? Is it an unnatural or unreasonable constraint, when applied to him, in a refined community, if
it be true that he is not capable of taking care of himself, as the social
and civil standards of the community require him to be taken care of?
Is it not as well that he should fill his place here, as any where else? If
he lives in an uncivilized country, he can take care of himself. He can
meet the requirements of fashion. An apron is all the clothing he wants
in Africa, and even this can be dispensed with. Is his condition made
worse when he reaches a civilized country, and adopts new modes and
habits of life? And if he would not adopt these new habits voluntarily;
if his tendency is back to barbarism; if he cannot take care of himself;
is it wrong to take care of him? Would it be better to send him back to
barbarism? It is certainly true that the negroes of the South are not
capable of governing themselves politically. They cannot make laws, or
execute them—only in the style that prevails in uncivilized countries.
What shall we do? Confer suffrage upon them, and allow the States to
go back to barbarism; or make laws for them, and require of them only
obedience? The latter course is pursued, even in one of the New England States. And if we may govern them, in this respect, because of
their inability to govern themselves; why may we not govern them in
other respects, if the same inability is apparent there also?

These questions have never been successfully answered by the abolitionists. They have ceased to agitate them. Indeed, they assert that it
is not worth while to discuss or decide them. They insist that slavery
is *sinful,* no matter whether it is a necessity or not. They deny that a
man is entitled to all the liberty he can enjoy with safety to the community in which he lives; but assert that one man is entitled to all the
liberty which any other man enjoys, without reference to capacity, disposition, or any other circumstance.

Another question which the abolitionists have lost sight of, is this:—
To what extent is it our right and duty to interfere with slavery in the
South[?] They have answered this question in very brief terms. They do
not recognize human law as at all binding, when it stands in the way
of their missionary enterprise. "Our country is the world; our countrymen are all mankind." This is the motto. And if the laws of any community says [sic], "Let us alone;" they answer, somewhat as did the
Jews of old, *"We have a law,* and by that law slavery ought to die. We
are appointed its executioners. We have a right to meddle with wrong

and oppression anywhere. We are prophets and apostles of the Higher Law."

The truth is, we have no more right to meddle with slavery in Georgia, than we have to meddle with monarchy in Europe; with the laws of descent in Prussia; with the school laws of Sardinia; with the restriction upon the press in France; or with the suffrage laws in England. How long could the peace of the world be preserved, or the peace of any part, if every nation were taking the same liberties with its neighbor's affairs, that the North, for thirty years, has been taking with the affairs of the South?

And what, we come back to ask, has been gained by all this intermeddling? Nothing. Who has been benefited? Nobody. Churches have been divided—communities have been embittered—hearts have been estranged—men have been taught to hate and curse each other—pulpits have been desecrated—infidelity has been encouraged—regard for law has been obliterated—the country has been kept in a *ferment* for thirty years,—and at last, the noblest, proudest, freest, and in many respects the most powerful nation on the face of the globe, has been torn asunder, and robbed of its greatness. For what? For nothing, but to gratify a few negro philanthropists. An abstraction—and unprofitable at that—is made the basis of a quarrel that interferes with every man's business and bread; that wrests the nation's glory; that robs us of all we possessed as a people. The *everlasting negro* is the rock upon which the Ship of State must split.

Will the people stand this much longer? Will they consent to a dissolution of the Union, and a civil war, merely to please the crazy fanatics who have managed this anti-slavery agitation? Will they make the negro their god, and give up their national greatness, their prosperity, their name, their firesides—everything for which, as a people, they have been proud—for the sake of worshipping according to the creed of Wendell Phillips? We warn the fanatics that they will not do it. The bands are being broken. Look out for a moral revolution at the North, and thank God, when it comes, that it is not such a revolution as came to France, as the consequence of allowing unprincipled priests to manage political affairs.

173. FREE NEGROES FROM VIRGINIA

(Columbus *Crisis*, February 7, 1861) [3]

Eighteen free negroes arrived in this city last week from Virginia, and we are informed that there are more to follow. We can not see how Ohio is to be benefitted [*sic*] by this process of making her a general depot for all the free negroes of the South. It is a new way of elevating the white working people, and it is very likely in the general breaking up of order and established government that those who labor will have something to say about this introduction of blacks amongst us.

What is of more than ordinary consequence in this matter is the fact, that Mr. GREELEY of the New York *Tribune* has all at once discovered that the present national troubles can be solved by purchasing all the negro slaves in the border States, by the Government, and setting them free.

This would turn nearly a million of negroes loose upon our borders to immigrate into Ohio to mix with the white population, and compete with the white laborers for a living, or steal from those who have got property, to suit their tastes and wants.—Ohio would be the general resort of these freed blacks, as the laws of Indiana and Illinois do not favor their introduction there.

In behalf of the farmers, mechanics and day-laborers we protest against this interference with their peace, prosperity and manhood. The next movement would be to elevate them to the right of suffrage, and hence of office and honors as well as competitors for labor.

Our Legislature being in session, their attention should be called to this evil, and such enactments should be placed upon our statute books as would protect their constituents from this evil and degradation.

The public feeling is becoming more and more excited on this negro question, and it will not now be quieted until the whole subject is ventilated, not as a party question as heretofore, but as one of self defence and self preservation. The South will find before it is over that we are not Abolitionists nor in favor of negro equality. We may lie under that stigma now, but the people will not be satisfied with it, and will rebuke, at the first opportunity, the idea that this population of white men desire to interfere with master and slave, and much less do they favor having these negroes introduced into their midst without a master to take care of them and keep them out of their way.

[3] This was the second issue of the *Crisis*. The proprietor and editor, Samuel Medary, was a former governor of Kansas Territory and a former editor of the Columbus *Ohio Statesman*. He founded the *Crisis* for the purpose of helping to avert civil war or, failing in that, to urge its early termination.

The whole politics of the country have run into the negro business as though there were no white men left amongst us. It is time this subject had changed—and it is time also that the white man had become of some consequence in politics and legislation.

The negro philanthropists have got our country into a pretty predicament, and it now becomes white men to get it out, even if politicians have to be discarded entirely. Every day produces evidence that the people are becoming disgusted with negro rule on the stump and in legislative halls, and in churches, and in lecture rooms as well.—The cry of "free speech" will result in "free votes," and "free negroes" must give way to *free white men*.

What benefits have resulted to the white men or black men either, from this ocean of troubled waters? Injury to both, and a most sorrowful evil to the country.

Of what value is this population to Ohio when brought here? Has any town, city or neighborhood been benefitted [*sic*] by their introduction? They are a source of weakness to the State in every point of view in which their introduction can be considered. Has Columbus been improved in morals or industry? Has Xenia, in Greene county, since becoming a common depot for them, been elevated, or in any way improved, or the condition of society raised to a higher state of security and advancement? We think but very few would bear witness to such a result.

The evil is becoming one of great magnitude, and in the general disturbances and disintegration of the States, we have got to look into the whole subject in self-protection. It is of lasting importance to the working population, and they cannot overlook the consequences to themselves if this process of filling up the avenues of industry with such a population of a lower race, continues. Where they are held as slaves they are less prejudicial to the rights and interest of the laboring white man than when running at large with no one to take care of them and look after their material interests.

It is no longer what we may think of the abstract question of negro slavery, but it is what we think of ourselves and what we should do to protect and advance our own personal interests and welfare. To this shape it must come at last, and the responsibility will rest on those who have forced the people to investigate it, and to settle it. If it is a war of races, the superior race will very likely take care of itself.

We have no reason to blame Virginia for sending these manumitted slaves into our midst. They have reason to believe, from the speeches of the WADES, BINGHAMS, SHERMANS, GURLEYS, &c., in Congress, that the public sentiment of Ohio is in favor of their introduction, and they think they are doing a service to the blacks of Virginia and the whites of Ohio.

Our duty will be to undeceive them, and to protest against any such public sentiment here. Thousands if not tens of thousands voted the Republican ticket, who never intended any such a construction to be put upon their votes. They never dreamed of such a thing as a dissolution of the Union, or the introduction of hordes of free negroes into Ohio, as the consequence of electing Mr. LINCOLN to the Presidency, and they are not prepared to follow leaders any longer who either knew the consequence of their party organization and refused to tell it, or who were ignorant of the effects of their own doctrines. Either horn of the dilemma condemns them, and they may choose their point of defense.

We say they were not ignorant, that such men as Senator SEWARD did know that their success must lead to the sad consequences that are now passing before our eyes. That he did look to a division of these States into two confederacies as the end, if not the aim, of the triumph of his party, and that he in part, as far as it was prudent at the time, gave out dark inklings of such a result. [sic]

We learn that the Virginians who accompanied these manumitted slaves have purchased a farm on which to place them near Hilliard's station, in this county, on the Urbana railroad.

Since the above was in type we learn that 79 free negroes arrived about the same time at Zanesville, from North Carolina.—Ohio is thus rapidly increasing in population!

174. THE REASON WHY

(Philadelphia *Morning Pennsylvanian* [Breckinridge], February 9, 1861)

Great stress is laid, by the Republican party, upon the fact that the Border States are less sensitive to the aggressions of the North than the Cotton States, although the Border States lose ten fugitive or stolen slaves where the Cotton States lose one. That the non-fulfilment of the fugitive slave law and the enactment of personal liberty bills by the Northern States, most injuriously affect the Border States; and that, therefore, the extreme sensibility should be on the part of the Border States. From this, the Republican leaders attempt to draw the inference, that the earlier secession by the Cotton States, is for cause other than anti-slavery aggression. By such uncandid statements and arguments have the minds of many thousand honest men in the North been prejudiced. We propose to correct this great error.

If the non-execution of the fugitive slave law, or the operations of the under-ground railroad were the only causes of complaint, there would be great force in the charge against the Cotton States.

But we assert, most distinctly, that were these the only causes for complaint by the South, or were they the chief ones, then neither the Cotton States nor the Border States would find secession the only remedy. The greater sensibility of the Cotton States arises from the fact that the negroes form a larger proportion of their whole population than they do in the Border States; that while in these last every day diminishes the proportion of negroes, in the Cotton States this proportion menacingly increases. That the aggressive action of the free States in restricting slavery within the existing slave States, presents the following certain future to the Cotton States.

The negroes in their midst, already alarming to prudence, will be augmented not only by a natural increase, but also by the flow of those now in the Border States, while the white population will be steadily drained, until the submerging of the whites by the negroes would be their inevitable fate.

This differing condition of the border and cotton States is of itself sufficient cause for the greater sensibility and greater watchfulness of the latter.

Yet in addition to these causes, enough of themselves to render any people sensitive, there stand revealed other alarming causes.

A sectional party is formed upon principles which necessarily exclude all whose interests are in the slave States. This party has exclusive control of the government of every Northern State, including their treasuries and their militia organizations, as well as of the Federal Government, with its army and navy, and with a tenfold more numerous army of civilians, studded in every corner of the slave as of the free States, all moved by one harmonious power.

This most formidable party avows the purpose of forever excluding slaves from territory, thus putting the cotton States in a position in which the public mind will feel certain that the condition of the whites in those States will be an assured process of submersion by the blacks.

Besides which, the President elect has declared that slavery must be put where "the public mind will feel satisfied that it is in a process of extinction."

Governor SEWARD, his Premier, has said, that "the election of LINCOLN is the downfall of slavery." He also said in his speech on his return from Europe, that no man henceforth must be sent a minister to Europe who will dare to vindicate the slave States—none but their slanderers are to be sent to Europe. A slaveholder is by him in that speech degraded as an unfit and unworthy representative of his whole country. The HELPER book, which Gov. SEWARD, in his written letter says he has carefully read and approved, is made the text book of the party. WEED, GREELEY, MORGAN and others, in a special card, recommended the circulation of this book *in the free States, "as being morally certain to cause the passing away of slavery and the triumph of the Republican party in 1860."* Many hundred thousand copies of this book, the sum of all villainies, were most industriously circulated to poison the Northern mind. The immense sympathy shown by leading men and assemblages for JOHN BROWN. Senator WILSON, claiming to have slavery under the Republican heel, and the purpose to keep it there as long as there was a slave. LINCOLN bidding defiance to the DRED SCOTT decision; other leading men threatening to augment the Judges on the Supreme bench by men of a character, who will record as constitutional the infamous edicts of the Republican party.

The claim made to establish Abolition journals throughout the South, to bring about emancipation, and the right also, through the United States Post Office, to disseminate insurrectionary matter, and that the Republican Government would sustain the claim. SUMNER's "Barbarisms of Slavery," was also made a text-book, and as a reward and the expression of her approval of his sentiments, Massachusetts again elected him Senator.

Every man who received popular favor was eminent for bitterest denunciations of Southern Institutions; this and this alone was the passport to Republican favor. We might swell to a volume the teeming and conclusive evidence of a mortal hatred to the institutions and the people of the Cotton States, by the *dominant* portion of the Republican party, including its ferocious, infidel clergy.

When we can verge to a focus all the hostile actions and threats of the Republican party against slavery and slaveholders—and bear in mind that *this party, fairly in power, would have the ability to execute its threats*—there can be no cause of wonder for the extreme sensibility of the Cotton States and of their taking the earliest and most efficient means to escape the dreaded calamities. Too weak to contend in the Union with this Anti-slavery boa constrictor, their only chance of escape is in getting beyond its reach, or by the interposition of some Constitutional barrier sufficiently strong to stay it in its purpose until time shall remove these bitter prejudices and restore ancient kindly feeling. Let only such as in similar circumstances would act more coolly condemn the hot haste of secession.

175. Negro Mania

(Syracuse Daily Courier and Union [Breckinridge], March 1, 1861)

There have been madmen in all ages, who on most subjects have seemed to the casual observer sane, and yet when the right subject was touched, have at once developed this particular frenzy which affected them. One poor wretch is monarch by right divine, another imagines himself to be the Lord Jesus, and another is a teapot or other fragile piece of crockery in constant peril of being broken up: and still another has his head turned so that he no longer looks ahead, but backward. But in this day, all these and other curious developments of madness seem to be superseded by the negro mania with large classes of fanatical men. Do they talk about liberty? It is the liberty of the blacks they mean, reckless of consequences to the whites. Do they demand the preservation [of] the Union? It means not the preservation of a natural Union founded on mutual good will and mutual toleration of fixed diversities of opinion, but a forced Union to subjugate the white and enfranchise the negro. Sambo is to these monomaniacs the type and model of American manhood, and they can see nothing except as it falls within his shadow. Sambo is the alpha and omega of freedom! They cannot rest content with the negro mania themselves but insist in forcing it on those to whom it is utterly revolting. They flaunt it persistently before the eye of the country and proclaim to the world as to this their black frenzy—

> "There is a pleasure in being mad,
> That none but madmen know"—

Proclaim it, even while the whole country and the great mass of their fellow citizens are suffering under the severest afflictions the direct and perhaps necessary results of their mania!

Of what consequence is the freedom and happiness of eight millions, aye of even twenty six millions of Anglo Saxons, so long as four millions of blacks are in servitude? Of what consequence is it to them that the non-restriction of slavery in the territories could make not one slave the more; nor its restriction therein by Congress not one slave less? Is it not a high moral and religious and political principle which therefore must over ride the Constitution and the laws as settled by the constitutional tribunals? Filled with a love for Sambo as their specialty, shall they not, for freedom of opinion's sake deny to Southern men their constitutional rights in territories and over-ride in his behalf judicial decisions in favor of the slaveholder? While all men unite in demanding submission to the decisions of the Courts as to all questions which come before them affecting only the white man and his interests, are not opinions which involve the status of the black man, principles of an order so much higher than those affecting the whites, that they can neither be submitted to the decisions of Courts, nor otherwise in the least degree compromised? Is there not a special privilege in this government to negro-philists, to organize the government on the basis of their theories, and to administer it in conformity to negro-philist principles, setting aside and trampling under foot all laws, and all the most solemn decisions and constitutional provisions which conflict with their opinions? While denying to eight millions of people their adjudicated rights, if these people refuse to acknowledge a government guilty of this denial, shall not the whole people under the penalty of being denounced and hung as traitors be compelled to unite with these repudiators of Constitutional rights in denouncing and harassing, and subjugating to the negrophilist yoke the men who demand in or out of the Union conceded rights? Are not the latter worthy of blockades and a halter, the desolating fire and the destroying sword?—Are they not unworthy even of propositions of reasonable compromise as to matters supposed to be clearly decided in their favor, until they shall first on bended knee sue for the forgiveness of those who supercede [sic] laws by substituting their own dicta in the high places where laws once ruled? And shall they not first submit themselves unconditionally to an administration supposed to be pledged to overthrow the principles established in their favor by the Courts, to men pledged to make the very opposite of these principles the rule of the government?

We trust no Republican will censure us for following the illustrious example of their President elect in his Indianapolis speech, especially when like him, we declare that we merely ask these questions that the people may consider them and answer them for themselves, according to their own sober convictions; and further that it is not our purpose to express any opinion upon them one way or the other!

But let us do more than Mr. Lincoln condescends to do on that occasion. While waiving an expression of opinion as to those questions, we will not hesitate to speak plainly on another. It is well known that the opinions of the Republican party, as avowed by them in their platform, are in direct antagonism to the opinions, not alone of one party at the South but of the whole people. It is equally well known that while the former are supported by no law, and by no legal decisions, the latter point to the decisions of the Courts and demand our assent not to their will or their opinion, but to the rights established by the decision of that tribunal which adjudicates and settles all other contested questions. If the Republicans who supported Mr. Lincoln on the anti-slavery grounds of the Republican platform can not honorably recede from their position; still less can the Southern people recede with honor, not alone from their own opinions but from their rights, settled and confirmed as firmly as any rights can be by any mere human tribunal, as they believe. Such secession can perhaps be reasonably expected from neither; least of all from the South! There can then be no adjustment except on some neutral basis, which while evading an expression against either opinion, or compromising both, shall yet, if not entirely satisfactory to all, give reasonable satisfaction to the mass of moderate and reasonable men of all sections. They who fight against all compromise therefore fight against all conciliation, fight for an indefinite continuance of the present disasters; for subjugation and the sword, for carnage and civil war; for the extension of what they call rebellion; and are the real authors of disunion.

176. A Question Settling Itself

(Troy Daily Times [Lincoln], March 2, 1861)

One of the most gratifying features of existing affairs, is the advance toward the development of comity and good feeling shown by rival parties to the great dispute which agitates the country. In the earlier periods of a heated controversy, when only the bald points of difference are prominently obtruded, men are apt to give way to excitement, and cool decision is rendered impossible by the heat of passion. They see only one side of an argument; they discover only one road to an honest opinion; they know no logic which justifies conclusions variant from those at which they arrive—and, therefore, all who differ from them are very naturally treated as enemies. As discussion advances, the various considerations which modify prejudice and disarm hate, one after another present themselves and are recognized,—parties begin to discover that those who oppose them may be as honest if not as well informed as themselves,—and ultimately, save in the case of the more bigoted and unreasonable, there is a general settlement upon the basis of a candid but not malignant disagreement.

There is no good reason why this should not be the case. Upon their broad and liberal bases, our institutions can present no conflicts which may not be determined by dispassionate discussion, and in a spirit of forbearance. The party which first resorts to malignant denunciation and bitter invective,—or which, still worse, abandons the arbitrament of logic for that of force,—in the very fact concedes the weakness of its positions, and invites failure. A good cause never is strengthened by a bad advocacy. And in the genius and spirit of republican polity, the traditions of our history, the character of our institutions, there is nothing which warrants an application here of the strong arm which is a necessity of the enforcement of ideas in less favored countries.

A dispassionate survey of the field of our present disputes brings with it a weakening of the prejudices which give them force. It is very natural for us, in the light of unbroken free institutions, to regard Slavery as a sin, and so viewing it, to denounce as inhumane and ill-deserving all who have part or lot in its perpetuation. But research and observation soften these asperities. We begin to see that, with an institution planted in their midst—not by their act, but without their consent; nurtured under and growing up with it; learning to look upon it as a necessity of political and social existence,—they are not altogether to blame for dreading anything calculated to disturb it. We find that all slaveholders are not villains; that all slaves are not abused and degraded as whipped spaniels,—that but [sic] there are honest and honorable men, holding property in their fellow-beings, whom they treat with undeviating kindness and consideration.—We cease to denounce all the fears and jealousies the upholders of slavery exhibit, when we consider the precarious nature of their position, and remember how assiduously partizans in the Free States cultivate their apprehensions. While therefore, we cannot concede the rightfulness of Slavery; while we cannot submit to the policy that would elevate it to political supremacy, we can at least deal with moderation with those who regard it as vital to their existence—and concede to their ineradicable prejudices whatever is not inconsistent with our honor.

On the other hand, the honest advocates of Slavery cannot fail to perceive its inherent weaknesses and inevitable descent to disintegration, in the more Northerly States where it exists. There is a tendency to the development and advancement of free labor interests wherever climate is in favor of them. The inroad has been rapidly made, in Virginia, Tennessee, Kentucky, Missouri and Maryland. It cannot be restrained. The climate of Virginia is no more favorable to Slavery than that of Pennsylvania, nor is it more desirable for Missouri than for Kansas. Commercially, it is impossible that for a great many years, slaves can be held North of thirty-five degrees—for Slavery is after all a commercial institution, and governed solely by considerations of profit and loss.

There is a constant movement of black chattels from the border States Southward, and a certain and progressive addition to their free labor forces. Missouri is almost regenerated already. Take from Southern Virginia, Maryland and Tennessee the advantages of slave breeding for the exclusively cotton States, and emancipation would immediately find supporters, in men who are now the strongest advocates of Slavery.

We grant the conclusions that logically follow from these premises. If Slavery is unprofitable above the 35th degree, there is a belt below that point where it is almost the only system of labor that can be made remunerative. If a Virginia or Missouri grain-grower can hardly work a hundred negroes to such advantage as to make both ends meet in his yearly accounts, an Alabama cotton planter or a Louisiana sugar-grower will work the same gang, under all the risks and disadvantages of a destructive climate, and net a profit of from twenty-five to fifty thousand dollars. White men could raise cereals in Virginia and Tennessee under conditions that would amply repay them, and add immensely to the wealth of the States; put an Anglo-Saxon on a cotton or a sugar plantation, and he would die in a year. The great mischief is, then, that there is Africanization where such a system has no business to be. Negro labor is not profitable in the border States. None other but negro labor can be made to pay in the gulf States. Under the operation of natural laws, dispassionately applied, the question must therefore settle itself. The black ban which retards the growth of Delaware, Maryland, Virginia, Kentucky, Tennessee and Missouri will be removed; they are to become Free States. The servile negro population they contain will for most part be shifted Southward, into the cotton States, and as a consequence they will become more intensely Slave.

What then? Suppose this operation of natural laws tends to a perpetuation of an institution we dislike—what have we to do with it? Clearly, nothing at all. We may deplore the fact, but it will not be for us to fight it. The whole question will, the moment present differences are healed, be relegated to the people of the States, for them to settle it as they think best, in the light of their own interests, information and consciences. With their judgments, we will have nothing to do. We have no more business to interfere with Slavery in Mississippi, than Mississippi has to intermeddle with the prison system of New York. The institution is local, and is to be governed by local laws. It did not require a resolution by Congress to settle the principle that there shall be no attempt by Free States to disturb Slavery where it exists—for that was incorporated into the Chicago platform, and is inwrought with the groundwork of the Republican party. The little knot of fanatics who maintain an opposite doctrine, are of no consequence, save as their importance is for base purposes magnified at the South.

The whole struggle, then, grows out of an attempt to give Slavery a control of national politics, because its supporters fear, if it has not this, it will be forcibly overthrown. The moment this is determined, and the point settled that it is a local and domestic institution, neither to be aggrandized or abolished by national legislation, but left to work out its own destiny under the operation of natural laws, that moment the existing controversies will cease, and, undisturbed by hatreds, jealousies, and conflicting passions, we shall go on as a concordant and prosperous people, to work out the great accomplishments which they have so seriously interfered with. To this result, let all good citizens lend their energies; and meanwhile, let the anger and personal malignity which so often grow out of conflicting opinions, be discouraged as unworthy our national character, unworthy our hopes, unworthy our institutions, unworthy the high and magnificent destinies we can even now, in the early morning gleams that break upon our dark night of political discord, see opening before us.

177. Nigger Worship and Its Consequences

(New York Herald [Breckinridge], March 7, 1861)

In the midst of a momentous crisis like the present, when there is no knowing what calamity a day may bring forth, or how soon the grand fabric of our constitution will be swept away, and the arm of brother be raised against brother in deadly strife, it becomes us to ponder gravely over the dangers that surround us, and, as men and patriots, to combine in the endeavor to avert the worst of those evils by which our country is menaced. To the anti-slavery propagandism which forty years ago swayed so violently the people of England, and thence found its way into New England and the Congress of the United States, and was years afterwards nurtured so warmly by societies and a portion of the press, we may trace all the causes that distract the United States. It has ever been a prolific source of disturbances, riots, family feuds and national discord. It has led to scenes which have disgraced our halls of Congress. It has caused the proper objects of legislation to be neglected, and the general interests of the country to be injured and mismanaged, and by its pernicious agitation has engrossed the public mind to an extent that is positively lamentable.

From its inception to the present time the question has undergone three phases. In the first instance it was a moral one; provoked by discussion and prejudice in England; in the next it was a social one, induced by the Northern States finding slave labor unprofitable, and, therefore, wishing to abolish it; and, in the third, it was a politico-religious one, which we may call "nigger worship." In this last phase we find it now. It has become a pulpit theme, and diverted the stream of religion from its course heavenward to the stormy sea of politics. We have a prominent example of it in the case of Ward Beecher. It has ruined churches, ruined parties, and now it is ruining the whole country. Anti-slavery fanaticism has stamped its character upon our Northern literature, and led away the minds of those who had not philosophy enough to withstand its subtle influence, which, for the thirty years of the forty it has been in agitation, has been gradually undermining the constitution of the republic and the best interests and liberties of our people.

With the secession of seven States, and the prospect of the eight Border States adding to the number, it may be said to have reached its culminating point. What will follow is uncertain as the wind, and it would be rash to hazard a conjecture on the subject. It may be the secession of the remaining slave States, and mayhap civil war. But the worst consequences staring abolitionists in the face would not turn one out of a thousand of them from their fatal purpose; for fanatics are deaf to reason, and, like the English Crusaders to the Holy Land, have only a single object to accomplish, and that whatever may be the sacrifice. The disruption of the Union is not enough for these men; they want blood, and they would callously exterminate every slaveholder, from Virginia to Florida, in order to realize their favorite, and we may add fiendish, purpose. And what is the actual condition of the slaves over which these rampant abolitionists are howling so insanely? Let them go down to the Southern States and look at the four millions of negroes they will find there, and see whether they are the ill cared for, abject creatures that they would make the Northerners believe. Let them remember that, at the time of the Revolution, the colored population of the same States amounted to less than an eighth part of what it is at present. The very fact of the immense increase of numbers within so short a time speaks for the good treatment and happy, contented lot of the slaves. They are comfortably fed, housed and clothed, and seldom or never overworked. They present in their condition a favorable contrast to the white slaves of Europe, who live in the utmost squalor, and are at once half-starved and overworked, and who only find rest in premature graves. Their condition is a far happier one than that of many of the white poor of the North, who are driven to seek refuge from want in the workhouses, or yet of many even outside of their walls, who vegetate in filth and hunger in the obscure parts of our cities. The heartrending accounts which are occasionally given to the English public of the miseries endured by the London poor show a far more deplorable state of things than could ever exist under slavery in America; and English travellers who have taken the trouble of inquiring, by personal observation, into the state of the slaves in the South, have acknowledged in print the superior comforts enjoyed by the latter over the white slaves of England. What the Garrisons and Phillipses, who pronounce the constitution "an agreement with death and a covenant with hell," may do next is more than man can tell; but they may rest assured that their fanaticism, although it may destroy the Union, will also destroy them. All that we pray for is that we may be spared the horrors of civil war.

178. The Great Controversy—Its Settlement

(Philadelphia Inquirer [Independent], March 11, 1861)

The question of the capability of the negro race for personal or political freedom among us is not solved, nor in any degree relieved by the case of Hayti, or the British West Indies. Hayti lies in the torrid zone, the proper residence of the negro. It never was, nor ever can be, at once under the political dominion and in the complete or available occupancy of the white races. France could hold it by the force of arms, she could garrison it, but she could not colonize, or, in any proper sense, occupy it. The political and personal liberty of the blacks there, is no more to the question of their enfranchisement here, than it is in Central Africa. As to the West Indies, they are there in a state of pupilage or wardship under the British Government, and the whites are not in strife with them for the occupancy of the country and the conduct of its municipal affairs. In all the British West Indies, at the time of their emancipation, the whites numbered about fifty thousand to eight hundred thousand colored inhabitants. The slave system in the Islands had so far failed that it became necessary to abandon it as an economic policy. Nineteen out of the twenty millions of pounds sterling given to the masters in compensation for the loss of their slave property, went to the payment of their debts in England! They were bankrupt, and nothing could be done with the Islands but put them to the trial of their fortunes as African states or provinces, under the care and protection of the superior race. The British hold of them now is only a political protectorate, and an absentee landlordism. Both Hayti and the West Indies are within the tropics. White men can get no home there, and no other dominion than that of foreign force. But our Cotton States are only semi-tropical; their white population is greatly in the majority numerically. They can, in the fullest sense of the word, occupy the domain, though they cannot cultivate its fields. Our question is, therefore, a different one from that which the islands are quoted to solve for us. Here it is:—Can the negro race enjoy our form of freedom in the presence, and consistently with the welfare of the white population? In our Southern States the staple products are those which require the unskilled labor of the negro. The whites occupy them for no other purpose than to avail themselves of such labor. They intend no such diversification of productive industry as Europeans in the temperate climates pursue. Cotton, rice, tobacco, and sugar, as objects of commerce, up to the quantity and value which gives them wealth and prosperity, will not be abandoned except under compulsion—such compulsion as would be a catastrophe to six millions of whites and four millions of blacks; and is, therefore, among the things improbable and inexpedient, and even impracticable as an enterprise, in the present state of things; for we must remember that the settlement of this question according to the project of the philanthropists, involves the Africanization of the country, the expulsion of the white population, and all the risks to the world's business that there is [sic] in negro self-government there, as well as the risks to themselves.

Thinking men must pause upon the fact that in the Free States, where the number of free colored people does not amount to the ratio of paupers to population in most civilized countries, the destiny of these people is not yet settled, or the disposal of them determined. They are not admitted in[to] the government or into society. As they have increased in numbers so as to press their presence and influence upon consideration, they have been politically disfranchised by those States which once, by mere neglect or oversight, allowed them some participation in our political privileges.

Freedom in the present age means, not only *self-government,* but an equal share in the government of the whole community—the government of others. The people of the Northern States do not invest the negroes among them with this power, but, as they are very inconsiderable in point of numbers, find no difficulty in governing them. It might not be expedient or safe to reserve the right of political mastership over four millions of emancipated men, leaving them free and irresponsible in the conduct of their material and personal affairs, with the whites at the same time dependent upon their industry for the wealth-producing power of the country. The peace and prosperity of States demands, not only harmony between the employers and the employed, the capitalist and the laborer, but requires besides, such a spirit of enterprise, and such a capacity and ambition for their own prosperity in the laborers as shall answer the demand upon them for productive labor. If these millions were held at wages no larger than the expenses of their keep, would they freely produce cotton enough to sustain the cultivation? And if they could, by exercise of their liberty, compel the rates of wages that freemen require, would the profit of its culture sustain the enterprise? Can these people be induced to work in freedom to the measure and effect required to keep the business in prosperity? If these questions must be answered in the negative, emancipation implies an industrial and economic revolution, with the wreck of the fortunes and callings of the white population—in a word, a surrender of the country, below the line of north latitude, thirty-five degrees, to the African race.

The impracticability of such a project is settled already by the dissolution of the Union upon a mere alarm that it is to be attempted. And to meet and allay that alarm the party suspected of the purpose has already disavowed it. It is not among the things allowable or feasable [sic], and ought not to have a feather's weight of influence upon our conduct, or objects in any principle or policy of our national conduct. The idea must no more color our administration of the Territories capable of, and requiring African labor, than in the States where it is acknowledged to be beyond our jurisdiction; for, whatever makes non-interference right in regard to the sovereign States, applies with equal force to the public domain, which falls within the reason of the rule. The mere possession of force for the disposal of a question does not carry with it the right or the responsibility of exercising it. The reason of the thing must rule it.

For conclusive authorities in support of our doctrine, so far as such authorities apply to the construction of the constitutional rights and duties of the Federal Union upon this matter, we may quote President LINCOLN. To the question, "May Congress prohibit slavery in the Territories?" he answers:—"The Constitution does not expressly say." But he has been anticipated by the party of which he has become the exponent. On the MONTGOMERY-CRITTENDEN amendment to the Kansas act, every Republican in the House voted to admit that State into the Union with or without slavery in its Constitution; and at the session just closed, the same party passed three territorial bills, without inserting the prohibitory proviso. In practice, as in principle, the doctrine is abandoned, upon the clear conviction that it settles itself without, and even in defiance of, national legislation, as to all the public domain clearly above that line of climate which appropriates the earth to its varied industries, the same overruling law as obviously applies to all the regions unquestionably below that line. The rule of non-interference by positive legislation rests upon the same reason equally in both cases, and is tacitly conceded and practically obeyed. But the uncertain belt of country which lies between these plainly distinguished divisions is in doubt. That doubt of itself should determine us to let natural causes decide it, for the doubt shakes at once the duty, the responsibility and the practicability, while it proves the inexpediency of assuming them. But the principle admitted in the government of the far North and far South territories, applies just as well to the intermediate domain. It commands us to remit the whole matter to the operation of the natural causes which must decide it. Principle and prudence both allow us to anticipate the issue, wherever that is known, and by agreement, called compromise, put all that is clear and certain out of dispute; and every consideration which should have place in the settlement of the great strife requires from us an equally explicit and binding agreement, to abstain from all controversy about that portion of the common property whose destiny is still uncertain.

We will not detain our readers with a resumé of the points presented and argued in the five articles which we have devoted to this subject. They lead us to an entire agreement with the resolutions of the Peace Conference; and we trust that the country will be speedily composed by a virtual adoption of them in the settlement of the great controversy which is now trying our capacity for republican government, with all our interests and hopes involved in the issue.

179. The Niggerism of the Secession Movement

(Cincinnati Daily Commercial [Lincoln], March 16, 1861)

The influence of the negroes of the South upon their masters is much greater than is generally understood, and appears in many traits of character, and in customs, social and civil, where we are not accustomed to give it recognition. The intimacy of the association between the whites and blacks in the slave States, the sensibility that exists among them as to mutual interests, and the interchange of sympathies between them, are not appreciated fully in the Northern States. The analyst of the phenomena of Southern Society, will find a remarkable vindication of the humanity and force of the negro race in the impress which the slaves make upon their masters. While the distinctions that we find marked between the white men of the South, and of the North, are not altogether to be attributed to the permeating presence of the negro in one section, and his comparative absence from, and isolation in the other,—much being due climatic influences, and much more, aside from the relation of races, to the relation of slavery—we will find, after the most cautious discrimination, the African elements of character appearing largely among the whites, who are brought into the closest contact with Africans. Men cannot be associated on any terms, without reciprocating influences. The slave imitates his master, and wears his manners as well as his clothes, at second hand; and the master, notwithstanding the superiority of his will and mental force, receives from the slaves, who in their humble capacity, are his play fellows in childhood, and his companions in manhood, impressions that give coloring to his character, and shape his life, as certainly as the Southern sun embrowns his complexion.

It has not escaped any intelligent person's observation that even the best educated Southerners have something of the African accent and dialect. We have heard Southern members of Congress, when it would be difficult to decide by the sound, whether the speaker was a white man or a negro. There is something too of Tropical taste displayed in dress by the Southern people. There are more bright colors in apparel, and richness of ornament, seen in the South than in the North. A New York merchant sending dry goods to be sold on commission to Southern and Northern points, would select a larger proportion of glittering patterns for the South than for the North. In Southern newspapers we find even greater intensity of style than in the sensation sheets of the North; and there are more fantastic and grandiloquent figurative efforts and a greater exhuberance [sic] of adjectives, in Southern speeches and editorials than in the Northern staples of that sort. This is especially true of the speeches of rural politicians and the writings of the editors of newspapers published in villages. In accounting for these things, while we should not forget the temperament induced by the Southern sun, we must not overlook the part of the sons of Africa in popular education.

It was, however, left for the secession movement to show the negroism of the politics of the extreme States and the extreme politicians of the South. The strained dignity and vainglorious sensitiveness of South Carolina, have an unmistakable flavor of the ragged pomp of Hayti; and the boasted revolution in the seven cotton States, bears far more resemblance to a negro insurrection than to the revolt of the thirteen American colonies, with which it is so complacently compared. It is unlike a servile revolt because there are no disabilities that would be removed by a success. But there is a want of foresight, an improvidence, an incapacity to understand the plainest relations of things—a dim, giddy notion that a pyramid should stand upon its apex—illustrated in the history of secession, that is glaringly African. The idea of rushing out of the Union to secure slave property—of making mighty war and conquering the cities of the North—of seizing the forts of New England and thence commanding the seas—of conquering Mexico, Central America and the West India Islands;—the policy of taking empty forts by storm —of incurring enormous expenses now borne by the Federal Government in protecting the frontiers, and furnishing postal facilities—of expelling from their communities all whose opinions do not square with their own;—the fussy war excitement when there is no danger—the financial policy of getting rich by becoming bankrupts—the cultivation of fierce, clannish local prejudices—the presumption that each particular spot of cotton soil is the center of gravity of the commercial world— the oracular and pretended original statement of crude and silly theories of government and political economy, exploded by the experience of mankind centuries ago;—the taste displayed in banners bearing crescent moons, snakes, trees, and other strange devices—these things point to Congo as the Father land. There are no terms in which the spirit and form, history and philosophy of the secession movement are so well condensed, as to say that it is an outbreak of *niggerism*.

180. What Shall Be Done for Them?

(Philadelphia *Public Ledger* [Independent], March 27, 1861)

However much the general condition of the free people of color in the United States may have been ameliorated, yet there exists a constant tendency to withdraw the few privileges heretofore accorded them. Many evidences of harsh legislation have occurred during the past winter illustrating this same tendency. The Legislature of Kentucky passed a law, which stipulates that no slave shall hereafter be emancipated, unless removed from its limits; and any free person of color entering the State shall be liable to an imprisonment for not less than one, or more than five years. A bill passed the Georgia Legislature, which provides that every free person of color found therein after the first of May, 1862, shall be liable to seizure and sale as slaves [*sic*] for life. The Governor of Delaware recommended the repeal of the law of 1855, allowing this class in Maryland to remove and reside in New Castle and

Kent counties, in that State; and the Legislature enacted that any free person of color may be sold to the highest bidder for debt. The same element of population in Alabama have been warned to leave at once, or submit to extreme measures. The City Councils of Charleston, S. C., have so heavily taxed the free colored people of that city, as must speedily result in universal abject poverty or their sale into slavery.

Thousands of these people will flock to the North for shelter and the means of living. How will they be received? Their brethren are very generally refused a fundamental right of freemen—that of voting for their rulers. Several States either forbid their acquiring and holding property, or prohibit their entrance and residence by severe penalties. Even in Ohio, an effort was made to move the Legislature to expel such of the Arkansas exiles as took up their abode in that State, and to prevent the admission of other such unfortunates. With this popular feeling existing and likely to exist, this increasing element of population can find no encouragement to regard this country as a permanent residence. Hence, the friends of the Colonization Society propose their settlement in Liberia, not because unfriendly to their improvement here, but because it appears certain that it is neither in the power of benevolence or legislation to remove their disabilities, and to save them from influences which must repress hope and weaken exertion. Causes will operate there to develope the talents, invigorate the faculties, and dignify their purposes. There they will not be depressed by the consideration of their past condition, and by the presence of another race of superior powers and attainments.

Upon this high and unexceptionable ground, the wise, the patriotic and religious of every portion of the Union may cordially unite. The citizens, the States, and the General Government can join in its intent upon accomplishing a great and good end by virtuous means. The latter is estimated to have appropriated to help the Indians in this country $200,000,000 within the last thirty years. These disbursements have arisen now to over $5,000,000 annually. If Congress can thus constitutionally grant money to remove and settle the Indians, why can it not pursue the same course for the Africans? The people of color are beginning to appreciate the fact that invaluable as freedom is to others, it is comparatively of little value to them. They are looking to Africa as their ultimate home, and where the whites will be dependent upon them for missionary and commercial agencies. One hundred and eight of the colored residents of Pennsylvania were colonized in Liberia during the years 1859 and 1860, and as large a number are now desirous of sharing in the same bounty. Let all aid the Colonization Society in the settlement of these people in that Republic. Help will be required only until the commerce which is rapidly growing between Africa and this country will furnish facilities for the same emigration from America to Africa, that is now taking place between Europe and this continent.

181. The Effect of the Present Revolution upon Slavery in the United States

(Paris (Maine) *Oxford Democrat* [Independent], April 26, 1861)

We are in the midst of a revolution, and that revolution has been caused by the institution of slavery. It is a struggle on the part of its advocates to perpetuate it. What logical results will follow this conflict? This is an important question for the North, but a more important one for the South. We start with this proposition, that whatever settlement may be made between the two sections, the final abolition of slavery will be hastened by the movement.

A re-construction of the government, giving slavery new guaranties, as contended for now, by which the cotton States would be brought back, would do more than any other settlement that could be made to strengthen and perpetuate the curse. If the cotton States undertake to maintain their own independence without the border slave States, their new confederacy will inevitably be the scene of numerous slave insurrections, and these will increase from year to year, until a large standing army will be required to protect them from violence from their negroes. If the border States remain in the Union and the cotton States stay out, the latter will re-open the foreign slave trade and ruin the domestic traffic in slaves, raised in the former. If the border States go out, Mason and Dixon's line will hereafter be the Canada line, between freedom and slavery. The constitutional provision for the rendition of slaves will become a dead letter. The moment their slaves step into a free State they will be free, and no power can carry them back except mob violence, and that would not be permitted by the general government.

The cotton States, as between them and the border States, in one confederacy, will have the control. The foreign trade in negroes will be opened, and negroes raised in Virginia, formerly worth from eight to fifteen hundred dollars, will be reduced down to two hundred. This will ruin slavery in the border States, and ruin the slaveholders themselves. Its operation will be the extinction of slavery from a direful necessity, for slave *labor* in the border States alone can never keep the institution in running order a single year.

Another thing, slavery will be hemmed in. There will be no new territory outside the States to give it expansion. Girdle it and it will die out. The new confederacy will be cut off from the acquisition of foreign territory. If it makes war on Mexico to acquire new territory, it will fail, because our government will interfere to prevent any such negro stealing, fillibustering [sic] operations.

Slavery in the border States *out* of the Union, would be an uncertain institution. Negro insurrections will be common occurrences, and will finally settle down into a reign of terror. The Southern Confederacy will be hated and despised by every civilized government upon the earth. Barbarism would be its chief corner stone. Its whole basis would be a magazine of death, liable to be touched off by any John Brown or Nat Turner that has the courage to apply the fuse. Say what you will, the general government is the great protection of slavery in this country. A separation, on a line dividing the free from the slave States, will be the greatest agency that can be brought into existence to extinguish slavery in the United States. We therefore come to this conclusion, that a confederacy composed of the cotton States will hasten the abolition of slavery; that a confederacy, embracing *all* the slave States, will utterly work out its entire extinguishment in a few years.

What will become of the African race in this country, who in such a contingency will escape from their masters, or who may gain their liberty by insurrections or otherwise, is a question not legitimately belonging to this discussion. We may speak of it hereafter at length.

182. THE PINE AND PALM

(Boston and New York *Pine and Palm,* May 18, 1861) [4]

This journal will be devoted to the interests of freedom, and of the colored races in America.

It will seek to array against Slavery, and the prejudices it has engendered, not the moral powers exclusively, but the physical forces of the age.

It will advocate action, rather than the promulgation of ideas.

It will expound a programme of associated action, having for its chief object the complete and abiding triumph of the Democratic Idea on this

[4] The issue of this date is marked as follows: New Series Volume I Number 1 Whole Number 96. There appears, however, to be no extant earlier issue; Gregory, *Union List of Newspapers,* lists none. The *Pine and Palm* is here included because its surviving files, unlike those of the *Liberator* and *National Anti-Slavery Standard,* are rare and incomplete. The Boston Public Library has a copy of the issue of May 18 and Gregory indicates that there are possibly two other copies in the United States. The proprietor and principal editor of the *Pine and Palm,* James Redpath, was a well-known English abolitionist.

Continent, and its Islands; and, with it, the elevation of the colored races inhabiting America, to a position of perfect social, political and National Equality and Power with the whites.

This programme will embrace:

I. The immediate eradication of slavery from the soil of the United States, by the authority of the Federal Government; or, failing in that, by John Brown expeditions, and simultaneous and extended Negro Insurrections.

II. The calling of a National Convention for the revision of the Federal Constitution, to place it unmistakeably [sic] and forever on the side of freedom; to erase from it its lingering remnants of royalist ideas; to enable the North to share the taxation and new duties, (as they have shared the guilt and the folly of Slavery,) which must necessarily result from a forced emancipation; and, finally, believing that the people of the Cotton States east of the Mississippi are, in every essential respect, a different and hostile nation to us, to take measures for their temporary secession from the Union, *after* the abolition of Slavery in their Territory; that is to say, if by a fair vote, their inhabitants shall decide, as we believe they would decide, in favor of an independent Government.

III. A Union with the British North American Provinces.

IV. The establishment of two Tropical Confederacies—the first to be organized by a union of the West India Islands; the second, by the colonization of Central America by the whites of the North, and the blacks of the country.

V. The promotion of the material unity of the North, by an enlightened and continental system of internal improvement.

VI. The destruction of political corruption by the withdrawal of the other than protectoral powers of the Federal Government; by the establishment of absolute free trade, and the substitution of direct taxation; and by the abolition of all manner of exclusive privileges, by which, under the fallacious hope of relieving labor, a monied aristocracy is rising in America, threatening the purity of its democracy, and extinguishing the aspirations to which free institutions give birth.

—As a preliminary series of measures aiming at these results, THE PINE AND PALM will advocate—

The building up of Hayti, by an enlightened and organized emigration, into the rank of a great American Power. We hold this measure to be now essential for the dignity of the African race and its descendants wherever they exist. The foundation of respect is *power*. As long as the negro is everywhere a subordinate, he will nowhere be treated as the equal of races which are "lords of human kind." Right or wrong, this is the fact; and practical minds must act in view of it. What, then, is to be done? *We must create a great Negro Nation.* Where? Hayti alone affords us a foundation near enough to influence Slavery and its brood of prejudices here, broad enough to establish a nationality of the necessary importance and durability there.

Let us not be misunderstood. We do not believe in a distinctive Nationality, founded on the preservation of any race, as a *finality.* We believe in Humanity, not in Black men or White men; for the fusion of the human races is the destiny of the future. We stand by man as man; not by the Saxon because we are Saxon; nor by the Negro because we are an Abolitionist. What we assert, as our belief, is this only—that, at this stage of the world's progress, the fact of a powerful Negro Nation is a lesson imperatively needed in order that the African race, wherever it exists, may be respected as the natural equal of other families of man. We do not believe that the inculcation of the doctrine of fraternity alone will accomplish this result; for without a physical basis, this class of truths require centuries for their universal acceptance.

The rapid physical development of our tropical regions, (which includes the West Indies and Central America) is necessary for another reason: because there alone can American free labor be brought into competition with the slave system of our Southern States. As long as the Cotton States supply England, Old and New, with their great manufacturing staples, just so long will they hold a mortgage on the votes, the pulpits, the presses and the consciences of Englishmen and Yankees. Thus the shadow of the whipping post of Charleston is often seen in the streets of London—oftener still in the factories of Manchester and the counting rooms of Liverpool. In our North, alas! it forms everywhere the sable cloud which obscures from our souls the rays of the sun of fraternal truth.

The recognition of the Confederate States might partly, but it would never wholly, drive this cloud away. *We must create other Southern Confederacies to save us from the cotton-growing and conscience-eating conspiracy of our bottomless-Gulf States.* Let us colonize the fair West India Islands and the rich regions of Central America, and make Cotton, not a tyrannical King, but a democratic Priest; let us call up, from their exhaustless fertility, cotton enough to clothe all the world in the robes of freedom, and sugar enough to sweeten the other products of the earth, without clarifying it in the blood of the Negro, or drying it with the sighs of the broken-hearted bond-mother.

This policy, of course, involves the expulsion of the Spaniards from America. They have long enough corrupted and blood-be-smeared our soil—sacred soil set apart by the Divine Father for Democracy and Fraternity. At any cost of blood and treasure, this pitiless people should be banished.

—To carry out this programme, we elect Fraternity as our Representative Idea. Henceforth, as equals, in harmonious union, the white and black races must work together, remembering their origin only to provoke emulation in effort, and in willing self-abnegation.

Yet we will not forget that, while the creation of a great Negro Commonwealth in the Antilles is necessary for the elevation of the African race here, and while the formation, also, of free tropical Confederacies is indispensable for the arraying of the physical forces of freedom against physical slavery, there is a higher possibility for humanity still—to which the world is tending, which America must inaugurate—THE COSMOPOLITAN GOVERNMENT OF THE FUTURE, which, superceding [sic] Nationalities and rendering war unnecessary, shall establish and secure forever, the "reign of peace on earth and good will to men."

—Our policy, therefore, is Continental in its scope—it embraces both the North and the South—the Arctic regions and the Torrid Zone—the land of THE PINE AND PALM.

JAMES REDPATH.

XI

THE MORALITY OF SLAVERY

183. "The Equality of the States, and the Equality of White Men"

(Concord (N. H.) *Democratic Standard* [Breckinridge], September 8, 1860)

We take for the text of this article an expression contained in the able letter from our Portland correspondent published in our issue of last week. It contains in a nut-shell, the political axiom upon which the democratic superstructure should be raised.

There are few who will not, in terms, assent to the first proposition which it enunciates. Whatever may be the practical action of politicians and parties in this country, none dares to affirm that the sovereign States constituting this Union, are not equal in dignity, power, and privilege, under the constitution. That proposition is admitted by all in the abstract, although denied and trampled upon in practical policy and action. When the people of one portion of the States assume to sit in judgment upon the institutions of another portion, it is denied and trampled upon. When they undertake to say that the various objects which *they* define to be property, shall be recognized as sacred and entitled to protection in the domains of the Union, and other objects defined to be property by another portion of the States, shall not be so regarded, and shall not be entitled to protection in the domains of the Union, they again deny and trample upon the proposition. Thus they violate the spirit of the constitution, and assault and invade the rights, powers, privileges, and dignity of their sister States.

The people also of one portion of the States, we mean, of the North, are guilty of an error equally great in their practical denial of the second proposition of the axiom which stands at the head of our article, viz: The Equality of *white* men; or rather, the Superiority of white men over black men. And in this error is to be found the cause of the present dissensions which agitate the people of this Republic; and of the great peril which impends over the Union.

We cannot blink out of sight the fact, that a great portion of the people of the North actually believe, that the negro is by nature the equal of the white man. The entire Republican Party so believe; and a good proportion of the Democratic Party supporting the heresy of Squatter Sovereignty, have been deluded into the same error.

To us, the proposition that the negro is equal by nature, physically and mentally, to the white man, seems to be so absurd and preposterous, that we cannot conceive how it can be entertained by any intelligent and rational white man. The facts of nature and history contradict the assumption of the equality of races. In form, in physical structure, in mental development, there appears to be a wide distinction between the different races of mankind. The Caucasian, or white man, in beauty of person, and in mental power, stands pre-eminently above all the other races of the earth. It is he who subdues all and controls all. It is he who is the pioneer of civilization,—who is ever progressive in art, and in government. He is ever advancing toward the solution of the problem of perfect civil liberty. He is the great interpreter of nature, the high priest of science. He is everywhere the architect and improver, ever enlarging the boundaries of human comforts and enjoyments.

The same cannot be affirmed of the inferior races of men. They remain stationary in barbarism, or ascend to an inferior civilization, and there they stop. The Chinese, the Japanese, and Hindoo races, have reached the acme of their civilization, and there they remain. In contact with the white man, they and their systems succumb and fall. That is their inevitable destiny.

The disparity between the negro and the white man, is still more obvious and striking. The normal state of the negro is barbarism of the most abject kind. Left to himself, all history shows, that he cannot rise above his normal state. Aided by the white man, and only through the medium of slavery, he becomes partially civilized and Christianized. He is the parasite man, and cannot flourish except in a state of dependence upon, and in subjection to, the white man. He is the mere infant of the human family, ever needing nurture, restraint, and correction. Hence, in all ages and countries, he has been the servant and slave, suffering the most cruel and revolting slavery among his own kith and kin. Rescued from the barbarism of his own home, his condition is immensely improved and ameliorated by his connection with the white man in the relation of a slave. If he ever appears in the anomalous and unnatural condition of a "free negro," he is still under the dominion of the white man—still controlled and restrained by the surrounding circumstances of civilized life. Without the restraints and discipline of the master, or of the superior civilization of the white man surrounding him, he would quickly relapse into barbarism.

And nature recognizes and proclaims this distinction between the white and black man,—the superiority of the one, and the inferiority of the other,—even in the configuration of countries and the differences of climate. The white man cannot endure the hot sun and the sickening miasma of the tropics. The black man is peculiarly adapted to those regions. He can live there and flourish. He can snuff its pestilence, and eat its spontaneous fruits, and grow fat. But, being a mere sensualist, after supplying his physical wants, he has no more aspirations for the higher and better life than the wild beasts which dispute with him the dominion of the forest and the desert. Therefore, under his dominion, the warm regions of the earth would forever remain in a state of nature. Their rich products, which so greatly administer to the comforts and luxuries of mankind, would never be evoked from the fertile bosom of the earth. Therefore it is necessary, in order that the warm regions of the earth, should be subdued, and made available to the wants of man, that the intellect and the energy of the white man, should be connected with the physical powers of the black man. And this union can be effected only by the establishment of the relation of master and servant, on a basis which would enable the master at all times, to control the labor of his servants. In other words, by slavery, if that term better defines such a relation.

Such is the relation which exists between the white man and black man, in the Southern States of the Union. And that relation lies at the basis of the civilization and prosperity of the South. Nay, its beneficial influences are felt at the North, indeed, throughout the civilized world. Without it the rich fields of the South, devoted to the production of sugar, cotton, rice &c., would again relapse into swamps and wilderness, and become the haunts of reptiles and wild beasts. Without slavery at the South, the North would lose half its prosperity. The immense interests founded on cotton, employing the industry of vast numbers of human beings covering the ocean with commerce, supplying wealth and revenue to empires, and contributing to the comforts of millions upon millions of human beings,—would all be annihilated. Such would be the results if slavery in the South were to be abolished, by the action of abolitionism operating in the open and direct form of Garrisonianism, or under the more specious guise of squatter sovereignty.

And why should rational men exercise themselves so much about slavery,—should display so much unnecessary sympathy for the "poor negro?" What is slavery? It is only a modified restraint or coercion. In the absolute sense no man is free. The master himself is not free. The father of the family is not free. The wife, the children, the servants, are not free. All have duties and obligations to observe and to perform. All, indeed, are dependent. There is no relation between human beings, in which there are not mutual duties, obligations, and dependence, on both sides. In the great system of social order, established by God himself, this is decreed. No man is absolutely free. No man is a sovereign even in a pure democracy, except jointly with his fellows, and in subordination to the State. No man can disconnect himself from the social compact, or community. Subordination is the fixed and inexorable destiny of every human being, and he cannot escape from it.

Subordination in the relations of life, exists in every community of human beings. God has impressed this fact upon the nature of things, as he has the law of gravitation. Subordination, which implies the superior and the inferior, power and submission, has existed in every community throughout all time. It was established in the polity of the Hebrews by the direct command of the Supreme Being, even in the form of *perpetual slavery*. And it will ever be so. The superior intellect will ever control the inferior. The superior man will ever control and coerce the inferior man. The Oriental will have to succumb to the European. The negro, while in contact with the white man, will be the slave of the latter in some form or other. And this very fact that the superior man will control the inferior, that the superior race will control the inferior,—lies at the basis of the industry, commerce, and prosperity of nations, and the advancement of civilization. He, who in the pursuit of the Utopian idea of absolute individual liberty, or absolute equality of races, would attempt to subvert this state of things, is a fool and madman. He can never accomplish his purpose.

Let us then, meet this great question of slavery just as it should be met, on the ground of philosophy and reason. It is the true way for the politician and statesman to treat it. The ignoramus, and the demagogue, only take a different view of it. Let the wisdom and intelligence of the North enlighten the one, and crush out the other. Then will come peace and tranquillity to the country, and not before.

184. Position of the Black Race

(*Boston Daily Courier* [Bell], September 24, 1860)

The paradox of our Declaration of Independence, that all men are born free and equal, has obtained such firm possession of the American mind, that it seems to many of us absolute blasphemy to contradict or even to doubt it. We do not feel bound, however, to ignore altogether the instincts of our organization, the observations of our experience, and the convictions of our understanding, and bow in submission to the authority even of the signers of the Declaration, upon a superfluous assertion of theirs in morals and politics. It is quite as much a matter of conscience with us to dispute the dictum, as it was with them to make it, and we think we can make the truth evident to the common understanding, if we only have time and space enough given us to accomplish such an achievement. We do not propose to enter upon that discussion to-day. We will simply suggest one or two hints for consideration, and reserve our arguments upon the subject for a separate and elaborate treatise.

We amalgamate all white races, however distinct, well enough with our own original English race. Numerous instances are known to everybody of the successful union of the Celtic and the German varieties of the *genus homo* without the slightest injury, but rather with decided and great benefit. The animal man is certainly improved by the combination. Far otherwise is it, however, with the African. Mixture of blood with that race does not improve the species. On the contrary, we believe the mulatto to be inferior in capacity, character, and organization, to the full-blooded black, and still farther below the standard of the white races. Amalgamation cannot be effected, therefore, except at the cost of a depreciation of the character of the Caucasian man. And we hazard little in predicting that no amalgamation will ever take place. The small extent to which a breed between the two races has been produced thus far, is sufficient evidence, one would think, that a general mixture is utterly improbable, as well as undesirable. A most pertinent question to be put to the Abolitionist, then, is, "What do you propose to do with the African, when he is freed from his bonds?" If he is left to obtain a subsistence by labor, with no one to direct it, he will soon perish, except in that climate, and in those fertile regions adapted by Providence to precisely his organization. It seems to be imagined by the generous, philanthropic, wise and considerate Abolitionist, that the negro is endowed with the same love of freedom, the same ambition of distinction, the same passion for haranguing his fellow mortals, that is so conspicuous in that single-hearted band of brothers. Unhappily for the theory, but happily for the race, these motives are all wanting in the black man, at least to the extent and with the power they exert over the white man. A trace, as the chemists call an immeasurably small amount of a substance, may be found in their constitutions, of ambition, or of enterprise; but a glance at the condition of Hayti, or Jamaica, where they have had all their own way for a quarter to a half century, is quite sufficient to exhibit with unmistakable distinctness the difference between the white man and the black.

It appears, then, that neither will they mix, so as to become one race with the whites, nor have they the power to compete with the Caucasian blood. It is sufficiently obvious, therefore, that the answer to the question, what is to be done with them, is not an easy one; that it is not for us to say to our brother, you *shall do* thus and so with your negroes. We know as little what is the best course to take as he does; and let us remember the ancient saw, "When you don't know what to do, don't do you don't know what." When you have nothing practicable to propose, do not be angry because others do not take up your vague notions and more vague theories. Wait for the development of the Divine plan, and do not imagine that because your scheme is not instantly adopted, it is because everybody else is blind and perverse. Abolitionism, as exhibited here at the North, is the very essence and quintessence of self-conceit and arrogance. Without the smallest practical experience, we coolly sit down in our closets to speculate and theorize about one of the most difficult problems of human thought; and because all men do not at once agree with us, we set ourselves to work to turn the world upside down, to scramble over the heads of the rest of mankind, and proclaim ourselves the only true Christian philanthropists. It is time that such preposterous delusions were dispelled, and that we looked at our own position, our own character, as well as at those of our neighbors, with a little discrimination, modesty and reserve.

185. JUSTICE APPLIED TO SLAVERY

(Providence Evening Press [Independent], October 25, 1860)

We have once in the most formal manner, and many times by implication, expressed our antipathy to slavery. But we do not desire to belong to that loud-mouthed class who make their hatred of slavery, or their pretence of it, the staple of their professions and proceedings, the great subject of their political, social, and moral relations. Indeed, as we observe the vast amount of unreasoning fanaticism exhibited in regard to the institution, and the immense quantity of hypocrisy generated concerning it, we are rather persuaded to keep our own opposition to slavery decidedly in the back-ground until we see some signs that it threatens to invade our own neighborhood.

We hear so much, and so continually, of the *in*justice of slavery,— by which we mean here, not its abstract unrighteousness as a principle, but rather its policy and practice as a system,—that it would seem to us, in the absence of striking proofs to the contrary, that no good thing could possibly come out of it, that it is a very Nazareth of evil. Inasmuch as this system is, at the present moment, incorporated into the Constitution[s] of nearly half the States of our great Confederacy, and was, until a very recent period, part and parcel of the civil and political organization of several of what are now called Free States, and inasmuch as thousands of patriotic citizens of this great Republic, including able statesmen, keen logicians, humble and earnest Christians, and in short, the noblest kinds of men, are involved in all the responsibilitie[s], political, social and moral, which grew out of this system, and however mistakenly, still conscientiously vindicate their relations to it; inasmuch as these things are true, it is not a matter of small moment that the public mind should be fully and correctly informed as to the true and actual out-workings of the system. It cannot be denied that the blemishes and blots, the excrescences and enormities of Slavery are far more eagerly and diligently displayed and discussed by the Northern press, than are the features which relieve it of some of its worst attributes.

There are those who will even sneer at the idea that there is any such side to slavery as this better one, while a much larger class of persons, perhaps honestly, but still ignorantly, believe that the moralities of the system are not only exceptional, but so exceedingly rare as to be quite inconsiderable in the task of solving the true character and results of the institution. It is bad enough at best; let us not exaggerate its deformities.

At the risk of being charged with assuming the unthankful character of apologists for slavery, we insist here that the system should be honestly and intelligently judged; that it should be credited with all that belongs to it of humanity, generosity, justice and other noble virtues. He who asserts that none of these belong to slavery in any degree, knows not of what he affirms; or wilfully falsifies the records of daily life. And let us add that ignorance on this point, considering the magnitude of the question involved, is hardly less criminal than deliberate falsehood. It is this reckless assertion of the unmitigated, unrelieved horror and guilt, and selfishness and cruelty of the system, and of its supporters no less, that has so naturally and deeply irritated and maddened the Southern feeling against the North. It is just this indiscriminate denunciation of the whole system, theoretical and practical, that has opened a breach of misunderstanding between us and the people of the South, which has at length broadened and deepened into a yawning gulf of enmity.

Now, slavery is not so invariably hideous as it is made to appear by those who look at it from one side only. It sometimes developes great virtues. It achieves great victories over the wrong principle that inheres in it. It clothes itself, not for low ends, but with generous impulses, so as to be more tolerable in our sight. It is occasionally benevolent, self-denying and noble in its workings.

At this moment, however, we mean simply to offer a proof of its *justice*. It is one that some of our papers have brought to public notice. It will not be found in all of them, since there are many to which such proof of the possible *justice* of slavery would be unwelcome, as tending to refute their theory that it is unqualifiedly bad. The case we allude to is this: An old man in Virginia,—the State whose soil is still red with the blood of anti-slavery violence,—whipped his slave to death, with the inhumanity, not of slavery exclusively, but of moral depravity. This old man has been tried for his crime, and by an incorrupt, al-though a Virginia judge, has been found guilty and condemned to eighteen years imprisonment,—which, as he is now seventy years of age, will inevitably carry him into his grave. We do not propose to dwell upon the case. It carries its significance upon its face. It establishes, by one instance, in circumstances that greatly enhance its moral force, the capability of slavery to be *just* to its subjects and even to its unhappy victims. We will only add that the most faithful and intelligent ob-servers of the times know that this is not an isolated example, but one of a multitude of proofs that slavery has its punishments for the brutal master, as well as its privations for the slave.

186. THE NEGRO RACE

(New York Journal of Commerce [Breckinridge], October 26, 1860)

There are certain great facts in reference to the negro race from which there is no rational or logical escape. A morbid philanthropy may attempt to pervert them; but they stand out so clearly and distinctly on the records of science and history, that a sensible and unprejudiced man cannot deny them.

He who has studied the difference between the natural races and families of men, knows that a superior and an inferior race cannot con-tinue to occupy the same territory on terms of equality. Either the in-ferior race will be enslaved, and in that condition increase and multiply, if treated with reasonable kindness,—or, in the attempt to compete with the superior race, be ultimately wiped out of existence by their greater skill and strength. We use the words *races of men* in a strictly ethnographical sense; and mean that kind of superiority of race which the Circassians and Anglo-Saxons manifest over the Indian, negro, Malay and Mongolian races. We do not recognize in the Norman and the Saxon,—the Gaul and the Oriental,—the Celt and the Russian,—any positive or absolute superiority of race, as compared with each other, for nature has marked no great or controlling differences in their physical and mental structure. But we can define, by means of physiological and anatomical science, the difference between the white man and the negro, or the Indian; and we know also, that neither the Indian nor the free negro can contend successfully against the white man, when they occupy the same soil and compete with each other. All history proves that the inferior race, in order to survive the aggressions and greater activity and energy of the superior race, must be brought to a condition of servitude, serfdom, or slavery.

These principles may not be in accordance with the belief of many who think they are guided by the purest spirit of philanthropy; and yet they are founded upon facts which are indisputable. And there is another natural law which applies to these races, particularly to the negro, and which is equally unsatisfactory to some who fear to meet the truth face to face. Negroes and whites cannot perpetuate a new race; the Divine laws are indestructible barriers against such unnatural experiments; and we have the direct testimony of acute and honest travelers in Central America and the West Indies, that the mongrel or hybrid races are incapable of perpetuating themselves, and have greatly deteriorated in mind and body. Anything, then, like equal social relations between the two races, is physically impossible.

We do not make these incontestable statements from any dislike to the negro, or from any partialities for the institution of slavery. But in these days, when distinguished statesmen, and public journals representing a powerful and vigorous party, are constantly teaching the people theories which inculcate violent and hostile opposition to an institution recognized by the Constitution and by the framers and fathers of this Republic, and promise, in substance, that an "irrepressible conflict" is to result in overwhelming humiliation and decadence of the South, it is time to grapple the question boldly, and not to dodge the pending issues, or to mince matters too much, or to confess that there is but one side to this irritating and dangerous slavery controversy. There are four million reasons in the South, clad in flesh and blood, against the wild political crusade now going forward, and which becomes more obstinate and reckless as it advances. If history and science tell the truth, the immediate, or unprepared, or hasty freedom of these slaves, will produce their extermination, accompanied by a train of events most horrible to contemplate.

And we advise, also, the professed philanthropist whose sympathies have got the better of his judgment, to reflect upon the great barriers which have been placed by nature between the whites and blacks, and that whatever may be the ultimate destiny of the latter, they are infinitely better off than if they had been born and bred in their native land. The records of travelers in Africa tell a sad but true tale of the negro race as it appears at home, and especially in Eastern Africa. The native African is an habitual drunkard, a thief, a liar, revengeful, licentious, groveling in his habits, almost destitute of natural affection, unprogressive in character, and in religion a devotee of the obscene mysteries of Fetichism. Moreover, the great bulk of the population is made up of masters and slaves. Indeed, slavery is almost universal. The principal occupation of the Africans, and the real object of almost all their wars, is the kidnapping of slaves; while the treatment and condition of negroes in our South, is benevolence itself compared with the cruel system which prevails in Africa. This is the picture drawn of the native African by disinterested and reliable travelers; and a more disagreeable one is not to be found in the history of barbarians. In truth, the negroes held in slavery in the United States, are much better off, physically and morally, than their ignorant and degraded brothers in Africa. Everybody knows this; and believes in his heart that the condition, prospects and character of the negro improve under the refining influences of civilized life. We may safely say, also, that scarcely a fraction of the people of the United States are in favor of now freeing the slave. Why then, in the face of the well-authenticated facts we have stated, do the abolitionists, fanatics, and many leaders of the Republican party, persist in their wild and reckless theories, whose development is dragging the Union to the verge of the precipice? To raise up the great African race from serfdom to a condition of advancement and civilization, or to place them in a position where every favor and liberty and right, social and political, shall be allowed them, just as it is allowed to the whites, is a possibility of which we may dream for coming ages. But in the present posture of affairs, and with our present knowledge of the insurmountable difficulties in the way of such an event, we know, first of all, that only those who own slaves can abolish slavery, and then, that every imprudent, or concealed, or violent opposition on the part of Northern men, does more injury than good, and impedes the advancement of genuine humanity.

187. Northern Error as to the Character and Necessary Permanence of Negro Slavery the Cause of All the Sectional Difficulties

(Newport Advertiser [Breckinridge], December 5, 1860)

The dangers, which now menace the existence of the Union are the result of ignorance of the true nature of the slavery question.—If the North could only be made thoroughly to understand that the negro labor, which the climate makes it impossible for the white race to perform, is demanded by the interests of the whole civilized world, and that the continuance of the relations of master and servant, substantially as they now exist at the South, is essential to the maintenance of the African race and required by every humanitarian consideration, as regards the slaves themselves, we should have a radical cure for sectional difficulties.

As to the connection between negro slavery and the industry of the world, we have heretofore said sufficient. It will be remembered that even the French ideologists, whom we last week cited, uncompromising abolitionists as they are, admitted that emancipation could not be attempted in our cotton States, without being attended with universal ruin both to Europe and America—that general bankruptcy and political revolutions every where would be the consequence.

Unfortunately, the true nature of domestic slavery in general, as only varying, in the mode of compensating labor, from the relations necessarily existing every where, in civilized life, between the employers and employed, is misapprehended. Moreover, the inapplicability to a slave population, between whom and the families of the masters no amalgamation can take place, of those principles of emancipation, which prevailed where pecuniary embarrassment or the accidents of war determined the position of the parties, are [sic] not appreciated. It is, we conceive, from disregarding the cardinal fact that, owing to that perpetual separation, which race creates, the same rules that applied to the countries of Western Europe in the middle ages, and which are now leading to the abolition of serfdom in Russia, cannot extend to negro slavery, that our Southern fellow-citizens are exposed to those assaults on their institutions, which are driving them to seek in an independent government that safety, which the doctrine of an "irrepressible conflict" would deny them. The abolitionists wholly overlook the circumstance that no act of legislation can make a citizen of an African negro. We do not refer to any controverted question as to elective franchise, but we speak of that civil and political, as well as social equality, in which it essentially consists, the idea of which is perfectly ludicrous in a State, which prohibits intermarriage between people of different colors. We need not go beyond the experience, which the affranchisement in the Northern States exhibits, to show that the only result of emancipation is the extermination of the inferior race. Nor are the States of the West, which are the most clamorous against Slavery, even willing to await the natural course of the extinction of the free negroes, but while annoying, in every way, the Southern planter, for holding Slaves, they refuse to admit within their territory the liberated blacks. Until the public mind of the North comes to recognize the domestic authority of the superior over the inferior race as a permanent, and not as a mere transitory institution, there can be no end of the sectional difficulty. If Northern Senators, disregarding all ethnological as well as economical facts, proclaim as barbarous the people of fifteen States of the Union on account of institutions essential to the prosperity of all, there can exist none of those relations, which should characterise the citizens of one Republic. If ministers of the gospel overlook not only the authority of history in general, but of the holy scriptures, and teach their hearers, (from whose very ancestors in many cases the progenitors of the negroes were purchased,) that Slaveholders cannot be Christians, there can be no such sentiments, as ought to prevail between people of a common origin, religion and language.

The fact is that it is rather the stigma attached to the word, which indicates, at the South, the connection between master and servant, than any intrinsic difference between the employers of labour and labourers elsewhere, that constitutes the great anti-slavery weapon. Of the force of terms, indeed, France and England seem fully aware, and while we are bound by a treaty with the latter power to keep up a squadron, at a great expense, to suppress the African slave trade, they, by calling their victims *apprentices* or substituting Asiatic Coolies for negroes, legalise, for the benefit of their Colonies, a slave trade infinitely more obnoxious to humanity than that which, with us, is subject to the penalties of piracy. From the first moment of the division of labor, from the time that every man did not cook his own dinner and make his own clothes, the relation of master to servant, in a sense more or less absolute, has existed. The earliest annals also show that, instead of a compensation in money or wages, the master gave, in return for services, protection with food and raiment. Not only were slaves made from captives, it being deemed a mitigation of the extreme rights of war to substitute servitude for death, but the Roman law, as well as the usages of the middle ages recognised, as a valid title, the perpetual right to a person and his offspring based on his voluntary enslavement. Where there was no diversity of race, no insuperable difficulty prevented either a total affranchisement, of which history presents several distinguished instances, where the ignoble birth was lost in the subsequent fame of the emancipated slave, or the substitution of a compensation for labor, with the privilege of seeking employment elsewhere. Because, however, the demand for labor, in a community like ours, always exceeds the supply and our institutions offer to the meanest immigrant the prospect of social elevation, it is not to be inferred that that condition of things is universal, or that those who are nominally free to make their own contracts are always better off than those who are permanently provided for. Speaking of the Celtic population of Ireland, as it was so late as 1847, and where what is called domestic slavery did not exist, a late eminent English writer says; "No more deplorable condition could be imagined than that of the Irish-speaking peasantry who, by their ignorance of the English tongue, were cut off from civilization. They were worse lodged, clothed and fed, than the peasantry of any other civilized country, or even than the savage or heathen races in Central Africa.— Their cabins were inferior to the habitations of any other human beings. Families slept in the same narrow chamber—at once a cause of disease, and an offense against good manners. The damp, the filth, the vitiated and corrupted vapours arising from the want of drainage and ventilation, in periods of epidemics, caused a terrible mortality. In such pestilential abodes, the most robust constitutions were weakened; natures more delicate succumbed; generations were decimated, and the survivors languished through life enerved. The roofless walls of those miserable hovels are now seen all through Ireland, I trust, (says Dr. Heron) they will never again be roofed for human beings." Contrast the condition of the negro slaves on a well ordered plantation with that of the above described tenants of English abolitionists and who by the theory of the law might make their own bargains for wages. In the case of the latter there was, moreover, no insuperable difficulty, from diversity of race, for that intellectual development, which the presence of a superior race renders impossible to the negro.—In the eye of humanity, the question is not what, in a different state of circumstances, in the case of a homogeneous people might be desired for the slave of the South, but what their actual condition requires. On that point—even among the most intelligent of their own race many of whom have so frequently resisted the intrigues of Northern abolitionists, there is a concurrence of opinion, that no change of their relations with the whites, either now or at any future day, is to be desired—that their condition is not only the best for the interests of the world at large, but for their own happiness. This conviction is an infinitely more potent fugitive slave law than any that can be passed by Congress, and if the well intentioned fanatics of the North could only realise its truth, the Union might yet be preserved. Nothing, indeed, is wanting but that we should look to "the beam in our own eye," instead of regarding "the mote in our brother's eye." At all events, if we do intermeddle, we must, like Sampson, be prepared to have the building tumble down on our own heads.

188. THE LAST STRUGGLE OF SLAVERY

(*Springfield* (Mass.) *Daily Republican* [Lincoln], December 22, 1860)

Turning aside from the political aspects of the great question now before the American people, and looking at it in the light of history and divine Providence, there are in it matters for most serious consideration. Slavery seems to be gathering itself up for a decisive struggle. The moral forces of the world have long assailed it, and everywhere religion, morality and politics are against it. Its stronghold is in the southern states of this Union. Spain tolerates it in her colonies, but does not justify it, or attempt to surround it by moral sanctions. Some of the most barbarous of the African tribes practice it, and sell captives taken from each other to the Christians, because they want the trinkets and the rum the Christians offer in barter, but we are not aware that the king of Dahomey attempts any other justification than the old axiom, "might makes right." All the nations of the world, civilized and uncivilized, agree in the denunciation of the system that chattelizes men, buys and sells them, compels their unrequitted [*sic*] labor by the lash, and makes them the unwilling ministers to others' welfare instead of their own. It is the unanimous verdict of Christendom and heathendom alike, our southern states and the kingdom of Dahomey excepted, that the institution of slavery is the worst possible perversion of human relations and the most entire violation alike of natural and divine law. Only in this country is an attempt made to throw around the system the sanctions of religion and to uphold it as a good and proper thing in itself and worthy to be cherished, protected and extended over other lands, and this defense of slavery is not a quarter of a century old, even here. But notwithstanding the assumed confidence of the people of the South that their theory of slavery is correct, they evidently feel uneasy and annoyed under the verdict of mankind against it. This feeling has shown itself often in the heat of the present controversy, and there is no plea the secessionists make with more effect than this, that it is impossible to live under the same government with a people whose prejudices are so strongly against the southern institution. It is the desire to throw off, and get out of the reach of, this moral sentiment against slavery that accounts in part for the disunion feeling, and in no one class is this more apparent than among the clergymen and Christian professors of the South. Slavery thinks to hedge itself in, to shut out the great influences that are moulding society and government everywhere, and to set universal opinion at defiance.

We do not believe it can be done. Popular opinion is becoming more and more the great power in this world. Kings bow before it; bloodless revolutions are achieved by it; the European governments yield to its demands and confess its right to be heard, and even the most absolute, like Russia, formally acknowledge that the ultimate appeal is to the popular will. No man can fail to see that the popular judgment is becoming more and more respected, and that the great idea of the right of all men to "life, liberty and the pursuit of happiness" is fast becoming the universal doctrine. We do not believe that any human power can destroy this great element in the world's progress, and we look upon the triumphal march of ameliorating ideas and events as certain to go on to the grand consummation, the foresight of which has been the inspiration of prophets and poets from the beginning. The world will move straight forward in its course, and all the petty obstacles interposed by the will and wickedness of men and nations will be ground to dust beneath it.

Suppose the slaveholders should induce the politicians to give slavery all the new guaranties it can ask, even to the extent of declaring the right of property in men sacred and of divine authority. That declaration would not change northern opinion on the subject. On the contrary it would arouse it to new vigor and zeal for the moral assault upon the institution, and neither the general government nor the slave states would henceforth have a moment's rest from "irrepressible conflict" till the new guaranties were swept away. Suppose the southern states go out of the Union to escape northern aversion to slavery. That would not diminish, but rather intensify that aversion, and would set it free from all the constitutional restraints that now limit its action, and the crusade against the institution would environ the South on all sides, and while the slaves would have a free door of escape, the entire circuit of the slave states would be exposed to the inroads of popular opinion against slavery, and in the border slave states the progress of emancipation and deliverance from slavery would inevitably be greatly accelerated. Neither would the schemes of indefinite extension south-ward and westward be realized. The northern states would agree with the European powers in resisting all attempts by the slavery propa-gandists to appropriate Mexico or Central America. The same powers would prevent the acquisition of Cuba by the slaveholding confederacy, and the institution would find itself more effectually and more rapidly hemmed in and circumscribed than it could be in the Union. For what-ever respect and toleration it now gets from other nations, it is chiefly indebted to the influence of the free states. Let it isolate itself and at-tempt to stand on its own merits, and it will find no aid and comfort from any Christian or civilized power.

Whichever way, therefore, the present struggle terminates, either in union or disunion, we look upon it as decisive as to the supremacy of slavery. In the Union, it must be content in its present limits and with its constitutional rights, and can never again subject the general government to its despotic control. Out of the Union, it will stand defenseless and exposed on all sides to the moral hostility of mankind, which it vainly seeks to evade. In the Union, it will live longer and die more gradually and quietly; out of the Union, its life will be one of constant peril and strife, and, like all great criminals, it will be pretty certain to come to a violent and bloody death. The day or the manner of its end no man can tell; but he knows little of human nature and human history, and lacks faith in the final reign of justice and truth on the earth, who does not see that no such institution can plant itself defiantly against the onward march of events and hope to escape col-lision and wreck. To see this and to say it frankly implies no hostility to slaveholders. It does not follow that they are the worst of men be-cause born into the worst of institutions. With the most kindly and fraternal feelings towards them as men and fellow citizens, it does not follow that we should suppress our convictions of truth, or conceal what seem to us important facts; nay, it is the highest fidelity and the only honest style of kindness to tell them exactly what we think and to warn them frankly of the dangers that seem to lie in their present course. If they indignantly close their ears and rush on, it cannot be helped. Whatever befalls them, we have confidence in the final result, and can only doubt it when we renounce our faith in God, and abandon this world to the control of the powers of evil.

189. Problem of Slavery

(Hamilton (Ohio) *Telegraph* [Douglas], December 27, 1860)

Without taking an extreme theory and afterwards paring down to fit, we begin by assuming what some may please to call Southern grounds as the basis of our comments. We shall see how liberal pro-slavery doctrine sounds to a northern ear. We deduce the fact that the negro was intended by God to be the servant of the white man, as much as children are intended by nature to be subject to and dependent on their natural guardians; that the natives of Africa are no more able by a spontaneous effort to raise themselves from their debased social, moral and religious condition, than a newly born infant is capable of supplying itself with food and raiment without the care of its parents; that every Christian man must recognize the responsibility which God's providence has laid upon the superior race to provide for the wants of the inferior; that to accomplish this end the white race must exercise a certain amount of authority; and that as a natural sequence, negro slavery, in some form or other, is part of the harmonious system established by God. We assume, further, what we presume no sensible men will deny, that there can be no civilization, no improvement in any race of men without labor, and if this be true of mankind, it is doubly true of the black race, who, by their physical and mental conformation, is [*sic*] less inclined to labor than any other race of men. The British experiment of emancipation of the negro slaves in the West Indies, that tribute paid by the British nation to fanatical sentimentality, which, under a monarchical government has produced the results towards which the despotism of democracy is now hastening us, proves it beyond a doubt. Here in the most fruitful country in the world, the negro, on an equal social footing with the white race, would be the most favorable for attaining the higher degree of civilization. But we find those born free and never compelled to work have fallen off from the civilization attained by their slave fathers, that they have degenerated into a barbarism not much in advance of their race in Africa. The permanent happiness of the negro can only be effectually promoted by making him labor. We say, *making him labor,* because, not only is his peculiar organization, as a human being, such as to indispose him, of his own will and accord, to labor, but his being without labor is a great cause of his degradation and misery. This appears to be the only true and sensible view of the subject, whether looked at from either a secular or religious stand point. All history and experience prove that labor is a necessary means of civilization. Revelation so teaches. No object can be accomplished, either in our natural or spiritual life without constant labor, and no race of men can advance without ceaseless and well directed labor, without work. Granting, then, the absolute necessity of labor, taking in conjunction with this proof of the constitutional distaste for labor, inherent in the negro, constitutional laziness for which he is no more accountable than for the color of his skin, and it follows that if he is to be raised, it must be by some power external to himself, that he must be reduced to a condition of slavery in some form or other, however much it may be modified by circumstances. Now is it justifiable in the white race so far as to act in contrariety to abstract notions of justice, so far to set aside what are generally known as the "natural rights" of the negro race, as to bring that race into subjection? In other words, is it not desirable that large bodies of our fellow creatures sho'd be raised from the degradation in which the negroes of Africa are now sunk, and placed in a state of society where the right of man in a savage state would be changed into adventitious rights, those only national rights which possess the power to make laws for the maintenance and welfare of society? It is all very fine to speak of God making all men free, but after all it is nothing more than mere sentimentalism. The question answers itself. It is doubtless our duty to bring this degraded and brutalized race under the influence of Christianity, *even in spite of themselves.* The theory of abstract right to liberty is at once proved false by the facts which can be brought to bear upon it. It is altogether useless to say that the negro has a right to liberty, when it can be conclusively demonstrated that he is physically unadapted for it. God has given no rights to man that He has not adapted man for exercising, and the fact of the negro being as a consequence of his fallen and miserable condition, thus unadapted, proves that he is incapable of enjoying liberty. The present system of slavery may be regarded as *an important advance* toward the realization of our views. Indeed, we hold that in order to inaugurate the humane system in the slave States it is only necessary for those States, each of them, to adopt some restrictive enactments for removing objectionable features, evidences of human weakness rather than results of the institution, for it is undeniable that isolated cases of cruelty and oppression reacting upon minds peculiarly constituted for promoting the work of sedition, gave rise to the organization and action of that reckless and therefore dangerous clique of pseudo philanthropists and politicians known as the northern Abolitionists. It is also undeniable that whilst these fanatics were striving to turn the exception into the rule, and inconsiderately concocting schemes for the accomplishment of inhuman designs, the Southern mind, as a whole, was patiently examining the slavery question, devising liberal Christian-like plans for the improvement of the moral condition of the negro, and discussing with fraternal kindness the great problem which we have attempted to solve. We see and lament that the institution of slavery like other God ordained institutions, is liable to many abuses, and we would universalize the condition which even now exists, much more largely than persons living in the free States are generally aware of, where the negro forms an humble, but still an integral portion of a Christian household, a fellow member of the church with his master, and an heir to the same hope of immortality. We have thus stated the case, we may err, but it is well to form correct opinions upon this momentous question, momentous not only to the millions sunk into the depths of barbarism, but to ourselves, who must one day answer to him who, for making out his own ends, has placed this great question in our hands.

190. This Is an Enlightened Age

(Dubuque *Daily Times* [Lincoln], January 12, 1861)

If the position now universally taken at the South on the subject of slavery be the true one, then does that part of the Confederacy owe a debt of gratitude for the anti-slavery agitation which they have been slow to acknowledge. Instead of up[b]raiding and reproaching the North for its war upon the institution, they should confess the greatness of their indebtedness, and in view of the benefits they have derived from the agitation of the subject, willingly pardon us any temporary inconvenience they have experienced from it.

A few years since the institution of slavery was quite generally, we may say universally regarded even by those implicated in it, as an evil in all respects. It was especially the habit of all Southern Christians to apologize for its existence, throwing the blame upon others, professing to ardently desire its extinction at the earliest practicable moment. Its removal was averred to be surrounded, indeed, with great practical difficulties, out of which it was hoped the Providence of God would at no very distant day deliver them. In the meantime they must bear with patience their burden, and endeavor by the moral and social elevation of the enslaved to prepare them for the enjoyments of the rights of manhood. We are bound to believe that this was an honest statement of their views. No one who knows anything of the sentiments of the great men who founded the Republic, is ignorant that this was substantially their

THE MORALITY OF SLAVERY 487

view of the institution. The opinions of Washington, Jefferson, Patrick
Henry, among other Southern statesmen are on record. I[t] cannot be
mistaken.

Especially was the African Slave trade execrated, till quite recently,
by all good men, South as well as North, as abhorrent to all sentiments
of religion or humanity.

How entirely the tone of the South has of late changed on this whole
subject, need not be shown. We no longer hear from any class there the
language of apology or deprecation, but the pulpit unites with the
rostrum and the religious with the secular press, in affirming the righteousness of the system of bondage, as it stands upon our Southern soil.
We hear not now from *any* quarter of a gradual and final emancipation, nor even of any attempts at modifying the system to remove from
it those barbarous, inhuman features which renders [*sic*] its existence in
a nominally Christian land the wonder of all Christendom outside of
itself. On the contrary, it is preached from the ablest and most influential
pulpits at the South, that her peculiar mission at the present time is to
perpetuate and extend to the full measure of her ability, the system of
negro slavery *as it now exists.* And though there are still some found
to oppose feebly the re-opening of that traffic, which the nations of
Christendom have united in pronouncing piracy, yet this too, with
more logical consistency, indeed, has found its advocates in the pulpit,
as well as in other quarters. Beyond reasonable doubt, it will soon be
the only orthodox sentiment among all parties, should a Southern Confederacy become a fact.

Then it is naturally asked—whence this vast change in Southern
sentiment on the moral character of this system? Nor is the answer withheld. It is distinctly replied that the agitation of this subject at the
North has forced upon its supporters a new and more thorough investigation of the subject, as the result of which they discover that all
their former views of it, as a system socially and morally, as well as
politically evil, hostile to the spirit of the gospel, and which the gospel
in its progress must eventually abolish, have undergone a radical change.
Their eyes are now opened to its real character, they clearly see that
it is a divinely appointed, divinely supported institution, benificent [*sic*]
in all its aspects, happy alike in its influence on master and servant, and
by no means to be restricted or abolished.

Now if this revised judgment be correct, it is very evident that the
South has gained immensely from the discussion of this subject. A vast
property interest, hundreds of millions in value, has been rescued from
the precarious footing it necessarily occupied, while the earlier view

of the institution obtained, and placed upon a foundation as lasting as the great eternal principles of rectitude. This alone were an incalculable gain, especially in view of the rapid increase of the number and aggregate value of slave property.

But, again, by this correction of opinion a much higher than any pecuniary gain whatever is achieved. What was before supposed to be a gigantic wrong, is now clearly seen to be a just and beneficent Right. And when the magnitude of the system and the mighty scope of its influence, for good or for evil, as the case may be, is taken into account, it becomes impossible to overestimate the importance and worth of the new discovery.

And yet again, by means of this revolution of opinion, the South is at once relieved of any necessity or obligations to devise ways for the removal of slavery, and put to the much easier and more grateful task of strengthening its defenses, and enlarging its areas. So long as it was an evil all men were in duty bound to earnestly and persistently seek the best method for the earliest practical abolition of the institution. Now, it is quite otherwise and a great burden must have been removed from all tender consciences.

It is true there are some facts which militate against the probability that this avowed change of sentiment has come of a more thorough investigation of the whole subject, and better understanding of the teachings of the Bible. It does not appear that any new principles for the interpretation of that book have been recently discovered, giving it a different aspect toward human bondage.—None of its denunciations of wrong, injustice and oppression are known to have been cancelled. Nor have any new canons of others come into general acceptance, which give countenance to the new doctrine. On the contrary, while this change has been going on among those implicitly in the offense, the whole christian world beside has been steadily advancing toward the deep-rooted sentiment and conviction that this same system is a gigantic crime against God and humanity, and a stain and disgrace to our civilization and our christianity. On the other hand the immense increase in the value of this kind of property, and its great prospective value suggest a possible reason for the change which most men find it far easier to comprehend than the one assigned.

However, since our Southern friends insist that this wide-spread and radical change has actually arisen out of the more thorough investigation which the North has compelled them to institute, we repeat that they owe to the anti-slavery agitation of the North a debt which is poorly paid in tar and feathers and the other tokens of their regard which our friends of the sunny land are just now so liberally bestowing upon all their Northern guests, indiscriminately. Nor does it greatly alter the case, that the North did not anticipate the result reached, since she is quite ready to subscribe to any new views which can be shown to be in accordance with justice and truth.

191. POPULAR MISAPPREHENSIONS

(Cleveland Daily Plain Dealer [Douglas], January 12, 1861)

The Northern mind has become educated to believe that the African race in this country is a down-trodden people. The reverse is true. They are already morally, socially and religiously, far above what they would have been had they been left in their native wilds. For six thousand years they have been known as an inferior race, incapable of progression, and as BAYARD TAYLOR, a Black Republican himself, says in his celebrated lecture on Man and Climate, "They are the lowest type of humanity known on the face of the earth." Had they emerged from their savage and cannibal state, and made any progress in the arts and sciences, they might now be considered an oppressed people. What most excites our sympathy for this colored race is the mixture we meet within this Northern country. The Celt and the Saxon often see their own white blood mixed with the ebony. Here is progression from visible admixture which appeals to us for protection; but these are exceptions to the race.—They should not determine the rule of our action as they evidently do with the Northern masses. Should an unprejudiced person travel the earth over in search of subjects for humanitary aid, he would find a multitude of inferior races quite as worthy of sympathy as the negroes. But should he visit Africa, as many are now doing, and run the gauntlet of life through its benighted and barbarious regions, witnessing the petty tyrannies and savage cruelties of its native Kings, the heathen sacrifices and hectacombs [*sic*] of human skulls raised to appease the wrath of imaginary Gods; observing too, the want and suffering for the physical comforts of life and the extinction of whole tribes by fammine [*sic*] and infectious diseases, millions of men, if so they may be called, of no use to themselves or to the world, wasting away in their own intestine wars, such a person could then visit the same race of people as transplanted in this country, go through the plantation States and find them with enough to eat, drink and wear; their young provided for and their aged taken care of; with labor enough to keep them healthy, and discipline enough to keep them peaceable; the whole earning an honest livelihood for themselves according to the great command and contributing at the same time to the general wants of man and the wealth of the world. Such a person, we say, thus posted from actual observation of actual facts, could come to no other conclusion than that the system of American slavery is a God-send to the *African Race!*

In point of personal comforts, of civilization, of morals and religion, *American* slavery is a Paradise compared with *African* slavery, and American sympathy should be exercised more about the latter than the former.

Another popular error is, that in case of dissolution of the Union the slaves can be counted on to help the cause of coercion. This is a Black Republican dogma and dangerous as a fact to found any public policy upon. It is a great mistake. In case of anarchy consequent upon the present revolution, no class of beings will be less troublesome than these blacks. Docility is the leading feature of the race. Do not judge the millions of these people now scattered throughout the plantations of the South, by the mulat[t]oes and others of mixed blood in the North. They are more happy and contented than any other race of people on the earth, because they are better provisioned, provided, and cared for than any other race of working men. A pure blooded African when let alone has no aspirations for liberty as we understand it. He never had any at home. He knows nothing about it and cares less. He is content with plenty of "hog and hominy," something he could not get in Africa and which he is glad to get here. He looks to his master as his provider and protector, a sort of patriarch who in the hour of danger he will defend with his life. We know this is not the picture found in "Uncle Tom's Cabin," nor in the New York *Tribune,* but it is the truth nevertheless, and the time has come to speak the truth whether men will hear or forbear. The slaves South are kept in submission by a system of municipial [*sic*] regulations suggested by the mutual interests of master and servant. It is a patriarchal system unknown to the statute laws of these States. Blot out all Legislative enactments there and the system would go on unmolested. Slaves know no law but their master's will.— This is the condition of all inferior races, and they will be found true to their masters, when laws and constitutions are done away.

Not so with the laboring classes in the North. Here every man feels that he is a Popular Sovereign, and his condition if unequal is in his opinion rendered so by partial laws and an unjust government. Let anarchy come, take away the restraint of law and that large and ag-[g]rieved class will be very apt to make conditions equal. We have a thousand times more to apprehend from mobs of starving and desperate men in the North than the South have from their slaves. Our large cities are full of dependent people; poor men with large families who live from hand to mouth by the earnings of their daily labor. Stop the government and you stop the manufactories, the shops and the trades that give them employment. This stops their pay and necessarily stops their food. Starvation will do and be justified in doing what no other condition in life would. No parent[s] can see their innocent offspring perishing in want so long as there is anything to sustain life within their reach. The rich man's gains heretofore protected by law will have to succumb to the general need, and might will make right. So these Republican agitators who have been sowing seeds of disunion by appealing to the hearts of the people instead of their heads; playing upon their passions, arousing their sympathies, all to get their votes for places of pelf and preferment, had better look to their own homes and hearthstones when the evil days which they have brought about shall come.

He that is wisest can penetrate the future deepest.

192. IS SLAVERY SIN?

(Ithaca *American Citizen* [Bell], January 23, 1861)

Within the last forty years a great discovery has been made in theology. It has been discovered that slavery, as existing in this country, is a sin *per se*—a sin in the same sense, that murder, larceny and piracy are sins. It has been discovered, that it is one of those obvious and glaring sins, which admit of no doubt of their character, and that it is only necessary to open the Bible to find it condemned in almost every page.

The discovery was first made by a club of Boston infidels; but a portion of the pulpit followed in the wake of these wise sceptics [sic], and became agitators on the subject. There was indeed, no negro slavery in their congregations, though there was plenty of other kinds of slavery —slavery to avarice, lying, cheating, and so on to the end of the interesting catalogue. There was negro slavery however at the South, which weighed with a more grevious [sic] burden, upon the tender consciences of these men, than the breaches of Divine law in their midst. They became *agitators*. It became their *mission* to engender the elements of sectional strife. They could wear cotton shirts, and sleep between cotton sheets, and eat rice pudding, and cane sugar, but they could not stand it, to live in a Union, in which some of the States were tolerated as slaveholding. Their consciences were too tender.

Men of over heated zeal, and who are righteous over much, are generally vain men. These clerical agitators, who have been so ready to be co-workers with infidels, fancy themselves leaders in the great work of rescuing the age from conservatism. They accordingly deal in high sounding phrases such as "the progress of the age," "modern civilization," "humanitarian interests," and others affording the surest evidences of arrant charlatanism.

The greater the stock of vanity, the more overbearing the intolerance. This in some localities has manifested itself to such degree, that a member of the church is in danger of expulsion, if he happen to *express* the belief, that the South should be let alone in the management of their own institutions. He is regarded as a "pro-slavery" man, and needs looking to. He is as unlucky, as the man who some years ago ventured to swallow a spoonful of brandy—*he* was a decided enemy of temperance. Indeed, so far has this intolerant idea obtained a foot hold, that men begin to talk of *anti-slavery* christians, leaving it to be charitably inferred, that all who differ from them on this question are not christians. We think the term *infidel* christians would be quite as appropriate.

Of course the memory of our fathers—Washington, Jefferson, Madison, &c., is brought into disrepute, either directly, or by inference, and the constitution which they framed for us, is little better, than "a league with hell and covenant with death." The oath to support the constitution, is not binding upon a tender anti-slavery conscience.

The sin of covenant breaking is merged and lost, in the higher sin, of living on the same continent with slavery. Our fathers were pirates and man stealers, and John Brown will go down to posterity as a hero and martyr, while Washington will be forgotten.

This is no exaggeration, and if necessary we can quote from high authority, in the anti-slavery church, to bear us out.

These same men, in their over weening vanity boast of large heartedness. Their benevolence ranges over a great field. Common sins are too vulgar to be noticed. The drudgery of attending to them must be left to smaller minds. They have looked into the frame work of society and find it out of joint—hence they are generally found in attendance at, or correspondence with "womans rights," and other kindred conventions, the object of which is to turn things upside down, under the plea of *progress.*

The bitter fruits of all this agitation, are now being realized, in the terrible crisis, through which our country is passing. The times are too dangerous to be mealy mouthed on this subject. The foundations of our government, are now rocking in the earthquake throes of revolution. That portion of the clergy, of whom we have been speaking, have contributed largely to this lamentable result, and it is time for men to speak out plain. It is high time, a political preacher should be regarded as *a nuisance*. It is time this question of negro slavery should be regarded, not as a religious question, but purely one of political economy. It is time the people should understand that anti-slavery preaching is not drawn from the inspiration of the Bible, but is, in some, the offspring of fanaticism and vanity, and in others the effect of blindly following the lead of other minds.

Our duty is plain, and we intend to perform it, however limited may be our sphere of use, let the consequences individually be what they may. We are thoroughly opposed to slavery, as a question of political economy here and elsewhere. Here, we have abolished it, in the exercise of our own sovereignty. The Southern States have the right to disregard our abstract opinions upon the subject, and abolish or retain it, as they shall decide for themselves, and we clearly have no right, nor can we without *sin,* enter upon a systematic agitation against them, because they see fit to remain slaveholding. We believe Washington was a christian man. We believe there are christian men in the Southern States, who are slaveholders, yea, *more* christian, than those by whom they are so loudly assailed.

One of the great leaders in the anti-slavery crusade, was Theodore Parker, who has lately passed from the stage. The present active leader, is Henry Ward Beecher, whose uncommon gifts, as a popular speaker, have imposed his notions, upon minds less gifted. But it is dangerous for men to yield their independence to the showy and glittering generalities of the orator; and this has been fully demonstrated by the sermon of Mr. Van Dyke, published by us some weeks ago. He proves by Bible references, that slavery was recognized and regulated by Divine law. He also proves that the Saviour did not interfere, by precept or example with slavery, although it existed throughout the Roman empire.

How does Beecher answer this? In his fast-day sermon he says:

"American slavery is not Hebrew slavery; it is Roman slavery. We borrowed every single one of the elemental principles of our system of labor from the Roman law, and not from the Hebrews. The fundamental feature of the Hebrew system was that the slave was a *man* and not a *chattel,* while the fundamental feature of the Roman system was that he was a *chattel* and not a *man*.["]

Now we humbly beg to know, how we are to understand all this? Does Mr. Beecher mean to admit that Hebrew slavery was *right?* Does he mean to admit that negro slavery, would be *right,* provided his master admitted him to be a *man* and abstained from selling him as a *chattel?* Can Mr. Beecher purchase a heathen African and hold him as a slave, and clear his skirts from sin, by proclaiming every Sabbath that his *slave* is a *man?* This distinction without a difference, shows how much easier it is to be superficial, than candid or profound. In another of his sermons his vanity sticks out in comparing a controversy with men of the class of Mr. Van Dyke, as equal to the cruelty of firing grape shot into a flock of pigeons. In other words the great man could do great execution, if he only put forth his great powers, but he abstains in mercy. This dodge will do very well, for the gaping congregation in Plymouth Church, but will hardly go down outside that admiring conclave.

193. Dipping up the Atlantic with a Spoon

(New York *Evening Day-Book* [Breckinridge], January 24, 1861)

The most imaginary thing, to us, in these abnormal and unhealthy times, is the stupendous empiricisms that are proffered on every head to "save the Union," and the wide-spread, almost boundless, display of tomfoolism that is exhibited in every direction. The nation is sick— sick unto death—not with natural disease, for it never was better, but from a purely fancied disorder—a thing of the imagination; in short, a mental delusion, but it may, nevertheless, prove fatal. We have in our midst four millions of negroes, men, it is true, but different and inferior men, who are in a social position in accord with the nature God has given them, and that is best adapted to our own welfare. The presence of these negroes—the relation they bear to the white citizenship—the products of their labor—in short, the *tout ensemble* of what, by an absurd misnomer, is called slavery, is one of the happiest things that has ever occurred in human affairs. The negroes themselves embody more of good, happiness, well-being, than *could* occur to that race in a million of years, while as regards ourselves, it has given origin to such men as Washington, Jefferson, Jackson, Calhoun, Benton, &c., and secured liberty to the white laboring classes; in short, we repeat, this thing, this so-called slavery, is at this moment the most natural, healthy, beneficent, and, in its consequences, the most desirable thing that has existed in human affairs. But a theory is set up that it is an evil to keep negroes in a subordinate position, and consequently a good to "abolish" this condition, and force these negroes into the position of the white man; indeed, a party has sprung up that assumes he is a white man—a Caucasian—a creature like ourselves, except in color, and it proposes to use the government for reducing this theory to practice, not by direct interference with the States, but by penning up this population within existing limits, and thus force the citizenship of the South to abolish their supremacy over their negroes. This, then, is the national disease—this monstrous delusion that fancies negroes are white men, and that would destroy the life of the nation in its mad efforts to carry out its theory—its stupid, impious, disgusting and obscene idea of negro "freedom."

Now, what should be done to cure this disease, to explode this delusion, to abolish this madness, and indeed to punish this monstrous treason to the white man, this abhorrent impiety to God? Why, enlighten the people—demonstrate to them that white is white and black is black—that the negro is a negro and is not a white man—that he is in his natural position of social subordination, and therefore the man or the party that seeks to thrust him into the position of the white man, to use this Government to force negroes into the position of white men, or "impartial freedom," deserves the execration of posterity, and will be doomed to everlasting infamy. But what do we witness? Why, every conceivable quackery and tomfoolery to delude the people still further and more hopelessly. Even the Jews are called in to prescribe in this momentous affair. Dr. Raphall, in a learned lecture, has shown that the Jews had slavery as well as polygamy, and other barbarous customs, four thousand years ago, and respectable and otherwise intelligent citizens listen to this as if it offered a solution for the wide-spread delusion about negroes that threatens to destroy the Republic. What a strange delusion has taken possession of even the opponents of delusion! Why not grapple at once with the stupendous folly that is sweeping over the land? Why not summon up the manhood to declare that this is a republic of white men, and negroes are in their normal condition, before it is "too late?"

194. The American Question

(Buffalo Commercial Advertiser [Lincoln], March 6, 1861)

The subject which now divides the nation has so many aspects, its nature is so mixed, and its relations so complicated, that its discussion and adjustment are attended by perplexities that baffle the wisdom of the wisest, and by difficulties that test the firmness of the most energetic. —Whether the gordian knot is to be cut by the sword of civil war, and [or?] loosened by fraternal compromise, remains to be seen.

Slavery may be looked upon in various lights and from different points of view. It may be regarded as a mere matter of *political economy,* of dollars and cents, affecting the material and productive interests of the country,—as an instrument for the culture of the soil, and other services.

It may be looked upon simply as a *civil institution,* ordained and regulated by positive statute, and put on the same footing precisely as other
establishments, that are created by law and legalized by local and municipal authority. It may, again, be contemplated and treated as a *social*
organization, modifying the manner of life, the morals of the community, the domestic habits and the estimate of labor in places where
it prevails. It is viewed by others from a higher standpoint. They regard
this as an institution of *Divine* appointment, clothed with all the sacred-
ness of religious sanction, and sustained by Scriptural authority. They
treat it as belonging to the normal condition of society, as part and
parcel of the original constitution under which man was placed. We
do not now discuss the truth or falsity of this view. We merely state the
fact as an important item to be weighed in the fair consideration of the
subject. While some thus make it a part of their religion to uphold
slavery, there are others, who, with equal conscienciousness [*sic*], deny its
claims to Divine support, and maintain that this institution is opposed
to the original and best state of society, and utterly at variance with
the laws of God and the precepts of Christianity.

And here is the issue. Here lies the gist of the question. One party,
the defenders of slavery as an ordinance of God, take the ground that
their opinions and practices in relation to the subject are right. It is to
them a matter of conscience, of religious obligation and sacred right,—
a bounden duty to maintain this institution at all hazards. To trench in
any way on its prerogatives, or to prevent its prevalence, is to touch the
apple of their eye, to assault the palladium of their liberties, and to lay
violent hands on the Ark of God. On the other hand, those who differ
from them feel equally constrained by conscience, and by all the dictates
of justice, humanity and religion, to condemn an institution which they
regard as radically wrong and inimical to the best interests of society.
In short, as President Lincoln states in his Inaugural Address, "One
section of our country believes slavery is *right* and ought to be extended,
while the other believes it is *wrong* and ought not to be extended." All
questions about the economical, social and civil aspects of slavery, however important they may be, are merged into the higher ethical and
religious bearings of the subject.—Both the South and the North appeal
to the tribunal of conscience, and the leaders in this conflict of ideas
make it a matter of sacred and imperious duty to maintain their respective grounds. All discussions of the subject, in its lesser and lower
relations, are mere skirmishings on the outside of the battle-field. The
real conflict is not concerning words or modes of society, but about ideas
of right, and convictions of duty. No subject, which does not involve

the conscience and the most sacred principles of men, could produce results such as we now witness.—The real moving cause of this violent agitation is a question of ethics in relation to government,—of deeply seated convictions with reference to their bearing on the fundamental law of the land. If it were a mere abstract enquiring into the right or wrong of Slavery, and if the discussion were limited to a single State, it would be difficult to reach a satisfactory conclusion. The question is embarrassed and complicated by its relations to the Constitution of the country.—Does this instrument ignore or recognize it? Does it condemn or justify it, either expressly or by implication? Is slavery placed under the broad ægis of the Federal compact, and entitled to its protection and patronage in the common domain, where it has never been legally established? Mr. LINCOLN puts the question in his Address: "Must Congress protect slavery in the territories?" To this he answers: "The Constitution does not expressly say."

In the cursory analysis we have given of this much-mooted subject, it is evident that it is a mixed and complex one, involving grave questions of freedom of conscience and of constitutional interpretation. We find that it is that phase of it which makes it a matter of right or of wrong, of human or of Divine authority,—a serious question of conscience and of religious duty,—that it is this view of the topic, which gives the clue and coloring to our interpretations of the Constitution, and modifies all the opinions that are held in relation to it, whether as an element of material prosperity, or as a mere civil and social institute. The question is, then, in fact, one of conscience; and as it now stands before the nation, summoning the contending parties to peaceful adjustment or to the arbitrament of arms, it is in reality, at its basis, a question of religious liberty. The South openly declares this; and while they contend that the plea of conscience on the part of the people of the North is a mere pretence, the deep moral convictions of the Northern people are as much a reality as the alleged conscientiousness of the South. This conflict is only another form and development of the great contest, which has agitated the nations for ages, and involves the fundamental inquiry: What is the proper and legitimate province of civil government in matters of conscience and religious freedom? The exigencies of the case force this enquiry upon us; and it becomes the parties now at variance calmly to consider and fairly to answer this question, before proceeding further. We will then be better prepared to consider what are the guarantees or prohibitions of the Constitution —the obligations of Government and the duty of the people in the premises.

195. A Plain View of Slavery

(Washington (D. C.) *States and Union* [Douglas], March 21, 1861)

It is an unfortunate circumstance for the peace of society and welfare of our country, that radical Northern Republicans do not make themselves familiar with our Southern neighbors by friendly intercourse and a social interchange of sentiment. They have not even returned the friendly visitations made to their streets by gentlemen with their families, who, during the summer season, visit the Northern States. Excepting those who are drawn to the South in the capacity of traveling mercantile agents, and a class of Abolition lecturers, preachers, and tract distributors, no Northern man is ever seen in the South. It is, therefore, impossible that a correct knowledge of the institution of slavery can be claimed by those citizens North and West who have so violently opposed the system, denounced the slave-owners with degrading epithets, and driven them to the foolish act of secession.

In corroboration of the fact that there is a bright side to the institution, and one which should rejoice the heart of the Christian, and cause anti-slavery fanaticism forever to abate its heartless epithets against slave owners, the following statistics, from a reliable source, will have their weight. The negro *slaves* connected with the different churches is 465,000, viz: Methodist, 215,000; Baptist, 157,000; Presbyterian, 38,000; Episcopal, 7,000; Campbellites, 10,000; other sects, 38,000. It is a safe calculation, adds the same authority, (Georgia Educational Journal,) to say that for every colored member three other negroes attend church. In the extreme Southern States, where owners and overseers requires [*sic*] their negroes to attend church, the proportion is larger. These 465,000 multiplied by three, gives 1,395,000 slaves in attendance on Divine Service in the South every Sabbath.

There is food for reflection in these facts. England and the United States engaged in one of the greatest Christian enterprises the world has ever known, when they embarked in Christian missions. In that work vast sums of money have been expended, and many valuable lives have been sacrificed. Yet their labors have been blessed to the conversion of 200,000 souls. But in all this great success, the figures show less than half the number of conversions that have taken place among the colored race in the South, at a cost of no lives, and with a comparatively insignificant outlay of money. These men came originally from among the degraded tribes of Africa, where the climate almost forbids our missionaries to venture; they have been elevated from abject ignorance to a knowledge and belief in the Saviour; some of them are now returning to the shores of Africa, where they have established the Republic of Liberia, introduced good government, schools, churches, seminaries, manufactories, agriculture, &c., and are prospering and disseminating the great principles of civilization and Christianity. Do we not see a providence in these things? Is it right, then, for our Republican neighbors to destroy the Union over an institution that can show so glorious results in the progress of civilization?

196. ROTTEN FOUNDATION

(*Niles* (Mich.) *Republican* [Douglas], March 30, 1861)

There is nothing stable or good on earth built upon a rotten foundation. Bad results must flow from perseverance in falsehood and error. There is no people on earth but can be taught to believe a lie if its reiteration is steadfastly continued for a longer or shorter time. Error is common to finite beings, and many possess a false pride which induces them to persevere in error, even though their country crumbles before them.

The republican party is founded upon error. It starts out with the false idea that all men are born free and equal. If this were so, holy writ would be a bundle of absurdities, and Jesus Christ an impostor— They construe this passage of the Declaration of Independence to mean negroes, and all other tribes of the earth. A greater absurdity never entered into the minds of men. By this they make out that Washington, Jefferson and the host of patriots that brought this government into existence were hypocrites, for neither of them ever aimed to make their slaves equal to themselves. It is certain that our fathers had in view the race of white men, the Anglo Saxon. This government was made for the benefit of the white race, to be governed by them and not by negroes or any other inferior race.

Another error is, that slavery is a great moral sin, and many believe the nation is to be cursed for it—that God will scourge them by fire and sword. This class of men believe that God foresees all things, regulates all things and shapes every thing to his own glory. Thus they will make out God a cruel and inconsistent being, for he led the old thirteen colonies to victory and independence, and, with a single exception, slavery existed in them all. If slavery was such an ungodly institution as many fanatics of the present day believe, how is it that God could establish such a government as this, when he knew a portion of it would be dedicated to slavery? Truly, these fanatics are wiser in their own eyes than God himself. They censure God and many of them kick the Holy writing under their feet, and even go so far as to give a reason why Jesus Christ (who came into the world to rebuke sin), did not rebuke slavery, but commanded them to be obedient to their masters. They say he was fearful of bloodshed and civil strife, thus making him out a coward. They censure St. Paul for sending back a runaway slave to Philemon.—Their whole fabric is on a rotten foundation. Nothing but clear plain truth can stand the test of time. Errors have ruined nations before ours. Blind guides have caused the destruction of millions of precious lives and filled the world with mourning. Nation after nation has been blotted from existence by falsehood and deception. The northern people have been led by political demagogues to believe a lie, and we now see before us a ruined nation. We see no more the glorious American flag unfurled in the seven States in this Union, and ere long six or seven more will have left to try their destiny with their southern sisters. We witness all these things with pain and sorrow. We cannot see our once glorious Union going to pieces without weeping at the sight. We cannot see it without calling upon every father to use his efforts to stay the wreck for the sake of his children.

We say the republican party of the North is founded in error. The crusade against the South is unjust, unholy and must result in our total ruin as a nation. God has a purpose in view in American slavery. It cannot be to pull down this great nation which he has blessed beyond all others, for he would be inconsistent. We see the good effects of American slavery on the African race. We see them among civilization christianized. We see American slavery sending back missionaries to Africa.—We see them much more happy in this than in their native clime. God['s] purposes are to send the Gospel to every creature, and prepare the way for the coming of the King of Kings. American slavery is more mild than any which has existed in all history. Behold this race—who can elevate the masses of them? Are they your equals, you republicans? God has not so ordered it. They can never be made your equals. Some men were born to govern, others to be governed. "The servant is not equal to his master."

We say the republican party rests upon a rotten foundation. It assumes that Congress has sovereign power over the people—that it must tell the people of all our national domain what they shall not have— that they shall not have slaves. The people are sovereigns, under our constitution, and it is for them to determine this matter. In the language of Clay, on this subject, "Congress must abstain, Congress must remain passive and let the people decide."

The republican party is in error inasmuch as it has departed entirely from the principles laid down in holy writ. The Pharisees thanked God they were not like other men. The republicans are Pharisees, pretending to great righteousness, set themselves up as models of perfection, intolerant, bigoted and impervious to truth. [sic] They see great faults in their neighbors, but cannot see their own. The leaders shout, "hurrah for freedom every where and equality," and the cry is echoed by their followers, as a thousand wolves will send back an answering howl to their leader, and with equal greediness they devour all before them. They have no respect for the opinions of their neighbors. They talk flippantly now of hanging democrats who do not agree with them, and suppose it would be as easy a task as it was to hang the witches of Salem.

The principles of the republican party are wrong in every particular, and carried out, must be fatal, and such men as Seward know it. They have obtained power under false pretences. They said they would prohibit slavery in the territories, and just so soon as they had the power they organized three territories, viz: Dacotah, Nevada, and Colorodo [sic], and never attempted to engraft the Wilmot proviso in the organic acts—showing clearly their hypocrisy.—The South believed they were in earnest.—The South saw the powerful array against them. They heard their speeches and declarations, their slanders, and believed they would wage an "irrepressible conflict" against them, and when the government itself fell into their hands, they left them. It was a hard thing to sunder the ties which bound this Union together, and it was useless, too, for although they obtained power they dare not carry out their avowed principles. The government can never be administered upon any other than the principles contended for by the democracy, and Mr. Seward and Mr. Lincoln know it well.

They have already abandoned their darling project of Congressional prohibition of slavery in territories. They have adopted the popular sovereignty policy, and the South have nothing to fear. Let them but remain in the Union and all will be well, for the republican party rests upon a rotten foundation, and it cannot stand. It must fall. There must, and there will be a revolution in the North, and when it comes it will sweep like a whirlwind.

197. THE WRONG ARGUMENT

(Wabash (Ind.) *Plain Dealer* [Lincoln], April 5, 1861)

Among the many arguments advanced by the South in support of their peculiar institution, is, that society demands as a necessity demands, as a necessity, to work in its various departments of labor men of every capacity, running from statesmen down to ditch-diggers. [*sic*] The fallacy lies not in the assertion that society must have[,] like the human body, feet and hands to do menial service, as well as an intellect to guide and direct and control, but rather in using these facts as an argument in behalf of slavery. No one, we think, who has exercised the slightest observation in reference to the formation of society, will for a moment deny that its great and magnificent purposes are and must be reached by the instrumentality of men of inferior mental endowments as well as of men of the most transcendant genius. Inferior men are a society [*sic*] necessity. Society must have a foundation, a basis, men to do its drudgery, dig its ditches, build its railroads and canals; and let us remark here, *en passant,* that labor in the humblest walks of life is as honorable as labor in the highest. If God has seen fit to deny us the endowments with which He has gifted others, our honest efforts are as commendable as those of the most brilliant and daring genius. There is, there can be nothing criminal in the decrees of Providence.—The poor Irishman, who follows his wheel-barrow and gains but an humble livelihood by the sweat of his brow, is as noble an object in the sight of Him in whose hands are the sublime destinies of the world, as he who sits imperious and enthroned at the head of a kingdom.

But to return. Because society must have a basis, because there must be cotton cultivators in the South, does it logically follow; is it a legitimate conclusion, that Slavery in the South is right? Or is it, therefore, even a matter of political necessity? We are persuaded that it is neither. It neither establishes the morality of servitude, nor does it dictate its necessity. The North demands railroad builders. Is this want ground for the servitude of all railroad builders? Heaven has left this question as to who shall be the head and who the feet of society, to the comparative capacities of men. It is the pride, the boast of free institutions to throw nothing—no obstacle, no law—in the way of a fair and honorable solution of this question. The boat hand may rise to be a Judge. He who to-day splits rails for an humble support, tomorrow rules the destiny of a mighty nation.—But the institution of slavery, indiscriminately, without regard to capacity, fixes forever the condition of men, as soon as they are one by one ushered into the world. Heaven has declared that all of these men may grasp after, and some of them reach the noble purposes of life.—The law with a profane assertion of superiority, declares that all shall be slaves! and all die the death of vagabonds!

But it will be urged that the hot, sultry climate of the South forbids white labor, and that black labor will not exist except by compulsion. Let us admit this with referance [sic] to a narrow strip of country running across the extreme South—Mississippi, Alabama, and those extreme Southern States. The proposition is, that society in the Cotton States cannot exist without the cultivation of cotton, and that cotton cannot be cultivated without slave labor. Suppose this all be true. Does it justify human bondage? Is the liberty of innocent human beings to be balanced in the scale with bales of cotton? We, of the boasted European caste, are accustomed, in the toasts and orations of our Fourth of July celebrations, to prize our liberty next to honor and life. Is this merely declamatory extravagance, or is it truth; and if truth, is it not so as applied to all races of men? Or, is the Caucasian face the passport to political freedom—the royal stamp which distinguishes the freeman from the bondman? The regaining of our liberties justifies the spilling of human blood, excuses the terrors of revolution and the crash of empires.—But the liberty of the African must be measured by the loss of a single paltry product of the earth! Stating the position is sufficient to refute it.

All this demonstrates that slavery in the South has but one excuse. The institution has grown by time and ingenuity combined, into the permanency and stability of an establishment. Those in possession of it now inherited it. They are in no manner responsible for its being ingrafted upon the political tree of the South. It was morally wrong at first; it is morally wrong now. To cut away suddenly, however, from the parent tree, would no doubt bring about a greater wrong than now exists. We are persuaded that these considerations are a sufficient apology for Southern slavery, without attempting to sustain it on the ground that it was originally right, and is now, and also that it is necessary to the successful growth of cotton, inasmuch as its cultivation is a drudgery, and beneath the scorching rays of a tropical sun.

Let the idea of fixed conditions and caste never creep into our text book of beneficial, political principles. The Chinese and the Indian Empires are stupendous examples of warning to us in this respect. They demonstrate, in terms not to be mistaken, that if the conditions of man are fixed and unchanged—that if the hope of rising and the fear of falling in the world, are not permitted to operate upon their minds, life is an unceasing inactivity, a dull monotony, without progress, and society an unending, eternal rest!

198. The Highest Status of the Negro

(New York Daily News [Breckinridge], April 10, 1861)

That socially and politically the negro is not the equal of the Caucasian is admitted generally at the North. Black Republican New York, when voting for Lincoln, repudiated the idea of negro suffrage, and some of the States of the West, that committed the same blunder at the last election, actually exclude the negro from their borders. Such a condition of inferiority, though in accordance with natural laws which have stamped on the negro a deficiency in mental vigor and in the faculty of will, is far from satisfactory. It leaves the negro an alien in the land of his birth, and a Pariah and outcast from society.

Very different is that relation which gives him a patron and protector in the dominant race who stands sponsor for him to society and who is responsible for him to the laws. The position of the negro is there defined; his duties are plainly recognized; he is relieved from the struggle for existence with a strange race, and from the influence of prejudice and oppression; he has but a single master to whom he is responsible, who watches over his well being and comfort, and in old age and sickness supports and protects him. His existence, it is true, is not idle; though relieved from the cares which belong to a highly artificial state of society, he shares in its benefits and enjoys the blessings of civilization without being subjected to the sufferings and calamities that befall so many of the dominant race. The increase of the race and the longevity of individuals attest that slavery is the best possible condition of the negro. To emancipate is to destroy the negro, unless it would, at the same time, separate him from contact with the more powerful family. Emancipation is death—slavery is life. Freedom for the negro is that of the savage—to elevate, ameliorate and Christianize him is the work of slavery. True philanthropy and respect for the happiness of the negro teach that slavery, as it exists at the South, confers the greatest good on his race. It is the highest and happiest status he has ever reached, and the true friends of the African are the supporters of this institution which makes him the companion and friend of the white, and links the latter, by the potent ties of self-interest, to watch over and protect him and his. Who would sever these friendly, confidential and pleasant relations in which the superior and inferior assume so naturally their position with respect to each other, and for it substitute an intolerable tyranny on one side and bitter hatred on the other? None but the crazy Abolitionists of the North, now ready to destroy the happiness of the country that four millions of blacks may starve and die in wretchedness and indolence.

199. The Ethics of Our Political Faith

(Rockford Register [Lincoln], April 13, 1861)

The Republican doctrine as set forth in the Chicago Platform, involves a vital principle in ethics, which makes the party consistently acting therefrom a living body, whose growth and maturity must be commensurate with the ultimate perfection of our political system.

By refusing to incorporate the institution of slavery into our national polity, and determining to regard it henceforth as the temporary creation of local law, which an advancing civilization will modify, ameliorate, and finally altogether repeal, a way is opened for the descent into the public mind of the pure principles of Divine Justice, which shall yet bring our national government into full accord with that immutable order which rules throughout the universe, and secures the stability of the kingdom of Heaven.

The vital principle referred to is that of the Equality of Man—a truth not obvious to the senses, but one that is hidden in God, and revealed to those only who in all sincerity approach Him. This vital truth, even though it be the central thought, the pivot upon which turns the whole system of free government, was yet but dimly recognized by the men who put their signatures to that immortal Bill of Rights which first gave it a political expression. Its light flashed forth for a season, and all well-disposed minds gave it an unquestioning assent; but the magnitude of its importance could not be fully disclosed in that day. If, then, those earnest, self-sacrificing men, the fathers of our Republic, could see the truth but dimly, how altogether obscure must it have been to the self-seeking politicians of a later period? And how totally must it have been eclipsed, when, during the administration of Mr. Van Buren, the presiding officer of the U. S. Senate solemnly affirmed that he would not recognize any higher law than the Constitution, and that whoever did so in that body was a traitor! From that hour commenced the decline and fall of the Democratic party, which, having lost the rule, is now madly striving to effect the ruin of our government. Who can fail to perceive that this wonderful transformation is the direct effect of political atheism?

In referring to these events we have no purpose of casting censure or reproach upon any person connected with them. Far otherwise. We know that the light of that primary truth, of which we have spoken, had disappeared, like a star that had sunk below the horizon, in the first evening of our political existence. But now, as the morning dawns, and we are entering upon the "first day" of our national genesis, its light re-appears with seven-fold splendor, and the great doctrine of Equality stands forth a perpetually shining orb in the sphere of natural science. The truth is now beginning to be understood that no mere man can be said to be possessed of an underived life, or to have *life in himself*, for the reason that this is an exclusively Divine attribute; and it is this great truth that makes each one of God's human creatures the equal of every other; for when life in all is derived from God, no one can have a claim to superiority over another. It matters not what may be the endowments of an individual—however brilliant in intellect, or pure in morals—there is no merit in the case, upon which to found a claim to individual superiority over the merest profligate and vagabond on earth. All such claims are founded upon the sensuous fallacy that the life of a man is his own, and is not derived from God.

Hitherto we have, as a people, been sadly blind to these truths, and consequently devoid of that genuine humility which is an inseparable accompaniment of true dignity. We have been inflated with pride at our supposed superior endowments over the people of other nations and tribes, and have been filled with contempt toward such as are of less lofty pretension than we are. Witness, for instance, the boasting, self-glorifying, spread-eagle style of oratory that has been so popular in this country until very recently; and bear in mind, also, the cruel treatment and gross injustice which four millions of helpless, unresisting, service-loving Africans are constantly receiving from our people. Before the testimony of these two witnesses we must bow our heads in shame and deep contrition, and perform the works of true repentance, before we can be enabled to see the light which Revelation and Science unite in offering for our relief. That work has been begun, and will no doubt be carried forward, either with or without our individual co-operation. Let each one remember, however, that it is his privilege to co-operate in the great and good work, and thus be borne along to those mansions of rest which are open for the reception of all who shall have worked earnestly and faithfully in the cause.

In this work our political action is made conformable to, and sanctified by a truly religious life; for we are laboring in an unselfish cause, even that of rescuing the creatures of God, whom He designs shall receive the impress of His own image, from that perpetual degradation to which a false, atheistic policy is endeavoring to consign them. We are laboring to establish Justice in our political affairs, which alone can secure for ourselves and our posterity the blessings of Liberty. We are, in short, but pursuing that straight-forward course of duty toward God and our fellow man that shall open our hearts and understandings for the reception of a larger measure of the Divine life, and thus be enabled to beautify the earth, by substituting good for evil, blessing for cursing, good-will toward all, and hatred of none.

This is the high purpose for which we are to-day called upon to devote ourselves—a purpose which includes all earthly good, and reaches beyond into the whole future. We believe that the leading men of our country are animated by this purpose, and that they are and will be endowed with wisdom and strength to firmly pursue it, offering no concession or compromise to its enemies, and regarding no event as a calamity but such as would weaken, turn aside, or thwart this holy purpose. We believe it to be in accord with the Divine purpose, and therefore to be pursued at whatever cost. This is the sentiment of a majority of the people, and we rejoice that we have at last attained to a political faith based upon sound principles of ethics.

XII

THE "CHIVALRY"

200. THE ERA OF LIBERTY

(Chicago Daily Democrat [Lincoln], October 31, 1860)

When one reflects upon the long and grievious [*sic*] oppression under which the people of the Free States of this confederacy have lived for nearly forty years, and remembers that the days of this oppression are numbered, and that the era of Liberty has already dawned, it becomes difficult to express the feelings of exultation and joy to which these thoughts give birth.

Who are these men who have lauded [*sic*] it so long and so despotically over the freemen of the North? They are men who dreamed of freedom in a slave's embrace, and waking, sold her offspring and their own to slavery. They are men who prated of freedom for the sake of establishing and perpetuating slavery; who boasted of liberty that they might exercise despotism; who vaunted their own prowess and chivalry that they might conceal their in[n]ate cowardice and meanness. Wedded to a system so barbarous that its reflex influence had made barbarians of them, they assumed for themselves the possession of all the graces and virtues of life, and dictated to the rest of the nation what should be considered the tests of refinement and gentility. Sneering at the honest free-laborers of the North, and stigmatizing as "mud-sills" and "white slaves" the men who earned their own livelihood by their own industry, they pilfered from the unpaid laborers on their plantations the products of their unwilling toil, and urged them by the whip, to new exertions, whenever their coffers ran low. Boasting of their chivalry and manliness, they answered arguments against the system which made them the reproach of the civilized world, by cowardly and murderous attacks, with bludgeon and pistol, upon an unarmed and defenceless Senator. Extolling themselves as masters of logic and as proficients in the theory as well as the practice of government, they reply [*sic*] with blackguard abuse and pot-house ribal[d]ry to those who exposed the rottenness of their social and political life upon the floor of Congress.—They attempted to suppress freedom of petition and of debate; they succeeded

508

in abolishing the freedom of speech and of the press in fifteen of the States of the Union; they placed their tools in every Federal office in the country; they bent the whole force of the government, legislative, executive, and judicial, to their purposes, until at length no one who did not recognize and defend slavery as the National Institution of the country, and as defended by the constitution as a sacred and invaluable thing, could hold the meanest office in the land.

And now all this is to be changed. Liberty, and not Slavery, is henceforth to be the end of the government. It is to be administered for Freedom and not for Slavery. The fitness of an applicant for office will be estimated, not by his devotion to Slavery, but by his devotion to Freedom. The government will return to the policy of the fathers, and slavery will be placed in the process of ultimate extinction.

The Constitution of the United States is the bulwark and foundation of the Republican party. We stand by it, and accept it as the rule of our action. It is an Anti-Slavery Instrument. Its framers were careful to avoid the introduction of a single word that should intimate the recognition of the right of property in man.—Wherever the constitution of the Union exerts undivided sway, there Freedom reigns with complete and undivided dominion. But it also saves to the several States their own individual rights, and we have no desire to interfere with them. The slave States can keep their barbarous system of slavery to themselves, but they can no longer force it upon us. We will let them alone. We will surround them with a cordon of Free States, as with a wall of fire.—We will hem them in, on all sides, by free and happy communities, rejoicing in perfect liberty, and progressing toward national and social greatness. Deprived of the aid of the general government, and thrown in upon itself for support, slavery must gradually die out— and the child is now born who will live to see the emancipation of the last slave upon the American Continent.

201. Secession Not Favorable to the Luxury of Safe Violence

(Daily Boston Traveller [Lincoln], November 20, 1860)

There is one point in connection with the general subject of secession, which it would be well for those unfraternal gentlemen, "our Southern brethren," to take into serious consideration, before they shall proceed to destroy the Union for the purpose of forming a Southern Confederacy. Has it ever occurred to them that by withdrawing from the Union they would cut themselves off, forever, from the inestimable privilege of lynching Yankees with impunity? As things now are, they have it in their power to torment every man from the free States who is foolish enough to go among them, and also every woman, which is the greater luxury of the two, particularly if she happen to be ill, and has sought "the sunny South" in search of health, but without any idea of finding the country too hot to hold her. All the delights that come from tarring and feathering defenceless Northrons, and of hearing the more timid of them scream, must be given up with the Union. Now, when a Yankee at the South becomes "suspect," he can be bullied, beaten, banged, and bruised with perfect safety to the bullies, beaters, bangers, and bruisers who take him in hand. His countrymen may become angry at the language that is addressed to him, and they may wince at the lashes laid on his innocent back, or they may think that for five hundred creatures to torment one man is not precisely correct; but what can they do about it? They can't help themselves or the victims, and the knowledge that they can't increases the enjoyment of their "sport" by the "Southern brethren" aforesaid. But there will come a change over all this, should the Union be broken up, and should Yankees stand to Southern Confederates in the position of foreigners. As the Southrons have now to refrain from the luxury of lynching Old Englanders, so then would they have to refrain from that of lynching New Englanders. The first abuse of a Yankee at their hands would be the signal for war upon them, and they would have to pay dear for that which they now have *gratis,* greatly to our shame. Or, we might retaliate by seizing upon such members of "the chivalry" as should be wandering about in search of adventures, and mete to them the measure received by our citizens at the hands of "the chivalry" at home. This matter is one that the Cotton States would do well to think of, or they may find their free trade in flogging abolished, and their illustrious people punished with many stripes.

202. AMERICA, OR AUSTRIA?

(Cincinnati Daily Commercial [Lincoln], December 1, 1860)

The recent proscriptive and despotic treatment to which many Northern citizens have been subjected in the South, is one of the most serious and deplorable effects of the present political excitement. If not speedily arrested, it threatens to lead to the most disastrous consequences. It is impossible to maintain harmony and good feeling between the different sections of the country, where any considerable number of the people of one section are liable to continual outrage and persecution whenever they set foot in the other. The freedom of transit and the liberty of opinion must be preserved at whatever hazard, or we are no longer one people, possessed of equal rights to life and liberty. If such outrages are to go on, as have recently disgraced certain localities in the South, this nation is no longer a Republic, where the rights of all citizens are respected through all its borders, but a semi-despotic country, a part of which is controlled by an organized tyranny, and ruled by the despotism of a mob.

It is the disgrace of the absolute governments of the Old World, that a continual espionage and inquisition are kept up on the movements of all who come within their borders. Men are here watched and guarded, inspected and vise[e]d, their movements noted, their words reported, and their opinions scrutinized by an omnipresent and all-penetrating system of espionage. Go where they may, on business or pleasure, the sleepless eye of despotism is upon them. It has its informers in every village, its spies in every hotel. An incautious word, or the suspicion of entertaining liberal sentiments, may at any moment subject the traveler to arrest or insult at the hands of the meddling officials of this political inquisition.

In America, it has hitherto been our proud boast, that all men were free from any scrutiny of this kind, either at the hands of the government or of individuals. Wholly freed from the cumbrous and burdensome system of traveling passports which prevails abroad, the people of all sections of this country, as well as aliens and foreigners from all parts of the world, were free to come and go, unquestioned and unchallenged. Security of person, and liberty of opinion, have been in the United States something more than a name—they have been a reality. That which our Revolutionary fathers established, and our Constitution guaranteed, has also been, in practice, an established fact. This entire immunity from interference with the personal freedom and natural rights of men, has been the crowning glory of our institutions. We have stood before the world, a proud example of a Republic, where freedom of action and liberty of speech were guaranteed to every citizen. It has been our boast that the normal principle of our social order and governmental polity was LIBERTY, GUARDED BY LAW.

We repeat—this *has been* the happy distinction of our Republic. Recent events in many parts of the Southern States, taken in connexion with the new threats that are made, and the new tests that are attempted to be imposed, threaten to interrupt all freedom of intercourse, if not to destroy utterly the good name of our Republic as a free nation. Citizens of the Northern States, peaceable, inoffensive, and attentive to their own business, have been subjected to repeated insult and outrage at the hands of a portion of the people of the South. Men with no political associations whatever, pursuing the quiet tenor of their journey, without the slightest offence by word or deed, have been rudely interrupted and turned back by threats of violence, if they pursued their way further. Merchants who themselves contribute largely to the prosperity and material interests of the South, have been insulted and warned off, without the smallest provocation on their part. Travellers from the North, even in advance of any expression of their opinions, have been waited upon by unlawful and irresponsible "vigilance committees," and bidden to leave on the first train.

Not only so, but many of the residents of the South itself have been persecuted and expelled. Teachers have been driven from their schools, ministers of the gospel from their parishes, and merchants and mechanics from their lawful pursuits, on mere conjecture and suspicion of entertaining "unwholesome opinions." A system of inquisition and espionage has been inaugurated, wholly without precedent in this country, and without a parallel, save in the worst and most absolute despotisms of the old world. Men have been arrested on mere suspicion, condemned without a hearing, and subjected to the infamous and savage punishment of tar and feathers, or riding on rails, or barbarous flogging on the bare back. Not only have these things been done without color of law, but the most lawless and violent proceedings have been openly approved and sanctioned by the officers sworn to execute the laws, and protect the liberty of the citizen.

This infamous inquisition rules in some regions of the Cotton States as with a rod of iron. So far from being held in check by public opinion, it has succeeded, apparently, in sweeping public opinion headlong in its own direction, and it claims the omnipotent sanction of the majority as its defence. It is merciless, unscrupulous, truculent, reckless, audacious, and false. Its leaders are impervious to argument, deaf to the voice of justice, insensible to pity and lost to shame. With the iron hand of irresponsible power, it executes its swift decrees, and with fanaticism absolute and unrestrained, it riots in the violence and disorder it has created. It tramples upon individual rights, tears down every muniment of personal freedom, and threatens to destroy the last safeguard of constitutional liberty.

These statements are borne out by facts, numerous and well authenticated, which are reported by most recent visitors to the Southern States, and find their way into the papers of the South themselves. The question arises—and it is one of an importance which cannot be overrated—where are these things to end? Are we to surrender the distinction of being a free country? Shall we quietly see established and fortified in our midst a worse than Austrian despotism? Are we to behold an American inquisition, having its head-quarters in the capitals of the South, and its ramifications in every village, which, like the Revolutionary Tribunal of FOUQUIER[-] TINVILLE and ROBESPIERRE, shall establish one universal reign of terror in the land?—Are all the rights and privileges of American citizenship to go for nothing, and all our constitutional guarantees to be trampled pell-mell under foot? Are we to understand, that the privileges and immunities of citizens are henceforth annulled, so far as a part of the States are concerned, and that if we go there, we have got to hold our personal security and our opinions at the dictation of a mob?

If these are the liberties of American citizens, then they are not worth preserving. If these things are to continue, no man with a spark of manhood in him will ever again hold up his head in pride, when he hears the name of the United States of America. He will rather hang his head in shame and sorrow that the only Republic on the globe has gone backward—that intolerance and fanaticism have triumphed over liberty and intelligence—that American citizenship is become a mockery, and American freedom a name.

But we will not, for the credit and honor of our common country, yield to such melancholy anticipations as these. We will not relinquish the hope, that the voice of reason and justice will prevail over the temporary terrors of bigotry and inquisitorial power. When the counsels of moderation have been heard, when the windy gusts of the tempest of fanaticism have exhausted their violence, when the evil spirit has gone out of our Southern brethren, we shall trust to behold them once more calm and in their right minds. Our liberty and our union have cost too much, and endured too long, to be thus lightly sacrificed or thrown away. When the returning reason of our fellow citizens of the cotton States shall have shown them these things in their true relations, we may hope that our national peace and harmony will return, and all sections of the country will see more clearly, from the sad experience of this divergency, that the only bond of our union, as well as the sole guarantee of our personal rights, is LIBERTY, GUARDED BY LAW.

203. SOUTHERN ATROCITIES UPON NORTHERN MEN

(*Chicago Daily Tribune* [Lincoln], December 13, 1860)

The people of the North have not been in the habit of calculating the value of the Union. Love for the Republic as represented in the confederacy of *all* the States, has been, and is to-day, a sentiment which all the men of the North rightfully claim to share. They do not ask themselves, Is this confederation profitable in a pecuniary sense? Is the maintenance of this partnership the best thing that we can do? Have we not hopes of profit and gratification elsewhere that we may pursue? Does not our continuance in this Union make us in part responsible for the guilt and sin of human slavery; and is it not our duty to withdraw and leave the institution to its fate? No discussion of these things in the North has been permitted, save by an inconsiderable faction. The Union sentiment has overridden everything else. The Union as our fathers made it—the representative of our national pride and power; the Union as the hope of the friends of free institutions and self-government the world over; the Union as a compact to which we have agreed, and which public policy and common justice will not permit us to dissever—this Union has been the watchword of all political parties, and, in some way or another, the hope of all patriots. The devotion to it has been idolatrous. The desire to preserve it intact, and hand it down to them who should come after us, has many times stifled the voice of justice, over-ridden the dictates of humanity and nullified the beneficent purposes for which it was originally formed. During all the years in which returning despotism, or, as Mr. Lincoln has it, "re-appearing tyranny" has been making its stealthy advances, sapping one after another the guarantys [sic] of personal freedom, and, one after another, the principles upon which all rational liberty rests; in which the purpose if not frame work of our government has been radically changed from a Democracy, the protector and benefactor of the many, to an Oligarchy, the insolent guardian of the interests of the few—during all this time, in all the political changes and the vicissitudes of parties, there has been no murmur against the Union. Men have seen and watched the approach of the dangers, but have hoped that, whatever might occur, the Union would remain untouched. No party in the moment of triumph has had the hardihood, if it had the desire, to assail it; no one smarting under the stings of defeat has dared to attempt the recompense of its losses by assailing it. It has been the symbol of political faith which nothing but treason has questioned.

The inquiry has been started— How long under the provocations which daily come upon the North from half a dozen States of the South, will this devotion last? How long shall the people of these infected places remain in an attitude of antagonism to the fundamental idea upon which the government is built— The majority shall rule; how long shall we be compelled to note the daily violations of the Constitution as well as of common decency and common sense in the treatment of

Northern men in the South; how long shall these manifold lynchings, hangings, maimings, whippings and tarring-and-featherings of white men for suspected political opinions, continue in the Cotton States; how many more men will be barrelled up alive and rolled into the Mississippi River, for having voted for Lincoln; how many more, as guiltless as babes of all just cause of offence, must be maltreated in their persons and injured in their estates, because they happen to be of Northern faith; how long will a mob with demoniac passions usurp the functions of legislatures, judges, executioners, and keep up a reign of terror in the South; how long must the mails be closed against Northern letters and papers, or, the mails being open, how long will the system of post-office *espionage,* which no European despotism dare practice, be in operation, before this devotion to the Union will be overcome and an irrepressible desire for separation take its place? We are ready to answer now. Unless citizens of this Republic can be citizens everywhere within its limits, and be protected fully and cheerfully in the rights which belong to them as free men, and which are guaranteed in the Constitution; unless this wholly barbarous business of beating, burning, hanging, drowning American citizens who are innocent of offences known to the laws; unless, in a word, the men of the North are placed on an equality in the States with men of the South, and unless they, in pursuit of peaceful, laudable and legal purposes, can enjoy the immunity from violence which is granted to the pro-slavery brawlers and fanatics who visit us, and unless it be definitely agreed that, in the maintenance of public order, the majority, expressing its will and doing its acts in obedience to the forms and spirit of the fundamental law, are to govern, this Union is not worth preserving; and the sooner the semi-barbarians who are now within it, betake themselves to other political associations and other forms of government, be the consequences to us and them what they may, the better will the interests of all parties be served! We demand justice in the Union; and failing to obtain it, would ignominiously expel the States which deny it, and afterward persuade them into decency as a foreign power.

This is strong language; but it will square exactly with the sentiments which full three-fourths of the Northern people entertain. They want, furthermore, all the questions involved in this matter to be settled now, and in such a way that no like abuses and outrages will occur again; and they will submit to no compromise, no adjustment, that does not cover and protect the rights of white men in the South to their lives, their liberty, and their property, against not only mobs but that mob-law which has the form of legislative enactment. We listen to no suggestions of peace until this thing is done, and the honor of the North is restored. We should be cowards to ask and traitors to accept less. Let no one say that the demand is unnecessary and the threat one that the free States will not back up by deeds. The times require just this plain talk; because, within the month past, depending upon the forbearance of the North and her unwillingness to disturb or jeopardize existing relations, for the protection of her sons, the business of lynching, always too brisk, has become so common and so wide spread, and is pursued with such evident malice and intention to wound and insult, that it can be submitted to no more. We take up no paper printed in the Cotton States in which accounts of these pro-slavery *auto-da-fes* [*sic*] are not found; we see no traveller from that region, who, if a Northern man, does not return with a sense of thankfulness that his life has been spared; we see no letters that do not refer to scenes which make strong men clinch their hands and set their teeth in a burning rage, that such things should be on American soil. Talk of the escape of negroes and Northern disregard of law! Since election day, the number of white men who have suffered death or punishment hardly less severe, or expulsion or degradation of some sort, at the hands of slave-holding mobs, far exceeds the aggregate of all the slaves that have been rescued from the hands of the officers of the law since the government was founded. Talk of Northern insults to the South! We talk of injuries more irreparable than those which words inflict—of atrocities which make our government, and the Union a sham, and which, as the indispensable prerequisite to anything else, *must be* suppressed!

204. War in the Event of Secession

(Bellefontaine (Ohio) *Republican* [Lincoln], December 15, 1860)

Whatever may be the opinion respecting the right of any of the original States, signing the confederation, to secede, there can be no doubt respecting the absence of any right to secede, belonging to the states subsequently admitted.

As for the Carolinas, little needs to be said. South Carolina was Tory during the revolution. She had no "revolutionary fathers." She is *bastard* —politically speaking. Excepting Marion, and Sumpter, with a handfull of followers, there were no friends of Washington in South Carolina, during the times that tried men[']s souls. She has been always Tory ever since that time. The men of the north conquered the State of Carolina during the war of the revolution. We may do so again; and will do so, if there can be any evidence produced, that her people are capable

of self government, and are worth the trouble of being licked into
decency.

As for North Carolina, it is known that she is the most ignorant and
degraded of all the States. In North Carolina in 1850, there were 73,566
white inhabitants over twenty years of age, who could not read and
write. And of those who could read and write, how many could read
without spelling, or write legibly? And this is one of those States that
purpose to dispense with the schoolmaster altogether, rather than hire
one from the north! Their politicians object to the north sending books
and newspapers amongst their citizens, to enlighten them. They will
soon have no cause of fear from that source, for ere long, there will be no
body down there, who can read them.

They eat mud in North Carolina.—They have a kind of blue clay
that the denizens devour. They stuff their bellies full of this, till their
eyes goggle out, so you might knock them off with a stick.

The people are like oysters—without brains, but bellies full of mud.
It might be supposed that this habit of dirt eating, had rendered them
idiotic, if it were not certain, that they must have been idiotic in the
first place, or they would never have begun the practice. There is not
a single "son of chivalry" in North Carolina, (nor South Carolina either,)
who can speak the plain english [sic] word "there." "Dar," he will say—
or possibly "dah." They are all fully africanized [sic] in intelligence and
morals, and are fast becoming so in blood. The Carolinas may go in
welcome, so far as we are personally concerned. But we have no doubt
it would be good policy, after the niggers are done with them, to drive
what may remain into the swamps of Florida, as food for al[l]igators.
You should remember the Helots, and the fate of Messenians. But away
[sic] do we talk to you thus; you cannot read.

As for Florida we have a word to say, applicable to many other States.
We bought the *claim* of Florida from Spain on account of her geographical position. We bought it without reference to the wishes of those who
inhabited it. We afterwards conquered it from its rightful owners, the
Seminoles. Florida cost the Confederation more than a hundred millions
of dollars. Florida had in 1850, 39,314 slaves. Counting those as a whole
—old grizzly's young cubs yet unlicked, the lame, and halt, and blind,
at $700 a head, we would have twenty-seven million 3 hundred and
nineteen thousand eight hundred or about *one-third* of the amount the
country cost us. Is it a very likely thing that we are going to all that
expense, in bringing the miserable little abortion into existence, and
then permit her to dictate to us, what we must do? We let her into the
Confederation it is true, but upon *our terms*. She now says she don't

like the terms. Very well; go out again; but remember you return to
just the position you occupied, before we admitted you, upon your own
petition. You are a territory—a *province,* ruled by a governor appointed
by the Confederation, and are brought into submission, if necessary,
by the military arm. That is all you are. We never expected to get our
money out of you; we did'nt [*sic*] buy you, because we had any particular love for you. We bought and paid for you for our own convenience,
and we expect to use you accordingly.

It is a nice thing truly, if you or any other purchased territory of this
government, can come into the Confederation one day—become a sovereign State; exercise your sovereignty the next day, and convey yourself—our property, away into the arms of England or France, or any
other foreign power. If you think you can do it, try it. We have reasoned
with you, coaxed you, giving you coppers and sing[ing] pretty baby
songs to you, but you must be licked, that is plain to see.

205. SOUTHERN TREATMENT OF NORTHERN CITIZENS

(Davenport Daily Gazette [Lincoln], December 19, 1860)

Right glad are we that public attention is being turned earnestly to
the treatment of Northern citizens when in Southern States. For the
sake of peace between the rival sections of the Union, much has been
left unsaid which should have been uttered long ago. Now, it is time
to speak out, not only with a feeling of indignation which has long
been smouldering, but agreeably to the stern determination of free men,
to submit no longer quietly to such outrageous wrongs as have been
perpetrated. The evidence comes pouring upon us—and, be it understood, not mere sensation evidence—that Northern men cannot travel
in the South upon their ordinary business without they are prepared,
at all times and upon all occasions, to clothe themselves with cursing
as with a garment, upon the mere utterance of the name of Abraham
Lincoln—that the faintest shadow of having exercised a freeman's right
in the North in favor of free soil, free speech and human liberty, brings
the lash, tar and feathers, and perhaps the hangman's rope or banishment, into requisition, in accordance with the supposed magnitude of
the offence. In fact, no man can be a man in the South, or rest with a
reasonable assurance of continued existence, unless eating dirt at the
feet of the all-controlling influence of the Slave Power. Men high in authority, and of acknowledged social position, countenance this state of
things, and interested and ignorant satellites at every cross-road take
the initiative from their superiors, and with a recklessness of purpose

which has scarcely a parallel in history, acts are perpetrated which should not only be discountenanced by any civilized community, but meet with a severe, swift and certain retribution.

We believe that, at the bottom of this matter, there is a prominent moving cause, which is not permitted to come fairly before the American people. Bankruptcy is staring the South in the face. A huge indebtedness hangs over them, the liquidation of which is beyond present, or perhaps prospective control. Accredited agents, traveling for commercial houses, discover all this, and in connection therewith, the minutiæ is obtained by which legal remedies can be instituted having in view the recovery, or partial recovery, of just obligations.—This, to the South, is grinding, galling, insufferable; and as a dernier resort, the cry of Abolitionist is raised upon every one from the North. We are willing to admit that an intense hatred of the free and progressive population of the North, arising from the conflicting relations of adverse social systems, is and has been an ever-abiding cause of discord—but what is stated above, we are fully convinced, gives a momentum to Southern proscription and acts of aggression which should receive serious consideration. That the South, the pink of chivalry and the very embodiment of honor, should adopt the questionably honest mode of getting clear of Sheriffs' executions by moving the body politic in opposition to the enforcement of law, and by maltreating and murdering the agents of inquisitive creditors, may perhaps be somewhat of a novelty, and many will be loth to believe it; but the evidence comes to us strong and convincing, that the Southern mind has also come to this pass in connection with its other acts of insanity.

Whatever the operating causes, it is time some measures should be set on foot to stop this career of villainy. We would not recommend acts of retaliation upon unoffending citizens of the South, for then we should be placing ourselves upon a moral level with those whose criminal actions we so heartily deprecate—upon a level with those whose constant and meditated perversions of human and divine laws have brought them within range of the public executioner. True, could we catch on the soil consecrated to freedom the immediate and active agents in any case of causeless lynching, a stout cord and short shrift, without the benefit of clergy, might be the consequence. The responsible scoundrels, though, take good care to remain far away from our Northern clime, or if compelled to visit us, do any thing else but boast of their nefarious deeds.

Of course, with the present imbecile Administration, nothing of a general character can be done to mitigate the existing and growing evil.

We suppose the North must submit a few months longer to the tyranni-cal exercise of irresponsible despotic power over the persons of American citizens, whose interest, duty or pleasure calls them South. With the advent of a new government, this policy must be changed, and South-ern men must be taught, in a manner that will admit of no possible mistake, that scenes of violence, bloodshed and aggression upon any of the citizens of our common country will henceforward meet with no toleration, but be punished. The name of American citizen must be a panoply of protection to every one within the bounds of a united re-public, guaranteeing not only freedom of action, but freedom of thought and speech. The insolence and cruelty of a mere section must be abated under the overshadowing influence of the Central Government, if re-turning reason shall not dictate the abandonment of the course at present pursued on the part of the South.

206. Lawlessness on a Gigantic Scale

(Philadelphia *North American and United States Gazette* [Lincoln], February 4, 1861)

The world must regard with profound astonishment the spectacle of national lawlessness which the southern States of this Union now ex-hibit. The Gulf States are large enough in area, and have a population great enough to make their follies and crimes almost national. They are now swept by a storm of rebellion such as has never been seen before. They are actuated by a spirit of resistance to law, by contempt for order, and by defiant rebellion against the entire structure which we call the United States government. It is not the election of Lincoln, or the existence of any grievance whatever, that moves them to these extraor-dinary proceedings, and the leaders and organs of the movement every-where avow that they act as they now do simply because they have the will and the power to do so. They spurn the idea of obligation to assign causes for rebellion, and have only to say that they will not submit to the laws of the general government, nor ask its consent to the establish-ment, first, of absolute independence for each State, and next, the es-tablishment of a confederacy of these revolted members of the old Union. In pursuance of this hostile policy, Louisiana has made haste to seize everything held in the name of the United States within her limits, and after taking forts and arsenals with impunity, has now seized the custom house and the mint. Actual war upon everything liable to violence was undertaken by the insolent band who control the power of that State, without waiting a moment to see whether a different course might not get them ultimately out of the Union they have hitherto lived upon, yet now traitorously turn upon, despise, and assail with arms.

This course of lawless outrage we do not believe to be the will or the deed of the great body of the peaceable citizens even of the Gulf States, but it is no longer doubtful that it is the policy on which alone the leaders there and the present holders of power are determined to act. This determination is also one of long standing. For many months before the late election it was deliberately planned and pre-arranged. In this purpose the democratic convention at Charleston was broken up, and, when broken up, it was known precisely what the issue of the Presidential election would be. Everybody knew that a President would be elected by the Opposition, and the arch traitors of the Cabinet set themselves vigorously to work to destroy the power of the general government, in order to insure the success of the grand revolution. Desperate and unscrupulous beyond all precedent, these men only defeated themselves by robbing too largely, and by ordering war material to the aid of traitors on a scale so unusual as to attract attention and awaken resistance. Nearly a year since, we are informed, it was exultingly claimed by many leaders of the expected movement in the South Carolina Legislature that they had the majority of the Cabinet pledged to aid the revolution, and that they confidently relied on the President not to lift a hand against it.

This case is, when all its aspects and conditions are considered, the most astounding spectacle of criminality which the civilized world has yet seen. Whatever may be its issue and end, it is now a most gigantic mass of causeless treason—of treason to law, to liberty, to humanity and to the interests of even the worst local community as well as State yet involved in it. No pretexts are offered except that the full will of a set of men cannot be gratified whose chief thirst is to open the slave trade. It is to free men from restraint whose name and character are a terror to every people of the foreign States surrounding the Gulf of Mexico—men whose raids on Nicaragua, on Cuba and on Mexico, have for years been the chief stain on the honor of the United States. These men now control the policy of a whole tier of States along the Gulf coast, and they have, as they think successfully, thrown off the restraints which the laws and government representing twenty-five millions of people in the States north of them impose. While fitting out hostile expeditions in Mobile and New Orleans against some one or other of the countries they hoped to colonize or conquer, we supposed them but an excres[c]ence which time would wear off. While pushing in new slave-trade ventures from Savannah and Charleston, we thought the palpable criminality of their demonstration would itself produce a healthy reaction. Now we find them in power in five or six States, and fostered as they have been by traitors in high place, they have risen to a height of aggregated force which it may well stagger the wisest to know how to meet.

The world must look on in amazement, as we have said, while this unprecedented drama is going forward. No revolutionist of Europe will know or recognize the horrid, misshapen monster which assumes a name honored in European struggles for liberty. Holders of despotic power in the Old World have not for centuries seen a government overthrown in order to found such a despotism as that which the ascendant party has already founded in the south. Not only is our own structure of law and order overturned, but the very foundations of all order are destroyed, to set up the violent wills of a handful of men who will rule or ruin whatever they are associated with. They revolt because they can no longer rule us of the more populous States; because the frame of the government does not provide for the possession of power by a minority. They profess no other reason in Charleston, the headquarters of treason. They spurn the idea that any special injury to slavery in South Carolina moved them. In no other State is there reserve or hesitation felt. Florida, Mississippi and Louisiana, alike entrench themselves in the vast dignity which characterized them as independent sovereignties before they entered the Union, and resume the powers they then delegated without condescending to assign a reason. It is lawlessness, in fact, it is rebellion in its worst sense, it is almost piratical defiance of the rights and peace of the whole world which actuates those who are, within the last twenty-four hours, reported to us to have seized the mint and custom-house at New Orleans, as the forts and arsenals of Louisiana, and the forts of the United States in other States were seized at various times within the past two months. A tremendous responsibility rests on this government and nation in view of these painful facts. The world outside is not alone the judge of us or our duty—the vast future, and our duty to the millions whose happiness we may guard and insure if we will, or may wreck in the greatest ruin the world ever saw, also appeal to us.

207. THE TREASON AND THE TRAITORS

(*Quincy* (Ill.) *Daily Whig and Republican* [Lincoln], March 7, 1861)

The inaugeration [*sic*] of Mr. Lincoln has revived the hopes of patriotism every where. Old Imbecility is out and talent, integrity and courage are installed in his place. The new *regime* will soon be established and will determine in a short time who are and who are not the friends of the country. And this will not be the *least* of the benefits produced by this crisis. It is well that the wolves be stripped of their wool. Let the line between traitors and patriots be destinctly [*sic*] drawn. But first let us take one more look at the grounds on which we decide, and see with whom we go.

The South are the accusers of the North. They charge us with violating their rights, and the laws. They do this in general terms and make out no case. Some of them are aware of this and of the groundlessness of the charge, and frankly indicate Northern sentiment and opinion as the sole offence. But they do not tell us by what article in the constitution "sentiment" is made criminal.

How is it with them?

Thus: They have been in open violation of the laws of our country, as well as the laws of nations, for years and make their boast of it in National Conventions and elsewhere. They have kidnapped the free citizens of other states, and reduced them to a state of slavery without *pretending* to justify their conduct by law. And when men go to test—in their courts, the lawfulness of their action, they are driven away by mobs. They have repeatedly violated the rights of Northern men in speech, person and property. They have insulted, maltreated, scourged, tarred and feathered, hung, shot and brutally butchered our fellow citizens without even the mockery of legal proceedings. They have headed them up in barrels with stones and rolled them into the Mississippi River, for the "crime" of differing in opinion, or even being suspected of it.

'But it is the mob that does this.' Yes, it is the mob, and it is the mob that now controls the action of the South. It is the mob that precipitates treason, and secession; it is the mob that demands concessions of the North—that demands the surrender of principles; and it is to this very mob, insane with conceit, arrogance and fury that we are now expected to make the surrender demanded.

They have suppressed the business of the country, destroyed its credit, robbed its treasury, ruined thousands of business men, and thrown tens of thousands out of employment into want and distress; they have disrupted the Union, seized the federal property, fired into American ships, insulted the National Flag, plundered the National Mint, stolen Government vessels, interrupted commerce, threatened the country with bloodshed and civil war, and are now using the most infamous means to overthrow the Government itself. And as climax to these atrocities add the unspeakable hypocrasy [*sic*] of charging the responsibility upon the North!

There is not a man in the country but knows, or might know if he desired to, that this action of the South from begin[n]ing to end, from the expulsion of Hoar from Charleston to the fraud and treason of Floyd, and the seizure of the Mint in New Orleans, has been one unmitigated piece of scoundrelism—without any warrant from the laws of God or man or anything but the basest motives of depraved and barbarous selfishness. Yet it is with these worse than Arnolds that the Democratic leaders of the North are, by the chagrin of a political defeat, put in sympathy. It is to these pirates, ruffians, thieves, plunderers, cutthroats, traitors and political debauchees that we are required to make concessions, surrender principles, political rights, the Constitution of our Country, and with it the hopes of the oppressed in all the world. It is with such unscrupulous rebels and robbers that we are to parley about Compromises! And the corrupting tendency of the last thirty years of politics has demoralized us nearly to the point of doing it. But peradventure there be five upright men in this Sodom it shall be saved.

Let reckless and disappointed "Democrats" fly; let frightened Republicans yield, but let all true men who are not prepared to dishonor their names, their sires and their race, by pawning their souls to oppression, barbarism and slavery, stand by their principles and their rights, trusting in God for the blessings of that peace and prosperity which are the inheritances of the good and the just, and which tyrants and the abettors of tyrants can never know.

208. "Blood Will Tell"

(Detroit Daily Advertiser [Lincoln], April 4, 1861)

Until Texas was admitted into the Union, it was considered the Botany Bay of America—the chief difference between the former and the British penal colony being, that one was the *compulsory,* and the other the *voluntary* resort of criminals. Every horse thief, murderer, gambler, robber, and other rogue of high and low degree, fled to Texas when he found the United States too hot longer to hold him. The pioneers of that State were cut-throats of one kind or another, with some honorable exceptions. Those of them who have escaped hanging or the State prison, and their descendants, are the men who have led the secession movement in that State. It is not strange that, with such antecedents, they should turn out traitors when all other crimes had been exhausted.

If the population of the State had not been of such an origin, we might have looked for some slight show of gratitude from them towards the United States, and even towards the North. But as it is, the world will hardly be disappointed, infamous as their ingratitude and treachery has been. In their war for independence, Northern men fought gallantly and contributed largely to its ultimate emancipation from Mexican rule. The United States Government has not only indulged the people of Texas, but it has paid their debts and involved itself in a war which cost the country three hundred millions of dollars.

Since 1848 nearly three-fourths of our active army have been employed in protecting the State of Texas from the Indian and Mexican incursions. We have maintained forts and garrisons at an enormous expense, to protect the Texan people, and the return which their potent demagogues make us is the confiscation or seizure of United States property, and the impudent declaration that Texas has seceded from the American Union. A hoary-headed old traitor, Gen. Twiggs, who had grown rich upon the favors of the National Government, tried to betray the army under his command in Texas; but there was not a man, and but few of his officers, mean enough to follow his dastardly example.

209. SOUTHERN CHIVALRY

(New Haven *Daily Palladium* [Lincoln], April 29, 1861)

The people of the North have heard so much of southern chivalry for many years, that they have been impressed, in a rather indefinite way it is true, with the idea that there is somewhere in the South, a very considerable amount of chivalry which would neither brook a wrong or purposely commit one, and that this chivalry in defense of its honor would as soon walk into a grave as to sit down to a good dinner with a hungry appetite. While our people have never been in the slightest degree intimidated by their impressions of the existence of this fiery element of our national character, they have always been disposed to look upon it forbearingly, even when severely provoked by it, and to regard it as the result of climate and education, for which the impatient gentlemen under such influences should be very much indulged. Hence they have had pretty much their own way in the government for more than seventy years. Personal apologies and national compromises have been tendered them whenever they required them, except when their demands were too outrageous to be even considered. These concessions have been imputed to wrong motives, and as the North grew more and more forbearing, the chivalry grew more and more arrogant and domineering, until a crisis has been reached in which they are to learn how they are really estimated at the North, and how erroneous have been their ideas of the northern character.

But we think the chivalry and even the bravery of the South, has been altogether over estimated. No one can doubt that there are brave men, and true hearted men in that section of the country. We have had proofs enough of that from the days of George Washington to this time. But at the same time, they have in all their communities, more cowards and mean men, in the proportion, probably, of twenty to one, than any other portion of our land. This fact has been illustrated from the days of the Revolution to this hour; and this character is found among their educated men as well as among their ignorant slave drivers. It is exemplified in their large and small towns as well as in the halls of our national Congress.

Their assault upon the National Government was as cowardly as their conspiracy was wicked. They believed they were assailing an impotent power, which, through the treachery of its pretended friends, they could surprise and overcome by a well-devised conspiracy, without any special hazard to themselves from bullets or scaffolds. They had so long trampled with impunity upon the rights and interests of the North; so often maltreated our citizens without atonement, that they imputed our forbearance to fear, and our desire to avoid a conflict with them, to an admission of their superiority in all the elements of a governing people. They did not[,] like the brave men of the American revolution— or like the lovers of liberty in Poland, in Hungary, in France, strike for their rights in the face of despots armed to the teeth, and regardless of all consequences to themselves; but they have been stealthily and gradually sapping the foundations of the Government, creeping into places of trust in order to betray them; hanging, whipping, and otherwise outraging unarmed and helpless men, and turning to their own account the passions of the ignorant multitudes that follow them by falsehoods the most malignant ever devised by the most wicked of men. Such is the *chivalry* of the South, as it now is, and has been at least for the last dozen years.

The brutal attacks from behind of these men upon an unarmed Senator in Congress, is a specimen of this kind of chivalry. The invariable flight of one hundred to two hundred of their number in Kansas, before thirty or forty free State men, is another proof of their valor and chivalry. The dastardly attacks upon Fort Sumter of the braggarts of South Carolina, with ten thousand men to back them, and the numerous batteries which they had been forbearingly permitted to erect for that purpose, is another illustration of their chivalry. The insolence of Pryor, the Virginian, in the House of Representatives, and his sneaking cowardice when he found that Potter, the man he insulted, was ready to meet him on his own terms, is another specimen of this kind of chivalry, which betrayed the last Administration, and which intended to usurp the present Government by a stolen march upon it.

The whole proceedings of these traitors, from the beginning of their last conspiracy to overturn the Government, has been characterized by the most contemptible cowardice. They have never threatened to attack any fortifications that were not almost in a defenceless condition for want of men and supplies. They have valorously assaulted Custom Houses and Post Offices, public mints and even a hospital of sick men, where there were none to defend; but we venture the prediction that they will not fight anywhere during the present contest, unless their advantage shall happen to be as ten against one.

If the Government maintains itself with the same energy and determination that it has exhibited since the attack upon Fort Sumter, we venture the further prediction, that this rebellion will be entirely suppressed with little or no fighting. The more troops we rally, the less prospect there will be of the loss of many lives in battle, for no battle will be fought unless we carry the war into the enemy's country, and *that* should be done. Our troops should protect the South from servile insurrection, from plunder, and from every evil not justified by the recognized rules of modern civilized warfare; but the traitors should be thoroughly *subjugated,* and at least a dozen of their leaders should grace a gallows within twenty-four hours after their capture. Fort Sumter should be voluntarily restored, or Charleston should be leveled with the ground after the women and children have had sufficient time to depart. Armistices and border State interference should have no consideration now, and in six months this warfare will be over; the honest people of the South who are now under a reign of terror from the conspirators, will deliver over their leading traitors for trial and execution, and the Union will have passed the fiery ordeal, and come out better and stronger than it ever was before.

210. Northern Homage to Southern Humbug

(Peoria Daily Transcript [Lincoln], May 8, 1861)

Come what may of the Slave State rebellion, one point it has already established—that the high-bred and chivalrous "Southron" of whom we have all heard so much, and read so much, and seen so little, is an absolute and universal humbug. This long-haired model of good breeding and honor has been held up before us on all occasions—when we have engaged in trade, or tried to collect our dues, or tilled our fields, or objected to being tarred-and-feathered, or claimed any portion of our constitutional rights, or intimated that we should like to elect our own rulers. Compelled, as we of the North nearly all are and have been, to earn our bread by our own labor—to struggle with a Siberian climate on the one hand, and with a sharp competition on the other—it could not reasonably be expected that we should exhibit all the grace and polish of a courtly and imperial race fed by the labor of slaves, and able to devote an elegant leisure to self-culture. Constantly reminded of our inferiority, we came at last to recognize the superiority of the Southron. He made laws for us, and unmade them, at will. Compromises were binding only on us; he could violate them at pleasure. We built great war vessels—armed them—manned them,—and then, with a commendable distrust of Northern ability, gave up the command to the ruling caste. The cavalier got drunk and beat his quadroon concubine; and we looked upon the act as somewhat strange, but as inseparable from the very highest refinement. He swore on the way home from church; and we thought that never did blasphemy sound so harmless before. He left his hotel bill unpaid; and the patronised and admiring landlord set it down as an established custom with distinguished men.

It is perhaps worthy of a passing notice, that some obstinate Northern fanatics refused to concede the superiority of the Southron, and would persist in talking about Free Labor, Liberty of Speech, and the Rights of Man. They even denied that there was any evidence of true manliness or superior culture in the long-haired, loose-jointed, strangely-clad person with pea-green gloves and superabundant watchchain, who wrote his name on hotel registers or college records as a native of the Sunny South; they insisted that the sallow face, the languid manner, and the love of ease, were proofs that he had become familiar with all the vices of maturity before he was fit to leave the nursery; and they scoffingly pointed to his smattering of foreign dialects, and his ignorance of the geography of his own country. In the rude men whom they met in Washington—armed like assassins, dressed like outlaws, with the air of ruffians, speaking the language of blackguards, arguing after the fashion of pirates, rioting, drinking, incessantly chewing tobacco—they failed to recognize the greatest statesmen of the age, whose learning and refinement had so often put Northern ignorance and awkwardness to the blush. But aside from these bold and dangerous fanatics, our people had, as a general rule, quite resignedly come to the conclusion that they had themselves no manners, no cultivation, no sense of honor, and that the noble Southron had all three.

What a change has four months wrought in the public sentiment of the North! The conduct of the "noble Southron" in the cabinet, in the army, in the navy, filled our people at first with astonishment, next with shame, then with anger, followed by disgust and abhorrence, and by a strong conviction that they had been deceived and bullied by a humbug and a cheat. A Southron was Secretary of War [Secretary of the Treasury?]. With a deliberate and circumstantial villainy unknown in the previous history or traditions of men, he robbed, wasted, and destroyed the public treasure and resources, in order to smooth the way for treason, and then cast himself upon the bosom of his beautiful and virtuous South. Another Southron was Secretary of War. He literally disarmed the loyal North, and bared its throat to the knife of the rebel South. Another was Secretary of the Interior. He held his commission, affected loyalty, and all the while acted the part of a spy and emissary for the traitors. This man now goes about boasting of his shame. A majority of the Southrons in the last Congress were perjured traitors, who, while they swore allegiance to the Constitution, did all in their power to insure its speedy overthrow—telegraphed false dispatches and treasonable advice to the South—enjoined the necessity of attacking the Government, and in their seats whined about coercion.

But it was reserved for the Southrons in the army and navy to show how low it is possible for man to descend in infamy. Never before was the military character so disgraced. A white-headed old man—for fifty years petted by an indulgent country—heads the role of shame. And then comes a startling list of captains and lieutenants. They surrendered vessels; they opened the gates of fortresses to worse than common enemies of their country; they bound themselves by solemn oaths to convey private government dispatches to exposed points, and revealed the contents to the rebels; they resigned, they surrendered without fighting, they deserted; they brought sorrow upon their country, disgrace upon their profession, and then went among their confederates and fairly wallowed in their own shame. Never was treachery more infamous, more unpardonable, or more general. One wretch, who had been excused from service on the ground of illness, was so far restored to health by the inspiration of treason, that he led an attack on a navy yard which he had pledged his sacred honor to defend. Another, after notifying the rebels that they must attack his post immediately in order to take it, as he was in expectation daily of being re-inforced and superceded [*sic*], hauled down the national flag with his own hands and cast it into the midst of a drunken rabble, where it was spat upon, trampled in the dirt, and torn in pieces. And all of these scoundrels, save Twiggs, have been promoted by the rebel junto. We expected to find this type of the Southron both vain and overbearing; but we feel ashamed for our country's sake to find him a perjured sneak; and we feel still more ashamed that his infamy is openly approved by the exponents of Southern public sentiment.

211. The Sepoys of Montgomery

(*Albany Evening Journal* [Lincoln], May 10, 1861)

While the government has carried conciliation and non-interference to its farthest verge, and loyal millions looked on with indignant but law-abiding patience, the traitors have hastened to heap every possible indignity upon the Constitution under which we have grown to be the most intelligent and prosperous nation in the world. They have done their best to turn constitutional liberty into anarchy and license. They have disgraced the name of the United States, and put our people to blush before the world; and, with the piratical glee of mutinous Sepoys, they have made it their first aim to tear down and trample into the dust those stars and stripes to which no foreign foe has ever dared to offer the slightest affront.

—*N. Y. Evening Post*

The epithet is as forcible as it is just. The Rebels are exhibiting all the lawlessness and ferocity of Sepoys. Their conduct reminds us rather of barbarians, maddened by the scent of blood, than civilized and Christianized men. Their atrocities would be too flagrant for belief did they not occur before our eyes. It seems incredible, that men who were but yesterday the patterns of "law and order," should be now transformed into lawless ruffians.

The tone of the Southern press reflects the popular madness, and the popular fury. The most conservative journals breathe nothing but war and rapine. The more extreme organs are filled with the most ferocious assaults upon the Government and the people of the North. Dictionaries are exhausted in the demand for epithets expressive of their contempt, their hatred, their loathing of us. The *patois* of the fish-market is Chesterfieldian in comparison with the style in which they speak of us. "Black hordes," "Northern barbarians," "Goths and Vandals," "brutal mercenaries," "besotted hirelings," "hogs," and "cattle," "frowzy fanatics," and "imbecile ruffians" are a few of the more popular titles with which they honor us when they happen to be in their more playful moods. The language of their sterner moments—the *soubriquets* which they shower upon us when they get really vexed—are quite too expressive to be repeated in these decorous columns.

Upon one point the Southern papers are agreed. It is that we are "cowards." While they denounce us as "invaders of their soil," they are morally certain that we don't know how to fight. There is no question in the minds of these valient [*sic*] scribes that one Southerner is, on an average, a match for at least three Northerners. It was only the other day a prominent New Orleans journal made a proposition to settle the difficulty between the two sections by a pitched battle between fifty thousand of the Chivalry and one hundred thousand Yankees. Thus the Rebels, not satisfied with hating, pay us the further compliment of despising us!

Ferocity, however, in most instances, gets the better of contempt. Deep, intense, implicable [*sic*] hatred of the Northern people, seems to be the prevailing animus of those who assume to speak for the South. Their rage at our attitude of resistance knows no bounds. Having dared us to meet them on the "tented field," they are scandalized at our exhibition of "blood-thirstiness," for taking them at their word!

The present temper of the Southern people affords a pregnant commentary upon the "Barbarism of Slavery." None but a people who had played the tyrants all their lives could become thus maddened because their revolutionary schemes were met and rebuked. None but men who believed they were "born to rule," could thus forget all the decencies of life at the prospect of being compelled to accept a divided empire.

212. ARE WE ONE PEOPLE?

(*Burlington* (Vt.) *Daily Times* [Lincoln], May 14, 1861)

We are not a homogeneous people. We never have been so. What is distinctively denominated American civilization has streamed across the continent on parallel or nearly parallel lines, from the two centers, Plymouth Rock and Jamestown. Other elements have, from time to time, been worked in, to be sure, but they have been leavened and molded by the controlling and primary power that set the whole movement agoing. A large foreign population is of no material account. If reckoned by the head, they would present a formidable army, but when estimated by the juster and proper standard of the *power* they exert in shaping our affairs and the destiny of the nation they shrink at once to an inappreciable value.

These two great currents of civilization were radically different on the start. Plymouth Rock had little sympathy with Jamestown. The plain, stern, reverent Puritan could not fraternize with the extravagant, profligate and courtly planter of the "old Dominion." These new and representative settlements were made under different circumstances with totally different aims in the settler. They took their root in entirely different ideas,—which were as widely apart in character as the two localities settled. While the sturdy Puritan braved the bleakness of winter, the fierce enmity of Indians, and starvation, wresting from a sterile soil but a scanty subsistance that he might be *free,* that he might exercise the prerogatives of manhood; the profligate gentlemen who settled Virginia, colonized that territory only to recruit their exhausted fortunes. They were greedy speculators. They were tyrannical masters; lazy and luxurious themselves, they ground hard the faces of the indentured servants or more luckless Africans who fell under their sway. They came to Virginia not to remain, but to make an estate to maintain them in easy extravagance at home.

Plymouth was always democratic—inside of the Church. Virginia was the theater of a struggle between the aristocrats and the democrats from her early settlement. The genius of Jefferson put the democrats in power for a time, but aristocracy gained the control after a while and has kept it up to to-day. The "first families" rule Virginia now. No man ever has been able to rule the sons of the Mayflower's passengers. They have always remained essentially true to the primary principles that were the beacons of their fathers. "God and Liberty" have been the pillars of fire that have lighted their grand march across the continent. The same sturdy loyalty, the same unswerving fidelity to Justice and human right, the same cheerful stout-heartedness and trusting faith in God, characterizes the son of New England who turns the furrow on the prairie of Kansas or Minnesota to-day, as animated the men who trod the snows of Plymouth in the dreary winter of 1620 and 21.—These men can be followed across the States. The church and school-house and town-house mark their course. Freedom and the love of it has gone with them. Thrift has followed them. Wealth and peace and happiness have flowed from the free play of their energy, exercised under the beneficent principles whose glorious promises sustained the faith of their exiled fathers.

Virginians congratulated themselves at an early day on the superiority of their country, over that of the settlers at Plymouth. They promised soon to excel them in all that was desirable in a State. They are farther from the realization of their hopes than they were then. Virginia and Massachusetts were never so far apart as they are to-day, both in resources and in ideas and sympathies. What we say of Virginia is true of the States South of her. They are all alike now as they have been from the outset. South Carolina, North Carolina and Georgia, of the early colonies and States, were settled by the same class of men. They were all possessed with the same instincts, the same aims and aspirations. They were all of a class—indolent, domineering, bragging, dissolute, poor and vicious. They swindled those whom they could. They wrenched from the soil and the labor of indentured apprentices, servants and slaves, enough to maintain them in their profligate luxuriousness. The feelings of superiority, which they had, have been intensified by the institution of slavery. This vanity, natural to them, has been flattered. Their spirit of arrogance and domination has been fostered. Their reckless contempt for the rights and claims of other men has culminated. The shoots planted early by the bragging and *gentlemanly* settlers of the Southern States have gone to seed now—and most villainous seed they are too.— As their fathers laughed to scorn the plainness and reverent spirit of the Puritans, they despise the sons of Yankees.—There is no bond of sympathy between us now. As always, we have different aims and different institutions. The principles of the one are not those of the other. What is dear to the former is hateful to the latter. We started off on diverging tracks. Apparently we have kept along side by side as yoke fellows, with only a little crowding now and then, but in truth we are very far apart. There is a gap that only time can breach. One must come to the other. Massachusetts must go down to Virginia, or Virginia come up to Massachusetts. Which shall it be? Which is toughest, most tenacious—has the most vigor and the greater power of resistance? As God reigns Virginia must come to Massachusetts, and there shall be *one people.*

213. The Ashes of Washington Stolen!

(Boston Herald [Douglas], May 17, 1861)

The record of Southern chivalry might now be closed. The Southern madmen cannot outdo their last recorded act. In the person of a representative mercenary scoundrel and thief who bears and defiles the name of Washington, they have, if we may trust the telegraph, entered the sacred precincts of Mt. Vernon and stolen the ashes of the Father of his Country! The instrument of this deed of unspeakable desecration was a perfectly fit one. Although bearing the name of Washington, we rejoice that none of the blood of that immortal patriot courses in his veins. He is only to be tolerated as an illustration of how extremes may meet in one name. While WASHINGTON stands before the world as the incarnation of all that is admirable in manhood, the living representative of his name will go down to posterity as the embodiment of all that is execrable in a human soul. Holding possession of the home of Washington until his niggardly neglect of it inspired the women of America to redeem it and hold it as the property of the nation, he scarcely yields his dishonored proprietorship before he steals back upon the premises, enters the solemn tomb of Washington, and removes those cherished relics which have made Mt. Vernon the Mecca of the civilized world!

It is said the contemptible scoundrel had reserved a proprietary title to the *tomb;* but it was clearly the understanding of the American people who paid for Mount Vernon, that the remains of Washington should never be removed from there. It was implied in the nature and spirit of the contract; but that was nothing to John A. Washington, who, doubtless, now proposes to enter into further negotiations with speculators in relics. If the report is true, and it is too characteristic to be improbable, a duty devolves upon the American people scarcely less noble and inspiring than the redemption of the Holy Sepulchre from the hands of the Infidel. To restore these sacred relics to their natural depository and custody should be the firm and unflagging purpose of every American heart.

214. The Morality of the Cotton Confederacy

(Paris (Maine) *Oxford Democrat* [Independent], May 31, 1861)

The Montgomery Confederacy has by its acts forever stamped itself with eternal infamy. Judged by its acts it is a disgrace to civilization. In the first place, the key stone upon which the whole structure rests is *slavery* and oppression in all its most damnable forms. Upon this foundation stands the whole fabric. The Davis dynasty first make civil war upon one of the best governments in the world. They then turn pirates and invite the pirates of the whole world to join them in preying upon northern commerce. They are not only pirates, but thieves and robbers, everywhere stealing the property that they have sold and received their pay for. They don't stop here, but advance another step, and publish themselves knaves and liars, by repudiating all their northern debts.

Their Governors send out their proclamations, commanding their subjects to cheat every man in the north, who has trusted them with goods and other property, and that people respond like loyal subjects of a banditti of pirates. More than this, they are a dynasty of murderers —cruel, cold-blooded murderers of men, women, and children. Not a mail comes from the south that does not contain the most revolting accounts of men, lynched, whipped, tarred and feathered, hung, shot and butchered in cold blood, only because they would not swear fealty to the pirate government of Davis, Beauregard & Co. Female innocence is no protection against southern rapacity. Women and children are grossly insulted and even murdered by the boasted chivalry of the Cottonocracy.

There is not such another despotism on the face of the earth as the Jeff. Davis oligarchy. No man in it is allowed to have an opinion, much less to express one. Terror, worse in all its forms than the horrors of the French Revolution, reigns supreme. Men are forced to bear arms against their will, and their property is stolen and confiscated at pleasure. If they utter a single word of remonstrance, up they go upon the limb of the first tree they meet, or sudden death overtakes them in some other violent form, no less revolting or terrible. Such are the morals of the Southern Confederacy, as shadowed forth in their acts.

Travel creation over and you can find nothing in savage or civilized life, that for attrocity [sic], moral debasement, and unmitigated total depravity, will for a moment compare with the hell-born confederacy at Montgomery. Sodom, Gomorrah, and the "cities of the plain," in point of morals, would go into the kingdom of heaven before it; and if the christian men of this nation, both North and South, do not wipe it out, there is not an attribute of the Almighty that does not point directly to its complete and final destruction.

215. CHIVALRY

(Columbus *Daily Ohio State Journal* [Lincoln], June 3, 1861)

Some of the best words in our language have been prostituted to the basest uses. What term is in such bad odor as "affinity," for instance, since its adoption into the vocabulary of the pestilent Free Lovers. Yet no more corrupt office does it perform than the word written above. "Chivalry" once had a noble meaning. We naturally associate with it the high tone of the ancient warriors, who disdained to strike an unarmed antagonist, and who would defend to the last even a foe who had eaten salt with them. But in the progress of time, with its changes, we find the import of words accommodating itself to the habits, the thoughts and vices of men even. The civilization of slavery, which gilds treason into "peaceful separation," humilitating concessions into "compromises," and theft and robbery into an "accumulation of means," readily transforms cowardly ruffianism, simply, into "chivalry."

From the time Virginia first made negro breeding her forte, South Carolina furnished a fine crop of poltroon tories for Marion's bullets, and Louisiana opened her arms to receive the harlots and cut-throats of France—our Southern brethren have monopolized all the chivalry of the entire Western Continent. They couldn't hear to the possession of a lingering spark of this element in the pleb[e]ian masses of the North, who work for a living, build churches and school-houses, construct railroads, pay their debts and fear God. These base Puritans never swagger. They have no servile population to bully. They consume a less amount of coarse tobacco and poor whisky, and have failed to reach the apex in brutal profanity and general beastliness. Hence their want of chivalry. Could these pitiable creatures be induced to embrace the saving grace of African slavery, repudiate their just debts, conspire against the Government, steal its property, the merchants turn their trading vessels into pirate ships, abolish the free school systems, devote themselves to dissipation, not forgetting the amusement, when maddened with "tanglefoot," to stab or shoot some unoffending, unarmed neighbor in the back, they might yet possibly redeem themselves.

This Southern chivalry takes on many shapes. It is as various as the different degrees of ignorance and brutality of its champions. To cudgel a United States Senator in his seat, off his guard and with no means of defence, beating him with a bludgeon within an inch of his life, while other armed ruffians stand near to see that the job is thoroughly executed, is the height of South Carolina chivalry and daring. It made a hero of the perpetrator of such a deed, and had not Providence so signally shown his hand, this same drunken bully would now doubtless be occupying a high seat in the rebel synagogue of the South.

The chivalry of Missouri assumed a form in Kansas which is yet fresh in the public mind. There Clark and Gardner, vieing [sic] with each other in the display of valor, stole behind one Barber, guilty of entertaining Free State notions, and fired their rifles at his back. He fell dead, but it was impossible to determine which hero had taken him off. A pro-slavery President got along with the matter, however, by appointing one Post Master and the other Purser in the Navy. In Kansas, too, was where Hopps, another Free State agitator, was scalped by Murphy, who was rewarded with an Indian Agency; where a Free State town was battered down and pillaged, everything portable being carried off; where a son of the old martyr Brown, a prisoner and unarmed, was hacked to pieces by a hatchet in the hands of one Gibson—where, in short, butchering Free State men and laying waste their property was the chief employment of the Missouri braves for two or three years.

Later we find the chivalry of Texas—after that State has committed the most disgraceful treason, and resorted to the most dishonorable means to capture the loyal soldiers of the Federal Government—cropping out in the paying of respects to a Massachusetts woman. It was discovered by the chivalric citizens of San Antonio that this unprotected female was guilty of the heinous offense of having been born in Boston. It was inferrable from this, of course, that she did not regard the system of African slavery as a little ahead of the atonement in the regeneration of a fallen world, and she was surrounded by the daring sons of the South, who led her into the public streets, stripped her bare, applied a soothing, unctuous plaster of tar to her naked person, set off with an outer covering of down, rode her in state round the public square on an unpolished rail, with a secession flag on either side, the march accompanied by the musical yells of an excited mob. It is not uncommon for slave women to be stripped and lashed, in the South; and the above incident but shows that Southern character is progressing in the natural direction. We are constrained to believe there is yet some show for Sodom and Gomorrah in the last day.

After this chivalry has thieved and robbed until there was nothing else to lay its hands on, and plotted the most damnable treason, setting up its vileness against the Federal Government, it asks to be recognised as an independent power, and intimates a desire to carry on war after the civilized programme. It commences this war, however, by setting seven or eight thousands of its bullies on a starving garrison of seventy soldiers, and when discovered that the post the latter held was wrapped in flames, the braves plied the red-hot shot the more furiously. The Southern chivalric plan of warfare continues as it began, and is, in fact, but an expansion of its ruffianism and assassinations in time of peace. Bribes have been offered our faithful soldiers, who were guarding entrances to forts, and sentinels have been shot down at their posts by concealed foes. The lives of entire regiments have been attempted through poisoned liquors, dealt out as if from friendly hands.—The slaveholding Indians of Arkansas and North Carolina have been instigated to visit their savage atrocities upon the loyal citizens of the United States when fitting opportunity should offer.

The assassin's dagger and bullet, the savage's tomahawk and scalping knife, arsenic, prus[s]ic acid and strychnine are to be the weapons of chivalry in this war. Oh, Dahomey! Ye cannibal realms of the South Pacific! hold up your heads!

INDEX

Abolitionism, and disunion, 92-96, 140-141, 143-144, 147-148, 151, 259-261, 280, 355, 365-366, 385, 430-431, 443, 454-456, 686, 713, 717, 772-773, 780-782, 783, 786, 798, 980

    and England, 978, 980, 983-985

    folly of, 94-96, 280, 430-431, 441-443, 449-451, 454-456, 468-471, 473, 491-494, 505, 686-687, 780-782, 783, 786, 825

    of Greeley, 1003-1004

    Republican party and, 31-35, 37, 143-144, 250, 259-261, 298-300, 349, 405, 408-409, 447-448, 635, 686, 713, 771, 782

    secession and, 92-94, 96, 98-99, 143-144, 299, 365-366, 686-688

Adams, Charles F., minister to England, 963

    peace proposal of, 303, 311, 319-320, 645

    on slavery in the territories, 655

Alabama, and secession, 85, 98, 108-109, 123-124, 875, 925, 974

Albany *Journal*, suggests waiting policy toward disunion, 666

Alexandria, Va., and Ellsworth murder, 1088-1089

Anderson, Robert, and Beauregard, 720

    and southerners, 721, 1083

    and strategy of Fort Sumter, 720-722, 727

    support of, by Buchanan, 205, 220-221, 748; by Lincoln, 639, 653, 703, 707, 708, 714-719, 729, 748-749, 767, 784

Anderson case, England and, 960

Anthony, Susan, abolitionist speaker, 280

"Armed neutrality," proposal of, 877-879, 883-885

Arnold, Benedict, Maury compared with, 1021

Articles of Confederation, defects of, 169, 181-182, 193-194, 685, 790

    principles of, 174-175, 337, 352, 685

Athens, democracy of, 886

Baker, Edward D., and Chicago platform, 654

Baltimore, and Civil War, 753, 842, 872, 1026, 1054, 1083

    and Massachusetts troops, 1054, 1055, 1083

    and secession, 872, 886-887, 1054

Baltimore and Ohio Railroad, and secession, 872, 887

Bangor Daily Evening Times, 757 n.

Banks, Nathaniel, overthrown at Chicago, 34

Barbary States, and Confederacy, 860, 955-956, 962

Bates, Edward, and Lincoln, 861, 995

    overthrown at Chicago, 34

Beauregard, Pierre G. T., and Fort Sumter, 720, 723

Beecher, Henry W., fanaticism of, 455, 789

    on morality of slavery, 493-494

    on secession, 591

Bell, John, change in attitude of, 1019-1020

    and Constitutional Union party, 73, 1019-1020

    and southern vote, 107-109, 113

    and Tennessee, 1019

Benjamin, Judah P., on secession of Louisiana, 558

Bennett, James G., seeks dissolution of Union, 986-988

Black, Jeremiah S., and Buchanan, 861

    on enforcement of revenue laws, 122-123, 620

Blackwood's Magazine, on disunion, 938-939

Blockade of southern ports, and Civil War, 816, 826, 874

    and disunion, 591, 602, 714-716, 724, 874

    and England, 967, 977, 979, 985

Border states, advised by Davis, 614-615

    and "armed neutrality," 877-879, 883-885, 894

    and central confederacy, 395-396, 416-417, 657, 855-856

    and coercion, 669-670, 675, 767,

Republican Party (*continued*)
609, 710, 712, 761, 765-766, 775,
778, 783, 785, 869, 924
and slavery, 31, 33, 42-43, 54, 76-
77, 84-85, 119, 143-144, 250-254,
261, 295, 298-300, 329, 447-448,
453-454, 469, 498-501, 504-507,
509, 635, 686, 836, 858
and slavery in the territories, 31,
66-68, 209, 259-260, 276-278, 289-
292, 310, 313, 316, 501, 858, 924
sole principle of, is slavery, 37,
59, 84, 88, 686
and southern political aggression,
54, 223, 251, 775
on tariff, 62-63, 81, 603-605
underestimates secession danger,
83-85, 86, 195-196
and Union, 51-53, 78-79, 122, 143-
145, 173, 184, 189, 224-226, 235-
236, 239-240, 248-250, 270-276,
298-300, 306, 329-330, 337, 349,
448, 451, 619-620, 633, 648, 664-
666, 687, 692, 706-714, 717-719,
765-767, 769-771, 775-776, 778,
782-783, 850-852, 869-870, 906
Revenue collections, Constitution and,
678-679
and president of U. S., 678-679
and secession, 598-602, 617, 623,
632, 642, 644, 659, 678-679, 715,
747, 828, 859
Rhett, Robert B., editor of Charleston
Mercury, 53-57
and secession, 107, 108, 439, 612,
639, 731
Richmond, and treatment of western
Virginia, 904, 907-908, 910
Richmond *Enquirer,* on payment of
southern debts to northerners, 565-566
Russell, Charles W., on division of Virginia, 895-897
Russell, Lord John, and English policy,
963, 968, 972-975
Russell, William H., on attitude of
northern people, 724
on danger to self-government, 939
Russia, and American self-government,
934
Great Britain and, 964
Rynders, Captain, and slave-catching,
428, 1046-1047

Sabbath, war and the, 1080-1081, 1087,
1094

St. Louis, disunion in, 376-377, 842
San Domingo, and Spain, 962
Schurz, Carl, and Chicago platform, 52
Scott, Winfield, and civil war, 784, 1021-
1023, 1047, 1096
conduct of, on Lincoln inauguration, 1016-1017
and Fort Sumter, 346, 347, 699-
700, 714, 767
leadership of, 1021-1023
and secession, 226, 724
Secession, and abolitionism, 92-94, 96,
98-99, 143-144, 299, 365-366, 686-688
acquisition of Mexico and, 957-
959
and African slave trade, 106, 439,
463, 521, 698, 728, 853-862, 864,
868
Baltimore and, 872, 886-887, 1054
and Baltimore and Ohio Railroad,
872, 887
and border slave states, 106, 110,
200, 235, 272-274, 287, 298, 312,
322, 329, 334, 374-376, 398-399,
416-417, 420, 446-447, 463-464,
591, 612, 634, 649, 657, 666-667,
669-671, 674-675, 696, 705-706,
733-734, 747, 773, 776-778, 786,
809, 842, 853-911, 919-921
Buchanan policy toward, 128-129,
131-132, 134, 137-140, 154-157,
205, 215, 221, 234-241, 378, 547,
636, 664-666, 719, 748, 875,
932, 974, 977, 993, 998, 1015-
1016
Buchanan on right of, 125-126,
128-129, 130-131, 134-141, 144,
148-149, 151, 153, 154-155, 998
causes and remedy of, lie with the
North, 98-104, 128, 143-144, 159,
276-278
Cincinnati and, 585-589
and Constitution, 158-159, 163-
170, 172-173, 175, 177-180, 182-
184, 189-190, 196-199, 227-228,
234, 322, 332-333, 335-337, 346,
352-353, 646, 683-685, 748, 776-
777, 808-809, 828, 849, 894
and cotton, 562-563, 580-582, 598,
617-618, 816, 866-871
of cotton states, motive of, 853-
855, 861, 862, 863, 866-869, 887
Davis and, 611-618, 661, 722-726,
743, 858, 893
and disunion, 104-106, 195-196,

xxiv INDEX

Union (*continued*)

laws, 216-220, 367, 513-516, 665, 673, 704, 741, 748, 752, 810-811, 884

designed and defended by God, 931-937

differences between Douglas and Breckinridge on preservation of, 39-42

dissolution of, and Bennett, 986-988; impossible, 49-50, 88-91, 96-97, 184-186, 191-192, 207, 212-214, 216, 344, 443, 657-658, 725-727, 729, 735-737, 739, 740, 747, 749-751, 757-759, 813, 815-818, 843-847, 849-850; dissolution of, and Mexico, 957-959

Douglas Democrats and, 392, 722, 730, 731

economic aspects of, 241-246, 283-286, 386-388, 391, 434, 562-564, 567-575, 578-582, 585-605, 816-817, 848-849, 871-873, 885-889, 901-902, 904-905, 924-930, 937-945, 947-948, 951-952

endangered, by abolitionism, 92-96, 140-141, 143-144, 147-148, 151, 259-261, 280, 298-300, 365, 429-431, 441-443, 454-456, 780-782; by partisan extremes, 1045-1049, 1052; by Republican administration, 270-273, 337, 349, 448, 451, 619-620, 633, 664-666, 687, 692, 706-714, 717-719, 765-767, 769-771, 775-776, 778, 782-783, 869-870, 906; by Republican extremists, 51-53, 78-79, 143-145, 184, 189, 239-240, 248-250, 270-276, 298-300, 329-330, 349, 450-451, 648, 706-714, 717-719, 765-767, 778, 782-783, 850-852, 869, 883, 906

and enforcement of laws, 216-220, 367, 513-516, 665, 673, 704, 741, 748, 752, 810-811, 884

and geographical integrity, 848-849, 904-905, 909, 951, 976

impending dissolution of, 383-392, 394-422, 683-688, 692, 695-696, 706-708, 711

Kentucky and, 797, 842, 873-875, 877-882, 891-894

Lincoln policy toward, 76-77, 299-300, 367, 368-369, 375, 378, 420, 421, 618-627, 630-651, 658-668,

671-674, 676, 679-681, 687, 690-692, 700-722, 725-728, 733-734, 747-749, 765-768, 771, 778-779, 783-784, 798-800, 804-807, 825-826, 831, 850-852, 869-870, 873-874, 905-906, 937, 974-975, 991, 1052

Maryland and, 885-889

might be restored after peaceable separation, 356, 358-359, 671, 952

misrepresented in South, 295

must be preserved, 121-122, 173-176, 194, 207, 256-259, 304, 344, 591-592, 648-650, 657-658, 671-673, 704, 726, 727-729, 733-742, 747, 751-753, 757-759, 763, 809, 810-811, 813-818, 825-830, 833, 839-850, 857, 859, 865-866, 894, 937, 965, 976

no reason for quarreling over, 38-39

northern benefits from, 244-246, 386-388, 562-564, 571-575, 591-592, 751-753, 871-873

northern and southern attitudes toward, 513-516, 518-520, 528-530, 592-596, 639-640, 659, 682-683, 695-696, 710, 722-723, 731, 741, 751-753, 762-764, 813, 831, 837-839, 843, 844-847

pleas for northern devotion to, 98-104, 110-111, 141, 143-144, 149, 151-152, 159, 165, 183-184, 241-247, 258, 275-278, 283-287, 314-315, 429-431, 591-592, 682-683, 744-746, 768-769, 850-852, 870

preservation of, and attitude of England, 960, 963-965; and attitude of Europe, 975-976; and civil war, 331-334, 338, 341, 355, 359, 363, 367, 372, 638, 648, 668-671, 674-676, 683, 685, 687, 692, 706-708, 711, 719, 734, 736, 738-742, 747, 770, 773-774, 779, 788, 789, 792, 793, 800, 801-804, 809, 810-811, 813-820, 825-826, 828-833, 839-852, 865, 873-875, 893-894, 906, 930-931, 935-937, 952, 965, 976, 1071; possible evils of, 334, 338, 342, 355-359, 363, 670-671, 675-676, 709, 940-941, 951-952; and self-government, 922-952, 954-956, 965

principle of, incompatible with